Bannockburn

Bannockburn

Battle for Liberty

John Sadler

But that the Scot in his unfurnish'd kingdom,
Came pouring like the tide into a breach,
With ample and brim fullness of his force;
Galling the gleaned land with hot assays,
Girding with grievous siege castles and towns;
That England being empty of defence,
Hath shook and trembled at the ill neighbourhood.
– William Shakespeare, *Henry V*

Pen & Sword
MILITARY

First published in Great Britain in 2008 by
Pen & Sword Military
an imprint of
Pen & Sword Books Ltd
47 Church Street
Barnsley
South Yorkshire
S70 2AS

ISBN 978-1-84415-673-3

A CIP catalogue record for this book is
available from the British Library

Typeset in 11/13 Ehrhardt by Concept, Huddersfield, West Yorkshire
Printed and bound in England by Biddles Ltd

Pen & Sword Books Ltd incorporates the imprints of Pen & Sword Aviation,
Pen & Sword Maritime, Pen & Sword Military, Wharncliffe Local History,
Pen & Sword Select, Pen & Sword Military Classics and Leo Cooper.

For a complete list of Pen & Sword titles please contact
Pen & Sword Books Limited
47 Church Street, Barnsley, South Yorkshire, S70 2AS, England
E-mail: enquiries@pen-and-sword.co.uk
Website: www.pen-and-sword.co.uk

Contents

Dedicated to My Wife

Preface

O God of Battles! Steel my soldiers' hearts;
Possess them not with fear; take from them now
The sense of reckoning' if th' opposed numbers
Pluck their hearts from them
— William Shakespeare, *Henry V*

This book has been a long time in the making, the product of a lifetime's obsession with Scotland, with its history and landscapes. There is, perhaps, no more epic contest than Bannockburn itself, a battle which seems to typify the Just War, the struggle by a sovereign nation to free itself from a ruthless foreign domination. The events of 1314 have a particular resonance which has never faded and have been brought even more sharply into focus in recent years by the whole devolution debate, even if this is, in part, fuelled by Hollywood fantasies such as the film *Braveheart*.

As a schoolboy is the 1960s, when history was still taught in the traditional, now no doubt unfashionable way, I learnt, at an early age, the moral of Bruce and the spider and the epic duel with de Bohun before the hosts. Bruce was the very stuff of legend, the freedom fighter, the man who liberated his countrymen from the yoke of English oppression. The reality is, of course, a good deal more complex. Bruce established himself only after a ruthless and bitter civil war and, following Bannockburn, visited a systematic and relentless reign of terror on northern England.

Apart from high drama the story of Bannockburn and the years of strife from 1296, have much to teach us today. The nineteenth-century German military philosopher Carl Philipp Gottlieb von Clausewitz, whose epic treatise *On War* extends to a hefty eight volumes, hails the concept of the 'remarkable trinity', that is the state, the army and the people harnessed to a common strategic purpose. Clausewitz was much influenced by both Napoleon and Gerd von Scharnhorst, a fellow Prussian and noted military reformer. His writing predates the modern age of industrial warfare but occurs after the dawn of the age of mass conscription, the *levee en masse*.

Clausewitz's understanding was that the prevailing mode of warfare, introduced by Bonaparte was 'the massive military event with a decisive outcome'.[1]
I think it likely he would have accepted Bannockburn as falling within this
concept. Nonetheless, the battle was not one which Bruce, given a prior choice,
would have chosen to fight. He had, hitherto, maintained a careful policy of
reliance on 'low intensity' guerrilla type warfare, avoiding a general engagement as being too risky.

The siege of Stirling and his brother's arrangement with the castellan is
traditionally regarded as having been the catalyst, one which had pitched the
king onto a course he did not relish, (this, however, is open to question) This
would, of course, be entirely sensible: the English could field an army that was
both larger and far better furnished with heavy cavalry, then still regarded as
the prime arbiter on the field. At the decisive moment, when urged by his
captains to stake all on the hazard of battle, the king, after initial misgivings,
chose to seize the moment. By careful generalship and inspired leadership his
inferior army won a momentous victory. This, of itself, did not end the war,
which was to drag on till 1328, a bitter, savage and inglorious attrition of
raiding and destruction.

But, without the victory at Bannockburn, the Peace of Northampton would
not have been possible. King Robert secured the national identity of Scotland.
After the battle the English, previously the aggressors, were constantly on the
back foot, their northern shires at the mercy of Scottish spears. Further
victories at Mytton and Byland followed, the northern English were utterly
cowed, the pride of their chivalry run ragged and humiliated in the course of
the abortive Weardale campaign of 1327. Even the crowning triumph of the
Treaty of Northampton, which set the seal on a remarkable lifetime's achievement, did not mark the end of hostilities between the two realms which sparked
with dire frequency until 1568. This legacy of strife was only brought to an end
by the Union of the Crowns in 1603 when, with fine irony, it was a King of
Scots who ascended, unopposed, to the throne of the southern kingdom.

Over a century later, the Act of Union finally and fully unified the two
realms. At the time of writing, there appears to be a growing and insistent
clamour for this process to be reversed; for the two kingdoms, once again, to
seek separate destinies. Should this come to pass it is to be hoped that not all of
the lessons of past history will be forgotten. At present the battlefield is com-
memorated by the excellent Heritage Centre, managed by the National Trust
for Scotland, though much of the field is obscured by modern development,
the quality of which does little for the historic environment.

John Sadler, Northumberland, Spring 2007.

Acknowledgements

Thanks are due to Rupert Harding, my editor at Pen and Sword; to Dr David Edge of the Wallace Collection; Winnie Tyrell of Glasgow Museums; Ailsa MacTaggart of Historic Scotland; Shona Corner of National Galleries of Scotland; Chloe Rodham for the maps; the staff of the Royal Armouries, Leeds and of the National Trust for Scotland at Bannockburn Visitor Centre; Rosie Serdiville of the Society of Antiquaries of Newcastle upon Tyne; Alex Speirs, 'The Time Bandit'; Philip Walling for help with the photographs; Graham Trueman and the staff of the DLI Museum and Art Gallery in Durham.

Timeline

1286 Death of Alexander III of Scotland.

1292 John Baliol ascends the Scottish Throne.

1296 Beginning of the Wars of Independence: capture of Berwick upon Tweed and the Battle of Dunbar.

1297 Battle of Stirling Bridge, Wallace appointed as Guardian.

1298 Wallace defeated at Falkirk.

1302 Battle of Courtrai in Flanders: defeat of the French chivalry.

1304 Siege and capture of Stirling.

1305 Capture and execution of Wallace.

1306 Killing of the 'Red' Comyn by Bruce; crowning of Robert Bruce as King Robert I of Scotland; Bruce defeated at Methven by Aylmer de Valence.

1307 Death of Edward I of England ('Longshanks'); accession of Edward II; civil war in Scotland between Bruce and Comyn factions.

1308 Battle of the Pass of Brander.

1314 Battle of Bannockburn.

1315 Scots besieging Carlisle.

1320 Declaration of Arbroath.

1322 Battle of Boroughbridge; execution of the Earl of Lancaster.

1326 Edward II is dethroned by Isabella and Roger Mortimer.

1328 Treaty of Northampton.

1329 Death of Robert I; accession of David II.

List of Maps

List of Plates

List of Abbreviations

Barbour – *The Bruce* by John Barbour
Baston – Baston's verses (as quoted in Bower)
Boece – *The History and Chronicles of Scotland* by Hector Boece
Bower – *Scotichronicon* by Walter Bower
Brut – *The Chronicles of England*, edited by F. W. D. Brie
Fordun – *Chronica Gentis Scotorum* by Johnannis de Fordun
Froissart – *The Chronicles of Froissart*
Guisburgh – *The Chronicles of Walter of Guisburgh*
Lanercost – *Chronicon de Lanercost*
Le Baker – *Chronica Galfridi le Baker de Swynebroke*
Scalacronica – *Scalacronica* by Sir Thomas Gray of Heton
The Life of Edward II – *Vita Edwardi Secundi*, edited by N. Denholm-Young.
Trokelowe – *Annales of John of Trokelowe*
Wyntoun – *Andrew of Wyntoun's Orygynale Cronykil of Scotland*

Chapter 1

Being Introductory

*We are bound to him for the maintaining of our freedom both by his rights and
merits, as to him by whom salvation has been wrought unto our people, and by him,
come what may, we mean to stand. Yet if he should give up what he has begun,
seeking to make us or our kingdom subject to the King of England or to the English,
we should strive at once to drive him out as our enemy and a subverter of his own
rights and ours, and we would make some other man who was able to defend us our
king.*

– Declaration of Arbroath, 1320

As sparrows, eagles; or the hare, the lion,
If I say sooth, I must report they were
As cannon overcharged with double cracks,
So they doubly redoubled strokes upon the foe:
Except they mean to bathe in reeking wounds,
Or memorize another Golgotha, . . .

– William Shakespeare, *MacBeth*

Robert Bruce

In 1996 the body of Robert Bruce was formally exhumed and forensic sculpture
techniques, applied to a cast of the skull, were employed to reconstruct the
features of the king, for whom no contemporary likeness otherwise exists.[1] In
the visitor centre at Bannockburn there is an image of how the ageing paladin
may have appeared in later life, scarred by old wounds and ravaged by terminal
illness.[2] It is, of course, not possible to gauge the accuracy of the reconstruction
against portraiture but it is naturally tempting to accept the image as true. It is
thus a very wondrous thing to look upon the face of Scotland's greatest king,
not viewed since his death in June 1329.

Robert was born on 11 July 1374, possibly in the castle of Turnberry in
Ayrshire.[3] His father was Robert de Brus, sixth Lord of Annandale (c. 1250–
1304), and his mother Marjorie, daughter of Niall, Earl of Carrick, by all
accounts a formidable chatelaine, though she died in 1292 when Robert was

eighteen. The union of the houses of Carrick and Annandale provided a considerable legacy. From his mother Bruce would inherit the Gaelic earldom of Carrick and, from his father, his claim to the crown of Scotland. His grandfather, the fifth Lord of Annandale, is known to history as 'Bruce the Competitor', an active claimant in the Great Cause (see Glossary), despite the weight of his four score years! His son, Robert's father, is said to have served on Edward I of England's crusade from 1270–74, though he returned to Scotland earlier, as he wed Marjorie in 1271.

She, perhaps five or six years younger was already a widow, her first husband, Adam de Kilconeath, had fallen in battle against the infidel. Legend asserts that it was Robert's sad chore to return and advise the young countess of her loss. She, for her part, was so taken by her messenger that she consigned him to the cells till he agreed to become her second husband! The marriage was a fruitful one, Robert junior had four younger brothers and as many surviving sisters. Of the boys, three, Thomas, Alexander and the doomed hero Neil, defender of Kildrummy, perished in the cause of resistance. The fiery Edward met his fate in Ireland in 1318. His sisters, as might be anticipated, married well, two to Scottish earls and one to Eric II of Norway.[4] On his mother's death, the earldom of Carrick passed directly to the young Robert, making him, still in his teens, a leading magnate.[5]

Galloway was something of a rough and ready fringe on the Scottish polity at this time, the Galwegians having a considerable reputation in war. They particularly impressed the English at the Battle of the Standard in 1138 when warriors, unprotected by harness, drove toward the English lines, even when stuck thick with arrows. Their language, a variant of Gaelic, was a survivor from their days of semi–independence, when links to Man and Ulster were strong. The Lordship was only dissolved after the abortive rising of Gille Ruadh in 1234. The Bruce family were relative latecomers of Norman descent who became successors in title to Gaelic predecessors, in their case Gilla Brigte mac Fergusa. Their later rivals, the Balliols, could claim their inheritance from another paladin, Uchtred mac Fergusa. English chroniclers were particularly censorious – the Galwegians serving under Wallace, during the raid on Hexham in 1296, were identified as desecrators of the Abbey.

Feudalism

These Norman lords were, in their day, a new breed. Scotland had been spared the more predatory attentions of land hungry freebooters unleashed by the Conquest of 1066 and the process had been more filter than invasion. The Norman influence did not really begin to grow significantly until the reign of the Anglophile David I, when the influence of feudalism had begun to be felt.[6]

The feudal pyramid had the person of the king at its pinnacle, lands were then parceled out to the great magnates as 'tenants-in-chief', The grant was usually made by charter and by way of a perpetual heritable lease. Land never belonged absolutely to the magnate, that is to say, in fee simple, but the reversion was held by the Crown. The magnate, in turn, sub-let parcels of land to the gentry who, in their turn, under-let to farming tenants. The pyramidal structure relied, therefore, not on a commercial or mercenary relationship between the parties but upon an interlocking raft of obligations, determined according to rank.

The magnate owed military service to the king and the knight was similarly obliged to his lord; the period of service was traditionally forty days per annum. Further down the scale husbandry supplanted war, the farmer thus laboured, whilst the gentleman offered his sword. The agricultural classes sweated in the fields to sustain their betters, who provided the shield that girded the land. Knight service was unwaged, although if the period was to be extended, then a monetary arrangement would arise. In the course of the Edwardian wars in Wales, many of the upper tier elected to forgo remuneration, not from loyalty but self-interest, as mercenaries could expect a far lesser share of the spoils. Each lord had a fixed quota of armoured or 'harnessed' men, mounted and un-mounted, which he must bring; two mounted sergeants (men-at-arms) were an effective substitute for a knight. Waging war was an expensive undertaking, the cost of arms and armour high. This grew during the late thirteenth and early fourteenth century as harness increasingly made use of plate as opposed to mail defences. It became possible to contract out of knight service by paying a fine or premium, described as 'scutage'.[7]

For his part, the king carried on the business of governance through the various officers of the royal household. Military resources were organized and admin-istered by the constable, whilst the chamberlain was charged with finance and audit. It was the office of chancellor which presided over the king's chapel and had conduct of religious matters generally – usually a senior figure from the clergy he was responsible for the drafting and sealing of state papers, including charters and treaties. When the monarch led his host into the field the maris-chall led the feudal elite, the heavy horse, while the steward generally oversaw the running of the royal household. By the thirteenth century tenure of these high offices had become largely hereditary.

Beneath this upper tier clustered a scrum of lesser positions, each with its own defined role (perhaps 'job description' in the modern idiom): the Door-ward was to ensure no undue rowdiness at feats when the drink flowed too liberally, the senior clerks of provend and liverance, the pantler, forester, the royal huntsman, sergeants of Spence (their role was to procure adequate supplies of food and beverage). In Scotland, the leading magnates held their rank from the old line of Celtic *mormaers*; of these Fife was senior and enjoyed the privilege of placing the crown. These *mormaers* enjoyed vice-regal powers within their own wide lands with full conduct of defence, taxation and the administration of justice.[8] In England the old Anglo-Saxon earls had similar status which, post conquest, came to equate more with the French comital precedent. In the southern kingdom, magnates might end up with many of their holdings scattered, whilst in Scotland, where feudalism was integrated rather than imposed, estates were more concentrated.

From the reign of David I, administration of the judicial system was entrusted to three senior officials, the justiciars, each of whom was responsible for a wide span of territory: north of the Forth and Clyde; the Lothians and southeast; Galloway and the southwest. In the discharge of their responsibilities the justiciars were served by a network of sheriffs, some twenty-six in total, each of them a crown appointment.[9] This Norman framework was grafted onto Celtic precedent, there was no ruthless supplanting as had been the case in postconquest England, but the imported influence proved pervasive. In the lowlands particularly, people turned their back on a Celtic inheritance, becoming increasingly anglicized until the old ways retreated into the west, where the Norse Gaels still held fast.

Increasing centralisation and the Norman influence fuelled the spread of urban development, with most of the royal burghs being clustered in the east: Stirling, Edinburgh, Leith, Musselburgh, Haddington, Roxburgh and Berwick. Towns did exist in the west, flourishing seaports such as Renfrew Glasgow, Rutherglen, Irvine, Ayr and Dumfries. Growth along the eastern seaboard was stimulated by the burgeoning trade in hides, wool, timber and fish, which were exported to the Low Countries and Baltic states. Inverness was renowned as a centre for shipbuilding. Successive Scottish kings created a web of commercial marriage alliances with Brittany, Holland, England, France, Flanders, Norway and Denmark.

Perhaps the most purely physical manifestation of feudalism was the castle, be it an imposing magnate's hold or a knight's more homely motte. As the Normans brought their motte-and-bailey fortifications with them and spread a rash of these across England after 1066, the impact of castle building on Scotland was delayed and, as the Norman chivalry came by invitation rather than conquest, more diluted. The classic motte comprised a raised earthen platform, surrounded by a defensive palisade wherein were located the usual range of domestic offices. An adjacent bastion was constructed atop a steep conical mound, gained by a causeway. This was the garrison's final redoubt should the bailey below fall to escalade.

In function, the castle performed a wider role than simply providing defensible accommodation for a lord, his family and retainers. It was a palpable symbol of status, of power and authority, a centre for administration, taxation and the dispensing of justice. In war it served for defence, as a muster point and secure base for offensive operations. A small, mobile garrison could hold down a great swathe of territory from beneath its walls. Macbeth may have been the first King of Scots to import Norman knights as mercenaries, his mesnie knights fell around him during the final stand at Lumphanan. It was, nonetheless, David I whose Anglophile inclinations fuelled the process, which quickened after 1130 when the king effectively suppressed local disturbances in Moray and parcelled out attainted lands to his Norman followers.

One of the principal beneficiaries of this process was a Flemish knight named Freskin who already held manors in West Lothian. He received a grant of Duffus where, in 1130, he constructed a motte – 'the perfect model of a Norman motte and bailey castle'.[10] Duffus was but one of perhaps as many as 250 mottes which spread over the land. Many, like Freskin's, were subsequently rebuilt in stone. Huntly Castle, in Strathbogie, was constructed toward the end of the twelfth century and Castle Urquhart, which still guards the shores of Loch Ness, was thrown up by Duncan of Fife, who, significantly, was of Celtic rather than Norman birth. Soon the bare volcanic plugs of Dumbarton, Stirling and Edinburgh were freshly crowned with fine, stone castles, whose successors still glower over the surrounding lowlands today.

By the early decades of the thirteenth century, many of the earlier timber mottes were being consolidated in stone and these new constructions were influenced by prevailing French style. John de Vaux, steward to Alexander II's French consort, Marie de Coucy, used Coucy le Chateau as the model for his splendid fortress of Dirleton, an influence which also extended to the building of Bothwell Castle on the Clyde. Often heralded as the 'noblest of northern castles', Kildrummy, near the Don, was constructed by the Earl of Mar, in part, at least, a feudal response to fresh disturbances which had erupted in Moray in 1228.[11] As the Norman influence had arrived by stealth, feudal practices tended to be simply grafted on to the existing Celtic framework; ruthless supplanting, secured by force of arms, occurred only in those areas, such as Moray, which exhibited fissiparous tendencies. Nonetheless, through the twelfth and thirteenth centuries the Norman influence became so pervasive as to drive out the Celtic, a trend particularly conspicuous in the rash of urban settlements. The English tongue also came to predominate, especially in the lowlands and royal residences, at Stirling, Edinburgh, Roxburgh and Berwick, which were all situated in the east.

Society and economy

The decline of Celtic influence extended to religion; until the thirteenth century Columba (Columcille) was the unchallenged Patron Saint, his reliquary, the *Brechennach*, providing the talisman for Scottish armies in the field. But, latterly, the east coast saints Andrew and Ninian, who deprecated the Celtic tradition, supplanted Columba; Canmore's English Queen, Margaret, had been canonised in 1250. Celtic laws also retreated, the ancient traditions clinging on in the remoter fastnesses of Galloway and the west, where Norman influence was much slower to intrude. Tanistry was steadily supplanted by primogeniture.[12] Despite this move away from the ancient Celtic past, Scottish kings continued to boast of their impressive genealogies, their descent from the fabled Irish heroes of old. If Celticism lost its hold on the church and on the law, it perhaps never quite lost its grip on the imagination.

Growth in urbanization notwithstanding, the majority of the population, which never at this time exceeded half a million souls, lived in scattered rural settlements. The commons dwelt in cruck-framed timber houses with wattle-and-daub panels, the superstructure supported on several foundation courses of masonry, roofed with heather or thatch. Despite the increase of feudalism, a widespread proprietary estate, the 'ferm-toun' survived – an agricultural holding in the ownership of a number of heritors whose rights passed by will or survivorship to their children.

The knight might boast a timber hall or even a motte, the hamlets linked by a network of miry roads. Oats and wheat, together with barley, were staples, the latter accounting for perhaps as much as thirty per cent of production. Cattle were also grazed, the ratio of beasts to crops increasing in marginal areas. Most produced 'small-beer', a weak ale that formed the essential beverage, water supplies, for the most part, being unfit. If life was, in the main, pastoral, it was far from idyllic. Poverty, disease and lawlessness abounded. Good lordship went to the very heart of the feudal web, the essential core that bound lord and commoner. The duty of the gentry was to fight, for the crown and to protect husbandry. Those who grew crops and laboured did so under their lord's protection. Where good lordship faltered or failed, anarchy lurked; an interregnum of minority kingship was to be feared; without a strong head, the pyramid became unstable as the magnates squabbled for supremacy.

Robert Bruce was born into an established Anglo-Norman dynasty, his great-grandfather Robert Bruce IV had wed the daughter of the Earl of Huntingdon (also brother to the king of Scots). His grandfather, the redoubtable

'Competitor', had married Isabel de Clare, a daughter of the English Earl of Gloucester. The formidable marriage alliance between Robert's father and Marjorie had combined the holdings of Bruce and Carrick, the latter coming to Robert at eighteen, though his father still lived. The Bruces thus held cross-border estate as did many Scottish magnates, (the Northumbrian Umfravilles were lords of Angus). As such it was perfectly proper, indeed obligatory, that they did homage to the king of England for the lands they held within his realm. The whole, pernicious matter of cross-border estate would complicate the allegiances of the magnates throughout Robert's life and reign and would form a serious obstacle to a lasting peace. It was the one overriding factor which contributed to the outbreak of fresh hostilities in 1332.

Throughout the early medieval period the kings of Scotland had been advised by a collective body of magnates and senior clerics. From as early as 1235 this formation, *colloquium,* becomes identifiable as a wider forum or parliament, having both a political and judicial function. By the time of Bruce, membership had been extended to embrace those of the equestrian and bourgeois classes, with three tiers or 'estates' – clergy, lay magnates and (after 1326) burgh commissioners. Parliament controlled taxation and had a voice in war and foreign policy, together with most aspects of domestic policy. During the course of the Wars of Independence, the Scottish parliament was to prove a robust and resilient institution with a strong patriot core.

David I, despite acceding to the throne in middle age, proved an effective and vigorous ruler. Though he had spent much of his life at the English court and was something of an Anglophile, the temptation offered by the civil wars between Stephen and Matilda, daughter of David's patron, Henry I, proved too compelling. Malcolm III (Shakespeare's Malcolm Canmore), had cherished the dream of creating a 'pale' or buffer state in Northern England. William I had compelled his submission in 1072 and, in 1093, he struck once too often and was killed at Alnwick. David's attempt enjoyed some success, though he too was finally seen off by the Northern English in a great battle beneath the holy blazon at Northallerton in 1138.

The shorter reign of Malcolm IV (1153–1165) was marred by internal strife and disturbances in the west. The increasing power of the Scottish throne was at variance with the fissiparous tendencies of the Norse-Gaels in the west, where Somerled, the great patriarch of what would become Clan Donald, held sway over the seaboard and a necklace of islands. It was the Scottish king's Norman knights who, at Renfrew in 1164, chastised the impudent Gaels and deprived their great chieftain of his life. Malcolm was largely overawed by Henry II of England, acknowledged the southern king as liege lord and was even commanded to perform knight service.

Malcolm was succeeded by the martial William II ('The Lion', 1165–1214) but he, too, found campaigning in Northumberland uncongenial, being captured in a skirmish at Alnwick in 1174. By the subsequent treaty of Falaise, the captive Lion was also obliged to do homage for his kingdom of Scotland. This question of sovereignty was an ancient feud. Henry of Monmouth has Brutus of Troy divide his Iron Age realm into two parts, the dominant south going to his elder son Locrinus and the lesser north to the sibling, Alba. The kings of Wessex, extending their sway to the north, bent the early northern kings to their will and compelled their allegiance. As early as 973, King Edgar was ceremoniously rowed along the Dee in a barge oared by half a dozen client kings, including Kenneth II of Scotland (971–955).

A complex situation was further clouded when Richard I of England, 'Lionheart', needing to fund his crusading venture, sold out his right by means of a formal quitclaim for a consideration of £10,000. As trade and thus prosperity grew during the early and middle years of the thirteenth century, the two kingdoms appeared to have reached a plateau of understanding. Alexander II (1214–1249) married King John's daughter Joan and, in the next generation, the English princess Margaret, daughter of John's son and successor Henry III, wed Alexander III (1249–1286). Despite this apparent accord, there was still some cross-border bickering. Alexander II led six major raids into Northern England, accepting the hazard of inevitable retaliation that periodically left the Lothians and southeastern ports smouldering.

In retrospect and in the light of the subsequent horrors and vicissitudes of the war with England, the reign of Alexander III came to be viewed as something approaching a golden age. There was, in the main, peace and prosperity; trade with Scotland's commercial partners on the far side of the North Sea was booming. Vast herds of sheep were grazing the southern uplands and the fine wool from their backs found a ready market in Flanders. Berwick-upon-Tweed was sufficiently important to merit two overseas centres, the Flemings' Red Hall and the White Hall of the German merchants. The former were sufficiently committed to enter into an undertaking to help defend the town from the English as a term of their tenure. In 1266 the king of Norway ceded both Man and the Hebrides, thus extending the bounds of the kingdom.

The pernicious question of overlordship had gone into abeyance but had not vanished. The cordial state of relations meant the king of Scots held lands in the southern realm from the king of England. For these holdings he was obliged to do homage, to acknowledge his fellow monarch as feudal superior. This was not uncommon, for his part the English king was obliged to swear fealty to France for his territories there. The question of whether the king of Scots was a free prince in his own lands or remained a vassal of England for the wider holding remained unresolved.[13] If Alexander III was fortunate in the condition of his realm, he was less lucky in the all important matter of securing his dynasty. A king needed sons. His English wife had duly provided three lads, which should have been sufficient, but she died in 1275 and all three of her offspring followed her into their early graves, leaving the middle-aged king without male issue.

The succession, therefore, fell upon his infant granddaughter, the Maid of Norway, who was formally recognised in 1284. This was far from satisfactory, so the king decided to find a new wife, the teenage Yolande of Dreux. In the late winter of 1286, the forty-four-year-old king could yet expect to produce a further male child and live long enough to avoid the uncertainties of a minority kingship. So anxious was he to perform his dynastic chore that, on Monday 18 March, in foul weather, he chose to ignore the warnings of his counselors and hazard the crossing of the Forth to bed his nubile consort at Kinghorn. Despite the filthy conditions he would not be gainsaid and headed off for Inverkeithing. Here, the baillies issued further dire predictions but, undeterred, the king, with only a small retinue, rode off along the wild, storm-tossed coast, into the gathering cloak of winter darkness. He was destined never too see Yolande again, for sometime in that awful dark his horse stumbled and he was thrown, his stiffening body undiscovered till the pallid light of dawn revealed the dread certainty.

The realm was without a king.

Chapter 2

The Dogs of War

I called for armor, rose, and did not reel,
But, when I thought, rage at his noble pain
Flew to my head, and turning I could feel
My wound break open wide. Over again
I had to let those storm-lit valleys heal.

– Thom Gunn, *The Wound*

Hang out our banners on the outward walls,
The cry is still 'They come'. Our castle's strength
Will laugh a siege to scorn: here let them lie
Till famine and the ague eat them up

– William Shakespeare, *MacBeth*

Of arms and men

In 1181 Henry II of England, founder of the great Angevin Empire and notorious as the instigator of Archbishop Becket's murder, made statutory provision for the arming of the nation. The Assize of Arms specified the arms and armour to be carried and worn by each degree in society from the knight to the commoner. This legislation was revised by Henry III in 1242 and then substantially modified by his son Edward I 'Longshanks' forty years later. To compensate for a shortage of knights, Henry ordained that all those having £20 or more, be they gentlemen or yeomen, be knighted (it was possible to commute feudal service by means of a cash subsidy, a form of war tax).[1] At the same time the militia were re-organised by the introduction of commissioners of array. These officers were charged to review all able-bodied men in the shire and to select a handful from each vill deemed fit to serve, their rations usually funded from the communal purse.

The Assize of 1242 established the social distinctions which would obtain for recruiting: any who had in excess of £15 per annum were obliged to provide their own mounts; £2 freeholders were to have their own bows.[2] There was no attempt, at this juncture, to standardize kit, nor were arms or harness provided by the crown, each recruit must shift for himself. Inevitably, this led to wide discrepancies with the poorest remaining the most ill-equipped. For his initial Scottish campaign of 1296, Longshanks extended a form of conscription, which he had devised the year before, whereby all those who held property to the value of £40 or more were to be ready to do service on three weeks notice; wages would be paid but each was responsible for arms and equipment appropriate to his standing. The move, like all such measures through the ages, proved less than popular.[3]

Edward I also expanded the role of the Royal Household as the primary state engine of war, the only military elite that represented a form of standing army. The Household acted as more than simply a kernel of dedicated professional warriors bound to the king's service; its function extended to the administrative and logistical. The chosen organ of the Household which accepted responsibilities for the logistical sinews of war was the Wardrobe. For his Scottish campaigns of 1298–1300 the king retained some 1,300 knights (*milites*) and perhaps 3,000–4,000 sergeants (*serviens*) plus men-at-arms.

In prosecuting his expensive wars of conquest Edward was the beneficiary of a significant boost in royal revenue generated by a booming economy, though by the end of the reign he was in serious difficulties, the Exchequer emptied and heavily in deficit. The cost of the king's great castle-building programme in occupied Wales drained off cash resources at a staggering rate. Partly as a consequence of this, there was no money for an equivalent scheme in Scotland, which by virtue of its size and topography, would have posed a significantly more onerous exercise. In the reign of his son, Edward II, a king unhappily noted more for his defeats than his triumphs, further efforts were made to improve the quality and composition of the crown forces by requiring both magnates and towns to muster suitably-furnished heavy infantry ('the foot') in addition to their established obligation to supply cavalry ('the horse'). Such a levy was called out to march to the relief of beleaguered Norham Castle, the 'queen of border fortresses', in 1319.[4] The unsettled conditions in the northern marches meant that there was a continued reliance on locally-raised militias, including men-at-arms, archers and light cavalry ('hobilers').

A contemporary chronicler has left us with this stirring vision, fit for the pages of Scott or Malory, of the English host on the march northwards from Carlisle in the campaign of 1300:

There were many rich caparisons embroidered on silks and satins; many a beautiful pennon fixed to a lance, many a banner displayed. The neighing of horses was heard from afar; the mountains and valleys were covered with packhorses and wagons with provisions, tents and pavilions.[5]

In practice, the east coast route, along the line of Dere Street, the old Roman road, was the favoured path for the English invader, used by Longshanks in the Falkirk campaign of 1298 and followed by his son on the way to his nemesis at Bannockburn. The advantages of using Dere Street were that it was flatter than the west coast route and the fleet could more easily keep station with the army – this was essential for adequate supply and revictualling. Professor Barrow, distinguished biographer of Robert Bruce, citing the apparently well-informed chronicler of *The Life of Edward II*, records that such was the magnitude of the royal baggage train snaking its way towards Stirling in the hot June of 1314 that the column of wagons, had they been lined up one behind the other, would have stretched for over twenty miles!

Troop types

We may therefore summon up an impression of an Edwardian army on the march which is somewhat less heroic than the poet might have us believe. The knights, divided for the 1300 campaign into four divisions, would not mount their precious destriers until taking the field; they would rather amble on lighter palfreys whilst grooms led the valuable chargers. Most armour and trappings would be stowed in the pack or baggage train, colours would be muted rather than flamboyant, the whole seeming more like a migration. The foot, clad in a riot of gear (there being no standardisation of kit), would slouch in uncomfortable columns, clouded by the vast quantities of dust stirred by their betters, ill shod, generally ill provisioned and frequently unwilling. These infantrymen were clearly socially inferior to the knights, though drill and training were by no means absent. De Montfort is said to have remarked as he saw his doom march up at Evesham 'By the arm of St James, they have not learned that for themselves, but were taught it by me!'.[6] The foot were divided into platoons of a score led by a vintenar, companies of a hundred captained by a centenary and battalions of a thousand led by millenaries.

Here and there we might see a well-drilled troop of continental mercenaries, though the use of these had declined markedly in the course of the later thirteenth century, or specialist troops such as engineers, their carts loaded with timbers and tools. The army was a sprawling host that required an array of trades to keep it functioning – carpenters, wheelrights, farriers, armourers, bowyers, fletchers, surgeons and sutlers, with a motley trail of wives and whores plodding in its wake. Add to this diverse mix unwieldy herds of beasts and flocks of sheep, driven by drovers and churning the way still further, and we see a huge column stretching for mile upon mile, the very sight of which must have terrorised local inhabitants for whom the passage of a medieval army could only spell ruin.

Despite the number of full-scale invasions and counter-invasions mounted by both English and Scots, the more usual form of warfare featured infinitely smaller mounted columns, raiders rather than invaders, relying on mobility and surprise rather than numbers. It is unlikely that a beleaguered peasantry would be able to draw much solace from such alternative tactics. Behind the army in the field stood a complex logistical effort that sorely taxed the resources of the medieval state. To underpin every campaign it was necessary to establish a series of forward supply dumps; Berwick in the east and Skinburness near Carlisle in the west, both of which were victualled from the sea. These supplies were usually collected by the royal prerogative of 'prise', a form of compulsory purchase guaranteed, at least in theory, by promissory note. The ships that were employed to transport the supplies were often equally unwilling, being private merchantmen pressed into the royal service.

The Wardrobe, which was the engine driving the war effort, kept full and meticulous accounts of its undertakings. The cofferers and controllers were in effect senior civil servants; they travelled with the army, bringing their own extensive trail of clerks and retainers. Their task was never easy for the forces deployed in the field consumed vast quantities of food and drink. As most water was unfit, the soldiers relied upon 'small-beer', a weak brew carried in barrels on carts. Foodstuffs comprised staples such as bread and potage (a mix of beans, peas and oatmeal). Poor milling left grit in the flour, which wore down teeth, and the basic diet was enlivened by fresh or salted meat and dried fish. The risks of too much ale on empty bellies can be judged from the fracas which occurred on the eve of Falkirk, Jean le Bel reporting a similar riot at York at the outset of the ill-fated Weardale fiasco.[7] An army of 30,000 men would consume some 4,500–5,000 quarters of wheat per week (800 imperial tons); 5,000 horses would need 2,000 quarters of oats and fodder.[8]

The king had power to issue commissions of array which, as mentioned, empowered his officers to call up local militias, who, at least in theory, were to be the best armed and accoutred men from each village in the county. This system was open to much abuse, a tendency Shakespeare was later to parody in *Henry IV*: [Falstaff] 'If I be not ashamed of my soldiers I am a soused gurnet. I have misused the king's press damnably'. In 1294 the king empowered Hugh Cressingham, Roger Brabazon and Peter Malore to raise men from six northern counties.[10] This was a shift from established practice which relied upon the sheriffs; clearly the magnates were better placed and perhaps less open to corrupt practices. Where numbers were needed, the sheriffs were likely too few, using the men who would lead the recruits would tend to promote a more judicious selection!

During the period in question, the early fourteenth century, the mailed horseman, the flower of chivalry, was still the prime arbiter on the battlefield. The roots of knighthood lay in the mist-shrouded past. Chivalry was a creation of the early Middle Ages which, on paper at least, provided a code for the behaviour, on and off the field, of the military elite. The profession of arms was the only career open to a man of good family and he trained assiduously from an early age, usually being placed in the house of another noble to receive his training among other young men of his class, squires (from *ecuyer*, bearers of the shield or *ecu*).

The horse may have been comprised of a basic ten man unit or *conroi*. Though this was being replaced by a larger grouping, twice that size, this was certainly the basic mounted, tactical formation favoured by the Templars. By the early fourteenth century the cavalry were likely massed in squadrons of one hundred, comprising four bannerets, sixteen knights and eighty squires. Following Templar practice the knight may have mounted with one squire in the line, carrying his lance, and the other more to the rear, leading the spare horses. The senior would hand the lance to his master when the squadron was ready to ride and follow him in the charge.[11]

To Longshanks the Scottish Wars were in the nature of a police action rather than a glorious endeavour. Those against whom he campaigned were mere traitors, rebellious vassals, not entitled to the courtesies of war as between equals. Even though, by the later fifteenth century, chivalry was felt to be in serious decline, authors still extolled its virtues:

> What a joyous thing is war, for many fine deeds are seen in its course, and many good lessons learnt from it ... You love your comrade so much in war. When you see that your quarrel is just and your blood is fighting well, tears rise in your eyes. A great sweet feeling of loyalty and pity fills your heart on seeing your friend so valiantly exposing his body to execute and accomplish the command of our Creator. And then you prepare to go and live or die with him, and for love not abandon him. And out of that there arises such a delectation, that he who has not tasted it is not fit to say what a delight is. Do you think that a man who does that fears death? Not at all; for he feels strengthened, he is so elated, that he does not know where he is. Truly he is afraid of nothing.[12]

The *schiltron*

Throughout the earlier period of the Wars of Independence the Scots continually fought at a disadvantage. True, they had the benefit of interior lines, but as the poorer nation they suffered a constant deficit in terms of both heavy cavalry and missile troops. The response to this, first seen on the field of Falkirk in 1298 under William Wallace, was the hedge of spears, the *'schiltron'* or *'schiltrome'*. The term appears to mean something akin to a 'shield wall' as might have been deployed in the Viking era, but under the leadership and inspiration of 'the Guardian' it became a mobile formation, bristling with steel. The idea of the phalanx of pikemen was hardly a novel concept – Alexander's phalangites had helped him overcome the might of Persia and win victories throughout the breadth of Asia Minor in the fourth century BC.

A *schiltron* was formed by a line of spears several ranks deep bending at the flanks till they met in what was then a circular formation. The points were thrust outwards to form a formidable barrier which, unless breached, could resist any assault by the horse. Unsupported cavalry recoiled before the *schiltron* in the opening moves at Falkirk and again on the first day of Bannockburn. The numbers employed were variable but each formation seems to have formed a tactical unit with a commander who most likely remained in the centre with the reserve, which was fed in to the lines as casualties mounted. When facing horse, the leading rank would tuck the butts of their spears in front of the rear foot, grasping the staves in both hands, points facing upward. This formation with the rear ranks closing up provided an impenetrable, bristling forest of points. For all their weight and fury the horse could never hope to overcome such an obstacle. The weapon itself was cheap and easy to produce, a steel head fixed to an ash stave some fourteen to eighteen feet in length.

In general the Scots fought at a considerable disadvantage, theirs was a much poorer and less populous country, riven by nearly a generation of war. King Robert could not afford mercenaries, he would struggle to find any means whereby he could retain men by paying wages. Scotland had fewer magnates and knights; numbers of both remained loyal to the king of England. A ravaged economy could not bear the groaning burden of increased taxation. King Robert's tactics, when he took the war into Northern England, proved effective in several ways. Raiding and waste weakened the north of England and led to a drop or elimination of revenue; the constant levying of blackmail obliged the English to bear the fiscal burden of continuing the war against them!

This was a form of economic warfare which, though apparently crude, was also highly effective. Good lordship was destroyed. The frustration of knights like Gilbert de Middleton and even Andrew Harcla appears palpable. 'Frightfulness' – the exertion of terror tactics as a means of pursuing policy – was honed in the Anglo-Scottish wars. Edward III and later Henry V exported this harsh doctrine into France with, in many regions, dreadful consequences for the inhabitants.[13]

Pike tactics were later developed to a fine art by the Swiss who relied upon a formidable mix of momentum and discipline. Their victories were facilitated by a clever use of terrain, concealing the troops in dead ground or woodland until contact was imminent, then sweeping forward with great *élan* to steam-roller the opposing forces, who, if they received the charge whilst static, would be swept away, trampled or impaled. The Swiss recognised that the formation had to both keep moving and avoid prolonged exposure to the shooting of missile troops to which they could not respond. This was the main weakness of the *schiltron*, as the events on the field at Falkirk showed. If immobile and un-supported by horse or archers to keep enemy missile troops at bay, the for-mations were horribly vulnerable. Wallace had to endure the agony of watching his men shot down in droves by relentless longbows, so weakening the strength of each unit that they were inevitably overcome when the horse swept down upon them once again.

At Bannockburn, Bruce had quite clearly learnt from Wallace's mistakes. As we shall see, his formations retained their momentum, attacking in echelon so that each division in turn crashed into the enemy with sustained impetus, a tactic favoured by the redoubtable Swiss. Later commanders, however, dis-regarded or failed to appreciate the lessons of Bannockburn where Keith's light horse rode down the few archers Edward managed to deploy. These light horse or 'prickers' were used for scouting and reconnaissance, but once battle was joined there was little direct control that a commander could exercise. Armies were marshalled into three divisions or 'battles' – the van or vaward, the main battle and the rear – which deployed for combat in line, the knights and men-at-arms with archers to the fore standing beneath the unfurled banners of their captain or lord. On the march the army advanced in columns, conforming to the three divisions.

Hobilers, specifically Scottish light horse, a fast moving force of mounted infantry carrying their meager provisions, were ideal troops to deploy in cross-border raiding. Jean le Bel, the Hainaulter who took part in the abortive Weardale campaign of 1327, comments on how ill suited heavy cavalry were to warfare on the marches. The English blundered through mire and over barren moss in search of a will o' the wisp foe, which would never stand and fight, yet mounted continued alarums. The commissariat swiftly broke down. The men, mail rusting in the dismal rain, suffered many discomforts, mocked by their fleeter enemy.

Commanders
War is and has always been a hazardous business. In the medieval period a commander had limited forces at his disposal, a defeat in the field was likely to

be fatal to his cause, and quite likely to his person. Communications were dependent upon gallopers and, where possible, signalling with flags; supply and victualling were a constant headache and treachery waited around every corner. In terms of command structures, the army was traditionally divided into three or four corps, each commanded by a man of rank. That a magnate should lead was almost an essential as the chivalry were loath to take orders from one of inferior status (and not infrequently equally recalcitrant when receiving orders from a feudal superior). The king, as commander-in-chief, would lead one corps, exposing his person to the chance of battle, though surrounded by his household men. These sub-commander's appointments were not fixed or of long duration, indeed the responsibility might well be entrusted on the very eve of battle.

A commander of rank, where demonstrably inexperienced, might lead in name only. Edward II, whilst prince, commanded a force in the campaign of 1301, though actual authority appears to have been vested in the experienced Earl of Lincoln. Edward I was not averse to delegating local commands to those from the knightly class. He tried, at one stage, to replace the absentee Earl Warenne with Brian Fitzalan of Bedale, but the knight took fright at the likely costs of his appointment! Those officers who proved unsatisfactory or dilatory in their offices might find themselves rebuked.[14] In 1315 Edward II sought to delegate the defence of the north to a quartet of local knights, but they clearly lacked the authority and the resources, being replaced by Aymer de Valence and, latterly, by Thomas of Lancaster, a political rather than a military choice as the earl had no martial credentials.[15] Smaller commands were frequently and successfully entrusted to men of middle rank, particularly household knights, tried fighters such as John Botecourt, who lead a *chevauchée* (mounted raid) into Nithsdale in 1304 and repeated the exercise three years later.[16]

Once battle commenced it is probable that a commander could do little to influence events. Nonetheless for purposes of morale a leader was expected to display both valour and prowess. Bruce's triumph over his impetuous challenger, de Bohun, in front of the lines at Bannockburn, was a tremendous boost to his beleaguered men, particularly the Highlanders to whom such a Homeric display was the very epitome of valour.

Grand tactics

In the mid-thirteenth century the bulk of the fighting was done by the mailed knights who clung to their destriers. In the Evesham campaign of 1265, Longshanks had found himself facing two armies: that of the elder de Montfort west of the Severn, and that of his son which had been before the walls of Pevensey. Edward, gathering forces, had barred the line of the Severn, pinning Simon in the west. Bridges were broken, Gloucester secured and the rebel fleet slighted at Bristol. Alerted to his father's peril the younger de Montfort, also raising men, reached Kenilworth. Longshanks, at Worcester, was roughly half way between his enemies. He struck swiftly, annihilating the younger Simon in a well-mounted dawn raid, before turning back to confront the elder at Evesham.

With his army marching in three columns, Edward was able to corral de Montfort at the base of a slope, the river bending on three sides with a detached corps blocking any avenue of escape. Simon the elder thus had to try and fight his way clear of the trap. In the mêlée, he and many of his supporters were cut down. Edward used his archers to shoot regular volleys against the relatively-unarmoured Welsh spearmen in de Montfort's ranks, causing loss and panic.

Those embarking upon knightly service were customarily provided with letters of protection, in effect amounting to an indemnity from legal proceedings which might arise whilst they were away from home and thus unable to respond. The Holkham Picture Bible, produced in the early years of the fourteenth century, contains a pair of striking images, placed one above the other. The upper shows mailed knights fighting on horseback, the epitome of chivalry, whilst the lower shows the commons in action in a furious mêlée involving bows, falchions, swords, bucklers and axes.[17]

For the first of his Welsh wars Longshanks recruited some 15,000 foot, over half of which were from the southern rim of the principality, though numbers did fluctuate according to tactical requirements. For the Falkirk campaign of 1298 Edward raised a staggering total of 26,000 foot, the largest muster of his long reign. In subsequent expeditions the numbers of foot present fell dramatically. In 1300 he took perhaps 9,000, three years later 7,500 and perhaps half this in the final campaigns. Experience showed that fighting in the inhospitable reaches of the border and the southwest did not favour the deployment of large forces, the country too bare and the foe too elusive.[18] By the closing years of the reign, the king's finances were slipping steadily into the red. Taxation, customs dues and generous lines of credit from his Italian bankers had all helped to fill the war chest but the cost of the Welsh and Scottish campaigns had been enormous and the meagre revenues from captured lands offered no real return.[19]

The indifferent quality of kit demonstrated by the bulk of the foot did stimulate some attempts at central procurement. Edward II appears to have entertained the notion he could create a corps of heavy infantry and efforts were made in this direction after 1316. Temporarily abandoned, further attempts were launched after 1323. The best equipped were to be paid at 4d per diem, those with some gear 3d, and for those with the worst kit a miserly 2d.[20] Heavily-armed foot soldiers were restricted in terms of mobility, it was the introduction, in the 1330s, of the mounted archer that was to fuel a mini revolution in warfare.

Good intelligence was, as ever, vital in the conduct of military operations. Edward I had knowledge of his enemy's dispositions before Evesham, which he put to good effect and, when an army was operating in unfamiliar country, the scouts, 'scourers' or 'prickers' were its eyes and ears. In the course of the Falkirk campaign Edward had been considering abandoning the advance and leading his hungry army, still unblooded, southwards. It was at this nadir that his scouts brought news of the Scottish army deployed nearby, intelligence which was to dramatically affect the outcome.

As a rule, armies deployed in a linear formation, with opposing divisions aligned. There was little scope for sophisticated manoeuvre prior to the advance to contact. Later in the century, in 1388, The Earls of March and Douglas mounted a bold flank attack in the moonlight at Otterburn, with decisive results. Troops being assailed by arrows tended to bunch up, sheering away from the missile troops loosing the rain of death; by so doing, of course, they presented an even finer target, a fate which befell the Regent Mar's army at Dupplin Moor in 1332.

On the field trumpets were employed for giving standard orders, much in the way bugles were used later. At the first blast, the horses were to be saddled; at the second, the men would don harness and make ready their battle gear. On the third summons they would mount, ready for action. Order and cohesion were important. The advance would begin at the slow (*petit*) pace, the men keeping in their divisions. Although Edward's reign did not witness any large-scale employment of mercenaries, a number of continental knights fought throughout the Scottish wars – these were usually renowned paladins, seeking further laurels.

An eye for ground is an invaluable, even essential attribute in a commanding general. The use of dead ground such as the English commanders employed at Neville's Cross (1346) to hide Edward Baliol's mounted reserve, allowed the horse hitherto unseen, to deploy unhindered at a critical point in the fight. Medieval captains were usually literate and familiar with their trade. A modern writer has, however, summed up the likely approach of most professional soldiers and even though he is writing with reference to the Italian mercenary *condotierre*, his remarks ring true for most armies of the earlier period:

> The fifteenth-century captain learnt the art of war as an apprentice to an established condotierre, not from books. He may have been gratified to learn from one of the humanists in his entourage that his tactics resembled those of Caesar in Gaul but it is unlikely that he consciously intended

them to do so. It was not a study of the Roman republican army which produced a revival in infantry, but the practical necessities of fifteenth-century warfare.[21]

We should not forget that despite the supposed influence of chivalry, 'frightfulness', the deliberate harrying of an enemy's lands and civilian population, was an accepted tactic: conquest by terror and waste. As a form of economic warfare this was undoubtedly effective, destroying the enemy's crops and indeed the tools needed to produce them. Such tactics also struck at the social order. Good 'lordship' was an essential element in the baron's relationship with his tenants; if this was damaged or destroyed the lord's position became increasingly tenuous. Plunder was a prime incentive to medieval soldiers and such robbery also reduced the economic wealth of the enemy.

Atrocity breeds atrocity. The Scots were the first to taste Longshanks' ruthlessness with the fall of Berwick in 1296. Wallace and later Bruce retaliated by striking into the English border counties. In the wake of the defeat at Bannockburn, this pressure was increased to the extent that the Scots were able to levy large amounts of blackmail from the northern shires, converting frightfulness to commercial advantage.

Jean II, king of France, after signing the humiliating treaty of Brétigny in 1360, explained his willingness to agree to such terms in the following manner:

> Because of the said wars many mortal battles have been fought, people slaughtered, churches pillaged, bodies destroyed and souls lost, maids and virgins deflowered, respectable wives and widows dishonoured, towns, manors and buildings burnt and robberies, oppressions and ambushes on the roads and highways committed. Justice has failed because of them, the Christian faith has chilled and commerce has perished, and so many other evils and horrible deeds have followed from these wars that they cannot be said, numbered or written[22]

The knight and his weapons
In Longshanks' day the mounted knight relied mainly upon chain mail for bodily defence, together with a flat-topped helmet with narrow eye slits ('the sights'), the cheek pieces perforated for limited ventilation, with arming cap and a mail hood or 'coif' worn underneath. His mail would consist of two garments: a long-sleeved, thigh-length shirt called a hauberk, and leg defences or hosen. Mail is both flexible and, when compared with plate, quite light. It may, however, not protect the wearer against a crushing blow, which can cause severe contusions or fractures even if the links hold. That vulnerable area around the neck received extra protection from a stiff, laced collar, a form of

gorget, and possibly reinforced with steel plates. Occasionally the coat of plates, (a descendant of the *lorica squamata* of the classical age), was preferred; mailed gauntlets or mittens were carried to protect the hands. By the dawn of the fourteenth century the thighs were further protected by tubed defences worn over the mail and linking to knee guards or 'poleyns'.

As the need for greater protection grew it became commonplace, following continental fashion, for the horseman to secure additional protection in the form of a poncho–like garment reinforced with steel plates to back and breast. Shoulder defences, or 'ailettes', were also added, often bearing the wearer's heraldic device. Shields, shaped like the base of an iron and curved to conform with the contours of the body, were also still carried. The increasing use of the longbow after 1300 spurred the need for further improvements – mail could not resist the deadly bodkin point – and gutter-shaped plate defences to the arms and legs were introduced, strapped on over the mail.

For the knight, aside from his harness his biggest investment was in his war horse or destrier. Good bloodstock came from France, Spain and Hungary. A sound horse could cost up to £30, a considerable sum. The animals were not as large as modern hunters, typically between 15 and 16 hands but with good, strong legs, deep chest and broad back. As a rule the destrier was reserved for the charge, on the line of march the knight would ride the lesser palfrey whilst his followers jogged along behind on inexpensive rounceys.[23]

With its high bow and cantle, the knightly saddle provided both additional protection against slashing cuts and also gave support which, coupled with the use of the stirrups, gave the knight the necessary platform for combat. The valuable warhorse was itself, to a degree, armoured, with two sections of protective covering, before and behind the saddle. The fore part covered the head with openings for nose, eyes and mouth; the longer rear portion reached as far as the hocks. This leather and quilted harness was stiffened by the chanfron, a plate section shaped to the horse's face – striking at the face was a standard footman's tactic. As he prepared himself for combat the knight would keep his lance in the upright position. The lighter weapon of the Conquest era had given way to a stouter, heavier model that was carried in the couched position under the arm, held securely against the rider's flank and angled to the left over the neck of his mount, resting on the shield. The amount of movement was circumscribed, a wider arc could only be created by 'aiming' the horse.

When he trotted forward, approaching the canter, he would lift the lance clear of the rest and wedge his backside firmly against the cantle, he would lean forward with his knees fixed. In this position the shock of impact, which could otherwise result in an ignominious and potentially fatal tumble, was dispersed from the shoulders, through the rider's chest and buttocks onto the solid bulk of the mount. The position also favoured the use of the sword once the lance, essentially a 'one-shot' weapon, was expended. In terms of its symbolic potency swords were the very emblem of knightly rank, blades imbued with the legendary spirit of Excalibur. By the early fourteenth century the knightly sword was a long-bladed, predominantly single-handed weapon, double-edged with a broad, straight, full-length fuller. 'Hand-and-a-half swords', or 'swords of war', had longer blades (there is record, from Longshanks' day of a sword from Cologne with a blade length of forty-five inches and a five inch hilt). Quillons, the cross-piece protecting the hand, were long and either straight or turned up toward the point.

Daggers were a preferred accessory, fashioned like miniature swords and intended for stabbing. It was standard practice to dispatch an armoured foe, once brought to the ground, with the point of the knife driven in through the sights of the helmet or into the armpit or groin, as the *coup de grâce*. The commons might carry the heavy broad-bladed falchion, a cleaver-like weapon which could deliver a cut of tremendous force. A very fine example, the Conyers Falchion, survives in Durham Cathedral. While Danish axes mounted on six-foot shafts were still very much in evidence for the infantry, mounted warriors might use the shorter horseman's axe or a mace.

The knights, paragons of chivalry, represented shock and awe on the field. It is unlikely the charge ever reached the speeds represented by Hollywood knights on film, probably never faster than a moderate canter. Even so, the sight of these caparisoned horsemen, grimly anonymous in their crested helms, their lance points bristling, a ton and more of mailed rider and horse bearing down inexorably would be terrifying, particularly to raw foot. Once tumbled from his horse, however, the knight forfeited his apparent invulnerability. William the Lion, surprised before the leaguer of Alnwick in 1174, boldly charged his mounted opponents and unhorsed one, but, his horse then being killed beneath him, he was hopelessly pinned beneath the carcass. A generation earlier the fearsome Richard Marshal, son of the famous William, Earl of Pembroke, a lion in the mêlée, hacked both hands from one attacker who sought to grapple him, fighting off all challengers till unhorsed and swiftly brought down by common footsoldiers, sustaining injuries that proved mortal.[24]

In terms of distinguishing English and Scots the chivalry of both sides would wear similar armours. The fourteenth century grave slab of Brice Mackinnon on Iona shows an effigy wearing a basinet over a coif with a mail collar or 'pisane'. He also wears a pleated fabric outer garment, or 'aketon', which was waxed and stiffened, stuffed with rags or tallow, to provide protection and, though less effective than plate, was considerably cheaper and lighter. He is armed with a hand-and-a-half sword which has a distinctive, lobed pommel.

Footsoldiers

Whilst knights and men–at–arms would wear full harness, archers tended to favour padded 'jacks' or 'brigandines'. These were fabric garments reinforced with plates of steel or bone riveted to the leather or canvas, sometimes just stuffed with rags. Much lighter and cheaper than plate, these afforded surprisingly good protection and were sometimes finished with sleeves of mail. Though archers generally did not wear leg protection, billmen and men–at–arms might wear full or part leg harness. By this time the crude peasant's bill had been refined into an elegant killing implement, with a long head tapering to a point, the blade furnished with a hook and a handy spike on the back edge. When the bill and spear collided, the latter had the edge in length, but when momentum was lost the bill could quickly develop the upper hand in a mêlée.

Billmen, like their more esteemed contemporaries, the archers, practiced long and hard with their weapon. The English became renowned in its use. In close combat the axe blade could lop the head off the spear, unless, as was rarely the case, the point was fitted with steel strips or languets. Then the holder was left with a rather unwieldy stick. Perhaps the most famous instance of a mass duel of this nature occurred in the course of the Battle of Flodden in 1513, when the Scots pike formations, having lost cohesion in a disorderly advance, were bested by English bills.[25]

The fierce and proud Norse-Gael warriors from Galloway, the Western Highlands and the Isles fought in their traditional attire and with their own weapons under the leadership of their chiefs. United by blood and honour, skilled in raid and foray, their fighting skills honed by endemic clan warfare, they were fearsome opponents. The sixteenth-century Scots historian, John Mair, has left us a fine description of a contemporary clansman and we may assume that this appearance had not much altered from the preceding centuries:

> From the mid leg to the foot they go uncovered; their dress is, for an overgarment, a loose plaid and a shirt, saffron dyed. They are armed with a bow and arrows, a broadsword and small halbert. They always carry in their belt a stout dagger, single edged but of the sharpest. In time of war they cover the whole of their body with a coat of mail, made of iron rings and in it they fight. The common folk amongst the Wild Scots [Highlanders] go out to battle with the whole body clad in a linen garment sewed together in patchwork, well daubed with wax or with pitch, and with an overcoat of deerskin.[26]

Yew was the timber most favoured by bowyers, though ash, elm and wych-elm were also employed. In length the stave was around six feet, in section akin to a rounded 'D'. An average draw weight might be anywhere from 80 lb to 120 lb (as a comparison, a modern sporting bow has a pull of about 45 lb). Momentum, which is defined as mass multiplied by velocity, was considerable and the stout yeomen of England could, it was said, punch a hardened bodkin point through several inches of oak at distances of up to two hundred yards. Mail was not sure protection and the lesser-harnessed foot would suffer terribly. The damage wrought upon Wallace's spearmen at Falkirk is ample testimony to the killing power of the bow deployed in massed formation.

Arrows were made from a variety of woods. Roger Ascham, Elizabeth I's tutor and a noted authority from the much later sixteenth century, advocated aspen as the most suitable, though ash, alder, elder, birch, willow and hornbeam were also utilised. The shafts were generally a 'cloth yard' (thirty-seven inches) in length, the fletching made from grey goose feathers. Arrowheads came in a variety of forms: flat hammer-headed, barbed, or wickedly sharp needle points (bodkins) to punch through plate. Arrows were described as 'livery' (being issued to retainers), 'standard' (made to a universal specification) and 'sheaf' (as they came in bundles of twenty-four).

The bow was tipped at each end with cowhorn, grooved to take the linen string. When not in use, the stave was carried, unstrung, in a cloth bag. To draw, the archer gripped the bow with his left hand about the middle, where the circumference was around four-and-a-half inches, then he forced the centre of the bow away from him to complete the draw, using the weight of his body to assist rather than relying on the strength in his arms alone. Such expertise required constant training, and practice at the butts was compelled by statute. Long-range shooting was preferred and the bow was effective at over two hundred yards, distinctly superior to the later matchlock musket, which was seldom effective beyond fifty paces. A leather or horn 'bracer' was strapped to the wrist to protect the archer from the snap of the bowstring.

Traditional siege engines, whose design remained unchanged from classical times, such as the ballista and the mangonel dominated siege warfare during the earlier period. The ballista was, in effect, a giant crossbow which hurled a bolt or occasionally stones at the enemy's ramparts. It was intended as an anti-personnel weapon, flensing unwary defenders from the walls and used to cover an assault or escalade.

On both sides of the line, as warfare became endemic in the fourteenth century, gentlemen rebuilt or fortified their residences. A good example is Aydon, near Corbridge in Northumberland, where the Reymes family in the course of the early wars of independence, added a substantial stone curtain wall to their fortified manor house, finished with several strong towers. The era of the border reiver in the sixteenth century saw the development of the Scots' tower house and the distinctive English 'pele' or 'bastle'.[27]

Naval actions certainly took place at this time; the merchantman of the day, only twice as long as it was broad, fat bellied, slow to steer with fixed square mainsail, was the jack of all trades. For the conversion to man o' war, timber 'castles' were fitted fore and aft. Tactics were usually restricted to grappling and boarding, missile power being provided by archers. Even ramming was near impossible and just as perilous for the aggressor. It was not until the fifteenth century that the earlier medieval vessel, the 'cog', which had been fitted with a steering oar, was replaced by the more sophisticated 'nef' steered by rudder. By the thirteenth century the use of crossbows as on-board missile weapons was commonplace in the Mediterranean, while regular contingents of retained marines were also in evidence. However, both these trends were slower to catch on in northern waters. As fleets engaged with limited man-oeuvring, lime was used to blind opponents and soap was employed to render the enemy's decks slippery and treacherous underfoot; thereafter it was a case of grapple and board.

The face of battle

Time and much romantic fiction have cast a shroud of pageantry over the harsh realities of medieval combat, but the truth is somewhat less comforting. Though lacking the scale and devastation of modern wars, devoid of the horrors of machine guns and high explosive, warfare in the middle ages was every bit as frightful. Commanders might, as Bruce did, seek to exhort their men through inspiring oratory, though this is probably much exaggerated by chroniclers, as a general, even if he rode up and down the line, would only be heard by a small proportion at any one time. Morale was, as ever in war, paramount, as the Scots demonstrated at Mytton and other skirmishes after Bannockburn, where their discipline, cohesion and faith in their officers created in their forces a formidable instrument of war. The knight had his years of training, pride in his lineage, the scorn and excoriation of his peers should he waver, to sustain him; the commons had less, much less. Faith too was important, the fourteenth century was an age where faith was paramount. Christendom had yet to be rent by the fires of schism. Early heresies, Bogomils and Cathars, had been ruthlessly and effectively suppressed.[28] However cynically men might act, this did not affect the integrity of their belief. Battle was seen as a manifestation of God's divine will; hearing mass and taking the sacrament were considered imperatives to a man embarking on the hazard of combat.

Our present age, mired in arid secularism, has lost the compelling nature of medieval religiosity, but the validity and importance of faith should not be overlooked. Clerics, though banned from bearing arms, were frequently to be seen in harness; Anthony Bek, the Prince Bishop who held office from 1283 till his death in 1311, was a significant leader in war.[29] Once battle was joined in earnest the combat became an intensely personal affair, a hacking, stamping mêlée of bills, spears, swords and axes. Men, half blind in armour, soon assailed by raging thirst and fatigue, would swiftly become disorientated. Few would be killed by a single blow, but a disabling wound, bringing the victim to ground, would expose him to more and fatal blows, most likely to the head or the dagger thrust through the visor, a horrible, agonising and by no means speedy end.

Images from the period show fearful injuries as helmets are split and men riven to the navel. More modern tests have shown a stout steel skullcap will resist a shearing blow; nonetheless the carnage at close quarters will have been utterly fearful. Many men died not from blows but from suffocation in the press, as at Dupplin Moor in 1332, or by drowning as they sought to flee over watercourses – hundreds of English corpses clogged the Bannockburn and the Swale at Myton five years later. A battle could be divided into a number of phases. It might commence with an archery duel, with the side that came off worst being forced to advance to contact. The horse would then advance and engage with their opposite numbers or, as at Falkirk and Bannockburn, assault the Scottish spears. When one side broke, dissolving in rout, then the pursuit might be both long and bloody. Men who had staunchly held their ground, giving way to the contagion of panic, casting aside arms and harness, easy meat.

These horrors were repeated on many fields in the Scottish wars, Halidon Hill and Homildon being just two examples. A fourteenth-century work describes how the man–at–arms' bravado rapidly diminishes, the closer to contact he comes:

> When we are in taverns, drinking strong wines, at our sides the ladies we desire, looking on, with their smooth throats … their grey eyes shining back with smiling beauty nature calls on us to have desiring hearts, to struggle awaiting [their] thanks at the end. That we would conquer … Oliver and Roland. But when we are in the field, on our galloping chargers our shields round our necks and lances lowered … and our enemies are approaching us then we would rather be deep in some cavern.[30]

By our standards, medical services were rudimentary and unreliable. The perceived presence of evil humours was the source of much bleeding of patients; quacks cast horoscopes and prescribed bizarre potions; wounds were cauterised with hot pitch. However, the use of forms of anaesthesia, derived mainly from herbs, was not unknown and surgical techniques were perhaps more advanced, at least in the hands of competent practitioners, than may be imagined. One of the dead from Towton, recently exhumed from a grave pit on the site, showed evidence of a prior and massive facial injury which had been skillfully repaired. Nonetheless, throughout the period northern European medical services lagged far behind those available to both Byzantine and Islamic armies.

As we have seen, most fatal injuries were caused by blows to the head, as the mute remains from grave pits testify: the bodies of the English dead from Otterburn, whose remains were found beneath the nave of Elsdon church in the nineteenth century, from Visby in Sweden (1361), and from Towton. Slashing and stabbing wounds, though ghastly, were not always fatal and more victims probably recovered than might be expected. Complications such as peritonitis or blood poisoning, however, were invariably fatal – many injured would be left lying on the field exposed to the rigours of climate and the tender mercies of scavengers. Campaigns of the period tended to be highly mobile and of relatively short duration, which was undoubtedly a major blessing for the participants for, in medieval wars as a whole, far more men died of disease, particularly dysentery, than from enemy action. Henry V's tattered band that stood at Agincourt was but a pale shadow of the host he had brought from England, the ranks thinned dreadfully by dysentery, rampant in the foetid confines of the siege lines around a beleaguered town or castle.

The lessons of Courtrai

Bannockburn should not be viewed in tactical isolation. Falkirk had shown that effective pairing of missile troops with the shock of heavy horse could break spearmen, even when these were well posted on good ground. The abortive first onslaught by the English cavalry demonstrated how the spears could, if not subjected to a murderous barrage of arrows, more than hold their own. The failure of the Scottish horse, however, left their own missile troops horribly and fatally exposed.

One engagement which bears striking similarities to Bannockburn is the field of Courtrai (1302). The facts of this battle are worth considering in some detail. A dispute between Philip of France and the worthy burghers of Flanders arose when the former imprisoned Count Guy on a charge of treason and sought to forfeit his lands. The gaoled magnate's son, Guy of Namur, and his cousin, William of Julien, raised a rebel army which ousted most of the French garrisons. This force was mainly comprised of citizens and the rural peasantry, the chivalry of Flanders largely remaining aloof. Robert of Artois, the king's brother in law, was handed the task of recovering the lost towns and suppressing the rebellion. Count Robert commanded a substantial host, the feudal levy in its chivalric glory, supported by mercenary Genoese missile troops and foot from Gascony and the Basque provinces. On 2 July the host crossed into Flanders, obliging the rebels to abandon the leaguer of Cassel and fall back upon a defensive position before the walls of Courtrai, whose garrison remained defiant.

Count Guy had chosen his ground well, though his position backed onto the formidable ramparts with only a couple of very narrow causeways for escape should the position be lost. Retreat was not therefore possible; the Flemings must triumph or face annihilation. Their front was traversed by the Groeninghebeke, not in itself a major water obstacle but the ground around was soft and miry. The line stretched along the Menin–Courtrai road. On the left, the Lys and the bulk of a Franciscan Friary covered the flank, whilst to the right a ditch feeding into the city moat gave protection. The ground down to the river was studded with traps and pits, '*trous de loup*'.

With virtually no cavalry, the foot were formed into a vast phalanx of spears, perhaps a thousand yards across and up to ten men deep. Another 1,200 were left to keep the line of the entrenchments and counter an attempt from the garrison to mount a sally. A small mounted reserve was hidden in dead ground to the rear, a cloud of skirmishers to the fore. Robert of Artois, despising the petty bourgeois flaunting their challenge, disdained manoeuvre and decided upon a frontal assault delivered by the heavy horse. His Genoese crossbowmen scrimmaged with the Flemings and drove in the skirmishers. Guy pulled his line backwards, no mean feat in itself, to keep the phalanx out of range. The French van, comprising ten squadrons, deployed in three waves and forded the stream, quickly losing cohesion in the wet ground and maze of obstacles.

Now the rebel foot moved steadily forward, driving back the swirling knots of horsemen, who could achieve nothing against the mass of serried points. Robert next committed his main body, himself in the lead. This intervention stemmed the imminent rout of the van and sheer weight of men and horses began to exert pressure on the phalanx as the crisis point approached. Forcing their way in a gap that was opened, victory seemed within the Frenchmen's grasp, but the Flemings' reserve came up and sealed the breach. An attempted sally by the defenders was seen off and the crisis passed. With all impetus lost, the horse were hustled back toward the stream, carpeting the ground with dead men and horses. The burghers fought for a cause rather than reward, no prisoners of rank were spared and the pride of French chivalry fell beneath the stabbing points. Count Robert, three score and more of the gentry and at least seven hundred knights were left dead upon the field.[31]

As an exercise in tactics Courtrai threw up a number of important matters: heavy horse, however valiant, could not best a determined body of spears contesting a narrow front; the defenders must be at pains, to secure their flanks and must keep out of range of missiles. Choosing ground that offered obstacles to the front and augmenting these with fieldworks clearly paid handsome dividends. Robert of Artois, when ordering the advance, commanded his cross-bowmen to withdraw. Some, as at Crecy forty-four years later, were ridden down by the exultant chivalry. As the attack developed his cavalry were without missile support so they were constrained to face well ordered lines of spears, an impenetrable obstacle, which confounded all their best and bravest endeavours.

The Count of Artois showed himself to be a poor general, he eschewed any thoughts of tactical manoeuvre in favour of the charge, an advance over such unfavourable ground as would ensure the horse barely moved faster than a walk and forfeited all cohesion and mass. Shock and awe turned to muddied confusion. Courtrai demonstrated clearly how vital for the attacker were the lessons of Falkirk, the importance of co-ordinating missile troops with the horse; neither could, of themselves, procure a victory, but used together they would be irresistible. We may surmise with some confidence that Robert Bruce had studied the lessons of both battles, and we may aver with equal confidence that his opponent, Edward II, had not.

Chapter 3

The Longshanks

> *For those Scots,*
> *I rate 'em as sots,*
> *What a sorry shower!*
> *Whose utter lack*
> *In the attack*
> *Lost 'em at Dunbar*
>   – Contemporary doggerel[1]

The Great Cause

According to the annals of Waverley Abbey, it was in 1291 that Edward I 'Longshanks', informed his council that he intended to assume direct rule of Scotland, to reduce the northern kingdom to the inferior status of a mere province, much as he had done with the Welsh.[2] There were numerous precedents for such authoritarian control; the kings of Wessex had exercised sway over the lesser princes of Scotland and Wales. Edward therefore may have seen himself as a successor to Athelstan or perhaps a new King Arthur, whose cult was already flourishing. It may be, however, that the king merely intended to gather up the reins of power and ensure a smooth transition whilst the interregnum lasted, as a prudent overlord might be expected to do.[3]

Prior to the events of 1291 there appears to have been no suggestion that Edward had any ambition to exert sway over Scotland. Alexander III was his brother-in-law, having married Edward's sister Margaret in 1251, and their relationship was entirely amicable. Indeed the English king seems genuinely to have shared Alexander's grief over the loss of both his sons; the younger boy, David, had died in 1281, aged only eight, and Alexander had barely made it out of his teens when, three years later, he too died. His daughter, Margaret, had been married to Eric II of Norway in 1281 and had departed sorrowfully for her short life in Bergen, which she found cold and depressing.

Margaret was not destined to see her native land again, dying a mere two years after her marriage, leaving an infant daughter. This sickly child, named after her mother, and clearly no more robust, was the last of the Canmore line and now became Queen of Scots. To ensure a smooth transition in the event of his death (which in 1284, Alexander had reason to hope might lie some years distant), the king, at Scone, had formally confirmed the child as his successor.[5] He would also have reason to hope that his marriage to the nubile Yolande of Dreux, solemnised on the 14 October 1285, ending a decade of widowerhood, might yet produce another male heir.

The king's untimely death, following so soon upon his marriage, confirmed the popular and pessimistic view that a day of judgement was at hand, that what would be seen in retrospect as a golden era would come violently to a close:

Quehen Alysandyr our King was dede
That Scotland led in lure and le
Awaye was sons of ale and brede

Of wyne and wax, of gamyn and gle
Our gold was changed into lede

Chryst born into vyrgynte
Succour Scotland and remede
That stad in perplexite.[6]

For the medieval kingdom, to be without a strong adult ruler was to open the doors to factionalism. For a brief interlude Yolande was able to maintain she was pregnant, but this was soon disproved and the sickly infant in Norway remained the only viable heiress. As an interim measure the governance of the realm was entrusted to a committee of 'Guardians', drawn in pairs from the higher clergy, the magnates and gentry.[7] In the southwest, Bruce's grandfather, the octogenarian 'Competitor', was squaring up to John Baliol, raiding his lands and entering into a band or recognizance with several of his fellow magnates, including from Ireland the 'Red' Earl of Ulster, Thomas de Clare and the MacDonald Lord of the Isles.[8] This accord, the Band of Turnberry, was ostensibly confined to affairs in Ireland but included a politic nod to Edward I and to 'whoever' became ruler of Scotland.[9]

The Guardians realised they needed the steadying influence of a strong external arbitrator to curtail the incipient violence simmering in the west. There were two obvious candidates. The first was Eric II, king of Norway and the father of the young queen. Eric was, however, distracted by a dispute with Denmark and the favoured choice was, inevitably, Edward I of England. In the circumstances this was a perfectly logical conclusion. Longshanks had experience of acting as an arbitrator in the difficult area of disputed kingship. Unfortunately the Scottish emissaries found the king on the point of departure for Gascony where the deteriorating situation, as he advised, required his full and immediate attention.

Matters therefore were to be left in the hands of the Guardians who took steps against the Competitor's aggression. Faced with such resolve his challenge quickly cooled. Upon his return from France in 1289, Edward proposed a dynastic union between Margaret, 'the Maid of Norway' and Edward of Caernarvon, the Prince of Wales. At a stroke Edward I would have united the whole of mainland Britain as a Plantagenet empire. In that November the pre-nuptial negotiations began in earnest at Salisbury and an early draft of the proposed treaty, whilst not directly mentioning the marriage alliance, did provide for Edward's intervention in Scotland as mediator and 'honest broker' when matters of such weight as surpassed the competency of the Guardians arose. Eric II had stipulated that his daughter's rights as to sovereignty should not be interfered with.

As the two young people were blood relations, a papal dispensation was needed before any marriage could be finally agreed.[10] In 1290 the Scots Parliament sitting at Birgham approved the draft treaty, though the union could not be solemnised until 1298 when both children were of age. The key question of sovereignty was left rather in abeyance at this juncture; guarantees were expected in terms of territorial integrity and the privileges of the senior clergy. Anthony Bek, the Prince-Bishop of Durham, acted as Edward's senior negotiator.[11] The resultant agreement provided the requisite assurances in relation to Scottish independence which was to endure 'without any sub-jugation to England'.[12]

If Edward had intentions to bring Scotland directly under his sway then these were far from obvious. The fact that he clearly placed greater emphasis upon matters in Gascony would tend to suggest that he did not, at that time, have ambitions in Scotland. However, with the marriage treaty now sealed he had no need for haste – with a Plantagenet as her consort the young queen would soon find herself under the powerful influence of her father-in-law. In the king's mind, therefore, the establishment of Plantagenet rule was possibly already a matter of fact.

Edward now wrote to the Guardians intimating he had appointed Bek as his lieutenant in Scotland.[13] The term was perhaps ambiguous; was the Prince Bishop merely an ambassador or a viceroy? The intention was that Bek would hold the administration of Scotland on trust jointly for both Margaret and Caernarvon. On 4 June Edward appointed Walter de Huntercombe as custodian of Man on the basis that the Earl of Ulster had offered the place to the English crown. Later that month Bek was empowered to admit the fis-siparous Islesmen into the king's peace.[14] None of this appeared to augur well for the Scots' continuing independence and the Guardians must have been rendered uneasy. They presently had other concerns, however, for the Maid of Norway never saw her throne. In the autumn of 1290, whilst still in Orkney, the unfortunate child sickened and died. There was now no clear heir to the vacant throne and the spectre of civil war emerged, like Banquo's ghost, from the shadows.

On 7 October, Bishop Fraser of St Andrews wrote to the king with the dire news and in fear of civil strife. The magnates, including Bruce the Competitor, had gathered at Perth to await the arrival of the child queen. The Bishop urged Edward to come north to the border with the English host as a deterrent to rival factions, particularly those of Bruce and Baliol. The king was soon presented with another tragedy when, on 28 November, Eleanor of Castile, his wife of thirty-six years, also died. Edward was wracked with grief. The great warrior king turned his back on affairs of state whilst he tried to come to terms with his loss.

It was not until early in the new year that Bishop Bek presented the suggestion to the Guardians that Edward should decide upon the matter of the succession in his capacity as feudal superior. In the meantime, Bruce proposed an allegedly ancient and highly dubious process referred to as 'the Appeal of the Seven Earls of Scotland', a form of collegiate election. Cannily, the Competitor also hastened to confirm his loyalty to Edward. The Scots Parliament most likely found that arbitration by the king of England was the best means of avoiding internecine conflict. Edward was widely regarded as a leading jurist and the legal procedure which followed marked the beginning of the 'Great Cause', the dispute over not only who should be king of Scots, but whether that king owed homage to the king of England as feudal superior.

The hearings lasted for a full eighteen months, with the court actually in session for a third of that time. Edward ordered that a full record be kept – he did not intend that posterity should accuse him of any partisan leanings. The proceedings were convened at Norham on 10 May 1291, with John of Caen maintaining the record.[15] In his opening address Robert Brabazon, Chief Justice of the King's Bench, required the Scots present to formally recognise Edward as overlord. This request undoubtedly caused consternation and yet from the king's point of view was entirely logical – for him to arbitrate according to feudal custom, his right to act in that capacity had to be accepted by all parties to the dispute. Robert Wishart, Bishop of Glasgow, might have protested at this point and the hearing was adjourned for the Scots representatives to consider their position.

Bishop Wishart may have been the author of the carefully politic response that they were not able to respond on behalf of the nation as such matters were the preserve of the king himself. Edward was therefore required to seek an appropriate undertaking from each of the rival claimants, on the basis such a recognition would, by definition, bind the Guardians. It would, nonetheless be plain that the Scottish polity as a whole did not necessarily consider itself subject to England. The wording of the reply, though diplomatic, carried more than an undertone of defiance: the Guardians 'have no knowledge of your right, nor do they ever see it claimed and used by you or your ancestors'.[16]

In spite of any reservations, Edward seamlessly assumed control of key royal castles. Again there was sense in this for an English presence would deter rival factions. He was also nominally a competitor – even though he sat in judgement, he had not conceded his own, albeit more remote, claim.[17] The Guardians could hand bastions to the king of England in his guise as a candidate and other claimants could do so in acknowledging Edward as their feudal lord. With the matter of his overlordship still undefined, Edward opened the main court hearing at Berwick in August, with his final judgement not handed down until 17 November 1292. The weight of legal argument was considerable. Both Bruce and Baliol, as leading contenders, were permitted teams of forty representatives or auditors each whilst Edward retained twenty-four. After exhaustive deliberation Edward decided upon Baliol. In law this decision was incontestable, his claim was demonstrably the strongest and, on 19 November, the king instructed that possession or seisin of the realm be given to him.[18]

'Toom Tabard'

John Baliol was now to be crowned king of Scotland, having recognised Edward as his sovereign lord. On 26 December he performed homage for the realm of Scotland. At the coronation Anthony Bek was in attendance whilst John of St John acted as proxy for the infant Earl of Fife. The seal used by the Guardians, now discharged, was formally broken up and the fragments sent to Edward in recognition of his rights. Scotland now had a king but he was not his own man. This act of submission has earned King John almost universal opprobrium from subsequent writers yet, at the time, he really had no alternative. Other competitors, notably Bruce, had shown indecent haste to offer their allegiance to the English king and there was ample precedent: Malcolm Canmore had sworn fealty to William I and the oath had been renewed from time to time by his successors.

It also appeared that Edward was content to allow the governance of Scotland to remain in the hands of the king and his ministers and to refrain from meddling. Even as feudal superior it was assumed Edward was still bound by the guarantees stated in the Treaty of Northampton. On 7 December, before Baliol had even sworn the oath, a Berwick burgess, Roger Bartholemew, appealed to Edward against three judgements found against him in the Guardians' courts. On hearing the appeal the king upheld two and overturned one. The decision sent ripples of alarm back to the Scottish Parliament but Edward made it plain he would continue to hear cases on appeal as he saw fit, even summoning the king of Scots as a party to proceedings if appropriate. As though to underline his own inferior status Baliol agreed to the annulment of the Treaty of Northampton on 2 January 1293.

If Edward was technically correct in exercising his powers as overlord he showed a total lack of understanding of the Scots and of how fiercely they valued their independence. By the end of the year he had indeed summoned King John to appear before the English courts. The matter was an action brought by MacDuff, a younger son of Malcolm Earl of Fife, alleging false imprisonment and theft of his inheritance. If this was not sufficient provocation then in the following summer Baliol, together with eighteen Scottish magnates, was summoned to perform military service against Philip IV. Such summonses were by no means unprecedented. Edward had previously requested knight service of Scottish nobles in the Welsh wars as a condition of their homage for lands they held in England.[19] From Edward's perspective, Baliol's position was now the same, though service was now due for the kingdom of Scotland. Malcolm IV had served Henry II on the same terms in 1159. In the event a general muster proved unnecessary when the Earl of Warwick defeated the Welsh rebels in March 1295.

Fresh disturbances, arising in Wales, frustrated Edward's plans to campaign against Philip but the fact he had demanded service from Baliol undermined the latter's position in Scotland. King John's inability to stand up to the king of England had begun to anger the representatives of the community who, at a Parliament convened in Stirling in July 1295, appointed a council of twelve (four bishops, four earls and four barons) to better advise the king or rather afford him that measure of backbone which appeared to be lacking. The council were undoubtedly the driving force behind overtures for a treaty of mutual support to be entered into with Philip IV. The delegation which travelled to France to negotiate comprised the bishops of St Andrews and Dunkeld, John de Soules and Ingram de Umfraville. The terms of the accord were agreed on 23 October and included provisions for mutual defensive and offensive action.

As an incentive there was the offer of a marriage alliance, King John to marry Jeanne de Valois, the king's niece. Even accepting the difficulties of his position there has to be some question as to Baliol's suitability for kingship. Furthermore there is doubt as to whether he was imbued with any great desire for the role. Later, in comfortable captivity, he is said to have admitted to Bek, his host that 'When he possessed and ruled the realm of Scotland as king and lord of the realm, he found in the men of that realm such malice, deceit, treason, and treachery, arising from their malignity, wickedness, and stratagems, and various other execrable and detestable actions'.[20]

To anyone as literally minded as Edward this dealing with France was treason. Baliol had yet to appear to respond in the MacDuff case and he had failed to hand over the three key castles demanded as a surety for his non-attendance. In law, Longshanks was now justified in resorting to force of arms. As proof of his resolve he appointed Bek and Earl Warenne as his deputies for all of the counties north of the Trent; Warenne was also given custody of Berwick (still in Scottish hands at this point) and Bruce, the Earl of Carrick, clearly no supporter of Baliol, was entrusted with Carlisle. On 16 October, Edward I as feudal superior formally demanded the surrender of the fortresses of Berwick, Roxburgh and Jedburgh. He also confiscated Baliol's lands in England. In December the king sent out writs summoning the host to appear at Newcastle by 1 March 1296. A state of open war was now imminent.

Open defiance was the Scottish response. Early in 1296 a general muster or *wapinschaw* (i.e. 'weapons show' or 'show of weapons') was proposed and the host called out for 11 March at Caddonlea near Selkirk. A wave of anti-English sentiment swept the country. English clergy were ousted and merchants harassed. At Berwick some sailors were said to have been murdered. Through his arrogance and high-handedness Edward had produced a degree of political unity in Scotland not seen since the appointment of the Guardians. The Bruce faction and the other pro-English magnates had no popular support; the political revolution of July 1295 illustrates just how determined the Scots had become to assert their independence.

The army which Edward I mustered to deal with his troublesome vassal was doubtless a large one. His expenditure incurred in the raising and maintaining of forces amounted to the very considerable sum of £21,443 12s, although this figure also included the costs associated with the troops then operating in Gascony.[21] On 23 January he had requested sufficient funds from the Exchequer to recruit 1,000 men-at-arms and a staggering 60,000 foot. If this were not enough, the Red Earl was commanded to provide a further 400 men-at-arms and 30,000 foot (in fact the Irish who mustered at Roxburgh on 13 May were barely ten per cent of this requirement).[22]

On 5 March the English army marched north out of Newcastle. Edward had arranged for the collection of the sacred banner of St John of Beverley to provide the requisite spiritual uplift. The Scots, wary of the size of the host coming against them and equally wary of the king's formidable military reputation, (in fact the last pitched battle in which Edward had led had been Evesham in 1265), had opted for a defensive strategy based on holding the border line itself. James the Steward held Roxburgh whilst William Douglas commanded at Berwick. The Scottish army was most assuredly not led by King John, now relegated to the role of hapless spectator. Command was in the hands of a general staff comprising seven earls: John Comyn of Buchan, Alexander Stewart of Menteith, Malise of Strathearn, Malcolm of Lennox, William of Ross, John Strathbogie of Athol and Donald of Mar. Prior to what would now be termed a pre-emptive strike the army moved into Annandale, Bruce's confiscated estates having been passed to Buchan. On 26 March, advancing in three columns, the Scots entered the English west march. From the outset this war was marked by a degree of merciless savagery that was to become all too familiar to marchers on both sides.

The land around Carlisle was thoroughly wasted and the city itself imperilled when a Scots spy managed to start a fire within the walls. The flames spread to a dangerous extent but the women took position on the ramparts whilst their menfolk fought the blaze. Two days later the Scots withdrew. Beyond burnt thatch and empty byres the raid had achieved nothing; moreover it had provided the moral justification Edward needed to assume the offensive. It was also on 28 March that the English crossed the Tweed and appeared before the walls of Berwick. The castle was formidable and Douglas, a name to reckon with, was no mean soldier.

Berwick's ramparts comprised nothing more substantial than a hastily repaired timber palisade with earthen ramparts and ditches. Despite the paucity of their defences the townsfolk remained defiant in the face of Edward's formal demand for unconditional surrender. Their replies were at best pithy, enlivened by obscenities and familiar gestures. Such conduct might provide inspiration for modern film makers but it was not the stuff of chivalry and such brimming overconfidence in the face of so potent an invader was to prove fatal. Edward was not a ruler noted for his sense of humour.

> King Edward wanne thu havest Berwick pike the
> Wanne thu havest geten dike the[23]

With due formality thus concluded the English host moved to leaguer the walls. In accordance with custom the king dubbed a number of new knights. The associated cheers and flaunting of banners persuaded the fleet lying in the Tweed estuary that an escalade was in progress and several vessels moved in to support. This proved unfortunate. The first ship ran aground and was promptly set on fire by the defenders, the crew cut down to a man, while the second was also engulfed in flames but the sailors managed to get off in the boats. First blood to the townsmen, but they did not have long to savour their success. A general assault from the landward side swiftly exposed the inadequacy of the wooden palisade, which was overcome, and the defenders pushed back into the narrow streets amidst scenes of frightful slaughter. Edward's men-at-arms, experienced in the Welsh and Gascon wars, had been quick to spot a weakness in the makeshift ramparts: 'where the townsfolk had made a path along the fosse, [the English] entered pell mell with those on horseback, whoever could get in first'.[24]

Resistance collapsed. Only a squad of determined Flemings, no more than thirty strong, held out in the Red Hall until it was burnt down around them. The attackers generally suffered few casualties although the young Richard of Cornwall, a son of the king's uncle, was amongst them, having unwisely lifted his helm to obtain a better view of the progress of the assault and receiving a fatal bolt for his pains. Although the women and children who survived the initial holocaust were permitted to depart, a significant proportion of the male population was left dead in the ashes, an atrocity which the Scots were never to forget. The castle surrendered on terms but the intransigent Douglas was to remain a captive.

Despite the fall of Berwick, Northumberland was not to escape unscathed. On 8 April, Ross, Menteith, Athol and Comyn of Badenoch launched a raid from Jedburgh against Redesdale, Coquetdale and Tynedale. The attack was stopped at Harbottle where the Umfraville castle resisted two days of assault but the Scots proved themselves the equals of the English in terms of frightfulness:

> They imbued their arms, hitherto unfleshed, with the blood of infirm people, old women, women in childbed, and even children two or three years old, proving themselves apt scholars in atrocity, in so much so that they raised aloft little span-long children pierced on pikes[25]

Having achieved no more with their second raid the Scots withdrew, falling back through Lothian and Teviotdale, gathering their resources to attempt to relieve the siege of Dunbar being undertaken by Earl Warenne. The castle was in the ownership of Patrick Dunbar, Earl of March, an English sympathiser serving with Edward at Berwick, but his defiant countess, a patriot, had taken advantage of his absence to open the gates to a Scottish force.

Undeterred by the prospect of facing the relieving army, which appeared around noon on 27 April, Warenne drew up ready to accept battle, leaving a masking force to contain the defenders. The Scots appeared over the brow of Spottismuir and Warenne, whose men were mainly mounted, moved forward to seek contact at the crossing of the Spot Burn which ran along the anticipated front line of both armies. The Scots mistook this manoeuvre for flight and whooped down for the chase. Warenne's charge smashed home, scattering the Scots and capturing most of their leaders. The fight dissolved into a rout and the Scottish army disintegrated.

For the hapless King John, this reverse, following upon the fall of Berwick, proved fatal. The English advance was now unopposed and Baliol was made to digest the full weight of his humiliation at Montrose, his coat of arms torn from him and flung to the ground, earning him the enduring sobriquet of 'Toom Tabard' – in the words of the chronicler Wyntoun:

This Johun the Balliol dispoyilyeide he
Offal his robis and ryalte.
The pellour that tuk out of his tabart,
Tuyme Tabart he was callit efftirwart;
And all other insignyis

That fel to kynge on any wise,
Baythe septure, suerde, crowne and rynge,
Fra this Johun, that he made kynge,

Hallely fra hym he tuk thar,
And mad hym of his kynrik bare[26]

Scotland was now no longer a kingdom, it was to be an English province, administered by a crown officer with vice-regal powers. Warenne was to be governor and the relics of kingship, the Stone of Destiny and the Black Rood of St Margaret were to be carried off to England as the spoils of conquest. A timid approach from the Earl of Carrick was met by a snarling royal rebuke[27] and the king is credited with a short, telling summary of his feelings towards Scotland when finally handing over the reins of government to Warenne: 'A man does good business when he rids himself of a turd'.[28] Before Edward left, all men of rank were obliged to swear an oath of allegiance at Berwick, the 'Ragman Roll'. The name of Malcolm Wallace of Elderslie is not on the roll, nor is that of his younger brother William; the estate of the elder brother was not a large one and William as the junior had no lands of his own. It is quite likely that Edward had never heard the name of William Wallace. If he had not then he would be hearing it a great deal in the following year.

Braveheart
William Wallace's earliest biographer was the poet Blind Harry, who died around 1385 but who likely relied upon more contemporary sources now lost.

Blind Harry's version of his hero's life is written on an epic scale as befits his subject and may tend to sensationalise certain events. It is not possible to determine the exact year of William's birth though it is certain he was still a young man, possibly very young, in 1297. Wallace simply erupts onto the political scene in May of that year with the slaughter of the hated William Heselrig, the English sheriff of Lanark. This may have been a calculated act of terrorism designed to unsettle the invader or an act of vengeance for the death, at Heselrig's hands or by his order, of the hero's lover, Marion Braidfute. She perished horribly with her family and retainers when the sheriff, frustrated in his efforts to capture the daring young outlaw, ordered her house to be burnt down.

> Gathering together a band of desperate men, he fell by night on the sheriff and his armed guard, hewed the sheriff into small pieces with his own sword and burned the buildings and those within them ... For the first time one of the high officials of the hated conquerors had been slain and a ripple of jubilation spread throughout the oppressed.[29]

Wallace was beyond doubt a born leader, a doughty fighter and a savage opponent. Physically strong, morally resolute, he did not shirk frightfulness. He was a dark warrior in a dark time.[30] Warenne was the king's lieutenant, assisted by Hugh Cressingham as treasurer and Walter of Amersham as chancellor, with the chief justiciar being William Ormsby. There is evidence that Warenne was less than zealous in his duties, preferring the relative comfort of his English estates. He was also ageing and his reactions during the coming conflagration were at best sluggish and lacking in that dash and élan he had displayed at Dunbar.

Having been the first to raise the flag of rebellion, Wallace unleashed the stirrings of discontent which had hitherto lacked any focus. Bruce was one who joined with both Wishart and the Steward. Responsibility for cowing these rebels was given to Henry Percy from Yorkshire and the Cumbrian knight, Robert Clifford.[31] Theirs was an effective partnership and before June was out they had penetrated as far as Ayr, both Bruce and the Steward sought terms; neither had struck a blow. Undeterred by this craven collapse, Wallace and his growing band of bandits cum guerrillas were sallying out from their lair in Selkirk Forest to wage war on English outposts. In the northeast Andrew Murray, son of Sir Andrew Murray of Petty, one of those knights who had been taken at the rout of Dunbar, also raised the flag of freedom.

Initially these outbreaks were not coordinated but by August Wallace was strong enough to take on the English garrison of Glasgow, commanded by the redoubtable Bishop Bek. After an extended skirmish the English came off worst and the Prince Bishop was obliged to retire behind the walls of Bothwell Castle. The English were to be expelled from Scotland, driven from their offices and benefices. Few who did not reach the shelter of the occupying garrisons were to leave alive. In the words of the English chronicler:

> They [the Scots] took old men, priests and women of the English nation (whom they had specially kept alive for the purpose) to bridges over the rivers; and when they had tied their hands or feet together so that they could not swim, they threw them or pushed them into the water, laughing and jeering as they struggled and went under.[32]

Warenne was obliged to begin a muster of troops to confront the swelling tide of revolt. By late summer Wallace and Murray had joined forces at Stirling and it was to be there that the inevitable confrontation took place. The Scottish forces, devoid of magnate support, were under the joint command of both guerrilla captains. Though their partnership was not destined to be a long one it appears to have been entirely amicable. In the first week of September the English, led by Warenne but with the increasing meddling of the obese treasurer, Cressingham, reached the town to find the patriots strongly posted to the north of the Forth. It is likely that the Scots had deployed a mile or so northeast of the wooden bridge spanning the river; this stood perhaps fifty yards upstream from the later sixteenth-century structure.

The bulk of their forces were drawn up on lower south-facing slopes of the Abbey Craig, which dominated the crossing point. From the high ground a timber causeway ran down to the bridge, the flatlands about being waterlogged meadow pasture, while a loop in the river covered the Scottish left. The position was a very strong one, ideal for defence, the bridge narrow and unsuitable for heavy horse. It is not possible to estimate with any semblance of accuracy the number of patriots Wallace and Murray commanded or even how many English they were facing. The Scots might have been three to four thousand strong, their opponents perhaps twice that number. Muttering about cost savings Cressingham had sent a detachment back!

When writing earlier to Edward, the treasurer had intimated that he had collected a force of three hundred horse and ten thousand foot, though the latter is very likely an exaggeration.[33] On past performance there was every reason to suspect that the patriots would not fight: the magnates, these men's feudal superiors, had crumbled easily enough in the confrontation at Irvine, they lacked heavy cavalry and had few men-at-arms. It is no mean testament to the grit and determination of these two young men that they refused to be cowed by the presence of an English field army. Murray had witnessed the

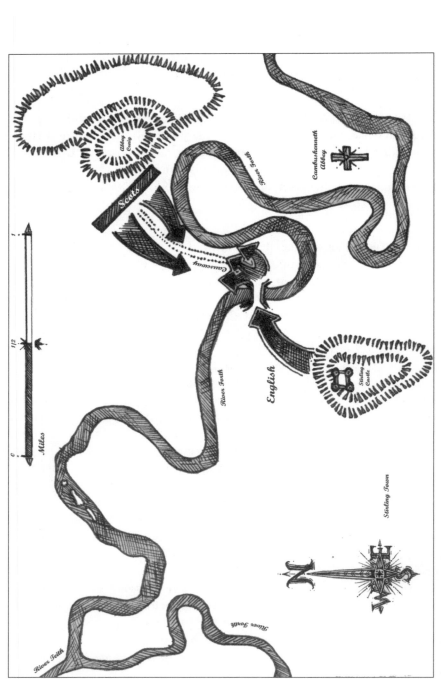

Stirling Bridge, 11 September 1297.

debacle at Dunbar, neither had ever commanded troops in pitched battle, the nobility had scarcely created an encouraging precedent.

Conflicting orders were given and a commanded party of mounted and dismounted men-at-arms was dispatched over the bridge. Presumably it was hoped that this manoeuvre would either tempt the Scots into abandoning their strong position and attacking or, being overawed, they would flee. Instead, the Scots launched a brilliantly-executed charge, hacking down knights and men-at-arms as they struggled to gain a lodgement. The Welsh, less encumbered, took to the water.

The press of men now trying to cross to succour their doomed comrades may have sufficed to bring down the wooden structure or the patriots might already have carried out some sabotage, but the wooden bridge collapsed beneath the great weight of armoured men and horses. Those already on the north bank were, for the most part, slaughtered. Cressingham, the hated tax gatherer, never lived to make the final audit, his gross carcass flayed by the vengeful patriots. Warenne seems to have lost his nerve completely, falling back upon Berwick with almost indecent haste, leaving Tweng to hold Stirling castle.

Edward had seriously misjudged the extent of the Scots capitulation. Insofar as the Community of the Realm was concerned, his domination of the magnates was unchallenged, the brief flurry of revolt that ended in humiliation at Irvine showed he was on firmer ground with the nobility. The notion of a popular rising led by sons of the minor gentry is unlikely to have featured in his calculations. Uppermost in his mind during the spring and summer of 1297 were the difficulties he faced in Gascony. Here two brigades were operating and these had had no reinforcement since being dispatched in the preceding January. One of the commanders had since died and the survivor, the Earl of Lincoln, was now hard pressed. Pushed onto the defensive he had been worsted at Bellegarde at the start of 1297. Anxious to relieve this pressure, Edward signed an accord with Guy of Flanders for mutual support but was desperately short of cash from which to fund additional troops.

The cost burden of the king's wars had severely squeezed the exchequer and increases in taxation were resented. In February 1296 Pope Boniface had issued a bull entitled '*Clericis Laicos*' which purported to prohibit the crown from taxing ecclesiastical revenues. Such a measure was bound to produce such howls of pain from impecunious monarchs that it had to be withdrawn, but the spirit of the edict was kept alive in England by the Archbishop of Canterbury, Robert Winchelsea. Edward ruthlessly countered the prelate's intransigence by outlawing the entire clergy who were then obliged to purchase a return to the umbrella of state protection, the consideration being equal to the amount of tax otherwise due. Such bullying cowed several of the leading clergy but not the archbishop, who remained boldly defiant.

The senior clergy were not alone in expressing their resentment of the king's autocratic style. Secular opposition was led by Roger Bigod, Earl of Norfolk, and the Earl of Hereford, Humphrey Bohun. Hereford, hereditary Earl Marshal and Constable, refused to serve abroad, despite threats from the king that his life would be forfeit. The earls knew this belligerence to be mere bluster as the king could not and almost certainly did not intend to make good on these threats. At the Salisbury Parliament in late February the rift widened to include Norfolk. Longshanks' position was increasingly untenable; he could not seek to prosecute foreign adventures and quell disturbances in Scotland whilst at war with both barons and bishops. In the end he was obliged to temporise, to seek an accommodation and be reconciled with his archbishop whilst promising the magnates that service overseas would be a matter of contract rather than obligation.

For Edward, the disaster at Stirling, whilst a signal humiliation, was not entirely devoid of benefit, the shock wave convinced both clergy and laity of the need for recompense from these upstart rebels. When Parliament met early in 1298 at Bury St Edmunds, Edward was voted a twelfth from the shires and an eighth from the towns. The clergy, asked for a fifth, vacillated. In Scotland, Wallace had not been idle. One of the casualties of Stirling was Murray himself who suffered wounds which were to prove fatal before the year was out. His injuries were such that he was unable to play any real part in the governance of the country in the wake of the English collapse. Wallace's strategy was now to capitalise upon victory and carry the war into northern England.

In the autumn he struck at Northumberland. Each man mounted on a sturdy garron, carrying everything he would need, fast moving, able to live off the land, strong enough to discourage any sporadic local opposition, fleet enough to avoid organised pursuit. These tactics, the hallmark of the successful guerrilla fighter, were totally effective. Terror, like a rampant virus, spread throughout the marches:

> the service of God totally ceased in all the monasteries and churches between Newcastle and Carlisle, for all the canons, monks and priests fled before the face of the Scots, as did nearly all the people.[34]

Tynedale was hard hit, as were both Coquetdale, and Redesdale. The Priory at Hexham had not been totally abandoned; it is said that three of the canons had remained, possibly in hiding. When discovered by Scots they were jostled and abused as the raiders demanded the surrender of the abbey's valuables. The harassed clergy retorted that there was nothing left to steal. Shamefaced

Wallace could only offer the canons' a letter of protection. He suggested he would like to hang the culprits but admitted such elements of his army were hard to control.[35]

It was then Cumberland's turn to feel the heat of the Scots passage with empty byres, smouldering thatch and the corpses of the slain stiffening in the ruins of their pastures. Wallace did make a demonstration against Carlisle, his emissary a priest who boldly summoned the city to surrender: 'William the Conqueror whom I serve, commands you to give up this town and castle without bloodshed; then you may leave unharmed with all your goods'.[36]

The citizens were not impressed. The Scots had no engines of war and though formidable in the field lacked the specialist skills and resources to crack so tough a nut as Carlisle. The bluff having failed, Wallace moved south of the city to beat up the settlements in and around the Inglewood Forest before swinging eastwards to fall upon Durham via Stainmoor.

Wallace, now dubbed as a knight, became sole Guardian. His task was not an easy one. He owed his position to the prestige of his victory at Stirling and all that he did was in the name of King John. This was not likely to appeal to the Bruce faction and Wallace was without a political faction of his own. From the start of the year he was keenly aware that the test of his office would come in the summer when the English invaded. To prepare for such a conflict required a major effort on a national scale – a field army had to be created and made ready to withstand Longshanks himself, the greatest commander of his age whose experience of warfare vastly exceeded that of Wallace and who, baronial and ecclesiastical dissent notwithstanding, had a far greater pool of resources.

It was inevitable that the backbone of the army would be infantry, spearmen for the most part, lightly armoured if at all, who would stand in their '*schiltrons*' to withstand the charge of mounted chivalry. Magnificent as the triumph at Stirling had been, Wallace would be well aware that the incompetence of the English command, their lack of cohesion and contempt had all played a part in delivering his enemy to him. He could hope for no such boon in the coming campaign.

The English muster was listed for Roxburgh on 25 June and the numbers were impressive, perhaps as many as 3,000 cavalry, 10,900 Welsh foot and 14,800 from England.[37] It was one thing to get men on the payroll, quite another to keep them there. Edwardian armies suffered very high levels of desertion; wounds and disease accounted for others. Precise numbers are, of course, impossible to provide, but in terms of suggesting how many actually took part in the battle to come, it would not be unreasonable to halve the totals for the English and Welsh foot. The king was also careful to ensure the army was not without spiritual leadership – he raised the banner of St John of Beverley and that of St Cuthbert.

By July the English army was lumbering through the Lothians, the fleet keeping pace off the east coast. Bek had been detailed to capture Dirleton and a couple of outposts but the Scots did not appear to offer battle. Despite the habitual thoroughness of Edward's logistical planning, food began to run short – a large army on the move is a hungry beast, needing fresh meat and corn, small beer, ale and wine (the former was scarcely a luxury as most water was unfit for drinking). At one point the fleet was able to offload several tuns of wine. Strong drink and empty stomachs are a bad mix and contributed to an unseemly fracas between the English and the Welsh. By the third week of the month matters had become serious and Edward, facing a will o' the wisp opponent, would have to start thinking of retreat.

Two Scottish lords in his service, Gilbert Umfraville and Patrick Dunbar, Earl of March, brought intelligence that they had espied the Scottish host encamped less than fifteen miles away by Callendar Wood.[38] The English spent the short summer night bivouacked to the east of Linlithgow, confident that battle would be joined the following day. In the night Edward's destrier broke free and trampled its master, severely bruising his ribs. A lesser man might have taken this as an ill omen; the king, as one might suppose, merely gritted his teeth.

To commit to the full hazard of battle is always dangerous. Wallace, in reality, had never fought a major engagement in open field. The victory at Stirling, impressive as it was had been opportunistic, brilliantly so, but represents an extension of guerrilla activity. Now he chose his ground with care, his forces deployed on the southern flank of the wood, their front crossed by the fast-flowing burn which at its confluence with another stream running downhill from Glen village created a marshy plain, difficult to detect but largely impassable to heavy cavalry. The foot, made up from the general levy of adult males aged between sixteen and sixty, were formed into four commanded brigades of perhaps fifteen hundred men each. These *schiltrons* bristled with a hedge of iron-tipped twelve-foot spears, front rank kneeling, second rank with staves levelled over the shoulders of the first. Each was encircled with a line of stakes, roped or chained together, creating a makeshift palisade.

Perhaps the prime purpose of these defensive formations was to resist the English chivalry. Wallace did have horsemen but they were few. He also had a contingent of bowmen under Sir John Stewart whose function was to provide missile troops to shield the spearmen from the lethal volleys from Edward's English and Welsh archers. The Scottish horse were there to protect the missile troops deployed in the open between the *schiltrons* from being ridden down. These dispositions were all sound but suffered from several telling flaws. The mounted arm, regardless of their subsequent conduct, were, from the outset, at a significant numerical disadvantage. In the shock of impact, as the mounted charge thundered home, their survival was precarious. Without them, however, the bowmen were exposed – if the archers were routed then the *schiltron*s, who need not fear cavalry if they held firm, were, in turn, horribly vulnerable to the arrow storm.

The bristling hedgehogs of spears were protected to their front by the morass but this, in turn, would impede them if they tried to advance. The *schiltron*, like the Macedonian phalanx, was intended as an offensive as well as a defensive formation. Indeed, when faced by missile troops, the spearmen had to be able to advance swiftly to contact or be shot down where they stood. It may be that Wallace did not feel sufficiently confident in the training of his men to contemplate offensive manoeuvring.

A brace of English earls, those of Norfolk and Hereford commanded the van – a politic selection as these magnates had been amongst the king's most vociferous opponents, Bek led the centre whilst Edward himself commanded the rear. The earls, hungry for glory and not mindful to attend upon the baser bowmen as they loosed, spurred into a precipitate charge. The morass rather spoiled their move and similarly discommoded the Prince Bishop, both wings being obliged to echelon sharply to avoid the obstacle. Once the horse came to contact they met a resolute hedge of spears, the attack faltered.

Bishop Bek, in similar difficulties, began a very public row with his second in command Ralph Bisset, who would have none of his superior's caution. Although these attacks could not budge the *schiltron*s, the weight of English horse served to unman the Scots knights who promptly turned tail and fled the field. Sir John Stewart and his gallant bowmen were slaughtered. Edward now took control, recalling the cavalry and advancing his archers and Gascon cross-bowmen. These had a perfect target: though they had seen off the horse, the spearmen had no protection against missile troops and the arrow storm burst upon them.

Untried, largely untrained, mostly unarmoured and now unsupported, the *schiltron*s nonetheless held their ground, even as their casualties mounted, gaps appearing in the line as men fell and reserves were used up. By mere valour they stood firm but, judging the moment, Edward called a halt to the barrage and sent the cavalry back into the assault. The *schiltron*s, dreadfully thinned, could no longer maintain their unbroken line. The knights hacked and battered their way through the spears, slashing and trampling. Hundreds died: 'they fell like blossoms in an orchard when the fruit has ripened'.[39]

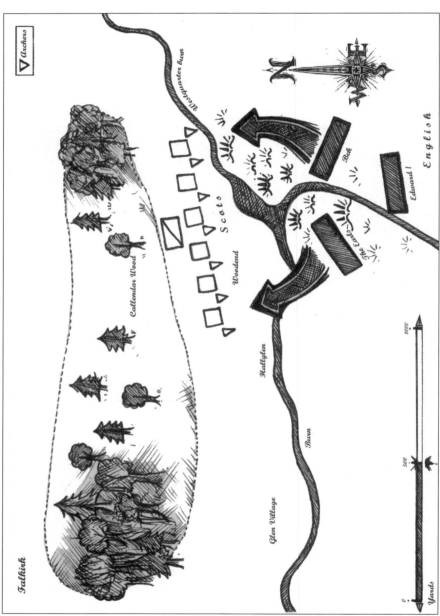

Falkirk, 22 July 1298.

Failure was palpable and costly but not shameful, not a debacle such as Dunbar. Wallace's untried militia had fought well and died hard, the *schiltrons* had succeeded in holding off heavy cavalry, a significant achievement and one which the English were to forget. The 'what might have been" was probably not much considered in the rush of victory but the heavy horse had little to celebrate. The spears had, in reality, been broken by missile troops. Had the *schiltrons* been able to move forward rapidly and attack, the outcome might have been very different. The Scots learnt from the defeat at Falkirk, the English did not.

A great battle had been won, the disaster at Stirling avenged and the upstart Wallace driven back into the hills. This did not imply that the war was necessarily over, however. The Guardian was neither dead nor taken and Edward himself was not free of political difficulties. His earlier opponents, Norfolk and Hereford, had agreed to serve only on the understanding that the king would honour his earlier concessions – both men knew Edward of old and probably suspected that, in the flush of success, the king might be tempted to renege on his earlier undertakings. This tension was exacerbated when, still at Carlisle, Edward granted the lordship of Arran to Thomas Bisset, an Irish peer from Antrim. Both magnates now left the army but the king was bent on further distributions of confiscated Scottish estates. He did refrain from granting lands in Annandale and Galloway so as to avoid further alienating Norfolk and Hereford, but he still gave Caerlaverock to Clifford and the Steward's estates went to the Earl of Lincoln. A number of these dispositions were made more in expectation than in reality.[40]

After sustaining so great a defeat as Falkirk, Wallace could not hope to remain in office as Guardian and he relinquished the post. As a commoner he could not fall back upon an established affinity, who might still form the nucleus of a viable faction. His position rested upon prowess and prestige, without one he must lose the other. His relationship with Bruce is uncertain, as indeed is the latter's role, if any, in the battle. The defeat had robbed him and Scotland of a viable field army. This did not operate in any way to prevent Wallace resuming the life of a bandit cum guerrilla which he had pursued so successfully before. The immediate following of diehards who clung to him would not desert him now. The next year he left Scotland on a form of diplomatic mission to the continent, first attending the court of Philip IV and in 1300 perhaps journeying as far as Bergen for an audience with Haakon V.

Despite the earlier accord between France and Scotland, relations had now cooled and Philip had come to an agreement with Edward in June 1299 at Montreuil-sur-Mer incorporating a proposed union between the widower

Edward and Philip's sister Margaret. There is a suggestion therefore that the French king found the Scots emissary something of an embarrassment and even offered to detain Wallace in France.[41] If this proposal was made then perhaps the Scots got wind of it and wisely decamped beforehand. At this time there is no particular evidence to suggest that Edward bore Wallace any marked ill will – the furious vengeance he was to pursue seems to have arisen later.

In 1299, Longshanks was aware that the victory at Falkirk had not entirely crushed resistance and whilst the patriots might be cowed they were not yet submissive. His plans for a further campaign in that year were frustrated by politics in both England and France, leading up to his accord with Philip which would leave him free to pursue a more proactive role in 1300. Bruce and John Comyn of Badenoch had been appointed as joint guardians, a partnership that veered between covert and outright antagonism. Comyn was a Baliol partisan, as Wallace had been, whilst Bruce was considerably less enthusiastic, being far more concerned with his own advancement. During August, at a meeting in Peebles the hostility between these volatile lords erupted into violence, with blows exchanged and daggers drawn. The argument had been fuelled by a dispute over the legality of Wallace's departure for France. His brother Malcolm was present and clearly seems to have been aligned with Bruce, notwithstanding that the Steward was his feudal superior.

Once tempers had cooled it was recognised that the continued partnership had no future and Bishop Lamberton of St Andrews was elected as Guardian, with Bruce and Comyn acting as deputies under his direction. William Lamberton was a determined patriot, an ally of Wallace who, as Guardian, had lobbied for his elevation when the existing incumbent had died in 1297. Lamberton was also closely identified with Bishop Wishart of Glasgow. He leaned more towards Bruce than Comyn and indeed had grappled with Buchan in the course of the unseemly fracas at Peebles.

At the time his sponsor Wallace was suffering disaster at Falkirk, the Bishop of St Andrews was on a diplomatic mission to lobby support from the Pope. He was regarded as sufficiently dangerous to merit an unsuccessful attempt to intercept and capture him whilst on the return journey. Patriot sentiment was therefore divided between those who wholeheartedly fought for King John and those who despaired of their king but accepted his role as a necessary figurehead. In one respect the eclipse of Wallace strengthened the patriot cause in that the nobility, who would not deign to serve under a commoner, would be easier with guardians drawn from the magnate class and more likely to relinquish their allegiance to the king of England.

Under the 'Hammer'

In reality the English grip was truly effective only in the southeast, the Lothians and the Merse, with a powerful garrison stationed at Berwick – as many as one hundred men-at-arms, a thousand foot and a further hundred crossbowmen.[42] Wallace's chevauchée in 1297 had shown the vulnerability of the English marches and Edward had been at pains to prevent a repeat. Successful captains such as Robert Clifford, William Latimer, Robert Hastangs, John of St John and Patrick Dunbar were appointed to key positions. The Scot, Dunbar, Earl of March, was given a commission to hold down his countrymen south of the Forth whilst Clifford held the English west march and Walter de Huntercombe the east. Nonetheless Caerlaverock fell to the patriots which left Lochmaben isolated. There was a skirmish between the two garrisons in which the Scots appear to have been worsted and an attempt to besiege Lochmaben came to nothing.

Frustrated by being unable to control events, Edward rather rashly determined upon a winter campaign in November 1299. Support from the magnates was lacking and the king's summons for a muster of 16,000 foot at Newcastle produced no more than 2,500, most of whom quickly deserted. The projected campaign proved farcical and failed to prevent the fall of Stirling, a major boost to the patriot cause. Edward resolved upon a major effort during the summer of 1300 and the summons sent out from Carlisle at the end of the year show that some forty knights and 366 sergeants were called up for unpaid feudal service, these were augmented by some three score of gentlemen volunteers with their affinities, perhaps ten–twelve men per squad or 'lance'. The Royal Household contained over 500 on retainer, boosted by recruitment to perhaps 850, all mounted.[43]

The army was marshalled into the usual four divisions, the first under the Earl of Lincoln, the second Earl Warenne, next the king's brigade and lastly that under the nominal command of Edward of Caernarvon, then only sixteen years old. Actual command in the field was exercised by John of St John.[44] The foot contingents were raised by commissions of array from Nottinghamshire, Derby and the four northern counties. A total of 16,000 infantry was required but perhaps just more than half of that number actually mustered at Carlisle. No Welsh were recruited. The king could clearly recall the difficulties of the Falkirk campaign and his remarks concerning his Welsh subjects, heavy with irony, do support the view that he was not entirely devoid of humour: 'We have given them leave to remain at home, because of all the great work which they have done in our service in the past'.[45]

This great array was fed by an enormous logistical effort. Thirty ships from the Cinque Ports responded to the feudal summons but their unpaid service was limited to a fortnight and thereafter the 1,106 men who crewed these vessels were to be retained on wages. A further squadron of fifteen lighter vessels and a couple of galleys were also chartered. Provisions from Ulster were carried in a further flotilla of eight Irish craft which plied the narrow sea to Carlisle. The link between England's westerly bastion and Northern Ireland was well established and the ports of Ulster were a major source of re-supply for the Carlisle garrison (the Irish vessels also conveyed 300 tuns of wine).[46]

The field army marched from Carlisle on 4 July, advancing by Annan to Ecclefechan, swinging westward to Lochmaben and Dumfries before approaching the red sandstone walls of Caerlaverock, held by a patriot garrison. For five days Edward's men-at-arms made repeated and totally futile assaults and each escalade was thrown back. This was mere knightly horseplay: the real work was done by the siege engines. These great trebuchets hurled hundred-weight boulders clear over the ramparts to smash down into the courtyard and buildings below, pulverising timber-framed structures and sending lethal slivers of stone flying like shrapnel. The sixty-odd defenders capitulated. No terms were offered and most were imprisoned – rebels did not figure in the chivalric code.

Capturing the castle of Caerlaverock, important as it was, amounted to a very poor return for such heavy expenditure, but the campaign was dogged by foul weather and the patriots cannily refused battle. Buchan, together with his kinsman Comyn of Badenoch, attempted to open negotiations for a truce when the royal army, wet, filthy and with the foot deserting in droves, tramped into Kirkcudbright. Their demands reflected a not inconsiderable level of confidence – they required the return of King John together with restitution of forfeited estates.

The talks stalled as the English infantry continued to melt away – fresh recruits, en route to Carlisle were deserting before they even saw the marches![47] The cavalry managed to win a skirmish against a Scots force led by Robert Keith the Marischal whose attempt to 'beat up' a foraging party by the banks of the River Cree was forestalled and he himself was taken captive. After the negotiations foundered the Scots appeared in force and a further confrontation took place, with both armies facing each other over the Cree. The Comyns were joined by Ingram Umfraville. The stand-off continued for a while, with neither side taking the offensive. Ironically it was the despised and depleted English foot who began the action by advancing, presumably without orders. The horse was drawn in after and a desultory combat ensued.

This was not an occasion when Scottish arms earned distinction, rather they fled like a summer haze, leaving their baggage and supplies, melting back into the sheltering hills and mosses. It was perhaps at this point the king missed his nimble-footed Welshmen who could have turned the precipitate withdrawal into a costly rout. If the Scots were embarrassed they were certainly undefeated and there was little more for Edward to do. As the fine rain continued to fall the army moved, on 16 August, to Wigton, but the campaign was effectively over. By the end of the month the king was back in Carlisle with little to show for his efforts.

Though neither side could claim any substantive edge in the military stakes, the Scots were enjoying some success on the diplomatic front. Their pleas to the Curia resulted, on 27th June 1299, in an admonition delivered by Boniface VIII – '*Scimus Fili*' ('We know my son'). This rejection of Edward's claim flew in the face of an earlier recognition, though, due to the envoy's persuasive entreaties, it made reference to the guarantees provided within the Treaty of Birgham–Northampton. The unwilling messenger was Archbishop Winchelsea who knew the weight of the king's wrath all too well, threatened with suspension from his see if he prevaricated. Having finally tracked Edward to the northern frontier the archbishop was kept waiting and faced the inevitable explosion when the king comprehended the full measure of papal disfavour.

Longshanks was never either more wily or more resolute than when facing a crisis. Age had robbed him of neither grit nor guile. The marches were a long way from Rome and matters might be favourably resolved before the intervention could bite. In the autumn of 1300, however, the Patriots' political and military situation was far from promising. The Scots had lost a major bastion and their army had been seen off with only the whisper of a fight. Equally, Edward's expensive campaign had entirely failed to cow the patriots, who were honing their skills as guerrilla fighters, learning to exploit English weaknesses without exposing their own. A further round of talks was held at Dumfries, but again these failed to reach any consensus. Philip IV had proposed a truce, to last until 21 May the following year; the king was glad to agree. Putting the lull to good use, Edward concentrated on mending his fences with the disaffected magnates. Although he procrastinated endlessly, the king was eventually forced to give way and reaffirm both Magna Carta and the Charter of the Forest.[48] The swell of opposition had been growing more vociferous and Longshanks was an old hand at recognizing the moment for compromise, however insincere his utterances might subsequently prove.

As an immediate riposte to '*Scimus Fili*', an embassy was dispatched to the Curia in November, led by the Earl of Lincoln and Hugh Despenser. The advertised purpose was to caretake the Anglo-French dispute but the matter of Scotland had been thoroughly researched and a detailed rebuttal of the patriot case prepared. This defence was approved by the Lincoln Parliament. Let the advocates haggle in the corridors of the Vatican; Edward was resolved on a fresh campaign in 1301. Summonses were issued in late winter for a muster on 24 June. The assault would involve two columns, one from Berwick under the direct command of the king, the other from Carlisle under the nominal leadership of Caernarvon, guided by the experienced Lincoln.

As in the previous season, recruitment of adequate numbers of foot proved problematic. Some 7,500 appeared at Berwick, rather more in the west from whence the main offensive was to be mounted, while from across the water the Justiciar, John Wogan, mustered an Irish brigade. The king's brigade marched westward from Berwick along the banks of the Tweed in mid-July, crossing at Coldstream before moving via Traquair to Peebles, whilst the prince advanced on Glasgow, probably through Nithsdale.[50] Caernarvon was on Clydeside by 23 August and the following month laid siege to Bothwell Castle. As ever the English were able to demonstrate first-rate engineering skills: a movable siege tower or belfry was erected *in situ,* the various sections having been disassembled and transported on carts. By 24 September the castle had fallen, followed soon after by Turnberry.

The king went into winter quarters at Linlithgow where he was joined by his son once the bulk of the army had retired to the border. Edward's great scheme for the winter was the construction of a bridge over the Forth, the 'Scottish Sea'.[51] But the attempt foundered through lack of funds. Had the project gone ahead, 'we would have achieved such a success against our enemies, that our business in these parts would have been brought to a satisfactory and honourable conclusion'.[52] Not only did the engineering vision evaporate for lack of funds but troops were again deserting in droves – the prospect of a winter campaign in Scotland failed to enthuse and the lateness of the season may also have prevented Edward from seeking to recover Stirling.

Any plans for a renewed offensive in the spring had to be postponed due to the difficulties the English ambassadors were encountering at the Curia. Thomas Delisle and Thomas Wale had found His Holiness polite, outwardly accommodating, but totally non-committal. Edward was by no means the only master of prevarication. In the meantime, their Scottish counterpart, Baldred Bisset, appeared to be doing rather better. He and his colleagues had submitted a counter-history of relations between the two kingdoms with an equally Homeric royal lineage beginning with a Princess of Egypt.[53]

Bisset was able to argue that the English were by no means in possession of the realm; John de Soules was now Guardian and whilst he avoided direct confrontation with the invader and won no battles, neither did he suffer any defeat. With no progress being made in Rome, Edward was prepared to agree to a truce to endure from 21 January until November. Baliol had already, in the course of the previous summer, been released into the care of Philip IV and subsequently fades into genteel obscurity. The negotiations with the French, who were also instrumental in brokering the Anglo-Scottish truce of 1302, had begun at Canterbury early in the preceding year. A powerful team of English negotiators comprised the earls of Surrey and Warwick, Aymer de Valence, John of St John and Hugh de Vere.

Though the French might have won the concession over custody of John Baliol, they could not extract any recognition that he was still King of Scots – that thorny question remained open. The talks continued across the Channel at Asnieres, where the lead negotiator on the English side appears to have been Walter Langdon, Bishop of Coventry and Chester, a highly skilled diplomat who had held a series of important royal posts including those of Treasurer and Keeper of the Wardrobe. If the French held Baliol and the Pope was undecided, Edward still had the loyalty of the Bruces; their claim could always be dusted down and re-glossed. Although there was no campaign on the border in that year there was action in Flanders, where the chivalry of France was severely checked by Flemish spears at Courtrai.[54]

Faced with such a serious reverse on his own doorstep, Philip could not afford continued enmity with England. In these changed circumstances support for the Scots became a burdensome luxury and was cynically put aside. Pope Boniface was also losing interest in the whole tangled business so the patriots suddenly found themselves cast adrift.

The Scots were sensitive to the shift in the weather vane and in 1303 sent a powerful embassy to Philip to try to bolster their position. The Guardian, Bishop Lamberton of St Andrews, Bishop Crambeth of Dunkeld, Buchan and the Steward hastened to Paris. The king of France remained distracted by the consequences of the debacle at Courtrai, his own difficulties with the Curia and pro-English disturbances which had arisen in Bordeaux. The final draft of the treaty with Edward was sealed in Paris on 20 May 1303.

In terms of strict protocol Philip had not abandoned the Scots; he held a power of attorney from Baliol to act on his behalf and on behalf of his country as he thought fit. Five days after completion of the alliance the Scots ambassadors wrote to their countrymen advising them of the situation. John Comyn was acting Guardian during de Soules' absence; it was very bad news indeed and the pragmatists in the patriot ranks began inevitably to think of coming to terms with Longshanks. Lamberton wrote privately to Wallace, no doubt to urge him to continue the struggle.

Whilst the truce of 1302 held, the English had been able to maintain garrisons, perhaps a thousand men all told, guarding the key bastions of Berwick, Roxburgh, Jedburgh, Edinburgh, Linlithgow, Dumfries and Lochmaben.[55] Still short of money, Edward could not hope to repeat his feats of castle-building. His programme of military architecture might have sealed the conquest of Wales but without adequate cash resources could not be replicated in Scotland. In the autumn of that year the patriots took the field led by John Comyn and Simon Fraser. Sallying out from Selkirk Forest they took the nearby tower and briefly encircled Linlithgow. Edward's lieutenant in Scotland, John de Segrave, had been ordered to lead a reconnaissance which, early in the year, was to advance as far north as Kirkintilloch.

To counter the patriots a force was mustered at Wark under the army paymaster Ralph Manton, marching in search of the Scots in three disparate columns. Comyn and Fraser seized the moment and the initiative fell upon the battalion led by Segrave at Roslyn. In the fight the commander, his brother and sixteen other knights were captured, including Manton. Ralph Neville brought up his men to relieve the survivors. An order was given to put the prisoners to the sword but in the event only Manton was slain, apparently after trying to bargain for his life, offering the army's pay chest as a ransom. Fraser was not moved and killed the paymaster, 'cutting off his hands and his head'.[56]

These alarums were not permitted to distract the king from his intentions. The campaign of 1303 needed fewer troops than in previous years, perhaps 7,500 foot in total, and a correspondingly low turnout of mounted men-at-arms. Edward realised that the Scots would be likely to decline battle and that a large field army would merely consume additional resources to no advantage. He did get his bridge across the Forth: not the grand affair he might have envisaged but a series of pontoons, designed and built at King's Lynn and floated up the east coast.[57] Safely over the Scottish Sea, the English laid siege to and took Brechin Castle.[58]

Continuing his Fabian tactics the Guardian offered no serious resistance and Edward's advance proceeded unchallenged as far as the Moray Firth, setting the stamp of royal authority along the length of the northeast coast. In September the army turned south from Kinloss to Lochindorb and thence to Boat of Garten, following the banks of the Spey towards Kildrummy. By 5 November the king had established winter quarters in Dunfermline.

Whilst Edward was conducting his leisurely chevauchée north of the Forth, Aymer de Valence was active in the Lothians. Here the English power did not go unchallenged. Wallace had returned to Scotland and, along with Simon Fraser, was actively raiding the outposts with Segrave, Clifford and Latimer in fitful pursuit. More violence flared in the west when the formidable Red Earl, with a force of some 3,457 Irish kerns carried in 173 ships, mounted an amphibious attack on Bute aimed at securing Rothesay Castle, before striking at Clydeside and scrimmaging with patriot forces at Inverkip.[59]

It is hard to gauge the effect, if any, on patriot morale of Wallace's return. Emerging from his old stamping grounds in Selkirk Forest he was still potent, but command appears to have been shared with Fraser and John Comyn. Annandale and Liddesdale were targeted, as was the English west march, the former undoubtedly harried to chastise Bruce for his defection, though Fraser himself had only reverted to his patriot allegiance despite having taken part in the siege of Caerlaverock in 1300.

In January 1304 and still acting in concert, Segrave, Clifford and Latimer led a commanded party out of Dunfermline seeking to beat up patriot forces south of the Forth. The raid was planned meticulously and in total secrecy. At Happenrew the English encountered both Wallace and Fraser, inflicting a sharp reverse and, though both leaders escaped the carnage, their position was greatly weakened. The increasingly isolated position of these diehard patriots was further marginalised when, at Strathord near Perth, the majority of the magnates submitted to Edward. They had accepted that without French support and without a second front in Gascony the king was free to concentrate his resources wholly against Scotland. The result of this was inevitable: Scotland would be conquered; Edward had already promised that the time was ripe, as he put it for 'an end to the business'.[60]

Only John Comyn refused unconditional surrender. As acting Guardian he demanded that all who submitted should be spared life and lands, that the laws of Scotland should be preserved as they had stood in the reign of Alexander III and not be varied or set aside without the consent of the Community of the Realm, a brave attempt to preserve the ideal of an independent kingdom. Edward had at least learned that savagery would achieve nothing and, with victory in his grasp, he could afford a show of magnanimity.

Those who submitted escaped without forfeit; those who had been dispossessed had an opportunity to buy back the lands they had lost, the tariff fixed by a sliding scale according to the perceived gravity of the buyer's intransigence. The Steward, Ingram Umfraville and de Soules were excluded from the general amnesty. They were not to be included in the general amnesty until William Wallace, that persistent thorn, was finally dealt with. Thus the problem of this most constant patriot became a problem for the nobility of Scotland. De Soules, not deigning to submit, preferred exile in France. The guarantees Comyn required were not forthcoming, although the king did advise he would give consideration to constitutional matters once Comyn had made his submission.

Edward had won – only the mopping up remained. True, Wallace and Fraser remained at large and the defenders of Stirling under William Oliphant still held out, but the king's authority was otherwise unchallenged. Leaving his winter quarters at Dunfermline, Longshanks summoned a Parliament at St Andrews which promptly outlawed these remaining patriots. Wallace was an outcast in his own country. The victor of Stirling Bridge, who with Andrew Murray had effectively re-invented the patriot cause, was not only abandoned but was to be hunted by his countrymen. Such were the bitter dregs of defeat.

The king could not claim to control Scotland fully whilst the garrison of Stirling Castle continued in defiance. The siege began in April. Oliphant's position was a delicate one – the Scots Parliament had disowned him but, in the course of parlay, he observed that his command had been conferred directly by de Soules and thus only the absent Guardian could order a capitulation. This was a neat argument and not without merit – as de Soules was in exile no early reply could be expected and the leaguer commenced in earnest.

Edward's master artillerist, Reginald the Engineer, had pulled together an impressive siege train with engines brought in sections, two from Brechin and one from Aberdeen. Caernarvon was commanded to oversee the stripping of church roofs at Perth and Dunblane to provide sufficient lead for the counter-weights needed to balance the massive trebuchets. A major logistical exercise was undertaken to tighten the net on Stirling's defenders; as well as carpenters, joiners and skilled labourers, arms, armour, crossbows and the components of Greek fire (sulphur and saltpetre) were supplied from across the counties of England.[61]

Great engines such as 'Segrave', 'Forster' and 'Robinet' rained a constant barrage of missiles down upon the defenders. Open spaces within the enceinte became killing grounds as crashing boulders spat a blizzard of lethal shards. The defenders survived by crowding into caves and cellars burrowed into the living rock on which the fortress stands. Edward was very much in his element, revelling in the fury of the siege, disdaining fire from the walls even when a bolt struck his saddle.

More successful was the manufacture of the massive trebuchet, 'Warwolf'. This great engine required a team of five master carpenters and fifty journeymen to assist. The building process was so laborious that the device was not ready to shoot until 20 July, by which time the garrison were already suing for terms. Not to be denied the spectacle of his creation in action Edward refused to allow a formal surrender until Warwolf had fulfilled its function. No terms were offered and Oliphant and his men must have feared the worst, but despite dramatic posturing, the king allowed himself to be persuaded towards leniency and their lives were spared. By the high summer of 1304 Edward had returned south to England, the 'business', as he had predicted, having been concluded.

Almost concluded – William Wallace was a brutal and vengeful man in an age of total war and all its attendant horrors. Alone of all the Scots patriot leaders he had never compromised. More resolute than Fraser, Comyn and certainly Bruce, he would remain defiant to the last. That end came in August 1305 when he was finally captured by John of Menteith near Glasgow. He was taken to London and tried at Westminster Hall on the twenty-third day of that month. 'Trial' is perhaps something of a misnomer for the accused was permitted neither voice nor representation. As an outlaw he could not expect the benefit of due process. The verdict was never in doubt and he suffered the full rigours of the sentence.[62]

In September 1305 the English Parliament debated the constitutional position of Scotland, nine or ten peers meeting with a score of the king's councillors. John of Brittany was appointed as lieutenant of the 'land' The use of the term 'realm' was carefully avoided and a series of administrative appointments were made. Most of the key bastions remained under English castellans; only Stirling and Dumbarton were given local commanders. There was to be a thorough overhaul of the Scottish legal system, with many of the more ancient and anachronistic processes deleted – in fairness to Edward this was probably overdue.

Edward's proposals for the governance of Scotland were neither harsh nor arbitrary – there was consultation, even if the matter of sovereignty was closed to debate. Edward had learnt that a gentler hand was needed, the arrogance of the earlier settlement of 1296–7 was avoided. As one modern biographer has observed: 'It was no small achievement for this elderly, conventional, conservative, unimaginative man that he had learnt anything at all'.[63]

In the end, the Edwardian conquest failed, but not while Longshanks lived – it was his uninterested, self-obsessed son who was to fail. Whilst the old king remained active he seemed invincible in the field. Indeed, he appeared to hold the magnates of Scotland in thrall; they seemed incapable of resisting him for any length of time:

> Edward I failed in his Scottish Wars. The task of conquering Scotland was an immense one, and failure is perhaps less surprising than the degree of success which the king achieved. His armies proved invincible in large scale battles, as Falkirk showed, and his engineers had an impressive record in siege warfare.[64]

That the durability of the conquest should prove so fragile derives from a number of factors. Edward had circled Wales with a ring of great concentric castles, Rhuddlan, Harlech, Conwy, Caernarfon and Beaumaris, even if the latter remained in its incomplete state due to a lack of funding. There was no more money to achieve a similar effect in Scotland so the king was obliged to rely on maintaining existing castles, supported by rather ad hoc outposts, invariably thrown up in timber and earth.

By the end of 1305 it must have appeared to English and Scots alike that the business was indeed now at an end, with Scotland's future as a province of the Plantagenet empire confirmed. That the settlement, not even a year old, should be destroyed by the chain of events unleashed by a brutal murder in the hallowed precincts of Blackfriar's Kirk in Dumfries would have seemed inconceivable. Scotland's greatest paladin was about to take the stage.

Chapter 4

Robert Bruce

*It was indeed a mighty undertaking that the king began, taking unbearable burdens
upon his shoulders, for not only did he raise his hand against the mighty king of
England and all his confederates and flatterers, but also devoted himself to a
struggle against one and all in the kingdom of Scotland . . . like a drop of water
reckoned against the waves of the sea.*
  – Walter Bower, *Scotichronicon*[1]

*Yet something fixed outlined the impulse.
His very health was dressed to kill.
He had an acrobat's love of self
Balancing body was his skill
Against the uniform space of death.*
  – Thom Gunn, *The Corporal*

Murder and sacrilege

The rebellion of Robert Bruce, Earl of Carrick, which was to change the entire
direction of the war with England and ultimately lead to the triumph of the
patriot cause, a success so telling that the flame of nationhood could never
thenceforth be extinguished, began with an act of murder. Worse, the killing
was compounded with sacrilege as the victim's blood was spilt on consecrated
ground. Quite why Bruce, on 10 February 1306, decided to stab to death John
Comyn of Badenoch, 'the Red Comyn', in the Greyfriars' church in Dumfries
has never been fully explained.

It cannot be that the killing was premeditated for only a fool would choose to
slaughter his victim in church. There had always been bad blood between the
two and this had erupted into violence before. It is possible that Bruce and
Comyn had entered into a pact or band between them whereby Comyn would
support Bruce as a candidate for the throne in return for the broad acres of his
earldom, whereupon Comyn had promptly confessed the scheme to Edward.
Bruce, when confronted with the damning evidence, could only temporize, re-
questing a night's respite to consider his position.

As he repaired to his lodgings, a page of the Earl of Gloucester's household brought him the gift of a shilling and a pair of spurs – a broad hint to be on his way as speedily as he might. Using the coin to reward the messenger, Bruce galloped north by forced stages to reach the temporary sanctuary of Lochmaben Castle. He arranged to meet Comyn in the Franciscan convent in the town, where the latter was accused of treachery. Harsh words and a blow struck in anger followed and the wounded man was bloodily dispatched by one of the earl's affinity.[2]

The affair is reported tersely in the English king's diatribe to Rome in condemnation of Bishop Lamberton of St Andrews:

> When Lamberton was made chief Guardian, Bruce rose against king Edward as a traitor, and murdered Sir John Comyn, lord of Badenoch, in the church of the Friars Minor of the town of Dumfries, by the high altar, because Sir John would not assent to the treason which Robert planned to perpetrate against the king of England, namely, to resume war against him and make himself King of Scotland.[3]

Comyn's violent demise was not a beacon to rekindle the patriot cause; on the contrary it ensured a vendetta with his surviving kin. It need not detract from the achievement of Robert Bruce that his rebellion was sparked by a need for self-preservation rather than a loftier ideal of freedom from the English yoke. The move was daring to the point of foolhardiness. Bruce had received few tokens from Edward since his defection from the patriots four years earlier and he may have chafed at this. It is uncertain when his wife Isabel, a daughter of the Earl of Mar, had died but he had, in 1302, married his second consort, Elizabeth de Burgh, child of the Red Earl of Ulster, an advantageous match, though as yet without issue. At twenty-eight Bruce may have felt the time was ripe for him to raise his standard. Edward was nearly forty years his senior and would be unlikely to live for much longer.

A blood feud with the powerful Comyns was not an enticing prospect, Bruce would have ample cause to regret the circumstances if not the act of his enemy's taking off. So damaging was the fact of the murder that he sought a pardon from the king, but Edward's days of indulgence toward Robert Bruce were over, he was on his own, rebellion the only course left open. In June 1304 Robert had entered into an agreement with Bishop Lamberton which may have been intended to keep the spirit of the patriot cause alive. The English supremacy was the triumph of Edward I, his relentless aggression and towering charisma had kept the Scottish lords in thrall. Bruce had obviously met Caernarvon and would have swiftly discerned that the son was altogether less formidable than the father.

King Hobbe

At the outset Bruce's insurrection caught the English unawares. He moved to ensure control of certain key bastions in the west: Caerlavenock, Dumfries, Ayr and Dunaverty, Dalswinton and Tibbers soon fell to him. By the end of March, supported by the Bishop Wishart of Glasgow, Bruce was making plans for his coronation. The most threadbare of ceremonies (much of the royal regalia and, of course, the Stone of Destiny, had been pilfered) was mounted at Scone on 25 March, the feast of the Annunciation. At the high mass, held two days later on Palm Sunday, the hereditary office of the heir to the kingdom of Fife had to be performed by Isabel of Buchan. The new queen was something less than fully supportive, rather deriding her husband's regal pretensions: 'King of Summer' as she cruelly christened him.[4] The English sneered at 'King Hobbe':

> Now King Hobbe to the moors has gone,
> To come to town he has no desire.[5]

The new king would indeed require all the support he could muster. Reaction in the realm to his elevation, and the spectre of English retaliation which it invoked, was lukewarm. There could be no immediate prospect of a rapprochement with the Comyns and their MacDougall allies despite the fact that Wishart had granted absolution for the murder of John of Badenoch. The bishop had already encouraged his protégé, James Douglas, to seek out the new king and proffer his sword. And a mighty blade this would be, despite the fact the Bruce, whilst in Edward's service, had harried Douglasdale; the young knight was keen to strike a blow at Clifford who was currently enjoying his family lands.[6]

With the west at least partially secure and the doorway to Ireland open, Bruce did not find himself without supporters. The earls of Athol, Menteith and Lennox attended the coronation and others such as Thomas Randolph, Gilbert Hay, Reginald Crawford, Robert Boyd, Neil Campbell and now the formidable Douglas, rallied to the colours. From Selkirk Forest, Simon Fraser sallied out to harass the English garrisons. The court progressed through the counties of the northeast, not on a leisurely tour but a whirlwind advance. The king used flattery, cajolery and, when these failed, threats and intimidation to coerce the magnates and secure the vital supply line through the east coast ports. Robert's grip on power was, at best, tenuous. Comyn and MacDougall alike were baying for vengeance and others such as Patrick Dunbar and Malise of Strathearn found the odds too great to risk reverting to the patriot cause.

Retribution was not long delayed. In February, Clifford and Percy took Tibbers and by the beginning of March had secured Dumfries.[7] On 5 April,

Aylmer de Valence, later to be Earl of Pembroke, was appointed to command in the east and began to build up his forces. By the middle of July he could deploy some 300 horse with a detachment of hobilers from the west march supported by 1,300 foot.[8] A fuller muster was arranged for Carlisle with Edward of Caernarvon in charge. King Edward was slowly, and by now very painfully, making his way north, his physical condition deteriorating. The prince did not leave the west march until July but, by then, de Valence had routed the patriots in a bold attack at Methven, near Perth. The Scots were caught totally unprepared on the evening of 19 June. So total was the defeat that the Scottish knights reversed their blazons to conceal their identities, there was no vestige of honour for a traitor.[9] King Robert, surprised and routed, fell back towards the west but suffered further reverses by Loch Tay and at Dail Righ (Dalry), near Tyndrum, where he was assailed by the men of Lorn led by MacDougall.

For the fugitive king of Scots, the hunt was now on, his slender forces scattered and demoralised. By the end of August his castle on Loch Doon had fallen and, far worse, the redoubtable Simon Fraser had been captured near Stirling. Bruce may have rested in the temporary haven of Dunaverty but, by September, this too was under siege. John Botecourt and John of Menteith brought engines from Carlisle by sea and battered their way past the crumbling walls, but Robert was already gone.

Worse was soon to follow. Having taken the surrender of Lochmaben, Caernarvon advanced as far as Perth, and as the summer waned in September, he reached Kildrummy, held by Robert's brother, Neil. The Queen and the Princess Marjorie (Bruce's daughter by his first marriage) were within. Though they sought to flee to sanctuary at Tain, both were captured by the Earl of Ross and delivered to Edward. Neil Bruce, following his surrender, endured a traitor's death at Berwick. The Earl of Atholl, Herbert de Morham, Thomas du Boys and Simon Fraser suffered a similar, dreadful fate in London, while Christopher Seton died at Dumfries.

Although Queen Elizabeth, as a daughter of the Red Earl, and Marjorie, on account of her tender years, were spared ill treatment, Robert's sister Mary, the Countess of Buchan, was forced to live, exposed to the mob and the elements, in a specially-constructed timber cage suspended from the walls of Roxburgh and Berwick. The ageing English king, aware of the inexorable advance of mortality, was savage in his haste to crush this pernicious germ of patriotism. After the fall of Kildrummy, Caernarvon's knights grew restive in the uncongenial Scottish autumn, so twenty-two of them simply upped and left to tourney in France or seek other, more lively diversions. Such gross dereliction, all the more heinous because it went unpunished by the hedonistic prince, drew forth a mighty groan of royal wrath and dire consequences were promised for the offenders, although Edward allowed himself to be converted to leniency.

By the turn of the year it was rumoured that Robert Bruce had sought refuge in Ireland, though he might expect short shrift from his father-in-law; more likely he was hiding on Islay.[10] Angus Og MacDonald was sympathetic; no friend of the MacDougalls, he had fighting men and fast-oared Hebridean galleys, so more men could be hired in from Ireland. Nonetheless the season began badly, with Thomas and Alexander Bruce defeated and captured by Domnal MacDougall when they attempted a seaborne raid on Galloway, having landed from eighteen ships with Sir Reginald Crawford and Malcolm fitz Lengleys, the lord of Kintyre. The Galwegians spared few; just a handful escaped. Fitz Lengleys was immediately put to death, Thomas was taken to Carlisle, drawn through the streets and then killed. Alexander Bruce and Crawford were hanged and then beheaded, the severed heads sent post haste to Caernarvon.[11] Only one of Bruce's siblings, Edward, now survived.

In those early months of 1307 Robert Bruce lived a precarious existence, the partisan, hunted by his enemies, liable to be betrayed by those he might call friends. It is often assumed that support for the king began to snowball at this time, from a thin trickle to a swelling torrent, but this is probably flawed, Bruce was on the run. The MacDougall, John of Argyll, was relentless, using tracker dogs to beat the bracken, as though in pursuit of game. This was, nonetheless, a dangerous prey and for the patriots there were some successes. They came off best in a skirmish in Glentrool in April, even if the planned ambush failed in its prime objective. At Loudon Hill, on the tenth of the following month, Bruce bested de Valence, who was seen off with some, albeit minor, loss.

Edward I, failing in body if not in spirit, swiftly grew restive at the lack of decisive action. He was acutely aware he did not have time enough for a protracted guerrilla campaign. At the start of the year the sheriff of Cumbria had been instructed to gather a fleet for service on the west coast whilst the king summoned the last physical reserves, dredged up by an iron will, determined to lead a summer offensive in person. But Longshanks had harried the Scots for the last time, dying at Burgh by Sands on 7 July.

With its guiding genius dead the English presence in Scotland faltered. The patriots were still few in number, short of arms and cash, but the initiative now passed to Bruce, who had learnt the rugged lessons of successful guerrilla warfare, who knew how to use the hostile terrain of Galloway and the wild uplands of Selkirk Forest to his advantage. Even before Edward I was dead the mood amongst English commanders, perhaps particularly at the local level, was becoming increasingly pessimistic. Correspondence survives from May 1307, most probably written by the English castellan at Forfar, which appears to sum up the prevailing gloom:

> I hear that Bruce never had the goodwill of his followers or of the people generally so much with him as now. It appears that God is with him, for he has destroyed King Edward's power both among English and Scots. The people believe Bruce will carry all before him, exhorted by false preachers from Bruce's army ... May it please God to prolong king Edward's life, for men say openly that when he is gone the victory will go to Bruce. For those preachers have told the people that they have found a prophecy of Merlin, that after the death of 'le Roy Coveytous' the people of Scotland and the Welsh shall band together to the end of the world.[12]

As his forces grew in numbers and his reputation swelled, King Robert developed means of waging war that maximised his strengths; castles, when taken, were often not garrisoned but slighted, denying their use to the foe and avoiding the need for static garrisons. Frightfulness, the deliberate use of terror, was not scorned. Intimidation and blackmail went with the ruthless harrying of enemy lands, economic and social destruction, forcing the northern counties of England to repeatedly buy off the Scots. Filling the war chest by extortion, pitched battles were avoided, Fabian tactics prevailed; the rugged terrain of the west provided ample refuge.

With his father at last gone, Caernarvon, now Edward II, had pressing concerns other than Scotland. Besides, the war was Longshanks' obsession, not his. With the old king dead, the mainspring of the English effort was removed. In July, the new king followed the body of the old as far as York before returning to Carlisle to resume the summer campaign. Edward now led an expedition, marching in three columns, into the western marches. Bruce was temporarily contained in Carrick and Galloway, whilst the English proceeded to Dumfries where the king received the homage of those magnates who remained loyal. The advance continued through Nithsdale as far as Cumnock and Edward kept the field until late August, after which he retired to Carlisle. To all intents and purposes this was to be his last major effort for the next three years, during which the initiative lay wholly with Bruce and his supporters.

At the end of August de Valence was appointed as the king's lieutenant but was speedily replaced by Edward's cousin, John of Brittany. This has been viewed as a political shift, inspired by the counsels of the young king's boon companion, Piers Gaveston. Edward's relationship with the Gascon knight had raised eyebrows during his father's lifetime but, free of the austere straitjacket of parental control, the king lavished honours and affection on his favourite. Whether the relationship between the two men was explicitly sexual is unclear but most contemporaries seem to have felt that it was and, as such, grossly repugnant. Additional appointments of march officials or 'conservators' were also made for the counties of Cumberland, Westmorland and Northumberland. These measures were entirely defensive in nature. No new expeditions were planned, the garrisons in Scotland were left exposed, as indeed were the king's Scottish allies. Unfettered by English aggression Bruce could assume the offensive.

Winning the realm

In the autumn of 1307 the patriots broke out of the southwest, supported by the MacDonalds and MacRuairidhs. They advanced by way of the Great Glen to confront King Robert's enemies the Comyns. Catching his foes before they could muster against him, Bruce compelled their submission. His methods were by no means gentle and when Buchan fought back during the winter his lands were thoroughly ravaged, the 'herschip of Buchan'. The Earl of Ross spelt out the grim reality of his and Buchan's position in a letter to King Edward which was probably written in the last weeks of 1307:

> Be it known that we heard of the coming of Robert Bruce towards the parts of Ross with a great power, so that we had no power against him, but nevertheless we caused our men to be called out and we were stationed for a fortnight with 3,000 men, at our own expense, on the borders of our earldom, and in two other earldoms, Sutherland and Caithness; and he would have destroyed them utterly if we had not made a truce with him, at the entreaty of good men, both clergy and others, until Whitsun next.[13]

The few English garrisons were too scattered to offer much support and the Comyn was decisively defeated by King Robert at Inverurie in May 1308, even though the Bruce, dangerously ill over the winter, could barely stay upright in the saddle. In the west, Bruce's MacDonalds bottled up John of Argyll, sick and despondent, in Dunstaffnage. By March he was writing despairingly to Edward, partly to show how desperate the odds had become and partly to explain why it had been expedient to agree to a truce:

> I was confined to my bed with illness, and have been for six months past, Bruce approached these parts by land and sea with 10,000 men they say, or 15,000. I have no more than 800 men, 500 in my own pay whom I keep continually to guard the borders of my territory. The barons of Argyll give me no aid. Yet Bruce asked for a truce which I granted him for a short space.[14]

Douglas too had been active over the winter, recovering his castle from Clifford's garrison, the celebrated mayhem of the 'Douglas Larder'.[15] This satisfying slaughter was followed by a thorough 'herschip' of Galloway in the company of Edward Bruce, Alexander Lindsay and Robert Boyd, causing many to flee in panic into the English west march. A skirmish was fought late in June 1308 in which the rebels were again victorious. By August, high summer in the highlands, King Robert was ready to settle with the MacDougalls, who, like all his native foes, were without recourse to English support and forced onto the defensive. Still not fully recovered, John of Argyll directed operations from a galley anchored on Loch Awe.[16]

His kerns sought to contest the Pass of Brander, massing on the steep slopes of Ben Cruachan, from where they launched a storm of boulders onto the patriots toiling through the narrow confines. Douglas, however, swift footed and ever valiant, led a commando against the defenders, scrambling up the heather-clad slopes and putting the MacDougalls to flight. By autumn Dunstaffnage had fallen, John of Argyll was in full retreat south and his father, Alexander, who surrendered with the garrison, bowed to the inevitable and offered his homage to Bruce.

By the latter part of 1308 the fortunes of the patriot cause were utterly transformed: the hunted had now become the hunters. From a few precarious toeholds Bruce had extended his sway over the western highlands, the Comyn lands in the northeast, Argyll and Galloway. Robert I was now king for all seasons. The main English garrisons still remained as it was mainly the lesser, timbered fortifications that had fallen, but these increasingly isolated outposts were perennially under strength and under supplied, neglected by an indifferent throne wrapped up in domestic difficulties.

Edward II is one of England's least-regarded medieval monarchs. Professor Prestwich finds he

> was one of the most unsuccessful kings ever to rule England. The domestic history of the reign is one of successive political failures punctuated by acts of horrific violence ... Personal hatreds and jealousies were more important than constitutional principles, as was demonstrated in the final overthrow of the incompetent king by his queen, Isabella.[17]

As prince he had formed his close relationship with Piers Gaveston which, regardless of any sexual connotations, was heartily disapproved of by his father, who had ordered the Gascon abroad. Isabella was a daughter of Philip IV of France, a woman of beauty, spirit and considerable courage, if also haughty, avaricious and ruthless. She was not of a temperament to be openly passed over in favour of the king's masculine intimates.[18]

The king undoubtedly reacted, at least in part, to the austerity of his father's reign. He was hedonistic, indolent, bored by matters of state and much given to rustic pleasures such as ditching and thatching, 'lazy and incompetent'.[19] Physically he was tall and well proportioned, graceful in speech and manner, an accomplished horseman, but lacking in the single mindedness necessary to make a soldier. Edward's marriage to Queen Isabella was solemnised in Boulogne in January 1308 but by then Gaveston was already returned and installed as Earl of Cornwall whilst rumblings of discontent, though still muted, were already beginning to sound. A group of senior magnates, all men of proven loyalty in the days of Edward I, entered into a band of agreement pledging themselves to strive for the reform of 'things which have been done before this time contrary to his [the king's] honour and the rights of his crown, and the oppressions which have been done and are still being done to his people'.[20]

A rising clamour to be rid of Gaveston began to swell mightily and the king, his position weakened by the parlous state of the exchequer, was finally, in 1311, obliged to concede the appointment of a supervisory council of twenty-one 'Ordinancers' to co-ordinate necessary reforms. Throughout all this the English position in Scotland continued to decline; defeating and subjugating the Scots had been Edward I's obsession; his son was, at best, uninterested and became increasingly preoccupied with the baronial opposition.

In June 1308 he had gone through the motions of launching a campaign, issuing writs of military service and ordering a muster at Carlisle for 22 August, though he easily allowed political developments in England to take precedence and the proposed army never materialised. Left to hold the line in Scotland south of the Forth were Robert Umfraville, Lord of Redesdale and Earl of Angus, Henry Beaumont and William Ros, with a troop of forty men-at-arms apiece. North of the river Alexander Abernethy, Edmund Hastings and John Fitzmarmaduke jointly held office with a force of one hundred and twenty men. In the southwest, Buchan, John Mowbray and Ingram Umfraville held sway, again with forty men-at-arms for each.

Clifford had replaced John of Brittany as Lieutenant, his office alternating with John Segrave, and he had his own retinue comprising a hundred men-at-arms, sixty from his own affinity and a further forty knights drawn from the Household. By the end of 1308 negotiations for a truce, at the prompting of France, were under way. In January 1309, Gloucester, with the mediation of two papal envoys, agreed a ceasefire to hold until the next All Saints (1 November). The agreement provided that both sides should withdraw to the lines they had held on the Feast of James the Apostle (25 July) in 1307. Needless to say King Robert had not the slightest intention of abandoning the extensive and hard-won gains he had amassed and the truce was, to all intents and purposes, an admission by Edward that he was in no position to resume the offensive.

Throughout 1309 the English remained largely on the defensive. Gloucester, who had succeeded Clifford, relieved a siege of Rutherglen castle, only to see the place fall to Edward Bruce later in the year. In July, the Stamford Parliament resolved to renew a campaign that had been proposed for June then cancelled. A muster subsequently ordered for 29 September was deferred until October, before being finally abandoned altogether.

Bruce had already held his first major Parliament, at St Andrews in March. His father-in-law, the Red Earl of Ulster, who had remained unshakeable in his allegiance to Edward, did mount an offensive, of the purely diplomatic sort, from Ireland, intended to try to relieve the pressure on John of Argyll. The mission produced no tangible results but Ireland remained a major source of supply for the remaining English garrisons of the southwest.[2]

In November, Edward's commissioners entered into negotiations for a proposed extension of the existing truce. At the end of the month Segrave was dispatched to Berwick, Clifford with the Earl of Hereford and John Cromwell posted to Carlisle, their brief to seek an extended truce until 14 January 1310. For his part Clifford was anxious to stretch this still further, till March at least or even into the early summer. Bowing to expediency, the king had empowered the castellans of the most exposed garrisons, excluding only those in the southwest, to agree local arrangements into early June, till Whitsun (which fell on 7 June).

Discerning the way the wind was now blowing, numbers of senior magnates hastened to submit, including Ross, the Steward and, significantly, the powerful Earl of Lennox, who brought the key bastion of Dumbarton as a potent token of his revised allegiance. Since his capture in the shambles at Methven, Thomas Randolph had served England; taken now by the Scots he voiced a deep abhorrence of the unchivalric nature of guerrilla-style warfare. Bruce won him over, however. Created Earl of Moray in 1312, Randolph was to become one of the great captains of the age and a stalwart of the patriot cause.

In his dealings and ordinances Bruce referred to Alexander III as his predecessor, Baliol's kingship being effectively overreached. The Scots Parliament was more than willing to expunge the luckless King John. Bruce was able to demonstrate the qualities required to match the four 'pillars' of inheritance: succession, inheritance, virtue, election and conquest. The Scottish Church provided a 'Declaration of the Clergy' in forceful terms which stressed Bruce's role as deliverer.[22]

Philip IV of France, Edward's father-in-law, publicly referred to Robert as Earl of Carrick, whilst in private correspondence addressing him as King of Scots.[23] The campaign which Edward II now planned for the summer of 1310 was largely a device intended to frustrate the growing ranks of the opposition and to snatch the reins of government from the grasping hands of reformers. Philip was also pressing his reluctant son-in-law to perform full feudal homage, a humiliation the king was anxious to avoid.

With the exchequer now removed to York, Edward and Gaveston might feel less threatened and, if the king had any doubt as to the seriousness of his affairs in Scotland, he received a sharp reminder in the form of a brutally frank letter written by four of his Scottish lords, Alexander Abernethy, Ingram Umfraville, Alexander and John of Argyll, addressed to Aymer de Valence, now, since 1308, Earl of Pembroke: 'We should lose both the land and those who still remain faithful to us by reason of our default and our laxity'.[24]

Edward's negligence was affecting northern England. Patriot success inevitably meant the northern counties were exposed. As far back as September 1307 'keepers of the peace' had been appointed to the English west march; in that November Gilbert Umfraville and William de Ros were given a similar role in Northumberland.[25] The ruthlessness of the patriot campaigns in Scotland had, by 1310, already swelled the marches with a desperate host of refugees. Dispossessed Gallowegians crowded their beasts into Inglewood Forest. Locals probably divined that worse was to come and in this they would have been entirely correct.

There was scant enthusiasm in England for a Scottish campaign. Magnates such as Pembroke, Hereford, Arundel and Thomas of Lancaster, ignored the summons.[26] Only Gloucester and Warenne were prepared to join the royal catamite for a muster at Tweedmouth. Bartholomew Badlesmere was appointed Constable with Nicholas Segrave as Marshall; Lincoln was to act as regent.

King Edward commanded a host comprising some 300 men-at-arms, fifty knights of the Household and perhaps 3,000 foot, Welshmen in the main with a company of elite crossbowmen raised and equipped by the City of London and intended for service in the Berwick garrison. The outposts on the Tweed and through the Merse were stripped to provide additional manpower. The delinquent earls had sent their basic feudal quota and the plan was for a combined assault, Edward in the east and the Red Earl from the west, leading a force out of Ireland to Ayr where they would act in concert with John of Argyll. De Burgh was to provide a force of 500 men-at-arms, 300 hobilers and 2,000 foot.

Ships were ordered up from both the Irish ports and the west of England, but on 2 August the Irish arm of the offensive was aborted. The declared reason for this cancellation was the difficulties caused by a poor harvest, but this is less likely than the fact that the MacSweens, clients of Edward, had been driven out of Knapdale by Menteith. In July, the king had granted the area to John MacSween, though his enjoyment was subject to him being able to expel Menteith. This feud over the local lordship was nothing new and had been festering for the best part of half a century. Patriot success in the west may have inspired fears of a possible attack on the Isle of Man and the Red Earl's knights were deployed to bolster Simon Montacute's garrison there.[27]

On 1 September the royal army forded the Tweed at Wark and carried out an initial sweep through Selkirk Forest. Meeting no opposition, the king turned west on 21 September to advance along the Clyde Valley as far as Renfrew. From here the army returned eastward, reaching Linlithgow by 23 October. A week or so later King Edward was back in Berwick. The expedition, though it had failed to bring on a general engagement, had secured the vital garrisons south of the Forth and demonstrated that the English still had teeth. The king remained on the borders until June 1311, a convenient distance from his critics, whilst Gaveston was safely installed at Roxburgh, Warenne held Wark and Gloucester the Prince Bishop's castle at Norham.

Throughout the campaign of 1310 Bruce was too canny to accept the hazard of battle. He relied, as ever, on the guerrilla-style tactics which had served him so well to date, denying sustenance to the invader, hanging on his flanks and cutting up isolated detachments. Thus the campaign was by no means bloodless:

> One day, when some English and Welsh, always ready for plunder, had gone out on a raid, accompanied for protection by many horsemen from the army, Bruce's men, who had been concealed in caves and in the woodlands, made a serious attack on our men. Our horsemen, seeing that they could not help the infantry, returned to the main force with a frightening uproar; and immediately leapt to arms and hastened with one accord to the help of those who had been left amongst the enemy; but assistance came too late to prevent the slaughter of our men ... Before our knights arrived, up to 300 Welsh and English had been slaughtered, and the enemy returned to their caves. From such ambushers our men suffered heavy losses.[28]

No sooner had the English departed than Bruce launched a retaliatory strike into the Merse. Edward led out the Berwick garrison to see him off and the Scots again fell back without engaging. One of the problems which confronted the English in 1310 arose from King Robert's policy of slighting the captured forts. This increased the isolation of the remaining garrisons in the larger holds and made the reoccupation of territory impossible without rebuilding, which was both time consuming and expensive. Longshanks had been able to maintain forty or so outposts and by 1310 Bruce had perhaps recovered a quarter of these.[29]

Edward now sought to consolidate the position by entering into a series of contracts or indentures with his nobles, appointing Robert Umfraville as his lieutenant in the far north, based at Perth, where Beaumont commanded the immediate garrison and with Percy and Pain Tiptoft in support. Umfraville could count on a couple of hundred men-at-arms plus the retinues of sympathetic Scottish lords. Clifford was given the southern command based at Berwick, Roger Mortimer took over from Cornwall at Roxburgh, John Segrave became warden of Annandale and, whilst Dungal MacDougall still clung on at Dumfries and Ingram Umfraville held Caerlaverock, the west was effectively ceded to the patriots.

In the meantime, the regent Lincoln had died. His beneficiary Thomas of Lancaster[30] was to become the focus of baronial opposition, a man of limited ability, much taken with private feuds, lacking in charisma or serious political acumen, 'sulky, vindictive, self seeking and vicious'.[31] He was, nonetheless, by far the wealthiest of the barons, with vast estates in the north. The earl journeyed north to meet the king and do homage for his inheritance, but being very much of the reform party, he refused to cross the Tweed and, after some procrastination, the king met with the earl at Haggerston on the English side.

With the tide of opposition swelling alarmingly there is the suggestion that Edward was prepared to consider a permanent peace with Bruce in return, possibly, for military assistance against the dissenting magnates and a safe haven for Gaveston north of the border. The reformers or 'Ordainers' were echoing the demands first aired in the constitutional crisis of 1297, but the opposition was now more broadly based. The rebels comprised a number of those peers who had opposed Edward I then but others, like Lincoln, had not been involved in the earlier crisis. The list of demands, not surprisingly, included the expulsion from the realm of Gaveston and a greater degree of control over the crown's finances.[32] The king's poor grasp of magnate politics and his abundant abuses of royal patronage had alienated many and thus deprived him of a solid affinity. The Ordainers' demands included not only the removal of Gaveston but a purge of the Household.

The year 1311 was to prove a difficult one. The king could not remain isolated in the north forever; he was without troops and had not the means to pay the hire of more. He feared calling Parliament as this would be to play into the hands of the Ordainers. Casting about for expedients he attempted to levy a local tax from the marcher communities and, on 20 May, tried to organise a general muster without Parliamentary sanction. His attempts to raise mounted contingents from the magnates were no more successful. A muster was planned for 5 July, a still-born thing: the king conceded beforehand that he had no choice but to square up to the opposition. Edward reluctantly summoned a Parliament then king and court rode south from Berwick at the end of July, leaving Gaveston at Bamburgh.

At Westminster the king was obliged to submit the governance of his affairs to what was, in effect, a regency council. His finances were restructured and the services of his current Italian bankers, the Frescobaldi, were superseded by the Genoese Antonio Pessagno. The odious Gaveston was sent into exile. Having learnt nothing from the wrack of his power the king procured his lover's return and by November Gaveston was restored to the realm. Facing new demands from the Ordainers for further expulsions from the Household, Edward, having kept Christmas at Westminster with his paramour, determined on defiance and fled north. Civil war now appeared inevitable.

From this point the situation began to deteriorate rather rapidly. The magnates were united in their opposition. Edward may have made further overtures to Bruce at this point but found his own officers on the border holding the line, not only against the Scots but also against him.[33] Having briefly rested at Newcastle the pair split up, with Gaveston sailing from the Tyne to the imagined safety of Scarborough Castle where he presently found himself besieged by superior baronial forces. With no hope of relief, the Gascon surrendered on terms to Pembroke, one of the more moderate Ordainers.

Though the earl guaranteed the favourite's personal safety, matters were taken irrevocably out of his hands when the besiegers were themselves ambushed by the Earl of Warwick, frequently a victim of the royal catamite's waspish tongue.[34] Having learnt nothing, the Gascon now insisted on insulting his captors, who were most certainly not bound by any oaths regarding his continued wellbeing. Presently he was handed over to a tribunal comprising the earls of Lancaster, Arundel and Hereford. Judgement was swift and Gaveston's final journey was to Lancaster's property at Blacklaw Hill, where he was executed without further ceremony.

Meanwhile, the patriots in Scotland had not failed to take advantage of these alarums in England. They now held the vital port of Aberdeen which served as a flourishing base for privateers, preying on enemy vessels in the North Sea. There were stirrings within the fastnesses of the border wastelands. Gloucester and Warenne mounted a sweep through Selkirk Forest before the former returned to England to take on the regency, vacant since Lincoln's death.

By now King Robert had gathered a fleet of sleek Hebridean galleys. John of Argyll was impotent and imploring at Berwick. His plight possibly motivated Edward to launch a fresh expedition from Ireland in the early months of 1311, comprising some 300 men-at-arms, ten times as many foot and a screen of 500 hobilers[35], the English king was

Greatly desirous that the fleet which he had ordered to set sail for Scotland and the coast of Argyll under the orders of his liege Sir John of Argyll should be ready as soon as possible, seeing [that] it is one of the greatest movements of the Scottish war[36]

This last, bold assertion proved somewhat optimistic; the response, in terms of ships, was less than encouraging. The expedition was inevitably scaled down but seems to have met with some success, including actions at sea.[37] Of infinitely greater import was the Scottish reaction when Edward finally quit Berwick. Bruce launched two devastating *chevauchées* into northern England. Lanercost Chronicle states the relevant dates were 12–20 August and 8–23 September. In the first of these raids:

Having collected a great army, he [Robert] entered England at Solway on the Thursday before the feast of the Assumption; and he burned all the land of the lord of Gilsland and the vils of Haltwhistle and a great part of Tynedale, and after eight days he returned to Scotland taking with him a great booty of animals; nevertheless he had killed few men apart from those who wished to defend themselves by resistance.[38]

In the following month the pattern was repeated:

About the feast of the Nativity of the Blessed Virgin, Robert returned with an army into England, directing his march towards Northumberland, and passing by Harbottle and Holystone and Redesdale, he burnt the district about Corbridge, destroying everything; he also caused more men to be killed than on the former occasion. And so he turned into the valleys of the North and South Tyne, laying waste those parts which he had previously spared, and returned into Scotland after fifteen days; nor could the wardens whom the king of England had stationed on the marches oppose so great a force of Scots as he brought with him.[39]

Despairing of any assistance from their king, now so thoroughly enmeshed in his squabble with the Ordainers, the Northumbrians bought local truces, to hold until Candlemas the following year (2 February). This handy blackmail was sufficient to fund a three-month siege of Dundee, which fell to the patriots in April 1312.

A mite more terror

Wasting Northern England was not merely blind revenge bent on destruction, it was a finely honed strategy of economic warfare. The intention was to attack the concept of 'good lordship' which went to the very core of the feudal pyramid. If the magnate and the knight beneath him could not defend their tenants then why was allegiance owed?

The raids either wasted or impoverished the northern counties, in part thereby weakening their capacity to support a renewal of the war and also funding the patriot cause, paying for men, engines of war and material. There was little that King Edward could offer in response, his own border officials having turned against him, his magnates wholly bent on hunting down his detested favourite. King Robert's war was a new type of conflict aimed at long-term damage to the economy of northern England rather than the winning of castles or battles in the field. His armies rode to war astride shaggy little garrons; these were not cavalry but mounted infantry, having the mobility of the former and the steadiness of the latter.

They travelled light these swift hobilers, no lumbering baggage trains struggling through the miry roads, no great straggle of camp followers and whores stumbling behind. The raids were of short duration but well co-ordinated and clearly targeted, each man carrying his supply of meal in his pack and a flat stone for cooking under the saddle. Such swift-moving forces could confound and overawe any local opposition and then outwit or outrun any conventional forces mustered against them. With northern magnates such as Clifford distracted by the hunt for Gaveston, Bruce struck again in that desperate summer of 1312:

> When Robert Bruce heard of this discord in the south, having assembled a great army, he invaded England about the feast of the Assumption of the Blessed Virgin [15 August] and burned the towns of Hexham and Corbridge and the western parts and took booty and much spoil and prisoners, nor was there anyone who dared to resist. While he halted in peace and safety near Corbridge he sent part of his army as far as Durham, which arriving there suddenly on market day, carried off all that was found in the town, and gave a great part of it to the flames, cruelly killing all who opposed them, but scarcely attacking the castle and priory.[40]

It is perhaps unsurprising that the Scottish chroniclers gave little thought to the sufferings of the English:

> The fruitless English nation which had unrighteously racked many a man, by God's righteous judgement, made to undergo awful scourges; and

whereas it had once been victorious, now it sank vanquished and groaning.[41]

In the wake of Scottish raids, with order and community wracked, lawlessness swept into the vacuum, the genesis of the 'riding' culture that would reach its dire apogee in the sixteenth century. A pattern of life would gradually be created in the northern counties, particularly in the upland dales, where warfare, raiding and the blood feud or 'feid' became endemic. Even the buying of truces was no guarantee of peace; local incursions such as that which witnessed the razing of the settlement at Norham early in 1312 still sparked, in this instance, possibly as a retaliation against forays by the garrison.

In addition to the other benefits the continuance of the war in northern England left Bruce unhindered in his efforts to reduce the remaining garrisons still holding out on Scottish soil. Though these were much diminished, the English presence was still formidable. With Dundee now recovered, Perth was the single major bastion north of the Forth; south of the divide the castles of Edinburgh, Stirling and Bothwell secured the Forth-Clyde isthmus, strengthened by outposts or peles at Linlithgow and Livingston.[42]

The Tweed was strongly held from Berwick along to Norham then Wark with the outlying fortresses of Roxburgh and Jedburgh in Teviotdale. In the west, though the English grip had been prised free over large areas, they still held on to castles at Lochmaben, Dumfries, and Caerlaverock with peles at Tibbers, Dalswinton, Buittle and the chain of forts in the English west march behind: Carlisle, Bewcastle and Harbottle.

As the Scots were still lacking both the means and the experience to conduct full-scale sieges of major castles, they were thrown back upon their ingenuity allied to boldness and cunning. On 6th June 1312 an attempt was made, by stealth, upon the walls of Berwick. Rope ladders fitted with grappling hooks were heaved over the parapet by a brace of sappers wielding a long pole. Only the providential barking of one of the dogs, clearly more alert that its master, gave the game away and roused the garrison in time to beat off the escalade.

A further consideration was that the protracted siege of a major citadel might tempt even the supine Edward into intervening in force. This was something Bruce wished to avoid at all costs. His campaign of attrition had been hugely successful, he had recovered vast swathes of ground, secured strongpoints and eliminated outposts without provoking an engagement in the field against superior forces which could so easily prove disastrous; the example of Wallace and Falkirk would still be fresh.

Nonetheless, by January 1313, the siege of Perth was under way. With a fine irony the English castellan was that same William Oliphant who had so valiantly held Stirling against Longshanks nine years earlier. Though Bruce had already been bolstered by the defection to the patriot cause of the Earl of Athol, Oliphant defended Perth as resolutely as he had Stirling. As the place was not likely to fall to a direct assault, Bruce resorted to a Homeric ruse worthy of the creators of the Trojan Horse. He caused his engines to be dismantled, his trenches and works levelled, and departed with all of his men, only to return a few nights later and, under cover of darkness, wade the moat and secure a section of parapet sufficient to allow the storming party to open the gates and admit the host.

He then moved on to Dumfries, held by Dungal MacDougall, the killer of two of his brothers. That notwithstanding, he permitted the garrison, in February 1313, to surrender on terms and depart. Both Caerlaverock and the pele at Buittle fell soon after. MacDougall withdrew into Rushen Castle on Man, soon to find himself once again besieged by the patriots. After five weeks this final bastion also capitulated and MacDougall was constrained to flee to Ireland. In the autumn the patriots seized Linlithgow.[43] The northern counties of England had sought to buy a further immunity from August 1312 to hold until the following midsummer. Spring still brought an invasion scare; in the east, the marchers were struggling to raise the requisite funds from their wasted lands. In April, a desperate plea to the king for military assistance met with the curt and less than helpful reply that the Northumbrians must shift for themselves. All that Bruce had to do was amass sufficient forces for an attack and the demoralised marchers paid up without a blow being struck. This time they scraped together enough to pay for the truce to be extended until Michaelmas (29 September) 1314.

Due in part to the brilliance of their tactics and the ruthless energy with which they were employed, and in part to the feebleness of Edward II, the Scots had achieved a complete domination of the English marches, which lacked the means, the will and above all the leadership to respond effectively. Matters were little improved in the west. As early as 1311 the inhabitants of the west march had struggled to meet the Scots' demands. At Carlisle, Andrew de Harcla was proving the kind of energetic warden who could be capable of resisting, but in 1313 the march suffered from fresh inroads as the Scots determined to administer a sharp reminder to the marchers:

On Tuesday after the octave of Easter [16 April] Edward de Brus, Robert's brother, invaded England by way of Carlisle, contrary to agreement, and remained there three days at the bishop's manor house, to wit, at Rose, and sent a strong detachment of his army to burn the southern and western districts during those three days. They burned many towns and two churches, taking men and women prisoners, and collected a great number of cattle in Inglewood Forest and elsewhere, driving them off with them on the Friday [19 April]: they killed few men except those who made determined resistance; but they made an attack on the city of Carlisle because of the knights and country people who were assembled there[44]

This kidnapping of victims for ransom was a handy means of waging economic warfare whilst maintaining additional pressure through deliberate terror. In the last dark days of the winter of 1313 Randolph stood before the formidable ramparts of Edinburgh itself. Though the great crag seemed to render the castle perched on its summit impregnable, the besiegers were offered a way up the cliffs by one William Francis who had pioneered the route, spurred on by a physical attachment to a lady within.

Randolph, with a 'forlorn hope' thirty strong, guided by Francis, made the perilous ascent of the crag. The garrison were distracted by a sham attempt on the east gate whilst, with the aid of the invaluable rope ladders, Randolph's commando climbed the wall, swiftly silenced the sentry and proceeded to open the gates. The defenders were put to the sword and the great castle slighted. Douglas, not to be outdone, planned to seize the great bastion of Roxburgh by an equally daring *coup de main*. He and his commando disguised themselves, unlikely as it seems, as black cattle, which guise enabled them to approach the walls unchallenged. The handy rope ladders with grapnels secured access to the parapet and an alert sentry was swiftly dealt with '*stekit upwar with ane knyff*' before he could cry the alarm. The garrison was overpowered and their Gascon commander mortally wounded. As before, the captured works were not held but slighted 'lest the English should ever hereafter be able to lord it over the land through holding the castles'.[46]

This war of outposts was an important element in the struggle, not only in terms of winning back that which had been lost but also in winning the confidence of the Scots themselves. Many of those who had declared loyalty to both Edwards had done so through fear or resignation. The patriot resurgence and the taking of the war into England won over many of the waverers:

All those [Scots] who were with the English were merely feigning, either because it was the stronger party, or in order to save the lands they possessed in England; for their hearts were always with their own people, although their persons might not be so.[47]

The English garrisons were frequently their own worst enemies, despoiling and abusing the populace, extracting ransoms and generally presenting what might now be described as a 'negative impression'.

In England, the death of Gaveston split the baronial opposition and at the same time removed the greatest obstacle to a 'rapprochement' with the king. By October 1313 an understanding of sorts had been arrived at. The Ordainers, in consideration for an apology over the killing, were received back into the king's grace. Earlier in the year, in May, Edward had attended his father-in-law in France to resolve his difficulties over homage for Gascony. This was particularly important as the king had negotiated a substantial advance from the papal coffers, secured on the ample revenues of the province.

Parliament, mollified by the truce, however shaky, with the Ordainers, was still absorbed by the effects of Gaveston's fall; matters in the north came a very poor second. Nonetheless the members were minded to vote subsidies for the maintenance of the Berwick garrison and to establish a commission under Robert Umfraville to look into the state of affairs on the marches. Hostage taking was an area of singular concern. In November it was agreed that a major offensive should be launched the following spring and the host was to muster at Berwick on 10 June.

Adam Gordon, one of the king's loyal Scots, had made the journey south to present Edward with the dismal facts concerning the infamous conduct of his remaining garrisons. For his pains he was arrested at Roxburgh. It is generally supposed that the threat to Stirling was the major factor influencing King Edward's decision to take the field in 1314. The castle is said to have been under siege by Edward Bruce from the summer of 1313 and that he had agreed with the castellan, Philip Moubray, that if the fortress were not relieved by midsummer's day the following year, 1314, it would be surrendered.

Had this been the case then King Robert would have been mightily put out, for a major trial of arms was the very last eventuality he desired. A long and protracted siege sufficient to draw a large English army north flew in the face of his entire strategy to date. It does now seem, however, that the leaguer of Stirling did not begin until the spring of 1314. After the fall of Edinburgh and Roxburgh, Philip Moubray very likely did come south to press for the castle's relief and this added urgency to the planned offensive.

Perhaps a far more telling imperative was Bruce's proclamation in the Scots Parliament at Dundee in November 1313 that his enemies in Scotland had the space of twelve months within which they must offer their submission or suffer the irrevocable forfeiture of their estates. This ultimatum left Edward with no real alternative; if he failed to march then his adherents in Scotland would be forced into submission or be perpetually ruined. To ignore the reality was to lose Scotland forever. The die was therefore cast, the matter would be decided according to the hazard of battle.

Above left: A replica of a single-handed double-edged broadsword.

Above: A replica of a mail shirt.

Left: A horseman's axe.

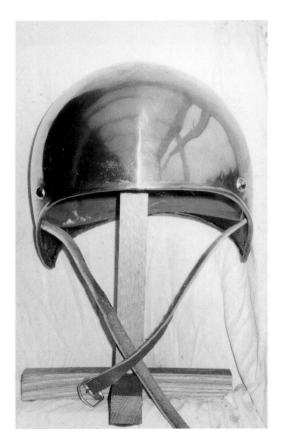

Above left: A replica small shield, or buckler, of the type carried by archers.

Above: A replica of an archer's single-handed sword.

Left: A replica of a simple infantryman's helmet.

The view northeast from
Stirling Castle, across the Forth
to the Wallace Tower, perched
on the Abbey Craig which
played a role in William
Wallace's victory at Stirling
Bridge in 1297. The intervening
ground was more miry in the
fourteenth century.

The current,
unspeakably
dreadful Wallace
statue at the base of
the Abbey Craig.

Two views of Stirling Castle, one showing the statue of Robert Bruce. Very little of the fourteenth-century enceinte remains; most of what is visible dates from the reign of James IV and after. Nonetheless, the fortress remains impressively perched on its volcanic outcrop and continues to dominate the town and its environs.

The bronze statue of Bruce located outside the present visitor centre off the A872 (Glasgow Road). It stands on the Borestone, where the Scottish standard is said to have been located during the Battle of Bannockburn. Behind, to the northwest, Coxet Hill rises.

The view of Stirling Castle, looking north from the Borestone.

Two views of the Bannockburn. The first is eastwards from New Road, looking down from the Telford Bridge, whilst the second looks westward towards the bridge. Each illustrates the sharp descent from the southern side, impossible for heavy cavalry.

The Carse, looking southeast (above) and southwest (below) from the A91, which bisects the field. This was the ground over which the main battle was fought in June 1314.

Looking north and west from the present A91. The Pelstream Burn runs by the trees to the left centre, across the intervening open ground. The line of the road and the frequency of the traffic do little for the study of the ground.

The Pelstream Burn, which witnessed the climax of the fighting on 24th June.

Chapter 5

Trial by Battle (1) – 23 June 1314

The water of my land, find her disease,
And purge it to a sound and pristine health,
I would applaud thee to the very echo,
That should applaud again – Pull't off I say –
What rhurbarb, seena or what purgative drug
Would scour these English hence? . . .
    – William Shakespeare, *MacBeth*

The Constable of Stirling came too and pointed out to the king how he had been
compelled by necessity to enter upon the truce. He persuaded the king to lead an
army into Scotland to defend his castle and the country.
    – *The Life of Edward II*

The Road to Bannockburn

Here was a challenge even Edward II dare not shirk. One of the Household, Edmund de Mauley, was appointed as castellan at Cockermouth and provided with rents to sustain his role. In the east, the trusty and experienced Pembroke was made the king's lieutenant in Scotland with a primarily logistical responsibility. Antonio Pessagno, the capable Genoese banker, was placed in charge of the commissariat in England. Thomas of Lancaster and twenty-one other peers were summoned to appear at Newcastle by 1 June. By 27 March arrangements had been put in hand for the recruitment of those tradesmen vital to the army's continued success: masons, carpenters, joiners, smiths and farriers.

When all the necessaries had been collected the king and the other magnates of the land with a great multitude of carts and baggage-wagons set out for Scotland. When the lord king had reached Berwick he made a short halt there to await the arrival of the army. But the Earl of Lancaster, the Earl Warenne, the Earl of Arundel, and the Earl of Warwick did not come but sent knights equipped to do their due service for them in the army. On the sixth or seventh day before the feast of St John the Baptist our king with all his army left Berwick and took his way toward Stirling.

The cavalry numbered more than two thousand without counting a numerous crowd of infantry.[1]

With the muster fixed for Berwick on 19 May, the magnates' quotas were to be supplemented by a further levy of 10,000 foot. John of Argyll was appointed as commodore of a squadron detailed to patrol the western approaches; Robert's father-in-law, the Red Earl, was commanded to produce a brigade of 4,000 of his kerns. The king wrote to the Anglo-Irish lords and to the native chieftains urging their support and the final requirement was to total 22,140 foot. Neither Lancaster nor Warwick responded but Gloucester and Hereford both agreed to serve; their affinities might have swelled the cavalry arm to perhaps 2,000 lances, a formidable force.

The Lanercost chronicler takes a pejorative view of Edward's preparations, blaming the lack of support from key magnates and the subsequent disaster on the king's impious attitude:

Now about the feast of Pentecost the king of England approached the March of Scotland, also the Earl of Gloucester, the Earl of Hereford, the Earl of Pembroke and the Earl of Angus, Sir Robert de Clifford, Sir John Comyn (son of murdered John), Sir Henry de Beaumont, Sir John de Segrave, Sir Pagan de Typtoft, Sir Edmund de Mauley, Sir Ingelram de Umfraville, with other barons, knights and a splendid and numerous army, if only they had had the Lord as ally. But the Earl of Lancaster and the other English earls who were of his party remained at home with their men (except those whom they were bound to send to the king in war) because the king had still refused to agree with them or to perform what he had promised. And while his noble father when he went on campaign in Scotland used to visit on his march the shrines of the English saints Thomas of Canterbury, Edmund, Hugh, William and Cuthbert, offering fair oblations, commending himself to their prayers and bestowing liberal gifts upon monasteries, this king did none of these things. But marching with great pomp and elaborate state he took goods from the monasteries on his journey and did and said things prejudicial to the saints. In consequence of this and other things it is not surprising that confusion and everlasting shame overtook him and his army ...[2]

The Scots, inevitably, could not muster anywhere like these numbers and, as ever, they were notably deficient in the cavalry arm. Professor Barrow estimates the Scottish host at somewhere between 5,000–6,000 in total and this is very likely correct (see appendix II). The bulk of the Scots comprised relatively light infantry:

Each was furnished with light armour, not easily penetrable by a sword. They had axes at their sides and carried spears in their hands. They advanced like a thick set hedge, and such a phalanx could not easily be broken.[3]

When the English army finally mustered at Wark on 10 June it included a leavening of Scots still loyal to Edward: Comyns, MacDougalls and MacNabs. A vast and cumbersome train of 200 carts was required to feed this monster. A logistical feat of no mean proportions, the marshalling and transport of the army and its great tail of supply wagons, livestock and followers was an epic in itself. It would be hard to imagine a greater contrast to the lean and hungry wraiths of Scots raiders who had so effectively terrorised the marches. This great and numerous army marched north from the Tweed in a dazzling array, the hot spring sun glancing from plate and mail, a veritable forest of pennons heralding the pride of the English chivalry. Victory must have seemed assured. For all King Robert's successes the patriots had yet to win the field in a major fight. Edinburgh was attained and occupied without opposition.

After a short halt to allow the fleet to attend for re-victualling, the host, on 22 June, advanced as far as Falkirk. Next morning the old Roman Road echoed to the tramp of thousands of marching feet and the ring of iron-shod hooves as the English set out to advance upon Stirling. Moubray had undertaken to surrender in two days' time if the castle was not relieved. Having marched over twenty long and wearing miles the day before, the English were still stirring and ready for the next stage at dawn on 23 June. As the drummers beat out reveille and the sergeants cursed in the penumbra of vanishing darkness, men tumbled from the sleep of exhaustion and girded themselves for possible contact. Prickers and spies would have brought news that the Scots were in force between the host and their goal of Stirling. Would the Scots fight? Surely the odds were too great; Falkirk a grim reminder of English prowess and might.

In the vast sprawling encampment, servants would be scurrying with sustenance for the lords and magnates in their gilded pavilions, bright flashes of opulent colour, a dazzling of silk, amidst the tan humdrum of the tattered canvas and hastily constructed shelters. Many would have spent the warm spring evening wrapped in their cloaks. The ring of armourers' hammers 'gives dreadful note of preparation'. For the army's vast tail of artisans, sutlers and whores, this was a busy time, priests moving amongst the companies, barbers shaving lords and gentry, whilst the commons swigged small beer and took a mouthful of bread.

By the time the sun had risen, the tents would be struck, the fires extinguished, baggage stowed and horses saddled. As today might bring a general engagement the army would move in a guarded column of march: a screen of hobilers and prickers scouting ahead, whilst the mounted van marshalled beneath the pennons of their unit commanders. Men would ride fully harnessed, for fear of ambuscade. The van was the place of danger and therefore of most coveted honour. Hereford and Gloucester were joined by John Comyn with a core of tried and experienced knights.

As the van moved off at the walk, the main body prepared to march on; further squadrons of horse with the foot toiling in their wake. These were a deal less colourful, mere 'warriors for the working day', some harnessed, some with gambesons, a forest of bills and the slung bows of the archers. The king with his household and heralds brought up the rear battle, a gorgeous parade of blazons and silk, polished harness, proud, chafing destriers.[4] Behind them, the great, toiling workaday convoy of carts and wagons, an untidy mass of camp-followers with a stiffening of foot to guard against intruders. A final, mounted detachment acted as rearguard.

If there was a likely perception that the Scots might not risk a general engagement, there was every expectation that they might launch an ambush or series of ambushes against the exposed flanks of the great sinuous column. An army is vulnerable on the line of march, especially where the going is narrow and hemmed by trees. Today, a more concentrated deployment of parallel forces moving over open ground was denied by the topography, for on this fine Sunday in June, the English were constrained by the sylvan confines of the great Tor Wood.

This was a dark primeval place. Not the ordered acres of regulated pines we see at Kielder and other plantations but a great sprawling wildwood of birch alder and oak, dense undergrowth clogging the verges of Dere Street as it drove through the canopy of trees, a thin ribbon of rutted track. The deep silence of the woods would descend like a blanket, leaves cutting out the strengthening sun, birdsong drowned by the tramp of marching men, the jingle of harness and the groaning axles of the transport. Those at the rear would be forced to avoid the spreading carpet of horse dung, and a rising cloud of choking dust, men dry-mouthed and sweating as they marched. Scouts from both sides were ranging ahead, Scottish horse under the Earl Marischal, would have been spotted by the English hobilers and word sent back, a stiffening in the leading ranks of the van, thrill of contact passing like a current. Keith sent word back to Bruce who trotted to meet his lieutenant, contact more imminent than perhaps they perceived. It was by now near midday and the English van would soon be clear of the woods.

Philip de Moubray had sallied from Stirling with a guard of mailed knights, a Scots safe conduct in his pouch. Cheered by the mass of horse and foot, he trotted down the great column till he reached the royal standard, there to bend his knee before the sovereign and offer congratulations upon relief of the garrison, now technically accomplished. King Edward appeared to have achieved his primary aim, the succour of Stirling, but whom was he to fight? Where was the foe? Would the Scots give battle? From the king's perspective a fight was needed, otherwise the outlay of treasure incurred in raising the vast array and marching thus far was mere show and nothing more.

His concern, at this point, would not be whether he could defeat the Scots but whether they would accept the hazard. Bruce had hitherto taken pains to avoid just such an encounter; as a guerilla he was brilliantly successful, but there was nothing to indicate he could command a large army in open field. Wallace had tried, had done so valiantly and had suffered ignominious if not ignoble defeat. Would Bruce now chance all his gains on a single throw? If indeed he was so resolved, then how and where would he fight?

For the van, such a debate on grand tactics had declined in importance. At last they were clear of the woods, before them a shallow incline led to the Bannockburn, before the road was again swallowed in the trees of the New Forest. It was not the ground which excited their attention, rather it was the Lion of Scotland blazoned in silk, floating above a knot of mounted knights, supported by a company of foot. They were gazing at Robert Bruce, King of Scots, King Hobbe himself.

As yet, neither side had had the opportunity to judge the mettle of the other. From the Scots perspective this was probably just as well for they were heavily outnumbered and completely so in terms of available cavalry. King Robert was well informed of the march and prior muster of his foes. For a month and more his own more workaday host had drilled in the sheltering confines of the Tor Wood, through which their adversaries had just passed.

The time had not been wasted, men drilled relentlessly in their spear formations till they became as one with their staves, officers and men able to deploy and manoeuvre with practised ease. Indeed the English would have passed the tell-tale signs of occupation without, however, gaining a glimpse.

To drill in woodland had a number of advantages. The place teemed with game and training could be conducted virtually in secrecy, difficult for a spy to get close enough to make an accurate assessment of numbers. The trees provided shelter and fuel but it would be difficult for Bruce to feel any over-powering sense of confidence, quite probably the reverse.

Whether it was his brother's rashness or other factors that had provoked this crisis the fact of its arising placed all the patriots' previous gains in mortal jeopardy. Wallace had drilled his men, had chosen his ground well, but this had not been enough. He had been unable to form a tactical response to the deadly partnering of missile and shock troops. His own heavy horse had failed the test and his archers paid the price of that failure. King Robert would have to do a great deal better if his cause was to prosper in the face of such odds.

Stirling Castle on its rearing volcanic spur is the cork in the bottle that guards the narrow neck between lowlands and the rugged west beyond.[5] The town lies to the east of the fortress and the River Forth loops and bends along its eastward course. The Bannockburn, a lesser tributary, rises in the west and follows its own wandering flow into the swollen waters of the Forth. A second burn, the Pelstream, flows into the Bannockburn, its course forming a line, not unlike the head of a pitchfork, with the tines pointing at the Bridle Path.

West of the old Roman road the ground rises towards those vigorous fastnesses that form the highlands of Scotland, but to the east lay a flat, alluvial plain, the Carse of Stirling.[6] In the fourteenth century this low ground was a patchwork of small fields, cut with expanses of peat bog. The New Park, which marks the western rim of the flat land, was the remains of an ancient hunting reserve. To the south the Tor Wood spills over a range of undulating folds and hills. The Carse itself becomes markedly wetter as it extends toward the Forth, a stretch of ground known as the 'Polls' or 'Pows'.[7]

King Robert had ordered his engineers to dig a line of man (and horse) traps along the north bank of the Bannockburn and covering both the existing crossings. This meant, in practical effect, that an attacker would be obliged to advance by Dere Street or the lesser way that ran parallel through the hamlet of Bannock, cross the burn, say half a mile to the east, before angling to join the main road by St Ninian's a mile or so further on. These pits were simple holes or 'pots' concealed beneath foliage and sown with sharp pointed stakes or caltrops, a serious menace to man and mount.

Meandering in its small valley, the Bannockburn separated the two densely-wooded areas. By noon on the 23 June the English army occupied the more southerly, the Tor Wood, whereas the Scots held the forested New Park to the north. This dense belt of trees stood between the invaders and the great rock of Stirling Castle.

Immediately north of the Bannockburn, the hills of New Park and the local eminence of Coxet Hill crowded the west, descending again to more level and cultivated ground, farmed by the inhabitants of St Ninians and Bannock. East of this fertile shelf the ground again descended sharply toward the spongy wetlands of the Carse.

Bruce had been faced with attempting to divine his enemy's intentions and then making his dispositions accordingly. He was not, at this juncture, committed to the need for a major battle. If the English were obliging enough and so tactically unimaginative as to attempt simply to batter a passage through to the castle along the line of the Roman road, they would deploy over the relatively level ground that lay to the east, Balquhidderock, terrain that would not unduly impede cavalry. By 'mining' the lower reaches adjacent to both crossing points, Bruce would do much to inhibit this, but he also needed to dispose his foot brigades in such a manner as would suffice to block the available approaches whilst retaining tactical flexibility.

With the army of King Robert holding the higher ground and overlooking Balquhidderock, the road to the castle wound around the lower reaches, inside the New Park, the actual trackway passing between the Borestone and the Bannockburn. The line occupied by the patriot forces was, on the right, protected by the untamed spread of forest and scrub; the left clung to the natural line of the escarpment running rearward to St Ninian's Kirk.[8] Randolph commanded the first of four Scots brigades and this comprised the men of the northeast, from Moray, Ross, Inverness, Elgin, Nairn and Forres, and he was posted by St Ninian's Kirk toward the northern Flank of the New Park.

Edward Bruce led the patriots of Buchan, Man, Angus, the Mearns, Strathearn, Menteith and Lennox, his brigade livened by a torrent of wild Gallowegians. Walter the High Steward was, at least in name, the general of the third brigade, but, as he was of tender years, his role was effectively filled by the redoubtable Douglas, followed by men from the border marches and Clydesdale. These two brigades were initially deployed between the king's own division and that led by Moray, though Douglas may subsequently have been moved to form a more effective rearguard behind Randolph.

The last and most powerful division was under the king's direct command and beneath his proud banner were also mustered the Highlanders brought by Angus Og – his MacDonalds, Camerons, Campbells, Frasers, Gordons, MacKintoshes, MacLeans, MacGregors, Rosses and Sinclairs. Bruce's division was stationed to cover the crossings of the Bannockburn, the most likely axis of attack ('The Entry'). Bruce had his 500 light horse under Keith, who operated as a screen of skirmishers whilst the patriots laboured to improve their defences. The miry course of the Bannockburn with the Pelstream was a sufficient barrier and this natural obstacle was augmented by the minefields of 'pots'. The King's Park forms the western flank of the approaches to Stirling Castle; it is habitually dry and cavalry can ride quite freely along the line of the road. East of the road lay a stretch of open ground, mainly under the plough, but at its easterly limit this ground dips sharply down toward the much wetter ground of the Carse itself.

Keith's Horse, though potentially formidable, were not viewed as a counter to the weight of the English chivalry, most would be light cavalry or hobilers; tactically their role could be to engage English archers should these, as would be likely, deploy on the flanks of any attack. Bruce could trust in his spears to frustrate the horse but they could only continue if they were protected from missile troops, otherwise any engagement had the potential for a repeat of the debacle at Falkirk, sixteen years before.

By the time the English were completing their long march through the confines of the Tor Wood, King Robert's initial dispositions were complete. His own brigade, which had been stationed by Torwood, had now been moved up to deploy along the line of trees crowding upon the New Park; his brother's command was stationed on the rising ground to the left. To his left, Randolph was positioned around St Ninian's, overlooking the Carse, whilst Douglas now occupied the rearward by the Borestone. The reserve of camp followers and lightly armed kerns took up dead ground to the rear, Keith's hobilers ranged in front.

That morning the Scots, like their adversaries, would have risen early and consumed a frugal meal. Almost certainly they would have heard mass and the king would have held a conference with his principal officers. Even before the English van hove into view it was clear they had only two choices, to advance through the New Park or attempt a longer, flank march across the uncertain ground of the Carse, an option scarcely likely to carry much appeal. As the approaches over the higher, dry ground were 'mined' nearest the crossings the intention was to herd the enemy into narrow lanes.

Preparations were thus well in hand, it remained only for the king to walk amongst his men, radiating reassurance. For medieval man the presence of his king on the field ('a touch of Harry in the night') is powerful medicine, when a man's throat is dry and his bowels uncertain. This army had trained and drilled for weeks, its soldiers were veterans of a score of skirmishes, it had many successes to its name but it had yet to best an English army in open field. Both sides would remember Falkirk. Now the patriots were positioned to completely dominate the approaches to the castle. Edward, if he wished to dislodge them, would be obliged to execute a frontal assault oven the generally-unfavourable ground. If he was to seek to outflank their position then he would be forced to pick his way over the treacherous slime of the Carse. Neither was an inviting prospect.

King Edward, acquainted with de Moubray's welcome intelligence, convened a hasty council of war. Despite the obvious strength of the patriots' dispositions, he nevertheless may have resolved upon an immediate attack, involving horse and foot combined whilst a commanded party of cavalry under Clifford and Beaumont attempted a flank march around the rim of the Carse to slip between the Scottish host and the castle. They would thus be placed to complete the technical relief of the fortress and equally handily deployed to deal death and ruin upon any stragglers if the patriots broke beneath the main assault. Whether the twin advance of the van and the commanded party of horse proceeded as a result of command decisions or by accident remains unclear. To probe your enemy's front whilst feeling around the flank is not without sense. If your van runs into solid opposition the flanking party might unnerve the defender sufficiently to cause a withdrawal, though, as the chroniclers assert, it does appear that neither force was aware of the actions of the other.

If Edward II of England was not a great commander, nor even a particularly good one, he was not the fool many subsequent writers have claimed. His resonance through history is generally viewed entirely in pejorative terms. It must be conceded that he had, technically at least, succeeded in effecting the relief of Stirling Castle, thus securing his immediate tactical objective. In terms of the wider grand tactics, he was seeking a decisive encounter with the Scots. There was no obvious folly in this, he was aware his army was the superior force in terms of numbers and with a very marked, seemingly invincible advantage in terms of heavy cavalry.

He undoubtedly viewed the situation as similar to that which had faced his father before Falkirk, the greatest risk being that the Scots would revert to Fabian tactics and rob him of a decisive engagement in the field. Given the odds it would be very likely they would do so. The combined arms at his disposal – horse, foot and archers – had, when properly and effectively combined, won a resounding triumph in the earlier battle. Neither the king, nor his officers would, however, be unmindful of the lessons of Courtrai; that the pride of the French chivalry should be at first confounded and then destroyed by spears provided a telling antidote to vaunting hubris. Edward would have certainly believed that he could win but not necessarily that the victory would be easily gained. In no place was the ground ideal and the Scots had held station for weeks, ample time to acquaint themselves with every nuance of the terrain and how to use this to their full advantage.

First blood

As the English van debouched from the dense woodland to espy their enemies in front, Bruce was mounted on a humble palfrey, his intention was to confer with Keith and steal a glance at his enemy's strength. Should the English, however, come on along the line of the road, hemmed onto the narrow way by the lethal scattering of pots, then an opportunity might arise to deploy his spears and turn them back with a bloody nose.

The great lion banner proclaimed the presence of the King of Scots and proved a certain lure to the hot-blooded chivalry on the far side of the valley.

A posse of knights, including Gloucester and Hereford, touched spurs; the latter's nephew, Henry de Bohun was with them.[9] Here indeed was a prize, the chance to end the conflict and win the day with a single thrust. De Bohun, mounted on his fine destrier, his lance couched and held across the saddle, gathered momentum and bore down on the king. Sensibly, Robert should simply have withdrawn; he was not fully attired for war, mounted on a mere palfrey and armed only with a timber-shafted horseman's axe.

At the very last moment, or fraction of a moment before impact, the king turned his mount to avoid the lunge and, rising in the stirrups, dealt his adversary a fearful blow with the battleaxe, cleaving both helmet and skull. 'I have broken my good battleaxe,' was his dry observation when his officers, rightly, remonstrated with him for taking so great a risk.

> The Earl of Gloucester and the Earl of Hereford commanded the first line. On Sunday, which was the vigil of St John's day, as they passed by a certain wood and were approaching Stirling Castle, the Scots were seen straggling under the trees as if in flight and a certain knight, Henry de Boun [Bohun] pursued them with the Welsh to the entrance of the wood. For he had in mind that if he found Robert Bruce there he would either kill him or carry him off captive. But when he had come hither, Robert himself came suddenly out of his hiding-place in the wood, and the said Henry, seeing he could not resist the multitude of the Scots, turned his horse with the intention of returning to his companions; but Robert opposed him and struck him on the head with an axe he carried in his hand. His squire, trying to protect or rescue his lord, was overwhelmed by the Scots.[10]

The luckless de Bohun was not the only one to miscalculate, for the whole advance was presently in difficulties, very serious difficulties. Whilst on the road the attackers could advance at a steady pace; once they were required to deploy against the massed ranks of the Scottish spears from King Robert's division now arrayed against them, it was a very different matter. The dense belts of hidden obstacles that constituted a threat to both horse and man and the serried points of the waiting *schiltron* combined to frustrate even the most ardent valour. Command of the van was exercised jointly by Gloucester and Hereford, complicated with the usual chivalric rivalries.[11] The charge, which can never have ridden faster than a slow trot, was soon in difficulties. Stung by obstacles and unsupported, the horse could achieve nothing. Gloucester, attempting to reform, was ignominiously unhorsed and obliged to retire on foot, the attack faltered and stalled.

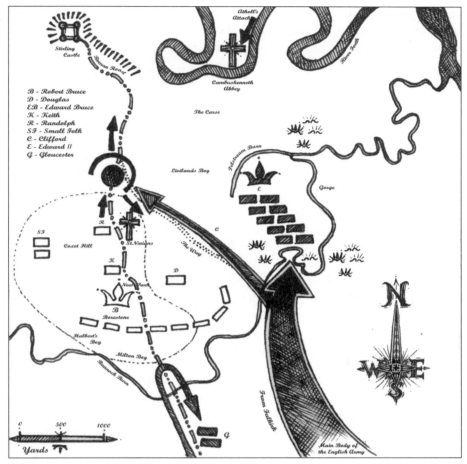

Bannockburn, 23 June 1314.

At first it appeared that Clifford and de Beaumont might fare better.[12] They commanded perhaps three hundred horse and cleverly followed the line of the bridle path on the eastern flank – the course of which lay below the sharp decline. The going was relatively dry and the great bulk of the castle reared ahead, the plain before apparently devoid of any enemy. The second water obstacle of the Pelstream was gained and traversed without hindrance, the column continuing its line of advance, heading northwest along the bridle path to a point almost due east of St Ninian's, which lay half a mile or so to their left.

King Robert, ever watchful, spotted the English pennons and was obliged to issue Randolph with a sharp order to engage forthwith. As the phalanx, its hedgehog points bristling, descended to cut the line of advance, the English knights swung around to meet the challenge. Gray takes up the story; his father, Sir Thomas, a border veteran was on the field, so we may assume the author had his account from one who was present:

> While the advanced guard were following this road, Robert Lord de Clifford and Henry de Beaumont, with three hundred men-at-arms, made a circuit upon the other side of the wood towards the castle, keeping the open ground. Thomas Randolph, Earl of Moray, Robert de Brus's nephew, who was leader of the Scottish advanced guard, hearing that his uncle had repulsed the advance guard of the English on the other side of the wood, thought that he must have his share [of glory] and issuing from the wood with his division marched across the open ground towards the two afore-mentioned lords.[13]

Gray goes on to report that Beaumont attends upon Moray's convenience calling to his riders that they should permit the Scots to fully deploy before charging. Sir Thomas observes that this is unwise, to which de Beaumont retorts that if the knight is leery, he may retire![14] A fierce mêlée now developed, the horse lapping around the *schiltron*, lances clashing with resolute spears, swords and maces hacking and slashing as the horsemen sought to break these impudent foot. They could make no headway. Sir Thomas, throwing himself boldly upon the foe to scorn de Beaumont's taunt, was unhorsed and taken, Sir William Deyncourt slain; other saddles were emptied.[15] Time and again the swirling mass of horsemen broke off and reformed, seeking the crucial breakthrough and entry that momentum must surely provide. It did not, the circle of spears remained unmoved.

As their predecessors had discovered in the opening charges at Falkirk, the knights, however valiant, could not break the *schiltron* unless the spears were first thinned by the clothyard storm. As the English attack ran out of steam Randolph pushed his infantry on to complete the unthinkable, tenant farmers and tradesmen besting the pride of English chivalry. Moray's men stood firm, like an island in the eye of the hurricane, buffeted but not at any point broken. The somnolent air of a warm late spring afternoon was bruised by the clangour of war, blades hacking on points, the sweating foot choking now on the great clouds of dust and steam. The men would have been taught to strike at the horses' faces, causing the mounts to rear and throw their mailed riders. Once on the ground the knight was very much more vulnerable, a man of rank could expect to be grabbed and dragged within the circle of points as a captive, the less illustrious might feel the dirk's cold point enter through face or genitals.

As the battle eddied and swirled, Douglas suggested he might advance his banners to Moray's relief, though the king demurred as Randolph was holding fast and appeared in no need of aid. The combat, however, was finely balanced and Bruce would be fully aware of the carnage that could ensue if the spears wavered and a gap appeared – the horsemen would ride through and over like the spilling of the dyke. The order for Douglas to march was given and the second *schiltron* moved up. The sudden appearance of fresh numbers did not immediately dismay the English, some of whom turned to meet the new threat, but the fury had gone out of the attack, men and beasts were tired and bloodied, some, though perhaps not many, had fallen and there was no sign of the enemy wavering. Moray, timing the moment to perfection, ordered his men to march on and they rose as one, steadied their staves and began to push forward.

This was enough; the English broke off, one group riding for the castle, the second and larger formation retiring by the route they'd come, the jeers and huzzas of their jubilant opponents ringing in their ears, more than a few saddles empty. Twice the English cavalry had advanced in different sectors of the first day's field and twice they had been checked and discomfited. De Bohun and Deyncourt were dead, Gray and others taken. Scottish losses had been trifling. If the Scots required proof of their prowess, the solid boost to morale that only victory can bring, then this was it; for Bruce and his officers, a moment of quiet self congratulation. The battle was not yet won but they had made a most satisfactory beginning.

So thoroughly had the English been chastened that Moray's weary men received a rapturous welcome from their comrades. Bruce too was impressed, to the extent that he was prepared to dilute his customary caution and ask the men outright if they thought they could win the larger fight that lay in prospect:

> I am full well assured that many an [English] heart shall waver that seemed erstwhile of mighty valour. And if the heart be dismayed, the body is not worth a mite. I trow therefore that a good ending shall follow this beginning. Nevertheless I say not this to you in order that ye shall follow my desire to fight; for with you will rest the whole matter. If you think it expedient that we fight, we shall fight; and if ye will that we depart, your desire will be fulfilled. I shall consent to do in either fashion right as ye shall decide. Therefore speak plainly your desire.[16]

The decision
In the long lines of English horse and foot, still stretched out along the line of the Roman Road, there was little cause for celebration, both initial skirmishes had ended badly with the flower of the invaders' chivalry vanquished. Losses,

in all probability, had been light but the dents to prestige were not inconsiderable. It must be questioned to what extent the morale of the rank and file suffered as a result of their betters' chastisement, perhaps less than might be imagined. It would not be unnatural for the foot, 'the poor, bloody infantry', to enjoy a quiet smirk at the discomfiture of the valiant horse, perhaps even a sly sense of admiration for those doughty Scottish spearmen.

For King Edward and his generals, Pembroke, Gloucester, Hereford and Clifford, several of whom had experienced the mettle of their foes at first hand, there was some serious thinking to be done. It was clear that the direct route to Stirling, passing through the Entry, proceeding along Dere Street and then through the New Park, was impassable. By mining the road and using his brigades effectively King Robert had barred the door; the attempt to outflank, if that had been Clifford and de Beaumont's purpose, had also foundered.

On this basis, the only viable approach was over the Carse, by no means an attractive prospect, given the nature of the ground and the prevailing wetness. Logistical considerations were now pressing: men and, above all, valuable horses needed fodder and refreshment, even those who had not been engaged were wearied by their fatiguing marches. The afternoon was, by now, well advanced and it appeared inconceivable that the army could mount any further offensive action that day.

To get the army from its present position, strung out along Dere Street and hemmed by trees, onto the Carse would be no easy matter; quite the reverse, it would be a major exercise in controlled manoeuvre. To advance toward the Entry, or the lower crossing at Bannock, would be to invite a repeat of Wallace's earlier triumph, defeat in detail as the Scottish spears swooped like hawks upon the extended lines and their great tail of carts and *bouches inutiles*. The only safe option was to swing the entire column to the right, move northeast over the bridle path and cross by the lower fords. This had the added advantage that the steep banks would have levelled out and the crossing would be easier for both horse and man.

Moving by companies, the foot began to filter through the trees, the horse picking their way over footpaths and tracks, sergeants and the marshals hoarse with bellowing, red-faced and doubtless evil-tempered in the afternoon sun. Once clear of the trees the army would have to negotiate the steep decline onto the Carse and pick their way across its damp and miry surface. We can imagine the difficulties this operation entailed: the vast English host, debouching from the trees in groups that would coalesce and swell over the tiny fields beyond, great tramping legions, kicking up a confusion of dust and noise, laced with the pithy exhortation of officers and NCOs. Manhandling the cumbersome train over the difficult ground and down the incline would be no easy matter, something of a logistical feat.

Men and beasts would have sought refreshment at St Peter's well or from the waters of the burn, but the crossing places would quickly be turned into viscous quagmires by the passage of so many. The chroniclers advise that English pioneers made free use of building materials stripped from the hapless town of Bannock, the common view being that timbers and doors were used to bridge the many streams and pools of the Pows. More recent analysis has suggested that the despoliation was more systematic and the purpose was to reinforce the fords, to use timber and boards to create what would be a crude form of plank or 'corduroy' road.[17] A similar process would be adopted to shore the crossing of the Pelstream.

As this great lumbering avalanche of armoured men, barded horses and palfreys, wagons, carts, the sprawling caravanserai of camp followers, descended onto the plain, someone had to decide what to do next, to select a safe and suitable camping ground. This singularly unenviable chore fell upon the provosts or harbingers who were responsible for billeting. The job of the billeting officer has never been an easy one. In this instance they were charged to find dry, level ground, where the lords might pitch their pavilions, with water for the horses and as secure as might be found.

Security was key given the considerable reputation which the Scots now possessed as guerrillas. There was every reason to suspect they would seek to capitalize on their earlier successes by launching a series of spoiling raids against the English lines. Such concerns were hardly fanciful: the Scots knew the ground, they were highly-skilled fighters, led by dynamic and aggressive officers, their morale was boosted by success and there were many throats ripe for slitting. Time and again the Scots would demonstrate a flair for 'beating up' enemy quarters. Tellingly in the course of the ill-fated Weardale campaign in 1327, they would come within an ace of capturing Edward III.

These harassed harbingers, therefore, had three primary considerations: security, the approach to Stirling and comfort. The ground adjacent to the ford would have been churned and muddied beyond immediate repair; the more easterly reaches of the Carse were studded by the polls and bisected by a myriad of small brooks and watercourses, equally unsuitable. That area which lay in the deep bow of the Bannockburn and the Pelstream, the two streams forming an inverted 'U' offered the best available prospect.

In terms of comfort it was the ease of magnates and gentry that counted, the commons could shift for themselves; tents would have to be unloaded and pitched, harness stripped and burnished, squires sweating to remove rust and oil the links. Fodder for the destriers was provided from the wagons, the forage on the Carse would not impart the same vitality as oats and the beasts were better mettlesome if a fight was coming. Fuel was sparse and any available timber not sequestered by the pioneers would be pressed into service.

Nobody was expecting a quiet or relaxed sojourn on the Carse, the foe was too close, the conditions too cramped and there were those who sought solace in strong drink and waxed raucous as the long summer evening wore on. The whole spreading panoply would have resembled an entire people on the march: the great clutter of carts, the *bacaudae* of artisans, whores, sutlers, vintners and opportunists who made up the tail, selling each of their wares. Amidst the endless ranks of the foot, few of whom would have stripped off their harness or jacks for fear of Scots attack, the smells of cooking, stale sweat, the odours of unwashed men and beasts, competed to pollute the clear air. 'But there was no rest', complains the Life of Edward II, 'for they spent it sleepless, expecting the Scots rather to attack by night than to await for battle by day'.[18]

The king may have entertained his senior officers but the mood cannot have been jolly. Surrounded by a glitterati of pretty young knights, Edward was expecting, next day, to resume his advance upon Stirling, his army set in proper battle array, horse in the centre with archers, *en masse*, on both flanks. Such a formation could cope with whatever offensive the Scots might decide. What had patently not occurred to him was the possibility the Scots might launch an all out pre-emptive assault on the present position. With the inestimable benefit of hindsight it is clear this was grossly negligent and yet there was no existing precedent for such bold action.

Wallace's victory at Stirling, though brilliant, was opportunistic and gifted by the incompetence of the English officers. Longshanks, at Falkirk, had demonstrated that the partnering of shock and missile troops, properly harnessed, was a proven battle winner. Bruce had no novel troop types, possessed no new reservoir of heavy horse. That the English had been worsted during the day's encounters could not be gainsaid, there were empty places at the king's board, De Bohun, Deyncourt and Grey but, in the grander scheme, these reverses were mere pinpricks, the potency of the host not even dented. The Scots could surely not expect to repeat their successes in open field.

Not all were sanguine, Gloucester undoubtedly spoke for many officers when he bravely opined that the advance should be postponed for twenty-four hours to allow the men to rest and recuperate. He was scornfully shouted down, the king, in his shallow hubris, even going so far as to accuse the earl of faintheartedness, a bitter and underserved slur. If any of the other magnates secretly agreed with Gloucester they kept their opinions to themselves. The king would have his advance on the morrow and the army must accept whatever hazard the foe chose to offer. Gloucester may have been suspect as it was he who had warned Bruce years before after the Red Comyn had 'spilled the beans' to Longshanks. Certainly the author of *The Life of Edward II* feels that Gloucester's advice reflected widely-held concerns:

> Wherefore our men [the English] , the veterans that is, and the more experienced, advised that we should not fight that day, but rather wait for the morrow, both on account of the importance of the feast [that of St John the Baptist] and the toil they had already undergone. This practical and honourable advice was rejected by the younger men as idle and cowardly ... The Earl of Gloucester counseled the king not to go forth to battle that day, but to rest on account of the feast, and let his army recuperate as much as possible. But the king spurned the earl's advice, and growing very heated with him, charged him with treachery and deceit.[19]

What of matters on 'the other side of the hill?' The Scots too were in hurried council. Bruce was disinclined to fight again – the day's combat had achieved its objectives. Randolph and the ever-valiant Douglas were all for moving onto the offensive. Bruce had remained steadfastly opposed to an attack – the risk was enormous: all that he had won by patience, skill and guile could be lost in an hour.

> For Robert Bruce, knowing himself unequal to the strength of the king of England in strength or fortune, decided that it would be better to resist our king by secret warfare rather than dispute his right in open battle. Indeed I might be tempted to sing the praises of Sir Robert Bruce did not the guilt of homicide and the dark stain of treachery bid me keep silent.[20]

Douglas, Randolph and Edward Bruce were all for seizing the moment and committing to an all out offensive; stirring sentiments but Bruce had cause to think long and hard. He was an experienced commander, it was obvious his opponent was not. His men were fresh and buoyed by victory, in the mêlée they had more than proved their worth. Yet the fact was no Scots army since Stirling had beaten the English in open field, and that only in exceptional circumstances; neither Dunbar nor Falkirk offered encouragement. If he attacked and won, the entire nature of the war would shift, no longer would he be the under-dog rising from the heather to bite the enemy's ankles, avoiding the lure and hazard of battle. If he lost, then Scotland was ruined, plunged back into the desolation of defeat.

It is said that Sir Alexander Seton who had just defected to the patriot cause convinced the king that the moment was right: 'Now's the time'. This enthusiastic admonition from one so newly arrived from the English camp finally swayed the cautious King Robert to hazard all. 'It greatly pleased his [Bruce's] heart and he was persuaded that men of such mind, if they set their strength to it, must indeed be night hard to vanquish'. At this time of year the northern nights are usually both short and mild. Sunrise on Monday 24 June, the feast of St John the Baptist, would be around 3.34 am. Gulping down a mess of oats (those who had the stomach, doubtless fortified with a dram), the Scots had, by 2.00 am, heard mass. Half an hour later dawn's pale outriders were visible in the sky and the *schiltrons* were on the move, the four brigades advancing in echelon. Edward Bruce took the van on the right, followed by Randolph and then Douglas. The king's strong brigade formed the rear, with Keith's horse in reserve. Posterity had cause that day to be indebted to Bernard, the Abbot of Arbroath, who took down the text of the king's speech to the host:

My lords, my people, accustomed to enjoy that full freedom for which in times gone by the kings of Scotland have fought many a battle. For eight years or more I have struggled with much labour for my right to the kingdom and for honourable liberty. I have lost brothers, friends and kinsmen. Your own kinsmen have been made captive, and bishops and priests are locked in prison. Our country's nobility has poured forth its blood in war. These barons you can see before you, clad in mail, are bent upon destroying me and obliterating my kingdom, nay, our whole nation. They do not believe we can survive. They glory in their warhorses and equipment. For us, the name of the Lord must be our hope of victory in battle; if you heartily repent of your sins you will be victorious, under God's command.[21]

The die was cast.

Chapter 6

Trial by Battle (2) – 24 June 1314

Ring the alarum-bell! Blow wind, come wrack;
At least we'll die with harness on our back!
 – William Shakespeare, *MacBeth*

Sir Alexander de Seton, who was in the service of England and had come thither
with the King, secretly left the English army, went to Robert de Brus in the wood,
and said to him: 'Sir, this is the time if ever you intend to undertake to reconquer
Scotland. The English have lost heart and are discouraged, and expect nothing but
a sudden, open attack.

Then he described their condition, and pledged his head on pain of being hanged and
drawn, that if he [Bruce] would attack them on the morrow he would defeat them
easily without [much] loss.
 – Sir Thomas Gray, *Scalacronica*[1]

Advance to contact

Each *schiltron* was deployed in eight ranks with 188 spears in each, the men
removing one or both of their leather-soled shoes to ensure a firmer grip on the
sodden earth. A final reserve, or 'small folk', was moved forward to the line of
the ridge so that they might be engaged to exploit any opportunity as it arose.
The stage was thus set. History, as a rule, tends more to the insidious than the
dramatic, rarely do events move with the eloquence and drama of stage or
screen, as though scripted. 24 June 1314 is a marked exception, for this is one
of those days that change history. King Robert had taken the momentous
decision to give battle. That he should have hesitated beforehand is not to be
remarked upon, such prudence was well-founded. His army, though tested,
had never undergone the full rite of battle against a superior foe, one whose
numbers were greater and whose potency, at least on paper, was higher. That
the day would be decisive could not now be doubted and the fate of nations
would hang in the balance.

Edward II did not expect to be attacked, his dispositions were defensive
in that he sought to defend against hit-and-run raids rather than a concerted

tactical offensive. To date the *schiltrons* had not been deployed as attacking formations; it is much easier to dispose of large bodies of spearmen in defensive hedges than to marshal them to take the fight to the foe. The sight of the Scottish brigades debouching from the tree cover and deploying in line of battle must, in the growing light of the warm spring morning, have been distinctly unnerving.

It has been suggested that king Edward had prepared his army for battle but had assumed that the threat would come from the north rather than the west, and that his mounted brigades were facing across the Pelstream toward Stirling Castle.[2] As the traditional or likely deployment of the period would involve the mounted arm in the centre with knights formed in parallel bodies under their bannerets, and archers on the flanks, it is possible this is correct.

Alternatively such an interpretation might assume a greater degree of planning than was in fact the case, though the Pelstream would not form a particularly severe obstacle. In the event, the bulk of the fighting on the English side would be undertaken by the cavalry with initial support from a skirmish line of bowmen and, later, a more structured but flawed deployment.

In this version the English army forms front, ten squadrons of horse on the left, the van and the rear to the right, with the king's gleaming household taking the centre. In such a scenario the bulk of the foot would have to have stood on the right, bills, bows and the ubiquitous Welsh 'knife-men', as all accounts appear to agree that the English foot were barely engaged. The stolid Scottish spearmen who formed below the dip of the Dryfield to march on across the Carse appeared very workaday compared to the great blaze of colour from their chivalric opponents. But they were hardened by long service, purposeful in their files, muted hues of faded gambesons with only the proud banners of their immediate commanders raised aloft, their points a steel tipped forest.

> The Scots directed their course boldly upon the English army, which had been under arms all night, with their horses bitted. They mounted in great alarm, for they were not accustomed to fight on foot.[3]

Gray echoes the prevailing belief that English morale was low. This may not necessarily be so. True the knights, or a number of them, had been given a bloody nose but that was not a serious tactical defeat and the Scots had shown no prior signs of moving onto the attack. Trokelowe rather opines that the English horse were anxious to be revenged for the previous day's failure:

> Some of the English army, riding out in front of the Scots' formations, challenged them ferociously, but they, resisting manfully, killed many

nobles on that Sunday, viz. the Vigil of the Nativity of St John the Baptist. As a result the English were exasperated and firmly resolved to be avenged or be defeated on the following day.[4]

Bruce may have deployed a screen of missile troops, mainly his slender reserve of archers, as skirmishers.[5] This would be a sound move as their shafts would deflect their considerably more numerous opponents from immediately loosing onto the tightly packed files behind. Some English archers certainly replied, with or without orders and there was a burst of outpost bickering as the two sides traded volleys. Lanercost records the outcome:

> On the morrow – an evil, miserable and calamitous day for the English – when both sides had made themselves ready for battle, the English archers were thrown forward before the line, and the Scots archers engaged them, a few being killed on either side: but the king of England's archers quickly put the others to flight.[6]

King Robert had a further surprise in that he intended to deliver his attack with the brigades in echelon, a series of blows rather than one concerted push. This tactic, potentially devastating, required first rate discipline, cohesion and communication; that the manoeuvre could be successfully accomplished under battle conditions speaks volumes for the quality of training Bruce and his highly competent officers had imparted.

Edward Bruce led the Scottish van, his right anchored on the Bannockburn; to his left rear marched Randolph's men, and Douglas behind. This deployment produced the effect of pushing the English bows to their right, toward the Pelstream. The king's own brigade, the strongest of the quartet now on the field, brought up the rear, marching between Randolph and Douglas. It is unlikely that any observer in the English camp seeing the great strength and resolve of this steady advance could doubt their enemies were anything but earnest; the many professionals present must have grudgingly admired the steadiness of the Scots' brigades.

In the following century, beginning with their struggle against Burgundy, the redoubtable Swiss pikes would become the arbiters of battle on the continent, till gunfire destroyed them at Bicocca in 1522. Their success was due to rigid, almost fanatical discipline, first-class intensive training and sound tactical deployment. A later King of Scots, James IV, would seek to import Swiss tactics to replicate the great victory at Bannockburn, but James was not Bruce, nor were his men veterans. James IV, though he comprehended the theory of Swiss tactics perfectly, blundered over his choice of ground and led his men to disaster. For the spears to succeed, like the Macedonian phalanx before them, they had to retain both impetus and cohesion, loss of either was to court failure.

As James too would discover, the deployment once in motion could not be modified, the pikes were essentially a 'one shot' weapon. Once they were committed the die was very much cast, to recall and reform them nigh on impossible. The supreme commander's role was therefore to plan the attack carefully and select ground that would facilitate the momentum of the attack but would not expose the men any longer than was strictly necessary to the attentions of the enemy's missile troops. Like Bruce, the Swiss favoured attacking in echelon, covering the exposed ground at a steady pace, narrowing the gap between their points and the enemy line as swiftly as the need to maintain mass would permit. A disorderly advance, such as occurred at Flodden, was almost bound to fail, the men losing that vital impetus, the great hammer blow as the massed staves struck the foe like a veritable steamroller.

As the *schiltrons* advanced the tide was still high, filling the Forth, the Bannockburn and the Pelstream, thus enhancing the value of these water obstacles. Bruce, having taken the initiative, needed above all else to retain it. If he could advance to the mouth of the pocket occupied by the English, compressed in their encampment, he could prevent Edward from maximizing his superior forces over a wider battlefield. If the English were given sufficient ground to deploy as they would intend, their horse in the centre, bows and bills on the flanks, then they would achieve a decisive tactical advantage. Much would now depend upon how fast the English could deploy, if they could break out of the trap that was already forming.

Many in the Scottish ranks would be aware of the risk from archers, some would be survivors of the carnage at Falkirk who could regale their comrades with dire warnings of the clothyard storm; to advance to contact as swiftly as the line of march would allow, offered the best chance to avoid such a lethal deluge. King Edward II still appeared to have doubts; wedded to his romantic version of chivalric warfare, he seemed unable to grasp the fact the Scots were nearly upon him, just a few hundred yards to the west (the distance across the Carse was perhaps half a mile or so from the base of the escarpment).

With the monarch was Sir Ingram Umfraville, who suggested the English should decline contact and fall back behind their own exposed baggage train and allow the disorder of plunder to upset the Scottish plans.[7] There is a suggestion the Scots halted before contact and fell to their knees for a final unction. This gives rise to the tale that Edward exclaimed his enemies knelt to beseech his mercy and Umfraville gave the tart response that though they might kneel it was not the king's forgiveness they sought. Such a version, though tempting in poetic terms cannot be sustained. The Scots had previously seen to the welfare of their souls and the advance could not be stopped once begun, momentum and cohesion together were all.[8]

We may imagine that, as the phalanxes of serried staves marched on, seeming to devour the intervening ground, the English camp would have been the scene for frenzied activity: squires straining with harness; grooms throwing saddles on the mettlesome mounts, fumbling with bards and chanfrons; the air thick with curses and a blur of movement; grindstones sparking as blades were sharpened; sergeants already soaked in sweat bellowing orders; knights and bannerets, stomping and fretting to order by squadrons. It is most likely that many knights in the van were amongst those who had lain in full harness, wrists looped around the reins of saddled destriers. These would be the first to mount, following the imperative of the trumpets. The Earl of Gloucester was still smarting from the gross injustice of his uncle's conduct the night before.

He and Hereford exchanged fresh broadsides as to which, now, should lead. Hereford was Constable but Gloucester claimed precedence:

> For there was rivalry between him [Gloucester] and the Earl of Hereford who should take precedence in the line and the Earl of Hereford said that this was lawfully his, because he was Constable of England. Gloucester replied that his forbears had always led the van, and therefore this pertained to him by custom ...[9]

Battle

In a foul and violent temper, the Earl flung himself, without his blazon, into the saddle and set off at the canter, his *mesnie* knights streaming behind; King Edward would witness who was fainthearted and who was not. This conduct was not due to failing morale and there is clearly substance in the suggestion that the knights charged because they sought both the glory in the day and revenge for the upsets of the previous:

> As for the reason for this disaster, I do not know to what misfortune I can attribute it; unless perhaps because the English advanced rashly and in a more undisciplined manner than was appropriate. For their men were weary and weak from too much haste, debilitated by hunger and lacking sleep's restoration[10]

At least one other chronicler, le Baker, states that the English were overconfident, which he evidences with the assertion that the magnates had brought with them a veritable caravanserai of luxury items:

> they got together to bring with them vessels of gold and silver such as men of rank are used to indulge themselves with in times of peace. Never up to

that time nor later has been seen so much nobility so nobly equipped nor swelled with such arrogance.[11]

This precipitate rush was rank folly, the worst response to a measured advance of spears. The horse, to be effective without missile troops, would require maximum impact, steamroller to steamroller if they were to beat the *schiltrons*. Throwing tactics to the wind and flinging themselves forward in some Homeric gesture was tantamount to gross negligence. The spears just ate them up. Gloucester could not have fared worse if Bruce had dictated his tactics.

Thundering across the Carse, flinging themselves against the points of Edward Bruce's brigade, the Earl together with Clifford, Sir John Comyn, Sir Edward Mauley and Sir Pain Tiptoft, were unhorsed and slain. The pride of English chivalry fell to Scottish peasantry, their proud destriers impaled on hungry points; tumbled knights were hacked and stabbed, daggers thrust through visors, beneath the arms or into the groin. Gloucester, though worth a hefty ransom, was not spared; without his surcoat he appeared no more than an ordinary knight, a life without cash value did not qualify for clemency.

According to the Life of Edward II, Gloucester attacked Douglas' brigade and actually succeeded in breaking into the mass of spears and was there unhorsed and killed, due, as the chronicler avers, to the faintheartedness of his affinity:

> The earl withstood him [Douglas] manfully once and again penetrated their wedge, and would have been victorious if he had faithful companions. But look! At a sudden rush of the Scots, the earl's horse is killed and the earl rolls to the ground. Lacking defenders and borne down by the weight of his body-armour he could not easily arise, and of the five hundred cavalry whom he had led to battle at his own expense, he almost alone was killed[13]

Such conduct was inexcusable. However Gloucester may have been smarting, his experiences of the day before should clearly have shown that an ill-judged canter onto the spears would achieve nothing but oblivion. Even as they fell, the piled carcasses of men and beasts created a wall of impediment to those who must follow. More English cavalry streamed forth to take on Edward Bruce's brigade. Great clouds of dust and steam would obscure the struggling mass so that a man, his vision already clouded by the red mist of battle, would struggle to see even that which was directly before him. Lances glanced from spear shafts, keen-edged blades hacked at the points. Some horsemen, frustrated in their attempts to get to grips with the impenetrable hedge, hurled axes, maces, swords and daggers. All to no avail, the line could not be breached and the

king's brother had firmly anchored his flank against the Bannockburn, the trap
had begun to close.

As the *schiltrons* crashed, one after the other, into the milling mass of English
horse, a desperate mêlée ensued. The scene is reminiscent of Marshal Ney's
gallant but fruitless charges at Waterloo, great streaming knots of magnificently
caparisoned horses, spilling around the schlitrons, as the French would later
lap around the British squares. Furious in their impotence the imperious war
horses, reared and lunged, the dense hedge of points thrusting at chest and
eyes. Stricken animals keening in fright, shied violently aside or, dying, pitched
their mailed riders at their enemies' feet, so that daggers and axes could
complete their frightful travail. The Lanercost chronicler records the fury of
the initial clash:

> Truly, when both armies engaged each other and the great horses of the
> English charged the pikes of the Scots, as it were into a dense forest, there
> arose a great and terrible crash of spears broken and of destriers wounded
> to the death; and so they remained without movement for a while. Now
> the English in the rear could not reach the Scots because the leading
> division was in the way, nor could they do anything to help themselves;
> wherefore there was nothing for it but to take flight.[14]

Despite the frantic gallantry of these attacks, the momentum of the spears was
scarcely checked and the three brigades formed up, as though on parade.
Together they formed the cork in the bottle, the English were denied further
room for tactical manoeuvre, Bruce had decided on the ground and the trap
wherein his enemies now found themselves represented everything he could
have hoped for. For all this the battle was neither lost nor won, if the gap
between the Bannockburn and Pelstream was, say, 1,200 yards in width,
allowing for a yard of ground per spearman and assuming little space between
the brigades, the files could not have been more than four or five men deep, by
no means an overwhelming mass.[15]

> One slashes, one slays, one warns, one wounds, one is routed, one lurks,
> one swaggers, one shoves, one groans, one is worsted; one shrieks, one
> shrinks, one shakes, one shudders, one is roped, one picks, one cloaks, one
> plucks, one pokes, one is robbed. There is increasing hunger. Bodies and
> booty are ransacked. Sadly, warriors, women and heirs are affected.
>
> Earl of Clare, admired inspirer of courage, landholder of Gloucester,
> alas! You die, laid low in the carnage! Thus God becomes avenger. Fierce
> Clifford, the sword-tip has blunted you, by great blows you are cut down
> in the thick of the foe. William Marshal, brave knight in the battle lines,

Scottish hardness has wounded you to the death. Edmund Mauley, bold in your manliness, you are overwhelmed by ferocious hostile folk. Tibetot, distinguished soldier, like a blazing fire, you are put out by swords and pikes, your death a threat to the standards[16]

Bruce had not yet committed his own strong brigade, which he wisely kept in hand. The other three, despite the odds able to be ranged against them, were doing rather well, the English horse impotent and sustaining losses. The noise would be tremendous, a crashing symphony of discord that rang across the plain, clear to the mighty ramparts of the castle and beyond, the clarion of a nation's deliverance. Men swore and yelled, emptied their lungs in screams and howls of agony as wounds bit home, the spring grass slippery with entrails and gore, pumping in great arterial gouts from the shrieking bodies of the stricken.

King Edward II, if he was no general, would not be accused of playing the poltroon. Monarch and gilded entourage fought in the front, as more and more cavalry came into play. Numbers were of no advantage, however, for the thicker the press, the less momentum. Those at the front could make to impression against the hedge of spears, those at the back fought each other for space to deploy. The king, by riding to the fore, showed greater hubris than judgement. His army was effectively leaderless; the lowly foot, including the potentially decisive missile arm, was allotted no role in the struggle.

With the English host careening wildly against the log jam of unyielding spears and the rest packed like sardines behind, some without sufficient space even to free their blades, there was little prospect of the foot becoming engaged. The trap was working, for the king of England's great swell of numbers counted for nothing in the narrows. Some archers did shoot over the heads of the cavalry, hoping their shafts would plunge into the packed masses of spears. This was largely ineffective, the arrows falling beyond the Scottish ranks, with more than the odd shaft striking their mounted comrades in the back, something which did little to endear the despised foot to their chivalric betters. More ominously for Bruce, a commanded body of bowmen was ordered to the right where, splashing across the burn, they took station with the Pelstream on their left flank. This gave them a clear shot at Douglas' brigade which soon found itself in difficulties, the arrows scarcely able to miss their mark in the press.

Wallace's men had been flayed by the arrow storm at Falkirk, the dense packed ranks of spears a perfect target for the men of the grey goose feather, their shafts whistling and biting deep into largely unprotected flesh. For the Scottish foot this was a terrible ordeal, the men could scarcely move within their ranks, as the arrows smacked home. This was the nightmare; Bruce could

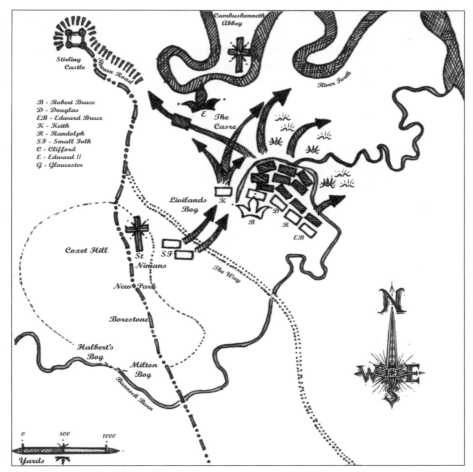

Bannockburn, 24 June 1314.

see the plan of attack unraveling if his men remained exposed, pinned by the horse in front, assailed from the flank. If one brigade gave way, then either the line would fold or the remaining *schiltrons* would become surrounded. Now was the moment for Keith's light horse to advance, to sweep down upon the archers, themselves unsupported, in a classic light cavalry action.

It was now that the doughty Scottish hobilers cantered over the Carse, their ponies' hooves flinging up clods from the damp earth, lances levelled. The archers, themselves taken in flank, had little time to react, even if they attempted to stand. This was no lumbering mass of feudal chivalry but swift, hard hitting and decisive. The surviving bowmen pelted back across the stream, Douglas was granted deliverance and the line held. The ranks on both sides were packed so tightly that the dead and wounded scarcely had room to fall. Once on the ground an injured man could likely measure his remaining span in seconds. English lances and Scottish spears lunged and parried, bit and thrust, the churned earth soon puddled in gore, spilt blood and entrails drenching the fighters.

Inexorably the Scots began to edge forwards, driving their mounted opponents back, Bruce now sent his own strong reserve in on the left to bolster Douglas, whose men were shaken and thinned by the arrows, Keith's hobilers still patrolling the far bank to deter any repetition. With his own brigade committed, Bruce had no viable reserves remaining; his men must win through or surely perish. None on the English side possessed the authority or the wit to attempt a full flank attack. Strong foot detachments, supported by the horse, could have crossed the Pelstream or, with difficulty, the Bannockburn, and come upon their foes from the flank or rear. Fortunately for the Scots, no such evidence of tactical competence emerged.

'Push, push, push' the Scots commanders urged as the fight continued, neither side having the advantage. For an hour or more the hosts remained locked, the dead and dying carpeting the mire. In the nature of medieval combat it would not be possible for the men to fight continuously for such a length of time. Wielding lance, sword or spear, particularly, as with the English, on an empty belly, is exhausting. It would inevitably be the case that, along the line, the leading files would draw back from time to time, to regain their breath and summon up the energy to continue. The hardy clansmen from Bruce's brigade either filled the gaps left by the arrows amongst Douglas' men or added their formidable brawn to the rear of the other formations, driving their tired comrades forward, akin to the press of a gigantic scrum.

These sons of Clan Donald were seasoned warriors, bearers of a proud lineage, who claimed their descent from Somerled and, through him, a distant line of Irish heroes. This day they did king and country good service, earning their coveted privilege to always hold the right of the line, the place of honour, a tradition that would be remembered even to that last grim charge over the bloody ground at Culloden. A battle is a finely-tuned affair, morale can fluctuate according to its tempo and, with all his forces now committed, there appeared little more King Robert could do to affect the outcome. This was now a soldier's battle, dependent not upon strategy and grand tactics but upon the grit and stamina of the individual, on the esprit de corps within units. The Scots, pushing forward, sensed a weakening; their archers, skirmishing on the flanks, were finding an abundance of targets; the great wedged mass of English was visibly wavering. With a great collective shout of triumph bursting from their lungs the spears drove forward, sloughing off exhaustion, adrenalin pumping.

> Let the pikeman strike like a snake with a deadly thrust. Let the smooth shafted spear pierce the commanders, spilling blood, causing anguish with lethal missiles! Let the billman with his axe sever leg from trunk, brandish shafts; thus he will overcome if he perseveres. The sword-tip stands forth. No one realizes that in combat nothing helps. Fortune overlooks those destined to have their places filled[17]

Bruce did have a single formation thus far uncommitted and this was the 'small folk', a *Volksturm* of those unfitted for service in the front rank, untrained or with skills more suited to the rear, leavened by the usual horde of varlets, camp followers, artisans and general looters. These now advanced, either by command or, more probably, on their own initiative and could be seen lining the Dryfield slope. Most were armed and flaunted a streaming of (rather *ad hoc*) banners. It is likely that these *bacaudae* were motivated by greed and opportunism, rather than love of country, spoil being the greater incentive.[18]

What appears certain is that this final reinforcement was interpreted by the hard-pressed English as indicating that the Scots still had reserves and that their full strength was not yet committed. Wavering in the ranks had accelerated to a steady trickle from the rear as thoughts of '*sauve qui peut*' sprang uppermost in men's minds. Courage is a collective as well as an individual resource, its sustenance is the commander's most valuable resource; lack of effective command is more likely than anything else to sap the collective and thus the individual resolve.

The rot always begins at the back, gathers momentum, swells from a bare trickle, to a stream, to a river, then the flood, the bursting of the dam. Once that point is reached then a rally is well nigh impossible. Men who have striven valiantly for hours, kept their faces to the foe and borne their arms with valour will be transformed, upon the fatal instant, into a panic-stricken rabble, casting aside honour and harness, fleeing for their lives like rabbits caught in the headlight's glare.

Rout

Edward II was not thinking in terms of defeat. He fought with manic courage in the thick of the mêlée. His household knight, Sir Roger Northburgh, had been unhorsed and taken, his glitterati bruised, bloodied and thinned. As the steam began to drain from the English effort, saving the royal person from capture assumed priority status. Edward, to his credit, would give no heed but his two paladins, Pembroke and Sir Giles d'Argentan, were mindful of their charge and virtually dragged the king from the press. This retreat, however, could not pass unnoticed, especially as a half a thousand chosen knights formed the royal escort. Even if he had to be removed by force the king's abrupt departure from the field sent a very clear message to his soldiers. The king's party splashed over the Pelstream, brushed Keith's hobilers aside and rode directly for the mighty walls of Stirling.

D'Argentan, having done his duty to the throne, proceeded to discharge his obligation as a knight and rode straight for the Scottish spears, dying on the points of Edward Bruce's men. Gray confirms the quixotic gesture:

> As those who had the king's rein were thus drawing him always forward, one of them, Giles de Argentin, a famous knight who had lately come over the sea from the wars of the Emperor Henry of Luxembourg, said to the king: 'Sire, your rein was committed to me; you are now in safety; there is your castle where your person may be safe. I am not accustomed to fly nor am I going to begin now. I commend you to God!' then setting his spurs to his horse he returned to the mêlée, where he was slain.[19]

The king's flight acted as a catalyst to transform fight into rout as though by dire alchemy, the entire English position dissolving into a sudden panic. Hundreds of the fleeing men, exhausted, many injured, weighed down with harness, died in the thrashing waters of the Forth. More drowned or were trampled under in the Pelstream and Bannockburn. The whole of the Carse became a giant butcher's yard, the narrow passage of the Bannockburn before the confluence was choked with dead and dying, men and horses piled in great shuddering, moaning piles. Barbour asserts the 'Bannockburn betwixt the braes of horses and men so charged was that upon drowned horses and men, man might pass dry over it'.[20] The Lanercost chronicler confirms the scale of the disaster:

> This account I heard from a trustworthy person who was an eyewitness. In the leading division were killed the Earl of Gloucester, Sir John Comyn, Sir Pagan de Tiptoft, Sir Edmund de Mauley and many other nobles besides footsoldiers who fell in great numbers. Another calamity which befell the English was that, whereas they had shortly before crossed a great ditch called Bannockburn into which the tide flows and now wanted to recross it in confusion, many nobles and others fell into it with their horses in the crush while others escaped with much difficulty and many were never able to extricate themselves from the ditch.[21]

How many died can only be guessed at, but the casualties on the English side would certainly be numbered in thousands. Over one hundred knights, to-gether with all their harness, horses and baggage, were taken – the triumphant

Scots would pick the field clean. Bruce had perhaps lost several hundred. The pursuit cannot, however, have being either long or intense, the exhausted Scottish foot were in no shape to endure further exertion and the paucity of their horse would restrict the scale of slaughter. For the English foot, immured in a hostile land, abandoned by their king, this was apt to be scant consolation.

We may assume that bodies of fleeing men were rallied and reformed for the long march home. The locals, previously cowed by the majesty of the unbowed host, would be a mite less restrained, prowling the shattered army like jackals, cutting off and cutting up stragglers, hungry for a share of the loot. And loot there was; all of the English king's chattels, the gorgeous baubles of his cata-mites, the silver and plate of the magnates, all these great riches fell into the hands of the commons. The haul would represent wealth beyond the imagin-ings of many of those who now rampaged unchecked through the wreck of the proud encampment.

> The knights shed their armour and fled without it; the Scots continually harassed their rear; the pursuit lasted fifty miles. Many of our men perished and many too, were taken prisoner. For the inhabitants of the countryside, who having previously feigned peace, now slaughtered our men indiscriminately wherefore it was proclaimed by Sir Robert Bruce that they should take prisoners and hold them to ransom. So the Scots busied themselves with taking prisoner the magnates in order to extort large sums from them. There were captured the Earl of Hereford, John Giffard, John de Wylyntone, John de Segrave, Maurice de Berkeley, undoubtedly barons of great power ...[22]

The Life of Edward II also makes it quite clear that is was the desire to rob the English baggage that distracted many Scots from the less lucrative business of the chase and that many English, who might otherwise have been taken or killed, escaped. The battered survivors mustered at Berwick where numbers would be much depleted. *The Life* asserts that as many as half a thousand of those presumed dead were in fact prisoners and whom, on payment of ransoms, were freed.[23] In assessing the pecuniary loss to the English of the valuables lifted by the victorious Scots, the chronicler puts the figure as high as £200,000: 'So many fine noblemen and valiant youth, so many noble horses, so much military equipment, costly garments and gold plate – all lost in one unfortunate day, one fleeting hour'.[24]

Edward II refused the temptation to seek refuge in Stirling (or perhaps the opportunity was denied to him), but fled south, with his five hundred knights guarding the royal person. He was accompanied by Hugh Despenser, his current lover, and de Beaumont. This was, in the circumstances, the only

viable course of action and Edward, who might be censored for poor leadership, cannot be criticised for taking such swift steps to avoid capture. As
serious as the defeat was, the loss of the king would have compounded the
disaster tenfold. Moubray bowed to the inevitable and surrendered the castle.
The Life of Edward II, however, makes it clear the king had no choice but to
ride on as the gates to the fortress were bolted against him:

> The king coming to the Castle and thinking to find refuge there, was
> repulsed as if he were an enemy; the drawbridge was raised and the gate
> closed. Wherefore the castellan was thought by many to be not innocent of
> treason, and yet that very day he was seen in armour arrayed as for battle
> as if to fight for the king. I neither absolve the castellan nor accuse him of
> treachery, but I think it was God's doing that the King of England did not
> enter the castle, for if he had then been admitted he would never have
> escaped capture.[25]

Edward II had embarked upon his first and only major test of generalship
and the result was the worst single disaster suffered by English arms in the
medieval period, on a par with the French defeat at Courtrai. Indeed the
parallels between the two combats are striking, and the fact that the example of
the earlier fight should have offered a valuable lesson merely increases the
weight of opprobrium.

The English king had seriously under-estimated his enemy, he had failed to
make a full tactical evaluation of the ground and consider possibilities beyond
the need for an all round defence. He failed to provide leadership and allowed,
even encouraged with his scandalous treatment of Gloucester, divisions
between his officers. Edward II was simply not fit to command. In contrast,
Robert Bruce had displayed fine tactical judgement. On the first day he had
fought primarily on the defensive having taken pains to create an impregnable
position. As his army was inferior in numbers and deficient in heavy cavalry,
this was entirely wise. His army met the challenge of the English horse, proving they were a match for the vaunted chivalry. With their morale thus buoyed,
the king, after much weighty consideration, took the momentous decision to
commit his forces to offensive action.

By so doing he shaped the destiny of both Scotland and England, he held
aloft that torch which Wallace and Murray had lit and dealt the death blow to
English hopes of outright domination. The echoes of the patriots' first great
charge, from the Abbey Craig against Cressingham's men, sounded in full
again that day and the business thus begun, if not ended, was at least guaranteed an ending. Whilst Bannockburn did not end the war, it changed beyond
recognition the nature of the conflict. From June 1314 and for nearly two

decades the Scottish commanders, particularly Edward Bruce, Douglas and Randolph, would carry on the war in northern England and Ireland, and the dwellers in the English marches would taste the full meaning of defeat; 'Maidens of England, sore may you mourn'.[26]

> Why should I beat about the bush? What can I sing about so vast a slaughter? Tragedy will scarcely answer the purpose to show the wounds left by this stroke. My mind has not skill enough to count the names of the fighters. How many and how awful the blows death has arranged to deal there. Many are mown down, many pierced by spears; many are drowned, many taken alive; many are bound in chains and held for ransom. Because of this some are now enriched and raised up who before had been humble and impoverished. All around are places heaped high with spoils. Words full of menace are shouted and reinforced with actions. I know not what to say. I am reaping a harvest I did not sow.[27]

Chapter 7
A Landscape of War

Richard and Robert began to tax the goods of the said men [of Northumberland] in the seventh year [of Edward II], and they sat at Morpeth in the said county; and suddenly there arrived Stephen Segrave and many others with him and they told them that the lord king was retreating from Stirling with his army and was coming towards England, and on this they were terrified. They fled and, like others of the county, stayed in the enclosed towns and castles and forts. And immediately afterwards, before the 1st August, there came Edward Bruce and Thomas Randolph leading the Scottish army[1]
– The Lanercost Chronicle

Harrying the north of England

For the northern English the defeat of the army at Bannockburn was a particular catastrophe. They were now fully exposed to the wrath of the victorious Scots. The battle, exceedingly important as it was, did not end the war. It ended only the period when Bruce felt constrained to rely mainly upon stealth and skirmish. It permitted him and his able captains to pursue a more aggressive strategy, taking the war far beyond the borders of Scotland, to the marches and as far south as Lancashire, into the waters of the North Sea and over the narrow passage to Ireland. From 1314 to the Treaty of Northampton, fourteen years later, the military initiative lay almost entirely with the Scots.

The objective of the subsequent Scottish campaigns was, above all, to wring recognition from Edward II of Bruce's sovereignty. Lesser but still important objectives were the recapture of Berwick and, if possible, of Carlisle, with the cost of the campaigns, as in earlier years, being funded by the cash extorted from the northern English counties. Hardship, famine and waste were to be their lot.

His dismal failure against the Scots was to haunt Edward II in the years that followed. His father had succeeded in diverting the opposition by glittering triumphs in the field. The spoils of war are mighty persuasive but Edward now had only the reverse, the bitter dregs of defeat. Victory in battle was the yardstick by which medieval kings might expect to be measured and he had spectacularly flunked the test.

Leadership of the opposition now focused on Thomas of Lancaster; Gloucester was dead and Aylmer de Valence, Earl of Pembroke, was discredited through his role in the débâcle. In September 1314 the king was obliged to stand by, impotent, as his administration was purged, household officials were sacked and a number of the sheriffs dismissed. The Lincoln Parliament of 1316 confirmed Thomas of Lancaster's role of chief councillor.[2] His appointees were by no means mere partisans. Merit was a clear denominator but half-hearted plans for a further Scottish campaign came to nothing. Edward never left the south and Lancaster proceeded no further north than Newcastle.

The two years from 1316–18 marked a brief flowering of amity between king and earl, their relationship consolidated by the Treaty of Leake. Edward was attempting to create an affinity by advancing certain younger lords such as Hugh Audley, Roger Damory and William Montague. Two of this new coterie of favourites scored handsomely when they were married to a brace of Gloucester's heiresses, thus each securing a slice of the late earl's great fortune.

Lancaster was being increasingly marginalised. He lacked political acuity and at this time was diverted by a private feud with Earl Warenne. The Leake agreement in 1318 provided for an advisory bench of seventeen councillors who were to deliberate all matters not otherwise requiring the assent of Parliament. The new favourites were distanced from the court whilst the earl and others received full pardon for all matters past. Leake was a triumph for the moderate reformers, of whom Pembroke was certainly the most influential. Lancaster certainly did not control the new panel; he had the right only to nominate a single banneret as member.

This entente was destined to be short lived, for amongst the king's new intimates was the younger Despenser, who was to be another Gaveston. Whilst the Gascon had been annoying, the Despensers, father and son, were alarming. Clever, manipulative, ruthless and avaricious, Despenser was to abuse the royal patronage to build up a vast estate. The main area of his ambitions lay in South Wales where he looked for a greater share of the Gloucester inheritance and his impatient greed brought him swiftly into conflict with the marcher lords, including Clifford, Hereford and Roger Mortimer.[3]

The marchers were not slow to assert their right and in 1321 they drove the upstart Despenser from South Wales by force of arms. Caught off guard, the king was obliged, in August, to agree to his creature's exile. It might seem that Edward had learnt nothing from the Gaveston years but he had come to appreciate the value of patience. His surrender in the summer was a mere device intended to lull his enemies into a false sense of security. Cannily, he had marked the cracks in the opposition and selected as his first target Bartholemew Badlesmere, an individual already renowned for duplicity and cordially detested by Lancaster. The latter would certainly not raise a hand to help, too blinded by his own conceit to realise that the lesser man's downfall presaged his own.[4]

Boroughbridge

After a cunningly manufactured *casus belli*, Badlesmere's castle in Kent was besieged and taken.[5] Having effortlessly sailed over this first hurdle the king then squared up to the marcher lords. Harrying the despised catamite was one thing but their collective nerve failed when confronted by the royal banner. Again Lancaster remained aloof, as though none of this concerned him. His turn was next. Isolated by his own hubris the earl soon found himself confronting a royal army. With the opportunity for concerted action gone, Lancaster had few friends left to call upon. The forces he could muster, however, were still formidable and the two hosts scrimmaged around Burton-on-Trent before the Lancastrians began to retreat north, almost certainly to seek sanctuary in Scotland.

In this they had not reckoned with Andrew de Harcla. Well advised by his own spies and raising a force of marchers from Cumberland and Westmorland, he executed a forced march to cut off the rebel's retreat at Boroughbridge. On 16 March Lancaster and Hereford found the bridge and crossing held against them. The tactics of this relatively-small encounter are extremely interesting, for, as Sir Charles Oman points out

> The first conscious attempt on the English side to use dismounted men-at-arms combined with archers may be Andrew Harcla's petty victory over the Lancastrian rebels at Boroughbridge in 1322 when we are told that he dismounted all his cavalry 'in the Scottish fashion' to assist his archers to hold a bridge and a ford.[6]

In terms of scale the action may indeed have been a small one but de Harcla did win a signal victory. Hereford and Clifford assailed the bridge head-on, whilst Lancaster attempted the ford. Both attacks were seen off with loss. Hereford, attempting to instill some fire in his men during the fight on the bridge, was mortally wounded by an ungentlemanly thrust from below; with his demise the heart went out of the Lancastrians. Foiled in their attempt to move north, the earl's army evaporated during the course of the late winter night. The next day it was de Harcla who followed up his advantage and advanced. Lancaster was forced to surrender. His subsequent condemnation and execution came as no surprise.

Edward's triumph was complete. He had isolated and mopped up all of the political opposition: executed with Lancaster at Pontefract were Clifford,

Moubray and a score of lesser fry, while perhaps a hundred others were quietly done to death or forced into exile. At York the Ordinances were finally annulled.

The Despensers now came into their own, father and son competing in ruthless rapacity. Both were universally loathed:

> For the brutal and greedy father had in the past wronged many; and promoted the excommunication of many: As a justice of the forest he had accused many from poaching from royal hunting grounds, many of these he vilely disinherited, some he forced into exile, from many he extorted unjust sums of money; and collected a thousand librates of land by means of threats ... By a general judgement he justly lost what he had accumulated from the losses of others.[7]

King Robert I might now appear secure in his hold over Scotland (John Baliol had finally died in genteel exile in 1313), but he was aware that without formal recognition by the crown of England his victories could still be reversed. After the defeat at Bannockburn Edward II had spent a fortnight at Newcastle, from where he sought to call up Henry of Lancaster (the earl's brother) and other magnates to restore his shattered army. He then fell back upon York, where Pembroke was appointed as captain of all royal forces north of the Trent. The earl was given wide powers, but in practical terms there was little he could hope to achieve.

By then the Scottish army was already ranging through the marches virtually at will. Northumberland was wasted as far south as the Tyne and the raiders crossed at Newburn to enter the Palatinate, compelling the terrified citizenry to buy a further truce. In the west, de Harcla was able to organise some resistance and clashed with the Scots at Reycross on or around 4 August.[8] During November he struck back at Dumfries, but these were isolated beacons in a sea of passivity. Already starved by earlier incursions, the Northumbrians had neither the resources nor the will to resist. For many the only remaining option was permanent fight and these murderous, desperate years saw a steady exodus from the upland dales.

Durham, richer, more populous, and further from the wild border, fared marginally better, being able to purchase successive truces. The years after Bannockburn witnessed a dramatic increase in long-distance Scottish raids, the flying columns moving through the northern counties effectively unopposed, extorting cash and ransoms, destroying crops and lifting livestock. Nothing was beneath the raiders' consideration – books, vestments, bed linen, pots and pans; iron, always scarce in Scotland, was much prized.[9] In tandem with this policy of extended *chevauchées* was the pressure exerted on the two key bastions of Berwick and Carlisle, plus the additional gambit of Edward Bruce's campaigns in Ireland.

A raid which extended as far south as Furness in Lancashire in 1316 was counted as a great success because it yielded a substantial haul of the precious iron. The policy of deliberate and thorough destruction, was so completely pursued that in addition to burning crops and cutting down fruit trees even the rabbit warrens at Bamburgh were systematically dug up.[10] On the march the army might be split into several columns. Randolph and Douglas were King Robert's most indefatigable captains. Fortified places were generally avoided, as was any general engagement; this was war fought for politics and economy, not for glory. The Hainault chronicler, Jean le Bel, has left a vivid description of the Scots as they appeared in the field, dating from the time of the Weardale campaign of 1327:

> one and all are on horseback, except for the camp followers ('*le ribaudaille*') who are on foot, that is to say the knights and squires are mounted on great rouncies, and the other folk of the country are all on little hackneys. And they do not bring wheeled vehicles, because of the various mountains through which they pass in this country.[11]

It was obvious that after the fall of Stirling, Berwick would be the Scots' next major objective and in anticipation of an attack the town's defences were overhauled in both July and December 1314. The walls and wooden palisades were pointed and repaired, timber outworks including a barbican were added, the whole entailing an expenditure of some £270.[12] The mood of the garrison was fragile, verging on paranoia.[13] Conditions were exacerbated by poor harvests and deteriorating weather, the spectre of famine adding to the townspeople's fears.

As Bruce had earlier threatened, all those who had held cross-border estates lost their lands (this included Bruce himself who had forfeited manors in Cleveland). The Umfravilles were now no longer earls of Angus or Baliols' lords of Galloway; Dirleton, previously held by the Vaux family from Gilsland, was also sequestered. The Umfravilles were lords of Redesdale and proved energetic in its defence, but the neighbouring upland valley of Tynedale, an ancient liberty, administered by the king of England since 1296, had previously been enfeoffed to the Scottish crown and, faced with the pressure of constant inroads, the inhabitants now tended to revert:

> At this time the people of North Tynedale, deserting the king of England and his faith, gave themselves up completely to the king of Scotland. They treated their neighbours the Northumbrians inhumanely, carrying

off their goods and taking them away as captives. The women too went riding in warlike manner, stealing the goods which their men did not care about, such as shorn wool and linen, and carried them off[14]

The creation of a brand of professional marchers, skilled in and dedicated to war, charged with local defence, did not always bode well for the inhabitants. The folk of Bamburgh complained that, having purchased an expensive truce from the Scots under Randolph, they found the castellan demanding an equal fee, plus he was happy to charge them for storage of their goods within the castle walls![15]

The Earl of Hereford was the Scots' most valuable prize at Bannockburn, one of the greatest English magnates and the king's brother-in-law. His release was negotiated in exchange for the ladies of Bruce's family along with Bishop Wishart and Donald, Earl of Mar.[16] King Robert also courteously returned the royal seal which had been overlooked in the rout. Bruce now held a parliament at Cambuskenneth where the lands of those who had fallen in arms against the crown were escheated. Others who were willing to submit, including Patrick Dunbar, the Earl of March and Ingram Umfraville, were permitted to swear the oath of allegiance.

John Comyn, Earl of Buchan, the king's inveterate foe, had died in 1308 with no male issue. One of his co-heiresses had married Henry Beaumont who thus gained a claim to the earldom, even though the lands were sequestered by the crown. Beaumont and others who were similarly deprived, the 'disinherited', would return to haunt the kingdom in the years after King Robert's death. Death was a subject much on the king's mind during the early months of 1315. Apart from his daughter Marjorie, now married to the Steward, the king had no legitimate heir.[17] For a monarch whose throne had been so precarious since 1306 and who was still at war with England, the lack of a male heir was a matter of the utmost gravity. The council which met in April to consider the situation determined that Edward Bruce would be heir apparent, the throne entailed in his favour until a male heir was born. Should he predecease and a minor be left as king on Robert's death (as proved to be the case), then Randolph should stand as Guardian.

In January 1315 the dearly-bought truce the citizens of Durham had negotiated was due for expiry. John de Eure was the king's lieutenant north of the Trent and it may have been he who facilitated crisis talks at York, where the leading clergy and magnates met to consider the defence of the northern frontier. The delegates resolved upon the appointment of four northern lords as captains of the marches with power to raise local forces. An appeal for assistance was dispatched to King Edward but met with no effective response.

It was suggested that the locally-raised militias could be funded by a form of local tax – this in an area already denuded of wealth by the Scottish inroads. Whilst the debate continued, the Scots harried the length of Tynedale, almost to the gates of Newcastle. In June it was the turn of the Palatinate:

> In the year [1312] Sir Robert Bruce came into the Bishopric of Durham with a great army and so secretly had he come that he found people sleeping soundly in their beds. He sent Sir James Douglas to the district of Hartlepool with many armed men while he himself remained in the vill of Chester[-le-Street]. Sir James despoiled the said town and he lead back as captives many burgesses and many women. Having collected much booty from the whole countryside they all returned to their own country[18]

Hartlepool was most likely targeted because it was a handy naval base for operations against Scottish privateers and perhaps because the residents had refused to recognise Bruce as their lord, the manor having previously been in his ownership. In spite of the thoroughness with which Durham was 'taken up', this raid was a mere diversion. Carlisle remained the prime objective. As a response to the attack on Durham, Pembroke was, on 5 July, appointed to command the northern shires and, together with Bartholemew Badlesmere, began to concentrate a contract army at York. By this time the Scots were before the beleaguered walls of Carlisle, though confounded by the spirited defence of de Harcla and the inhabitants.

By the time Pembroke was approaching the city the Scots had withdrawn and the earl joined with the castellan in the pursuit. By 21 August Pembroke was back in Newcastle and planning a raid into the Merse, though he advanced no further than Berwick. In due course he was succeeded by Henry Beaumont.

In the late summer King Edward was making what appeared to have been genuine efforts to base himself in the north for a major 'push' against the Scots in the autumn, acting on the advice of his most seasoned councillors, magnates of the calibre of Warenne and Hereford. These good intentions foundered on the grim realities of the king's previous failures and his lack of resources (Pembroke's contract army had consumed most of the parliamentary subsidies), the weakened state of the northern shires exacerbated by the effects of famine.

Edward Bruce in Ireland

The Irish intervention, which began in May 1315 and ended with the death of Edward Bruce in October 1318, eased the pressure on northern England. For the Scots it was a major logistical exercise to fight on two fronts simultaneously and the periods of intense activity oven the Irish Sea afforded corresponding relief to the marchers. Barbour's account presents the decision to open the new front thus:

The Earl of Carrick, Sir Edward
Who was braver than a leopard
Thought that Scotland was too small
For himself and his brother both
And therefore to one and all announced
That he of Ireland would be king.[19]

The presence of Edward Bruce in Ireland was 'to leave its mark on the country for generations'.[20] The bitter and destructive campaigns waged by the Scots ultimately achieved nothing other than to pile more death and destruction on a land already ravaged by famine and feud. The objectives of this intervention may have comprised the following: the opening up of a second front in the Irish Sea would put further pressure on the English and could result in the western seaboard becoming a Scottish 'lake'; Carlisle, that vital fortress, the gateway to the west, could be dramatically weakened and isolated if its supply route from Ireland was severed.

John of Argyll took Man in February 1315 and the suspicion that a major attack from Ireland might be launched that summer could imply the descent upon Ireland was, at least in part, a pre-emptive strike. The Scots' capability was bolstered by a substantial arms shipment from Flanders which docked on 18th February. More cynically, Edward Bruce would be removed from affairs in Scotland, his volatile personality could be channelled into the Irish adventure, thus reducing the risk of civil strife at home. The chronicler Fordun makes some telling observations on the character and temperament of the king's younger sibling:

The cause of this [Irish] war was this. Edward was a very mettlesome and high spirited man, and would not dwell together with his brother in peace unless he had half the kingdom for himself; and for this reason war was stirred up in Ireland.[21]

There is also the romantic idea of Bruce's appeal to notions of pan-Celtic brotherhood, a rising of the Gael against the tyranny of the Anglo-Saxon. Whilst such an approach might have a propagandist value, it was scarcely sustainable. Bruce, like most Scottish magnates, was Anglo-Norman, the Red Earl was his father-in-law. Nonetheless, the king was supported by the clans of the northwest and the manifesto he issued makes a strong claim to a common cause with the native Irish:

Since each Christian man is obliged to assist his neighbour in every difficulty, so also should those who proceed from a common root, who share
the same race, ancestors, and country of origin. On that account we have
now and for a long time been overwhelmed by sympathy with you in your
servitude and oppression. Affronted by the vexations of the English, we
are bound to attend to your plight, and with the help of the Most High, to
expel from the borders of your land with all force the unnatural and
barbaric servitude imposed by the English, so that, as from earliest times,
the Albanic and British people having expelled their enemies, should
become one in perpetuity.[22]

Edward Bruce could command a force of 5,000–6,000 picked veterans, a
formidable instrument of war. The expedition was ferried in a fleet of swift
Hebridean galleys and undoubtedly included a number of *galloglas* (Norse-
Gael mercenaries) from the Isles.[23] Randolph, John Soules and Philip
Moubray all accompanied the army, whose first objective was mighty Carrick-
fergus castle, under siege by 22 July.

About the same time as Bruce was investing Carlisle, Domnall O'Neill,
the king of Tyrone, offered Edward Bruce the vacant title of High King. The
Scots failed before the walls of Carlisle and made little initial headway against
Carrickfergus, which resisted stoutly. Their lack of expertise in siege warfare
was a major handicap and one which went some way to seriously offset their
prowess in the field. The first Anglo-Irish army sent against him, drawn mainly
from Connacht, was cleverly confounded when Bruce nimbly played off some
of the various contending factions. These divisions were to plague the native
Irish for years to come but the Red Earl, leading the Anglo-Irish, was scattered
at Connor in Antrim.

Bruce then marched south to defeat Roger Mortimer in battle at Kells in
Meath. Whenever the armies marched, wholesale despoliation followed:

Theft, famine and destruction of men occurred throughout Ireland for the
space of three years and a half; and people used actually to eat one another
throughout Ireland.[24]

In 1316 the Scots-Irish secured another victory near Athy in Kildare and, at
Dundalk, Edward was enthroned as High King. To consolidate his brother's
successes, King Robert brought a second force over early the next year, mainly
comprising more *galloglas* from the Western Isles. By 1317 the brothers' army
was able to make a demonstration against Dublin, the seat of English lordship,
marching as far south as Limerick before retreating north.

Such raids not only spread devastation through a starving and divided land but sowed a whole plague of local feuds in their wake. The O'Donnells beat up Sligo whilst the O'Moores, O'Tooles, O'Byrnes and O'Hanlons fought it out in Leinster. In southern Ulster the local warlord, Felim O'Connor, king of Connacht, turned against the Anglo-Normans but was crushed by William de Burgh and Richard de Bermingham at Athenry in August 1316.[25]

By 1318 Edward Bruce's campaign was rapidly running out of steam, the land exhausted by the ceaseless strife and wholesale destruction that followed the Scots-Irish like a pestilence. With perhaps no more than 2,000 men supported by the de Lacys, enemies of Roger Mortimer, Bruce again marched south. Richard de Clare, the Lord Lieutenant of Ireland, confronted him with a vastly superior force at Faughart, just north of Dundalk. Though his captains urged caution in the face of such odds Bruce would not countenance withdrawal. Like a punch-drunk fighter who doesn't see it's time to quit the ring, Bruce attacked. The Scots fought hard and well but the end was never really in doubt and Edward Bruce fell amongst the wreck of his army.

Berwick-upon-Tweed was the other crucible of war. The Scots had established an effective naval blockade which sealed off the harbour. With the port out of action, supplies had to be diverted to Newcastle and then carried overland. In the cold January of 1316 the Scots mounted a night attack, which, thanks to the fitful moonlight, was detected and the raiders seen off. On 14 February the Gascon knight, Raymond de Caillen, led a sortie, contrary to the express orders of Maurice Berkeley, the castellan. The raiders were intercepted by the indefatigable Douglas at Skaithmuir near Coldstream and a sharp action ensued. The enthusiastic de Caillen fell by Douglas' hand; a score of men-at-arms and three times as many foot were also killed. A second commanded party under Robert Neville who sallied out to relieve the first were also cut up and Neville, too, was slain.[26]

For the demoralised garrison the situation soon became critical. Relationships with the townspeople were strained to breaking point, desertion was rife and starvation imminent. A truce of sorts was negotiated to hold until Whitsun, but the Scots would not relinquish the pressure on the beleaguered town. With the concord between King Edward and the Earl of Lancaster now enjoying its brief flowering, plans were made for a full feudal muster, the numbers available to be augmented by a demand on the vills that each should supply and victual one soldier for a period of sixty days. These plans were frustrated by an outbreak of fresh disturbances in Wales.

In June, King Robert mustered his own forces around Duns. On the twenty-fourth day of that month the Scots struck through the wasted manors of Tynedale and down into Durham. The gentry of North Yorkshire, sheltering behind Richmond's formidable ramparts, were quick to buy a truce, so the raiders moved westward by Swaledale to Furness, where they lifted a quantity of iron. Any effective riposte was frustrated by the unhelpful row which erupted between King Edward and Thomas of Lancaster. The latter retired to his own stronghold at Pontefract, leaving the king to salvage what he could from any hopes of a campaign. A muster was planned at Newcastle for 6 October but fresh discord broke out over a disputed succession when the Prince Bishop died. Henry Beaumont was pushing for his own brother Louis to follow the late Bishop Kellawe; so bitter was the wrangling that the matter was decided only by papal intervention.

Increasing the pressure

The autumn campaign therefore never took place. Instead truce negotiations were entered into. By now King Robert, together with Randolph, was en-meshed in his brother's Irish adventure, leaving Douglas and the steward as guardians of the realm. With Scottish attentions thus divided it was possible to negotiate a ceasefire to hold until the following summer. Over the winter, matters in the north were left in the hands of the Earl of Arundel who was able to supplement the garrison outposts with a mobile field force raised under contract and including nearly 500 hobilers.[27]

Arundel proposed to keep his men's ardour sharp with a series of punitive raids, the first of which was aimed at beating up the area of Jedwood Forest. The raiders crossed over the high neck of Carter Bar. So thorough were the preparations that Douglas, in residence at his manor of Lintilee, was initially caught off guard. Never one to shirk a fight, Douglas mustered such men as he had available and struck at the English van under Thomas de Richmond, killing the knight and besting his men. Returning to Lintilee the Guardian discovered a company of English foragers making free at his table. These unbidden guests were soon dealt with and Arundel, perturbed by his losses, withdrew.

Undeterred by this reverse the resilient earl next planned a naval expedition against Fife. A squadron of five ships sailed from the Humber carrying men-at-arms who, on making landfall on the banks of the Forth, frightened off a local militia led by the sheriff, then proceeded to loot and burn at will. The timorous official, in full flight, ran into a commanded party led by the Bishop of Dunkeld. The prelate was made of much sterner stuff and turned the locals around to join in his attack. The English were again seen off with loss.

Events outside the British Isles now began to have an increasing influence, for in that year Pope John XXII was elected with a manifesto for a new crusade. Brokering a peace between England and Scotland was therefore very much on his agenda. He was prepared to exert pressure on Edward but also renewed Bruce's excommunication.

This was no trivial matter. King Robert was a pious man in an age of religion – to be cut off from the body of Christ was an anathema and something he would naturally strive to overcome. In practical terms, however, the king was not to be diverted from his objective of taking Berwick. A lasting truce would render this unattainable and he therefore resorted to prevarication.

In the summer a brace of cardinals arrived in England. In the autumn they journeyed north, their diplomatic mission coinciding with the proposed consecration of Louis Beaumont, now secure in his appointment. The combined party comprising the two papal envoys and both Beaumont and his brother were kidnapped by the piratical Gilbert de Middleton.[28] This incident may be viewed as a simple act of brigandage, exemplifying the breakdown of law and order in the north. Alternatively, subsequent writers have been tempted to see Lancaster's hand in the affair (he opposed the appointment of Louis Beaumont), and possibly also that of Robert Bruce, he being anxious to keep the cardinals from meddling in Scotland. The Bishop–elect and his brother were released in October. Middleton soon faced the gallows for his crimes, though he kept silent as to any encouragement he might have had in the affair.

If Bruce had somehow intended to frustrate the cardinals' mission then he was largely successful; when members of their entourage did finally locate the king of Scotland they would not address him as such. Bruce, as ever, was courteous but insistent: he would have his rank acknowledged. As for their suggestions of mediation he vacillated, intimating that the matter would have to be debated before a full council, which might not be expected to assemble before Michaelmas (29 September). The king was determined to bring Berwick under his sway before listening to terms. Again, however, the Scots could make no impression on the walls and by the end of November the siege had been abandoned.

The terms of the papal truce were pronounced by the cardinals in London; a public announcement in Scotland proved more problematic. The friar who was dispatched to complete the task had a difficult journey, being denied safe conduct and robbed. The cardinals had no option but to reiterate the sentence of excommunication against the king and place the realm under an interdict. Dire as this was, the state of English politics denied Edward any opportunity to exploit the papal ban. Relations with Lancaster had sunk to a new low and the constant wrangling between the king and the greatest of his magnates undermined plans for a campaign. Just how close the earl had become to the Scots at this point is open to question; clearly the divide was immensely beneficial to Bruce.

As the king sought to arrange a muster at York for early September, Lancaster mustered his own retainers at Pontefract and even went so far as to break down the bridges leading northward from the city. For all his belligerence, the earl lacked the stomach for a full-scale rebellion and the papal envoys were able to negotiate the bones of an accord.

If Edward had hoped that pressure from the Curia would compel Bruce to the negotiating table then he had, not for the first time, gravely underestimated his opponent. King Robert would have Berwick. In 1317 the defence of the town had been entrusted to the burgesses, largely as a cost–cutting exercise and one which might effect a reduction in the tensions between the garrison and the civil populace. By the spring of 1318, Wark, Harbottle and Berwick were all under siege. On 2 April Douglas led a surprise attack on Berwick's town walls by the Cow Port. It is said the Scots were assisted by one of the citizens, Peter or Sym of Spalding, who was a relation of the steward, and it was he who facilitated the escalade.[29] The Scots gained the walls and a fierce fight ensued as members of the garrison contested the ramparts and narrow streets.

At length, the survivors were bottled up in the castle, commanded by Roger Horsley, which continued to hold out until 11 June when finally compelled by hunger to capitulate. By that time both Wark and Harbottle had also surrendered. As might be expected, the English traders in Berwick were subjected to robbery, abuse and summary ejection from the town, though there was no wholesale slaughter. From now on Bruce tended to allow offensive operations to be conducted by his captains Randolph and Douglas: both were formidable and vastly experienced. By distancing himself from a direct involvement in raids the king could deflect papal criticism and blame attacks on over-zealous subordinates. He did not, however, distance himself from Berwick.

The capture of the town and castle was a major coup, marking as it did a return to the status quo of 1296. It provided the Scots with a major and secure base on the border, a vital seaport and a further boost to soaring morale. In the early months of 1319 the king was active in supervising the strengthening of the defences whilst also organising a spoiling raid against the partially finished works at Dunstanburgh. If the loss of the Tweed frontier were not sufficient, Mitford was sold out to the Scots by a traitor. With their rear now secure, Randolph and Douglas launched a great *chevauchée* down the east coast, sweeping through Northumberland and west Durham as far as Barnard Castle and the Tees. It is possible that this destructive sweep through Durham was intended to instruct the new Bishop, Louis Beaumont, in the wisdom of buying truces.

Beaumont was of a more aggressive temperament than his predecessor and the Scots perhaps reckoned that a mite more terror was required.[30] The raiders then made for Ripon by way of Richmond, a commanded party 'took up' Wensleydale before meting out similar treatment to Hartlepool. Both columns then marched south, converging on Knaresborough. It is unlikely that the town was selected at random. The garrison had, in the wake of Middleton's rising, turned against the king and royal forces laid siege to the place from October 1317 to the following January. It is highly probable that the Scots might have expected a 'friendly' garrison. In this they would have been disappointed, but the town was thoroughly taken up and razed before the Scots marched westward to cross the Pennines via Airedale, Ribblesdale and Wharfedale prior to turning north, replete with loot.

It was the fall of Berwick which drove Edward to seek a further accommodation with Lancaster and which then led directly to the accord of Leake. Harvests had improved and the loss, desperate as this might be, was compensated in part by the news of Edward Bruce's defeat and death in Ireland and the recapture of Carrickfergus Castle. In 1319, therefore, the king determined on a major campaign to recover Berwick. A muster of 24,296 foot was proposed, though barely a third of this ambitious total actually served.[31] Lancaster contributed half a thousand and Edward was able to call upon perhaps 1,400 horse, victualled by a fleet of seventy-seven ships. Harcla's marchers were employed to hold the remaining border garrisons. The recapture of Berwick would obviously help to restore local morale, it would re-establish the defensive line on the Tweed and perhaps draw the Scots out to fight.

Once the walls were invested and the engines in place, an amphibious assault was launched under the cover of an artillery bombardment, but King Robert's refurbished defences stood the test. The number of engines was increased to boost the effect of the artillery and fresh attacks launched. There was desperate and sustained fighting along the landward flank of the walls and the outworks changed hands several times, but still the defences held.

Mytton and Byland

Bruce, as ever, was too canny to accept the lure of a general engagement, regardless of the scope of the threat to Berwick. His strategy was to unleash the hounds down the eastern flank, Douglas and Randolph driving as far south as Yorkshire. It has been suggested that they might have hoped to kidnap Edward's queen, then inside York. This is not necessarily fanciful, with the 'She Wolf' as hostage Bruce would possess a valuable trump.[32]

It was said that a spy in York betrayed the plan to Archbishop Melton and also offered to reveal the location of the Scottish camp. The queen was packed off to safety in Nottingham and the archbishop, perhaps recalling the glorious episode of the Battle of the Standard at Northallerton in 1138, prepared to lead local forces against the raiders. As the majority of able-bodied men liable to muster had already marched to the siege of Berwick, Melton pulled together a scratch force of what remained. This motley assembly advanced upon the Scots, who were encamped at Mytton some three miles east of Boroughbridge on the banks of the Swale, near its confluence with the Ouse.

It is highly unlikely the Scots could be taken by surprise and they deployed in *schiltron* formation, setting fire to nearby haystacks to confuse the attackers. As the archbishop's force stumbled forward the raiders bellowed out their fearsome war cries and tramped towards them. It was enough: the citizens bolted, allowing the Scots to mount up for the pursuit. The 'Chapter of Myton', so called because so many ecclesiastics fell in the rout, was a complete disaster. The mayor of York was amongst the dead and many prisoners were taken, several of them members of the Royal Household, including the notary Andrew Tang.[33]

Having decimated the archbishop's rag-tag army, the Scots advanced to Castleford before, in their by-now-habitual manner, swinging westward through Airedale and Wharfedale. The raiders seem to have split into two marching columns and entered Lancashire by differing routes, some moving through Lonsdale, others along the Greta Valley. At 'Gratirhals' this second party was ambushed:

> In returning homewards through western parts of England, they were set upon by a throng of Englishmen at Gratirhals, a very narrow pass.[34] But the Scots prevailed and the English were scattered, and many were killed, including Sir Henry Fitzhugh, and they returned with great rejoicing to their own country taking many knights and squires with them.[35]

News of the disaster at Myton brought confusion to the siege lines around Berwick. The southern barons were all for ignoring the defeat and maintaining the pressure, the northerners favoured abandoning the siege, fearful of further Scottish inroads. Lancaster decided the day by withdrawing, which effectively brought the leaguer to an end. The English had barely been ten days before the walls, from 8–18 September. The earl's indecent haste to abandon the siege lines inevitably raised fresh doubts as to his loyalties. The king withdrew the remainder of his forces to York to consider how best to protect the marches. Whilst these deliberations continued, Randolph and Douglas struck again.

On All Saints Day (1 November) the Scots crossed into the middle march over Gilsland Waste. In a dozen days of mayhem they penetrated as far south as Brough on Stainmore, garnering a haul of beasts and ransoms as they 'took up' Cumberland on the return journey. Despite their string of successes and the retention of Berwick, the Scots were as much in need of a respite as were the battered English. Edward had exhausted his treasury with nothing but fresh humiliations to show and Bruce, having secured Berwick, needed time to mend his relations with the papacy. On 12 October safe conducts were issued to a dozen Scottish negotiators to attend at Newcastle where, on 22 December, the terms of a two-year cessation were agreed.

Not unsurprisingly in the circumstance, the terms favoured the Scots. Harbottle was returned but only on condition that the defences would be slighted and custody given back to the Scots if a permanent peace could not be agreed on the expiry of the current truce.

Negotiations with Rome were more difficult. The king's failure to recognise the papal truce was viewed as a most serious dereliction. Bruce and his bishops were summoned to the Curia to explain themselves. They did not attend but letters were sent by the king, the leading clergy and the nobility. The submission offered by the magnates contained a precise summary of reasons why the Scots should be free of English rule. It was clear, concise, yet heavy with heartfelt emotion. It became known as the Declaration of Arbroath and the simple grandeur of the language has rung down through the ages:

> For so long as a hundred of us remain alive, we will never in any way be bowed beneath the yoke of English domination; for it is not for glory, riches or honour that we fight, but for freedom alone, that which no man of worth yields up, save with his life.[36]

The passionate eloquence of this correspondence produced the desired effect. His Holiness was minded to refrain from further interdict against the Scots and urge both sides towards mediation. Notwithstanding the spirit of unity underlying the Declaration of Arbroath, within a few months of its submission a handful of the signatories were plotting King Robert's downfall. These were William Soules, Edward Moubray, David Brechin, Patrick Graham and Eustace Maxwell. Bruce was to be supplanted by Edward Baliol, the son of the disgraced and now forgotten 'Toom Tabard'.

After the death of Edward Bruce the king had drawn up a fresh entail or 'tailzie' in favour of his son-in-law, the Steward, but without a male heir he remained vulnerable. At the 'Black' Parliament held at Scone in August 1320, the conspirators were exposed. Several of the ringleaders suffered the full ghastly fate of the traitor, being hanged, drawn and quartered, a barbarity rarely practised in Scotland. Maxwell was cleared of complicity but Soules and his aunt, who was also implicated, received a sentence of life imprisonment. Moubray had already died, but in a grotesque parody his corpse was disinterred and condemned. Ingram Umfraville was tainted with suspicion but wisely absented himself from the realm; he never returned.

The truce, which held from November 1319 until January 1322, served the interests of both sides. It empowered Bruce to rebuild his forces after the losses sustained in Ireland whilst it also permitted Edward II to deal with the baronial opposition. Negotiations were conducted at Bamburgh. John of Brittany appeared for the English side as Pembroke was detained in France. He had the support of Bartholemew Badlesmere and the bishops of Worcester and Carlisle. William Soules, as yet free of the stain of treachery, and Alexander Seton deputised for Bruce. The debate ranged over the historic issues, the English harking back to Baliol's homage. Nothing was finalised, though there was the suggestion of an extended truce to endure for twenty-six years.

When matters with Lancaster 'hotted up' in the early part of 1322 the Scots struck, almost certainly in support of the rebels. It is alleged that treasonable correspondence confirming the collusion was discovered on Hereford's corpse after the fight at Boroughbridge, though there has to be a question of whether this was genuine.[37]

Through the second half of January, Durham was savagely raided to the extent that the episode earned the epithet of 'the Burning of the Bishopric'.[38] It may be that this was intended to proclaim Scots' support for the rebels whilst chastising Louis Beaumont for his defiance. Whilst Bruce ravaged the area of south Durham around Darlington, Douglas paid another visit to Hartlepool and the Steward terrorised Richmondshire. In order to march against Lancaster, Harcla had been constrained to negotiate a local truce in the west. Having won the battle against the rebels, he met Edward II at Gloucester with a request that the king take action on the marches. Edward advised that this would not be feasible until after Michaelmas, though Harcla was greeted with the title of Earl of Carlisle in recognition of his good service against the late rebels.

A muster at Newcastle was proposed for 13 June, but soon deferred until 24 July. The numbers the king intended to raise were, at least on paper, impressive.[39] Recruits were drawn from east and west, from Wales and Ireland. The largest contingent was to assemble at Newcastle, with a lesser muster at Carlisle and substantial detachments from Ulster. This was to be a conventional campaign of heavy and light horse with a host of foot and archers, victualled at least in part by the fleet. Edward had not learnt the lessons of hobiler warfare. The Scots would be bound to adopt Fabian tactics, wasting the land before the invaders and avoiding battle, the great host made vulnerable by the sheer weight of its logistical 'tail'.

With the lighter and infinitely more mobile forces under his command Bruce struck first, crossing into the English west march in mid-June, the raiders adopting their customary two-column formation, the first led by the king in person, the other by the well-tried partnership of Randolph and Douglas:

Robert de Brus invaded England with an army by way of Carlisle in the week before the Nativity of St John the Baptist [around 17 June] and burnt the bishop's manor at Rose, and Allerdale and plundered the monastery of Holm Cultram, notwithstanding that his father's body was buried there; and thence proceeded to lay waste and plunder Copeland, and so on beyond the sands of Duddon to Furness[40]

Lancaster was razed by the king's column. When the second detachment came up the army went on to destroy Preston before retracing their route back to Scotland.[41] By 24 July the raiders were safe home, unmolested by any relief, despite having enjoyed a leisurely spate of ravaging around Carlisle. It was not until 12 August that Edward's host marched into the Merse. By the nineteenth Musselburgh had been left in flames but the army was already beset by supply problems. The previous year's harvest had been insufficient and extra supplies of grain had to be imported by sea from Gascony, the lumbering, fat-bellied cogs at the mercy of Scots and Flemish privateers.

Two days later the English marched into Leith. Still the Scots would not commit to battle, but hunger, demoralisation and dysentery thinned the ranks just as effectively. A commanded party which descended on Melrose was intercepted and seen off by Douglas and, by 2 September, the English army was withdrawn south of the border. All in all, the campaign had been a very expensive fiasco.

The army was a hugely expensive beast to feed and maintain. Edward, having spent all available monies, had no choice but to disband his forces, retaining only the knights of the Household, including the younger Despenser. The king found time to vent his frustrations on the castellans of the major east march holds – Bamburgh, Warkworth, Alnwick, and Dunstanburgh – lambasting each for the poor state of their works and the inertia of the garrisons. Scapegoating the individual officers was a shoddy attempt to shift the blame for the parlous state of the region's defences. Conventional garrisons behind castle walls were no answer to hobiler warfare; the whole thrust of Bruce's strategy was to avoid attacking fixed defensive positions.

Even Louis Beaumont, the Bishop of Durham, did not escape censure, being rebuked for neglecting Norham. The Prince Bishop's northerly bastion was, in the event, soon put to the test for, by 17 September, the Scots appeared before the walls.[42] This was, however, nothing more than a feint intended, in all probability, to draw such royal forces as the king commanded into north Northumberland. The main blow fell, once again, in the west. On

30 September Bruce led his army back over the Solway at Bowness and the Scots spent a further five days ravaging the lands around Carlisle, presumably accounting for what little they'd missed in July.

The redoubtable Harcla was, unusually, caught off guard; he had disbanded his western army and the speed of the Scots' attack left him no opportunity for regrouping. He was obliged to retire into Lancashire and seek fresh recruits there. In the event, however, the west was to be spared. King Robert's objective was not mere plunder but to capture the person of Edward II. This was a bold plan for sure, but one which was both carefully conceived and cunningly executed. The Scots now reversed their habitual pattern and came on eastwards over the Pennines. The clearly-excellent spy network which Bruce maintained had informed him of the English king's whereabouts and the paucity of forces under his command.

Edward II was heading south from Barnard Castle when, on 2 October, he learnt of this fresh incursion. Orders were immediately sent to Harcla and numerous other northern magnates to join a muster of North Yorkshire levies at a moorland location known as 'Blakehoumoon', near Byland. The rather optimistic intention was that the barons would raise a conscription of all able-bodied males between sixteen and sixty. The king was much angered when Harcla failed to appear. Whether this was due to intentional tardiness or, as was quite likely, the difficulties the earl experienced in recruiting, he did, however, succeed in finding recruits in Lancashire:

> This he did, having taken command of the county of Lancaster so that he had 30,000 men ready for battle; and since the Scots were in the eastern march, he brought his forces by western parts to reach the king.[43]

Whilst he waited for the magnates to come in, the king established his headquarters at Byland Abbey where, on 12 October, he received the unwelcome news that the Scots were across the Pennines. In the immediate vicinity he had only Pembroke, Richmond (John of Brittany) and John de Birmingham with their retinues. The royal forces fell back towards Rievaulx with a view to mustering on Blakehoumoon. Randolph's division was already at Northallerton and Edward faced the very real prospect of being caught between the earl and King Robert who was marching to cut off his retreat.

Blakehoumoon has been identified as Scawton Moor, an area of high ground overlooking Sutton Bank and Roulston Scar.[44] Edward sent a most urgent summons to Pembroke, Richmond and Beaumont 'to attend with all possible power'.[45] Randolph was by now barely fifteen miles distant at Malton, whilst Bruce's brigade was storming through the Vale of York. The English, completely out-generalled, took up the best position they could along the summit of the ridge. The ground favoured the defenders in that the direct access to the higher ground was through a narrow approach.

Randolph and Douglas led the van against the pass which was hotly contested whilst the king sent his nimble Gallowegians to outflank the defenders on the ridge. Richmond, his meagre forces drawn up by Coxwold and Old Bylande, held on for as long as possible, allowing his king, 'being ever chicken hearted and luckless in war',[46] time to make good his escape before he and the other survivors, including the French knight Henry de Sully, surrendered to the Scots.[47]

The field thus yielded a fine crop of prisoners (Richmond and Robert I were longstanding enemies and the earl was not ransomed for two years) and an even finer haul of loot: for the second time all of King Edward's baggage and papers fell into the king of Scots' hands. This was to be Bruce's last battlefield command and though he had won another sparkling victory and further humiliated Edward II, the raid failed in its main objective of capturing the English king. As a result the war was to drag on for several more weary years. Edward was chased to the gates of Bridlington. From there, more sedately, he was able to progress to York. Here, belatedly, he was joined by Harcla who suffered the full range of royal fury for his laggardly advance. Having thoroughly beaten up the East Riding, the Scots, loaded with prisoners and spoil, re-crossed the border early in November:

And syne with presoneris and catell
Riches and mony fayr jowell
To Scotland tuk thai hame thar way
Bath blyth and glaid joyfull and gay ...
That thai the king off Ingland
Discumfyt in his awne countre[48]

Chapter 8

The Final Reckoning

Blood axeth blood as guerdom dew
And vengeance for vengeance is a just reward
For look what measure we to other award
Take heed ye princes by examples past
Blood will have blood, either first or last.

      – Contemporary Ballad

The she-wolf

Robert Bruce might reasonably have anticipated that, following the 'Rout of Byland', the English king would have been minded to discuss terms, spurred by a second humiliation. The military advantage now lay wholly with the Scots and their ability to range at will over virtually the whole of northern England was unchallenged (apart from Harcla's resistance in the west). Bruce still maintained his two principal strategic aims: to compel Edward to renounce his claims to overlordship, and force him to recognise Bruce as Robert I of Scotland. Even as crushing a win as Bannockburn and the successful outcomes at Mytton and Byland could not together advance the war beyond stalemate. The bulk of the English lived south of the Trent and remained unconcerned by Scottish raids; the north was effectively abandoned to its fate.

Throughout these crucial years 1314–1327 the Papacy continued to exhibit a strong pro-English bias. The Gascon Clement IV was an unashamed partisan and John XXII, his successor, saw 'The Scottish Question' as an avoidable distraction from his grand plan for yet another crusade. Edward II, meanwhile, had found in Hugh Despenser the Younger an ideal replacement for Gaveston: able, shrewd, utterly ruthless, vicious and avaricious. Despenser quickly alienated his fellow marcher lords by his single-minded dedication to increasing his holdings at their expense.

Having, by the summer of 1322, apparently mopped up all opposition, the king's position appeared impregnable, his coffers replenished from the loot of sequestered estates. When the redoubtable Pembroke died (possibly by foul play) in 1324, thus removing the final voice for moderation, the dead man's widow swiftly became a target for Despenser's avarice.[1] Queen Isabella was ignored and treated with contempt, particularly when fresh disturbances in Gascony flared into the War of St Sardos. The king did permit his consort to act as envoy to the court of her brother Charles IV, who was dangerously insisting that Edward should perform full homage for Aquitaine.

Edward and the Despensers feared what enemies might appear should the king quit the realm. For this Isabella had a ready suggestion: Prince Edward should be invested with the Duchy of Aquitaine and then do homage on his own account. This appeared entirely reasonable, neither king nor catamite saw the pit that was yawning. Once in France the lad was firmly under his formidable mother's thumb and she, disdaining her husband's summonses, was to become the focal point for a swelling group of exiles, dedicated to (in modern parlance) 'regime change'.

Prominent amongst these was Roger Mortimer, who had escaped from the Tower in the previous year and who now embarked on a scandalous liaison with the queen. Obliged to quit France for Hainault (Prince Edward was betrothed to the count's daughter, Philippa of Hainault), the exiles were gaining numbers and impetus. In September 1326, the rebels, bolstered by a mercenary corps, landed unopposed in Suffolk. King and paramour found themselves without friends; scurrying through their diminishing realm in a vain search for allies; presently both were made captive and Despenser reaped the full reward for his innumerable misdeeds:

> Hugh, you have been judged a traitor since you have threatened all the good people of the realm, great and small, rich and poor, and by common consent you are also a thief. As a thief you will hang, and as a traitor you will be drawn and quartered and your quarters will be sent throughout the realm ... Go to meet your fate, traitor, tyrant, renegade, go to receive your own justice, traitor, evil man, criminal.[2]

None of these developments, dramatic as they were, proved to be of any assistance to the beleagured Northerners, upon whom the full fury of the Scottish attrition continued to fall. Incidents such as the Middleton rebellion can be viewed as mere brigandage, yet they also express something of the desperation and frustration of the Northumbrians, seemingly abandoned by the English polity. Andrew Harcla, now raised to the earldom of Carlisle, took the perilous step of opening direct negotiations with King Robert and talks were entered into at Lochmaben.

Harcla, without sanction, was prepared to concede the matter of sovereignty, though it is difficult to perceive quite what wider result could be hoped for as there was scant prospect Edward would agree. The draft treaty contained a raft of assurances and provision for the payment of compensation by the Scots. Bruce remained obdurate on the matter of the 'Disinherited' – cross border estate was to be extinguished. The Lochmaben Treaty, which reached its final draft by January 1323, is remarkable in that it anticipates many of the conditions of the final settlement; at the time, however, it was a presumption too far. Harcla, something of an arriviste, had overstepped the mark and given his local enemies the perfect stick with which to beat him, and they did not refuse the opportunity. His particular rival, Anthony de Lucy, orchestrated the campaign which led to the Earl's downfall and subsequent execution.

Though the prospects for peace thus appeared diminished, the crowning irony was that the English king appointed his creature, Walter Stapledon, Bishop of Exeter (later done to death by the London mob) and his catamite, Despenser, to lead a team of negotiators. The unwillingness of the English to recognize Bruce as King of Scots proved a near fatal stumbling block and he wrote furiously to the French knight Henry de Sully, one of his own delegation:[3]

> On this matter we have received letters of yours and transcripts of the king's letters saying that he has granted to the people of Scotland who are at war with him a truce; and this manner of speaking is very strange to us, for, in the other truces which have been made between him and us, we have been named the principal on one hand as he has on the other, though he would not style us king ... And do not wonder therefore that we have not agreed to this truce.[4]

Though it proved impossible to agree terms for an enduring settlement, an extended truce for a period of thirteen years was negotiated. In the circumstances this was an achievement and would certainly bring relief to the hard pressed Northern English. All occupied territories were to be restored, the erection of new defensive works was curtailed, a form of diplomatic relations was established and Edward II, for his part, undertook to exercise best endeavours to have the sentence of excommunication lifted from his opponent's head.

Rising choruses of complaint against these seemingly reasonable terms was growing louder in England, especially from the representatives of the Disinherited. Henry Beaumont, who was voluble in council and unafraid to voice boldly his opposition to the terms. For once, many Scots agreed; war had become a trade for many of Bruce's veterans, its spoils a steady source of income. In correspondence Bruce confessed he was experiencing difficulties in restraining his more ardent followers. On 1 March 1324, Queen Elizabeth presented her husband with a son, the future David II. Edward was soon under pressure when his difficulties with France arose and spiralled into conflict.

Fresh talks were entered into in July 1324 when the Scots, emboldened, appear to have increased their demands to include the ceding of a pale or buffer zone.

Edward riposted by maintaining the question of English overlordship and brought forward some additional tactical gambits. Edward Balliol, son of 'Toom Tabard', was dusted off from obscurity and pressure piled on the Curia to extend the exclusion of the Scottish church. The courtship worked both ways, Randolph scored a personal triumph when he successfully argued the case for recognition of his master from the Holy See.

In April 1326 the Scots concluded an understanding with France, the terms of which were sealed by the Treaty of Corbeil. These embodied joint undertakings of mutual military assistance in the face of English aggression. This renewed entente led to a heightening of tension through the marches that summer, the prevailing truce notwithstanding. Some raids and skirmishes bickered along the line and a Flemish vessel, the *Pelarym*, with a complement of Scottish pilgrims was despoiled off Whitby. Both crew and passengers, regardless of age or sex, were butchered.

The Treaty of Northampton

By the end of the year the political landscape had undergone a major shift. Edward II was a prisoner of his wife; the Disinherited had joined the rebellion and, by 20 January 1327, the king had agreed to an abdication. A few weeks later, Edward III, at fourteen, took the throne in his stead. The Scots celebrated the accession with an abortive raid on Bamburgh; it was business as usual on the border.

Roger Mortimer, though nominally subject to a regency council headed by Henry of Lancaster, proved as ruthlessly acquisitive as Hugh Despenser. His and Isabella's regime remained inherently unstable. The pair lacked any constitutional position and, as both would discover, this young Edward was an altogether different character from his father.

Despite the support they had received from the Disinherited and marcher lords, Isabella and Mortimer could not afford to undertake a resumption of the war. It was time for further talks. These negotiations proved largely fruitless, the Scots commissioners finally abandoned their lodgings in York, leaving some choice suggestions nailed to the doors! Talk without compromise aided nobody and both sides spread alarums; Edward III, full of knightly ardour, wished to teach these Scots a lesson, something his mother and her lover found difficult to gainsay.

The result was the near farcical Weardale campaign of July 1327, when a force of English chivalry, led by the young king, was run ragged in the barren wastes of northwest Durham and Northumberland by a will o' the wisp commando under the joint command of Douglas and Randolph. The expedition proved an expensive fiasco, with the Scots launching a bold night attack on the English camp with the aim of capturing the king. In this they failed, but the English floundered through the peat bogs without bringing their enemy to battle; the campaign achieved nothing and Edward is said to have wept with frustration.

Scarcely had the miserable and chastened English crept back into York than King Robert burst onto the marches in his final grand chevauchée, planting his banners before the defiant walls of Norham, whilst Randolph harassed Alnwick and Warkworth. Once again the marchers were obliged to dig deep into their depleted reserves to buy the rampaging Scots off:

> The landis of Northumbirland,
> That next Scotland thar was liand,
> In fe and heritage gave he
> And thai payit for the selys fee[5]

Bruce, prior to his raid on Northumberland, may have successfully closed the 'back door' from Ireland, which had remained in turmoil even after Edward Bruce's death in 1318. Bruce, as the Red Earl's son-in-law, had a stake in Irish affairs. He negotiated a truce with the leading Anglo-Irish magnate, Henry de Mandeville; no blackmail this but a carefully constructed contract, respectful to both sides, with the Scots paying compensation for recent losses. Isabella and Mortimer had only the most tenuous grip on Ireland and this was shaken by fresh disturbances – quite possibly orchestrated by the King of Scots!

Bruce was thus able to exert pressure on the regime from several directions and may even have been contemplating a further diversionary raid on Wales. He would be acutely aware that, though he held the advantage, the inexorable progress if his illness might bring the game to an end before a lasting peace could be secured. Neither the English queen nor her increasingly unpopular lover could afford to delay a settlement. They had already galloped through the funds of Edward II and the Despensers and the cost of the abortive Weardale adventure added to their burden. On 9 October 1327 Henry Percy was appointed to lead the English commissioners. Bruce was still before Norham and presented the English negotiators with a list of six conditions precedent to any successful outcome:

1. The king and his successors should hold Scotland as free princes, with no homage to England;
2. Prince David would wed Edward III's sister, Joan of the Tower;
3. Cross border estate would disappear;

4. Both sides would provide for mutual military assistance (save for Scotland's current obligations toward France);
5. The Scots would pay compensation in the amount of £20,000, (a very sizeable sum);
6. Edward III would exercise best endeavours to secure the release of the papal excommunication and interdict.

Of these terms it was the matters of sovereignty and cross border estate that were to remain contentious. The former was conceded during bargaining in November and December – a formal quitclaim, the return of all charters and historic papers. Consensus over the pernicious question of the cross border estate could not be reached and indeed remained unresolved even through the final drafting of the proposed treaty.

This single division, the final bone of contention would be the maggot that ate away the fabric of the settlement that marred the crowning achievement of Bruce's life and reign. On 1 March 1328 Edward III appended his seal to a series of letters patent that finally spelt the demise of thirty years of murderous strife:

Whereas we and some of our predecessors, kings of England, have attempted to gain rights of rule, lordship or superiority over the kingdom of Scotland, and terrible hardships have long afflicted the realms of England and Scotland through the wars fought on this account; and bearing in mind the bloodshed, slaughter, atrocities, destruction of churches, and numerous evils from which the inhabitants of both realms have suffered over and over again because of these wars; and having regard also to the good things in which both realms might abound to their mutual advantage if joined in the stability of permanent peace, and thus more effectually made secure, within and beyond their borders, against the harmful attempts of violent men to rebel or make war; we will and concede for us and all our heirs and successors, by the common counsel, assent and consent of the prelates, magnates, earls and barons and communities of our realm in our parliament that the kingdom of Scotland shall remain for ever separate in all respects from the kingdom of England, in its entirety, free and in peace, without any kind of subjection, servitude, claim or demand, with its rightful boundaries as they were held and preserved in the time of Alexander of good memory King of Scotland last deceased, to the magnificent prince, the Lord Robert, by God's grace illustrious King of Scots, our ally and very dear friend, and to his heirs and successors.[6]

For Robert Bruce this agreement had been over two decades in the making, through tragedy, loss, heartbreak and despair; latterly through the creeping wastage of mortal illness. This was the final fruit of the field of Bannockburn, the relinquishment of English claims and the recognition of Bruce and his line as kings of Scotland. John Balliol was simply expunged from the record, relegated to a footnote in history. Bruce was entitled to date his accession from the date of Alexander III's fatal tumble, Scotland must now surely be secure.

As a final stamp on Scotland's triumph the treaty was to be sealed in Edinburgh, a clear and unequivocal acknowledgement of true nationhood. The final talks were conducted 'in a chamber within the precincts of the monastery of Holyrood in Edinburgh where the lord king was lying'. Bruce was bedridden but still able to negotiate the final draft which was agreed on 17 March. He was surrounded by the senior Scottish clergy and the lay magnates, even the Anglophile David of Mar.[7]

The Treaty of Northampton, as it was styled (to the English it was 'The Shameful Peace'), was formalized in a series of five deeds or indentures, the wording of which consolidated that which had been agreed beforehand, all dated 17 March 1328. By October a papal bull lifting the excommunication and interdict had been issued, whilst the royal betrothal had been formally contracted at Berwick on 12 July.

On 7 June 1329, at his fine new house at Cardross and in his fifty-fifth year Robert I of Scotland, Robert the Bruce, Scotland's greatest king, finally succumbed to his illness – '*La grosse maladie*'. His heart was carried, as he had wished, toward the Holy Land by the faithful Douglas, who met his own quixotic end at the Battle of Tebas de Ardales on 25 March 1330. The redoubtable Randolph was appointed as head of the regency council, though he lived only until 20 July 1332, having crowned the seven-year-old David II the preceding November.

Peace was not of long duration. Mar and his army was decimated by the Disinherited at Dupplin Moor, Berwick was lost the following year and the Scots army again routed at Halidon Hill. A second and equally-desperate war of independence was waged. When David II returned from protective exile in France he, too, led a host to fresh disaster at Neville's Cross.

The wars between England and Scotland dragged on over the decades and through three long and savage centuries, not finally resolved till, with crowning irony, James VI of Scotland ascended to the English throne as James I, on the death of Elizabeth in 1603. In this context, Bannockburn was but a rare victory in a series of conflicts wherein, in general engagements, the Scots were most often worsted, sometimes catastrophically as at Flodden in 1513 or humiliatingly as at Solway Moss nearly thirty years later.

And yet, it had not all been in vain. The Battle of Bannockburn, the Declaration of Arbroath and the Treaty of Northampton established beyond doubt that Scotland was a nation, a free and independent state, and that her sovereign was a free prince, not bound in fealty to the king of England. Bruce's struggle and that of the men and women who followed and supported him through the dark days of wretched flight and civil war, the long, hard years of attrition, the clawing back of castle and town, to the final great confrontation, was not a fruitless one.

The flame he lit in June 1314 made all that followed possible, gave back to his country its precious nationhood. In time the flame would falter but it was never extinguished. In the many dark days of the seemingly-endless grim conflicts, Scottish men and women would remember the men who fought at Bannockburn and the man who led them; and this perhaps, above all, is the test of greatness.

A Note on Sources

It is likely that the English source *Vita Edwardi Secundi* (*The Life of Edward II*) was written shortly after the battle by a monk of Malmesbury who has been identified with John Walwayn, a qualified lawyer who died around 1326. He may have had some involvement in the diplomacy of the period; his chronicle is well-informed and constitutes an excellent source.

The Lanercost Chronicle, named for the priory, was probably written else-where on the border but appears to be contemporary. It represents the work of a number of authors and was certainly completed before 1346 when David II gave the priory to the flames. The description of the battle may have benefited from eyewitness testimony.

Scalacronica was written by Sir Thomas Gray of Heton, son of the father who fought in the action against Randolph's brigade on the first day and was captured. The son was also captive a generation later, immured in Edinburgh from 1355 to 1357, when access to a good library and enforced leisure spurred his writing.

John de Trokelowe wrote his *Annales Edwardi Secundi* sometime after 1330. Trokelowe was a cleric, originally from Tynemouth, who found himself detained in St Albans for unspecified misdemeanours.

Geoffrey le Baker of Swinbrook compiled his chronicle probably prior to 1347 in Oxfordshire. He picked up from earlier authors and his account of campaigns suggests the original source had been personally involved or intimate with those who were.

Robert Baston was a Carmelite friar who rose to be Prior at Scarborough. A poet of some note, he is known to have accompanied English armies in Scotland during the reigns of the first two Edwards. His account owes a good deal to poetic licence and rather less to narrative history. At the time, apparently, the Scots derided his verses as wildly inaccurate.

Like Baston, the fragments in Bower's *Scotichronicon* are an early, if incomplete, source. Bernard of Arbroath was Bruce's chancellor and thus well placed to understand his subject matter, yet his version is lacking in detail.

Archdeacon John Barbour (1320?–1395) probably began work on his epic poem *The Bruce* sometime around 1375. The author is believed to have travelled to England to collect testimony from eyewitnesses on both sides, though there can have been few living three-score years after the event. His epic account is wildly inaccurate when giving numbers of combatants and rather vague on detail.

A number of later accounts are certainly worthy of mention. John Morris and William Mackay Mackenzie both produced works in 1913, on the eve of a very much more frightful conflict. Of these, Morris is meticulous in his researches and his conclusions, especially on numbers, have been accepted by later writers.

Particularly eminent amongst these is Professor G. W. S. Barrow, who has written widely on medieval Scottish kingship and on Robert the Bruce. Peter Traquair published an excellent account of the Wars of Independence, *Freedom's Sword* in 1998, followed by Peter Reese's comprehensive and readable study of the battle two years later. A short but highly illuminating account was written for the National Trust for Scotland by General Sir Philip Christison in 1965.

Appendix II

Orders of Battle

It is notoriously difficult to assess, with any degree of accuracy, the numbers of men engaged in medieval battles. All assessments, however painstakingly arrived at, must ultimately remain largely, if not entirely, subjective.

The Life of Edward II describes the Scots as fielding 'a great force of armed men', later assessing the number of these as 'about forty thousand'. This, of course, is a wild exaggeration as such numbers would represent something in the order of ten per cent of the entire population! What does appear likely, however, is that the English may have been taken aback insofar as the Scots could field more men than they'd imagined.

Trokelowe describes the Scots attacking in 'dense battle array'. Lanercost avers they were 'in all their strength' and later speaks of the English charging 'as it were into a dense forest'. Le Baker also speaks of a dense formation 'in a very solid fashion in ordered ranks'. Abbot Bernard states the English had 300,000 cavalry and 40,000 foot, the former preposterous and the latter unlikely.

Amongst more modern authors there has been much debate, most notably between John Morris and William Mackay Mackenzie, who wrote just prior to the First World War, and the eminent and influential Professor Barrow in the 1960s. There is some element of consensus between their varying accounts. Those authors writing within the last decade, notably Peter Traquair and Peter Reese, have broadly agreed with their immediate predecessors, though the former has tended to pare the numbers down yet further.

When speaking of the English horse, *The Life of Edward II* puts the total at 'over 2,000 cavalry'. Barbour opines the number was far greater with 'barded' horses (those ridden by knights in full harness) numbering 3,000 alone. John Morris put the total at 2,400, Reese agrees with this total and I see no reason to differ. Barbour gives the Scots a far more modest cavalry arm, not more than 500 strong and these essentially hobilers. Again, this seems a reasonable figure.

Barbour does, however, grossly exaggerate the numbers of foot. He gives the Scots 30,000 and the English over three times as many at 100,000; such numbers cannot be credited. Morris, writing in 1913, and having perused the muster rolls for Longshanks' campaigns in Wales, suggested that Edward II mustered, or sought to muster, nearly 22,000 infantry, including billmen, archers and some crossbowmen. Of these he estimates, quite reasonably, that no more than 15,000 were assembled on the field. With the cavalry arm, then, Morris gives the English a total of 17,500 men.

Added to these would be the Irish detachments, Scottish knights serving the English crown and continental adventurers. Mackenzie suggests a total figure of nearer 20,000. General Christison's excellent study of the field, which dates from the mid-1960s, agrees with Mackenzie.

How many Scottish foot opposed the English army? This is an even more difficult exercise. If we accept Barbour's ratio of three to one, this gives Bruce some 7,000 – Christison says no more than 5,500 'regulars', with perhaps 3,000 in the reserve. This would still not allow the *schiltron*s a deep deployment as they marched to their battle stations between the two watercourses on 24 June, but otherwise feels about right.

Barbour and other contemporary writers, whilst in any event prone to exaggeration, would also tend to lump in the non-combatants and camp followers. On the English side these (including grooms, sutlers, tradesman, women and whores) would be numerous.

If Christison suggests 5,500, Professor Barrow 500 more and Morris under 7,000, then a figure of around 6,000–6,500 appears a reasonable total. Peter Traquair's even lower estimate of 4,500 is rightly dismissed by Peter Rees as being too few to accomplish their deployment.

Taking these figures as a whole the following assumptions can be made in terms of numbers:

English heavy horse	2,400
English foot	17,600
(including all Irish and other elements)	
Total	20,000
Scottish light horse	500
Scottish regular foot	6,500
Reserve 'small folk'	3,000
Total	10,000

There can be little or no doubt that the 'small folk' included a number, perhaps a significant number, of females. Whilst the presence of women on the field is not generally acknowledged by chroniclers, they were almost certainly there, not as combatants but as water carriers and medical auxiliaries. A later Scottish battle, Harlaw fought in 1411, is remarkable as there is record that separate grave pits were dug solely to receive the bodies of female casualties, women who had fallen in the fight.

If we now try to assess casualties, our task becomes even more arduous. The contemporary accounts are irritatingly vague. If we look at Courtrai, and parallels always present difficulties, casualties on the French side, knights and gentry, amounted to perhaps 800, the Flemings escaping far more lightly. The loss of a comparable number of the English chivalry would have accounted for a full third of the force present.

This would be too many. It is likely that, given the thickness of the press, that relatively few knights were killed. Those who went down with Gloucester in that first intemperate charge were not numerous and at least one English chronicle speaks of the rest of the mounted affinity deliberately holding back. Even in the rout the Scottish force were not numerous enough to inflict real losses and the survivors, if they negotiated the water obstacles, would have a fairly clear run.

Whilst the English foot was scarcely engaged, some, perhaps hundreds together with more from the press of camp followers, would fall in the rout, either beneath Scottish spears or by drowning. The long march home through a hostile landscape would have seen many stragglers picked off and their carcasses picked clean. The total loss is impossible to estimate. Barbour claims 200 English knights fell and this may be pretty accurate, something under ten per cent of the total present on the field. We might guess that ten times as many of the foot also perished.

In purely economic terms the outcome of the battle proved a boon for the Scottish economy, struggling under the burden of nearly a generation of war. Hereford, with a sizeable affinity of mixed horse and foot had managed an orderly withdrawal from the field and sought refuge in Bothwell castle, where the castellan, Sir Walter Fitz Gilbert, previously leaning toward the English, experienced a politic conversion and promptly made his guests prisoners. Apart from the earl, himself a prize of great value, Beaumont, Umfraville, Sir John Segrave, Sir Anthony Lucy and Sir Maurice Berkeley all went 'into the bag'.

Aside from the earl's cash value, his ransom included the release of a clutch of Scottish captives, including the king's, wife, daughter and sister, together with aged Bishop Wishart. The Earl of Gloucester was the highest-ranking fatality, along with over thirty lords and men of rank. Numbers of English foot surrendered outside the walls of Stirling and would be liable for ransom according to their degree.

It seems that something in the order of sixty per cent or more of the commons who either followed the king to Stirling, or Hereford to Bothwell, failed to return through death or capture. If, as Peter Reese suggests, this figure is applied to the mass of English foot as a whole, then perhaps as many as 10,000 failed to survive as far as the border.

Scottish losses were obviously much lighter, the English archers, during their brief ascendancy, might have accounted for numbers of Douglas's men. The Scots lost only three knights: Sir William Vipont, Sir Walter Ross and Sir William Airth. Reese puts their total casualties at not more than 200 and I see no cause to suggest they would have been any higher.

Choosing Ground

There has, over the years, been some controversy as to where the main action on 24 June actually took place. One early favourite was the Borestone, located near the present bronze statue. Whilst this may have formed a handy vantage it can swiftly be discounted. Mackenzie, writing in 1913, rejected this location out of hand. He favoured a location by Muirton with the battle being fought by the English facing west and the Scots' east, the field being bounded by the Forth and the Bannockburn. Professor Barrow opposed this view, citing Mackenzies' confusion over the interpretation of the terms 'Poll'. It was Barrow who championed a site further west, nearer to the settlement of Bannock.

As Peter Reese points out, this leaves the historian with a likely site bounded by the Dryfield to the west and the Carse of Balquiderrock in the east. Barrow took the view that the clash occurred in the more westerly portion but General Christison looked to a location further east in the mouth of the 'U' formed by the course of the Bannockburn and the Pelstream.

The argument continues. Peter Reese favours the Christison site (as do I) but Peter Traquair supports Professor Barrow. He does so on the basis that this area offers Bruce a narrower frontage across which to deploy his more modest force; less distance would allow for a greater massing of the Scottish spears and the chronicles do talk of a dense concentration.

Traquair, as we have seen in appendix II, is of the view that Bruce's infantry were less numerous than other writers would suggest at around 4,500. This would not give sufficient mass to the deployment on the site chosen by Christison/Reese. If, however, we accept the Scottish foot were perhaps 6,500–7,000 strong, this argument becomes more difficult to sustain.

Reese, in his findings gleaned by extensive walking of the ground and a study of the older maps, finds the gap across the neck of the 'U' is about 0.7 of a mile in width, whilst Traquair feels it to be rather more than double this width.

Part of Barrow's argument is that the Scots were so confident of the ability of the *schiltron*s to withstand horse that they advanced regardless of protection on their flanks from the twin water obstacles of the Pelstream and Bannockburn. This is unlikely. Bruce, as we have seen, was extremely cautious; he would not wish to deploy on ground that might have left his flanks in any way exposed to missile attack.

Appendix IV
The Knights Templar

There has been some speculation that the Knights Templar fought on Bruce's side during the battle and that their stalwart support helped win the day. This theory suggests that it was their intervention rather than the commitment of the final Scots reserve, the 'small folk', that proved decisive. It must be stressed that there is no historical evidence to support this view, nor are their any references in the contemporary chronicles which could sensibly be interpreted as giving weight to the possibility.

Since the release of sensationalist fiction such as *The Da Vinci Code* and burgeoning interest in heresies such as Catharism and its attendant association with the legend of the Holy Grail etc., attention has focused on Rosslyn and the Templar connection.

The Order was founded in 1118 with the objective of protecting pilgrims to the Holy Land. Having overreached themselves and exposed their position through wealth and hubris, the knights were suppressed by Philip the Fair. Some of the order may have fled France for Scotland in 1304.

These refugees brought both treasure and specialist skills, particularly in the field of metalworking, that they had gleaned in the Levant. The site at Rosslyn and the career of Sir William Sinclair have been inextricably linked to the existence of the Order in Scotland. Given that the knights had been suppressed with the full backing of the church, any survivors would have needed to adopt a veil of secrecy.

Sir William appears to have been of the Douglas affinity and fell later in the Battle of Teba with his brother, on Douglas' doomed journey to the Holy Land. The Templars and Sir William Sinclair are also linked to the history of freemasonry in Scotland. However seductive the association, however, there are no objective grounds for associating the Order with victory at Bannockburn. That some of the Scottish knights may have been or remained members of what was, in effect, an underground organization is, of course, a possibility. The leap toward giving the Templars or former Templars a key, decisive role cannot be substantiated.

Those wishing to read more could consult *Rosslyn* by Andrew Sinclair (Edinburgh, 2005).

Appendix V

The Battlefield Today

Much of the ground over which the battle was fought has been subsumed by subsequent building and the drab urban sprawl of modern Stirling, little of which could be described as an improvement. The great fortress, much re-modelled since the fourteenth century, still holds sway, unchallenged on its rocky eminence, one of the most inspiring castles in Europe.

The National Trust for Scotland manages the heritage centre, which features the fine and much-copied image of Robert Bruce, sculpted in Bronze by C. J. Pilkington-Jackson. The centre and monument are on the left of the A872 as you head north toward Stirling. The left flank is now dominated by the line of the current motorway (M9) and most of the ground eastwards toward the Forth is heavily built up. Northwest of the centre is Coxet Hill, also developed, as is St Ninian's to the northeast.

West of the heritage centre would have been the area covered by the New Park, and the road to the south crosses the Bannockburn at what would have been the Entry. The actual site of the battle is bounded on the western flank by the railway and, running parallel, Pike Road.

Glossary

Aketon – a quilted garment, 'soft' armour, (derived from the Arabic word for cotton).

Arming cap – padded fabric hood or cap worn under mail.

Balinger – a smaller vessel, with single mast, part propelled by oars.

Ballista – a type of catapult, of classical provenance, shooting a projectile from an integral bow, tensioned by the operation of a windlass.

Banneret – a military rank, the holder rated above a knight and entitled to a square banner rather than a knight's pennon.

Barbican – an outwork, constructed so as to create additional protection for a castle or the fortified gateway of a town, this could be erected in stone as a permanent addition, or constructed in timber as a temporary expedient.

Battle (Battail) – a division of an army.

Bill – a polearm, that was born of a fateful union between an agricultural tool and the military spear, much favoured by the English.

Bolt – the short thick arrow or quarrel, shot from a crossbow.

Bracer – plate defence for the lower arms.

Brigandine – a type of protective doublet with horn or metal plates sewn in.

Buckler – a small round shield, usually fashioned of metal, used primarily for parrying.

Caltrop – a rather unpleasant form of spiked anti personnel or anti equine device.

Captain – an officer in charge of a particular position or location, whose responsibility did not extend beyond.

Caparison – a fabric horse covering, both decorative and, padded for protection.

Chevauchée – a large scale raid into enemy territory to wage economic warfare, taking livestock and destroying crops and villages.

Cog – a medieval sailing vessel, primarily a merchantman.

Coif – a mail hood.

Comital – pertaining to the estates of a senior magnate (from the French '*comte*').

Conroi – a mounted detachment.

Destrier – the knightly warhorse.

Enceinte – the circuit of defences for a castle or fortified place.

Enfoeff – to grant a feudal estate.

Escalade – an assault on the walls, akin to storming.

Falchion – a cleaver-like sword with a heavy blade, a fine survivor is the 'Conyers Falchion' in Durham Cathedral treasury.

Fief – a feudal landholding.

Fosse – a defensive ditch.

Fuller – the central groove or grooves running down the sword blade, more for balance and weight than channeling blood as has been fancifully suggested.

Great Cause – the matter of the succession to the Scottish throne following the deaths of Alexander III and the Maid of Norway.

Harness – a full armour of mail or plate or a combination of the two.

Hauberk – a form of mail overgarment, reaching usually to the knee, the shorter version being the **Habergeon**.

Helm – the Great Helm was the knightly headgear of choice in use at the end of the thirteenth century.

Herschip – a raid or harrying, 'taking up' an enemy's lands, not dissimilar to the chevauchée.

Hobiler (Hobilar) – a light horseman who could fight from horseback or on foot.

Jack – similar in some respects to the brigandine but more simple, stuffed with rags or tallow and usually sleeveless.

Kern – an Irish warrior of low status in the service of a chief or, often, serving as a mercenary.

Lance – a tactical unit, built around a knights retinue, not fixed in terms of numbers.

Leaguer – a siege or blockade.

Mangonel – an engine for throwing stones. The arm is held back under tension with the projectile being shot when the arm is released to spring forward and strike against a buffer.

Mêlée – usually a mass combat between opposing forces, often refers to a clash of mounted troops.

Mesnie – a household knight, i.e. of the lord's *demesne* or domain.

Motte and Bailey – a form of timber castle, introduced by the Normans, which features a yard or bailey constructed on a raised platform and containing domestic offices, guarded by a palisade, whilst the motte is a defensive tower built on a higher mound and purely defensive in function.

Palfrey – an everyday horse.

Pommel – the metal knob which completes the top of the sword hilt, contributes to balance, can be used offensively for striking a blow.

Pricker – a mounted scout or skirmisher.

Quillons – the bars or sections at the base of the sword hilt which afford protection to the swordsman.

schiltron – a formation of spears, particularly favoured by Scottish foot.

Surcoat – the long, flowing fabric garment worn over mail and bearing the arms or blazon of the wearer.

Tailzie – a form of legal entail (Scottish).

Trapper – padded horse protection.

Trebuchet – a large siege engine with a heavy throwing arm, the king of early medieval artillery.

Vintenar – an NCO in charge of a foot platoon usually twenty strong.

Notes and References

Preface
1. R. Smith, *The Utility of Force* (London, 2005), p. 57.

Chapter 1
1. This work of reconstruction was undertaken by the University Dental Hospital in Newcastle upon Tyne.
2. The King's malady has never been fully diagnosed but may have been paralytic leprosy.
3. A note on spelling: Bruce in old Gaelic is 'Roibert a Briuis'; in current Gaelic 'Raibeart de Bruis'; and in Norman French 'Robert de Brus (or Bruys)'. For the sake of clarity I have, in line with most authors on the subject used the anglicized version.
4. His sister Christina wed Gartnait, Earl of Mar, and another, Matilda, married Aodh of Ross.
5. Carrick is the comital district which now comprises most of South Ayrshire and Dumfries (in Gaelic 'Carraig' or 'rocky place'); the chief hold was Maybole Castle.
6. David I (1080–1153, King of Scots from 1124), was the sixth son of Malcolm III and the fourth of those siblings to rule.
7. From the Latin *scutum* = shield.
8. Mormaer = 'sea-officer'.
9. From the English Shire-Reeve (this function also tended to assume a hereditary aspect).
10. C. Tabraham, *Scottish Castles and Fortifications* (Edinburgh, 1996), p. 30.
11. Kildrummy Castle became the scene of the epic siege where it was so nobly defended by Robert Bruce's youngest brother, Neil, who paid for his defiance with his life. Edward I made certain improvements to the enciente, traces of these being the main evidence for Edwardian castle building in Scotland.
12. Tanistry was a Celtic system for inheritance whereby the successful candidate, or 'tanist', was elected from a particular class or category of eligible claimants. This may sound democratic but was the stuff of mayhem as claimants sought to level the odds by eliminating rivals, see F. J. Bryne, *Irish Kings and High Kings* (Dublin, 1973).
13. Feudal homage was the due owed by the vassal to his lord. The extent of this might vary according to the terms of the oath entered into by the parties, but

might extend to a full military obligation. See J. J. Lalor (ed.), *Cyclopedia of Political Science, Political Economy and the Political History of the United States by the Best American and European Writers* (New York, 1899).

Chapter 2

1. A. V. B. Norman and D. Pottinger, *English Weapons and Warfare 449–1660* (London, 1966), p. 60.
2. *Ibid.*, p. 60.
3. *Ibid.*, p. 60.
4. It was this period that gave birth to the story of Marmion, retold later by Scott.
5. M. Prestwich, *Armies and Warfare in the Middle Ages* (London, 1996), p. 2.
6. *Ibid.*, p. 9.
7. Jean le Bel recounts that a dispute arose between the English and the Hainaulters which led to a serious fracas, resulting in several hundred casualties, see Prestwich, *op. cit.*, p. 178.
8. *Ibid.*, p. 251.
9. Shakespeare cast Falstaff as the prime practitioner of such corrupt practices.
10. Prestwich, *op. cit.*, p. 123; Hugh Cressingham earned an unenviable reputation in Scotland, where he held the office of treasurer, it was largely his bungling which contributed to the disaster at Stirling, Wallace is said to have flayed his fat carcass and fashioned a belt from the flesh!
11. Prestwich, *op. cit.*, pp. 48–9. The effigy of Sir Roger de Trumpington (d. 1280), shows the knight reclining in full harness, his great helm attached to his belt by means of a chain or lanyard, the heater-shaped shield hangs from his right shoulder on a gigne strap. His sword belt hangs low, the preferred position for the draw from horseback. His arms are painted on the ailettes (these were intended mainly to cover the vulnerable neck area from a lateral cut). He has steel poleyns protecting his knees and his mailed hands are joined in prayer – his expression is altogether purposeful. A later effigy, that of Sir Robert de Servans (d. 1306), from Chatham, shows this knight with his mailed hood thrown back and his mittens hanging free. He wears a scalloped fabric or leather pad holding the poleyns in place against the mail and to prevent chafing.
12. A. Boardman, *The Medieval Soldier in the Wars of the Roses* (London, 1998), p. 173.
13. Henry V is reputed to have said that 'War without fire is like sausages without mustard'.
14. Prestwich, *op. cit.*, p. 165.
15. D. J. Sadler, *Border Fury* (London, 2004), p. 9. The knights in question were William Roos, John Moubray, Peter de Mauley and Ralph Fitzwilliam.
16. Prestwich, *op. cit.*, p. 168.
17. *Ibid.*, pp. 116–17.
18. *Ibid.*, pp. 116–17.
19. Aside from the improvements at Kildrummy, Edward attempted little serious castle building in Scotland, relying on garrisoning the existing holds and linking

these with outpost chains. This was clearly not ideal and left the defensive system vulnerable, but cash constraints prohibited any more ambitious schemes.

20. Prestwich, *op. cit.*, p. 134.
21. Sadler, *op. cit.*, p. 34.
22. P. Traquair, *Freedom's Sword* (London, 1998), p. 289.
23. Writer and explorer Tim Severin, as Professor Prestwich points out, attempted to determine the closest modern descendant of the medieval warhorse for a recreation of the route taken by Western European crusaders journeying to the Holy Land in the course of the First Crusade. He decided upon a breed of heavy horse from the Ardennes which, whilst robust, proved rather too broad in the back for long days in the saddle; in the event, the beast, like many of its forbears, never reached the Holy City.
24. Prestwich, *op. cit.*, pp. 1–2.
25. At Flodden in 1513, the Scots, descending from high ground to attack the out-numbered English below, completely lost momentum and cohesion when they floundered in wet ground. In the subsequent mêlée the bill proved a far superior weapon.
26. John Mair (Major) writing in the sixteenth century, see Sadler *op. cit.*, p. 41.
27. A pele may derive its name from the Latin *pilum* – a stake, implying the structure comprised a wooden palisade and a timber tower within, the term is later used to describe the stone towers of the border reivers.
28. The Cathar heresy had flourished in the Languedoc region during the twelfth and early thirteenth centuries, de Montfort's formidable father had been active in its brutal suppression, finally falling at the siege of Toulouse in 1218.
29. Anthony Bek owed his advancement to Longshanks and carried out a series of diplomatic missions on his behalf. A grand prince of the church, renowned for hubris and good living, he was every inch the worldly prelate. He enjoyed the chase and built castles at Eltham and Somerton as well as the magnificent Great Hall in Durham's castle. His elder brother was Bishop of St David's and another sibling, Thomas, held the see of Lincoln from 1321. Bek quarreled with the king over his dismissal of the prior of Durham and suffered a brief forfeiture. Although reconciled with the king the feud simmered. See C. M. Fraser, *A History of Anthony Bek Bishop of Durham 1283–1311* (Oxford, 1957).
30. From 'The Vows of the Heron.'
31. Sir Charles Oman, *A History of the Art of War in the Middle Ages*, vol. II (London, 1924), pp. 113–16.

Chapter 3
1. Prestwich, *op. cit.*, p. 478.
2. 'Longshanks', as in 'long legs', a reference to the king's height and cavalier build.
3. Prestwich, *op. cit.*, p. 386.
4. *Ibid.*, p. 469.
5. A 'tailzie', or 'entail' – see Glossary.

6. A. Fisher, *William Wallace* (Edinburgh, 1986), p. 17.
7. '*Custodes Pacis*', i.e. keepers of the peace.
8. Baliol was from a wealthy Anglo-Norman line with extensive holdings in England and Picardy, the castle at Barnard Castle in County Durham represents their endeavour. John Baliol seems to have been both inexperienced and unenthusiastic; one suspects the loss of his kingdom was not a particular source of lasting sorrow.
9. This was a cautious nod toward Yolande of Dreux, should she in fact be with child by the late king.
10. Edward of Caernarvon's grandfather, Henry III of England, was great-grandfather to the Maid of Norway.
11. Anthony Bek, churchman, soldier, diplomat, politician and practitioner of dubious property transactions. See chapter 2, note 29, above.
12. Prestwich, *op. cit.*, p. 361.
13. Bek had added the Liberty of Tynedale to his holdings, formerly a fief of the Scottish crown. This grant appears to have been in recognition of disbursements (bribes) to certain of the Norwegian delegates.
14. Prestwich, *op. cit.*, p. 362.
15. *Ibid.*, p. 364.
16. Traquair, *op. cit.*, p. 27.
17. Longshanks was, at face value, a good choice. He had an impressive record of similar adjudications at the very highest levels. Through Henry I of England he did have a direct, if somewhat remote, claim in his own right.
18. A stiff fine or premium of a hefty £100,000 (to accrue to the papal coffers as a contribution to the proposed crusade), due if the handover was delayed once a decision had been reached.
19. Malcolm IV had so conformed in the reign of Henry II.
20. Fisher, *op. cit.*, p. 23.
21. Traquair, *op. cit.*, p. 42.
22. The castellan of Wark, Robert Ros, was one who suffered from a divided loyalty, though his conflict was more romantic than politic and he was prepared to trade the castle to secure the favours of his Scottish paramour Christine de Moubray!
23. In very rough translation this means 'dig your way in and defend the town with a new ditch' – certain more pithy elements may have been lost in the translation.
24. Traquair, *op. cit.*, p. 46; Prestwich, *op. cit.*, p. 471.
25. Traquair, *op. cit.*, p. 49.
26. Fisher, *op. cit.*, p. 27.
27. 'Have we nothing to do but win kingdoms for you?' – see Fisher, *op. cit.*, p. 30.
28. *Bon besoigne fait qy de merde se delivrer* – see Fisher, *op. cit.*, p. 30.
29. Fisher, *op. cit.*, p. 37.
30. *Ibid.*, pp. 4–6.
31. Clifford was a long established Westmorland line. Roger de Clifford had died in one of Edward's few reverses in the Welsh campaigns. The dead man's son, also Roger, served constantly and with distinction in Edward's Scottish wars; he was

destined to fall at Bannockburn. See 'Military Service of the Cliffords during the Reigns of Edward I & II' in *Hobilar: the Journal of the Lance and Longbow Society*, no. 18 (1992).

32. Fisher, *op. cit.*, p. 40.
33. D. J. Sadler, *Scottish Battles* (Edinburgh, 1996), p. 41.
34. Fisher, *op. cit.*, p. 64.
35. These Gallowegians or 'Gallgaels' were particularly ferocious in attack; see Sir Charles Oman, *A History of the Art of War in the Middle Ages*, vol. I (London, 1924), p. 393. The wild men from the west, though useful in the attack, were notoriously difficult to discipline, as both David I and later Wallace discovered.
36. Fisher, *op. cit.*, p. 68.
37. Sadler, *op. cit.*, p. 41.
38. The Umfravilles were a Norman line who held the lordships of Redesdale and Prudhoe in Northumberland, as well as the earldom of Angus. Members of the family fought on both sides. See Hedley W. Percy, *Northumbrian Families*, 2 vols (Newcastle, 1970).
39. Sadler, *op. cit.*, p. 44.
40. Prestwich, *op. cit.*, p. 483.
41. Fisher, *op. cit.*, p. 98.
42. Traquair, *op. cit.*, p. 89.
43. Wages: magnate 8s per day; banneret 4s; knight 2s; sergeant or man-at-arms 1s. Rates for contracted service tended to be higher; see Prestwich, *op. cit.*, p. 485.
44. *Ibid.*, p. 484.
45. *Ibid.*, p. 486.
46. The supplies gathered included 7,000 quarters of wheat, 8,000 of oats, 4,300 of malt and 1,000 of beans and peas, with an additional 1,000 quarters of wheat from Ireland; see Prestwich, *op. cit.*, pp. 486–7.
47. Traquair, *op. cit.*, p. 95.
48. The Dissenters were agitating for additional constitutional safeguards to be inserted into Magna Carta. Eventually a compromise agreement was reached and codified as Confirmatio Cartarum; see Prestwich, *op. cit.*, pp. 427–30.
49. In Geoffrey of Monmouth's *History of the Kings of Britain* the author entertainingly dates kingship from the arrival of Aeneas' grandson, Brutus of Troy, who exercises sway over the entire island. On Brutus' death the northern kingdom is devolved onto Alba, the younger son who, nonetheless, owes allegiance to his elder brother holding what was to become England.
50. Prestwich, *op. cit.*, p. 494.
51. *Ibid.*, p. 494.
52. *Ibid.*, p. 494.
53. The Scots, to counter Geoffrey of Monmouth, produced an epic lineage for the kings of Scotland, tracing their origins to the pharaonic princess!
54. See chapter 2 for a discussion of this important battle.
55. Prestwich, *op. cit.*, p. 497.

56. Traquair, *op. cit.*, p. 11.
57. The cost amounted to some £938; see Prestwich, *op. cit.*, p. 499.
58. It is deduced from a record of quantities of sulphur supplied to the besieging forces that the use of gunpowder may have been current. See Prestwich, *op. cit.*, p. 499.
59. *Ibid.*, p. 499.
60. Traquair, *op. cit.*, p. 112.
61. A petroleum based incendiary. See David Nicolle, *Medieval Warfare Source Book* (London, 1999), pp. 294–5.
62. Fisher, *op. cit.*, p. 504.
63. Prestwich, *op. cit.*, p. 504.
64. *Ibid.*, p. 511.

Chapter 4

1. Walter Bower, *Scotichronicon*, quoted in Traquair, *op. cit.*, p.150.
2. G. W. S. Barrow, *Robert Bruce* (London, 1965), p.198. A taint of treachery clung to Gloucester and may have influenced the king's apparently pejorative attitude toward his nephew.
3. *Ibid.*, p. 199.
4. C. McNamee, *The Wars of the Bruces* (East Lothian, 1997), p. 29.
5. *Ibid.*, p. 32.
6. Douglas was a cousin of the steward's, son of the commander of Berwick in 1296. The elder Douglas, having later surrendered, refused to hand over the boy as a surety. He was therefore kept in custody and died in the Tower, possibly, as Barbour suggests, through foul play. The son met Lamberton when a student in Paris. The Bishop's efforts to reverse the attainder were unavailing, see P. Reese, *Bannockburn* (Edinburgh, 2000), pp. 86–7.
7. McNamee, *op. cit.*, p. 31.
8. Prestwich, *op. cit.*, p. 506.
9. *Ibid.*, p. 507.
10. McNamee, *op. cit.*, p. 36.
11. *Ibid.*, p. 38.
12. *Ibid.*, p. 38.
13. Traquair, *op. cit.*, pp. 152–3.
14. *Ibid.*, 252.
15. *Ibid.*, pp. 154–5.
16. *Ibid.*, p. 154.
17. Prestwich, *op. cit.*, p. 79.
18. French representatives attending Edward's marriage were deeply offended by the prominent role of the upstart Gaveston. See Prestwich, *op. cit.*, p. 81.
19. *Ibid.*, p. 81.
20. *Ibid.*, p. 83.
21. McNamee, *op. cit.*, p. 46.

22. Traquair, *op. cit.*, p. 164.
23. *Ibid.*, p. 164.
24. *Ibid.*, p. 164.
25. McNamee, *op. cit.*, p. 46.
26. Henry Bohun, Earl of Hereford, the hereditary Constable who was to play an important role at Bannockburn, died in the fight at Boroughbridge on the rebel side.
27. McNamee, *op. cit.*, p. 48.
28. Traquair, *op. cit.*, p. 166.
29. McNamee, *op. cit.*, p. 50.
30. Thomas of Lancaster was Lincoln's son in law; the demise of the latter left Thomas the wealthiest of the English magnates.
31. Prestwich, *op. cit.*, p. 84.
32. *Ibid.*, p. 84.
33. Bruce sent a fairly blunt response pointing out the king's perfidy toward his own countrymen.
34. Gaveston invented scurrilous nicknames for the magnates, a tactic not calculated to ensure popularity amongst a class who already despised him.
35. McNamee, *op. cit.*, p. 52.
36. *Ibid.*, p. 52.
37. *Ibid.*, p. 52.
38. *Ibid.*, p. 53.
39. *Ibid.*, p. 53.
40. *Ibid.*, p. 56.
41. Traquair, *op. cit.*, p. 168.
42. 'Pele' probably from the Latin *pilum*, for a stake or palisade.
43. Matthew Binnock jammed a haywain beneath the portcullis as the grill descended, enabling the eight commandos concealed amongst the straw to gain possession of the vital gateway.
44. McNamee, *op. cit.*, p. 60.
45. Traquair, *op. cit.*, p. 178.
46. *Ibid.*, p. 62.
47. McNamee, *op. cit.*, p. 60.

Chapter 5

1. N. Denholm-Young (ed.), *Vita Edwardi Secundi* (London, 1957), p. 52.
2. J. Stevenson (ed.), Chronicle of Lanercost (Edinburgh, 1839), p. 207.
3. McNamee, *op. cit.*, p. 62.
4. Heralds were an indispensable part of the Household, it was the herald's job to act as a diplomat and scout; he would arrange truces; count the tally of dead and wounded; negotiate ransoms. He was expected to possess a detailed knowledge of the lineage and arms of magnates and gentry. He could determine matters of etiquette and precedence whilst acting as his emissary's royal master. Heralds were to be treated with courtesy and held immune from violence.

5. Stirling Castle, the gateway to the highlands. The great fortress still glowers down from Castle Hill, a steep sided volcanic plug. Most of what now stands dates from far later than the fourteenth century; the buildings are, in the main from the fifteenth and sixteenth centuries, the outer walls from the eighteenth.

6. The 'Polls' or 'Pows' – these have been identified by Professor Barrow, one of the most eminent scholars on the subject of the battle, as meaning a slow moving, miry waterway. The confusion with the 'pots', i.e. the man made obstacles dug by Bruce's sappers is understandable but erroneous.

7. The Carse of Stirling – since the fourteenth century the process of continuous peat harvesting and subsequent drainage has changed the nature of the landscape; most of the ground is now built over.

8. Sadler, *op. cit.*, p. 48.

9. Henry de Bohun would have a particular enmity for Bruce, and vice-versa, as his family (he was Hereford's nephew) had gained lands in Galloway from Bruce's attainder; obviously in practical terms, these had since reverted.

10. N. Denholm-Young (ed.), *Vita Edwardi Secundi*, p. 24.

11. Gilbert de Clare, Earl of Gloucester, came from a distinguished line of Welsh marchers who had done good service under Edward I. Gilbert was the king's nephew and highly regarded by his contemporaries; despite his relative youth he had considerable experience of command. Humphrey de Bohun, Earl of Hereford, was Edward I's son-in-law, immensely wealthy, of a long and noble line. He was a noted figure in the opposition to the king's tendency to despotism and an enemy firstly of Gaveston and, latterly of the Despensers. He died on the bridge during the skirmish at Boroughbridge in 1322.

12. Sir Robert Clifford was from a distinguished line of Cumbrian knights and a proven commander. Henry de Beaumont was the king's cousin; he was married to Alice Comyn and thus inherited, through her, an interest in the earldom of Buchan. Bannockburn was by no means the end of his career, he was to become a prime mover amongst the 'Disinherited' in the 1330s and led a rebel army to victory at Dupplin Moor in 1332.

13. Sir Thomas Gray of Heton, *Scalacronica* (London, 1836), p. 7.

14. Gray, a Northumbrian knight from the manor of Heton (Heaton) and father of the chronicler, was no novice in the Scottish wars; de Beaumont might have done better had he heeded the advice being given!

15. Sir William Deyncourt – the unfortunate knight appears to be the only gentleman killed by the Scots during this combat.

16. John Barbour, *The Bruce*, bk 12, line 497.

17. A. Nusbacher, *Bannockburn, 1314* (Stroud, 2000), pp. 118–19).

18. Denholm-Young (ed.), *op. cit.*, p. 52.

19. *Ibid.*

20. Reese, *op. cit.*, p. 41.

21. *Ibid.*, p. 146.

Chapter 6

1. Gray, *op. cit.*, p. 7.
2. Nusbacher, *op. cit.*, pp. 130–1.
3. Gray, *op. cit.*, p. 55.
4. John of Trokelowe, *Chronica et Annales*, H. T. Riley (ed.) (Rolls Series, 1865), p. 87.
5. The Lanercost chronicle clearly records the archery duel but this cannot have been a full deployment of the English bows, far more likely an outpost line only.
6. Stevenson (ed.), *op. cit.*, p. 207.
7. The Umfravilles were lords of Redesdale and Prudhoe in Northumberland. William the Lion had invaded the county in 1174 to chastise them and was captured at Alnwick by a raiding party.
8. Lanercost does support this, saying the Scots fell tot heir knees to repeat the Paternoster before their final advance.
9. Denholm-Young (ed.), *op. cit.*, p. 52.
10. Trokelowe, *op. cit.*, p. 87.
11. E. Maude Thompson (ed.), *Chronica Galfridi le Baker de Swynebroke* (Oxford, 1889), p. 7.
12. *The Life of Edward II* implies Sir Giles Argentan fell in Gloucester's charge but in fact he perished later, in the rout, having first discharged his obligation to assist the king safely from the field.
13. The Life is in error here as a knight, even when in full harness, was not prevented from rising swiftly and fighting on foot, more likely he would simply be swamped by the press of footmen as he struck the ground and overborne.
14. Stevenson (ed.), *op. cit.*, p. 207.
15. Reese, *op. cit.*, p. 160.
16. Baston's verses, quoted in Bower, *Scotichronicon*, ed. and trans. D. R. Watts.
17. *Ibid.*
18. For a discussion of the role or supposed role of the Knights Templar, refer to Appendix IV.
19. Gray, *op. cit.*, p. 7.
20. Sadler, *op. cit.*, p. 82.
21. Stevenson, *op. cit.*, p. 207.
22. Denholm-Young (ed.), *op. cit.*, p. 52.
23. *Ibid.*
24. *Ibid.*
25. *Ibid.*
26. Prestwich, *op. cit.*, p. 81.
27. Baston's verses, quoted in Bower, *Scotichronicon*, ed. and trans. D. R. Watts.

Chapter 7

1. McNamee, *op. cit.*, p. 72.
2. Prestwich, *op. cit.*, p. 86.

3. The Mortimers were Welsh Marcher Lords, with a sound pedigree of supporting Longshanks in the Barons' War. The conflict had fostered a particularly rancorous feud with the Despensers so much in favour with Edward II. See I. Mortimer, *The Greatest Traitor* (London, 2003), pp. 7–8.
4. Prestwich, *op. cit.*, p. 54.
5. Mortimer, *op. cit.*, pp. 111–13.
6. Oman, *op. cit.*, p. 101.
7. Mortimer, *op. cit.*, p. 107.
8. McNamee, *op. cit.*, p. 72.
9. *Ibid.*, p. 75.
10. *Ibid.*, p. 76.
11. *Ibid.*, p. 76.
12. Traquair, *op. cit.*, p. 109.
13. Two local lads who'd strayed from the walls were arraigned as spies, so great was the prevailing terror. On enquiry they were found guiltless; their ages were 11 and 9!
14. Traquair, *op. cit.*, p. 200.
15. *Ibid.*, p. 201.
16. *Ibid.*, p. 201.
17. The issue of Marjorie and the Steward would, in his middle years, and on the death of the childless David II, ascend the Scottish throne as the first Stewart king.
18. McNamee, *op. cit.*, p. 79.
19. *Ibid.*, p. 166.
20. G. A. Hayes–McCoy, *Irish Battles* (Belfast, 1969), p. 39.
21. McNamee, *op. cit.*, p. 194.
22. *Ibid.*, p. 192.
23. *Galloglas* were Norse-Gael mercenaries attached to Irish magnates, a form of feudal *Samurai* – see J. Marsden, *Galloglas* (East Linton, 2003).
24. McNamee, *op. cit.*, p. 192.
25. Hayes–McCoy, *op. cit.*, p. 40.
26. Traquair, *op. cit.*, pp. 210–11.
27. *Ibid.*, p. 213.
28. Middletons: a Norman family with lands at Belsay and Mitford in mid-Northumberland; they still own Belsay to this day.
29. McNamee, *op. cit.*, p. 85.
30. *Ibid.*, p. 88.
31. Traquair, *op. cit.*, 220.
32. McNamee, *op. cit.*, p. 91.
33. *Ibid.*, p. 94.
34. *Ibid.*, p. 96.
35. *Ibid.*, p. 95.
36. Traquair, *op. cit.*, p. 224.
37. McNamee, *op. cit.*, p. 96.

38. *Ibid.*, p. 96.
39. The muster at Newcastle was to comprise 28,500 of all arms, that at Carlisle 11,000; over 7,000 were to arrive from Ireland with 10,000 being levied from Wales with the same number again being levied in June. The York Parliament significantly culled these impossibly optimistic numbers which were more paper strength than real. See Traquair, *op. cit.*, p. 228.
40. McNamee, *op. cit.*, p. 98.
41. Some resistance was offered but only in isolated pockets.
42. The legend of Marmion dates from the siege.
43. McNamee, *op. cit.*, p. 100.
44. *Ibid.*, p. 101.
45. *Ibid.*, p. 101.
46. *Ibid.*, p. 101.
47. Oman, *op. cit.*, p. 100.
48. Traquair, *op. cit.*, p. 230.

Chapter 8

1. It was rumoured that the earl had in fact been murdered 'suddenly on a privy seat', Prestwich, *op. cit.*, p. 94.
2. Traquair, *op. cit.*, p. 199.
3. This Henry de Sully was a French knight, captured at Byland.
4. Traquair, *op. cit.*, p. 200.
5. Hayes–McCoy, *op. cit.*, p. 40.
6. Barrow, *op. cit.*, p. 363.
7. Mar became regent and fell in battle against the Disinherited at Dupplin Moor in 1332.

Bibliography

Primary Sources

Andrew of Wyntoune's Orygnale Cronykil of Scotland, edited by D. Laing (Edinburgh, 1872).

The Bruce, by John Barbour, translated by A. A. M. Duncan (Edinburgh, 1997).

Calendar of Close Rolls.

The Chronicles of Froissart, translated Sir John Bourchier Lord Berners (London, 1901).

The Chronicles of Walter of Guisburgh, edited by H. Rothwell (London, 1957).

Chronica Galfridi le Baker de Swynebroke, edited by E. Maude-Thompson (Oxford 1889).

Chronica Gentis Scotorum, by John of Fordun, translated by F. J. H. Skene, edited by W. F. Skene (Edinburgh, 1872).

Chronicon de Lanercost, edited by J. Stevenson (Edinburgh, 1839).

Documents Illustrative of the History of Scotland, edited by J. Stevenson (Edinburgh, 1870).

Johannis de Trokelowe et Henrici de Blaneforde Chronica et Annales, edited by H. T. Riley, Rolls Series (1865).

Scalacronica, by Sir Thomas Gray of Heton, edited by J. Stevenson (London, 1836).

Scotichronicon, by Walter Bower, edited and translated by D. R. Watt (Aberdeen, 1991)

Vita Edwardi Secundi, edited by N. Denholm-Young (London, 1957).

Secondary Sources

Allan, J., 'The Borestone of the First Bannockburn', *Stirling Journal and Advertiser* (1904).

Anderson, A. O., *Early Sources of Scottish History* (Edinburgh, 1922).

Anderson, R. & R. C., *The Sailing Ship* (London, 1926).

Barber, R., *The Knight and Chivalry* (London, 1974).

Barron, E. M., *The Scottish War of Independence* (Inverness, 1934).

Barrow, G. W. S., *Robert Bruce and the Community of the Realm of Scotland* (Edinburgh, 1976).

Barrow, G. W. S., *Kingship and Unity 1000–1306* (Toronto, 1981).

Barrow, G. W. S., *Robert the Bruce* (London, 1965).

Barrow, G. W. S., *The Kingdom of the Scots* (London, 1973).

Bartlett, C., *The English Longbowman 1313–1515* (Oxford, 1995).

Becke, Major A. F., 'The Battle of Bannockburn', in G. E. C. Cockayne, *Complete Peerage* (London, 1949).

Bingham, C., *The Life and Times of Edward II* (London, 1973).

Blair, C., *European Armour* (London, 1958).

Boardman, S., *The Early Stewart Kings* (Edinburgh, 1996).

Bradbury, J., *The Medieval Archer* (New York, 1985).

Byrne, F. J., *Irish Kings and High Kings* (Dublin, 1973).

Caldwell, D. H., *Scotland's Wars and Warriors* (London, 1998).

Christison, General Sir Philip, *Bannockburn: the Story of the Battle* (Edinburgh, 1960).

Contamine, P., *War in the Middle Ages*, translated M. Jones (Oxford, 1984).

Crum, Major F. M., *Bannockburn* (Stirling, 1927).

Davis, R. H. C., *The Medieval Warhorse* (London, 1989).

Devries, K., *Infantry Warfare in the Early Fourteenth Century: Discipline, Tactics and Technology* (Woodbridge, 1996).

Ducklin, K. & J. Waller, *Sword Fighting* (London, 2001).

Duncan, A. A. M., 'Early Parliaments in Scotland', in *Scottish Historical Review*, 45 (1966).

Evans, J. (ed.), *The Flowering of the Middle Ages* (London 1998).

Ewan, E., *Townlife in Fourteenth Century Scotland* (Edinburgh, 1990).

Grant, A., *Independence and Nationhood, Scotland 1306–1469* (Edinburgh, 1996).

Gravett, C., *Medieval Siege Warfare* (England, 1990).

Hyland, A., *The Medieval Warhorse from Byzantium to the Crusades* (Stroud, 1994).

Hutchinson, A. F., *Edward II* (London, 1971).

Keegan, J., *The Face of Battle* (London, 1976).

Keen, M., *Medieval Warfare: A History* (Oxford, 1990).

Lomas, R., *Northumberland: County of Conflict* (East Lothian, 1996).

Lomas, R., *North-East England in the Middle Ages* (Edinburgh, 1992).

Lynch, M., *A New History of Scotland* (London, 1991).

Mackenzie, W. M., *The Bannockburn Myth* (Edinburgh, 1932).

Maxwell, Sir H., 'The Battle of Bannockburn', in *Scottish Historical Review*, vol. X (1914).

McNamee, C., *The Wars of the Bruces* (East Linton, 1997).

Miller, Rev. T., 'The Site of the New Park in relation to the Battle of Bannockburn', in *Scottish Historical Review*, vol. XII (1914).

Morris, J. E., *Bannockburn* (Cambridge, 1914).

Morris, J. E., 'Mounted Infantry in Medieval Warfare', in *Royal Historical Society*, 3rd series, viii (1914).

Mortimer, I., *The Greatest Traitor* (London, 2003).

Neillands, R., *The Hundred Years War* (London, 1990).

Nusbacher, A., *The Battle of Bannockburn 1314* (Stroud, 2000).

Nicolle, D., *A Medieval Warfare Source Book* (London, 1999).

Norman, A. V. B. & D. Pottinger, *English Weapons and Warfare 449–1660* (London, 1966).

Oakeshott, R. E., *A Knight and his Weapons* (London, 1964).
Oman, Sir Charles, *The Art of War in the Middle Ages*, vol. 2 (London, 1924).
Prestwich, M., *Edward I* (London, 1988).
Prestwich, M., *Armies and Warfare in the Middle Ages* (London, 1996).
Prestwich, M., *The Three Edwards* (London, 1980).
Sadler, D. J., *Scottish Battles* (Edinburgh, 1996).
Sadler, D. J., *Border Fury – The Three Hundred Years War* (London, 2004).
Scott, R. M., *Robert the Bruce, King of Scots* (London, 1982).
Scott, W., *Bannockburn Revealed* (Rothesay, 2000).
Smith, R., *The Utility of Force – The Art of War in the Modern World* (London, 2005).
Smurthwaite, D., *Battlefields of Britain* (London, 1984).
Tabraham, C., *Scottish Castles and Fortifications* (Edinburgh, 1996).
Traquair, P., *Freedom's Sword* (London, 1998).
Wagner, P. & S. Heiss, *Medieval Sword and Shield* (Highland Village, Texas, 2003).
Wise, T., *Medieval Heraldry* (Oxford, 1983).

Index

The Merchant Adventurers
General Editor: Ralph Davis, Ph.D.

Latin America and
British Trade 1806-1914

The Merchant Adventurers

Latin America and British Trade 1806-1914

D. C. M. PLATT, D. Phil.

Professor of the History of Latin America,
University of Oxford

Adam & Charles Black
London

First published 1972
A. & C. Black Ltd.
4, 5 & 6 Soho Square, London W1V 6AD
ISBN 0 7136 1309 2

Printed in Great Britain by
T. & A. Constable Ltd., Edinburgh

Contents

List of Tables

List of Figures

Maps

Acknowledgements

I AM most grateful, as always, to my wife, Sarah, for her assistance at every stage in the preparation of this book for publication. I am also indebted to Professor R. A. Humphreys, Dr R. C. Floud, Mr R. C. Trebilcock and Mr J. R. Wells for comments on the final draft.

St Antony's College
Oxford

D. C. M. P.

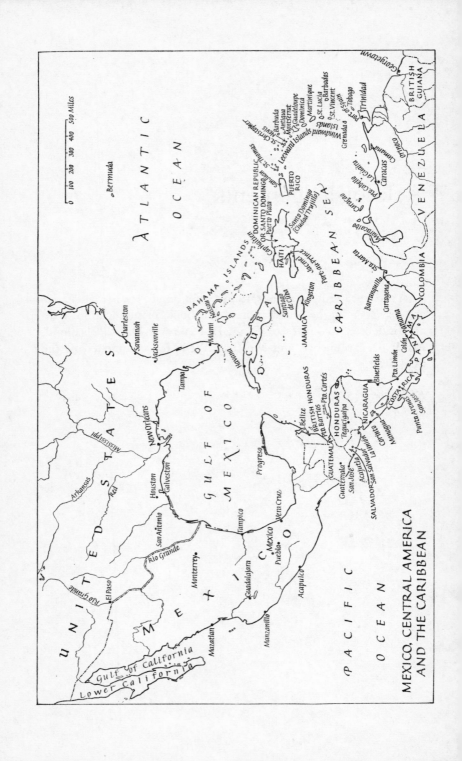

MEXICO, CENTRAL AMERICA
AND THE CARIBBEAN

PART I

1806-1860

describe Britain, technologically and industrially advanced, as becoming in these early decades 'as important to the Latin American economy as to the cotton-exporting southern United States'?[1] The explanation seems to lie in a natural tendency to find some economic reflection of a violent political change. Markets were 'thrown open' to the free importation of European manufactured goods which 'flooded' both seaports and the interior. Massive imports of British manufactured goods 'simply crushed local industry based upon primitive technology'. These, it seems, were the economic consequences, satisfactorily dramatic, of the struggle of peoples to be free. But is it pedantic to ask what volume of goods had already been reaching Latin America during the colonial period, what industry existed to be crushed? If no basic change had occurred in the distribution of wealth,where were the new markets to be found? Could it be that the inflow of goods simply satisfied the needs of a restricted area of colonial society accumulated over years of blockade, together with such new demand as may have arisen from access to European fashions in furnishings and dress? Did imports return later to a level not altogether dissimilar to that experienced under the Spanish Empire? Could it be that except in the major seaports and their hinterland, open directly to manufactured imports, the great mass of the population continued as always to consume the products of their own cottage industries?

*

Optimists saw in Latin America in the early nineteenth century, as in China in later decades, limitless opportunities for the expansion of trade. Thomas Ashe described it as 'embracing the finest country of the same magnitude in the world, peopled by 40,000,000 of inhabitants, abounding in riches, and wanting only our manufactures to possess every comfort of life'.[2] But the truth was that trading opportunities were limited, that the mass of the population was not in the market for imported manufactured goods, and that the purchasing power of the new Republics was dependent on an ability, not as yet evident, to produce commodities in demand in Europe or the United States.

[1] Stanley J. Stein and Barbara H. Stein, *The Colonial Heritage of Latin America* (New York, 1970), pp. 134-5.
[2] Thomas Ashe, *A Commercial View and Geographical Sketch of the Brasils in South America* (London, 1812), p. 8.

Accurate population figures are unobtainable for the early nineteenth century and the estimates are wildly out of line. However, it may not be too unrealistic, for the critical years of the newly reopened trade, to suggest a population for Rio de Janeiro (1808) of 60,000,[1] for Buenos Aires (1800s) of 30,000-40,000,[2] for Montevideo (1807) of about 10,000,[3] for Santiago (1820) of 40,000,[4] for Valparaiso (1820) of 3,000,[5] and for Lima (1820) of 64,000.[6] Away from the main cities and seaports the population was sparse, transport conditions appalling, and the marketing of imported goods expensive and unrewarding. In the white Republics of the South, population outside the main cities was exiguous. The total population of Argentina in the mid-'20s was probably less than 600,000, of whom nearly 150,000 lived in the city and province of Buenos Aires.[7] Schmidtmeyer, in what may have been too drastic a revision of suggested figures for the population of Chile, reduced the estimates from 1,200,000 to a maximum of 400,000 and a possible minimum of 250,000.[8] In the central and northern Republics, and in the Empire of Brazil, where there were larger concentrations of population, a preponderance of the population was Indian or Negro. Three-quarters of the population of Mexico, Indian and mestizo, could make no contribution to the market. Only about one-third of Rio's population in 1808 was white or white mulatto, and the proportion was far smaller outside the capital. Whatever its imperfections, Humboldt's estimate of the racial distribution within Spanish America in 1823 gave 7,530,000 to Indians, 5,328,000 to mestizos, 3,276,000 to whites, and 776,000 to blacks.[9] By contrast, in 1800 the total population of France was 27 million; of Germany, 25 million; of the United Kingdom, 16 million; of Europe as a whole, including Russia, 192 million.

---

[1] John Luccock, *Notes on Rio de Janeiro* (London, 1820), p. 41.
[2] Miron Burgin, *The Economic Aspects of Argentine Federalism, 1820-1852* (Cambridge, Mass., 1946), pp. 26-7.
[3] J. P. and W. P. Robertson, *Letters on Paraguay* (London, 1838), I, 102.
[4] Peter Schmidtmeyer, *Travels into Chile over the Andes in the years 1820 and 1821* (London, 1824), pp. 854-5.
[5] John Miers, *Travels in Chile and La Plata* (London, 1826), I, 446.
[6] R. A. Humphreys, *Liberation in South America 1806-1827* (London, 1952), p. 85.
[7] Burgin, *Argentine Federalism*, p. 115.
[8] Schmidtmeyer, *Chile*, p. 855.
[9] Alexander von Humboldt, *Personal Narrative of Travels to the Equinoctial Regions of the New Continent* (London, 1826), VI, 836.

A small population, well dispersed, had little to offer the trader, and even by the standards of the time the attractions of Latin American markets were limited. Buenos Aires, Rio and Valparaiso, centres for trade and some immigration, doubled their population in the first decade of independence. But for too many areas the devastation created by the struggle with Spain and by a succession of civil wars put an end to any hope of swift expansion. Every traveller visiting the northern Republics of Colombia and Venezuela in the '20s commented on depopulation and destruction. Colombia's population, said Colonel Francis Hall, had remained barely stationary, all its natural increase lost to supplying the waste of the Spanish and Republican armies; the population of Venezuela, worst hit of all, was, he reckoned, halved during the struggle.[1] John Hawkshaw, travelling in Venezuela a decade later, found destruction and decay still evident in all the large towns and in the country.

> Houses and streets are empty. Farms and cultivated estates are left to go back to a state of nature; and weeds and rank vegetation are covering up what once were scenes of productiveness and prosperity.[2]

Most of the Republics were battlefields at one time or another. J. A. B. Beaumont, who visited Montevideo in 1826, found it reduced to a third of its former population, sunk into a miserable state of poverty, while an extensive suburb, formerly the villas of Spanish merchants, still remained completely desolated and in ruins.[3] Although the ports of Peru were opened by the patriots to foreign trade in 1821, the Spaniards remained at large in the interior, and it was not until 9 December 1824, after the battle of Ayacucho, that the last Spanish viceroy laid down his arms. The expulsion or flight of the Spanish merchants created serious problems of shortage of capital and of breakdown in the traditional trading connections, particularly evident for cities like Lima which had taken so central a part in the Spanish trading system. But Mexico, according to the picturesque but exaggerated figure

---

[1] Francis Hall, *Colombia: its Present State* (London, 1824), p. 15.
[2] John Hawkshaw, *Reminiscences of South America* (London, 1838), p. 38.
[3] J. A. B. Beaumont, *Travels in Buenos Ayres and the adjacent provinces of the Rio de la Plata* (London, 1828), p. 69.

current at the time, lost \$100 million in the flight of Spanish capital, and loss of trading capital, together with the presence of a Spanish garrison at the castle of San Juan de Ulloa commanding the port of Vera Cruz, delayed the restoration of normal trading relations for several years after the formal break with Spain in 1821. Central and north-western Argentina took decades to recover from the destruction of the Spanish trade routes to Bolivia and from the extinction of the 'grand staple trade' of Córdoba and the west, the export of mules to Chile and Peru. 'Discord and Civil War', General Paroissien recorded in his Journal in January 1826, 'have indeed made a deplorable difference between the skeleton I now behold, and the industrious, the gay, the hospitable Tucuman I remember.'[1]

Whatever the local circumstances in Latin America—the ravages of civil war, depopulation, the flight of capital, the abandonment and flooding of the mines—further progress in international trade was limited above all by the nature of the consumer and of his needs. Wealth was concentrated in the hands of the few. In Brazil, Argentina, Peru and Mexico this group, which had paid the high prices of colonial imports, remained fully capable of meeting the cost of any luxuries obtainable from Europe. A small middle class existed on the proceeds of professional services and trade, and these too provided a market for the cheaper level of imports after the collapse of colonial monopolies. Outside the capital itself and the principal ports there was little prospect of any substantial enlargement of trade. £200,000 p.a. of woollen goods was as much as the Brazil market could absorb. The cities of Pernambuco, Rio and Bahia took the major part of the Brazilian trade. Adventurous merchants, trying to open markets elsewhere, found themselves helpless before a complete absence either of demand or of purchasing power. John Luccock, who arrived at Rio Grande do Sul early in 1809 with a mixed cargo of goods, found it impossible to dispose of them. There was a shortage of cash, bills of exchange were unknown, and trade, even by retailers, was largely barter. Luccock tried every known means to rid himself of that small portion of his cargo which he had landed. He opened a store larger and more variously stocked than anything seen before in the town. He filled several retail shops with his goods, employing their owners to sell

---

[1] Quoted in Humphreys, *Liberation in South America*, p. 147.

on his account. He sent hawkers through the neighbourhood and took a caravan of goods into the interior. He held an auction at which he employed a man to run up the prices, and found himself with not a single lot disposed of.[1] His experience was matched in any provincial town or small port. O'Gorman complained that for a place like Acapulco in the '20s, £10,000 of British goods would stock the market for three years.[2] The population of the hinterland of Maracaibo in Venezuela was miserably poor. As for the city itself, its population 'barely exists upon plantains and lake water; there are not three families that sit down to a regular meal, and a cloth is a luxury seldom had recourse to'.[3] The country people of Uruguay, even in the '40s, remained 'averse to improving their means of subsistence, and seem to wish for nothing beyond the bare necessaries of life'.[4] Whatever social luxury existed in the northern Republics was confined to Caracas, Bogotá, Quito and a few seaports; throughout the interior, 'the comforts and even the decencies of life are unvalued because unknown':

> The man who can eat beef and plantains, and smoke segars as he swings in his hammock, is possessed of almost everything his habits qualify him to enjoy, or to which his ambition prompts him to attain—the poor have little less, the rich scarcely covet more.[5]

Even in the comparative luxury of Lima, consumption of foreign textiles among the rich lagged well behind the generous habits of Europe. Robert Proctor noted, with proper disgust, that Society went to bed very late in Lima, 'and what appears very disagreeable to an Englishman is that both sexes sleep naked without so much as a covering to the head'.[6]

The truth was that manufactures of any kind, and above all

---

[1] Luccock, *Rio de Janeiro*, pp. 184-5.

[2] Despatch dated Mexico City, 10 August 1824, printed in R. A. Humphreys (ed.), *British Consular Reports on the Trade and Politics of Latin America, 1824-1826* (Royal Historical Society, Camden Third Series, LXIII, London, 1940), p. 333.

[3] Sutherland's report of 5 July 1824, in Humphreys, *Consular Reports*, p. 279.

[4] MacGregor's report on Uruguay, Parliamentary Papers 1847, LXIV, 307.

[5] Hall, *Colombia*, p. 37.

[6] Robert Proctor, *Narrative of a Journey across the Cordillera of the Andes and of a Residence in Peru 1823 and 1824* (London, 1825), p. 234.

imported manufactures, were far beyond the income of all but a few, concentrated in the major coastal or capital cities. Where the national capital was placed, like Bogotá and Quito, well away from the sea, even Society could not afford to import more than the smallest quantities of goods, since transport costs and the profits of intermediaries raised import prices beyond reason. In any case, an upper-class income in Bogotá could seldom have risen above £1,000 p.a.; middle-class incomes ranged from £30 to £140; agricultural workers, servants and unskilled labourers were lucky to get £14 to £15 p.a.[1]. And if, for one reason or another, a man found himself with cash to spare, he was unlikely, once he got beyond a small radius of the capital, to find anything on which to spend it. Hawkshaw described a typical Venezuelan *pulpería* as a cross between a German gasthof and an English huckster's shop, 'not formed, however, until both the said concerns had been sometime bankrupt, and all the movables, in consequence thereof, carried away'.[2] Luccock, travelling north from Rio to Minas Gerais in 1817, halted at Pampulia, an area market consisting of six or seven *vendas*. At the largest of the *vendas*, perhaps the best-equipped store for 150 miles, the shopkeeper's stock consisted

> not only of the articles commonly found at a venda, such as a barrel or two of poor wine, a few bottles of sour British porter, some garlic, cheese, and rosca [rusks], which is brought baked from the city, a little bacon, a few beijus and boxes of marmalade, with some rum and tobacco, but comprised also articles of linen and woollen drapery. He had a few coarse hats, a few yards of woollen and cotton cloth, half a dozen pieces of muslin, three or four pairs of cotton stockings, a piece or two of tape, and a little thread, the whole set off by a dozen of indecent French snuff boxes.[3]

A few imports always found their way into the interior, but it was not unnatural that until the interior itself developed a marketable export product, provincials continued, whether they liked it or not, to be self-sufficient. Primitive needs were met, easily enough, by primitive manufacturing, and it is the survival of cottage industry

---

[1] Frank Safford, 'Foreign and National Enterprise in Nineteenth Century Colombia', *Business History Review*, 39 (1965), 505.
[2] Hawkshaw, *South America*, p. 136.
[3] Luccock, *Rio de Janeiro*, p. 391.

in the interior which has to be considered in determining the scope for foreign trade.

The Spanish colonies had always met the great majority of their needs by domestic, handicraft production; prices, by the time imports had followed the tortuous routes and endured the extortions established and encouraged by Spanish regulations, were too high for it to be otherwise. Increased imports and lower prices of linens and woollens from Europe and cottons from India, more especially in the late eighteenth century, had already threatened such colonial textile mills as existed, and taken their market for the better quality cloths. The cotton and woollen mills of Puebla in Mexico, Cuzco in Peru, Cochabamba in Bolivia were reduced to the cheapest type of cloths, or shut down altogether. Handicraft production, in the late colonial period as in the early years of the new Republics, survived simply because it was in no sense in competition with expensive imports. Indian cotton piece goods, the coarse cotton cloth known on the Mexican coast as 'sanahs' and 'bafitas', might cost two Spanish dollars at Calcutta for each eighteen-yard piece. Eustace Barron pointed out that such a piece, 'after passing through all this ordeal of sales and resales, freights, commissions, respondentias [high interest loans] and profits, must be sold in South America at least for ten dollars in order to pay all charges [and is] often sold for 15 and even as high as 20 dollars'.[1] British cotton goods were still relatively expensive in the early '20s. When cotton manufactures left England for Mexico, their declared value at the Customs House averaged just over a shilling a yard, 1822-5. Commissions, interest on capital, insurance, freights, pushed up prices so that, according to one report for Vera Cruz in 1824, gingham was fetching four shillings a yard, calico two shillings, brocade eight shillings, printed cotton four, and Irish linen five.[2] By the time imported cottons arrived on the West Coast they were burdened not only with all the costs and commissions of their journey via Jamaica and Panama but also with a rate of duty which, with customs valuations still regulated by the old monopoly prices, could reach 200% on invoice cost. In colonial Mexico and after,

[1] Barron's report on the West Coast of Mexico, 1 January 1825, in Humphreys, *Consular Reports*, p. 337.

[2] Mackenzie's report on Mexico, 24 July 1824, *ibid.*, pp. 326-7. The total yardage of U.K. manufactured cottons leaving for Mexico, 1822-5 inclusive, was 23,108,645 with a declared value of £1,157,602: *Return relating to Trade with Mexico from 1820 to 1841*, P.P. 1842, XXXIX, 531.

the market for imported textiles on the West Coast was principally among high-class consumers for whom prices were relatively immaterial; the population as a whole continued to wear the products of domestic industry.

One source of confusion in estimating the effect of cheap imports on the handicraft industry is that for a period British prices did reach a level at which they seriously threatened local domestic production even far into the interior. Over-importation was a chronic problem in all markets in the first months, sometimes longer, of deliverance from the Spanish Crown. Surplus goods were sold off at prices at which it became profitable to ship up-country and undercut local producers. But such times were short-lived, and when the market returned to normal, imports had again to be priced at uncompetitive levels. Naturally, open accessible markets existed in Brazil and the River Plate where Lancashire's cheapest cotton goods made a real impression; the steady fall in British production costs widened these markets in the decades after 1820. Once away from the coast, transport costs, local taxation and trading commissions were felt more heavily for cheaper cottons than for the finer grades, so that importers found it difficult to compete with the stronger, more durable and familiar products of the local handicraft industry.

It would be difficult to argue otherwise than that *factory* production was uneconomic in Latin America, and that it had been so in most respects since the late seventeenth century. The ruins of textile factories observed by some travellers might have had several explanations, colonial and post-colonial. The factories could have fallen before competitive European and Indian imports in the eighteenth century. They might have suffered from the new trade routes and cheaper imports created by revised Spanish trading regulations in and after the 1760s. They might, as conspicuous objects on the landscape, have been destroyed by one or other of the royal and republican armies. If they had survived so far, they might have been unable to meet the competition of the new, less expensive generation of textile imports after the opening of the trade. They might themselves have suffered, when forced by competition to reduce the quality of their goods, from just that competition of local, domestic industry which was already limiting the field for imported manufactures. A shortage of skilled labour, the high cost of imported machinery, the absence of sufficient supplies of low-cost fuel, small restricted local markets separated from other market opportunities by expensive and difficult transport—all contributed to the failure of large-scale, factory production, while acting only as a partial check, if at all, on domestic production by cheap, otherwise unemployable female labour. The contrast is illustrated in the inland mining province of Minas Geraes in Brazil, where, despite nearly a decade of British imports, domestic textile manufacturing—the spinning and weaving of wool, worsted and cotton—was still reported to be in a flourishing condition in 1817. Yet the cotton and woollen cloth factory at Registro Velho, established fifty years before and producing cloth of excellent quality celebrated over a great part of Brazil, was visibly 'expiring' despite the efforts of the Brazilian government to maintain it. Its failure was in part due to its difficulties with the Portuguese government before the transfer of the Portuguese Court to Brazil in 1808, but in any case imported British fabrics had since reduced the price of such cloth to an uneconomic level.[1] Precisely the same was true of the Mexican textile industries at Puebla and Queretaro. The substantial cotton and woollen manufactories operating under Spanish monopolists at the end of the colonial period felt the cold draught of competition immediately British traders appeared at Vera Cruz and Americans at Tampico. But the handicraft industry continued to supply the greater part of popular needs outside the narrow governing class right up to the development of a low-cost, *national* textile manufacturing industry. Mayer calculated that there were as many as 135,000 spindles in Mexican cotton mills by the early '40s, but machine weaving was not economic as yet and there were said to be about 5,000 hand-looms in operation, which would 'work up all the spun yarn into *mantas* and *rebosos* as fast as it can be made'.[2] With few exceptions, the large-scale manufactories which survived into the Independence period were government-backed or financed—mints, arsenals, ship-building yards, gunpowder factories and costly experiments such as the Brazilian government's iron foundry at Ipanema.

Local factory production, then, could offer no real competition to foreign imports after 1808 and very little before. It rarely had more than a marginal place in the market. What is more at issue is

[1] Luccock, *Rio de Janeiro*, p. 535.
[2] Brantz Mayer, *Mexico as it was and as it is* (New York, 1844), pp. 313-15.

whether the handicraft industries of the continent left room for foreign imports, and the extent to which these industries declined in the face of foreign competition. Woodbine Parish explained how, during the colonial period, imported silks and linens were beyond the reach of the ordinary consumer, 'the poorer classes being miserably clad in the coarse manufactures of the interior'. When the port of Buenos Aires was opened, British cotton goods flooded the markets, prices were low, and a great and general demand was created to the extent that British manufactures, especially amongst the country people, became articles of prime necessity:

> The gaucho is everywhere clothed in them. Take his whole equipment—examine everything about him—and what is there not of rawhide that is not British? If his wife has a gown, ten to one it is made at Manchester; the camp-kettle in which he cooks his food, the earthenware he eats from, the knife, his poncho, spurs, bit, all are imported from England.[1]

Parish's remarks have been taken too readily as evidence of the total penetration of British manufactured goods in Latin America. But quite independently of whether what he said was true of Argentina, the diversity of conditions in each of the Republics and in Brazil— political, economic, social and racial—made it unlikely that anything said of one could be applied automatically to another.

In a primitive economy, textiles are obviously the most important branch of manufacturing. In Latin America, as elsewhere, no price had to be attached to female labour in the home so that where the raw material was at hand, home and local needs continued to be met by domestic manufactures almost at whatever price outside products could be introduced. In cotton- or wool-producing areas, the likelihood of imports touching the mass of society was small, more especially if the heavy transport costs and an element of protective tariffs common to the Republics were added to the first cost of foreign imports. Even in British India, where Lancashire piece goods enjoyed as favourable conditions as they were ever to experience for the penetration of an overseas market, Lancashire was never able entirely to displace the hand-loom weaver; the hand-loom industry was still supplying at least 25% of the cloth consumed in India at the beginning of the twentieth century.

---

[1] Woodbine Parish, *Buenos Ayres and the Provinces of the Rio de la Plata* (London, 1838), p. 338.

Thomas Stuttard, a partner in a large and long-established Lancashire cotton spinning and manufacturing enterprise, told a Royal Commission in 1886 that although the quantity of hand-loom work in India was very much less than it had been,

> in coarse counts, for example, in the sample under 20's twist, in the low numbers, owing to the low price at which it is sold, it is still possible for hand-loom weavers to make coarse open goods to successfully compete against power-loom made goods. I mean in the far interior. I mean places, say, 20 miles from any town 200 or 300 miles from any big port.[1]

In China, where habits of consumption were even more ingrained and transport less developed, Shanghai power-spindles made some progress at the end of the century in displacing a part of home-spinning, but power-loom manufacturing had no success. Chapman explained as late as 1906 that the system of home production was so deeply ingrained in the habits of the people and so low was the cost of their labour, that power-loom cloth could not easily supplant home-made at the price at which it could be placed on Chinese markets.[2]

For both China and India, import duties were set at a level where they did little to impede imports. In Latin America, after the first few months of freedom, tariffs were always a factor. The great majority of the Indians of Mexico, Central America and northern South America, remained clothed in local domestic textiles late into the nineteenth century. Many remain so to the present day, while in Mexico the development of a substantial and competitive local factory production did far more than imports to displace home spinners and weavers. The point has already been made that in the early years of post-colonial trade the prices of British cotton and woollen goods, even without the addition of high freights and commissions, were not low. Prices began to fall drama-tically after 1815, both as a result of increased mechanization and cost-reduction in the factories, and in response to a sharp decline

---

[1] Minutes of Evidence, *Report of the Royal Commission on the Depression of Trade and Industry*, P.P. 1886, XXI, Q.4959.

[2] S. J. Chapman, *The Cotton Industry and Trade* (London, 1905), p. 167. The strength and survival of the handicraft industry in China is interestingly confirmed in a recent article by Albert Feuerwerker, 'Handicraft and Manufactured Cotton Textiles in China, 1871-1910', *Journal of Economic History*, XXX (1970), 338-78.

in the prime cost of raw materials and in import duties into the United Kingdom. In 1811 James Thomson, a calico printer in Lancashire, paid a guinea a piece (28 yards) for his calico; by the early '30s the same piece cost him seven shillings or under. When Thomson first went into business in 1795, printed calico for home consumption and export was sold at 2s. 3d. a yard; in 1833 the same article could be sold with a very good profit for about 8d. a yard.[1] Freights, too, were lower in the '30s than they had been in the early '20s, when British products were making their strongest bid for Latin American markets. John Nickols, a shipowner and ship-broker, told the 1833 Commission that charter rates for the shipment of San Domingan coffee had fallen from £6 per ton in 1824 to less than £4. Rates for the River Plate were £2. 5s. in place of £4; to Rio, £2 instead of £3. 10s.[2] It was this fall in prices and freights which really opened up the market for British textiles in Latin America. Imlah has calculated that, on average, export prices of British yarns and cotton piece goods fell 72% over the period 1816-18 to 1849-51; in the woollen industry the fall was 63%.[3] But important though this was for the further development of British trade with Latin America, it was not a significant factor in the early years when British prices, except as sold off in a period of glut, were still too high for a mass market. The white or blue *bayetas*, a loose unfulled and undressed woollen cloth used universally by both male and female peasants in Chile in the mid-'20s, were woven at home by the women. Miers pointed out that the wife and daughters spun and made all the clothes for the family, and easily disposed of any surplus at a very cheap rate:

> It will, therefore, excite no wonder that our coarse cloths do not find a more extensive sale in Chile, when we find these bayetas, which are a yard wide and very durable, sell for two and a half reals the yard undyed, and four reals or two shillings when dyed blue.[4]

It was not only in *bayetas* that this competition was felt. The women were equally adept at weaving sashes, blankets, saddle-

---

[1] Minutes of Evidence, *Report of the Select Committee on Manufactures, Commerce and Shipping*, P.P. 1833, VI, Q.3824.

[2] *Ibid.*, Q.5842.

[3] Albert Imlah, 'The Terms of Trade of the United Kingdom, 1798-1913', *Journal of Economic History*, X (1950), 183.

[4] Miers, *Chile and La Plata*, II, 230.

cloths, ponchos of cotton as well as wool. Some of the Indian materials, of cotton, wool and especially *vicuña*, were of exceptionally high quality; they were always expensive, but their qualities of design and workmanship, the fact that they were very durable, warm and relatively rain-proof, secured the market against European substitutes. Domestic woollen goods, in any case, resisted foreign imports far longer than cottons. Hand-looms remained competitive even in the United Kingdom until late in the century. In certain ranges of fashionable or fancy goods, where only one or two pieces were required, a hand-loom could handle the order without trouble; a machine manufacturer would never execute an order unless he were asked to make ten, twenty or thirty pieces of a colour.[1] Even for poor quality materials, a light plain cloth was produced and exported by French peasant families in the late nineteenth century, known as *mousseline de laine*, with which no power-loom manufacturer could compete.[2] Similarly, all over Latin America, in the Indian communities in particular, woollen goods continued to be produced for local consumption and markets until the end of the period. As late as 1896, Lionel Carden, when commenting on imports of French light coatings and dress materials and British heavier qualities and broadcloth for the Mexican middle class, added that 'cheap "sarapes" and blankets are manufactured in the country at prices which defy competition from abroad'.[3]

As for the other needs of the community, most, if not all, were satisfied at a primitive level by local production—wooden chairs and tables, hammocks, coarse glass and earthenware, shoes and saddlery, iron and copper cooking pots and ironware generally, soap, candles, jewellery, knives. In inland settlements, the odd English earthenware mug or plate or green-glass porter bottle might appear on a country table, but there was little call for imports. Even in a city like Buenos Aires, as open as any to cheap imports, manufacturing establishments by 1830 included 68 carpenters, 33 tailors, 33 hatters, 16 tinsmiths, 16 harness makers, 11 candle makers, 35 shoemakers, 17 tanners, 14 cabinet-makers, 3 carriage

---

[1] Sir Jacob Behrens' evidence, 26 February 1886: Minutes of Evidence, *Report of the Royal Commission on the Depression of Trade and Industry*, P.P. 1886, XXI, Q.6979.

[2] Sir Joseph Lee's evidence, 10 March 1886: *ibid.*, P.P. 1886, XXIII, QQ.8261-2.

[3] Carden's report on Mexico for 1895, P.P. 1897, XCII, 187.

manufacturers and 8 lathe mechanics.[1] These and others, although mere workshops processing what were often imported semi-manufactured goods or textiles, were handling the basic needs of all but the upper levels of porteño and foreign society. There were, in fact, some 590 independent workshops in Buenos Aires in 1830.[2]

The price fall, though less evident than for textiles, applied also to British exports of hardware, tools and cutlery. A contemporary estimate put Sheffield goods such as scissors, saws, edged tools at 30-40% cheaper in 1833 than in 1815, and the fall for cutlery was even greater.[3] Undoubtedly, lower prices increased outlets for such goods overseas and by the mid-nineteenth century British and German hardware, glass and earthenware had spread far more widely into the interior of Latin America. But over the 1810s and early '20s imports were still too expensive to make much impact. The rough earthenware which Mrs Graham discovered in the market at Valparaiso—jars, plates, dishes, pots—was made by women and children in huts outside the town at prices well below anything imported. The fine earthenware from Melipilla still found a market, with water jars selling, on occasion, for as much as fifty dollars.[4] Chilean coppersmiths worked on a small scale and with crude implements, but their prices in the '20s were very competitive. Gallon pans, tinned inside with pewter, were sold for only six shillings. The pint pots used throughout the country for boiling water for *mate* were made and sold for a dollar (four shillings). Small soap factories, sited all over the country and on each big estate, sold a rough, black soap at about sixpence a pound.[5]

It is easy enough, in the absence of documentation or any kind of statistics, to ignore this large and competitive area of domestic industry. Marx found effective ammunition in the Governor-General's report for India, 1834-5, where the bones of cotton weavers were described as 'bleaching the plains of India'; he made similar, if less apposite, comments on the spinners and weavers of

---

[1] Burgin, *Argentine Federalism*, p. 43.

[2] Roberto O. Fraboschi in Academia Nacional de Historia, *Historia Argentina Contemporanea, 1862-1930* (Buenos Aires, 1966), III, 130.

[3] Minutes of Evidence, *Report of the Select Committee on Manufactures, Commerce and Shipping*, P.P. 1833, VI, Q.2850. Imlah's estimate is of a price fall of 45% for exports other than textiles over the period 1816-18 to 1849-51: *Journal of Economic History*, X (1950), 184.

[4] Maria Graham, *Journal of a Residence in Chile during the Year 1822* (London, 1824), pp. 133, 141-2, 261.

[5] Miers, *Chile and La Plata*, II, 294-7.

China. It is tempting—and it certainly would not be impossible—
to find some individual Latin American equivalents. But the evidence does not support any generalization. Travellers' accounts are
dangerous material, even if there is little else to help historians
through the economics of the early years of independent Latin
America. It was understandable that English travellers should be
inclined to pick out evidence of the spread of British products
throughout the Continent. The Rev. Robert Walsh, visiting Villa
Rica in Minas Geraes in 1829, found shops filled with cotton goods
from Manchester, broadcloths from Yorkshire, stockings from
Nottingham, hats from London, cutlery from Sheffield, on sale in
the heart of South America at prices little above those in the towns
in which they were manufactured. He confided to his readers that
when he saw all about him the produce of the labour of our own
hands, he was moved to exclaim, with Aeneas, 'Quae regio in terris
nostri non plena laboris'. But Walsh had just entered the town by
a long, almost interminable street 'where artizans chiefly reside,
and where are several workshops, in which braziers, smiths and
other operative mechanics were plying their trades, in different
home manufactures'; the braziers made pots and kettles from
sheet copper sent from England, while blacksmiths forged shovels,
hammers, hinges and a variety of domestic implements from local
Brazilian iron.[1]

The emphasis given to local manufacturing depends from which
part of Walsh, or any other traveller, one takes one's extract. Many
travellers, consuls or commercial men were by class and temperament disinclined to visit local markets and examine the goods on
display. When they took the trouble to do so, like Maria Graham
in Valparaiso, William Stevenson in Quito, Peter Schmidtmeyer
in Santiago, Charles Cochrane and John Hamilton in Bogotá, they
discovered two distinct levels of trade. At one level, in the shops
surrounding the main plaza or down the principal street, imported
textiles and all kinds of hardware and cutlery were on display.
These shops, since they catered for a small upper class for which
price was not everything, dealt in good quality goods of the latest
fashion. But in the market stalls in the centre of the plaza, down
the side-streets, or on the outskirts of the town were the local
manufactures—woollen and cotton ponchos, felt hats, boots and

[1] Robert Walsh, *Notices of Brazil in 1828 and 1829* (London, 1830),
II, 194-201.

shoes, gold and silver plate, *mate* pots, candlesticks, buckles, chains or ornaments, earthenware, iron and copper-mongery, haberdashery, saddles and bridles, furniture, stockings and coarse domestic textiles. The stalls in which these were displayed filled a large part of the plaza at Santiago. The palace was on one side, the cathedral on another and behind the market stalls, on the remaining two sides, were shops, kept, said Schmidtmeyer, 'by some of the most respectable people of Santiago personally, and chiefly filled with foreign and valuable goods'.[1]

Naturally, the success or otherwise of penetration by foreign manufactured goods during these early years varied from Republic to Republic, and from province to province within each Republic. Some of the remote areas remained virtually free of imports for decades. When John MacGregor reported on market prospects in Bolivia in the '40s, he explained that the great distance of its centres of population from the Pacific, to be reached only by mule over a 14,000-ft pass, had compelled the inhabitants to become their own manufacturers:

> Cottons and woollens are manufactured; tanneries are also numerous. There are also some glass-works, and manufactories of hats, cloth, etc.[2]

Ecuador, for the same reason, had continued to develop its manufactures; the inhabitants of the coast preferred British goods, but coarse cotton and woollen stuffs were woven at many places in the elevated valleys, and silk manufactories and some tanneries helped to meet local demand.[3] No prospect of an import trade existed with some of the inner Brazilian towns other than through barter. By the time foreign merchandise reached Diamantino up the Tapajos river from Pará, it was sold, according to Hadfield in 1854, at 850% on its price at Pará, which in turn was from 50 to 100% on New York prices.[4] The *llaneros* (plainsmen) of Venezuela, when visited by Charles Dance around the middle of the century, had no need for foreign products, and high duties in any case put imports out of reach of all except the very rich. For the *llaneros*, a pair of boots was manufactured in five minutes from two pieces of rawhide.

[1] Schmidtmeyer, *Chile*, p. 319.
[2] MacGregor's report on Bolivia, P.P. 1847, LXIV, 259.
[3] MacGregor's report on Ecuador, *ibid.*, 200.
[4] William Hadfield, *Brazil, the River Plate and the Falkland Islands* (London, 1854), p. 201.

C

Owners of substantial wealth in cattle and cultivated land made their appearance bare-footed and bare-legged, in cheap, uncouth shirts and short trousers, with coarse kerchiefs on their heads. Dance describes a call to dinner, the master and wayfarers sitting on benches and home-made chairs, eating off rough pottery dishes and plates. Immediately before dinner, 'two Indian girls bring calabashes of water, which answer for finger basins, after which the fingers may freely do the duties of knives and forks'.[1]

Foreign imports were more successful in a country like Argentina, where the flat pampas simplified travel far into the interior. The horses, bullocks and waggons, conveying cattle or carrying hides, wine and dried fruit from the western and northern provinces to Buenos Aires, took back cargoes of imported textiles and hardware. Even a small provincial town like San Luis, when visited by Samuel Haigh in 1817, had a few shops selling European articles of dress, hardware and crockery, while Mendoza imported all kinds of manufactured goods in quantity. The house in which Haigh lodged at Mendoza, one of the best in the city, was 'furnished with good taste, in the French and English style', and Don Manuel's breakfast service was of 'fine French porcelain, of a late fashion'.[2] Certainly, the more respectable women who came out to stare at Robert Proctor a few years later, at a post house in Central Argentina, were dressed principally in English manufactures, wearing printed calico gowns, with shawls over their bare shoulders.[3]

Domestic textile manufactures never disappeared altogether in Argentina, any more than they did elsewhere on the Continent. But the odds were weighted against anything other than production for home use or the manufacture of special types and qualities of fabrics for which custom, taste, or peculiar suitability to local conditions could always ensure a market. One of the problems, for Argentina in particular, was the price and availability of the raw material. The textile manufacturing of the Indian communities in Peru, Ecuador, Colombia, Central America and Mexico was not an activity which needed any economic justification; outlets for peasant produce were slight, and such land and resources as existed

[1] Charles Daniel Dance, *Recollections of Four Years in Venezuela* (London, 1876), pp. 18-20.
[2] Samuel Haigh, *Sketches of Buenos Ayres and Chile* (London, 1829), pp. 71, 79-87.
[3] Proctor, *Peru*, p. 37.

were turned to use as part of a self-sufficient village economy. The Argentines, on the other hand, were a pastoral people whose products, from the beginning, were at least of some interest to markets outside their own. The Indian population of Argentina, among whom the manufacture of the finer woollens and cottons was concentrated, were a relatively small and fast declining element in the population. As for the Argentines themselves, there were better ways of employing scarce labour and capital than in cotton, and when cotton ceased to be grown, cheap British manufactures swiftly took the place of local production. Furthermore, the growing popularity of Argentine wool in European markets raised its price locally to such an extent that the manufacture of ordinary cloth by the primitive methods available in the old centres of Córdoba, Mendoza, Tucumán, Salta and Corrientes ceased to make sense where British or French woollens were so much less expensive. Some very fine blankets were still being made in Córdoba in the mid-'60s, but they were 'enormously dear'.[1]

Even in Argentina, this process of substitution took some time to work itself out, particularly in the remoter manufacturing centres like Santiago del Estero. The British Committee of Merchants, commenting in 1824 on an annual import of nearly £400,000 of plain and printed calicoes and cloth, described them as of 'primary necessity' in Argentina; 'on British manufactures at large the *country* population is entirely dependent'.[2] But though this was certainly far more true of Argentina than it was of most of the rest of the Continent, the Committee's argument was exaggerated, based on a knowledge of the more accessible provinces and on a disinclination to look as far down as the bottom levels of society. Beaumont, who travelled in Argentina in 1826-7, spoke of cotton as cultivated successfully on a small scale in Catamarca and woven in sufficient quantity to satisfy the needs of the inhabitants of the province; coarse cotton and woollen cloths were still being manufactured in Córdoba and Tucumán; the woollen ponchos of Santiago del Estero and Jujuy, for which a satisfactory European substitute had yet to be developed, were still in universal use amongst the country people in the provinces.[3]

---

[1] Thomas Hutchinson, *Buenos Ayres and Argentine Gleanings* (London, 1865), p. 213.
[2] Humphreys, *Consular Reports*, p. 36.
[3] Beaumont, *Buenos Ayres*, pp. 52-3, 95-6.

Such evidence as there is for the impact of British manufactures is patchy, often contradictory and inconclusive, and no reliable figures are obtainable for the scale of local production over this first period. Yet the real position is shown clearly enough in the figures for the total exports of the United Kingdom to the entire continent of Spanish America and Brazil, which, even as late as 1841-50, averaged only £5·7 million per annum. With so large a part of this absorbed by one market, Brazil, it is obvious that the remainder, spread among the populations of every Republic, was likely to go only a short way towards meeting local demand for manufactured goods. Local demand, such as it was, continued very largely to be satisfied by local cottage and workshop production.

CHAPTER II

The Trade

THE inadequacies, ignorance and imprudence of many of the early trading ventures in Latin America are proverbial. The Brazilian customs officials, Walsh was told, 'could not contain their astonishment and mirth' at the incongruous things taken from the packing-cases in the first rush of imports in 1808. The shops and warehouses of Fleet Street and Cheapside had been ransacked for exports, the consideration being not what should be sent, but how soon it could arrive. The wool blankets, warming pans and skates which reached tropical Brazil ultimately found employment, the blankets as screens for gold washings, the warming pans (with their lids knocked off) as skimmers for the boiling sugar in the sugar *engenhos*, the skates as a source of well-tempered steel for knives and as latches for doors in the Brazilian interior.[1] Consignments of teapots reached markets where tea was sold simply in apothecaries' shops as a drug.[2]

Elegant services of cut-glass and china were offered to persons whose most splendid drinking-vessels consisted of a horn or the shell of a cocoa nut; tools were sent out having a hammer on the one side and a hatchet on the other, as if the inhabitants had had nothing more to do than to break the first stone they met with, and then cut the gold and diamonds from it.[3]

[1] Walsh, *Brazil*, pp. 443-5.
[2] William Walton, *Present State of the Spanish Colonies* (London, 1810), I, 235.
[3] J. R. McCulloch, *The Principles of Political Economy* (2nd edn, London, 1830), p. 330.

Luccock, as a general merchant in Rio in and after 1808, was sent a box of coffin furniture which, he told his partners in Leeds, was 'of all articles made in England and not saleable here . . . the worst'. He was later to receive a consignment of pocket-books and wallets, such as Englishmen used for carrying bank-notes. Why, he asked, was he sent these to a land where there was no paper money, and where the coin was so heavy that slaves were employed to carry it: 'Pray let no more absurdities of this kind be sent to us!'[1]

On the strength of this, it is commonly believed that Latin American markets were new and untested in the 1800s, that they were exploited by a group of ignoramuses, and that they were continuously swamped by every kind of British manufacture from the day the ports were opened to northern European trade. But there was, in fact, a long experience of Latin American markets dating back, on a substantial scale, to the late seventeenth century; a number of the merchants who set up branch establishments in Brazil or the Republics after 1808 were the same people who had handled the trade through the West Indies, Spain or Portugal during the colonial period; and the initial response to the markets of independent Latin America should be described rather as an *interruption* of traditional trading patterns, to be re-established on a slightly expanded scale after the enthusiasm had subsided.

In Chapter I the nature of the market was described. Nothing had happened which made any essential difference to its requirements or prospects for further development. Years of political troubles and blockade had allowed serious shortages to develop in colonial markets among those classes who might be considered as traditional consumers of European manufactures. In addition, the European wars had closed two of the normal sources of supplies for Latin America. French and German manufactured goods, previously imported legally through Lisbon and Cadiz or as contraband from the West Indies, were now under blockade, and the way was left open to British manufactures alone to satisfy accumulated needs after 1808. The warehouses in Rio, early in 1808, were filled with produce for export to Portugal, held up by the French occupation; but they were bare of imported goods of any kind

---

[1] Quoted in Herbert Heaton, 'A Merchant Adventurer in Brazil, 1808-18', *Journal of Economic History*, VI (1946), 14.

intended for consumption within Brazil. The same was true of every other part of Latin America. As each of the markets opened —Buenos Aires first at the time of Sir Home Popham's expedition and capture of the city in 1806, Montevideo in 1807, Brazil in 1808, Venezuela in 1810, Colombia and Chile in 1811, Peru and Mexico in 1821—consumers clamoured for the goods for which they had waited a decade. But with such a limited market, the demand was satisfied almost immediately. For Rio, the first fleet of merchantmen from England arrived in July 1808, and the market was overstocked even before the second fleet appeared off the coast; Luccock, at any rate, found himself sailing south to Buenos Aires later the same year with a cargo of goods unsaleable in Brazil.[1] Upwards of 5,000 tons of British shipping crowded Ancon Bay (Peru) in September 1821, awaiting General San Martín's permission to land manufactured goods for the markets of newly liberated Lima. The first arrivals alone far exceeded the capacity of a market once the richest in the Spanish Empire but now shattered by civil war.[2] Overstocked markets, where so few real, permanent customers existed, remained a source of anxiety until enough merchants had retired from business to restore supplies to normal. The warehouses at Valparaiso in 1825 were 'filled with European goods with which the market is overstocked.'[3] Lima, in 1826, was overflowing with British shawls and dresses; 40,000 muslin dresses had arrived in one vessel, consigned to a single mercantile house. A useful trade could be done, and 'when the shipments are in proportion to the demand, they cannot fail to ensure a fair profit'; but prices were now 'extremely low'.[4] Even as late as 1828, Walsh found the principal shopping street in Rio de Janeiro

> filled with all kinds of European merchandize, particularly Manchester shawls, handkerchiefs, cotton and calicos of the most showy colours, broad-cloths, silks, hats, boots, shoes, and stockings, all hung up in front of the houses, and covering the

[1] Luccock, *Rio de Janeiro*, pp. 139 ff.
[2] G. S. Graham and R. A. Humphreys (eds.), *The Navy and South America 1807-1823; Correspondence of the Commanders-in-Chief on the South American Station* (London, 1962), pp. 348-9; Humphreys, *Liberation in South America*, pp. 96-7.
[3] Miers, *Chile*, I, 448.
[4] Humphreys, *Consular Reports*, p. 196.

doors and windows with their rich drapery. These things were sent out in such profusion, and the market was so overstocked, that they were selling in the Rua dos Pescadores for less money than in Cheapside.[1]

A return to normal was visible in Lima by the mid-'20s where a few powerful resident merchants were holding back stocks and releasing them slowly at high prices as the demand warranted; a newcomer, without contacts in the market, found it difficult to dispose of his goods unless he made contact with retailers and consumers through the established houses. These established houses included Antony Gibbs and Sons, whose goods were well known in Lima long before it set up a branch establishment; Antony Gibbs had a tradition of business contacts and dealings with Limeños at its house in Cadiz.[2] Experienced houses did business in every nation. A merchant house like Maxwell and Wellwood Hyslop, prominent in the Jamaica trade at the end of the colonial period, moved naturally into direct contact with Latin America after the declaration of independence, placing a branch at Cartagena in 1813 and another at Maracaibo in 1821. Others were branches of English mercantile or manufacturing concerns, themselves with long experience in overseas trade. Frederick Brittain, a leading merchant in Buenos Aires, was one of the family interested in the Sheffield firm of Brittain, Wilkinson and Brownell. Luccock had been sent out to Rio on a ten-year contract by Luptons of Leeds. Henry Glover was the Rio representative of Abraham Rhodes, a Leeds merchant with a substantial business in the United States. Owen Owens, a Manchester merchant, did his first overseas business with Boston and Baltimore after 1806; in 1812 he opened a consignment account with Rio. Each of these firms was feeling the pressure first of closed markets in Europe during the Napoleonic

---

[1] Walsh, *Brazil*, p. 143.
[2] A substantial literature exists for the activities of the first mercantile houses. Antony Gibbs and Sons' early connections with Latin America are described in J. A. Gibbs, *The History of Antony and Dorothea Gibbs* (London, 1922); Hyslop's in R. A. Humphreys, *Tradition and Revolt in Latin America* (London, 1969), pp. 117-21; Lupton's in Herbert Heaton, 'A Merchant Adventurer in Brazil, 1808-18', *Journal of Economic History*, VI (1946), 1-23; Rhodes' in R. G. Wilson, 'The Fortunes of a Leeds Merchant House, 1780-1820', *Business History*, IX (1967), 70-86; Owens' in B. W. Clapp, *John Owens, Manchester Merchant* (Manchester, 1965).

wars, and then of a restriction and later suspension of trade with the United States before, during and after the war of 1812. Warehouses, docks and factories were idle. 'In moments embittered by such gloomy considerations', wrote Thomas Ashe in 1812,

> and where we see the access to the Continent of Europe so hermetically sealed up, we ought to be peculiarly grateful to Providence for casting open the doors of the West, and for disclosing to us the avenues of the New World; for giving us an influence in South America, which will invigorate our commerce, and ultimately take as much of our manufactures, or more, as are now denied to the oppressed nations which were once wont to purchase them of us.[1]

It is quite evident that even if this solid core of merchants existed, with experience of markets and manufacturing on which to base their business operations in Brazil and the new Republics, a large number of adventurers and speculators attempted, seldom successfully, to break into what seemed so promising a market. J. P. Robertson, in Montevideo at the time, estimated that about six thousand British subjects entered the city after its fall to Sir Samuel Auchmuty on 3 February 1807, 'of whom four thousand were military, two thousand merchants, traders, adventurers; and a dubious crew which could scarcely pass muster, even under the latter designation'.[2] They all left again when General Whitelocke evacuated Montevideo in September. But elsewhere, even when the political situation permitted, it was not long before the men were separated from the boys. As many as a hundred distinct British traders may have been in business in Rio in 1808. By 1814 they had fallen to nearly half that number, so that in imported woollens only six houses remained to share out the trade between them.[3]

The spectacular rush to the market has made it difficult to keep some sense of proportion about the importance of Latin American trade. The absurdities of some aspects made a deep impression on British merchants and manufacturers, and respectable Indian merchants, like Cockerell and Co., were still, a quarter of a century later, referring in horror to 'that hurried, harum-scarum sort of

[1] Ashe, *Brasils*, pp. 7-8.
[2] Robertson, *Paraguay*, I, 102.
[3] Heaton, *Journal of Economic History*, VI, 8-10.

shipment similar to those which occurred upon the opening of the trade to Buenos Ayres'.[1] It is true that the Latin American trade, for a short period, really *was* important to Britain. Between 1805 and 1808, the declared values of British exports to Northern Europe, including France, fell from £10·3 million to £2·2 million; over the same period exports to the Americas, other than the United States, rose from £7·8 million to £16·6 million, reaching a peak of £18 million the following year (1809) (Table I).

Table I

Exports of British Produce (real values), 1805-11
(£000)

Year	North of Europe, including France	Spain	Portugal	Gibraltar, Malta, Sicily, the Levant, etc.	Ireland, Guernsey, etc.
1805	10,320	50	1,850	1,410	5,000
1806	7,570	30	1,700	2,960	4,510
1807	5,090	30	970	2,920	5,070
1808	2,160	860	430	5,570	5,870
1809	5,700	2,380	800	6,960	5,450
1810	7,700	1,400	1,310	5,210	4,210
1811	1,500	1,230	4,650	5,450	5,020

	Asia	Africa	United States	Rest of America	Total
1805	2,900	760	11,010	7,770	41,070
1806	2,940	1,160	12,390	10,880	44,140
1807	3,360	770	11,850	10,440	40,480
1808	3,520	630	5,240	16,590	40,880
1809	2,870	800	7,260	18,010	50,240
1810	2,980	600	10,920	15,640	49,980
1811	2,940	340	1,840	11,940	34,920

Source: Eli F. Heckscher, *The Continental System, an Economic Interpretation* (Oxford, 1922), p. 245.

For a few years Latin America, with Spain, Portugal and Gibraltar acting largely as entrepôts for Spanish America and Brazil, was providing the main outlet for *new* trade during a period in which the important European and North American markets were particularly lean. British exports of cotton manufactures, official

[1] G. G. de H. Larpent's evidence, 6 June 1833: Minutes of Evidence, *Report of the Select Committee on Manufactures, Commerce and Shipping,* P.P. 1833, VI, Q.2149.

values, show the temporary influence of extensive and sanguine shipments to Latin America. Standing at £9,708,046 in 1807, exports rose to £12,503,918 in 1808, £18,425,614 in 1809; by 1810 they had fallen to £17,898,519, and by 1811 to £11,529,551.[1] It was a passing phase. British domestic exports to Central and South America, including Brazil, rose to £6·4 million (declared values) in 1825, having fallen as low as £2·1 million in 1816. In the '30s and '40s they remained steadily in the range of £4 million to £6 million, with Brazil alone accounting for between a third and a half of the trade.[2]

In the first years, then, of the British trading connection with Latin America, and again briefly in the mid-'20s when trade with Europe seemed relatively stagnant and British investments in Latin America were passing through a spectacular speculative boom, Latin America looked as if it might become a valuable addition to Britain's markets. But it was at this point that the limitations of such a market re-asserted themselves. Brazil continued to offer a generous outlet to British cotton manufacturers; she was in many respects the perfect market for cotton goods, with a warm climate, a comparatively large population, marketable commodities such as cotton, sugar and coffee to provide a return trade, and no trace of a competing local cotton textile industry. Brazil supported and inflated the total for British exports to Latin America in the first half of the nineteenth century much as did Argentina for British exports after 1880. But Figure I shows how dependent British exports were on the Brazil market, and how undistinguished was their record, for the '30s and most of the '40s, in the remainder of the Continent. Even the more impressive figures for 1848 and 1849 reflect merely a short-term movement of manufactured goods into Buenos Aires after the conclusion of the Anglo-French blockade.

*

No convincing estimate can be given for the value of British trade with Latin America during the colonial period; so much of the trade was contraband that the figures become almost pure

[1] Eli F. Hecksher, *The Continental System: an economic interpretation* (Oxford, 1922), p. 246.

[2] Figures from A. D. Gayer, W. W. Rostow and A. J. Schwartz, *The Growth and Fluctuation of the British Economy 1790-1850* (Oxford, 1953), I, 146, 182, 215, 251, 282, 314.

Figure I. British Exports to Latin America[1] (A) and to Brazil (B), 1831-1850 (declared values).

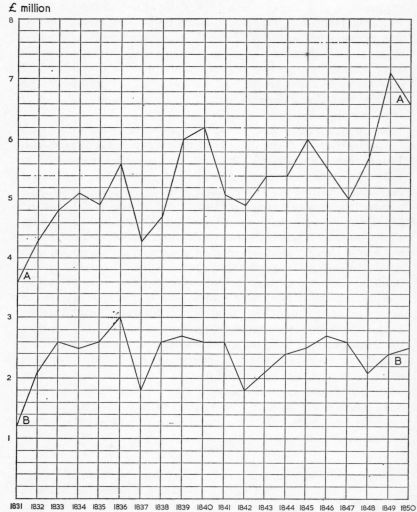

£ million

Source: Porter's Tables *and* General Statistical Abstract (United Kingdom) *rounded to the nearest hundred thousand pounds.*

[1] Brazil, Buenos Aires, Chile, Colombia, Ecuador, Mexico, Montevideo, Peru, Venezuela.

guess-work. But it is noticeable that in spite of the dominant position Britons had secured by the 1830s and '40s in cotton textiles, in linens, in silks, in iron, in hardware, in spite of the presence of British merchants in most of the main ports and in the capitals, in spite of the investment of British capital, and making allowance for the decline in British export prices, the value and volume of British trade with Latin America was not totally out of line with what estimates survive of the colonial trade.

In general, British trade to the Spanish colonies in the eighteenth century took three main routes, the contraband trade, the semi-legitimate trade developed around the 'asiento' and the South Sea Company, and the conventional trade through Spain and Portugal. The trade in Negroes and cloth through Jamaica was already important in the last decades of the seventeenth century. In 1691, the Governor of Jamaica reported that the last fleet had carried £100,000 in bullion back to England, and, at the turn of the century, the annual sum was estimated at between £150,000 and £200,000. The trade in merchandise, almost entirely cloth and wearing apparel, continued to increase rapidly; an estimate by one competent observer of the value of British goods sold to the Spanish colonists at Jamaica, August 1706 to August 1707, was £275,000, and in 1715 English Customs houses entered goods for the Spanish colonies valued at £196,000.[1] The Caribbean area remained the main focus of contraband activities, but the agents of the South Sea Company maintained, under cover of the traffic in Negroes, a considerable contraband trade all over Latin America in supplies of flour, pitch, tar, beef, pork, mercury, brass, iron-ware, woollens, cottons and canvas. It has been estimated, from the secret account books of the inner clique of directors running the South Sea Company, that between 1730 and 1739 goods and pro-visions valued conservatively at £6,000,000 must have been intro-duced in the Company's slavers and in the annual ship permitted by its contract, a figure which 'becomes even larger when to it are added unknown amounts of private trade carried on by individuals or groups associated with the South Sea Company and by others who had no connection with that organization.[2]

[1] Curtis Nettels, 'England and the Spanish American Trade, 1680-1715', *Journal of Modern History*, III (1931), 8, 28-9.
[2] George H. Nelson, 'Contraband Trade under the Asiento, 1730-1739', *American Historical Review*, 51 (1945), 64.

Throughout the eighteenth century no more than isolated estimates exist for the extent of the trade. The British interest in the
flotas which sailed from Cadiz may for the early 1760s have averaged £1,090,000, compared with the French share of £1,250,000.
The Spanish share was less than either.[1] As for the contraband
trade, in which Britons from Jamaica were by far the worst offenders, a report of a Spanish enquiry into the economic life of the
Empire (presented to Charles III in 1761) put a value to it of at
least 6,000,000 pesos a year, 'and this in contravention of the most
solemn treaties'.[2] Similarly, British exports to Portugal in the
middle decades of the century, 1730-60, were averaging over
£1,100,000 p.a.; in the five years 1756-60, they reached a peak of
£1,301,000. It is impossible to say precisely what proportion found
its way to Brazil, but the English Factory at Lisbon described the
Brazil trade in 1715 as the 'Basis and Foundation' of its whole
trade. Portugal herself had little part in the production of manufactured goods for the rapidly expanding Brazilian market. The
English Factory believed its own trade to Brazil in 1716 to exceed
the combined French and Dutch trades; British commodities
formed the 'chief part' of the Brazil trade. Furthermore, an estimated £200,000 annually was thought to be reaching Buenos Aires
in contraband through Southern Brazil by the middle years of the
century.[3]

Spain and Portugal remained a principal route for British trade
with colonial Latin America, although both trades fell off after the
early '60s. The West Indian trade continued to provide a substantial outlet for British manufactures. The figures remain as elusive
as ever, and mercantile estimates, as Frances Armytage says, are
inclined to be over-optimistic so as to inflate the merchant's own
importance. But, she continues:

> Thomas Irving, the Inspector General [of Customs], thought
> that the total value of British manufactures exported from the
> West Indies in 1792, before the war, in British and foreign

[1] Allan Christelow, 'Great Britain and the Trades from Cadiz and
Lisbon to Spanish America and Brazil, 1759-1783', *Hispanic American
Historical Review*, 27 (1947), 4.
[2] Allan Christelow, 'Contraband Trade between Jamaica and the
Spanish Main, and the Free Port Act of 1766', *Hispanic American
Historical Review*, 22 (1942), 313.
[3] H. E. S. Fisher, 'Anglo-Portuguese Trade, 1700-1770', *Economic
History Review*, 2nd ser. XVI (1963), 222, 227, 226.

vessels was about £400,000 to £500,000, but this may be an underestimate. The Governor of Grenada thought that about £330,000 worth of British goods had been sold in that island alone in 1792. Trinidad was supposed to have exported manufactures worth one million dollars (about £200,000) in 1805, while the total exports from Jamaica in 1808, before the great increase in trade, were believed to be five million dollars (£1,000,000).[1]

An extensive trade was also passing through the foreign entrepôts in the West Indies—Curaçao, St Thomas, St Domingo—some unidentifiable part of which, naturally, was British. Walton claims that in 1789 alone, 710 vessels of a combined 213,540 tons brought manufactured goods to the value of £4,125,610 from France to French Santo Domingo; in the same year, Spanish traders from the whole Caribbean area brought specie and products to the value of £2,450,115 to Santo Domingo to buy Negro slaves and European manufactured goods.[2] France herself would have supplied most, though not all, of these manufactured goods, but a table of British manufactures exported to the island of St Thomas in 1807 shows a total of £210,108, nearly all of which would have been re-exported within the Caribbean.[3]

No reliable comparison can be made between the volume of British manufactures reaching Latin America before and after the Emancipation. But what does emerge from such random estimates is that the pattern and the constituents of the trade between Britain and Latin America were well-established long before the breakaway from Spain. Once the excitement was over and the needs created by a decade of interrupted trade were satisfied, trade settled back into a familiar pattern, expanded for British cottons by their success in displacing Spanish cottons and German linens, swollen by new fashions and needs, supplemented by the demand of resident foreign communities, but not, in the final analysis, so very different in volume or content from the trade with the Spanish Colonies. Knowing what we do about the routing of the trade, the figures in Table II for British trade in the eighteenth century, taken from the British Customs records as summarized by

[1] Frances Armytage, *The Free Port System in the British West Indies* (London, 1953), p. 92.
[2] Walton, *Spanish Colonies*, I, 299-300.
[3] Armytage, *Free Port System*, p. 158.

Elizabeth Schumpeter, can at least suggest a comparison with the figures for the first half of the nineteenth century in Table I.

After all the high expectations which followed the capture of Buenos Aires in 1806, the meagre development of Latin American

Table II

Exports from England to Spain, Portugal and the West Indies, 1701-1800
(average annual values, £000)

Years	Spain	Portugal	West Indies
1701-05	120	610	305
1706-10	166	652	322
1711-15	406	638	393
1716-20	428	695	430
1721-25	582	811	471
1726-30	632	914	473
1731-35	780	1,024	383
1736-40	702	1,164	494
1741-45	87	1,115	728
1746-50	702	1,114	732
1751-55	1,038	1,098	710
1756-60	1,274	1,301	952
1761-65	1,023	964	1,119
1766-70	1,004	595	1,174
1771-75	1,009	613	1,353
1776-80	723	525	1,244
1781-85	434	622	1,272
1786-90	633	622	1,405
1791-95	589	594	2,486
1796-1800	109	811	4,379

Source: Elizabeth Boody Schumpeter, *English Overseas Trade Statistics 1697-1808* (Oxford, 1960), Table V.

markets over the period 1825-50 does need explanation. Ultimately, the barrier to further development was the impossibility of maintaining a sufficient return trade in Latin American produce. As Woodbine Parish pointed out in 1839, writing well after the first period of disillusionment, 'it is in proportion to the increase and multiplication of the native productions that we must look for the stability and improvement of this trade—the great difficulty being to collect returns for the importations from foreign countries'.[1]

Gold and silver specie, in the colonial period and later, was the main, sometimes the only, return product available for much of

[1] Parish, *Buenos Ayres*, p. 356.

Latin America. For a large exporter like Mexico over the last quarter-century of colonial rule, 1796-1820, $8,391,088 out of an annual average export of $11,181,369 consisted of precious metals.[1] If anything, the situation was *more* weighted in favour of precious metals and specie during the last years of the Spanish Empire. In the 1770s, the United Kingdom was still taking nearly all its indigo from Latin America. By 1808 the indigo came almost entirely from Asia. The export of raw materials generally from the Caribbean during this period was static, while imports of manufactured goods, paid for by increased exports of specie, advanced rapidly.

Exaggerated expectations were formed of Latin America's capacity both as an exporter of specie and of produce during the first, post-colonial boom. The great quantities accumulated under official restrictions at Buenos Aires and Montevideo were released in a rush as the markets opened, just at a period when wars in Europe and industrial expansion in the Uuited Kingdom were creating special demands for products such as hides and tallow. When J. P. Robertson first landed in Buenos Aires in 1809 he found the warehouses, large as they were, filled to overflowing with hides, with further hides stored in immense heaps in the corridors and courtyards—three million hides altogether, with horse skins, hair and tallow. The situation at Montevideo was much the same, while the country on both sides of the River Plate 'seemed as if groaning under the immense pressure of the teeming multitude of quadrupeds'.[2] In specie, too, the accumulation awaiting the first traders gave an entirely false impression of wealth. Goods were temporarily in great demand; gold and silver coins and ornaments were brought out from their places of concealment; there was pressure, among the *peninsulares*, to remit wealth, at whatever cost or commission, to lighten their exile in Spain. A British Consul General estimated, in a memorandum of 14 October 1824, that something like $40 million in bullion had been shipped to Europe from the Pacific coast over the past five or six years, half of it illegally.[3]

---

[1] Mackenzie's report, 24 July 1824: Humphreys, *Consular Reports*, p. 305.

[2] J. P. and W. P. Robertson, *Letters on South America* (London, 1843), II, 271.

[3] Thomas Rowcroft in Humphreys, *Consular Reports*, p. 116 fn. 2.

D

None of the Republics, in the early decades, could match imports with exports except by specie or by the attraction of foreign capital. Argentina and Brazil came nearest to doing so, the one with hides and tallow, the other with cotton, sugar and tobacco. But Rio, in 1828, was having to pay for her $24½ million of imports with $10 million of produce and $14 million of specie,[1] and Argentina, according to the Robertsons, had by the early '40s accumulated a debt to Britain, including the Baring Loan, of at least £2½ million.[2] In both cases, the return trade had been artificially boosted by war scarcities and by the closure of alternative sources of supply. Argentine tallow was shipped in considerable quantities during the last phases of the Napoleonic wars to replace Russian supplies, and shipments ceased when the Russian markets re-opened. The hide-trade, though more resilient, was in part substitution for an existing trade, interrupted by war, with Russia, Spain and Prussia. Hides were in demand throughout the nineteenth century for industrial purposes, where leather served functions now filled by rubber, plywood, plastics and elastic metals. British tanners for many years took nearly all South American hides before sufficient tanning industries developed in Europe and the United States. Over 3 million of the 5,653,761 hides imported into Britain between 1810 and 1815 came from the River Plate. But, as Professor Ferns explains, demand contracted with the end of the wars and the re-entry of Continental producers. Although hides remained by far the most important element in Argentine exports to the United Kingdom, the Argentine proportion of the British market had fallen to little over a third by 1825-9.[3] Over 20% of the cotton used by Britain from 1801 to 1810 came from Brazil, and with the American War the amount increased for the next decade to about 30%. By the '70s, the proportion was as low as 5%; production had not fallen nor had the amount received in Britain decreased, but the great expansion of demand in British industry was met by producers in the United States, Egypt and India.[4]

Over £20 million were raised on the British market for Latin American government loans in the early '20s, and a further £3½

[1] Walsh, *Brazil*, II, 536.
[2] Robertson, *South America*, II, 269.
[3] H. S. Ferns, 'Investment and Trade between Britain and Argentina in the Nineteenth Century', *Economic History Review*, 2nd ser. III (1950), 213.
[4] Phipps' report on Brazil, 24 June 1872, P.P. 1872, LIX, 647.

million paid-up capital was attached to the optimistic mining flotations of the same period. Some of this reached Latin America. It helped to redress the balance between imports and exports, and to encourage further imports of British manufactures by furnishing remittances which could not otherwise have been obtained for the English trader. But further investment was cut off abruptly by the financial crash of 1825. The British merchants themselves did all they could to develop satisfactory returns to finance the imports on which they depended. They took a large share in opening Continental markets to Latin American sugar, tobacco, coffee and cocoa. They developed a triangular trade in jerked beef to Cuba and in Latin American products to Continental ports such as Trieste and St Petersburg. But the problem still existed. Preferential duties in favour of British Possessions made it almost impossible for two of the main export products of Latin America, sugar and coffee, to enter the British home market; the sugar duties lasted until 1854, the coffee duties until 1851. The development of British exports to Brazil was checked by Britain's failure to offer any kind of a market for Brazilian sugar and coffee, and ultimately a large share of the export trade passed to those countries which could take Brazil's products in exchange. The difficulty in finding satisfactory remittances meant that capital was tied up unprofitably in Latin American markets, while creditors at home pressed export merchants for payment. It was this which forced Abraham Rhodes to recall his Rio partner, Henry Glover, in 1816. During 1813 Rhodes had been drawing on his bankers in Leeds at the rate of over £12,000 a month, which, as he told Glover on 8 March 1814,

> sums up very fast in our Bankers Books against us, when there is a stoppage of remittances to place on the other side, and except the £4,000 we have drawn upon you we have not had a farthing on account of any goods sent you in 1813. We open our hearts and tell you our sorrows, comfort and relieve them.

No comfort came; the capital was withdrawn and more profitably employed in the United Kingdom.[1]

Brazil and Argentina, none the less, had something to offer European markets. Others had nothing, and their ability to import, after the first resources were exhausted, depended ultimately on their success in attracting foreign capital (almost nil after 1825) and

[1] Wilson, *Business History*, IX, 81.

on the export of whatever precious metals they might extract from their mines or obtain in exchange for produce in trade with another Republic. Peru could supply nothing other than bullion and specie in the '20s. Wool and nitrates made some impression in the '30s and the 'guano age' opened in 1841. But in 1840 Peruvian exports consisted of bullion and specie to the extent of £1,562,149; wool was next on the list at £141,724, nitrates at £90,942, cotton at £85,889 and bark at £23,600.[1] By far the greater part of Colombia's exports to Britain even in the mid-century were in specie, declared or smuggled. Paraguay's products were of no interest to Europe. Cuba became Britain's main supplier of imported copper ores for a period after the late '30s, but until then her imports into the United Kingdom were generally in the range only of £200,000 to £300,000 (official values). Bolivia's exports were almost exclusively gold and silver, since transport costs over the mountains to Arica priced other possible exports, *vicuña*, cotton, cocoa, *mate*, bark, out of the market. Chile, except when copper came periodically into demand in Europe or India, could offer little except silver and gold, or wheat for trade on the Pacific coast; the long voyage round the Horn made speculations in Chilean hides, hemp and tallow unattractive. The interior provinces of Argentina suffered the same disability. The *Gaceta Mercantil* gave a table of estimates, in 1834, for the distances at which the cost of transportation equalled half the price of the commodities in the Buenos Aires market. Among the principal exportable commodities, the distance for jerked beef was 95 leagues, for tallow 226 leagues, for salted hides 240, for wool 400, for horsehair 426 and for dry hides 515. Only the last four, Burgin remarks, could bear the cost of long overland hauls. The interior provinces received from 20 to 30% less than Buenos Aires producers for their dry hides, wool and horsehair; they could take no share at all in the export of jerked beef or tallow.[2]

[1] W. M. Mathew, 'Anglo-Peruvian Commercial and Financial Relations 1820-1865', unpublished Ph.D. thesis, London 1964, pp. 76-7.
[2] Burgin, *Argentine Federalism*, p. 118.

CHAPTER III

The Traders

FOR the first half of the nineteenth century, the British impact on, and influence in, Latin America is easily exaggerated. Yet for a few years British subjects were conspicuous in the armies and navies of Brazil and the new Republics, in the ports and cities as traders, shopkeepers and artisans, in the mines, and even, in one or two areas, on the land. It is interesting to see where this effort was concentrated, what effect it had in the short term, and what happened to it once the first enthusiasm evaporated.

Naturally, the largest British communities were to be found in the few important capitals and ports, more particularly in Rio, in Buenos Aires and in Valparaiso. In the early days of the opening of Brazil, in 1808, there may have been as many as 6,000 foreigners in Rio.[1] Many of these dispersed almost immediately to more promising outlets, some to Brazilian ports to the north and south, others to the River Plate. But in the mid-'20s Mathison computed the foreign population of Rio, in which Britons formed the most prosperous though not the most numerous class, at between three and four thousand.[2] The British community in Buenos Aires, which stood at about 120 in 1810, the year of Independence, had risen to somewhere in the region of 3,000 by 1824[3]; in Argentina as a whole there were probably not more than an additional 500

[1] Luccock, *Rio de Janeiro*, p. 41.
[2] Gilbert Farquhar Mathison, *Narrative of a Visit to Brazil, Chile & Peru* (London, 1825), p. 129.
[3] Humphreys, *Tradition and Revolt*, pp. 113, 126.

British subjects.[1] Few British subjects lived in Santiago, perhaps a hundred in 1820, together with thirty North Americans, Germans or French.[2] However, at Valparaiso there was a large but fluctuating British community which, depending on what part of the visiting shipping was included, was estimated by the mid-'20s at between 400 and 3,000. Miers, who knew the place intimately, felt that 400 was nearer the mark, including seamen, and only a few 'respectable' families were in permanent residence.[3] The totals were much smaller elsewhere. British subjects were scattered in small numbers all over the Continent. In the larger mining enterprises, such as the St John del Rey mine in Minas Geraes, Brazil, or the English copper-mines at Aroa in Venezuela, between 150 and 200 Englishmen were employed. The usual British community consisted simply of three or four mercantile houses and a few artisans. Even in an important trading centre like Lima, there were only some 250 English residents in 1824, three years after the opening of Peru to foreign trade.[4]

British working men seldom took root in the Republics. A few had arrived and settled during the colonial period. Proctor met one who had come out via Panama at the beginning of the century 'in the quality of Mr. Merryman to a company of English mountebanks', and had decided to stay in Peru when the company disbanded. Several hundred soldiers from Beresford's and Whitelock's defeated armies remained in Argentina in the last years of the Empire. A few did well enough for themselves. A Scotsman introduced himself to Joseph Andrews in 1825 during Andrews' visit to the Jesuit ruins at Sinsacate in Argentina. He had been taken with other prisoners-of-war into the interior where, having obtained his liberty, he had married and settled. He was now a sort of major-domo on the local estate and described himself as 'very happy, having a good wife and five children, and also some thousands of dollars to leave them'.[5] But the majority, according to

---

[1] Parish estimated the foreign population of the Argentine Federation in 1822 to be 15,000, of whom 3,500 were British: E. J. Pratt, 'Anglo-American Commercial and Political Rivalry on the Plata, 1820-1830', *Hispanic American Historical Review*, XI (1931), 305.

[2] Schmidtmeyer, *Chile*, p. 236.

[3] Miers, *Chile*, I, 445-6.

[4] Humphreys, *Consular Reports*, p. 108 fn. 1.

[5] Joseph Andrews, *Journey from Buenos Ayres to Santiago and Coquimbo in the years 1825-26* (London, 1827), pp. 107-8.

Woodbine Parish, had 'sunk by the 1820s to the lowest scale of misery and moral degradation'. And this, unfortunately, was the more general experience. British working men arrived to serve in the Republican armies, to work in the re-opened mines, to try their luck in the cities, to settle on the land. They were not well-suited to the climate, the language, the conditions of work or the standard of living. They could have lived very cheaply anywhere in Latin America if they had chosen to live as others lived around them. Even in Buenos Aires, said the embittered Beaumont, beef and brandy were cheap, and peaches were to be had at the same price as turnips in England, with about as much flavour. But everything else, lodging, clothing, the foods to which Englishmen were accustomed, was much dearer than in London. Moreover,

> the climate is enervating, and disinclines a man from labour; the customs of the country—examples and invitations on every side, or the sneers and reproaches of idlers—all tend to produce drinking, idleness, and smoking. In these latter ways, the emigrant is soon brought to the level of the country. . . .[1]

It was in and through the mercantile houses that Englishmen made the greatest impression during the first decades. Englishmen served at all levels of commercial society, as tailors, saddlers, hucksters, shoemakers, as bakers and keepers of pot-houses and hotels. In the '20s English pot-houses lined the streets of Rio near the beach, and, 'Union Jacks, Red Lions, Jolly Tars, with their English inscriptions, vie with those of Greenwich or Deptford'. The same could be found near the landing-stages at Buenos Aires, Valparaiso and Callao. An Englishman ran a good inn at Buenos Aires in 1817. Mrs Walker kept the British hotel at Santiago where most Englishmen stayed and enjoyed 'at least a shadow of English comforts with an English landlady'. A steward off an English vessel had set up house on the road between Valparaiso and the capital, advertised by the legend painted on a board dangling from a high pole: 'Acomodaçion—Good beds for a gentleman and his horse'. Faunch's Hotel in Buenos Aires, built at considerable expense by Mr Thwaites, was where the 'higher sort of emigrants generally take up their quarters on their first arrival'.

The core of the community—the source of finance for the chaplain, church and cemetery, of subscriptions to the Benevolent

[1] Beaumont, *Buenos Ayres*, p. 255.

Fund and the English library, of patronage for the Commercial Rooms—was the British merchant. Woodbine Parish gave a total of 4,072 British subjects registered at the Buenos Aires Consulate between 1825 and 1831. Heading the list were 466 'merchants, traders and clerks'—the largest group after 'labourers' (667), women (595) and children (827).[1] Until the mid-'20s, British mercantile houses of all shapes, sizes and capital resources existed in some numbers at the principal centres of international trade. In Britain's most important market, Brazil, about sixty British houses were in business in Rio in 1820; there were nearly twenty houses at Bahia (eighteen, according to Maria Graham), sixteen at Pernambuco, five or six at Pará, and smaller numbers up and down the coast at ports like Parahyba and Maranhao in the north and Rio Grande do Sul in the south.[2] On the River Plate in the mid-'20s ten British mercantile houses were established at Montevideo and forty at Buenos Aires.[3] In Peru in 1824, there were twenty British houses at Lima, and a further sixteen at Arequipa.[4] Mexico City had fourteen British houses in 1826, eight of which had branches at Vera Cruz.[5] In Colombia, between one and three individuals were in business at Riohacha, Santa Marta, Sabanilla, Barrancas, Barranquilla and Mompós, while there were four British commercial establishments at Cartagena.[6] Many of these were simply commission agents, or branches of larger houses in the local capital, in Liverpool or in London.

It was not an exciting society, male or female, and it decidedly lacked *haut ton*. Maria Graham, the wife of an English naval captain and for all her charm a snob and a blue-stocking, found the English ladies in Bahia to be 'quite of the second rate of even colonial gentility'. The merchants in Santiago were 'very civil, vulgar people'. It was curious, at Valparaiso and at such a distance from home, 'to see specimens of such people as one meets no where else but among the Brangtons in Madame D'Arblay's

---

[1] Parish, *Buenos Ayres*, p. 394 (Appendix 3).

[2] James Henderson, *A History of Brazil* (London, 1821), pp. 91, 340, 390, 464; Maria Graham, *Journal of a Voyage to Brazil* (London, 1824), p. 146.

[3] Humphreys, *Consular Reports*, p. 76; M. G. Mulhall, *The English in South America* (Buenos Aires, 1878), p. 328.

[4] Mathew, 'Anglo-Peruvian Commercial and Financial Relations' pp. 14-15.

[5] Humphreys, *Consular Reports*, p. 303 fn. 2.

[6] *Ibid.*, p. 261.

Cecilia, or the Mrs. Eltons of Miss Austen's admirable novels'.[1] Yet, as Mrs Graham admitted, these were the people most likely to be there, and even if they did not reach her social standards they were, in general, young, vigorous and very interested in making money. Few places existed of any commercial importance on the Latin American coastline in which British interests were not, however marginally, represented.

*

In terms of the total trade, all this activity did not amount to much. The volume handled by many of the houses was small, and the trade itself was often merely a re-channelling of an existing trade away from the traditional Spanish or Portuguese monopolists and into the hands of a host of newcomers. One of the reasons for the relative infrequency of British houses in Colombia, other than the limited trading opportunities in the area, was the fact that the trade continued for many years to be handled through the traditional channels, by merchants in Jamaica acting through local Colombian houses. Where the colonial system had broken down entirely, as it had in Buenos Aires, Santiago, Lima or Vera Cruz, the number of foreign houses was bound to be much higher even if it did not represent a great enlargement of trade. However, the effect of so many new arrivals was undoubtedly to set new fashions, introduce new needs, and so, within that part of society which might be regarded as in the market for European imports, enlarge consumption. Indeed, the foreign community itself was one of the largest consumers of its own imports.

The opening of the ports of Latin America, the arrival of foreigners, and, for Brazil, the transfer of the royal court to Rio, naturally created the kind of atmosphere in which society was likely to look anew at conditions of living with which it had been satisfied for generations. 'The time of advancement was come', said Koster, comparing Pernambuco in 1811 with the city as he knew it two years before, 'and men, who had for many years gone on without making any change either in the interior or exterior of their houses, were now painting and glazing on the outside, and new furnishing within; modernizing themselves, their families, and their dwellings'.[2]

---

[1] Graham, *Brazil*, p. 142; Graham, *Chile*, pp. 179, 234.
[2] Henry Koster, *Travels in Brazil* (London, 1816), p. 189.

Colonial society had had little contact with changing European fashions. When Koster first arrived in Pernambuco in 1809 the women were dressed, on formal occasions, in heavy silks and satins; the men appeared daily in full-dress suits of black, with gold buckles and cocked hats. A few pieces of fine French furniture had been imported on the east and west coasts during the eighteenth century, and some English furniture in the north from the British West Indies. But the houses of the rich in Peru, Bolivia, Gran Colombia and Mexico were furnished in an antique style of large gilded chairs and sofas, crimson damask hangings, gilded bed-posts and table legs heavily carved and ornamented, large paintings of saints in richly embossed silver frames. At a lower level of society and in Argentina, Chile or southern Brazil, where there was no mineral wealth to buy ostentation, traditional furnishings were of the simplest kind— whitewashed walls, brick floors, a carpet over part of the *sala*, a line of chairs and sofas, sometimes barely more than a raised platform (the *estrada*) covered in mats and warmed, if that is the word, by a charcoal brazier. At Guayaquil Captain Hall was surprised to find the ladies reclining in immense grass hammocks, suspended from the roof twenty feet above. In one house, when the party of British naval officers arrived to pay a call they found the grandmother in one hammock, the mother in the second, and three pretty young daughters lounging in a third. All were

> swinging away at such a furious rate, that at first we were confounded and made giddy by the variety of motions in different directions. We succeeded, however, in making good our passage to a sofa at the further end of the room, though not without apprehension of being knocked over by the way. The ladies, seeing us embarrassed, ceased their vibrations until the introductions had taken place, and then touching the floor with their feet, swung off again without any interruption to the conversation.[1]

Fashions in dress and furnishings did not change overnight; at the end of the nineteenth century, in the pastoral provinces in particular, conditions were much the same as they had been centuries before. But the new style of life, imported by foreign mercenaries and merchants and by the exiled Portuguese aristocracy, was rapidly

[1] Basil Hall, *Extracts from a Journal written on the coasts of Chile, Peru and Mexico in the Years 1820, 1821, 1822* (Edinburgh, 1824), pp. 108-9.

apparent in the main cities and ports. Although this made itself felt in furnishings, imported furniture was still expensive, and in the interior prohibitively so, so that new styles were seldom visible outside the *sala*. The change was most noticeable in the smaller items, English and French prints for the walls, mirrors, ornaments, even English grates to replace the charcoal braziers. Table furniture changed most of all. Luccock, who mixed freely with the Brazilians, reported that he had never dined in a Brazilian house where part of the china, glass, silver and table linen was not British. Before the British arrived, Brazilians had eaten off pewter or rough pottery, drunk from small Portuguese tumblers or calabashes; each guest had supplied his own knife, usually broad, sharp-pointed and mounted in silver. Luccock explained how social intercourse between foreigners and residents was considerable in the early days, and how by degrees, after frequent visits on each side, British habits gradually came into general use. Some of the effects were unfortunate. The Brazilians, like other Latin Americans, drank sparingly. Some adopted the British habit of toasting, and Luccock had seen a whole bottle of wine swallowed without a pause. He was glad to report that such habits had not yet spread widely among the people of Rio. Toasting, indeed, was adopted chiefly out of regard for the British, of whom it had unfortunately been reported that they were much devoted to the bottle; 'the Brazilians, unused to such modes of complimenting, often exhibit scenes of beastliness, for which friendly intention is no adequate excuse'.[1]

Naturally, the interior provinces were the last to be affected. But Mrs Graham reported visits to sugar estates within riding range of Rio where the change in interior appointments, even by the early '20s, was 'most rapid and complete' from the rough conditions reported by the first British travellers.[2] General San Martín's study at Mendoza was furnished with English commodes, tables and chairs of rosewood inlaid in brass, on a Brussels carpet, although Miers' attention was caught more particularly by a large likeness of the Liberator, hung between prints of Napoleon and Wellington, all three framed in a corresponding manner.[3]

It was in dress that the new fashions spread furthest. At the top level of society, colonial Spanish America had always appreciated

[1] Luccock, *Rio de Janeiro*, pp. 123-5.
[2] Graham, *Brazil*, pp. 279, 289.
[3] Miers, *Chile*, pp. 159-60.

the more expensive fabrics, silks, woollens, linens, the jewellery, the lace, the millinery of France. All were imported in great quantities to support the heavy magnificence of colonial society. They were as popular in the new Republics. No expense was spared, and the evening-dresses of the ladies of Buenos Aires, at the balls and public assemblies, were made from 'the finest fabrics that England, France, or the "gorgeous East" can procure'. By this time English chintzes, muslins and ginghams were the common day-dress, from which the ladies changed into French fabrics and fashions for the evening. The smarter, city men were as well dressed as those of the same class in London or Paris. French and English tailors, dressmakers and milliners, settling in Buenos Aires after 1810, took pains to follow the latest European fashions, and when Samuel Haigh visited the city in 1817, he found it a considerable advance on anything in old Spain, with its manners and fashions far closer to those of the the two great capitals, London and Paris, than were those of many of the cities of Europe.[1] Much the same was true of Pernambuco, Rio and Santiago, but it was harder to displace the more distinctive national dress of the north-west. Fashionable Peruvians had abandoned the long Spanish cloak well before 1821, and ladies often appeared for evening occasions in English or French costume. But the *saya y manto* survived for day wear and were still worn in Lima when Hill visited Peru in the middle of the century.[2] The *saya y manto*, a picturesque costume well-adapted to amatory intrigue, consisted of a form-fitting dress with a mantle or hood of thin black silk drawn round the waist and then carried over the head, closed at front to reveal a single lustrous eye; Englishmen described it as bewitching or disgusting according to individual experience. Similarly, although the ladies of Bogotá wore French fashions adorned with a profusion of pearls, emeralds and other precious stones for their *tertulias* and balls, and English chintz or cotton gowns, a Norwich shawl and a pretty straw hat with artificial flowers for their evening promenades, it proved far more difficult to displace the national day-dress. Some bold ladies were parading the streets, even before Colonel Hamilton left Bogotá in 1824, in large French bonnets and gay-coloured silk gowns. But it took courage and time before Colombian society was weaned away from the morning walking-dress of ladies of rank—

[1] Haigh, *Buenos Ayres*, pp. 18-21.
[2] S. S. Hill, *Travels in Peru and Mexico* (London, 1860), II, 73.

a close-fitting black silk gown, a fine black or blue cloth covering head and shoulders, and a small black beaver hat. As Colonel Hall said, the effect was 'most singular and outré'; 'the ladies allow it to be a barbarous fashion, but want courage to break through the custom'.[1]

For the British merchant in post-colonial Latin America the problem was that 'articles are not wanted, because they are not known; and their necessities must be created before supplies for them can be asked for'.[2] To some extent, the free, expansive and receptive atmosphere created by the break with Spain, the arrival of foreign merchants and immigrants, the availability of new products, sometimes at glut prices, combined to enlarge the 'necessities' for Latin American society. The 'discordant jarring of the old half strung guitar' had given place to the piano in every house of quality in Chile, and Broadwood pianos found their way up the river and over the mountains to Bogotá. In the coastal cities, cheap, tawdry North American furniture and highly coloured French prints replaced the bare, white rooms of colonial Spanish America. Property values rose, and a second storey was added to fashionable Buenos Aires. The lower classes in Argentina, although they may have kept to their local cotton shifts for normal wear, now appeared for their holidays dressed colourfully in imported cloths and velveteens for the men, baizes and cotton stuffs for the women.

*

The expanded market offered new opportunities to British merchants to make or mar their fortunes. It was up to them to create needs and then to find the means to satisfy them, and for some this meant great wealth. Yet the general experience of the mercantile houses competing for what, to them, were the unexpectedly limited market opportunities in liberated Latin America, was rather different.

Windfall profits always attract attention. Antony Gibbs and Sons made 200% on their first cargo of textiles to Lima in 1806.[3] The first cargoes to reach Lima after its fall to San Martín in 1821

[1] Francis Hall, *Letters written from Colombia during a Journey from Caracas to Bogota in 1823* (London, 1824), p. 153.
[2] A British merchant comparing the state of the market in Paraguay, 25 December 1819, to that of the country around Buenos Aires in 1809: Graham and Humphreys, *The Navy and South America*, p. 290.
[3] Gibbs, *Antony and Dorothea Gibbs*, p. 195.

were said to have realized upwards of 400%.[1] One London merchant, on a consignment to Mexico in the early '20s costing £80, received in return £1,660, a profit of 1,975%![2] Handsome profits were obtained from the sale of arms and ships to both sides during the struggle for independence. Two old East Indiamen, the *Wyndham* (800 tons) and the *Cumberland* (1,200 tons), were sold to the Chilean patriots for $180,000 and $150,000 respectively, to be met in cash, bills on the Customs House, family plate, copper, jerked beef and tallow. Military accoutrements, condemned as unserviceable at the Tower of London, were bought at low prices and sold to patriots or royalists, whichever proved the more eligible. The claims of British merchants to ardent patriotism unmixed with views of profit in the cause of the Republics must, said John Miller, be disallowed: 'It is true that many of them displayed the liberality of feeling which is generally found to exist in the commercial world; but in this case their sympathies and their interests went hand in hand. When these became unhappily at variance, poor Sympathy often went to the wall. . . .'[3] Certainly, when the royalist army was approaching Santiago in 1817, the British merchants, after meeting to form a body of cavalry—for which they immediately designed a uniform (scarlet jacket, yellow pantaloons and a shako with a white feather in it)—lost heart and fled to the Cordillera. The departure of the English filled the Chilean patriots with gloomy forebodings. 'You may depend,' said they, 'that it is all over with our cause, for the English would never leave their property, whilst there was the least hope.'[4]

Good profits during the early years depended on swift arrival at the market or the wit to see a new opening when it came. The Robertson brothers made a fortune out of a war-created shortage of hides. For a few months in 1816 dried hides, priced at 1½d. a pound in Corrientes (Argentina), could be sold for 9d. or 10d. at Liverpool. The hide of a horse costing 3d. in Corrientes fetched seven or eight shillings across the Atlantic. It was a question of getting accumulated hides from an interior province of Argentina to the Buenos Aires market, and this the Robertsons were able to

---

[1] Sir Thomas Hardy to Croker, 14 September 1821: Graham and Humphreys, *The Navy and South America*, p. 348.

[2] W. F. Cody, 'British Interest in the Independence of Mexico, 1808-1827', unpublished Ph.D. thesis, London 1954.

[3] John Miller, *Memoirs of General Miller* (London, 1828), II, 221-6.

[4] Haigh, *Buenos Ayres*, pp. 203-5.

achieve by heavy and timely investment in credit to the landowners, in elaborate transport arrangements and in storage and shipping facilities.[1] But there was always more than enough competition. The forty English houses in Buenos Aires in 1823 brought profits down to those of 'an English chandler's shop', and English cotton goods were cheaper than in London. Real money came from lucky anticipations of demand in an unstable market, from intelligent investment in local enterprise, or from finance. The hundreds of thousands of pounds brought home by partners in mercantile houses in India in the '20s were not the profits of trade; they were drawn from an ability to lay hands on a great deal of money at 6% and lend it at 10%. Nothing equivalent came out of Latin America, although business of a similar kind made it possible for men like John Proudfoot of Montevideo, Thomas Bland Garland and Samuel Lang of Valparaiso, James Brittain of Buenos Aires to return to the United Kingdom with comfortable fortunes.

The handsome profits on the first shipments to Latin America encouraged a life-style among British merchants which, over a longer period, proved damaging to all and disastrous to many. The houses of the Spanish monopolists at Buenos Aires, 'most splendid and capacious habitations, built at an uncountable cost', were rented by the English merchants,

> men of the John Bull breed, and who all, more or less, carrying out with them John Bull's love of comfort, diffused among the people John Bull's love of hospitality, showed how little John Bull cared about expense, or even extravagance.[2]

One of the more splendid palaces in Lima was the home of 'a British merchant of great eminence'. British merchants occupied the choicest suburbs. The Cerro Alegre above Valparaiso was 'entirely monopolised by the British'. The charming Victoria, a suburb of Bahia, was almost exclusively British. The British consul received Captain and Mrs Graham at his garden house in Victoria, literally overhanging the bay, where 'flowers and fruits mingle their sweets even down to the water's edge', while

> Sea born gales their gelid wings expand,
> To winnow fragrance round the smiling land.[3]

[1] Humphreys, *Tradition and Revolt*, p. 115.
[2] Robertson, *South America*, II, 68.
[3] Graham, *Brazil*, p. 134.

At Rio the British merchants inhabited the elegant southern suburbs, Praia Flamingo and Botafogo, where the beach was 'edged with some of the neatest and most elegant houses in the vicinity'. Mr Harrison's house, in particular, exhibited 'all the beauty, elegance, and comfort of an English villa'.[1] Fanny Calderón de la Barca, the young Scottish wife of the first Spanish Minister to independent Mexico, found herself, at Vera Cruz, lodged nearly opposite a fine house in the principal street, particularly well kept and handsome, where they saw beautiful flowers as they passed. It belonged to an English merchant. A few days later, she and her husband started on their journey up to Mexico City. They fell much in love with Jalapa, up in the hills above Vera Cruz, 'so old and gray, and rose-becovered, with a sound of music issuing from every open door and window, and its soft and agreeable temperature'. In the few, steep streets stood some large and excellent houses, 'the best as usual belonging to English merchants'.[2] At every port, however small, Englishmen lightened their exile by a careful selection of the finest, coolest, most agreeable places to live. Mr R.'s *sitio* at Parahyba (northern Brazil) lay on the brow of the hill, within the bounds of the upper town. It enjoyed magnificent views over the ocean on the north, the Cape and Fort Cabedello, the mouth and course of the river, up to the shipping before the lower town. R. had spent a great deal of attention on the cultivation of his grounds, planting many coffee and orange trees and a vegetable garden. There were

> fine springs of water, a yard of cows, and other valuable appendages of rural life, so that he might be truly said to have *rus in urbe*, 'a farm in the city'. The house was large and airy, with brick floors, latticed windows, and no ceilings above, save in the parlour.[3]

Yet the volume of trade could support few of these pleasant, sometimes luxurious establishments. Most of the ships coming to Parahyba were in ballast, and the merchants of the town survived off commissions on an export trade amounting in the early '40s to about £100,000, mainly of cotton, with some sugar and hides. It

[1] Henderson, *Brazil*, p. 59.
[2] F. Calderon de la Barca, *Life in Mexico during a Residence of Two Years in that Country* (London, 1843), pp. 23, 31-2.
[3] Quoted in MacGregor's report on Brazil, P.P. 1847, LXIV, 663.

took little capital to set up in business simply as a consignee, selling consignments from British manufacturers on commission. The great majority of the young men reaching Latin America in the early days were commission agents. They could make a comfortable living without risk provided first that there were not too many competing for the same business, and then that British manufacturers continued to find it worth while to 'dump' their surplus products on Latin American markets. The first of these conditions was lost almost immediately, the second disappeared with the contraction of credit and difficult trading conditions in and after the mid-'20s. With the stagnation of trade and oversupplied markets, commission agents were in a critical position. They themselves, in order to dispose of consignments in generally impoverished markets, had had to be prepared to give ample credit to local dealers. Consignments had ceased to come in. The merchants at home were pressed by the banks for repayment, while their own money was lent out in advances to the manufacturers. They in turn demanded remittances from their agents in Latin America, whose unenviable task it became to collect money from local dealers in a glutted market with no sales in prospect.

Consul Ricketts estimated that there were not less than $2 million in outstanding debts to British merchants in Lima at the end of 1826, 'and the recovery is most tedious and a great part, I fear, doubtful'.[1] Antony Gibbs had about £45,000 locked up in its Lima branch house in 1826. But the firm was also committed heavily in large advances to British manufacturers. The crisis came in the middle of 1826, with trade in England at a low ebb and many failures particularly among the manufacturers. The debit balance of Gibbs' advance account stood at very nearly £100,000.[2] Naturally, firms without Gibbs' access to capital or credit went out of business. By the late '20s the days of the multitude of small consignees were already over. Many hung on in hope of a recovery, or turned their attention to local investments in land, mining or manufacturing. But the future pattern of a few strong, diversified houses sharing out the limited market between them was already established.

*

[1] Ricketts' report from Lima, 27 December 1826: Humphreys, *Consular Reports*, p. 130.

[2] Gibbs, *Antony and Dorothea Gibbs*, p. 384.

E

There are dangers in classifying a nineteenth-century merchant simply as an economic man. The element of chance and the possibility, almost probability, of disaster were enough to persuade successful merchants to sell up rather than battle indefinitely in the market-place. Sharp fluctuations in trade, in a period of uncertain communications, could make fortunes one day and lose them the next. All successful merchants passed through such crises, even to the point of bankruptcy, and there was every incentive to move out at the crest of some wave either to try another more promising market, or to withdraw into the comfortable status of a rentier. Quite apart from the difficulties of trade with Latin America, the commercial and financial world in England suffered crises of extreme gravity almost every ten years, in 1825, 1837, 1847, 1857, 1866, when, Sir William Forwood said, it was not a question of having to pay a high rate of interest on advances, but of not being able to get money at any price. Forwood well remembered the panics of 1857 and 1866, when 'many banks and honest traders were cruelly ruined', when bank bills could not be discounted, and produce was unsaleable. Forwood himself, although he made large sums out of shipping and cotton 'banking', retired completely from business at the age of fifty, and devoted the rest of his life to politics; he was 'tired with the fag and toil of twenty-five years' strenuous work'.[1]

The incentive to remain overseas, under such conditions, was slight. Many men had gone out to Latin America to seek their fortune. Some found it, most did not. There was no incentive to remain in business once the real extent of the market was evident to all. Since the normal merchant was simply a consignee, surviving off commissions on goods despatched by others, his capital stake was small, if it existed at all; he could return home at any moment, and did so once he found that profits were eluding him. In any case, he was compelled to withdraw when no consignments were received to distribute, and many British manufacturers and merchants in the United Kingdom, having suffered severely during the crisis of the mid-'20s, turned inwards on themselves, putting their money into home markets and investments or into the more familiar overseas markets of Europe, the Colonies or the United States. Luptons of Leeds were a case in point. For some years after

---

[1] William Forwood, *Recollections of a Busy Life, 1840-1910* (Liverpool, 1910), pp. 65-6, 77.

the return of the resident partner, Luccock, from Rio in 1818 Luptons continued to send out manufactured goods and to import Brazilian cotton through Luccock's former assistant, still in business at Rio. But the general collapse of 1825, at home and in Latin America, made it harder than ever to obtain remittances. Heaton explains how 'the Luptons therefore cut their losses, turned to less hazardous fields of enterprise, and let the trade with South America pass into the hands of those who had more of hope or less of experience'.[1]

More might have remained in business if there had been sufficient opportunities locally for the profitable investment of capital. A few merchants found good openings, and were able either to shift their interests altogether out of the import/export trade or to turn over their capital for long enough to be in at the revival of overseas trade after the middle of the century. But there was no prospect as yet of investment in communications, nor would there be until Europe developed a real need for Latin American produce. Local manufacturing, in which Britons might have invested, suffered from the same competition of the handicraft industry which so limited the market for imports. Money might yet be made out of advances to miners, landowners or peasants, but it was a precarious business, especially for a foreigner ill-acquainted with the politics, customs and character of the people with whom he dealt. Miers, who had had some embittering experiences in an attempt to establish an ambitious copper-smelting enterprise in Chile, was convinced that a merchant or foreign capitalist had no chance of employing capital profitably *except* in the import/export trade, and he was writing in the mid '20s just at the point where the import/ export trade itself collapsed.[2]

Many explanations may be suggested for the failure of the British mercantile houses to maintain their leading position in Latin American trade, a number of which are external to Latin America. Incompetence and extravagance, no doubt, account for some individual failures. But the explanation of what became a trend is to be found in the problems of particular trades. Traders were mobile, ready to open up business or close it down again as conditions dictated. Better opportunities elsewhere, or the charms of a gentleman's life at home, on the land or in politics, were

[1] Heaton, *Journal of Economic History*, VI, 23.
[2] Miers, *Chile*, II, 337.

perfectly respectable reasons for closing a trading connection in Latin America, even if it were paying a modest return on capital invested. Businessmen have always had a sharp eye to the relative rates of return for different forms of investment. Owens, before even considering a new trade to Buenos Aires in the early '30s, required an average of $17\frac{1}{2}\%$ advance on the invoice: 'The carriage, shipping charges and freight will average 4%, Insurance 2%, Interest (at least) 4%—making charges 10%—now the least profit we would think equivalent for the risque and trouble attending shipments to your place would be $7\frac{1}{2}\%$'.[1] John Ewart, a partner in the Liverpool firm of brokers and general commission agents Ewart, Myers and Company, explained that his firm, which dealt widely in the produce of the Western Hemisphere, used to calculate that 5% ought to be earned on money in trade, besides commissions and other profits, even if, with money as cheap as it was at the time, such a rate could not be hoped for in 1833. He added that if a firm were to invest money in goods on its own account, 6% on such a risk would be a very poor return; 5% might hold a firm together, but not many men would be disposed to give their capital and labour for such a return, and they would rather put it into something that was more easy and more certain.[2] William Graham, a substantial cotton spinner and weaver, giving evidence to the same Select Committee in 1833, felt that it was difficult to give a firm answer for foreign trade where profits were sometimes very large but where often traders were left with less than the goods cost them. As a manufacturer he would be glad to do business on the basis of a profit of from 3 to 5% on capital, over and above an annual depreciation of $2\frac{1}{2}\%$ and a standard interest of 4% (which his capital would have earned on the market without any exertion on his part).[3] A shipowner, at the time, would not have felt it worth his while to undertake new commitments under a 20% return—10% on capital invested, and 10% depreciation on his ships.[4]

This was the kind of calculation which a businessman made when deciding whether or not to retain his Latin American inter-

---

[1] John Owens to Hodgson & Robinson of Buenos Aires, 6 March 1833: Clapp, *Owens*, p. 40.
[2] Minutes of Evidence, *Report of the Select Committee on Manufactures, Commerce and Shipping*, P.P. 1833, VI, QQ.4033, 4153, 4158.
[3] *Ibid.*, QQ.5547-8.
[4] *Ibid.*, QQ.6521-3, 7030-1.

ests. Slow turnover, poor communications, high tariffs and commissions, might well have priced his lines out of the market at a level well below that at which the trade offered a satisfactory return, in which case he simply withdrew and used his capital to better effect elsewhere. There is nothing infinite about the resources available for a trade, and the decision how best to distribute them is a business decision. The cries of alarm from British consuls, and of triumph from our competitors, at the withdrawal of the British mercantile house from nineteenth-century Latin America, merely high-lighted their own inexperience. What might have looked like a defeat in one market was, often enough, a soundly argued decision to transfer limited resources to markets offering safer, more consistent, and higher returns.

Slow turnover accounted for a large part of the high prices charged on imports during the days of sail. Cockerell and Company, in the India trade, calculated that, taking the voyage out and home at ten months, allowing three months for sale, and calculating the remittance at six months, it was about eighteen or nineteen months before the manufacturer or shipper received his return. John Innis, another India merchant, believed it to be fifteen months.[1] Even as late as 1860 the British consul at San José, Costa Rica, argued that what with an average of six months' credit on the sale of imported manufactured goods, with the advances on coffee (which was the only produce in which returns could profitably be made), and with the long double journey round Cape Horn, at least two years would be required; a general cargo would have to produce a net profit of 20% before it could be considered worth engaging in the trade.[2] Turnover was far quicker on the east coast, in Brazil or in Argentina, and this was one reason why the trade with these markets was so much more attractive to Englishmen. But a long credit was as customary here as elsewhere on the continent, and it was most unlikely that a trade would bear less than nine to twelve months' interest on the capital employed. Insurance could be a formidable addition to costs. During the early years of post-colonial trade, when war and blockade added to the dangers of sail, rates could be anywhere from 6 to 12% on the value of the cargo. Insurance premiums were still high in the '20s, and many merchants

[1] *Ibid.*, QQ.2155, 3191.
[2] Report on Costa Rica for the five years ending 31 December 1860, P.P. 1862, LVIII, 652-3.

preferred to take the risks themselves, choosing first-rate ships and sending out small shipments in each.

Some of the heaviest burdens of all were met in transport. Shipping rates, on the whole, were not high; many merchants themselves owned, or held shares in, a number of ships, and tariffs generally were on the decline after 1825. The problem was the irregularity of shipments. In the small, easily saturated markets of Latin America, the timing of a speculative consignment was all important; one cargo alone might fill the market for months or years at a time, and a late arrival found no market at all. Even within a single cargo, good timing was often essential. Merchants jockeyed to bring their goods to the quayside as late as possible before sailing so that their shipments were the first to leave the holds at the other end and furthest removed from the bilges. Trade in Britain's main manufactured export, textiles, was normally seasonal, winter-weight clothes to reach markets in the autumn, summer-weight for the spring. Contrary winds could add months to voyages, and ships might wait weeks or even months at the Liverpool docks while a full cargo accumulated. It was not uncommon for a shipment of winter-weight clothing for Chile, intended for May, to reach Valparaiso after the winter market had closed, in August or September.

Delays were expensive in loss of interest and earning power both to the shipowner and the shipper. But the crippling freights were inland, within Latin America. We have seen already how the high costs of transport had helped to maintain the native handicraft industry against imported manufactured goods, while at the same time pricing Latin American exports out of world markets. Carriage roads barely existed. The northern Republics—Colombia, Venezuela, Ecuador—had none at all in the '20s. There were no railways in Latin America before the middle of the century, and nearly everything had to be carried on the backs of mules, sometimes of men. The waggon road between Mexico City and Vera Cruz, the main point of entry for all manufactured goods, for the machinery for the mines and cotton factories, 'would in any other country be called the bed of a mountain stream, so rough and jagged was its surface'. Brantz Mayer, who as United States Secretary of Legation, had had to travel up the royal highway in 1841, described the roads down to Mexico City, on the other side of the range, as unique in the world—

They were gullies, washed into the mountain side by the rains; filled, here and there, with stones and branches; dammed up, to turn the water, by mounds a couple of feet high—and thus, gradually serpentining to the foot of the declivity. You may readily imagine that there was no such thing as *rolling* down with our rapid motion over such a ravine. We literally *jumped* from dam to dam, and rock to rock. . . .[1]

Even on the plains of Argentina mud and dust could be axle deep in winter or summer. In Corrientes, Robertson reminded his readers, the operations and movements of his troops of carts were totally unlike the business of Messrs Pickford and Company in the United Kingdom: 'Ours might be more aptly compared to the dragging of heavy artillery through a difficult and harassing country'.[2] Woodbine Parish remembered seeing, in the streets of Buenos Aires, mire so deep that the oxen could not draw the country carts through it, while the animals, unable to extract themselves, were left to die and rot in the swamp.[3] Four hundred pounds was as much as a mule could carry, though the average was nearer 250. The freight of a single mule from Vera Cruz to the capital in 1824 was £8. 10s.[4] It cost between £4 and £6 to take two hundredweight of goods from Santa Marta, on the coast, up to Bogotá in the early '20s; European manufactures, often of very inferior quality, fetched extravagant prices—over £3 for a hat or a pair of boots, £6 for a coat of inferior cloth and £12 for super-fine cloth, £2 for a dozen common glass tumblers or as many poor-quality cups and saucers.[5]

Capital, credit, insurance, freights made Latin America, even at the best of times, an uncertain and expensive market. This was not an absolute disqualification since most of the more distant overseas markets shared the same problems, and Latin America, particularly in textiles, could still offer a comfortable business for a limited number of solid, experienced houses. But the continent had little, after 1825, to offer to newcomers, and even those who had been in the business for a long time were under pressure to look for better opportunities elsewhere. A central factor in the withdrawal of so

---

[1] Mayer, *Mexico*, p. 36.
[2] Robertson, *South America*, I, 183.
[3] Parish, *Buenos Ayres*, p. 42.
[4] Mackenzie's report on Mexico, 24 July 1824: Humphreys, *Consular Reports*, p. 320.   [5] Hall, *Colombia*, pp. 194, 152.

many of the remaining British houses was the insecurity of life and property, the political instability which, for the first decades of independence, seemed endemic in Brazil and the new Republics. Even a profitable trade could not compensate for the sacrifice of life or limb, while the profit itself might be cut off at a moment's notice by the arrival of a revolutionary army, the closing of communications, a collapse of local prosperity, the drafting of men and the destruction of export crops. Each of the Latin American nations suffered more or less severely from civil or inter-American wars, some for decades, Argentina for twenty years, Mexico for thirty. A British consul, reporting from Mexico in the early '60s, described how civil war had 'entirely destroyed the former path of trade, already obstructed by the decrease in the power of consumption in a country whose people are occupied with destroying instead of producing'. It was more difficult than ever to find the means of paying for the few articles of necessity imported. Total ruin, Kelly added, had been avoided only by the natural resources of the country and by the introduction of considerable amounts of foreign capital into the mines, and it was doubtful whether this investment could continue. Many of the inland towns in his part of Mexico were completely deserted and others reduced to ruins; the male population had been compelled to take up arms behind some political adventurer or common highwayman and to live, in turn, off pillage from the few honest working people who remained.[1]

Full political stability was never achieved in some of the smaller Republics. Even in the larger, although a few British mercantile houses might continue to do a reasonable business in the capitals and ports, they were reluctant to set up in trade in the interior. Religious differences, although normally tolerated, could lead to trouble, and incidents like the expulsion of an English merchant from Guadalajara (Mexico) at twenty-four hours' notice for speaking 'too freely' about the Church, or the public burning of Mr Wheelwright's Bibles along with a heap of immoral and indecent pamphlets in the main square of Quillota (Chile), gave Englishmen cause to wonder whether they might not be happier elsewhere, perhaps in their own colonies among people whom they knew and understood. The difficulty of obtaining justice from primitive magistrates and petty despots in the interior, the avarice created by any display of wealth, the risks in remitting

[1] Kelly's report on Mazatlan for 1861, P.P. 1863, LXX, 235.

returns through bandit-infested territory, all acted as substantial disincentives to inland settlement at a far remove from the comforting epaulettes and English cocked hats in the streets of Rio, Montevideo or Buenos Aires. The Robertson brothers, as enterprising a pair as ever made money in provincial Argentina, only 'began to breathe' as they rode through the streets of Buenos Aires. Expelled by the dictator Francia from Paraguay, imprisoned in Corrientes by the local police chief, in danger from Artigas's gauchos or the Indians, always an object of surveillance and suspicion, their most delightful sensation in Buenos Aires was being a 'nobody' in a city of a hundred thousand:

> Give us London or Paris, in the old world, and Buenos Ayres, Lima, or Mexico in the new, in which to refrigerate our overheated spirits, after the hot vapour-bath, especially in troublous times, of inland society.[1]

A bold and lucky man could make a fortune from the fluctuations in trade occasioned by political instability. A few, like the Robertsons themselves, did just that. The majority preferred the lower but safer returns of a stable society. An early-Victorian merchant looked for a standard 4% return on his capital; in addition, he required a 'fair' reward for his trouble and risk. He knew his trade, and he could judge the alternatives open to him. Latin America, because of its political and economic instability, its depreciating currency, was not a good risk. The Brazilian milreis, which stood at 6s. in 1815, was down to about 2s. 6d. in the early '30s; the Argentine peso, at 3s. 9d. in the '20s, was worth 7d. at the end of the next decade. Both went lower. The profits on a consignment of manufactured goods might be wiped out by depreciation long before a merchant found an opportunity to remit to the United Kingdom. In Latin America, the best profits went to the man who smuggled most or paid up generously to those in authority. Everyone took part, Britons included. A Venezuelan finance minister estimated that out of the $200 million of imports during the first sixteen years of independence, $129½ million were smuggled.[2] In Mexico, the contraband trade was carried on 'with

---

[1] Robertson, *South America*, II, 70-2.
[2] Edward B. Eastwick, *Venezuela; Sketches of Life in a South American Republic* (London, 1868), p. 60. The information seems to have been compiled, so far as possible, from the published exports of other nations to Venezuela.

the utmost audacity'. MacGregor considered that the $8 million difference in the early '40s between exports ($20 million) and imports ($12 million) was fully covered by smuggling.[1]

With so many smuggled goods on the market, it was often impossible to offer competitive prices through the official channels. William Parish Robertson described how he himself was drawn into the contraband trade at Buenos Aires. In one instance, a valuable cargo of linens arrived from Hamburg to his consignment. A high tariff was in force at the time, with venal officials, so that a flourishing contraband made the profitable disposal of the cargo, at full duties, inconceivable. Robertson was approached by a native merchant who offered to land the whole at half duties, but since this was smuggling he felt obliged to decline. The merchant then offered to buy the cargo as it stood on board, receiving it in the usual and legal way into lighters. Robertson agreed, and a few days later watched his linens, under cartloads of grass, entering Buenos Aires. On another occasion a large vessel came in with orders to load jerked beef for Havana. The export of jerked beef was prohibited at the time, and Robertson spent many days petitioning fruitlessly for a licence. One day, walking home at the dinner hour through the hot and deserted streets, he was beckoned into a shop where he discovered the first clerk of the Secretary of State for the Interior:

'Now, Mr. Robertson,' said he with an easy nod, 'I know whence you come, and what you have been about. You have been to the Fort [the Government offices] and you want a special licence to load a cargo of beef. Well, send us in a dozen of your good old port here, and you shall have your licence.' I nodded assent, withdrew, and—led away by considering how little could be lost, and how much might be gained by the transaction,—I became an agent in 'bribery and corruption.' and 'treated' the first clerk to *two* dozen of prime old port.[2]

Corruption at this level was easy enough. But there is no doubt that foreign traders would have welcomed a safe, open trade, even if they lost the windfall profits of successful contraband. Contraband undermined a trade. It took the certainty out of it. It could destroy an honest trade altogether. And it was not something in which a

---

[1] MacGregor's report on Mexico, P.P. 1846, XLVIII, 445-6.
[2] Robertson, *South America*, III, 152-3, 156.

foreigner had the advantage. The volume of contraband into Latin America during the first decades of independence undoubtedly forced many English traders out of business and persuaded others, for moral or practical reasons, to abandon trading in circumstances for which they had slight taste or expertise.

PART II

1860-1914

CHAPTER IV

The New Trade

THREE circumstances, in particular, held back the development of
Latin America's overseas trade in the first half of the nineteenth
century—sparse population, political instability, and poor to non-
existent communications. Francis Clare Ford introduced his first
report on the commercial condition of Argentina, 30 October 1866,
with the sensible observation that

> Scantiness of population, and deficiency of means of internal
> communication are the two pressing drawbacks to the develop-
> ment of the Republic; and until a decided tide of immigration
> sets in, and the energies of the native population are diverted
> from politics and fighting to peaceful pursuits, and until diffi-
> culties are removed from the path of such foreigners as may be
> willing and capable of devoting their time and money to the
> construction of railways, but little prospect can be held out of
> any material change for the better in the condition of the country.[1]

In practice, improvements in each direction, population, politics or
communication, encouraged developments in others. The railways,
commercially effective in Brazil and Argentina after the early '60s,
opened up land for settlement and brought the products of settlement to market. Immigrants, attracted by the opportunities offered
by the railways, settled the land and provided the traffic on which
the railways survived and expanded. Political stability, the pre-
condition of investment, was reinforced in turn by the unifying
effect of railways. The failure of General Mitre's attempt to over-

[1] P.P. 1867, LXIX, 289.

throw the new President, Avellaneda, on 24 September 1874, was, as Consul Joel said at the time, a useful lesson to old-style politicians that the arts of peace had become more attractive to the Argentine people than 'their once morbid desire for violent political changes'. In one day the Central Argentine Railway conveyed 2,600 soldiers, their arms and military train from Rosario to Córdoba, a distance of 246 miles; it was this, together with the energy of the government in reinforcing General Roca and furnishing supplies, which enabled Roca to march against and defeat General Arredondo, dealing a final blow to the revolution.[1] Civil war, which in Hutchinson's day (the early '60s) had been 'looked upon as an indigenous institution' in Argentina, and was still in the '70s regarded, at least among foreign diplomats, as 'a permanent feature in South America generally', was no longer perennial on the River Plate. Joel's superior at the Buenos Aires Legation, F. R. St John, observed how revolts in Argentina were not only less frequent than in the past, but less intensified in form. 'The wielder of the long knife and lasso', he added, 'has almost ceased to play a prominent part in the political history of the country, and the "gaucho" of the Pampas must needs give way before authority supported by the disciplined soldier and his breech-loading rifle.'[2] With the growth of the Argentine economy, with the inflow of a-political immigrants, with the relative decline of the gaucho class and the spread of railways, the disruptive effects of the violent political battles of the past were substantially reduced. The economy now carried itself along with its own momentum, and politics, even if they remained disturbed, could in future have far less effect on economic development.

Of even greater importance for the long-term economic development of Latin America was the effect of railway construction in opening up the interior of Latin America for the production of foodstuffs and industrial raw materials. Europe was already outrunning its own resources and traditional suppliers both for feeding its expanding population and for meeting the needs of new and massive industrialization. Latin America had met some part of these needs even before the middle of the century. The import/export trade, though slow, was never stagnant, and Brazilian cotton, sugar and coffee, Argentine wool, Cuban and Chilean copper,

[1] Report on Rosario for 1874, P.P. 1875, LXXVI, 315-16.
[2] Report on the Argentine Republic for 1874, P.P. 1876, LXXIII, 179.

Peruvian wool, guano and nitrates were among the products which had provided an element of expansion at least since the '30s, and in some cases before. Brazil in 1831 was supplying 11% of British imports of cotton. In 1850, Britain was taking 5% of her expanded demand for cotton and sugar from Brazil, 27% of her hides; 40% of her hides came from Argentina and 2% of her wool, while a further 4% of the wool was Peruvian.[1] But if Brazil and the Republics were to enter world markets competitively, on a large scale, they had to tap the interior. On mule-back or ox cart, this was virtually impossible outside a narrow radius of the main seaports. In the '30s the cost of moving a ton of goods from Salta, in the interior of Argentina, to Buenos Aires was thirteen times that from Buenos Aires to Liverpool.[2] To fit out a large Missouri waggon carrying about 5,000 lb between St Louis and Chihuahua (Mexico), cost $1,200 to $1,300; each waggon had its teamster at $25 a month and fifteen or twenty extra mules; a waggon train of twenty had a waggonmaster at $100 a month, and the round trip, Indians and river fords permitting, took ten months. This was in 1852. Thirty years later, when the railways reached Chihuahua, American goods flooded the market at slight advance over prices in the North.[3] The arrival of the Central Railway at La Laguna, in the States of Durango and Coahuila, made it the principal cotton-growing area of Mexico. Railways helped to create the great coffee-producing states of southern Brazil. They opened up the grain, wine and sugar production of Argentina. They were as important to the progress of Latin America's most traditional industry, mining. With only mules, donkeys or llamas to bring the ore down to the coast, the cost of carriage was so heavy as entirely to prohibit the export of any but the richest Bolivian ores; no copper could be sent down for shipment under 70%; no tin ore at less than 55 to 60%.[4] The Argentine mines, high in the mountains on the west, could never pay their way. The rich silver ores of the Mejicana range, 16,000 or 17,000 ft above sea level, had to be brought more than 10,000 ft down to the village of Famatina for smelting, after which the bars were sent to the nearest station on the Córdoba line, in 1880 still

[1] William Woodruff, *Impact of Western Man: A Study of Europe's Role in the World Economy 1750-1960* (London, 1966), Table VII/2.
[2] James R. Scobie, *Revolution on the Pampas* (Austin, 1964), p. 11.
[3] Frederick A. Ober, *Travels in Mexico* (London, 1887), pp. 582-3.
[4] Nugent's report on Arica for 1871, P.P. 1872, LVIII, 584.

F

over 100 miles away. The cost of carriage over the easier stretch, from Famatina to England, 'nearly equals that of the extraction and rough smelting of the ore'.[1]

There was nothing uniform about the economic impact of railway construction in Latin America. Gran Colombia, with formidable mountains which made it easier, said Captain Cochrane, for the inhabitants of Cumana, Barcelona and other distant parts of the Republic to go on a pilgrimage to Mecca than journey to their own capital, had still only an exiguous railway system by 1914. Argentina, on the other hand, with 20,726 miles, was operating one of the most complete railway systems in the world. Railway construction had a dramatic effect on the Argentine economy, and the railways themselves were central both to Britain's leadership in Argentine overseas trade, and to the unique position of the Argentine market, in relation to the rest of Latin America, in the decade before 1914. Argentine progress even over the first decade of railway development and mass immigration was remarkable. Between 1862 and 1872, the revenue of the Republic rose from about £1 million to over £3 million. Argentine bonds in 1862 were without a quotation on the European exchanges; by 1872, the 6% bonds were quoted at 98. In 1862 only 5,000 immigrants arrived; in 1872 over 40,000. Only 18 miles of railway were open in 1862; by 1872 there were over 700, and many more under construction.[2] Grain was first exported in the '70s, but as the railways opened up the wheat lands, Argentina, formerly an importer of flour, became over a couple of decades one of the world's great wheat exporters. Argentine wheat exports in 1880 amounted barely to half a kilo of wheat per head of population; in 1885 the figure was 5 kilos, in 1889 117 kilos, and in 1890 259 kilos.[3] The Central Córdoba Railway reached Tucumán in 1876; the area under sugar cane cultivation rose from 5,700 acres in 1874 to 180,200 acres in 1912.[4] The wine traffic on the Central Argentine Railway began in 1878; the acreage of vines, in Mendoza and San Juan in particular, rose from 9,200 in 1878 to 306,100 acres in 1909.[5]

[1] Egerton's report on Argentina, 10 April 1881, P.P. 1881, LXXIX, 181.
[2] Joel's report, Rosario, 31 January 1873, P.P. 1873, LXV, 11.
[3] Gastrell's report on the Economic Position of the Argentine Republic, 1892, P.P. 1893-4, XCII, 137.
[4] Mackie's report on Buenos Aires for 1912-13, P.P. 1914, LXXXIX, 540-1.
[5] Mackie's report on Buenos Aires for 1911, P.P. 1912-13, XCIV, 141.

Other developments contributed to the same ends. The new bulk export products required proper handling facilities at railway stations and docks; increased imports, though less of a problem because less in bulk, were still difficult or impossible to handle at such ports as existed in the middle of the nineteenth century. Until the end of the '80s Buenos Aires was an open roadstead, and steamers of any size were compelled to lie ten miles out to get sufficient depth of water. Montevideo, lacking a breakwater, was open to the *pamperos*, winds from the south and south-east which caused serious damage to shipping. At Valparaiso in 1900 all the shipping still anchored in the open bay, dangerously exposed to heavy winds and seas from the north; cargo was generally unloaded into lighters at a rate, for most sailing-vessels, not exceeding 60 or 70 tons a day. Vera Cruz, the main port of Mexico, was an exposed anchorage with a total absence of port facilities, so that the cost of handling for many classes of imports even when the ship was alongside was larger than the freight from the United Kingdom. Santos, already by the mid-'80s the second port in Brazil and the outlet for the rich coffee province of São Paulo, consisted simply of 'a few ill-constructed jetties, projecting from fetid and unsightly riverside mud-banks'.[1] The discharging of vessels at Rio at the turn of the century was entirely by lighter. Goods were transferred no less that four times in the course of landing: from ship to lighter, from lighter to trollies on the Customs quay, from trollies to elevators, from elevators to deposit, each time accumulating heavy charges.

Montevideo, Buenos Aires, Valparaiso, Vera Cruz, Santos and Rio were the leading ports of the Continent. In smaller ports and for the lesser Republics conditions could be far worse. The Pacific coast of Guatemala, for its whole length, was 'a surf-beaten beach without a single harbour'. Bolivia's two ports of entry were Antofagasta (Chile) and Mollendo (Peru). Antofagasta was a difficult port to land at, where all goods had to be transferred to launches; the route up to Bolivia was notorious for theft first at the launches, then at the Customs House, then on the railway, and finally at Oruro, the Bolivian terminus. Mollendo had an equally bad reputation both for safety in landing and for theft; huge rollers struck the rocks throughout the year and work had been known to be suspended for as many as forty days out of a possible sixty.

[1] Leay's report on Vera Cruz, P.P. 1903, LXXVIII, 261.

The goods then lay on the wharf, unprotected and at the mercy of anyone who chose to help himself; it was rare for a crate to reach Bolivia untampered with. As an illustration of what this could mean for imports, Vice-Consul Moore calculated for Sucre that a felt hat, costing four shillings in London, 'will cost here, in round figures, for freight etc. 4s 4d.; duty 40 per cent, 1s. 8d.; total 10s.; and on account of the great risk of its being damaged, stolen or lost, and allowing for interest during 14 months at 10 per cent, it is sold at 15s. wholesale and £1 retail, the actual price'.[1]

Towards the end of the nineteenth century, substantial sums were invested in modern port facilities, above all to cope with the export of Argentine grain and Brazilian coffee. The new port of Buenos Aires, the Puerto Madero, opened its first docks in 1890. Rosario, La Plata, and Bahia Blanca offered modern services from the '80s and '90s. Santos by 1908 had two miles of quay and a further half-mile in prospect. Elaborate docks were under construction at Rio and Montevideo in the first decade of this century, and both were in operation before the war.

The problem was to keep up with the needs of a rapidly expanding yet fluctuating production for export. Overloading of the railways and overcrowding at the ports were chronic complaints for every major producer. It is difficult to see how they could have been otherwise. The rapid expansion of agricultural and pastoral production was constantly overtaking the transport resources available for movement to the ports, and even if the railways were able to provide the rolling stock, the point of blockage was simply transferred to the ports where an accumulation of waggons waiting to be unloaded into ships blocked the docks and left shortages of rolling stock throughout the country districts. Even total control by the State was no answer. The Australian railways, under state ownership, experienced precisely the same problems of inadequate grain storage facilities at the stations or docks and of insufficient lines or rolling stock. Canadian railways were better organized, but in every case the fluctuations in production made forward-planning extraordinarily difficult. It was calculated for the early 1900s that shipping business at Buenos Aires was increasing at the rate of 30% per annum, which meant that whatever improvements were made to the port of Buenos Aires itself, there was no hope of a real

---

[1] Moore's report on Sucre (Bolivia) for 1907, P.P. 1908, CIX, 558.

solution short of developing several entirely new relief ports.[1] The scale of the problem is evident from the kind of calculations which had to be made for the movement of Argentine grain exports. *The Times* Buenos Aires Correspondent, estimating the quantities available for export from the 1911-12 harvest, calculated that for the early harvest (wheat, linseed, oats, barley) for which shipments began in December, some 3,800 ships, with an average loading of 1,500 tons, would be needed to carry Argentine grain to Europe. Nearly half as many might be needed for the maize harvest some months later.[2] The extension of Argentine grain production over a wider area of Argentina tended to iron out the extreme fluctuations in production of the early years, but locusts, hailstorms, rain, frost and drought could still play havoc with the best predictions. Taking the extremes, Argentine railways had to handle 237,865 tons of wheat for export in 1887, 22,806 in 1889, 1,608,200 in 1894, 101,000 in 1897, 1,929,676 in 1900, 644,908 in 1902 and 2,304,724 in 1904. Imports suffered, too, since a blockage at ports reacted on trade in any direction, and often itself added new dimensions to the problem. The Argentine Minister of Public Works explained that one of the reasons for the serious delay in transporting the wine production of San Juan to Buenos Aires was that the Argentine Great Western Railway, facing a 40% increase in production over the previous year, had twelve locomotives and a number of waggons sitting on a steamer outside Buenos Aires, which had been waiting its turn for more than a fortnight to enter the port to discharge.[3]

By the time the first portion of the extensive new port works at Rio were completed in 1911-12, well after the estimated date, the volume of imports had increased to such an extent that the docks were already inadequate to handle the shipping. Unfortunately, despite elaborate planning and heavy investment, congestion remained a problem for which no real answer could be found. It was not uncommon, in 1911-12, to see over 100 ships lying for weeks at a time in the outer roads at Buenos Aires awaiting berths. Further docks costing in the region of £5 million were contracted for, and other ambitious schemes were on hand for vastly increased harbour facilities at Mar del Plata, La Plata and Bahia Blanca,

[1] *The Economist*, 24 March 1906, 494.
[2] *The Times*, South American Supplement, 26 December 1911, 5c.
[3] *The Economist*, 9 June 1906, 962.

including the revival of an abandoned scheme to connect Buenos Aires with the deep water of the River Paraná by a canal, 30 miles in length, at the cost of something like £10 million. In Brazil conditions were as bad. Dock accommodation was inadequate at all the principal ports, and the delays to shipping were frustrating and expensive to importers and exporters alike. H. S. Birch, commenting on the situation in 1914, described how

at Pernambuco both passengers and goods are slung in cages, by means of the ships' derricks, into lighters, there being no docks. At Bahia there are shallow water docks, and deep water docks are now under construction. At Rio de Janeiro there are no docks, but only a wharf, which cannot cope with all the business of the port. Consequently many ships have to discharge into lighters in the bay. At Santos there is also a wharf, but as this is a private concession the dues are very heavy. At no port in the whole of South America is there one-sixth of the dock area at Liverpool.[1]

All the same, the modernization of Brazil and the Republics after the middle of the nineteenth century was bound to effect substantial changes in the volume and character of British trade. The construction of the railways, the opening up of new districts both agricultural and mining, the provision of docks and storage facilities for the new export products, the introduction of sanitation, water supplies, gas and electricity into newly prosperous communities, the development of new industries—all these, and more, created a market, in the larger Republics, far greater than anything dreamed of in the first half of the nineteenth century. Latin America, from its status as a slow consumer of British textiles, had become a substantial, expanding market for every kind of manufactured product, iron and steel as well as cloth, and for British coal to drive the railways, the mills and the shipping which visited Latin American ports. In 1818, 85·5% of British exports to Argentina were textiles, 3·9% fuel and metal manufactures. In 1858-62 textiles still accounted for 75·3%, with 11·2% for fuel and metal manufactures. But by 1886-90, at the height of the railway construction boom, textiles were down to 29·6%, and metal manufactures and fuel up to 49·8%.[2]

[1] Birch's report on Brazil for 1912-13, P.P. 1914-16, LXXI, 186.
[2] H. S. Ferns, 'Investment and Trade between Britain and Argentina in the Nineteenth Century', *Economic History Review*, 2nd ser. 3 (1950), 210.

This merely reflected a general redistribution of emphasis in British exports to all parts of the world during the nineteenth and early twentieth centuries. Textiles, which had formed 67% of Britain's total exports in 1830, accounted for only 34% by 1913. By contrast, metal and engineering exports had risen from 11 to 27%, and coal from 1 to 10%.[1] Again, for textiles this was a percentage decline, not absolute. Textiles were still overwhelmingly the most important commodity group in British exports just before the First World War. But metal manufactures and some of the new industrial products like chemicals and motor cars had made remarkable progress. The changing shape of British industry can be seen from Table III.

Table III
British Exports of Manufactures by Commodity Groups
(£ million)

	1880	1890	1899	1913
Iron and steel	21·5	24·3	19·5	37·5
Non-ferrous metals	4·3	6·7	4·7	7·7
Chemicals	8·0	11·6	12·6	24·0
Non-metalliferous materials	2·0	3·3	2·4	5·3
Miscellaneous materials	4·4	5·4	4·3	8·8
Metal manufactures	14·4	21·8	31·1	62·8
Ships and Railway material	9·8	17·0	16·0	24·3
Cars and cycles	—	—	0·7	7·6
Drink and tobacco	2·3	3·2	4·2	9·7
Textiles and clothing	119·8	124·7	109·9	197·7
Cultural and entertainment goods	2·3	2·8	3·5	8·4
Other finished goods	3·5	4·7	6·3	11·6

Source: S. B. Saul, 'The Export Economy 1870-1914', *Yorkshire Bulletin of Economic and Social Research*, 17 (1965), 13.

[1] E. A. G. Robinson, 'The Changing Structure of the British Economy', *Economic Journal*, LXIV (1954), 460 (Table IV).

CHAPTER V

Local Industry and Competition

TRADITIONALLY, much of the academic discussion of relative trade performance has been Eurocentric, with North America introduced as a new, competitive element in the last decades before 1914. Yet what was equally and often more important to the British traders at the time was the extent to which overseas customers were furnishing their own needs. The competitiveness of local industry and its ability to supply its own markets against foreign competition were the first points to establish in opening a trade.

In the conventional wisdom, Latin America developed no systematic protective tariffs before 1914; tariffs existed for revenue purposes, not protection, and without the benefit of protection, progress towards industrialization was insignificant. Yet it would have been surprising if the politicians of the new Republics had shown themselves insensitive to the need to protect existing local interests against foreign competition. Later in the century some statesmen subscribed, at least while out of office, to the *laissez-faire* economics of the day. But in the first decades after 1808 there was nothing disreputable about protective tariffs. The Spanish monopoly was broken and the barriers associated with that monopoly were removed with enthusiasm. But this did not mean that the markets were thrown open without restriction to every variety of foreign produce. General San Martín was careful to place a limit to any promise of access to Peruvian markets. If the campaign against the Spanish viceroy were successful, he told Britain's senior naval officer on the West Coast, Peru's ports would remain open to British commerce and 'the regulations of the duties shall be such as may prosper it in an evident manner *consulting the good of the inhabitants*'.[1] In the event, the provisional commercial code, published on 8 October 1821 at Lima as a first act of newly independent Peru, established a 20% revenue duty on the value of all imported goods; for protective purposes, all manufactured goods which might injure the industry of the country were to pay double duty.[2]

The problem for the new Latin American governments was to protect local interests and prevent distress, while at the same time meeting their pressing need for revenue from the only source readily available, taxation on foreign trade. Revenue considerations were often paramount, as they were for the Mexican national and provincial governments of the turbulent '30s, '40s, and '50s when, in spite of prohibitions or high nominal duties, privileged entry was sold to foreign merchants for cash. The rate of protective duty might be set too low, as it proved to be in San Martín's provisional code for Peru. But there is no doubt of the protective intention of the early tariffs, even if, at this stage, governments rarely felt it their duty to go beyond the protection of *existing* industries to the creation of conditions under which *new* industries might develop. The Peruvian tariff was revised upwards several times in the early '20s. The Commercial Code of 1826 set a 30% revenue duty on cotton, woollen and hardware goods such as were not produced locally. On imports regarded as 'prejudicial to the agriculture and industry of the State', the level was deliberately prohibitive—90% on sugar, *tocuyos*, baizes, hats, boots, shoes, saddlery, soap, candles and furniture; 100% on spirits; 114% on wheat.[3]

Precisely the same was true of other substantial markets, in Chile, Mexico and Argentina. In Mexico the moderately liberal tariff of 15 December 1821 was followed almost immediately by a protectionist reaction. Baur explains how within a month foreign flour imports were prohibited to protect the Mexican corn and wheat growers of the northern states:

---

[1] [My italics.] General San Martín to Captain William Henry Shirreff, R.N., Valparaiso, 7 July 1820: Graham and Humphreys, *The Navy and South America*, p. 305.

[2] W. B. Stevenson, *Twenty Years' Residence in South America* (London, 1825), III, 424.

[3] Mathew, 'Anglo-Peruvian Commercial and Financial Relations', pp. 50-1.

By May, 1824, the policy makers, now thorough protectionists, added rice, sugar, sugar cane, coffee, most green vegetables, rye, beans, and ham, bacon, rope, all types of leather, including shoes, and many more metals. Now, almost all potential agricultural and industrial goods were theoretically protected, but on November 16, 1827, one could count 54 prohibited import goods.[1]

Even under such conditions a few fortunes were made by British importers of the finer quality cloths, but William Graham, a Glasgow cotton spinner and weaver, was speaking for British manufacturers in general when he confessed himself, in the early '30s, 'afraid of the Mexican market from the extent of the duties'.[2] Certainly the coarser broadcloths, carpeting, serges, sack cloth and *sarapes* had been prohibited imports from the mid-'20s, and from 1837, possibly earlier, low-grade bleached or unbleached cottons were similarly prohibited, while heavy duties were leviable on cottons of superior quality and on all coloured goods.[3]

The Argentines, although without any extensive local industry to protect, were as sensitive to the demands of local handicraft workers. The first general tariff of 1 January 1822 established deliberately protective duties on a range of products—furniture, carriages, shoes, saddles, clothing, brandy, liquors and caña, etc.— which were manufactured locally or in the provinces, and the level of these duties continued to be raised throughout the '20s to provide more effective protection. The Rosas tariff of 1835 was totally protective. In the provinces, local taxation was similarly protective. The Córdoba tariff of 1822 levied 16% on all imported goods competing with domestic production, compared with a normal rate of 8%. In Entre Rios, by the tariff of 3 October 1821, imported shoes and wearing apparel paid 20%, compared with a normal rate of 4%; by the tariff of February 1836 a long list of manufactures were declared prohibited imports, including certain textiles and leather goods, footwear, hardware. The Tucumán 6% duty of 1826 was raised to 30% in 1834 for furniture, shoes, clothing, hats,

---

[1] John E. Baur, 'The Evolution of a Mexican Foreign Trade Policy, 1821-1828', *The Americas*, XIX (1962-3), 245.
[2] Minutes of Evidence, *Report of the Select Committee on Manufactures, Commerce and Shipping*, P.P. 1833, VI, Q.5558.
[3] Cody, 'British Interest in the Independence of Mexico', p. 277; Lionel Carden's report on the Cotton Manufacturing Industry in Mexico, 1898, P.P. 1898, XCIII, 485.

saddles and other manufactured goods produced within the province. The importation of footwear, clothing and certain varieties of textiles was entirely prohibited by the provincial government of Corrientes in 1831.[1]

A responsible government could hardly have behaved otherwise. Even Britain at the time was operating an extensive protective system for certain of her manufactures: 40% on linens of all sorts, 30% on lace, manufactured leather, brass manufactures, painted china or porcelain ware, and so on down the scale. British subjects in Latin America may have been indignant at the futility of some of the protective measures; they were not surprised by them. The new commercial regulations of Chile in October 1822 set duties which in many cases amounted to a prohibition. The fault in the regulations was not in their intention. Protection of local manufactures was understandable if Chilean resources could substitute for prohibited or high-priced imports. But there were many reasons, over and above cheap foreign imports, for the failure of Latin American manufacturing to progress beyond the handicraft stage. Because a man in Santiago had actually made a pair of stockings in a day, Maria Graham complained, no more stockings were to be imported, so that the ladies must learn to knit or go barefoot, for it was hardly to be expected that the single pair per day would satisfy the needs even of the capital:

> As there are literally no Chilean cabinet-makers, the prohibitions [in the 1822 regulations] of foreign chairs and tables will send the young ladies back to squatting on the estrada; and as it must be some years, perhaps centuries, before they will raise and weave silk here, or manufacture muslins, we shall have them clad in their ancient woollen manteaus; and future travellers will praise the pretty savages, instead of delighting in the society of well-dressed and well-bred young ladies.

Mrs Graham felt that the scarce labour resources of Chile were best employed in tilling the ground, digging the mines and manning the ships; 'it grieves one to see a parcel of rules well enough for a ready-civilised country in Europe—where the niggard earth yields not wherewithal to trade, and all must be laboured and fashioned, and the gold and silver must be made with men's hands—adopted here, when every circumstance is diametrically

[1] Burgin, *Argentine Federalism*, pp. 70-5, 134-5, 237-42.

opposite'.[1] There was a certain amount of truth in what she said, and it came to be appreciated more readily in Latin America first as demand for Latin American produce developed in Europe so that resources were profitably diverted to producing for export, and then as prices of European manufactured goods continued to fall so that Latin American industry, except in certain well-recognized fields, became too expensive a luxury to sustain.

In general, the issue between Protection and Free Trade was not fully resolved until the last quarter of the nineteenth century, and even then not openly admitted to be so. The Republics began as Protectionists, but in a spirit of revolt against the monopoly protectionist tradition imposed on them by Spain. Each of the early governments came to recognize the need to protect elements of their local industries, but they did so with more or less enthusiasm and effect. Protective clauses were added, almost as an afterthought, to tariffs designed primarily for revenue purposes. There was a noticeable cooling-off in enthusiasm for protected local handicraft industries in the middle decades of the century as they showed themselves incapable of keeping up with expanded home demand. Simultaneously, each of the Republics was feeling the pressure for more revenue, and for each, governed as it was by a landed oligarchy with a rooted distaste for direct taxation, the only obvious source of increased revenue was taxation on a larger import trade. Out of a total government revenue of $14,833,904 in 1870, duties on Argentine imports accounted for $12,092,122 and exports $1,860,083; the remainder consisted of Customs' storage receipts, post office revenue, dividends on the Government's shares in the Central Argentine Railway, and $27,334 of 'sundries'. A system of federal inland revenue was not developed in Argentina until as late as 1891, and in the mid-'90s the Customs House was accounting for between 70 and 80% of federal government revenues; about 50% of federal revenue was supplied by import duties in 1913. For Brazil and Mexico at the turn of the century import duties were averaging between 45 and 50% of federal revenue. For a small republic like Ecuador the proportion might be as high as 75% up to the First World War.

Whatever enthusiasm there may have been, in theory, for economic liberalism, for *laissez faire*, for free trade and classical economics among mid-century Latin American intellectuals and

[1] Graham, *Chile*, pp. 289-90.

politicians, trade could never be free while so much importance continued to be attached to import duties as revenue producers. Under the shelter of revenue tariffs, local industries took root. Their growth was promoted further by an artificial protection derived accidentally from the depreciation of most Latin American currencies in the last decades of the century, with its corollary of increased prices for foreign imports. Once local industries had established themselves, politicians found it as difficult to be a party to their destruction as to that of the handicraft industries of the independence period. The dilemma emerged time and again in the apologia of Latin American politicians in the '80s and '90s. Many continued to see the theoretical attractions of free trade while finding it inapplicable to their own circumstances. Porfirio Diaz's Finance Minister, Matías Romero, defending some modest tariff reductions on Mexican imports in 1892, put all the arguments in favour of Free Trade—the effect of tariffs in raising prices for consumers to the advantage of a few industrialists; the desirability of encouraging production in areas where Mexico had special advantages, like minerals and metals; the fallacy of developing 'artificial' industries dependent entirely on protective tariffs; the need to redistribute scarce capital and labour to products such as coffee which could command a world market. But, as he said, the government could not carry through so wholesome a doctrine. A sudden change in the economy could bring both immediate ruin to the capital already employed in manufacturing industry and mass unemployment, even if only temporary, to all those engaged in it.[1] The dilemma was summed up in what a British Secretary of Legation described as the 'cautious observations' of General Roca, President of the Argentine Republic, to the representatives of local manufacturing industries, 25 July 1899:

We are not in the position of one of the oldest and richest of monarchies, which, having arrived at its last economic evolution, may boldly proclaim free trade. Nor are we in the same position as the richest and most powerful of republics in the world, which, having given a great impulse to its industries, can afford to liberate itself from foreign demand, and entrench itself behind absolute protectionism. In this respect our condition must be

[1] Quoted in Daniel Cosío Villegas (ed.), *Historia Moderna de Mexico. El Porfiriato: La Vida Económica* (Mexico, 1965), I, 475-6.

that of the other nations of the earth. We have our own traditions
and an economic system which we cannot suddenly renounce
because under its influence very valuable interests have sprung
up, and because 1,000,000 of men ['This is a somewhat exaggerated calculation'—Sect. of Legation] earn their living under
that régime. National industry, which is mainly the result of
protection laws that have been in force for years, is to-day a
great power. It represents considerable capital and labour, both
of which the Government must respect because they are incorporated with the life and development of the country. But, as
you yourselves recognise, it will be necessary to moderate the
system and to remove whatever is exaggerated therein. Protection should be reasonable and fair, otherwise interests equally
worthy of respect would be injured, and industry would be
driven into wrong channels to its own detriment.[1]

What, then, was the effect of all this, translated into tariffs?
Most of the Republics, at one time or another in the middle years
of the century, went through a phase of relatively free trade. The
commercial laws of Brazil, Consul Cowper reported from Pernambuco in February 1857, were 'extremely liberal', and indeed
throughout Brazilian legislation there was 'a mildness and absence
of severity well worthy of imitation'.[2] The Peruvian tariff was
particularly liberal in the mid-'30s. The Mexican tariffs of 1853
and 1856 marked a temporary abandonment of protection and a
removal of prohibitions. Argentine protectionism subsided with
the fall of the dictator Rosas; apart from the question of revenue,
the British vice-consul reported from Rosario for 1858 that there
was nothing that could prevent Argentina from adopting the most
liberal of tariffs, since her staple products, from the cattle farms,
were all exported and competed in no way with manufactured
imports.[3] The Colombian tariffs of 1861, developed during an
interval of Radical government, reduced protective duties and
aimed simply at revenue.[4]

[1] As translated and quoted by Clarke in his report on the Finances of
the Argentine Republic for 1898-9, P.P. 1900, XCII, 98.
[2] P.P. 1857 (Sess. 1), XVI, 447.
[3] P.P. 1859, XXX, 380.
[4] The contrasting elements in Colombian tariff policy have been
described by David Bushnell, 'Two Stages in Colombian Tariff Policy:
The Radical Era and the Return to Protection (1861-1885)', Inter-
American Economic Affairs, IX (1955), 3-23.

The liberal phase could not last long. Tariffs, raised to a protective level by successive increases intended for revenue, provided the conditions under which the Brazilian and Mexican cotton textile industries made substantial progress. The opening up of communications within Latin America exposed what was left of manufacturing in the interior—after the steady fall in prices for imported manufactures since the '20s—to the cold blast of foreign competition, and demands for protection could not be ignored. Certain of the products of the interior, like Argentine sugar and wine, which were not likely to develop to the point of export yet which could make a bid to supply the whole of home demand, could challenge foreign competition only under protection. World opinion, which had seemed in the '60s to be moving towards Free Trade, had returned to Protectionism, and for Latin Americans the tariff policies of their powerful North American neighbour supplied unanswerable arguments for the protection of infant industries. 'My ideas,' said Marcos Avellaneda, Argentine Finance Minister in 1893, 'have completely changed on this point.'

A few years ago I was an enthusiastic Free-trader and could not understand how Dr. Lopez, on returning to his native land, gave utterance to such enthusiastic Protectionist ideas. I am now convinced that he is right and that Protection must triumph. A young country like this requires Protection to give root to its nascent industries.[1]

The conversion to Protection was not complete. The importers, naturally, put up a spirited defence of low duties, but, as foreigners, their views carried little political weight; their Commercial Defence Leagues were no match for the industrial pressure groups—the Unión Industrial Argentina, the Associação Industrial in Brazil, the Sociedad de Fomento Fabril in Chile. The mass of consumers, and the Radicals and Socialists who spoke for them, protested against the inflated prices which the sugar monopolists of Brazil and Argentina were able to charge under the shelter of tariffs. In a country like Argentina, for which imports were still so essential in the decade before the First World War, high protective tariffs had a serious effect on the cost of living for the working class, and in doing so, reacted on Argentina's most pressing need, immigration. The Argentine Minister of Agriculture, in a memorandum to

[1] *The Economist*, 29 July 1893, 909.

the Minister of Finance in August 1903, pointed out how a combination of high import duties and overvaluations at the Customs
House had brought import duties, on average, to 52·4% in 1902.
Among the articles of prime necessity the rate for sugar was 123%,
vermicelli 58%, cotton tissues 34%, woollen articles 43%, petroleum 111%, salt 52%, boots 60%, cooking utensils 36%. High
import duties and excessive municipal and provincial taxation, the
Minister argued, had pushed up the cost of living in the Republic
to such an extent that it had become a serious barrier to immigration.[1] The cost of living in Brazil, in part as a result of protection,
rose by 306% between 1893 and 1920.[2]

This kind of consideration helped to delay a complete application of Protection. But there is no doubt that the greater part of
influential opinion in all the Republics was by now converted. The
failure to take industrialization further before 1914 owed little
to *laissez-faire* economics. Where an industry showed signs of
developing, where a promising project for industrial development
came before the Minister, where political support was on call, the
required degree of protection was provided. An English hosiery
manufacturer, giving evidence before the Tariff Commission in
the early 1900s, explained how he had formerly shipped large
consignments to the Argentine; the Argentines had begun manufacturing for themselves and a high tariff was imposed, since when
he had done no trade worth mentioning.[3] His experience was shared
in every area where local competition developed.[4] The Brazilian
government, with respect to certain parts of the textile industry,
had been extreme protectionists since the early '70s.[5] The duties

[1] Quoted in Harford's report on Argentina for 1902 and 1903, P.P.
1904, XCVII, 13.
[2] Hambloch's report on Brazil for 1919, P.P. 1920, XLIII, 76.
[3] Tariff Commission, *Report on the Textile Trades* (*Hosiery*) (London,
1905), para. 2327.
[4] It has, as Carlos Díaz Alejandro says, been 'the nearly unanimous
opinion of students of Argentine economic history that before 1930 public
policy was either indifferent or hostile to the expansion of manufacturing,
unless it was directly related to exports of goods of rural origin'. This
opinion is clearly due for revision, not least as a result of Professor
Diaz's own work, recently brought together in his *Essays on the Economic
History of the Argentine Republic* (New Haven, 1970).
[5] Consul Lennon Hunt refers in his report on Rio for 1872 to the
'enormous duties lately levied on cottons', which had had the effect of
bringing into existence two large manufactories for the production of the
finer qualities of cloth: P.P. 1874, LXVI, 211.

collected on cottons, woollens and linens in Rio in the mid-'80s worked out on average at about 45% on official values. But the official values, when the tariff was first devised, were fixed very high. Real values had fallen substantially over the past years, with the result that the effective tariff rates in the '80s ranged from 35% to 80 or 100%.[1] Over the next years, and particularly after the overthrow of the Empire in 1889 and its replacement by a protectively inclined Republic, the range of protection in Brazil was spread wide, so that by the 1900s the fiscal policy of the country could be described generally as 'highly protective, and, wherever possible, prohibitive'.[2] A post-war comparison, in 1920, with the tariff rates in force in 1889 and 1890, showed increases of from 300 to 9,000%. Boots and shoes which had paid 2 $000 in 1887, paid 3 $200 in 1890, 6 $400 in 1896 and 9 $400 in 1919.[3] Similarly in Mexico the government of the long-surviving dictator, Porfirio Díaz, adopted a fiscal policy which favoured the importation of capital goods and of certain industrial raw materials, while maintaining high levels of duty for goods which might be produced locally.[4] The policy, as Consul Jerome explained in his report for 1906, was to manufacture in Mexico itself as much as possible of what Mexicans required; 'there is a considerable amount of industrial development quietly going on'.[5]

The degree of protection provided for infant industries in Latin America in and after the last quarter of the nineteenth century is commonly understated. It is not enough simply to look at the official tariff and compare it with those applied elsewhere. The incidence of the Russian tariff on British imports in 1903 was calculated at 131%, the German tariff at 25%, yet both were as effective in giving protection to the industries selected.[6] Governments, European or Latin American, set tariffs at the point at which they gave effective protection. In the case of Latin America, duties might be maintained at what now appear low levels over long periods of time either because artificially high valuations at the

[1] Ricketts' report on Rio for 1885, P.P. 1886, LXV, 333.
[2] Rhind's report on Rio for 1903, P.P. 1905, LXXXVII, 418.
[3] Hambloch's report on Brazil for 1919, P.P. 1920, XLIII, 76.
[4] Fernando Rosenzweig in Cosío Villegas, *Mexico: La Vida Económica*, II, 690. [5] P.P. 1907, XCI, 241.
[6] Board of Trade, *The Comparative Incidence of Foreign and Colonial Import Tariffs on the Export Trade of the United Kingdom*, P.P. 1903, LXVII, 469-70.

Customs House were in reality inflating those rates considerably, or because the heavily depreciated currencies had raised the price of imports to a point at which they were no longer competitive. Certainly, both Mexican and Argentine manufacturers benefited more from currency depreciation in the '90s than they did from official protective tariffs, and when this benefit showed signs of disappearing, the government stepped in to provide the same level of protection by different means—for Argentina by pegging the paper dollar at 44 cents gold by the Conversion Law of 1899, and in the case of Mexico, when she went on the gold standard in 1905, by introducing a new higher tariff, from 1 September 1905, to safeguard national industries. Naturally, no government sets a uniform tariff; it selects for special attention the industries which, for one reason or another, are most suitable for development. The Russian tariff, averaging 131%, rose to 246% on imported English printed cotton piece goods, 220% on woollen broad piece goods, and 310% on linen piece goods. The Argentine tariff, when calculated similarly for its overall effect on British imports, *averaged* only 28%. But Argentina, with her great railway system, her docks, her public utilities, her developing industries naturally taxed imports like machinery, iron, steel, chemicals and cotton yarn very lightly. For those 'national industries' which she hoped to develop, the rates on British imports, even without allowing for artificially high valuations at the Customs House, were high—40% on cotton piece goods, 50 to 60% on woollen manufactures, 67% on linen manufactures, 91% on leather boots and shoes.[1]

*

It is clear that by the last decades of the nineteenth century there were no serious institutional obstacles to the development of manufacturing. In Mexico, at least, import substitution had become a prime element in government tariff policy, and to a lesser extent the same was true of the other Latin American nations with industrial pretensions—Brazil, Argentina, Chile, Peru. There were good, practical reasons for lack of progress in manufacturing shared by all nations at a similar stage of development—shortage of capital and of local raw materials, a restricted home market, scarce

[1] Board of Trade, *The Comparative Incidence of Foreign and Colonial Import Tariffs on the Export Trade of the United Kingdom*, P.P. 1905, LXXXIV, 354.

and costly labour, poor and expensive communications, the high price of imported machinery and industrial raw materials, the absence of cheap power resources. The shortage of capital, though fundamental as a barrier to industrial progress, was less an absolute scarcity than a decision to invest quite considerable local capital resources in more promising openings elsewhere. The speculative booms in Argentina and Uruguay in the late '80s, in Brazil in the early '90s, in Chile in 1905-6, and in Argentina and Brazil in the years 1909-12 indicate that sizeable quantities of local capital were available where there was some prospect of a good percentage return and of heavy capital appreciation. But in years when cities were expanding rapidly and when railways were opening up immense opportunities for land speculation and development in the interior, it was obviously more sensible to put money into urban property, land, or high-interest mortgages. *El Industrial*, the organ of the Unión Industrial Argentina, complained that the capital invested in industrial expansion in Argentina during the '90s was largely foreign. Local capital was to be found easily enough for mortgages on estates, loans on jewels, and other good 'negocios' for sparrow hawks, but capital was lacking for the development of industry, the only enterprise 'que daría honor y gloria al país'.[1]

It took a great deal to change the pattern. In the mid-1900s, when Chile might have industrialized extensively, large investments were diverted to new sheep-farming enterprises in the extreme south and to the recently opened Bolivian tin-mines. Chilean capital and labour were closely interested in the nitrate and copper industries. Little was left for manufacturing. In Argentina, although cotton had been widely cultivated for local use in the early nineteenth century and efforts were made a century later to develop a home manufacturing industry based on local cotton, the counter-attractions of the profitable sugar and quebracho industries absorbed the capital and labour which might otherwise have been available for new enterprises of this kind. Local capital naturally looked for exceptional returns; if it wanted a standard return, there was always the national debt or the foreign railways and public utilities. The Mexican cotton-manufacturing industry, with profits averaging 20 to 30% during the '90s, had no difficulty in finding local capital for development. The Argentine textile industry, in

[1] Quoted by Roberto Fraboschi in Academia Nacional de Historia, *Historia Argentina Contemporanea*, III, 172.

the favourable conditions created by the cut-off in imports during the First World War, had the same experience. The distribution of paid-up capital in limited liability companies within the whole of Argentine industry in 1917 was £26,482,943 Argentine and £19,281,695 foreign; it was, as the British Commercial Secretary said, at least an indication that Argentina was not the 'capital-poor' country which it had generally been held to be.[1]

A deficiency of local capital has latterly proved far less of an obstacle to industrial development in the Republics than it was for the years before 1914. In the early decades of industrialization, the problem was one of counter-attractions, and with these counter-attractions removed, notably during the 1930s, local manufacturing found sufficient support for rapid development. The endemic problem was the size of the market, and it was a problem as acute for industrialists in Australia, New Zealand, South Africa and Canada as in Latin America. The British Trade Commissioner's report on New Zealand in 1911 might have been written for Argentina. He pointed out that the population was so small and labour so expensive that local manufacturing was not likely for the present to become an important factor in foreign trade. To manufacture for export was economically impossible, while the size of the market and the high quality and great variety of goods demanded put the local manufacturer at a disadvantage when trying to compete in the home market with highly differentiated manufactures of established industrial nations.[2] Even in the less developed Republics, provided that local industries operated on a small enough scale, they could be successful. Peruvian coarse cotton goods, bricks and tiles, beer, cotton-seed oil cakes, soap, candles, furniture, saddlery, lard, olive oil, were all making good progress on a workshop/small factory basis at the turn of the century. The trouble started when something more ambitious was attempted. The condition of a large hat-factory established in Lima in the late '90s was 'a source of great anxiety to the shareholders of the company'. A brick and tile factory was slow to prosper. An ambitious match factory at Callao saw little profit; its production was so large that it had been compelled to suspend work for the time being, and its attempts to open up further markets in the neighbouring republics of Bolivia and Ecuador met keen competi-

[1] Chalkley's report on Argentina for 1919, P.P. 1920, XLIII, 10-11.
[2] P.P. 1912-13, XCIII, 937.

tion from Norwegian manufacturers.[1] The usual result of large-scale manufacturing in a market like Peru, where even in the 1930s the average *per capita* income was $60 and where more than 3 million Indians and mestizos in the sierra region were relatively self-sufficient, was over-production. For the bigger markets of Brazil, Mexico and Argentina, the problem was not so serious, but it was bound to recur wherever production reached a specialized scale. However capable a local engineering industry may have been, it could never enter the market for substantial items for which local demand might not exceed two or three a year.

What, then, was the pattern of development for manufacturing in Latin America before 1914, and to what extent did it achieve effective import substitution? Although the handicraft industry still held on to many inland markets, the primitive state of factory production in Latin America in the middle of the nineteenth century is not in doubt. Mexico alone had a large-scale cotton manufacturing industry, consuming, in the mid-'60s, about $14\frac{1}{2}$ million lb of cotton wool and turning out between $10 million and $12 million of coarse cotton manufactures.[2] Cotton manufacturing was Mexico's only substantial industry. In the other Republics and in Brazil workshop production was reasonably extensive in the major cities. Scully discovered 'about fifty cotton, paper, hat, soap, glass, carriage, and other manufactories' in Rio.[3] But manufacturing in the sense of factory production barely existed. Bridgett was able to report rapid progress in the province of Buenos Aires by the early '70s, but he observed how remarkably dependent the littoral provinces continued to be on imports of foodstuffs and manufactures. With the exception of bread, meat and vegetables, there was hardly an article of daily consumption which was not introduced from abroad,

for, although this is essentially a grazing country, cheese and butter were last year imported to the extent of £66,000. Notwithstanding the high customs duties which protect native industry, there is scarcely a manufactory in this province. There are a few tanneries and soap factories, but both soap and leather are imported, the latter to the extent of £53,000 during the last

[1] St John's report on Peru for 1901, P.P. 1902, CIX, 112-13.
[2] Middleton's report on Mexico, 12 August 1865, P.P. 1866, LXXII, 231-2.
[3] William Scully, *Brazil* (London, 1866), p. 162.

year. A cloth factory has lately been started with approved machinery, but has not been working long enough to judge as to its result.[1]

In each of the main manufacturing countries, Mexico, Brazil and Argentina, the last two decades of the century saw rapid industrial development based on greatly expanded local markets. The foreign capital in railways and public utilities, the resources created by an enlarged export market, the interconnection of internal markets by modern communications, political stability, all contributed to the opening up of market possibilities quite distinct from those existing in the '50s and '60s. By 1912, Brazil was estimated by its 'Centro Industrial' to have 3,664 industrial establishments, with a capital value of £48,030,000 employing 168,764 persons,[2] and employment may have been understated by as much as a third since the 'Centro Industrial' took account only of the larger firms. The Argentine figures are not comparable since they include workshops of every size down to single masters. But the general industrial census of 1910 showed 31,988 'factories', with a capital value of £63,664,224 and a work force of 329,490.[3]

In Argentina, the really large industrial establishments were still the breweries, freezing plants, sugar mills and refineries, quebracho extractors, saladeros, electrical and gas works—that is, the big public utilities or the industries associated with processing primary products. In the industrial census of 1914, 53·3% of the manufacturing sector, employing 34·5% of the labour force, fell within the category of foodstuffs and beverages; next were wood products 8·7% and 12·9% respectively, clothing 7·9% and 10·5%, metals 6·3% and 9·9%, leather products 6·3% and 7·5%, and stone, glass and ceramics 3·8% and 7·5%.[4] Industrialization in Mexico and Brazil took a different pattern, dominated in both cases by the emergence of an important cotton manufacturing industry. In terms of capital invested, the Brazilian cotton manu-

[1] Bridgett's report on Buenos Aires, 14 November 1873, P.P. 1874, LXVI, 188.
[2] Quoted by Birch in his report on Brazil for 1912-13, P.P. 1914-16, LXXI, 208. Hambloch supplies some comparable statistics for a slightly earlier period. These give the number of industrial establishments 'of any size' as 3,258, the capital as about £42 million and the number of workmen employed as 152,000: P.P. 1911, XC, 413.
[3] *The Times*, South American Supplement, 25 February 1913, 11a.
[4] Díaz Alejandro, *Economic History of Argentina*, p. 212.

facturing industry accounted for £15,625,000, the Mexican for £10,416,000.[1]

These quantities may not look impressive alongside the manufacturing investment of contemporary Britain, Germany or the United States. But it is worth considering what effect they had on imports into what were still, even after a massive population increase during the nineteenth century, relatively restricted markets. Argentina, by far the largest market for imports in Latin America just before the First World War, had a population of under eight million, in which unskilled workers were earning, on average, only 35 cents (paper) an hour. And the working population of Argentina enjoyed living conditions and a purchasing power far in advance of the great majority of their fellows in Spanish America and Brazil.

Certain general tendencies in the import pattern need to be identified. In the first place, industry in the smaller Republics of Central and South America had made very little progress by 1914 beyond the handicraft stage; even today some are only beginning to develop basic consumer industries. Most had small industrial plants or.workshops manufacturing such articles as matches, candles, soap, boots and shoes, cigarettes. Colombia, Venezuela, Guatemala, Ecuador and Uruguay had small cotton-manufacturing industries, ranging from Colombia's 20,000 spindles and 300 looms down to Uruguay's no spindles and 300 looms.[2] They continued to import the great majority of such manufactured goods as they needed, but their needs were modest and their importance to British trade negligible.

For the larger Republics, few common consumer goods were not, in some form or another, manufactured locally by 1914, usually in the lower ranges of quality and price. The same applied to the more basic forms of machinery, for mines, for textile manufacturing, for processing coffee, sugar and cotton; to equipment for the construction industry; to military supplies; to shipbuilding and repairing; to railway locomotives, passenger carriages and goods waggons. Every big railway, public utility, manufacturing or processing plant developed its own machine shops, at first to cope with servicing and repairs, later often to manufacture. When Thomas Brassey built the new mole at Callao in the late '60s and early '70s,

[1] *The Times*, South American Supplement, 29 August 1911, 4a.
[2] Figures for 1910: *ibid*.

he had to develop his own concrete works, steam sawmill and foundry. Lennon Hunt, describing the opening in 1862 of one of the first of the Brazilian railways, the Recife and São Francisco Railway Co., commented on its 'very costly and complete range of locomotive workshops, where a staff of English and native artificers and labourers is employed in repairing the original rolling stock, and in constructing inferior vehicles such as goods' waggons, timber trucks, etc.'.[1] As the railway systems multiplied and lengthened, some of the repair shops developed into substantial industrial establishments. The Rosario Railway Company's repairing shop was building at the rate of a thousand 40-ton waggons a year in the early 1900s.[2] The arrival of the steam engine in Latin America in the first decades of the nineteenth century brought with it the need for foundries and metal workshops. By the end of the century there were several large metal manufacturers in Argentina, one of whom, Pedro Vasena, founded in 1872, was employing 400-500 operatives and selling more than £200,000 worth of products annually. Argentine manufacturers were 'principally occupied in founding supports, joists, bars, etc., including pieces of great size; they also construct machinery for general use, such as windlasses, winches, wheels, saws, as well as boilers and other smaller goods'.[3]

The effect of local manufacturing was often not so much to reduce imports as to divert them to different lines—to British cotton yarns instead of piece goods, to British machinery and machine tools instead of general manufactures, to iron, steel, industrial raw materials and semi-manufactures in place of finished products. The breweries, foundries, match factories, cotton and jute mills, clothing, boot and shoe manufactories were fuelled by British coal and fed by European or North American raw materials. A Brazilian official complained, with some reason, that 'instead of our preparing hides and skins here, thus stimulating cattle breeding, we undertake the creation of a boot and shoe industry, importing from abroad all the raw materials necessary for manufacturing these articles—leather, skins, silk, etc. Instead of trying to manufacture liquors and national wines from Brazilian

---

[1] Hunt's report on Pernambuco for 1863, P.P. 1865, LIII, 362.
[2] McLaren's report on Campana for 1904, P.P. 1905, LXXXVII, 18.
[3] 'Memorandum on the Leading Argentine Industries', included in Worthington's report on Argentina, P.P. 1899, XCVI, 523.

fruits and essences, we import barley and hops, and make beer.'[1] Argentina did the same. Her output of beer in 1911 was no less than 22,059,000 gallons, and her imports, formerly large, were reduced to insignificance. But she grew little barley, with the result that in 1912 she was importing 22,265 metric tons of barley valued at £222,600.[2] 77% of the raw material employed in Argentina's metallurgical industries in 1913 was imported; 47% for the construction industries; 45% for clothing and hats.[3]

Whatever the rights and wrongs of such a distribution of effort, and there were bound to be anomalies, the effect on the relative distribution of consumer and production goods among total imports was striking. Mexico was a consistently small market for imports with a very positive import-substitution policy. At the beginning of the Porfiriato in 1876, consumer goods formed 75% of imports, production goods 25%; at the end, in 1911, the proportions were 43 and 57% respectively.[4]

A further tendency, which had little effect on British trade, was for the importation of foodstuffs to decline as communications improved and land was developed within each republic. Stock raising in Rio Grande do Sul was, by the end of the 1900s, threatening to extinguish the trade in imported animal products from the River Plate; vineyards were making a bid for Brazil's home market. Mixed agricultural, dairy and fruit farming in the State of São Paulo had made great progress, and Rio was dependent on the rich agricultural and pastoral resources of Minas Geraes for its daily food. Argentina, formerly an importer of flour in quantity from the United States, Brazil and Chile, was now a major exporter; she supplied her home market for sugar and was rapidly replacing imported wine with the produce of her own vineyards. Jenner, in his 1889 report, listed '24 specific duties, chiefly devised for protective purposes and dealing with stearine candles, macaroni and pastes for soup, biscuits, flour, starch, sugar, beer, spirits, wine, and liqueurs, all of which articles might be, or actually are, produced in the country'.[5] By 1914 each of these was

[1] Quoted in Hambloch's report on Brazil for 1919, P.P. 1920, XLIII, 76.

[2] Mackie's report on Buenos Aires for 1912-13, P.P. 1914, LXXXIX, 552.

[3] *Third National Census* (Buenos Aires, 1914), Vol. VII.

[4] Cosío Villegas, *Mexico: La Vida Económica*, II, 637-8.

[5] Jenner's report on Argentina, 13 May 1889, P.P. 1889, LXXVIII, 32.

firmly established with a large or total share of the market. In the smaller Republics, a single railway could alter the balance of the economy. The Guayaquil–Quito Railway, completed in 1908, which opened the resources of the interior highlands to the hot, coastal strip, transformed Guayaquil from an importer of potatoes, vegetables, corn, hay, beans from Chile and Peru, into an exporter; Quito, in turn, was able to develop its textile manufactories with imported foreign machinery and supplies of raw cotton, wool and fibres from the lowlands. Consul Cartwright forecasted optimistically in June 1908 that the elevated regions of Ecuador would in the course of a few years lose their dependent status, become self-supporting, and begin exporting to foreign countries.[1]

In the traditional, consumer goods market of the larger Republics, British imports were facing serious local competition, part compensated for, at least in the short run, by an increased demand for high-quality products as yet beyond the capacity of local manufactures, and by the need for industrial raw materials, semi-manufactured goods, and coal to feed and drive the new industries. St John noticed how in Peru the total importation of articles similar to those locally manufactured—cloth, beer, boots and shoes, hats, candles, cigars, cigarettes, wines, clothing, soap and brooms—had fallen from £451,653 in 1877 to £97,619, in 1898; imported raw materials had risen over the same period from £27,787 to £47,786.[2] Hartley, reporting from Arequipa at about the same time, explained how the local cotton factory and brewery met almost the entire local consumption, while Lima factories were supplying the market with its requirements in safety matches and woollen hats.[3] This did not mean, of course, that the total value of British imports into Peru was falling before 1914. But it did mean that British imports were challenged in many of the traditional areas, that they made much less progress than might be expected, and that the emphasis and quality had to change. The same was visible in Chile where, as Muñoz has argued recently, industrialization had been taken much further before 1914 than is commonly supposed, and where there was an industrialization process 'of some importance'

[1] Cartwright's report on Ecuador for 1907, P.P. 1908, CXI, 141-2.
[2] St John's report on Peru for 1899 and 1900, P.P. 1901, LXXXIV, 102.
[3] Hartley's report on Arequipa for 1900, P.P. 1901, LXXXIV, 138.

in the second half of the nineteenth century.[1] Certainly, large sums were invested by the end of the 1900s in smelting works for copper and silver, corn mills, sawmills, tanneries, soap, biscuit, rope, cheese, candle, cloth, furniture and paper works, breweries and distilleries; substantial machinery works were manufacturing for the mining and nitrate industries, and large workshops were attached to the national and British railway systems.

As one might expect, import substitution was taken furthest in Mexico, Brazil and Argentina. Mexico was fortunate in her access to hydro-electricity, coal and, later, oil. She could call on a reserve of cheap factory labour, grossly exploited. Consul Jerome argued in 1905 that Mexico was fast becoming able to manufacture most of the commodities she required, 'and one does not need to be a prophet to foresee that the day is not far distant when her surplus manufactures will compete with those of other countries in the marts of the world'.[2] Substitution was most noticeable in textiles, where imports fell 30% between 1888-89 and 1910-11, particularly in plain cotton goods, where the decline was almost 85%. But it was evident, too, in the Monterrey steel plant, the only steel plant in Spanish America until the Second World War, which cost £1 million of local capital in the early 1900s and which had the capacity, never fully realized, to supply the whole of Mexico's demand for structural iron, rolled steel, rails, commercial iron, pig iron, etc. Cement production, which had barely existed at the beginning of the century, had reached 75,000 tons in 1911, 55% of national consumption, and local production of dynamite (for use in the mines) had reduced the amount of imported dynamite by 35% between 1903-4 and 1910-11.[3]

In Brazil the cotton-manufacturing industry had replaced imports of the lower-grade cotton goods in mass demand, and was encroaching on the better qualities. Most of the other basic consumer goods were locally manufactured largely, though not entirely, at a workshop level, and there were some promising developments in the production of equipment to meet demand from the armed services, the construction industry, the railways and ports, and the

---

[1] Oscar E. Muñoz, 'An Essay on the Process of Industrialization in Chile since 1914', *Yale Economic Essays*, 8 (1968), 175-6.

[2] Jerome's report on Mexico for 1905, P.P. 1906, CXXVI, 691.

[3] Cosío Villegas, *Mexico: La Vida Económica*, I, 325, 329; II, 693. Also Jerome's report on Mexico for 1903, P.P. 1905, XC, 755.

great coffee, sugar and cotton industries.[1] Nathaniel Leff has recently challenged the conventional view of Brazil in 1929 as still essentially an agricultural export country, with sustained industrialization dating only from the 1930s. He points out that as early as 1920 industrial output at São Paulo equalled coffee exports in value; that in Brazil as a whole by 1927 domestic industry was supplying almost 90% of the internal market for cotton textiles; that by 1938 local manufacturing accounted for 85% of the manufactured goods on the market. Leff is emphatic that this development was *not*, as is often argued, the result of exogenous shocks or of the limitation of imports during the First World War; war-time development was constrained by the shortage of imported raw materials and capital goods, and only the industries which could make larger calls on local inputs could expand rapidly to take advantage of import scarcities. All the giant economic groups of Brazilian industry, Leff adds, such as Matarrazzo, Votorontim, Jafet, Klabin and Lundgren, were in business well before 1914.[2] Warren Dean has reached the same conclusions in his examination of Paulista industry. He points out the deficiencies of the Centro Industrial census for 1907, and after taking into account small workshops, replaces the São Paulo census figures (326 establishments employing 24,186 workers with a value produced of 118,087 contos) with revised figures of 1,500 establishments, 30,000 workers and 155,000 contos. He concludes that *new* plants and *new* lines of manufactures were not significant during the First World War, and that the contrast between the scale of pre- and post-war industry has been exaggerated.[3] Admittedly, Brazil had far to go as a manufacturing nation. But British businessmen and officials were well aware of an import-substitution so evident in its impact on the import trade. H. S. Birch, Secretary of Legation, reported for 1912-13 that a large proportion of home consumption in Brazil was already provided for by the national industries.[4]

The high cost of fuel, the scarcity of skilled labour, and the

[1] Some details of these developments are given in Nathaniel H. Leff's *The Brazilian Capital Goods Industry 1929-1964* (Cambridge, Mass., 1968).

[2] Nathaniel H. Leff, 'Long-term Brazilian Economic Development', *Journal of Economic History*, 29 (1969), 474-6.

[3] Warren Dean, *The Industrialization of São Paulo 1880-1945* (Austin, Texas, 1969), pp. 83-104.

[4] P.P. 1914-16, LXXI, 208.

abundance of more attractive openings for capital elsewhere inhibited extensive development of the textile industry in Argentina. The Argentine cotton-manufacturing industry was sixth on the list of Latin American cotton manufacturers in 1910, with only 9,000 spindles and 1,200 looms.[1] But industrial development in other sectors had made remarkable progress since the first serious developments in the '80s. At the beginning of the '90s, the President of the Republic told Congress that Argentina was already defying competition in alcohol, wax matches, and the boot and shoe industry, and would shortly be similarly placed for sugar and wines. By 1897, *The Times* Special Correspondent, in one of a series of articles on the economic situation in Argentina, was able to report a rapid advance in local manufacturing. The financial crisis of 1890-91 and the depreciation of the paper currency put many of the imported articles in ordinary use out of reach of a large proportion of the inhabitants, and it was found, he said, that several of these articles could be manufactured in Argentina at a cost far lower than that at which they could be imported:

> For one factory existing ten years ago there are now 20 in full work. Beer, spirits, wines, hats, boots, cloth, matches, cigars, and cigarettes, paper, rope, sacks, and a dozen other articles are now made locally for consumption. Sugar is produced in quantities far in excess of the needs of the population; cereals and flour form one of the principal exports of Argentina, whereas ten years ago the importation of these products was an absolute necessity.[2]

The period of most rapid industrial growth, Ezequiel Gallo explains, was 1907-13; but each of the great export booms brought expansion not only to the export industries but also to all those industries connected with that sector or with meeting the needs of those profiting from it.[3]

The rapid expansion of meat and grain exports, continued immigration, spiralling land values, a large inflow of foreign capital into transport, public utilities and the processing industries, and a relative abundance of local capital for promising industrial projects

[1] *The Times*, South American Supplement, 29 August 1911, 4a.
[2] *The Times*, 18 August 1897, 6a.
[3] Ezequiel Gallo, 'Agrarian Expansion and Industrial Development in Argentina, 1880-1930' in Raymond Carr (ed.), 'Latin American Affairs', *St. Antony's Papers*, 22 (1970), 49-50.

protected by tariffs, gave every incentive to progress in local manufacturing. Argentina was already a nation of large cities. Buenos
Aires, at the turn of the century, was the largest city in the southern
hemisphere, and after Paris the second largest Latin city in the
world; it was said to be the Paris of the New World as New York
was the London. In 1914, out of a total Argentine population of
7,885,000, 1,576,000 lived in the federal capital and a further
458,000 in the outer suburbs of Greater Buenos Aires; over 3
million Argentines lived in communities of 10,000 and above.[1] It

Table IV
Argentine Industrial Production and Imports, 1911-15

Type of industry	Produc-tion ($ million m/n)	Imports, yearly average 1911-15 ($ million m/n)	Consump-tion ($ million m/n)	Percentage covered by domestic industry
Food	1,004·7	102·6	1,107·1	90·7
Clothing and cosmetics	160·3	21·9	182·3	87·9
Building	229·6	57·9	287·5	79·9
Furniture, cars, etc.	87·1	37·1	124·1	70·2
Objets d'art and ornaments	16·1	9·5	25·6	63·0
Household utensils, etc.	94·3	189·3	283·6	33·2
Chemicals	56·3	90·1	146·3	37·9
Graphic arts	39·7	6·2	45·9	86·4
Textiles	40·2	138·1	178·4	22·6
Various	147·7	101·8	249·5	59·1
Total	1,875·8	754·5	2,630·3	71·3

Source: Ezequiel Gallo, 'Agrarian Expansion and Industrial Development
in Argentina, 1880-1930' in Raymond Carr (ed.), 'Latin American
Affairs', *St. Antony's Papers*, No. 22 (1970), 50.

was hardly surprising that so large an urban population should have
supplied many or most of its basic needs for manufactured goods.
Of an active population of 3,069,000 in 1910-14, 1,051,000 were
employed in the rural sector. But there were 633,000 in manufacturing, 218,000 in construction, 426,000 in commerce and finance
and 170,000 in transport.[2] For Buenos Aires itself, the National
Census figures for 1914 give 10,275 industrial establishments

[1] Díaz Alejandro, *Economic History of Argentina*, Statistical Appendix,
Tables 21 and 23.
[2] *Ibid.*, Table 30.

employing 149,289 persons. Gallo has published a table (Table IV) taken from the National Census, which illustrates more clearly than for any of the other Republics the extent to which domestic industry was contributing to local consumption during the five years 1911-15.

The percentages would be larger still if volume rather than value were the measurement, since local production made a bid for the lower end of the market. Import substitution, as Gallo says, had made real progress in the general area of consumer goods, especially foodstuffs. Argentina was still a large importer of British coal and cotton goods, as it was of more sophisticated products. But her industrial production had increased by 130% between 1900 and 1913, and it was to double again by 1930.

Competition between local manufactures and imports will be studied more closely for individual trades in Chapter V. In general it was limited to the lower ranges of quality, to such bulk products as would not easily bear high transport costs, and to the products for which a sufficient local market could be developed. For many of Britain's traditional exports to Latin America, especially such items as hardware, china and glass, British products were replaced by European competition long before local manufacturing became significant, and it was Belgian or German industry which found itself deprived of a market. But in many areas and particularly for cotton piece goods, themselves so critical an element in British exports to the Republics, local manufacturing was certainly a factor to be reckoned with in British trade before 1914.

CHAPTER VI

International Interest in the Markets of Latin America

Up to the last quarter of the nineteenth century Britain's leadership in the international trade of Latin America is not in doubt. Consul Drummond-Hay was speaking for Latin America as a whole when he boasted that British trade with Chile in the early '70s, both imports and exports, nearly equalled the trade with all other countries; 'the consumption of English manufactures is above that of other countries, and British shipping visiting this coast exceeds in number and aggregate tonnage that of all other nations'.[1] What is less certain is the competitive position of Britain for the period after 1880.

It is obvious that wherever Britain traded, the emergence of industrial competitors in world markets in the last quarter of the nineteenth century would diminish the percentage of trade which had fallen to her while she was still the workshop of the world. In particular areas this percentage decline was considerable. From the leading position in Mexico's import trade which Britons had enjoyed since the end of the colonial period, they found their share equalled by the United States in the early '80s. By 1910-11, United States imports were nearly five times as great. Even in the three big markets of South America—Argentina, Brazil and Chile —Britain was not able to maintain her percentage of the import trade. British imports, which had accounted for 36·9% of Argentine imports in the quinquennium 1896-1900, were down to 34% in 1901-5, and 30·6% in 1910-12. Comparable percentages for

[1] Drummond-Hay's report on Valparaiso for 1872-3, P.P. 1874, LXVI, 529.

Brazil were 29·7, 31·4 and 27·4; for Chile, 39·6, 37·4 and 31·8. But before we jump to any conclusions about Britain's industrial and commercial decadence, we might ask ourselves whether it is reasonable to expect to maintain a fixed percentage of a vastly increased trade—an import trade which, for Argentina, had risen from $49 million (gold) in 1870 to nearly $500 million (gold) in 1913—in an age when Germany and North America, in particular, were making a strong bid for overseas markets. We might also ask whether a serious decline in certain markets represented a total defeat, or simply a decision to transfer limited resources to markets or products which offered better returns. Is it sensible to make generalizations about British competitiveness on the basis of figures for the condition of trade in Latin America? Was South America, 'the most truly competitive area of all'?[1]

*

For the quarter-century before 1914 the only serious competition in Latin American markets came from Germany and the United States. The United States had taken the lead in the neighbouring markets of Mexico and the Caribbean, and was challenging Britain in the northern Republics of South America. Germany met Britain in every market and in every type of product. In the early decades, the '70s, '80s and '90s, British traders and manufacturers were obviously more concerned with the threat of German competition. But it was becoming clear to them, even by the end of the '90s, that the United States was likely in the long run to be the more dangerous rival. British exports of manufactured goods in 1893 amounted to £185,934,000, German to £98,235,000 and United States to £37,293,000. In 1913 the figures were £411,572,000 (British), £332,839,000 (German) and £247,292,000 (United States). British exports had increased by 121%, German by 239% and American by 563%.[2]

Germany's great strength was in the protected, neighbouring markets of western and eastern Europe; 75% of her increased exports, 1890-1913, went to Europe, as compared with only 34%

---

[1] S. B. Saul, *Studies in British Overseas Trade, 1870-1914* (Liverpool, 1960), p. 38.
[2] Board of Trade, *Return showing Trade Development (U.K., Germany and the United States*, P.P. 1914, LXXVIII, 13-15.

H

of Britain's.[1] But her position outside Europe was far less secure. For the period 1880 to 1902, which was the first of serious competition, Table V indicates the position for all the markets outside the principal protected markets (Russia, Germany, France, Belgium, Holland, Spain, Portugal, Italy, Austria-Hungary, United States). It is clear that by 1880 the United States was already a more substantial exporter than Germany, and was increasing her share by a comfortable margin.

Table V

British, German, French and United States Exports to Destinations outside the Group and other than the Principal Protected Countries, 1880, 1885, 1890, 1895, 1900 and 1902
(£ million)

Year	United Kingdom	Germany	France	United States
1880	125·3	24·8	28·7	25·0
1885	126·5	27·9	26·1	30·4
1890	155·9	36·2	34·5	37·0
1895	129·7	37·2	30·0	37·7
1900	167·5	51·5	36·9	77·0
1902	176·8	51·7	37·0	80·8
Average 1880-2	132·8	25·5	29·3	28·8
Average 1900-2	172·7	50·9	36·9	78·1
Increase	39·9	25·4	7·6	49·3
Increase %	30	100	26	171

Source: Board of Trade, *Memorandum on the Course of the Export Trade of some of the chief Commercial Countries with Protected and other Markets*, P.P. 1905, LXXXIV, 456.

A number of qualifications should be made as to the content of these domestic exports, since for the United States they include a large element of non-competitive primary products. But the point is that these were British official figures, and that British officials were well aware that although Britain was positively declining as an exporter to Europe and the United States, her exports to 'neutral' markets were increasing faster than Germany's (in absolute, though not percentage terms), and slower than the United States.

[1] W. Arthur Lewis, 'International Competition in Manufacturing', *American Economic Review*, XLVII (1957), 581.

What is so striking, in fact, about Germany's trading position before 1914 is the limited range of opportunities open to her outside Europe and Russia. German exports were showing signs of levelling-off at a point still below that of the United Kingdom, and her long-term prospects for expansion, without a colonial empire, were far less promising. Back in the '80s, Britain's commercial attaché had reported Germany's special efforts to produce more cheaply than France or Britain in order to capture a share of the 'neutral' markets, since unlike Britain 'she has no colonies to fall back upon, and she has not that old custom in neutral markets which the French have'.[1] Germany was able to keep expanding on a substantial European base, but by 1914 she too, like Britain some decades before, was finding herself losing these markets to new, protected local European industries. Overseas, the development of a system of imperial preference threatened to close the rich markets of the British Dominions. North America was locked behind high tariff barriers. Germany was left with only four geographical areas in which she might win her way in competition —the Near and the Middle East (especially Asia Minor, the Levant and the Persian Gulf); Equatorial Africa; South and Central America; China and the Far East. In each of these, she was meeting strong competition and making little headway in the decade before 1914. It was not surprising, as Sir Francis Oppenheimer remarked, that particularly from the second half of 1913 the need for larger German exports seemed uppermost in the public mind, and the whole press suddenly overflowed with articles on Germany's economic mission abroad, her *Weltwirtschaft*.

Again and again it was pointed out that among the three leading industrial countries of the world Germany found herself by a long way in the least favourable position. The United Kingdom had her vast colonial empire as a natural national market; the United States had a whole continent, while Germany, as the last comer, had no such privileged territories. As her colonies could, at best, be regarded in the light of future sources of supply for various raw materials, she must regard the world as her trading empire and rely exclusively upon her energies and

---

[1] J. A. Crowe's evidence, 16 October 1885: Minutes of Evidence, *Report of the Royal Commission on the Depression of Trade and Industry,* P.P. 1886, XXI, Q.1032.

enterprise to conquer it. Sometimes the limits were drawn somewhat more closely, and South America, Asiatic Turkey and the Chinese Empire were pointed to as her special trading areas.[1]

Germany, then, had good reason to pay particularly close attention to Latin American markets. The United States was similarly placed, restricted in Europe and Europe's colonial empires, and on the watch for long-term outlets in the Far East, in Oceania, and, above all, in Latin America. Although the United States made an ambitious attack on the markets of Europe in the hope of establishing demand for her manufactured goods, the vast proportion of her exports continued to be in raw materials and foodstuffs. The percentage of finished manufactured goods in her total exports to Europe in 1910 was 15·1, compared with 69·9 to South America, 68·0 to Asia and 71·8 to Oceania. 'It is in Asia, Africa, South and Central America and Mexico, Australia and Oceania', said the Secretary of Commerce in 1905, 'that the great market for finished manufactures exists.'[2] And it was Latin America which caught the public imagination. American exports to Latin America in 1910 totalled $258,581,000, of which just under a half went to Cuba and Mexico, and a fifth to a group of northerly Republics (Haiti, San Domingo, Central America, Venezuela and Colombia), leaving only about $90 million for the rest. The largest items were food products (13%), steel products and railway material ($8\frac{1}{4}$%), lumber and office furniture ($6\frac{3}{4}$%), petroleum products ($4\frac{3}{4}$%), agricultural implements and twine (4%), boots, shoes and leather (3%), electrical machines and instruments ($2\frac{3}{4}$%), cotton and cotton goods ($2\frac{1}{2}$%), typewriters, phonographs and sewing machines ($1\frac{1}{2}$%) and naval stores (1%), with the remaining $52\frac{1}{2}$% made up of a great variety of manufactured articles headed by 'builders' hardware' amounting to $5\frac{1}{2}$% and including all kinds of tools, cutlery and general hardware. O. P. Austin of the Bureau of Statistics estimated that, in 1910, the United States supplied Latin America with 24% of all the goods which it imported, in contrast with the 14% average for the rest of the world. He added

[1] Oppenheimer's report on Germany for 1913, P.P. 1914-15, LXXII, 805.
[2] David E. Novack and Matthew Simon, 'Commercial Responses to the American Export Invasion, 1871-1914', *Explorations in Entrepreneurial History*, 2nd ser. 3 (1966), 138, 141.

that trade with the Latin American countries represented 19% of the entire foreign trade of the United States.[1]

The situation for the United Kingdom was rather different. She too was finding herself compelled to look outside Europe for expanding markets. Like Germany, she faced the heavy tariff barriers surrounding American industry. Like Germany and the United States, she looked to Latin America, Africa, the Middle East and the Far East for new opportunities. But she had her own back-yard to cultivate, and it demanded more and more of her available resources. Between 1880 and 1902, British exports of manufactured goods to the principal protected markets (in Europe and North America) declined from £81·9 million to £71·6 million; over the same period, exports of manufactured goods elsewhere rose from £115 million to £150·1 million.[2] Over the longer period 1860 to 1938, the percentage of total British exports destined for France fell from 8 to 3, for Germany from 11 to 4, for the United States from 14 to 4. The percentage to Latin America rose from 7% in 1860 to 11% in 1913, falling to 8% in 1938 and 6% in 1960. To the white Dominions, Australia, New Zealand, South Africa and Canada, the 9% of 1860 rose to 18% in 1913 and to 26% in 1938; it was 28% in 1960.[3]

One of the themes to which witnesses before the Royal Commission on the Depression of Trade and Industry (1886) returned again and again was the contraction of the old markets in Europe and North America and the need to look further afield, particularly to India, the Colonies and China. 'On India we rely,' said Thomas Stuttard, a cotton spinner and manufacturer, 'and if we lose India, Lancashire is practically ruined.' George Lord, speaking for the Manchester Chamber of Commerce, agreed on the importance of the Indian market; Manchester was now excluded from her main European markets, and it was to India and before long China that she must look for the disposal of her steadily increasing production; India in 1884-5 had taken as much as a third of Britain's total exports of cotton goods and yarns. The Master Cutler of

[1] Figures quoted by William C. Downs, "The Commission House in Latin American Trade', *Quarterly Journal of Economics*, XXVI (1912), 120-6.
[2] Board of Trade, *The Course of the Export Trade of some of the chief Commercial Countries with Protected and other Markets*, P.P. 1905, LXXXIV, 452.
[3] Woodruff, *Impact of Western Man*, Table VII/14.

Sheffield spoke of competition in neutral markets and exclusion from the home markets of rival manufacturing nations; but 'in most of our local industries we still hold our own for colonial demand'. Samuel Osborn, a Sheffield steel and tool manufacturer, made the point that although Sheffield had lost, as a result of protective tariffs, the markets of the United States, Germany, France and Spain, she had to a certain extent made up the loss over the past twenty years by developing new markets in the Colonies, India and China. John Ellis, chairman of John Brown and Co., spoke of the loss of nearly all Britain's former foreign markets in Germany, France and the United States, where needs were now satisfied by home manufacturing. But British manufacturers had nothing to fear from competition in iron and steel construction in India and China.[1]

Latin America helped fill the gap in British trade. The Tariff Commission was told in 1905 that the South American trade had in part replaced the markets lost to Bradford dress goods on the Continent and in the United States. A witness from the electrical industry spoke of being able to do nothing anywhere abroad except in the Colonies, Japan and South America, but it was the colonial market, he added, which was the most important to retain. 'If it were not for our Colonial trade,' said a witness from the woollen trade, 'our works would not be running three days a week', and many firms told the Tariff Commission that within their experience the home and colonial trade had, to some extent, taken the place of the lost foreign markets; they had been driven on to the colonial markets by the loss of their foreign trade. Sir Andrew Noble, speaking for the whole engineering trade, told the Commission that the colonial trade was the only part of the engineering trade which was still increasing.[2]

It is worth emphasizing, at any rate for the '90s, that before the great revival in foreign trade and investment in the 1900s, the home market was providing a strong counter-attraction for British manufacturers and investors. As far as Latin America was concerned, British investments fell off sharply after the Baring Crisis

[1] Minutes of Evidence, *Report of the Royal Commission on the Depression of Trade and Industry*, P.P. 1886, XXI, QQ.4955, 5285, 2659, 2687-8, 3339-48, 3148-57.
[2] Tariff Commission, *Report on the Textile Trades (Woollen Industry)* (London, 1905), paras. 1430, 1434; Tariff Commission, *Report on the Engineering Industries* (London, 1909), paras. 475, 518.

of 1890-91, and did not revive until the early 1900s. The same pattern was visible in British imports into Latin America. But for the United Kingdom herself, net home investment nearly trebled between 1888 and 1902. A 10 million increase in population over the last decades of the century and the rising real wages created primarily by falling foodstuff and raw material prices, gave a promising market to the new products of the age, to bicycles, sewing machines, cheap watches, electrical goods, patent medicines, branded foodstuffs and textiles. Investment switched from overseas issues to house building in the United Kingdom, to breweries, to speculative loans in the electrical and cycle industries, to engineering and shipbuilding. Many of the new products, the more sophisticated engineering and chemical goods, the branded textiles

Table VI
Empire Share of Selected British Exports, 1931 and 1938

	1931		1938	
Products	Total exports (£ million)	Percentage to Empire	Total exports (£ million)	Percentage to Empire
Iron and steel products	35·0	52·6	42·2	62·8
Electrical machinery and apparatus	11·8	55·9	15·2	71·7
Other machinery	29·8	40·6	36·0	54·7
Motor cars and parts	9·1	59·3	16·2	69·7
Cotton piece goods	37·3	46·6	40·3	55·8

Source: Political and Economic Planning, *Britain and World Trade* (London, 1947), p. 24.

and foodstuffs, were unsuited to the markets of Latin America. Resources were diverted from the cotton goods, hardware and basic iron and steel manufactures, which had formed the major part of Britain's Latin American trade, to products which, by their nature, found better markets at home or in the Dominions.

Overseas, there can be no doubt of the strong attractions to Britons of empire markets. By the end of the 1930s, the Empire was taking about half of British exports, in comparison with some 35% in 1913-14. Table VI shows the increase in the percentage share of Britain's critical exports taken by the Empire between 1931 and 1938 over which years Central and South America's share of total British exports fell from 9·5 to 7·7%. At the same time, the proportion of Britain's imports drawn from the Empire rose from a level of 25% before the war to nearly 40% in 1936.[1]

A number of circumstances made British Dominion markets particularly attractive. In the first place, per head of population the Dominion trade was exceptionally large. Even the Argentine, which itself was well in advance of any other Latin American market, could not begin to match the concentration of Dominion markets (Table VII).

New Zealand headed the list, with imports of £19·3 per head, and Canada and Australia were not far behind. The share of South Africa would have been substantially increased if the white population had received its proper weighting as a purchasing group. Taking the purchasing power of the native population as seven natives to one European, the value of imports per head of population worked out at about £18·8.[2]

Then, it is quite clear that the familiarity of colonial markets to Englishmen, the similarity in tastes and needs, the existence of extensive import-export and financial facilities, the ample shipping services, the maintenance of law and order, and the encouragement of enterprise and investment were all factors especially favourable to the growth of trade within the Empire. Trade Commissioners in all the Dominions reported the 'strong and patriotic desire to keep as large a proportion as possible of the trade in British hands'. In Canada some restraint was imposed by the fact that market conditions, taste and proximity made Canada a natural extension of the United States market. But in Australasia there was no such check, and what G. T. Milne called the 'commercial and sentimental preferences in favour of the Mother Country' were strong.

> The community is thoroughly British in sentiment, and other things being equal, the individual buyer prefers to purchase goods of British manufacture. In some cases he is even prepared to pay a higher price for the British made article.[3]

No doubt the reputation of British goods for quality and durability had much to do with it; consumers were paying more for what

[1] Werner Schlote, *British Overseas Trade from 1700 to the 1930s* (Oxford, 1952), pp. 88-9.

[2] Sothern Holland's report on South Africa for 1913, P.P. 1914-16, XLV, 579.

[3] Milne's report on Australia for 1912-13, P.P. 1914, LX, 115.

Table VII

Foreign Trade of Selected Countries per Head of Population, 1912

	Estimated population at middle of 1912 (millions)	Imports		Exports		Total	
		Amount (£ million)	Per head £	Amount (£ million)	Per head £	Amount (£ million)	Per head £
New Zealand	1·1	21·0	19·3	21·8	20·0	42·8	39·3
Australia	4·6	78·2	16·8	79·1	17·0	157·3	33·8
United Kingdom	45·6	814·1	17·8	663·8	14·5	1477·9	32·3
Canada	7·5	140·7	18·8	81·9	10·9	222·6	29·7
Argentine	7·5	77·0	10·3	96·1	12·8	173·1	23·1
France	39·7	435·3	11·0	368·2	9·3	803·5	20·3
Germany	66·3	595·0	9·0	491·4	7·4	1086·4	16·4
South Africa	6·7	39·8	6·0	63·3	9·4	103·1	15·4
United States	95·4	400·7	4·2	544·8	5·7	945·5	9·9

Source: *Second Interim Report of the Dominions Royal Commission*, P.P. 1914, LX, 144.

was, or what they believed to be, the better product. But there was more to it than that. A manufacturer of wire, wire ropes and netting told the Tariff Commission that the export trade was now negligible outside the colonies, with the exception of Argentina. Argentina was enjoying a period of great prosperity and importing a large amount of wire for the purpose of fencing in new land, but at any moment the trade might go to the United States. Elsewhere, British manufacturers found it impossible to take orders for solid fencing wire in competition with the foreigner. The manufacturer frankly admitted that any ordinary wire would do for fencing, yet in Australia many merchants still preferred to buy British wire. In New Zealand consumers 'believe in English wire. They like to buy English goods, and for English goods they are willing to pay higher prices. That is one of the special cases where we can get orders for common wire indented home.'[1]

As R. W. Dalton pointed out after the First World War, a good deal of the trade between Britain and the Dominions had become 'routine' trade, where orders for certain lines of British products were repeated automatically through the usual channels without much thought as to the possibility of obtaining corresponding goods at equal prices from other sources.[2] This was a major source of strength for the British connection. British manufacturers were further assisted by government preference. The British government did not extend the system of Imperial preference to the Crown Colonies until 1933. Some of the colonies, however, had on their own initiative already given limited preference, and the system by which colonial governments did their purchasing through the Crown Agents in London gave Britons a solid and permanent advantage. Furthermore, H.M. Government was able to fix Colonial, Ottoman and Chinese tariffs at a level which did nothing to dissuade British imports while remaining insufficiently high to permit local industry to develop, so that important markets were kept open to British industry. The Dominions, with full tariff autonomy, gave a limited preference to certain ranges of British products well before the First World War, Canada from 1897, South Africa and New Zealand from 1903, Australia from 1907.

---

[1] Tariff Commission, *Report on the Iron and Steel Trades* (London, 1904), paras. 910-15.
[2] Dalton's report on New Zealand, July 1920, P.P. 1920, XXXIII, 648-9.

The preference was not large, but about two-thirds of British imports into Australia just before the war were receiving a remission of duty equivalent on average to rather more than a quarter of the ordinary rates; as for New Zealand, rather more than a third of British and Empire imports were benefiting from a remission of duties averaging a half of the ordinary rates.[1]

Probably more influential in developing British trade within the Empire was the decided preference given in government purchasing, both for the colonies and for the Dominions, to British products. This was a matter of government policy, and it extended to the full range of purchases by government departments. 98·05% of government stores imported into Rhodesia in 1907 came from Britain, and 79·42% of those imported by the Union of South Africa; the percentages for 1910 and 1911 were 90·19% and 84·26%, and 94·26% and 75·23% respectively. In 1913 the British Empire supplied 93·09% of South Africa's imports of government stores (£3,302,460), of which 84·05% (£2,775,680) came from the United Kingdom—which, as Holland said, 'shows a very healthy condition in regard to British competition in Government Stores during the year 1913'![2] The percentage for the normal range of British imports to South Africa was just under 60%.[3] The South African government was prepared to pay more for a British product. 'There is every desire on the part of colonial municipalities', Henry Birchenough reported in 1904, 'to meet manufacturers half way by paying an appreciably higher price for British work.' But he warned that the municipalities had obligations to the communities they represented and the price could not be too much out of line.[4] The Central South African railway system had recently placed a large contract in England for 80-lb rails, in spite of the fact that British prices were acknowledged to be from 10 to 15% higher than Continental or American. In a product like this, with such a formidable margin, it is obvious that British manufacturers were not going to waste their time and

[1] Dominions Royal Commission, *Second Interim Report*, P.P. 1914, XVIII, 147.
[2] Sothern Holland's report on South Africa for 1913, P.P. 1914-16, XLV, 624.
[3] Sothern Holland's report on South Africa for 1911, P.P. 1912-13, XCIII, 899.
[4] Birchenough's report on South Africa for 1903, P.P. 1904, LXI, 101-3.

money trying to compete for Latin American markets. Their best, or only, chance of a sale lay within the Empire.

The overall position of Dominion and British Indian trade with the United Kingdom for 1912 is shown in Table VIII. The table indicates the extraordinarily strong position which British manufacturing occupied in Dominion markets by comparison even with the best of their Latin American markets. Britain's share in Crown Colony imports was higher. Over 70% of Rhodesian imports in 1913 came from the United Kingdom.[1] To Nigeria Britain was supplying between 70 and 75% of imports between 1907 and 1912[2]; to the Gold Coast about 75%. The Acting Comptroller of Customs, in his report for the Gold Coast of 19 October 1912, felt that there was not the least reason for the British supplier to be dissatisfied with his position.

> He has held his ground in all his staple commodities, and he has taken the lion's share of all important increases. . . . For every pound the German has gained in the last three years he has gained seventeen, and there is every reason to believe that, in the future, he will increase rather than lose his advantages.[3]

So far as Empire exports were concerned, it is true that the percentage was swollen by Britain's position as a clearing house for Empire produce. To a lesser extent, Britain was acting in turn as a re-exporter of Continental produce to the Empire, although the import figures in Table VIII are in most cases for the country of origin, not simply of shipment. But in measuring the extent to which Britain had captured the market for products in which she was interested, it is fair to make a distinction between imports as a whole and the imports which she was in a position to supply. If, for instance, the 'non-competitive' items in Australasian and South African imports are excluded—bullion and specie, rice, sugar, tea, coffee, oil and kerosene, ores, timber, raw rubber, hides, fresh fruit, etc.—Britain's share of Australian imports in 1912 rises to

---

[1] Sothern Holland's report on South Africa for 1913, P.P. 1914-16, XLV, 632.

[2] Birtwistle's report on Southern Nigeria, 24 August 1912, P.P. 1913, LXVIII, 367.

[3] Mitchell's report on the Gold Coast, P.P. 1913, LXVIII, 384.

Table VIII

British Trade with Selected Countries, 1912

	Imports from United Kingdom		Exports to United Kingdom		Total	
	Amount (£ million)	Percentage of total imports	Amount (£ million)	Percentage of total exports	Amount (£ million)	Percentage of total imports and exports
South Africa	23·2	58·2	56·1	88·7	79·3	76·9
New Zealand	12·5	59·6	16·9	77·4	29·4	68·7
Australia	39·1	50·1	31·5	39·8	70·6	44·9
British India	91·7	60·2	45·9	26·8	137·6	42·5
Canada	28·9	20·5	37·1	45·3	66·0	29·6
Argentine	23·7	30·8	24·3	25·3	48·0	27·7
United States	61·6	15·4	124·4	22·8	186·0	19·7
France	41·9	12·7	54·5	20·3	96·4	16·1
Germany	48·5	8·8	59·0	13·0	107·5	10·7

Source: *Second Interim Report of the Dominions Royal Commission*, P.P. 1914, LX, 145.

62·58%, of New Zealand to about 73%, and of South African (1913) to 66·95%.[1]

Although it would have been unwise to dismiss competition altogether, British traders and officials had reason to be confident in Empire markets before 1914. Table IX shows the relative shares of the United Kingdom, Germany and the United States in Australian trade, 1909-12, distinguishing between total imports and 'competitive' imports. The stability of the shares is remarkable, and it indicates the difficulties with which the United States and Germany were meeting in challenging Britain in her Empire markets. There had been a slight decline in Britain's share in 1911 and 1912, which her Trade Commissioner put down in some degree to the industrial unrest in the United Kingdom during those years. But as he pointed out in the context of the slight rise enjoyed by Germany and the United States, it was important to notice that the value of the 'competitive' trade of Britain increased by over £12½ million in the period 1909-12, which was double the combined increases of Germany and the United States, and in excess by more than £4¼ million of the increase in imports from the rest of the world.[2] British investment in Australasia was helping the trend. The annual figures for new investment show a rise from £6·1 million in 1908 to £19·4 million in 1914. New investment in Latin America reached a peak of £45·8 million in 1912, but fell in the depression years of 1913 and 1914 to £36·2 and £28·2 million respectively, just at a point when Australasian investment, standing at £10·8 million in 1912, was rising to £18·8 million in 1913 and £19·4 million in 1914.[3]

Although a downward tendency had been noticeable in the British share of Dominion markets before 1902-3, this seems largely to have been checked by 1914. Even in Canada, where the United States enjoyed special advantages, Britain was holding on to a comfortable share of a valuable trade and German competition was insignificant. If the imports of 'competitive' merchandise are

[1] Milne's report on Australia for 1912-13, P.P. 1914, LX, 117, 120; Dominions Royal Commission, *Second Interim Report*, P.P. 1914, LX, 146; Sothern Holland's report on South Africa for 1913, P.P. 1914-16, XLV, 618.

[2] Milne's report on Australia for 1912-13, P.P. 1914, LX, 121.

[3] Matthew Simon, 'The Pattern of New British Portfolio Foreign Investment, 1865-1914' in A. R. Hall (ed.), *The Export of Capital from Britain 1870-1914* (London, 1968), p. 40.

Table IX

Australian Imports from Selected Countries, 1909–12

Year	Imports (£000)	United Kingdom		Germany		United States	
		Percentage total	Percentage competitive	Percentage total	Percentage competitive	Percentage total	Percentage competitive
1909	51,172	50·54	63·61	8·87	11·05	11·60	10·23
1910	60,014	50·68	63·43	8·69	9·58	12·76	10·59
1911	66,968	48·88	61·45	9·52	11·99	13·45	11·54
1912	78,158	50·06	62·58	9·15	11·42	13·77	11·76

Source: G. T. Milne's report on the Trade of Australia during the year 1913, P.P. 1914, LX, 117, 120.

taken for the fiscal year ending 31 March 1913, the trade was divided between the United States with 57% (£43,380,000) and Britain with 33% (£25,010,000); only 10% (£7,610,000) was shared out between other trading nations.[1] Ross Hoffman, whose book on Anglo-German trade rivalry is a strange compound of praise for German competitiveness with figures which prove the reverse of his case, is at least right in pointing to the fact that Britain's hold on her colonial markets was 'most certainly as strong on the eve of the War as it had been twenty years earlier'. He prints a comparison of British and German imports for 1913 into those Empire markets where German trade was making its strongest showing (Table X), and as he says, it shows British preponderance to be 'most overwhelming'.

Table X
British and German Imports into Selected Empire Markets, 1913

	British Imports £	German Imports £
British India	91,695,158	6,874,708
Straits Settlements	6,175,526	877,739
Ceylon	3,879,975	401,500
South Africa	25,059,933	3,546,594
Nigeria	4,938,243	811,350
Sierra Leone	1,138,683	174,191
Gold Coast	3,466,351	388,669
Canada	28,521,185	2,921,879
Australia	47,615,561	4,956,834
New Zealand	13,312,193	687,935

Source: Ross J. S. Hoffman, *Great Britain and the German Trade Rivalry 1875-1914* (Philadelphia, 1933), p. 201.

Britain's performance in India during the decade before 1914 was very creditable. She was holding her own in products like railway materials, machinery, tools and implements, electrical apparatus, cars and commercial vehicles, where she suffered marked failures in competition elsewhere. India, in 1913, was taking no less than 42% of British exports of cotton piece goods, in place of 23% in 1850. By contrast, the cotton piece goods to the Western Hemisphere, excluding the United States, had fallen from the 27% of 1850, to 10% in 1913, and to the United States from 10

[1] Hamilton Wickes' report on Canada for 1913, P.P. 1914, LX, 219.

to 1%.[1] There was no direct stated preference, outside government purchasing, for British goods in India; tastes lay in that direction, the main buyers were British, and most of the natural channels for India's foreign trade lay through the United Kingdom.

It was not surprising that the greater part of the drive and enterprise associated with British exporting should have been directed at these large and promising imperial markets; they were the 'naturals' for British manufacturers and merchants before the First World War. The total trade of British South Africa during 1912 amounted to £105,338,140—merchandise imports and exports, re-exports, specie and government stores. Of this, the United Kingdom handled no less than 78·9%, which, as the Trade Commissioner said, truly represented the great value of the South African market to the manufacturers, merchants, traders, shipowners and bankers of the United Kingdom.[2] The pattern of preference among British businessmen is evident from Figure II. The top curve (A) represents British exports to the 'white Dominions', to Australia, New Zealand, Canada and South Africa; it shows marked, dramatic progress from 1898. The second curve (B) shows British exports to Latin America as a whole, and its similarity with curve A until as late as 1910 suggests why commentators have tended to lump together these 'new' countries, Dominion and Latin American, in discussing Britain's competitive position before 1914. But if Argentina, which for British trade and investment was not unlike a 'white Dominion', is removed, the result is the flatter curve C, at a level by 1913 which, for the whole of Latin America less Argentina, was not much more than a third of British exports to the Dominions. And if Brazil, Chile and Uruguay (for which adequate commercial representation, the renewed competitiveness of certain lines of British manufactures, and large British investments after the early 1900s had inflated our trade) are also removed, we are left with curve D, the 'normal' pattern for British trading interest in the Republics. Curve D is the sum of British exports to all the remaining Republics—to Mexico, Guatemala, Costa Rica, El Salvador, Honduras, Nicaragua,

---

[1] C. P. Kindleberger, 'Foreign Trade and Economic Growth: Lessons from Britain and France, 1850 to 1913', *Economic History Review*, 2nd ser. XIV (1961), 296.

[2] Sothern Holland's report on South Africa for 1912, P.P. 1913, LXVIII, 338.

I

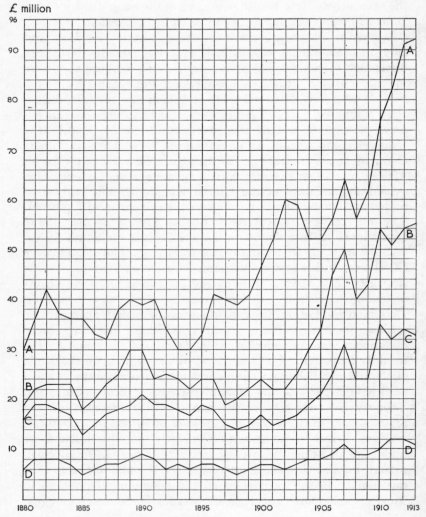

Figure II. Exports of the Produce and Manufactures of the United
Kingdom to the Dominions and to Latin America, 1880-
1913 (declared values).

£ million

Key: A – Australia, Canada, New Zealand, Canada and South Africa
     B – Latin America
     C – Latin America, less Argentina
     D – Latin America, less Argentina, Brazil, Chile and Uruguay.

Source: U.K. Trade and Navigation Accounts, *rounded to the nearest million pounds.*

Panama, Cuba, Puerto Rico, the Dominican Republic, Haiti, Colombia, Venezuela, Ecuador, Peru, Bolivia and Paraguay.

*

The point, so far as British manufacturers and traders were concerned, was that the greater part of Latin America was simply not in the running for such resources as they were prepared to put into the development of existing and new trades.

The *per capita* consumption of foreign imports for the majority of the Republics was extraordinarily low. Argentina approached nearest to the Dominions, with £10·3 per head in 1912 to New Zealand's £19·3. But an estimate for Venezuela in 1910 gave about a guinea a head, and Carden's calculation for the annual consumption of British imports into Mexico in the early '90s was a bare 80 cents per inhabitant.[1] At the end of the nineteenth century as at the beginning, a large proportion of Latin America's population could not be regarded as consumers of any kind of import. Jenner calculated, in the mid-'80s, that about 7 million, out of a total Mexican population of 10½ million, were still 'utterly indifferent to the needs and aspirations of civilised humanity'.[2] The small shopkeepers, artisans and minor professional men, who made up the middle class in Mexican towns, were poor and frugal in their tastes, and their contribution to imports was insignificant. This left only the upper classes to be supplied, the 6,000 or 7,000 families who shared out the entire lands of Mexico between them, and their political and professional associates in the cities. In the smaller Republics conditions were as bad or worse. What could one expect to import into Bolivia, where the Indian 'grows his own food, makes his clothes from the wool of his llamas and sheep, lives all day in the open air and goes to bed with the sun in a mud hut devoid of furniture'?[3] What market was to be found in Guatemala, where 'two or three yards of grey cotton each person per annum' met all their needs, other than for 'the rum, manufactured in the Republic, by which they destroy themselves'[4]; or in Haiti, where few had 'more than the clothes they stand up in and these are

---

[1] Milne's report on Venezuela, 1913, P.P. 1913, LXVIII, 612; Carden's report on the finances of Mexico, 1881-91, P.P. 1893-4, XCV, 201.

[2] Jenner's report on the finances of Mexico for 1886, P.P. 1887, LXXXV, 20.

[3] Smith's report on Oruro (Bolivia) for 1912, P.P. 1913, LXIX, 195.

[4] Scholfield's report on Guatemala for 1871, P.P. 1873, LXIV, 318.

rarely in a condition to cover them', and where 'there is a brisk demand for old condensed milk, preserve, butter and lard tins, of which are made practically all the cooking and table utensils they use'?[1] Great expectations had been formed of the agricultural wealth of northern Brazil, but, said Consul Cowper, 'imagine six months' heavy rain without any drainage, and then six months' of scorching sun without irrigation, and your Lordship may form an idea of how far commerce may be extended'.[2]

The United States, by the beginning of the twentieth century, was exporting more goods to Mexico than all the European powers put together, and as the British consul in Mexico City said at the time, there was no possibility of this being otherwise; 'Mexico, from the point of view of British trade, is not, as it were, on the main line'. The Mexican market, he added a year later, was small and unlikely to increase, 'as it is evident that a determined effort is to be made to make it into a manufacturing country'.[3] Britons were as pessimistic about most of the Central American and Caribbean markets, with reason. Venezuela's total imports, which had averaged £3,295,200 p.a. between 1892 and 1896, had fallen to an average of £2,503,500 between 1907-8 and 1911-12. In fact, the level of British imports back in the mid-'70s was higher than it was in the years before the war. The British vice-consul at Caracas pointed out in 1907 that although Venezuela was more or less equal in area to Germany, France, Italy and Greece put together, her annual imports were only about one-tenth of the value of all goods entering Norway in 1906; what is more, they were showing a steady decline.[4] British exports to Guatemala over the first decade of this century averaged £245,000. Averaged over July 1901 to July 1906, British imports into Honduras amounted only to £38,774 and her share of the Republic's exports to £5,603; the United States, by contrast, was importing £264,982 and exporting £355,129. Where British manufacturers retained a substantial share of the trade, the explanation is to be found less in any effort on their part to work the trade than in the acknowledged superiority of their cotton goods in an unsophisticated

---

[1] Murray's report on Haiti for 1908, P.P. 1909, XCVI, 8.
[2] Cowper's report on Pernambuco for 1859, P.P. 1862, LVIII, 423.
[3] Jerome's reports on Mexico for 1902 and 1903, P.P. 1903, LXXVIII, 225, and P.P. 1905, XC, 760.
[4] Gray's report on Caracas for 1906, P.P. 1907, XCIII, 829.

import trade of which textiles still accounted for a major part. In Ecuador and Paraguay, at the end of the 1900s, Britain retained between 30 and 35% of the import trade, in spite of being barely, if at all, represented among importers, wholesalers and retailers. But for each Republic textiles were by far the most important manufactured item on the import list, £497,923 out of Ecuadorean imports of £1,870,424 in 1909, £214,236 out of Paraguayan imports of £757,590 for the same year.

Many of these markets were simply too small to be bothered with, so long as an alternative existed. The tendency which Sir Francis Oppenheimer observed in 1913-14 for Germany to direct an increasing proportion of her foreign trade to the smaller countries, to Chile, Colombia, the Dominican Republic, Siam, Morocco, the Philippines, Venezuela, Bolivia, Uruguay, etc.[1]— was a reflection of Germany's exclusion from so many of the really promising markets outside Europe. Britain had those promising markets, in the Empire, in China and in Argentina, firmly under control, and her own inclination for many years had been to move out of the minor markets and to concentrate her resources on those which really paid. Why should Britons trouble themselves with shipping services to Rio Grande do Sul, in Southern Brazil, when there were such magnificent opportunities in the newly constructed port of Buenos Aires? British shipowners abandoned the Rio Grande service long before there was any question of German competition, and when representations were made to the shipping lines to the effect that the trade of the region would fall inevitably, without a shipping link, into German hands, they replied that since the trade no longer suited them such a result was immaterial.[2] British shipowners knew that their capital could be better employed elsewhere, as they did for similarly unpromising services to the west coast of South and Central America, and to parts of Africa and the Middle East. The Departmental Committee on Shipping and Shipbuilding, reporting in 1918 on German competition before the war, explained how German trade and influence had been increased in certain directions by the reluctance of British shipping, with its long record and established connections,

---

[1] Oppenheimer's report on Germany for 1913, P.P. 1914-16, LXXII, 808.
[2] Stanniforth's report on Rio Grande do Sul for 1899 and 1900, P.P. 1902, CV, 378-9.

to engage in unremunerative trades while the more lucrative trades in the world were still open.

> German shipping, being a late comer, had in a sense to be content with the leavings and to develop new spheres which might in time become profitable. It would appear that factors of this kind existed in the Persian Gulf, and in Eastern Africa, and that, when German competition became keen, the British companies did not think the trades worth fighting for.[1]

In terms of carrying capacity, quality and age of ships, the British mercantile marine had reason to think itself, before 1914, the most up-to-date and efficient fleet in the world. On 30 June 1914, with 11,538,000 tons of steam vessels, Britain had 44·4% of the world's steam tonnage, with Germany's 3,096,000 tons (11·9%) next in the line; the United States was third with only 1,195,000 tons (4·6%).[2] The British share of foreign tonnage at Buenos Aires rose from 56% in 1903 to 61% in 1912 (from 1·4 million tons to 3·6 million tons); Germany could only maintain a 12% share, 406,000 tons rising to 660,000 tons. Britain had 56% of the tonnage at Bahia and Rio in 1913, 65% at Pernambuco.[3] What did she care if she lost some trade in the smaller ports of southern Brazil?

British manufacturers and merchants made precisely the same calculation. Their efforts in Latin America were directed at the principal cities, and at ports like Pernambuco and Panama, which lay conveniently on a main trade route. They clustered round those towns which serviced the export products in which Britons or their capital were interested, Iquique, Pará and Manaos for Peruvian and Brazilian rubber, Rosario and Bahia Blanca for Argentine wheat, the Chilean nitrate ports, and Oruro as the centre of the great Bolivian tin-mining industry. Markets which lay off the main routes, or which served export products in which the United Kingdom had little interest, were left to those less fortunate or more interested in Latin American products for which Britain's sources of supply lay elsewhere. Back in the '60s, Lennon Hunt called attention to the fact that no less than 84 commercial

---

[1] *Report of the Departmental Committee on Shipping and Shipbuilding,* P.P. 1918, XIII, 573.

[2] *Ibid.,* 525.

[3] Figures from R. G. Greenhill, 'British Shipping in Latin America and the Caribbean: a case study (the Royal Mail Steam Packet Company)', unpublished Ph.D. thesis, Exeter, 1971.

houses (19 of which were British) shared the £3¼ million of import/export trade at Pernambuco. Yet at Puerto Rico, for which the trade was almost as large but which lay off Britain's traditional trade routes, there was not a single British mercantile house. The contrast, as he said, was 'a curious instance of the tendency of trade to run in particular grooves'.[1]

Britain was, in fact, in the position of any well-established trader or manufacturer. The question was not whether she could make a sale at all, but which sale offered the better return. She had to decide whether it was worth making a bid for certain kinds of markets when she was well-established in others and under no pressure to move. She had to allocate capital and skilled labour to best advantage, and since these resources were limited, she was bound to lose sales when her order books were full. British manufacturers might have sold many more locomotives to Argentina in the late '90s, or agricultural appliances to Cuban sugar planters in the early 1900s, or battle cruisers to Latin American navies before the First World War. But their order books were full, their terms were consequently inflexible, their delivery dates were distant, they would not go out of their way to alter plant to suit individual manufacturing needs, and they lost the sales to Germany or the United States.

As old-established traders and manufacturers, Britons had certain prejudices and preferences which set limits to the type of business which appealed to them. British merchants did not care to handle the smaller lines. They were not prepared, as were some Hamburg commission houses at the turn of the century, to make up cases and invoices of mixed goods in almost retail quantities, so that an invoice of £10 to £20 might frequently consist of all kinds of articles from cutlery to silks and laces.[2] The established English merchant, said Ernest Satow in his report on the trade of Uruguay for 1886-90, was

> not under the same necessity of offering inducements to consumers as those who aspire towards an equally good place in the commerce of the world. He does not care for the trivialities, the odds and ends of trade, but looks to large transactions of a simple kind in a few articles of extensive consumption. If he

[1] Hunt's report on Pernambuco for 1863, P.P. 1865, LIII, 356.
[2] Cartwright's report on Ecuador for 1899-1905, P.P. 1906, CXXIV, 78.

finds the remuneration inadequate, he turns his attention to more lucrative fields.[1]

In trade, as in all things English, a snobbery developed over lines of trade, qualities of goods. The travellers in Manchester piece goods, frequently seen even in the remoter Republics where nobody else in Britain cared tuppence for the market, were not themselves to be bothered with the umbrellas, pins, needles, shoes, shawls, silk handkerchiefs, knives, buttons and carpets hawked round by the Germans and the French. Their attitude was shared by the British trader in the Far East where the dealers in tea and silk were the commercial aristocracy, and articles other than these were known derisively as the 'muck and truck trade', suitable only for foreigners. When asked why they did not handle a certain type of product, British merchants declared it to be 'too small for them to look into' or 'not in their line', even if, as one consul said rather sadly, 'somehow there always seems to be a German in whose line it is'.

It was not only the range of products but the quality which set limits to British interest. In the early days of trade in Latin America, British manufacturers had been up to all the tricks. Cast-iron knives, hatchets, carpenters' tools, nails had been sold as wrought iron, and 'brought our hardware manufacturers into great disgrace'.[2] Cotton goods were adulterated with clay which, as a Glasgow manufacturer told the Select Committee on Manufactures in 1833, enabled British manufacturers 'to sell a very showy article very cheap, and the foreigners liked it'.[3] The reputation of British linen goods was such that the dictator Francia himself examined every piece of linen purchased by the Paraguayan government for soldiers' shirts and trousers. His Excellency, distrustful of Irish and Manchester manufacturers, would often unroll with his own hands the piece of goods submitted for inspection, and measure it out, yard by yard, to check it against the length, 25, 26 or 28 yards, marked on the ticket.

So quick-sighted did he become in the quality of manufactured goods, that finding a great many of them had wide interstices

[1] P.P. 1890-91, LXXXVIII, 692.
[2] Andrews, *Buenos Ayres*, p. 173.
[3] Minutes of Evidence, *Report of the Select Committee on Manufactures, Commerce and Shipping*, P.P. 1833, VI, Q.5463.

between the threads, filled up with starch, he had one end of the piece washed, and then viewing it through a microscope, ascertained the nature of its real texture. If he found, as it must be confessed he often did, the gaps between the thread to be rather yawning, he allowed the owner half of the prime cost for it, and told him to thank his stars, for that he ought to be imprisoned as a knave and imposter.[1]

In cotton goods Britain continued to make the full range, from the cheapest to the best qualities. Zimmern remembered his own firm, at the beginning of this century, selling 18-inch prints in Latin American markets at a penny a yard—'undeniably pretty poor stuff'.[2] But in cotton goods in those Republics which were developing their own industries, as in every other product meeting with foreign and local competition, the tendency was for British manufacturers to take refuge in higher quality production, beyond the skills and range of their competitors. The quality of goods demanded on the home market in the United Kingdom was also rising, and by the last quarter of the century Britain was generally a high-quality market, unprepared to tolerate shoddy goods.

The trend towards higher quality may have been primarily defensive, as it was for the Birmingham and Black Country flint-glass and gun trades. It would also, as Wickham pointed out in 1914, have been a serious error to divert skilled labour from making high-grade goods, for which there was a good demand and less competition, to the production of low-grade articles in which the competition was severe.[3] But there can be no doubt that a strong belief developed in British industry, more particularly in the hardware and engineering trades and in some branches of the textile trade, in the maintenance of high-quality production as an end in itself. Much of Latin America before 1914, with the exception of the rising markets in the cities of Argentina, Brazil and Chile, was still a low quality outlet. Few could afford to pay for quality. Heavy depreciation in most Latin American currencies in the late nineteenth century had inflated the price of imports, and consequently lowered the quality which all could afford. There

[1] Robertson, *Paraguay*, III, 227.
[2] W. H. Zimmern, 'Lancashire and Latin America 50-60 Years Ago', *Manchester School of Economic and Social Studies*, XXVIII (1960), 42.
[3] Wickham's report on New Zealand for 1914, P.P. 1914-16, XLVI, 660.

were clear signs of a return to a better quality of demand in most of the Republics in and after the turn of the century, but expectations were still generally low.

For the British Dominions, on the other hand, high-quality markets developed to replace similar markets in Europe now closed by tariffs, and British manufacturers turned naturally to Dominion consumers as outlets for the quality products on which they had come to pride themselves. 'There is perhaps no country in the world,' said Hamilton Wickes from Australia in 1911, 'where wages are higher and wealth more evenly distributed, and a population more ready to pay for an article, when its intrinsic value is properly demonstrated.'[1] Manufacturers were sometimes slow to become aware of this change, and consumers found it difficult to alter their habits or standards. But the trend was there, and alert traders and manufacturers were on to it before long. Britain's Trade Commissioner in New Zealand was confident, just before the war, that a considerable section of the community now put quality before price, although his predecessor, a few years before, had described New Zealand as still generally a market for cheap goods, except in such lines as tools, some woollen goods, electrical machinery and appliances, some hardware, ribbons, muslins and fancy goods.[2] The same tendency had been remarked rather earlier in South Africa, where Henry Birchenough saw signs in 1903/4 that the days were over when cheapness was, as hitherto, the first consideration; better goods were now wanted in almost every branch of trade, especially in 'soft' goods of all sorts. Birchenough had been 'assured over and over again by merchants and retailers that the level of quality in general goods was being raised all over the Colonies'.[3]

The decision not to go for the cheap-quality trades, to keep to the main lines of production, was quite deliberate. British manufacturers had lost the popular market for cheap cutlery in Argentina before the war; they consistently refused to meet the demand, first because they did not make the cheaper range, and then because if they did it would ruin their reputation for good work. This

[1] Hamilton Wickes' report on Australia for 1909 and 1910, P.P. 1911, LXXXVII, 565.
[2] Wickham's report on New Zealand for 1911, P.P. 1912-13, XCIII, 940; Jeffray's report on New Zealand for 1907, P.P. 1908, LXXIII, 309.
[3] Birchenough's report on South Africa for 1903, P.P. 1904, LXI, 40.

reputation accounted for the willingness of customers, in all markets, to continue to pay rather more for British goods, and it was worth preserving. After all, even if the popular demand in Argentina was for the cheaper cutlery, often manufactured locally,

the large English community in the country, as well as the wealthier Argentines themselves, who as a rule are extremely partial to English goods, from socks to agricultural machinery, still insist on Sheffield blades, which in the best shops are the only ones procurable.[1]

In the distant, inaccessible markets of Bolivia, Paraguay, the interior of Colombia, Ecuador and Brazil, prime cost was so small an element in the final retail price that it made little sense to pay fractionally less for the lower quality article. On the other hand, there was no technical obstacle which might prevent Germany from raising the quality of her goods once she had made an entry into a market, and this is what she often did. Whatever the rights and wrongs of the British manufacturers' decision, and this could only be argued for each individual case, there could, said Jeffray from Australia in 1907, be 'little doubt in the face of the evidence as to the fact of a deliberate choice'.[2] Even in Empire markets, Britons were content to leave the miscellaneous low-value trades to others. The 'Kaffir Truck' trade in South Africa, in cheap goods suited to the native market—beads, cotton blankets, brass, copper and steel wire, cheap cutlery—was left to Germany and Belgium. Belgium did a good trade in blankets, unbleached cotton with very bright coloured headings at each end, for sale to the natives of South Africa. The trade was large enough to tempt Lancashire manufacturers to compete, but after repeated trials they declared that it was 'not worth their while to pursue it, as they could use their looms to better advantage'[3]. British distillers made no serious effort to capture the West African gin traffic, a trade worth over £410,000 p.a. in imports into Southern Nigeria alone around 1910. C. A. Birtwistle reported from Lagos that there appeared to be a strong prejudice in some quarters against the business 'in what is commonly termed "trade" spirit, this

[1] N. L. Watson, *The Argentine as a Market* (Manchester, 1908), pp. 37-8.
[2] P.P. 1907, LVI, 802.
[3] Birchenough's report on South Africa for 1903, P.P. 1904, LXI, 89.

description being held in contempt as implying that the liquor sent out here from Rotterdam or Hamburg is generally of the worst possible type'.[1]

It was, to some extent, the universality of cheap foreign goods in every low-grade store throughout the world before 1914 that has given a misleading impression of competitive failure on the part of the British manufacturer. The fact was that these were markets for which, in most cases, Britons did not compete. Germany may have been making rapid headway in certain lines designed to suit particular markets, but, said the Departmental Committee on the Engineering Trades, 'our manufacturers do not turn out these cheaper articles, being content apparently to let the cheaper trade go'.[2]

*

The interest taken by European nations in Latin America and the advance of their trade were determined to a substantial extent by their respective contributions to immigration for each of the Republics. Immigration statistics are as difficult to handle as any before 1914. In the case of Argentina and Brazil, by a long margin the largest recipients of European immigration, the statistics are complicated by a heavy movement of seasonal labour between southern Europe and Latin America. Mallet estimated that no less than 150,000 men were needed to get in the Argentine wheat crop for 1883-4, and the demand for harvesters was so great that as much as £12 a month was offered, with board and lodging.[3] Machinery was already taking part of the burden, and there were over 4,000 reaping machines in the Santa Fé province alone by the mid-'80s. But grain production was rising all the time, and the Argentine cereal harvest in the years just before the war provided constant employment for some 130,000 men over a period of five months (December to February for wheat, linseed and oats; February to April for maize).[4] After the Argentine harvest was in, Italian and Spanish labourers could go up to Brazil to pick coffee cherries in São Paulo, and return to Europe in time for the harvest

---

[1] Birtwistle's report, Lagos, 24 August 1912, P.P. 1913, LXVIII, 380.
[2] *Report of the Departmental Committee on the Engineering Trades*, P.P. 1918, XIII, 394.
[3] Mallet's report on Rosario for 1883, P.P. 1884, LXXX, 11.
[4] *The Times*, 8 September 1911, 3d.

and two/three months at home with their families. A return fare of £5 or £6 falling as low at one time as £1. 6s. for a single passage, and an accumulated £50 to £60 of harvest wages, made economic sense to a Southern European. Yet even apart from this seasonal migration and from the effect it had on immigration figures, it was usual for Europeans to come out to Latin America with the intention of staying only for a few years, of saving as much as they could, and of returning to buy land in their native villages in Spain or Italy. Many formed attachments and stayed, but in a country like Argentina where landownership was concentrated in relatively few hands and where so much of the land was held primarily for speculation and leased out on a short-term basis for cultivation and conversion to alfalfa for grazing, it was often difficult to find satisfactory land to purchase. Whatever the reason, of the 4,758,729 immigrants entering Argentina between 1857 and 1916, 2,184,708 are estimated to have left the Republic.[1]

The numbers, then, have to be taken simply as an indication of an order of magnitude. So far as can be calculated, the net gain of Italians to Argentina, 1857-1916, was 1,112,086.[2] Foerster estimated that 2 million, or 30% of the Argentine population, were Italian or of Italian descent by the second decade of this century, and in Brazil he put the Italian element in 1919 at about 7% in a population of 20 million.[3] For Latin America as a whole, Rippy guessed at a population of over 6 million of Italian or part-Italian descent by 1900, rising to over 8 million forty years later.[4] For the period 1857-1916, 928,908 of the Spaniards entering Argentina remained in the country.[5] Total Spanish immigration to Brazil between 1841 and 1920 amounted to 510,814, compared with a Portuguese total of 1,055,167, an Italian of 1,388,893, a German of 131,441, and a French of 30,503—in no case, however, allowing for departures.[6] Spaniards tended to form the largest immigrant

[1] Figures from David P. Rock, 'Radicalism and the Urban Working Classes in Argentina, 1916-22', unpublished Ph.D. thesis, Cambridge 1971, p. 13 fn. 6.
[2] *Ibid.*
[3] Robert F. Foerster, *The Italian Emigration of our Times* (Cambridge, Mass., 1919).
[4] J. Fred Rippy, *Latin America, a modern history* (Ann Arbor, 1958), p. 365, and Rippy, 'Italian Immigrants and Investments in Latin America', *Inter-American Economic Affairs*, III (1949), 27.
[5] Rock, 'Radicalism and the Urban Working Classes', p. 13 fn. 6.
[6] Roy Nash, *The Conquest of Brazil* (New York, 1926), p. 151.

element in the northern Republics, Central America and Mexico, and 800,000 are believed to have settled in Cuba.[1] Some 750,000 immigrants of 'German' descent may have entered Latin America between 1850 and 1914, with the largest communities in Brazil and Argentina,[2] and French settlers in South America, again principally in Argentina and Brazil, were estimated at about half a million at the end of 1909.[3]

Each of these communities became an important element in developing trade with the homeland. Italians looked for the pasta, the wine, spirits, rice, oil, cheeses, the prints and engravings, the blue cotton dress of the Italian working class. Spaniards imported wines, olive oil, sardines and conserves, Barcelona cottons and clothing, cord-soled shoes, fire-arms, fans, tiles, casks, musical instruments, books and newspapers. The Portuguese and Brazilians generally retained a taste for the dried fish and sardines, the onions, chestnuts and wine, and the traditional clothing of the Portuguese people. O'Sullivan-Beare, in his report on São Paulo for 1911, remarked on the fact that twenty years before, when Italian immigration was only just beginning to flow into the state, imports from Italy had been insignificant. But Italian trade had doubled itself over the past six years, and was now worth over £1 million. 800,000 Italian immigrants had made their homes in the State; they had 'preserved their taste for the products of their native land, and it is their demand for these which supports the export trade of Italy with this State'.[4]

Italian immigration and trade were as strong further south in Brazil, in Uruguay and in Argentina. Intensive German settlement in the towns and agricultural colonies of southern Brazil, in the states of Parana, Santa Catarina and Rio Grande do Sul, gave German trade a solid advantage. Patriotism, national prejudice or taste are only part of the explanation. The fact was that once an area had become intensively settled by one nationality, the natural direction of trade passed through the home country. The ships which brought immigrants and seasonal workers carried out cargoes of manufactured goods; they brought back the produce of

[1] W. L. Schurz, *Latin America* (New York, 1942), p. 96.

[2] J. Fred Rippy, 'German Investments in Latin America', *Journal of Business of the University of Chicago*, XXI (1948), 65.

[3] *The Times*, South American Supplement, 28 December 1909, 46.

[4] O'Sullivan Beare's report on São Paulo for 1911, P.P. 1912-13, XCIV, 458.

the settlements. Uruguay was served by fast steamers from Genoa packed tight with steerage passengers and offering sea freight on goods at about half the rate from Havre or Antwerp. The German colonies of southern Brazil, abandoned by British liner services in favour of more profitable calls to the north and south, were supplied regularly from Hamburg. In southern Chile the German community, strong in resources rather than numbers (since only 7,049 Germans are recorded in the 1899 population statistics for Chile), did much to determine the pattern of shipping services and the general direction of trade. Vice-Consul Howard described Valdivia, at the turn of the century, as in a real sense a German colony, since the extensive tan-yards, the large brewery and a quarter of the 8,000 population were German. Of exports in 1898 valued at $2,900,000, $2,590,000 went to Germany and none to Britain; of the imports, $1,207,779 came from Germany, and a bare $270,000 from Britain.[1]

The same applied wherever British subjects were settled in sufficient numbers. The Germans monopolized Valdivia, but up north, in a Chilean nitrate port like Iquique where Britons staffed the nitrate companies, the orders from the *oficinas* (nitrate works), whether for foodstuffs, clothing or machinery, went home to the United Kingdom unless there were distinct advantages in placing them elsewhere. Edward Hudson explained that British subjects abroad liked to use articles with which they were familiar both in their houses and in their business, and if they could not obtain what they wanted from local importers, they sent for it from England. He concluded that wherever there was a British community established in a foreign country the importation of British-made goods in that district would be found to be considerable.[2]

Britons were as loyal or as conservative in their tastes as any others. But British settlement in Latin America was relatively insignificant. The great flood of emigration which left the British Isles, over 15 million between 1851 and 1920, was directed almost entirely towards the Empire and the United States. Although 21,000 British 'immigrants' are included in Brazilian statistics, the wastage was high and there were never more than a few thousand Britons resident in Brazil at any one time. If allowances are made for second-generation residents, who appear as 'nationals' on the

[1] Howard's report on Valdivia for 1899, P.P. 1900, XCII, 515.
[2] Hudson's report on Iquique for 1911, P.P. 1912-13, XCIV, 544.

census statistics, there may have been 11,000 British subjects in Chile in the mid-1900s (of whom perhaps 5,000 were of dual nationality, often more Chilean than the Chileans themselves), and perhaps a further 2,500 in Uruguay.[1] The statistics are complicated in the Caribbean region by the large numbers of West Indians, themselves good consumers of British goods so far as their incomes permitted, serving as casual or contract labour on plantations and public works. The 1911 census for Panama showed 23,062 British West Indians, while about an equal number worked in the Canal Zone; other British subjects amounted only to 567. The United Fruit Company employed large numbers of West Indians on its plantations all over Central America. There were 1,500 in Nicaragua in the early 1900s, and in the Orinoco region of Venezuela, next to Trinidad, about 8,000 West Indians were said to be settled before the war. The 5,198 British subjects listed in the revised Mexican census figures for 1910 included Australians, Canadians and Jamaicans; Spaniards headed the list for foreigners with 24,212 and North Americans accounted for 19,568. The only substantial British community in Latin America was in Argentina. Britons accounted for a bare 2% of immigration into Argentina during the nineteenth century, and many of those returned home again. But the official immigration figures conceal two factors of some importance, the arrival of many British subjects via Montevideo so that they appear on the statistics as 'Uruguayans', and the exclusion of first-class passengers (among whom so large a proportion were British). In the event, census figures are the only guide to numbers, together with the informed guesses of men on the spot as to the element of second generation Anglo-Argentines. The 1895 census gave 21,000 foreign-born Britons in Argentina, of whom 6,700 lived in the city of Buenos Aires and 8,700 in Buenos Aires province; Consul Ross estimated the British population at the time, counting the Anglo-Argentines, as not far short of 50,000. In his report of a decade later, Ross remained convinced that the British population numbered about 50,000, and there was no reason why it should have declined.[2]

---

[1] Leary's report on Chile for 1907, P.P. 1908, CX, 94: Kennedy's report on Uruguay for 1910, in which first-generation Britons are given as 1,324, P.P. 1911, XCVII, 746.

[2] Ross's reports on Buenos Aires for 1901 and 1910, P.P. 1902, CV, 138 and P.P. 1911, XC, 53.

The British community in Argentina was undoubtedly a strong element in maintaining the level of British trade, and its purchasing power was out of proportion to its numbers. The huge Italian community, while it contained many prosperous businessmen, industrialists and landowners in Argentina, Uruguay and Brazil, was generally working class—peasants and 'colonists' in the country, labourers in the cities and towns. The Spaniards and Portuguese, the other large immigrant groups, were also predominantly working class. The emphasis in the British community was quite the reverse, with the lead taken by merchants, landowners, engineers and businessmen, while few fell below the level of skilled labour, paid at relatively generous contract rates. Nothing, however, could replace numbers as a stimulus to trade, especially as the big foreign communities worked their way up in the commercial, industrial and professional circles of the Republics.

For Britons, Latin America could never offer the same incentives to emigration and permanent settlement. The working class, which found it difficult enough to settle in Latin communities, in hot climates, on the local diet of black beans or rice and yuca, could always find a more familiar and congenial outlet in North America or the white Dominions. They were under pressure, in fact, to do so from the Dominions themselves, from a large number of trade union and philanthropic societies in the United Kingdom, and from the government Emigration Commissioners. The experience of British working-class migrants to Latin America, on the occasions when a particularly tempting offer of subsidised passages, land, stock and implements had encouraged emigration, was almost universally unfortunate. The reports of the Emigration Commissioners and of the Emigrants' Information Office gave notice right up to the First World War of a steady stream of published warnings and advice against emigration to Latin America. The climate, yellow fever, sanitary conditions, diet, language, insecurity of life and property (particularly for men without the resources to buy protection), all militated against emigration. The Emigrants' Information Office explained, in its report of January 1891, that

> the common sense of the subject is, perhaps, adequately expressed in a leaflet issued by this Office during the past year to intending emigrants to foreign lands, which states that 'the

K

climate of most countries outside Europe is less suited to emigrants from the United Kingdom than the British colonies in Canada, Australasia, and South Africa, and the United States', and that 'in all foreign countries British emigrants will have to face the disadvantage of different government and laws, and, except in the case of the United States, language and mode of life and work from those to which they have been used'.[1]

It should be said that the emigrants had themselves to blame for many of their misfortunes, and the dislike of British working men for Latin Americans was returned. The Guatemalan government, anxious to encourage northern European settlement in the early '70s, went out of its way to get Germans in preference to Englishmen. The stray British workmen visiting the country had established for themselves the reputation of 'a contentious and intemperate race, constantly in trouble with the authorities, and a nuisance to everybody connected with them'.[2] Nothing in the traditional consumption of British working men was cheap in Latin America other than liquor, and it was to liquor that they turned for compensation for the heat and squalor which they found on their arrival. There was seduction, too, in an Indian proverb which many took to heart. Why stand when you can sit, and why sit when you can lie?—for the day is made for rest, and the night for sleep.

British contract labour was more successful, at any rate under the better employers, and skilled working men found a place at gold and silver mines all over the Continent, at copper mines and smelting works in Chile, in cotton factories in Brazil, on the railways and in their workshops, in the waterworks, gas and drainage companies, and on the docks, sometimes in communities of as many as two or three hundred men and their families. In the mid-'80s about 300 Cornishmen were still employed at the Pachuca mines in Mexico. As many Englishmen found employment in a single railway company, the Central Argentine, administered and

---

[1] *Report on the Emigrants' Information Office for 1890*, P.P. 1890-91, LVI, 152. I have tried myself to explain the failure of British working-class agricultural settlement in two articles, 'British Agricultural Colonization in Latin America', *Inter-American Economic Affairs*, 18 (1964), 3-38, and 19 (1965), 23-42.

[2] Scholfield's report on Guatemala for 1871, P.P. 1873, LXIV, 321.

staffed by Englishmen from Rosario to Córdoba. The largest community built on skilled, contract labour was the sheep rearing and shepherd population of the Magallanes Territory in Chile and Southern Patagonia in Argentina, where over 8,000 British subjects were settled in the early 1920s[1]; wages were much higher than they were at home, the contract was for only three to four years at a time, free passages out and home were provided, and opportunities existed for saving. Back in the '60s, a foreman, platelayer or engine-driver in Pernambuco could earn £14 to £15 a month, a smith, carpenter, bricklayer or mason, £12 to £14—rates half as high again as those paid to local skilled labour; a skilled mechanic at Coquimbo, the Chilean copper mining and smelting centre, could ask between £150 and £200 p.a.[2] The 250 engineers, carpenters, moulders and fitters employed by the Pacific Steam Navigation Company in its repair works and factory at Callao were provided with 'comfortable lodgings on the company's premises', good pay and overtime, a theatre for amateur dramatics, for concerts and the weekly meetings of the Mutual Improvement Society, a 'most commodious hospital', an 'unlimited quantity of the best quality provisions, consisting of soft bread baked on the premises, beef from bullocks bred in Chile, mutton ditto, vegetables, puddings, tea, coffee, and sugar, and all the condiments on the dinner table of the middle classes in England'. They worked from 7 a.m. to 5 p.m. (2 p.m. on Saturdays), and their souls were in the care of an Episcopalian clergyman, subscribed for by the Company at £400 p.a.[3]

Naturally British labour of this kind, while it existed, helped to promote British imports, but it was expensive, not always satisfactory in the tougher conditions of the Brazilian textile mills, and replaced as soon as possible by cheaper local men and women. Special skills alone could command a market up to the First World War. A rich mine of the standing of the St John del Rey Mining Co. Ltd, working at Morro Velho in Minas Geraes the deepest gold mine in the world, could afford to continue paying for imported skilled labour. The company in the 1900s still provided

[1] Department of Overseas Trade, *Report on the Financial and Commercial Condition of Chile* (H.M. Stationery Office, 1922), p. 70.

[2] Hunt's report on Pernambuco for 1863, P.P. 1865, LIII, 367; Gollan's report on Coquimbo for 1866, P.P. 1867-8, LXVIII, 5.

[3] Wilson's report on the Pacific Steam Navigation Co., 11 May 1878, P.P. 1878, LXXV, 302.

a hotel for 160 Englishmen, where they were fed daily at a charge of under £3 a month; their wages, for a British chargehand working underground, were £19 a month and overtime for the first four-year agreement, £23 a month for the second. The average agricultural wage at the time was 1s. 10d. a day.[1]

With these aristocratic exceptions, it was only an unfortunate accident which brought a British working man to Latin America. British communities in the Republics were small and middle class. The English equivalent of migrant Italian and Spanish labour, of the 'golondrina', was the East Ender who spent the summer in Canada and returned to London, as one official put it, 'to take the benefit of winter charity at home'. Latin America continued to offer opportunities for men of some capital, in land, commerce, mining, industrial enterprise, even if it had no attraction for the labourer. A Republic like Colombia, pleasant though it was in so many respects and liked by foreigners for its religious toleration and the fair treatment they received from its government, was 'a good place for a moderate number of merchants who have capital and connections at home, or for workmen who come out under contracts for high wages, but the day is distant when it can serve the purposes of emigrants in the usual meaning of the word'.[2] Argentina, Uruguay and Chile, on the other hand, had many openings for young men of energy and capital, prepared to put up with some hardship in return for the prospect of a handsome income or substantial capital gain. In the early '60s, great expectations were formed of the profits to be gained from sheep farming at settlements in Entre Rios or along the new Central Argentine line; young men 'of birth and education' brought out a capital of three to four thousand pounds expecting to realize enough in five to eight years to return home and live in comfort for the rest of their days. Droughts, Indians, locusts, flies, and above all the collapse in European wool prices 1867-9 put paid to those hopes in the short run. Many Englishmen returned home in disgust, and others, 'giving way to the vice of drink—more pernicious here than in a colder climate—sank to the lowest depths of degradation'.[3] But some turned to wheat production and others to cattle,

[1] Campbell's report on the Mining Industry in Minas Geraes, P.P. 1908, CVIII, 815.
[2] Bunch's report on Colombia for 1869-70, P.P. 1871, LXVII, 467.
[3] Egerton's report on Argentina for 1879, P.P. 1881, LXXXIX, 160.

and large fortunes were made from land in the '80s and again after the early 1900s. In the period of pure speculation between 1883 and 1887, land values appreciated by as much as 1,000% in the Province of Buenos Aires, 420% in Santa Fé, 750% in Cordoba and 370% in Entre Rios.[1] Prices collapsed in 1890, but an indication of the very real advantages of land investment is given in the data, in paper pesos per hectare, on the average for all rural property bought and sold. These show a rise from 14·1 in 1901-5 to 49·8 in 1916-18.[2]

Englishmen had always bought land, and Vazquez Presedo was probably underestimating when he put British holdings of Argentine real estate by 1914 at about 9 million acres, with a nominal capital value in excess of £13 million.[3] *The Times*, in a euphoric moment, thought that British investment in land might rise as high as £50 million.[4] But a feature of this period was the sale of land by Englishmen to Argentines and the investment of the increment either in real estate, stocks and shares in the United Kingdom, or in re-settlement in the promising, new (and British) colonies and Dominions. Similar fortunes might be made from city property, local industry and finance, and in each the capital of British residents was interested. But such opportunities were limited to a few, and their exploitation became even less natural for British communities in Latin America as men with capital followed the general drift of the working man to the white Dominions, to the many opportunities opening in the farm lands of Rhodesia and East Africa, and to the plantations of Ceylon, India and Malaya.

---

[1] H. S. Ferns, *Britain and Argentina in the Nineteenth Century* (Oxford, 1960), p. 424.

[2] Díaz Alejandro, *Economic History of Argentina*, p. 46.

[3] V. Vazquez Presedo, 'The role of Foreign Trade and Migration in the Development of the Argentine Economy', unpublished D.Phil. thesis, Oxford 1968, p. 155.

[4] *The Times*, 9 November 1909, 5f.

CHAPTER VII

Trading Practices and International Competition

AFTER the first inflow of speculators, of agents without capital, and of manufacturers interested simply in 'dumping' surplus products unsaleable in the traditional markets, the import/export trade between Britain and Latin America had settled into the hands of a few mercantile houses. This trend, visible as early as the immediate aftermath of the 1925-6 crash, continued after the '60s despite a vastly increased volume of trade. It took the form, more particularly, of the extinction of British import houses in the smaller markets; of the concentration of British business at the principal centres in the hands of a few large firms, themselves normally branches of partnerships back in the United Kingdom; of the growth of a direct trade between British manufacturers and Latin American consumers and between Latin American producers and European consumers, which by-passed the traditional mercantile house; of the decline of the import/export trade for even the few remaining mercantile houses, and the diversion of their resources into local finance and manufacturing. The process was slow and in many directions not completely operative until after the First World War, but it was a constant and substantial element in determining the volume and shape of British trade with Latin America.

The withdrawal of British houses from the smaller markets was unmistakeable after the mid-'20s. Warren Schiff calculated that some two-thirds of Mexico's wholesale trade was in German hands by the late 1850s. His statistics are suspect; it was he who explained the spread of German interests in Mexico by the observation that 'very importantly, most marriages between Germans and Mexicans seem to have been happy ones on the whole'![1] But it is true that by the end of the century there was not a British firm or merchant of any kind in Vera Cruz, nor a British wholesale house of business in Mexico City; the only representatives of British trading interests were a few firms undertaking agencies for home manufacturers.[2] A scattering of British firms survived in Central America: one large firm in Guatemala, another in El Salvador, and a few in Panama, with the remainder mere commission agents or retail stores. In Colombia just before the war only one British firm was operating on the Atlantic coast (at Barranquilla), and no British houses survived in Cartagena, Medellín or Bogotá. Not a single British house remained in Venezuela; none of any importance had existed since the middle decades of the nineteenth century, when H. L. Boulton transferred his trading connection to the United States.[3]

British trade would, unquestionably, have been larger in each of these markets if Britain had been better represented, but this was not the point. 'Our merchants at home doubtless know their own business best,' Hervey admitted from Guatemala in 1906, 'and if it does not suit them to establish branch houses or appoint agents here I take it that they find business more profitable and less risky elsewhere.'[4] Trading partnerships, often no more than commission houses, had little to gain and all to lose by staying in a market once it ceased to bring an adequate return on capital. It is probably true that the tidy fortunes of early years set a standard which was too high for normal, day-to-day trade, and that British merchants, remembering better days, were more inclined to pull up stakes than their successors, the young Germans who had so often started in business as their clerks. But it was not simply a question of relative competence. Britons had promising opportunities in the Empire, and it was as natural for them at this stage to move their sphere of operations to an expanding, English-

[1] Warren Schiff, 'The Germans in Mexican Trade and Industry during the Díaz period', *The Americas*, XXIII (1966-7), 280, 294.

[2] Leay's report on Vera Cruz for 1902, P.P. 1903, LXXVIII, 273; Biorklund's report on Mexico for 1900, P.P. 1901, LXXXIII, 588.

[3] Milne gives some details in his reports on Central America, Colombia and Venezuela for the Commercial Intelligence Committee, P.P. 1913, LXVIII.

[4] Hervey's report on Guatemala for 1905, P.P. 1906, CXXV, 719.

speaking community as they had found it, at the beginning of the century, to transfer their business from Cadiz, Gibraltar and Lisbon to the newly opened markets of independent Latin America. Antony Gibbs and Co. had closed their Cadiz branch in 1827 and their Gibraltar branch in 1833, by which time every ounce of capital and energy was required to maintain and develop the South American trade. Later in the century, following the pattern, they opened up a business connection with Australia; their Australian house, Gibbs, Bright and Co., developed a flourishing import business and took an important part in Australian shipping, mining and manufacturing. Gibbs opened a branch office at New York in 1912, and bought themselves into a large South African connection in the 1930s. Balfour Williamson, another leading British firm on the West Coast of South America, was already, by 1914, much stronger financially in California, Washington and British Columbia than it was in Chile.

Both Gibbs and Balfour Williamson remained deeply interested in Latin American trade, finance and manufacturing. But for many less well established partnerships the temptation was to get out while the going was good and set up in business under the British flag. In any case, there was room only for a few large businesses in most of the Latin American markets, while good prospects existed in the Dominions, in the Crown Colonies and in the Far East. With the exception of Canada, British mercantile houses were still overwhelmingly strong in the Empire before 1914. The 'coast houses' shared out the trade of South Africa between them. The relative importance of British to foreign merchants trading in Nigeria was as 85% to 15%.[1] British trade with New Zealand was still the preserve of New Zealand firms served by buying agents in Britain, of British export houses with their own retail distributing centres in the Dominions, and of the New Zealand agents of British houses.[2] Hamilton Wickes counted more than 200 British firms with offices both in the United Kingdom and Australia in 1910, acting as warehousemen and wholesale distributors, and as retailers and direct distributors to the consumer.

In addition there are a number of British manufacturers with their own offices in Australia, and the number of Australian

[1] Birtwistle's report on Southern Nigeria, 24 August 1912, P.P. 1913, LXVIII, 366.
[2] Jeffray's report on New Zealand for 1907, P.P. 1908, LXXIII, 308-9.

firms who have buying agents in the United Kingdom can be counted in hundreds. Besides these, there are the British Shipping Companies, and banks and insurance companies, with offices and staff in both countries. The traders of no other country in the world have a twentieth part of this number of firms of their own nationality to do their business for them in Australia.[1]

In Latin America, British mercantile houses gathered at the principal entry points—Pernambuco, Bahia, Rio, Santos, Montevideo, Buenos Aires, Valparaiso and Callao—which in turn acted as 'ports of deposit' for the smaller coastal communities and the inland Republics of Paraguay and Bolivia. Antony Gibbs, Duncan Fox, Balfour Williamson, Frederick Huth rank with but after the great mercantile houses of the nineteenth century, Jardine Matheson and Butterfield & Swire in the Far East, Guthrie in Malaya, Ralli Bros. in India. These were the houses which were able to defend and extend their businesses in face of a double threat, first from foreign and native competition and then from the growing inclination among British manufacturers to spare the middleman's commission and trade direct.

It was natural enough that as immigration increased after the middle of the century, the new German, Italian, Spanish and Portuguese communities should establish their own import firms to deal with their needs and with the products of their home countries. It was natural, too, that the decline of Britain's position as the main entrepôt of Latin American produce for the markets of Europe, and the development of direct trade with France and Germany, should encourage the establishment of foreign firms to handle the new trade. German merchants had, by the '80s, taken over virtually the entire export business of Bahia in tobacco and sugar. By the early '90s they were the principal exporters of Chilean nitrates. French and Belgian houses handled the major part of Argentine wool exports. During and after the last decades of the century, German and North American houses were responsible for the bulk of the Latin American coffee exports from Brazil, Venezuela, Colombia, Central America; except in Peru, sugar exports, too, passed out of British hands. The effect was

[1] Hamilton Wickes' report on Australia for 1909 and 1910, P.P. 1911, LXXXVII, 559.

felt not only in the export trades but also for imports, since it made as much sense for Continental and North American traders to get hold of both ends of the trade, with the opportunity for a double transaction and profit, as it had for British import/export houses similarly placed earlier in the century.

These were probably the leading elements in the destruction of the British houses' monoply, but there were others which sped it on its way. In the past, long voyages and large shipments had demanded considerable resources of credit to cover what might be a two-year interval between despatch and return. Obviously, it was difficult for any but the largest traders to survive in these circumstances, and then only with British connections or as branches of British-based partnerships. Merchant houses had to finance every service connected with overseas trade—the gathering of information on local markets, the purchasing of credit, the organization of transport—all in the most uncertain circumstances. But the development of local banking facilities after the middle of the century, the provision of regular steamer services handling packets of any size, the opening up of telegraphic communications, made it perfectly possible first for the smaller importer to encroach on the larger, and then for the importer to be replaced entirely by direct transactions between local wholesalers/retailers and foreign manufacturers. The middleman's business in the past had rested on his ability to carry large stocks in markets where replacements might take twelve months from the despatch of the order. Such stocks, though often still an advantage, were now no longer necessary, and a large number of individuals with small capital set themselves up in trade in competition with the established houses. The reaction of British houses in these overcrowded markets was either to give up in disgust and withdraw such capital as could still be salvaged, or to base their business on bulk products or high-value specialities. Houses in Chile imported bulk cargoes of gunny sacks from Calcutta, rice from Rangoon, lumber from the Puget Sound. Others specialized in machinery, in iron and steel. Britons were able to keep their hold over export products like copper, grain and rubber for which the United Kingdom provided a leading market, although even for these they were challenged by Argentine export houses for River Plate wheat and German and American houses for Brazilian rubber. Meanwhile, the low-value import trades passed to foreign or native houses prepared to trade on smaller margins. From as early as the '70s native retailers on the Atlantic coast, in Brazil, Uruguay and Argentina, paid periodical visits direct to European markets.

British consuls were right to draw attention to the fact that the complaints of displaced British merchants did not mean that Britain's competitive position had declined, merely that her trade had been re-routed. But business, except at the larger centres, was far less attractive than it had once been, and Lennon Hunt, surveying the unfortunate prospects for trade in Brazil in 1870, found it as difficult to discover a merchant who had acquired money in trade as a planter with an unembarrassed estate; he could remember the names of only four or five persons in the British communities at Pernambuco and Rio who had been able to quit business with very moderate fortunes over the past seven years.[1] Men of substance were unlikely to return to personal battles in the market-place, and they preferred to put their money into finance, land or industry, sometimes in Latin America, more often at home or in the Empire. In spite of greatly expanded markets, the drift continued. 'The old firms die out,' said Chapman from Brazil in the early 1900s, 'and no fresh ones appear to take their place. No doubt this is due, to some extent, to the fact that they have a greater choice of markets [than the Germans] and naturally withdraw from those where competition is severest and the means employed in such competition are not in accordance with the business principles they are accustomed to.'[2]

*

The other threat to the mercantile house arose out of the manufacturer's interest in developing a direct connection. As a broad generalization, the characteristic attitude of the British manufacturer in the nineteenth century was to regard his role as fulfilled when he had produced his goods at an acceptable quality and at the lowest possible manufacturing cost. It then became the function of the merchant or of the overseas agent to pack, market, advertise and promote sales. Even at the point at which British manufacturers first began to consider handling sales for themselves, some carry-over of the old attitude remained in the greater prestige attached to production rather than sales. The sales

[1] Hunt's report on Rio de Janeiro for 1869, P.P. 1870, LXIV, 238.
[2] Chapman's report on Brazil for 1902, P.P. 1903, LXXVI, 478.

department for many manufacturers was inadequately staffed, poorly equipped, and ill-housed; the effort and expense were directed at the introduction of technical experts, engineers and chemists on the production side.

The division of labour in Victorian trade encouraged intense specialization. At each stage of manufacturing, packing, shipping and selling, specialists were engaged. Specialization had its advantages. For the small manufacturing establishments characteristic of British industry before the '80s it made good sense to delegate. 'Never thou put salt water between thee and thy money' was the advice which the British manufacturer received from his cradle. As manufacturers grew in size and ambition, they began to look towards direct contact with the consumer, partly to save commissions but as much, perhaps, to gauge the market for themselves, without intermediaries, and to manufacture for it. Equally the trend was for the retailer and customer overseas to open up the same direct contact. By the beginning of the twentieth century, large combinations had developed in the traditional sectors of British industry, textiles, iron and steel, coal, shipbuilding and armaments, and others in the newer lines of chemicals, branded foodstuffs, tobacco, rubber tyres, furniture, wallpaper, soap and cement. In each of these, direct selling was likely to replace the traditional merchant.

The merchant might still hold his place in products where prices were flexible and where his expert knowledge could be brought into play. His position was strong in unbranded goods, obtainable at a wide range of prices and qualities from a variety of sources—cheap textiles, hardware, foodstuffs or pharmaceutical products. He was less able to preserve his hold over standardized, unbranded products such as cement, which could be obtained direct from a limited number of known manufacturers. Nor could he necessarily cope with high-value art and fashion goods, for which the individual taste was the prime factor, and in which, as it turned out, the first direct contacts between Latin American retailers and European manufacturers were made. The merchant's position was at its weakest in what had become, by the end of the century, two of the main lines of trade. The first was specialized machinery, constructional steel work, bridge work, railway and industrial equipment for which expert knowledge and servicing were required and where the high value of individual items or orders made direct contact between manufacturer and client practicable. The other was in branded goods—Horrockses' or Tootal's fabrics, Hollins' Viyella, Sunlight soap, Colman's mustard, Huntley and Palmer's biscuits, Clark's shoes, and all the household names in general consumer goods, electrical products, gramophones, typewriters, sewing machines, bicycles, motor cars which were so much part of the marketing scene at the beginning of the twentieth century. In each of these the purpose of the brandname was to establish a direct link at known prices and standard qualities between the manufacturer of a particular, competitive product and the consumer. The merchant had lost his function in determining prices and qualities; he became a mere commission agent, or found himself replaced altogether by the manufacturer's sales department and overseas sales offices.

*

The number of resident British mercantile houses in Latin America continued to fall. Yet the mercantile system, as conducted by German, French, Italian, North American, Portuguese and local houses in Latin America itself, and by the great Liverpool, Manchester and London wholesale and export houses in the United Kingdom, survived over a far broader range of products for British trade with Latin America before 1914 than it did for the more familiar markets in Europe, North America and the Dominions. The reason was simply that Latin America, with few exceptions, provided too small an outlet requiring too specialized a knowledge to be handled directly by the manufacturer. Direct sales were not cheap. Even in Europe in the '80s an agent could cost as much as £500 p.a., and expenses were rising. Outside Europe, the representatives appointed in 1911-12 by one of Britain's leading soap manufacturers, Joseph Crosfield and Sons Ltd., were drawing salaries ranging from £250 to £500 p.a. plus expenses, the total cost of each rising to between £800 and £1,000.[1] The price of a representative in Buenos Aires, quite apart from salary, was £16 to £20 a month in rent for a one-room office, a further £10 a month in expenses, and a tax of some £25 p.a.[2] High prices in Brazil made direct representation almost

[1] A. E. Musson, *Enterprise in Soap and Chemicals: Joseph Crosfield and Sons, Limited, 1815-1965* (Manchester, 1965), p. 185.
[2] *The Times*, South American Supplement, 31 January 1911, 9c.

prohibitive. Just before the war, the cost of living at Rio was said to be three times that of the United Kingdom, while it was five times as high at Pernambuco, Pará and Manaos. Business propaganda and promotion were very expensive; according to one estimate, for every £1,000 of capital required in the United Kingdom at least £3,000 were needed in Brazil.[1]

The result was that most manufacturers used a combination of selling methods, according to the size and accessibility of the market. J. H. Fenner & Co Ltd. of Hull, manufacturers of leather belting for machinery, covered the home market largely through direct personal contact and advertising; overseas, Fenners' main market, the Balkans, to which £20,000 worth was exported in 1913, was big enough to justify a full-time representative. Henry Fenner and other English representatives occasionally visited neighbouring markets in northern Europe, but most of the business was handled by agencies—independent firms at Riga, Oslo, Odessa, working on a commission basis. In the other substantial export market, Asia, Fenners did its business through one or other of the great London exporting houses, Matheson & Co. Ltd. for China, Jeremiah Lyon & Co. and H. C. John for India.[2] Pilkingtons, the British glass manufacturers, did much of its trade with the Continent through H. &. E. Lion of Hamburg. Merchants in London and Manchester exported Pilkington glass, but the company found it necessary to supplement these exports by direct sales handled by its own rapidly expanding export department. Pilkingtons had had its own agent in Australia from the 1850s, in Cape Town from 1882, in Egypt from 1892, in New Zealand from 1894. It opened a depot at Montreal in 1890 and Toronto in 1893, new warehouses at Vancouver in 1903, Winnipeg in 1906 and Calgary in 1912. By 1894 Pilkingtons had an office in Hamburg, depots in Paris and Naples, and agencies in Palermo, Bari, Rome and Turin.[3] For Latin America, neither Fenners nor the much larger Pilkingtons felt it necessary to deal other than through the established merchants and commission agents, although it is a sign of the special position occupied by

[1] Birch's report on Brazil for 1912-13, P.P. 1914-16, LXXI, 184.
[2] Ralph Davis, *Twenty-One and a Half Bishop Lane: a History of J. H. Fenner & Co. Ltd* (London, 1961), pp. 33-5.
[3] T. C. Barker, *Pilkington Brothers and the Glass Industry* (London, 1960), pp. 168-9, 196-7.

Argentina in British trade that, in 1907, a Pilkington warehouse was opened at Buenos Aires.

The strongest element in the trade was the large warehouseman/ wholesaler with a house in Manchester or London. Each house was served at home by specialized buyers; overseas, branch houses worked the sales territory with their own corps of travellers. Although the tendency was still to develop a direct trade if possible, the large British houses offered real advantages to foreign traders dealing in a wide range of textiles, hardware, china and glass, stationery and pharmaceutical goods. A prominent and powerful firm of fabric and clothing wholesalers such as Messrs Cook, Sons & Co. of St Paul's Churchyard, London, brought together in one place a full selection of English and Continental products; it could offer, through bulk buying, prices competitive with, and even cheaper than those which might be negotiated by an individual merchant or retailer in direct contact with the manufacturer. The wholesale houses were fully conscious of the threat of direct trade and took care to safeguard their sources. There was nothing to distinguish the nationality or origin of the goods in stock, nothing to put the shipper in contact with the markets or the consumer with the manufacturer. The British manufacturer was often, in practice, reluctant to open up a direct trade; he was afraid of jeopardizing the relationship he already possessed with the Manchester or London wholesaler on whom so large a proportion of his overseas sales depended.

Some of the large houses overseas were able to win much the same sort of position for themselves. A firm of Australian textile agents told the British Trade Commission in 1914 how the great bugbear of Australian agents was the London buyer of the leading Australian houses who objected to manufacturers having their own agents in Australia; 'we find that many British firms live in fear and trembling of this individual and are fearful of losing the trade they get through him'.[1] But the position of the overseas house, in Latin America as elsewhere, was soundly based on its specialized knowledge of complex marketing problems, on the uneconomic size of the individual markets, on the strength of established trading links and the conservatism of the consumer and, above all, on its ability to offer credit and discriminate between credit risks. In the smaller Republics, poor communications and

[1] P.P. 1914-16, XLVI, 126.

a general lack of contact between communities fragmented the markets for some lines of hardware and textiles. If a traveller were sent to cover the northern Republics together, the chances were that samples suited to Colombia would be so much waste baggage by the time he reached Venezuela, and indeed samples which might attract buyers in one Venezuelan town might find not a single buyer in another. 'I have been shown samples,' Gray reported from Venezuela in 1907, 'of agricultural implements, knives and other goods, apparently identical for all practical purposes but which are useless in one district and commanded a ready sale in another, owing to a slight difference in colour, bend, or shape of tool or handle, readily recognized by the buyer, but hardly perceptible to the "man in the street".'[1]

The complicated customs tariffs and regulations, with heavy penalties for the slightest infringement, put an additional premium on expert knowledge for most of the Republics before 1914, and in any small outlet the personal relationship built up over the years with local officials was one of the merchant's chief assets. Besides, the trade, even in some of the bigger markets, was seldom one-way. The merchant, whether in Latin America or in the United Kingdom, depended on a double return for each transaction. European houses, with which firm and long-standing relationships were established, acted both as salesmen for Latin American produce and buyers of European manufactured goods for Latin American markets. What was bought in Europe depended on what was sold to Europe, and both parts of the transaction were in the hands of a single firm. There was very little attempt, at least in the northern Republics, to break this 'relación', either on the part of the Latin American producer or of the merchant. Nor was it easy for a manufacturer to intervene. Messrs Fosters, one of the three substantial West Riding manufacturers of alpaca worsteds, gave thought to the possibility (in the late '50s) of buying the raw material direct from the only source, Peru. In a letter of 10 February 1863 Fosters described how

Sometime back we had the intention of trying a small shipment, but after thinking over the difficulties of the case and taking into consideration the competition of such established houses

[1] Gray's report on Caracas for 1906, P.P. 1907, XCIII, 836-7.

as Jack Bros. [Liverpool and Arequipa] and Gibbs [London and Arequipa] we concluded that no satisfactory business could be done, unless we carried out the same principles as that on which they are formed, viz., for consignment, as we understand the major part of the purchases of alpaca in the Interior are paid for out of the proceeds of Goods, etc. received, which of course leaves a profit both ways.[1]

The position for a limited outlet like Iquitos, the Peruvian rubber port, was precisely the same as late as 1914. The largest firms in Iquitos handling the export of rubber were branches of European houses and to a greater or lesser extent financed by them. The Iquitos firms naturally ordered any return imports through their European houses, and they handled between them a high proportion of all imports into the area. In the circumstances, it was obviously more sensible for British manufacturers wishing to open a trade to make contact with the London or Liverpool agents of the principal Iquitos firms, rather than try direct.[2] And this applied equally to the German houses with their Hamburg and Bremen connections, responsible for so much of the external trade of Latin America in the decades before 1914.

The survival of the mercantile house depended ultimately on its ability to extend credit and to judge credit-worthiness. Local knowledge was important in any sphere, whether in placing tenders for contracts or in keeping head offices at home supplied with the most recent information as to the condition and requirements of the market. But experience on the spot was essential for the system of four to nine-month credits universally applied to Latin American imports before the First World War. In the first place, the import house had itself to have access to credit to carry the trade, and in this respect British houses had an overwhelming advantage for the first three-quarters of the nineteenth century. Interest rates in Latin America remained high so long as local capital was scarce. In most of the Republics at the mid-century, and for the smaller Republics long after, it was not uncommon to pay 12 to 15% on a good real-estate mortgage, and 25 to 30% on personal security. By contrast the average minimum rate of

[1] Eric M. Sigsworth, *Black Dyke Mills; a history* (Liverpool, 1958), p. 238.
[2] Huckin's report on Iquitos for 1914, P.P. 1914-16, LXXIV, 541, 545-6.

L

discount charged by the Bank of England was 4 to 5% in the '50s and for most of the '60s, and 3% thereafter. 3% Consols averaged 93½ in 1855-9; in 1880-4 they were up to $100\frac{17}{80}$, and in 1889 H.M. Government was able to convert to a new $2\frac{3}{4}$% stock which had itself risen to over 110 by the late '90s.[1] Even in the United States the normal rate of interest on a first-class security was 7% in the late '70s, and generally much higher for commercial purposes and for the discounting of business paper. 'I have recently seen it stated,' wrote A. J. Mundella in 1878, 'by Mr Mudge, of Boston, and Judge Kelly (well-known authorities on American industry), that they have not so much to fear from the low rates of wages in England, as from the low rates of interest. With us it is sometimes 3% per annum, when with them it is said to be 3% per month.'[2]

The ease with which the British merchants could discount their bills, and later, in the '60s and '70s, the ready access they possessed to bank finance through credits and overdrafts with specialist banking houses such as Brown Shipley, the Liverpool Union Bank, the Merchant Banking Corporation, the Union Bank of London and the National Discount Co., gave mercantile houses a strong hold over foreign trade. It was an advantage which British merchants came to share with other respectable houses as banking systems developed both in Europe and in Latin America, but it was something which a small retailer found impossible to by-pass. If a retailer wanted to buy textiles or hardware, he could hardly avoid buying through a middleman, German or British, simply because a banking house would not give credit on his documents unless they bore the signature of some well-known merchant. Nor would the manufacturer, at the other end of the transaction, be wise to do business without the same guarantee. The condition of the law was such, even in the great Republics, that debt collecting was a hazardous and expensive business. Vice-Consul Rhind, in his report on Rio for 1903, spoke of the 'most discouraging element' to trade which was to be found in the commercial laws; the recovery of debts was uncertain, 'thus facilitating

---

[1] Board of Trade, *Comparative Trade Statistics*, P.P. 1903, LXVII, 774-7.
[2] A. J. Mundella, 'What are the Conditions on which the Commercial and Manufacturing Supremacy of Great Britain Depend?', *Journal of the Statistical Society*, XLI (1878), 93.

inequitable and secret settlement between unscrupulous traders, to the detriment of less favoured creditors, and particularly of such as are not resident, or are not adequately represented, in the country'. He advised manufacturers not to open up a direct trade, but to do their business, whenever possible, through resident merchant commission firms, many of whom had branches in the United Kingdom.[1] The Consul-General in Chile reported (1908) that it was almost impossible to collect a debt; in a market where credits were customary, great care had to be exercised before entering the trade.[2] As for the Caribbean, the great difficulty in collecting foreign accounts by legal process in Honduras enabled 'the Honduranean buyer to set his British creditor at defiance', and in Haiti, where one of the British houses had outstandings in 1891 to the extent of between £60,000 and £70,000, it was 'certain that sending goods indiscriminately to a market like this must inevitably be followed by loss'.[3]

Without the sophisticated systems of credit-rating which existed in the older markets, it was sensible to deal through a resident merchant, even at the cost of a commission. Reliable merchants could be found in most of the trading centres of Latin America. British travellers spoke highly of commercial morality among the Latin American houses with which they dealt, and one, in conversation with the British Minister in Venezuela in 1898, told how he had had to write off only £300 over the past ten years in the course of dealings which, for his last visit alone, had amounted to orders for over £25,000 of cotton textiles.[4] But it was important to discriminate, to deal through reliable merchants with well-established connections which they would not easily change. 'New houses,' Dickson reported from Colombia for 1901, 'send a traveller who finds it difficult to induce these old-established firms to enter into business with him, so that he is prone to open accounts with little-known firms, with the result that he eventually finds himself obliged to return to collect his accounts.'[5]

*

[1] P.P. 1905, LXXXVII, 416-17.
[2] Leary's report on Chile for 1907, P.P. 1908, CX, 28.
[3] Macklacklan's report on Omoa and Puerto Cortes for 1891, and Tweedy's report on Haiti for 1891, P.P. 1892, LXXXII, 686, 722.
[4] Haggard's report on Venezuela for 1898, P.P. 1899, CIII, 659.
[5] P.P. 1902, CVI, 359.

It was for reasons such as these that wholesale warehouse men and shippers in the United Kingdom and the mercantile house overseas, British or foreign, were able to hold on to what was still the major part of the Latin American import/export trade with Britain before 1914. Even in the high-value machinery trades, the reluctance of British manufacturers to give competitive credit terms and their insistence on cash against shipping documents at the port of departure, meant that the mercantile firm, although concerned at no other point in what was now a direct trade, was still often called upon to provide temporarily the capital required to bridge the transaction.

It is difficult to get any idea of the proportion of 'direct' trade between British manufacturers and Latin American markets, in part because the definition of 'direct' is so variable. In the distant markets of the West Coast, the resident mercantile houses were better placed to retain their share of the trade. British manufacturers certainly attempted to open up a direct trade, and even at a smaller outlet like Coquimbo in the mid to late '80s, travellers did good business in dry goods, iron and medical products, biscuits, mining appliances, boots and explosives.[1] But Worthington's report on Chile in 1898 showed that the mercantile houses still retained their hold over by far the larger part of the import trade. Worthington estimated, in fact, that only about a ninth of the goods imported were by direct sale on account of European producers to dealers in Valparaiso.[2]

The East Coast markets, however, were far more promising for direct representation from Europe, whether by travellers from the manufacturers or from the large European wholesalers and shippers. Worthington believed that between a quarter and a third of Brazil's total import trade was direct through travellers and/or local representatives, between European shipping houses or manufacturers and native dealers.[3] Again, very little of this business was actually direct between European manufacturers and Brazilian dealers; it was done chiefly on indents placed with European firms. In dry goods, Brazilian shopkeepers or merchants at a port like Pernambuco in the '90s, where the last British dry-goods

---

[1] Grierson's report on Coquimbo for 1887-8, P.P. 1889, LXXVIII, 342.
[2] Worthington's report on Chile, April 1898, P.P. 1899, XCVI, 461.
[3] Worthington's report on Brazil, November 1898, P.P. 1899, XCVI, 536.

importer had already gone out of business, bought direct from Manchester, Dundee and Belfast merchants; these were represented in turn by commercial travellers who called frequently and kept in touch with the requirements of the market and the state of trade. Although the traditional resident British house in Brazil continued to decline, there may have been a trend back to business transactions through the European house after some unfortunate experiences in direct trading during the '90s. The evidence suggests this to be so for many lines in the 1900s, and Pearson, in his report from Pernambuco for 1910, warned manufacturers of goods retailed in small quantities that it was more sensible either to furnish samples to a traveller who already had a good connection in Brazil, or to come to an arrangement with one of the exporting houses in the United Kingdom. Direct business, he pointed out, between the manufacturer at home and the shopkeeper in Brazil, meant long credits, unsatisfactory business, and bad debts.[1]

*

What is particularly of interest in the present context is the effect of this mechanism of trade on Britain's competitive position in Latin American markets. The common view was that the declining number of British mercantile houses resident in Latin America was a disaster for British trade. Consul Cowper explained how the trade supremacy of Great Britain, on land and sea, had been established by the enterprise and ubiquity of her merchants. Every merchant became a centre of introduction, distribution and transmission of the trade of his own country. 'As surely as the British merchant disappears from the commercial arena, so also will the magnitude of our trade diminish in its ratio to the trade of the world.'[2] Hervey felt that the principal cause of Britain's failure to obtain markets for her goods in Central America was the want of established British houses to take up agencies.[3] Milne explained how it had been repeatedly remarked to him, in the course of his 1912-13 mission to enquire into trading prospects in Central America and northern South America, that the most

[1] Williams' report on Pernambuco for 1894, P.P. 1895, XCVI, 448, and Pearson's report on Pernambuco for 1910, P.P. 1911, XC, 381-2.
[2] Cowper's report on Santos for 1888, P.P. 1889, LXXVIII, 233.
[3] Hervey's report on Guatemala for 1904, P.P. 1905, XC, 13.

effective means of increasing the sale of goods of British manufacturers would be the establishment of British import houses;
he himself had no doubt whatever of the general soundness of
this view.[1] 'No trade without representation,' said Beaumont of
Venezuela in 1921, 'might well be the motto of this market.'[2]

Beaumont was overstating his case. British trade could survive
very well without representation in products for which British
manufacturers continued to offer competitive terms, and even in
a market like Guatemala or Costa Rica, where American and
German interests were overwhelmingly strong, Britain maintained a satisfactory level of trade in the 1900s based primarily on
cotton goods, but also on coffee machinery, galvanized iron
sheets, tin plates and jute sacking. To a large extent, too, in the
South American markets if less so in Central America and Mexico,
extensive British investments in railways and public utilities kept
up the share of the import trade without requiring the presence of
British resident merchants; the orders were despatched direct by
British engineers to their customary suppliers in the U.K.

But this was a passive, take-it-or-leave-it attitude to Latin American markets from which others profited. No German merchant
would deny himself a profit in a competitive market by refusing to
supply such British goods as were in demand. Indeed, British
merchants had a worse record in this respect. British houses,
probably because they operated only at centres where British
trade was already strong, were slow to handle Continental goods;
German houses, universal in every market, almost invariably
took a fair part of their stock from the United Kingdom. But the
problem was not in the large, established lines of trade. It existed
in those for which there was no competitive advantage one way or
the other, where a German, an Italian or a French house naturally
made its purchases through its own traditional suppliers in its own
home market. This would apply to bulk products such as rice,
beet sugar, cement and fertilisers, or to the mass of smaller lines
in iron and steel manufactures, electrical apparatus, china, glass
and earthenware, matches, tools where convenience in filling
small orders outweighed any slight price differential.

---

[1] Milne's final report on his mission to Central America, P.P. 1913,
LXVIII, 612.
[2] Dept. of Overseas Trade, *Report on the Financial and Commercial
Condition of Venezuela* (H.M.S.O., 1921).

The preponderance of German houses created precisely the same advantages for German trade in Latin America as did British houses for British trade in the Empire and the Far East. The development of economic nationalism, of patriotism in international trade, meant that more trade, both for British and for Continental houses, followed strictly national lines in the years immediately before the First World War than in the first decades of serious competition, the '70s, '80s and '90s. But so long as there was competition at all, merchants could not be expected to do more than favour their own goods at equal or almost equal prices. Where better representation really made the difference, as Consul Jerome pointed out when he remarked on the existence of only two or three British exporting houses in the whole of Mexico in 1904, was in the exchange of commodities.[1] The average German or French importer in Mexico was also an exporter, buying from his customers in Germany or France, usually mercantile houses in Hamburg, Frankfort-on-Main, Havre, Bordeaux or Paris; it was the buyer in Europe who, able to secure more advantageous terms for himself from one supplier than another, decided if an order for his Mexican correspondent was to be given to a British or a foreign manufacturer. The chances were that he would deal with those with whom he was intimately associated. It was likely, too, that a Latin American retailer or producer would be more inclined to deal with German or French commission houses, or with North American houses in the Caribbean area, by reason of the credit facilities such houses provided for the purchase of their goods, the advances they gave on produce, and the banking services they supplied, especially in the smaller Republics where British overseas banks were not represented.

*

Britain could not be represented in *every* market, and where she was not represented, her interests were bound to suffer. She suffered less in markets where her mercantile houses were replaced, as in Canada, by large, national wholesalers with English prejudices, than she did in Latin America where the wholesalers— national, German, French, Italian, North American—had their own ideas and preferences. She suffered less by loss of direct contact and local knowledge in the Dominions, where her habits

[1] Jerome's report on Mexico for 1903, P.P. 1905, XC, 759.

and tastes were shared automatically, than she did in Asia Minor, where a Political and Economic Planning survey reported the marketing of British goods under trade marks 'highly offensive to the religious feelings of the country in which they were sold' while others sold under a British trade name which 'rendered phonetically represented a word in the vernacular seldom mentionable even in a near Eastern bazaar'.[1]

Under-representation affected the ability of British manufacturers to put new lines on the market, to build up new trades and create demand for products not already established or known in the smaller markets of Latin America. The loss was at the two levels, since Britain was not only poorly represented among the importing houses but almost totally unrepresented in the retail trade. Carden made the point, in his Mexican report of 1895, that with local manufacturers rapidly supplanting foreign goods in so many areas, foreign commerce in future depended on anticipation of needs. Foreign merchants were ready enough to handle goods well known in the country, but by no means as anxious to go to the trouble of creating new openings for British products, often in opposition to their own national interests or in competition with products for which they already possessed a comfortable trade. Canvassing by commercial travellers might have some effect, but travellers could reach consumers only through wholesale or retail firms, where they were usually met with the answer, when trying to introduce a novelty, that such goods were unknown to the market and there was no demand for them. 'The only means', Carden concluded, 'of inducing people to buy an article they do not know is to bring it before their notice in the most prominent way possible, and this can only be done through establishments which, if not exclusively retail, combine a retail with a wholesale business.'[2]

In the first years of independent Latin America, British subjects had taken an active hand in retailing at all levels, from the large import house trading direct from its warehouse to the keeper of a grog shop down at the water's edge. Following the usual pattern, they clustered round the main entry ports for British products, Rio, Montevideo, Buenos Aires, Valparaiso. Maria Graham described English saddlers, food stores (hucksters), tailors,

---

[1] P.E.P., *Report on International Trade* (London, 1937), p. 141.
[2] P.P. 1897, XCII, 190-1.

bakers, and pot houses at Rio in 1822.[1] No less than 193 'shop-keepers' were registered at the British consulate at Buenos Aires between 1825 and 1831, together with 66 tailors and 63 shoemakers.[2] But Mrs Graham was already noticing a tendency for Britons at Rio to sell their goods wholesale to native or French retailers. Merchants like John Luccock, who at one time carried on open shelves all kinds of miscellaneous hardware—cutlery, watchglasses and chains, seals, keys, mirrors, needles, trays, cigar cases, snuff-boxes, spectacles, candlesticks and snuffers, tools, canisters, teapots, mouse-traps—found that metal goods went rusty, glass was dropped and broken, thieves were 'uncommonly adroit and shielded by their numbers'.[3] They were happy, when they could, to pull out of the retail business altogether, and Walsh, visiting Rio in the late '20s, found the retail business dominated by the French, with a bazaar and about 140 shops handling every range of trade known to France, while the British goods were all packed up in warehouses and only exhibited in the shops of the Brazilians.[4]

Although a fair number of English retailers were still in business in Buenos Aires and Montevideo at the mid-century, and the English had the distinction of keeping the worst shops in Rio when visited by Mr Robert Elwes on his *Sketcher's Tour Round the World*, the tendency to abandon this kind of business continued. In a small isolated Republic like Paraguay, Britain was scarcely represented. At the end of the '80s between £8 million and £9 million of British capital was invested in Paraguay, chiefly in land companies and in the railway. But in commerce British representation was confined to a single grocery store, with a nominal capital of $1,000. The Italians, by contrast, accounted for 177 trading premises and shops, nine of which were importing houses, with a combined capital of $1,500,000; the French for 36, with two importing houses and a capital of $500,000; the Germans for 14, with three importing houses and $400,000 capital.[5]

One reason, unquestionably, for the insignificance of British representation at this level was the fact that the parallel class of Englishmen found better opportunities in the British Empire. The

[1] Graham, *Brazil*, p. 189.
[2] Parish, *Buenos Ayres*, p. 394 (Appendix No. 3).
[3] Heaton, *Journal of Economic History*, VI, 15.
[4] Walsh, *Brazil*, II, 467.
[5] Pakenham's report on Paraguay, P.P. 1890-91, LXXXVII, 326.

success of other European retailers, whether German, Italian, Portuguese or Spanish, was based often, in the first instance, on large resident communities of fellow nationals. The British equivalent might be found in North America or in the Empire, and it was only in a city like Buenos Aires, with its large British community and prosperous, fashion-conscious upper class, that English retailing made any impression. Ross found the retail trade of Buenos Aires, in 1909, to be almost entirely in the hands of foreigners, among whom Britons were conspicuous by their small number. English retailers were represented by eight machinery and hardware stores, eight tailors, five booksellers and stationers, three drapers, four furniture stores, five jewellers, five boot stores, seven druggists, and three wine stores. By contrast there were 'hundreds of shops run by Spaniards, Italians, French and Germans', and it seemed probable that, 'other things being equal, the nationality of the retailer may in many cases turn the scale in favour of non-British goods'.[1] Some impressive names were added to the British list shortly afterwards; Maple & Co. and Mappin & Webb had branch establishments in operation in Buenos Aires by 1910, followed by two large English-owned department stores, Gath & Chaves (1912) and Harrods (1913). But Britons were still handling only a portion of the higher class trade.[2]

*

No precise estimates can be given for the effect on the import trade of nationality among retailers, but much the same points of national preference, established lines of trade, knowledge of markets apply to retailers as to import houses. The link between import specialities and nationality is evident enough in the fact that Mexican retailing, in the early years of this century, was generally divided between the French in retail drapery, the Germans in hardware, and the Spaniards in foodstuffs. Similarly, in Argentina, with its large Italian immigrant population, the Italians were strong in the foodstuff trade. It was natural that each should look first to its own home market for wholesale service and supplies, no more surprising than that Albert Gettie & Co of Buenos

[1] Ross's report on Buenos Aires for 1909, P.P. 1910, XCVI, 126.
[2] Roger Gravil has recently examined the operations of the two department stores in his article 'British Retail Trade in Argentina, 1900-1940', *Inter-American Economic Affairs*, 24 (1970), 3-26.

Aires in the early '90s should advertise itself as holding special stocks of drapery imported from 'the first Manufacturers in England', that Wilson Sons & Co. should keep stocks of 'only the very best descriptions of South Wales steam coal', that E. E. Cranwell should always have on hand 'a large supply of the best classes of Drugs and Patent Medicines from the chief establishments of England and America', that Feeny & Co should boast the best assortment of English groceries in Buenos Ayres', and that the Victoria Tea and Luncheon Rooms at 742 Cangallo should offer the jaded shopper 'a good cup of Tea served instantly', 'English cooking and attendance in the real home style', and, as a special preliminary attraction, 'Porridge at 7.30 A.M.'.

The difference was in numbers, not in habits of trade. But the end effect of nationality among retailers could be considerable. Local tradesmen, in touch only spasmodically even with their own home markets, were simply unaware of competing foreign products. Britain was the first exporter of bicycles, but there was scarcely a British bicycle to be seen in Porto Alegre in South Brazil. The reason was that the craze had reached Porto Alegre in the '90s through a German retailer. The ninety-nine member cyclists of the 'Radfahrer-Verein Blitz' rode German cycles to the man, and 'English machines are quite out of it'.[1] Consumers had to be made aware of the possibilities now opening before them, and in the absence of satisfactory channels for advertising, it was up to the retailer to make the effort. The Bolivians at Sucre in 1905 never even knew of the existence of such a convenience as a portable india-rubber bath; until they saw a 'Sparklets' they never dreamed that a drink of soda water could conveniently be carried in the saddle bag for a fourteen-hour journey; until Vice-Consul Moore gave away a 6d. tablet from his own private stock, they never imagined that a certain brand of glycerine soap could remove in half a day 'the awful roughness of the skin on face and hands'.[2]

Once large wholesale and retail establishments had replaced the traveller and his order book for machinery and apparatus, the nationality of the retailer could be of importance even in the largest trades. In Brazil at the turn of the century it was still possible to do business in engineering products chiefly by catalogue

[1] Archer's report on Porto Alegre for 1898, P.P. 1899, XCVIII, 369-70.
[2] Moore's report on Sucre for 1904-5, P.P. 1906, CXXIII, 29.

and traveller. Ten years later, Rio retailers were carrying big stocks of every kind of equipment except the most specialized lines of engineering tools, drills, or armouring for concrete. Every conceivable item of electrical equipment could be bought out of stock, together with most of the minor classes of engineering articles such as pumps, ventilators and lathes. Wholesalers and retailers tended to be German, Italian or North American, and their preferences were naturally for their own products. Britain's business by catalogue and traveller was virtually dead in engineering products for Brazil. It lasted longer in a less sophisticated market like Bolivia where the mining companies, in the absence of local stocks and suppliers, continued in general to order their steam engines, boilers, stamp batteries, and aerial ropeways direct from British manufacturers. The absence of direct representation was more damaging in mining steel, steel rails and dynamite where there was not much to choose between suppliers and where trade followed the lines set by existing facilities. No British importer of mining materials was in business in Oruro in the early 1900s, and if British articles were required they had to be bought from one of the Valparaiso firms. Steel rails from Valparaiso, placed at Oruro, cost 8s 6d. per metre, whereas the same imported direct from Germany by resident German merchants were sold at 6s. 6d.[1] In British Empire markets, where Englishmen ran the engineering and electrical stores, the same pattern was seen in reverse.

The nationality of the retailer was felt more particularly in the smaller lines of trade, in low-value orders for the multiple items of haberdashery, hardware, groceries, pharmaceutical goods and perfumery, where the determining factor was a common order to a single wholesaler, dealing with his own sources in the home country. The wholesaler, if he were a German in Hamburg, would probably fill his orders for wines and cognac in France, for whisky in the United Kingdom, for cement in Belgium and Britain, for candles in Belgium, for cotton manufactures in Britain, for men's hats in Italy or France. But in all the small lines, where it made little difference where he went, he took his supplies from neighbouring producers in Germany—laces, embroidery and trimmings, ladies' and children's boots and shoes, ready-made clothes, silk textiles, perfumery and drugs.

[1] Ramsay Smith's report on Oruro for 1904, P.P. 1905, LXXXVII, 378.

The shelves of a Chilean haberdasher, chemist, grocer, 'novelties' store, supplied primarily from the Continent, must have looked utterly different from those of a similar store in Australia, supplied primarily from the United Kingdom. The distinction was much less obvious in the case of a draper, where in either country most of the goods on display before 1914 were British. Bolivia provides a convenient illustration, since the general import trade was handled almost entirely by Germans. Of the goods imported (through Antofagasta) into Sucre, Potosí and Oruro in 1903, Britain supplied £44,200 of woollens (Germany, £4,900; Belgium, £3,200) and £44,000 of cottons (Germany, £12,600; the United States, £22,250; Belgium, £3,250). Britain's manufacturers were holding their own in, even recapturing, the textile trade. But in hosiery they supplied only £300 to Germany's £1,200; in drugs and chemicals, £450 to Germany's £1,560 and America's £1,150; in general hardware, keys, bolts, padlocks, tools and iron manufactures, £420 to Germany's £5,100.[1] Sir Berry Cusack-Smith put the point succinctly when he explained that there was no English chemist in Santiago in 1901 and only one in Valparaiso: 'All the chemists are German. We are consequently behind in all chemicals.'[2]

The converse, so far as it affected British exports of small lines of trade, is true of a market like South Africa at the the beginning of this century. There British manufacturers almost monopolized the haberdashery and millinery trades; 96% of the total imports in 1902 came from the United Kingdom. In fancy goods the trade was mainly through London. The trade in medicines, drugs and medicinal preparations was predominantly British, and imports from the Continent were relatively small; the Americans supplied patent medicines but, practically speaking, Britain commanded the market in all except specialities and patent goods. Nearly 90% of the soap came from Britain; most of the best-known British brands were extensively advertised and the trade was well worked by home manufacturers. British manufacturers even had the bulk of the perfumery trade, although there was considerable competition from France in the best classes, from Germany in medium grades and in 'Kaffir truck', and from the United States in 'accessories'. Scotch and Irish whisky, much advertised, might

---

[1] Moore's report on Sucre for 1904, *ibid.*, 383-4.
[2] Cusack-Smith's report on Chile for 1901, P.P. 1902, CV, 722.

'almost be said to be the national beverage'. An ordinary grocer's stock contained a majority of English products. Sauces, condiments, table salt, golden syrup were British. Large items such as corned beef, ox tongues, Quaker oats, tinned salmon and lobster, maizena, canned fruit came from America and Australia, but 'the hundred and one food delicacies and groceries, which make up the diet of South Africans, are almost all of British origin.'[1] In each, 'British' imports concealed a large element of Continental or North American produce brought in through wholesalers in the United Kingdom. But the point is that the natural direction of Dominion trade was to Britain, as the natural direction for Latin America was to the Continent and North America. For one, as for the other, all the marginally competitive or unallocated trade went to the market and manufacturers of first resort.

*

With this general pattern in mind, rather different conclusions emerge for the competitive qualities, the trade methods and enterprise of the nations interested in the foreign trade of Latin America before 1914. Were British businessmen, after the 1870s, unable to call on their Government for the official assistance so freely offered by foreign Governments to their own traders? Were they peculiarly blind to the need to send out travellers to work Latin American markets, ignorant of the possibilities offered by advertising, prone to flood the Republics with untranslated catalogues illustrating products measured in yards and ells and priced 'f.o.b. Liverpool' in pounds, shillings, and pence? Were they unwilling to give credit, unable to pack goods, innocent and helpless in face of false-marking and 'dumping'? Obviously not. Each man has his favourite horror story, and a classic was the export of a 'Victoria' to Johannesburg *with its hood up*, so that the unfortunate consignee faced a bill for freight almost twice what it should have been. But the stories were by no means confined to British trade; they have appeared for every country at all times. Britons may have thought North Americans or Germans the last word in commercial dexterity. But aliens felt much the same about Britons. 'In this part of the world at least,' said Wardrop from Haiti in 1902, 'the British are held up to their American com-

[1] Birchenough's report on South Africa for 1903, P.P. 1904, LXI, 94-121.

petitors as models; they are said to study more carefully the local requirements and to pack their goods in a manner better suited to the market.'[1] Critics of Britain's performance might have found a familiar ring in the complaints of a French chamber of commerce at a Far Eastern port in the '90s, where manufacturers were urged, if French trade were to take its proper place in the East, to send out goods suitable to the country, to take more care in the choice of agents, to execute orders punctually and in conformity with what was asked for, to ship promptly, and to avoid the temptation to raise prices when orders were repeated after one success.[2]

The grass was always greener on the other side of the fence. Britons used to accuse their competitors of benefiting from active diplomatic and home government support, just as foreigners were convinced that British manufacturers and traders enjoyed the power and resources of a great Empire. When it came to the point, there was little to choose between the official support available to either. French or German government departments were more likely than British to insist on the 'tying' of overseas loans to the purchase of national products, but the effect of overseas investment in promoting national trade was much the same whatever happened, and Britons were by far the biggest investors. A French diplomat may have asked for a banking concession, a German for a railway, an American for a warship order. There was certainly no consistency, and in any case the sum total of such efforts was insignificant. 'What a lot you do for your British subjects', Harold Satow's German friends used to tell him at Trebizond just before the War; 'I wish our consuls would do as much for us!'

Allegations of greater government assistance to Continental trade usually return to government subsidies and the existence of preferential rates for exports on State railway systems. German railways quite openly offered special rates for all German manufactures to the ports. British railways, privately owned, were naturally less uniform in their practices and more guarded in quoting preferential rates within earshot of possible competitors. But there is no doubt that many British exports enjoyed preferential rates of one kind or another. It cost $1\frac{2}{3}$d. per mile in the mid-'80s to take a ton of starch between London and Leeds, $\frac{11}{18}$d. to

---

[1] Wardrop's report on Haiti for 1901, P.P. 1903, LXXVII, 744.
[2] Quoted in a consular report from Saigon, April 1898, P.P. 1899, XCVI, 659.

take it to Antwerp. The dock rate between Manchester and London was 25s. a ton, compared with a London city rate of 40s.—a differential which encouraged manufacturers to consign to the docks and then load into lorries for shipment back to the home market in London. This is clearly documented in the evidence taken by the Royal Commission on the Depression of Trade and Industry, and in particular in a paper on a 'Comparison of English and Foreign Railway Rates' compiled and handed in as evidence by J. S. Jeans, Secretary of the British Iron Trade Association. British railway rates for pig iron, for example, were certainly in advance of Continental, but whereas for inland markets they were higher than German and French by 102% and 68%, for exports the differential was only 43% and 40% respectively.[1] The lower rates often reflected competition between various British railway systems or ports. Sir Thomas Farrer explained that if the export rate from Manchester to London was lower than the home market rate, it was to attract goods which would otherwise have gone to Liverpool for export. But whatever the reason, the effect was the same. There was an element of special pleading in the 'fundamental difference' discovered by the Departmental Committee on Shipping and Shipbuilding between the British and German systems:

> If through rates in the United Kingdom are sometimes lower than inland rates, it is generally because special circumstances render it commercially sound for the railway companies to give such rates, and not because of a deliberate policy to afford special facilities with a view to furthering particular sections of the export trade.

In any case, as the Committee explained, although the German special through-rate system had operated openly to the Levant and East Africa, there was no evidence that it applied to German goods shipped by German lines to South and Central America.[2]

Both Britain and Germany operated a system of shipping subsidies, primarily for the carriage of mail. But subsidies elsewhere

[1] Minutes of Evidence, *Report of the Royal Commission on the Depression of Trade and Industry*, P.P. 1886, XXI and XXIII, QQ. 3285-6, 5010-13, 8089-92, 11,305-9, 11,594-611, 14,993, and Appendixes A(5) and C to *Second Report*.

[2] *Report of the Departmental Committee on Shipping and Shipbuilding*, P.P. 1918, XIII, 572.

were unknown. The Departmental Committee on the Engineering Trades, reporting towards the end of the First World War, explained that it had received allegations from a great many sources of direct government subsidy in support of German trade.

Except in the matter of railway rates above referred to [rebates on goods intended for export], we have failed to find any instance of direct assistance—unless, indeed, in the matter of German coal, where the State itself owns certain coal mines which are members of the coal syndicate. We have inquired as closely as we could into this question of direct Government assistance, and we have traced any likely statement to its source; but we have in each case failed to find any confirmatory evidence of direct Government subsidy. On the other hand, we have received direct evidence from an authoritative German source that no such subsidies are paid, and the Budgets of Germany and Prussia carry no such items in their accounts. We are on the whole inclined to believe that this is correct.[1]

In practice, government assistance was insignificant in determining the total and distribution of Continental and North American exports to Latin America before 1914; insignificant, that is, except for the few colonial territories and, intermittently, for U.S. government tariff policy. The explanation for any competitive 'failure' in British trade methods can be found more readily in the nature of business with Brazil and the Republics.

Germany, from as early as the 1860s, made serious efforts to cut into the Latin American trade. The obvious starting-point was to challenge British manufacturers in the lower reaches of the market. In the late '60s de Fonblanque, Consul in Cartagena (Colombia), felt sure that customers still looked to Manchester, Belfast and Sheffield for solid serviceable goods, but 'for cheap showy trash, and fraudulent imitations of well-known British trade marks, Hamburgh appears to distance all rivals'.[2] Britons, with their established outlets, were content to supply well-made and reliable articles for which they knew there to be a sure sale. The Americans, although aggressive enough in certain directions and described by one disgruntled consul in 1880 as descending 'like the vulture

[1] *Report of the Departmental Committee on the Engineering Trades*, P.P. 1918, XIII, 393.
[2] De Fonblanque's report on Cartagena and Barranquilla for 1868, P.P. 1868-9, LX, 284.

M

after the dying horse' as soon as they smelt the opening of a market, were merely disposing of the surplus of long production runs designed first and foremost to satisfy demand in a large home market. The Germans, without the advantage either of an established position or of a large, uniform home market, had to make the running in 'novelties', in the creation of markets where none had existed before. In time Germany was able to raise the quality of her goods, build up staples, and allow her exports to sell on their own merits without a 'Sheffield' or 'London' imprint. Meanwhile, her trading methods were bound to be very different, more accommodating to local circumstances in language, measurements, currencies, quantities, more obviously aggressive and competitive over a wider range of small items, with all the frauds, inferior qualities and 'dumping' which British manufacturers and traders had employed in an earlier generation of exports. The tin soldiers imported into Argentina from Germany at the turn of the century carried Argentine flags; those from Britain, British. Yet Britons had shown precisely the same adaptability when making their way in a new trade. Samuel Haigh told a sad story of an enterprising British manufacturer who had sent out a consignment of chamber-pots to Buenos Aires in 1817, with the patriot arms tastefully painted in the bowl; when discovered at the Custom House, the indignant administrator declared the pots an insult to the State and ordered the whole consignment destroyed.[1] As A. E. Bateman sensibly observed, in a covering letter to a collection of consular criticisms of British trading methods, the alleged disinclination of British traders and manufacturers in the '90s to supply cheap goods, to accept small orders, to give long credits, and to be responsible for loss in exchange arose in great measure from the fact that most of those firms already possessed steady and established businesses and were not anxious to take on additional, more hazardous undertakings. Foreign firms, by contrast, and especially German houses, were often in a smaller way of business; they had more to gain and less to lose by taking up new lines of trade under more risky and troublesome conditions.[2]

There is no denying that British manufacturers and traders were slow to react to the new challenge in the '80s and '90s, or

[1] Haigh, *Buenos Ayres*, p. 30 fn.
[2] *Opinions of H.M. Diplomatic and Consular Officers on British Trade Methods*, P.P. 1899, XCVI, 622.

that they lost many markets to the developing manufacturing nations. This was not unnatural in a period of general depression for world trade, when profit margins were cut to the bone and trade went to those prepared to take least and work hardest. As established traders and manufacturers, Britons could afford to hold back in hope of better times; others had to trade to survive.

Slow as Britain was to react, there is sufficient evidence of competitive recovery in and after the late '90s to suggest that many of the complaints of 'hide-bound conservatism', of refusal to adapt to foreign requirements, were themselves due, as Wickham pointed out from New Zealand just before the war, 'to the very fault that is condemned, namely a vision limited to a groove, an inability to face facts or to sift evidence first hand'.[1] A customer in a distant market often failed to appreciate the production problems created by requests for what might have seemed trivial modifications in style or design—problems which made some individual orders uneconomic from the start. It was as difficult for anyone, customer and British consul alike, to accept that his own particular market might not offer sufficient attractions to be worth competing for. Once manufacturing industry reached a certain size, some of its adaptability to individual requirements was bound to be lost. Germany was frequently cited as a manufacturing nation ready to meet any requirement. While this was true of the first decades of competition, German manufacturing naturally shared the trend towards replacement of expensive labour by machines, towards larger orders for standard patterns. It was becoming more difficult, before the war, to find a German manufacturer willing to accept individual orders for goods out of the ordinary patterns.[2] As for the United States, so often praised for the adaptability of her manufacturers and their willingness to fit products to individual requirements, Wickham may have been right in his suspicion that American manufacturers normally found markets suited to their goods, rather than suited their goods to markets entirely unlike their own.[3]

*

[1] Wickham's report on New Zealand for 1913, P.P. 1914-16, XLVI, 631.
[2] Sir Francis Oppenheimer's report on Germany for 1913 includes some interesting observations on this subject, P.P. 1914-16, LXXII, 804.
[3] Wickham's report on New Zealand for 1911, P.P. 1912-13, XCIII, 952.

A great deal of nonsense has been printed on the inferiority of one nation's trading methods to another's. In general, nationality had nothing to do with it; the distinction was between individual traders, different trades, distinct options, varying stages of development. Take the question of opening a direct trade. How much should be spent on advertising? Should the trade be canvassed by commercial travellers, or first opened by the circulation of trade journals, brochures, illustrated catalogues and price lists? Is it worth printing and circulating catalogues in translation? Should the prices be quoted in local currency? What measurements should be given, or manufactured for? Is it better to quote f.o.b. or c.i.f., and if c.i.f., to which port *en route* if it is impracticable to quote for the whole distance? Some of the answers to these questions may look self-evident, but any businessman could have explained what each decision entailed.

From the point of view of British traders and manufacturers, the emphasis in trade promotion was increasingly towards home and Empire markets. It was here that the first efforts were concentrated. Brochures and catalogues were printed and prepared for English-speaking markets. Advertising was best placed in the newspapers and 'illustrateds' which reached both home and colonial markets. An English manufacturer, faced with the heavy expense of promoting a branded product like Hollins' 'Viyella', or Crosfield's 'Perfection' and 'Pink Carbolic', directed the bulk of his advertising towards the home market, after which he went to South Africa, to Australasia, perhaps to the United States, Canada and China. The great cotton manufacturing combines, Horrockses and Tootal, marketing a branded product, did most of their trade with the home market; it was the home trade in branded products which made such rapid progress in the last years of the nineteenth century, partly because of the strength of the combines but also as an outcome of the introduction, after the mid-'80s, of direct sales to the draper. The most successful direct sales firms found their best outlets, obviously, in markets with which they could keep in close touch, at home and to a lesser extent in the Dominions, the Colonies, and neighbouring Europe. Advertising of brand names and the familiarity of the public with the standard quality of the brand were the key elements in trade strategy.

Beyond the handbills and placards distributed by commercial travellers, such advertising as appeared locally for British products in Latin America was handled almost entirely by the import house holding the agency for the manufacturer; the home manufacturer saw little sense in dispersing an exiguous advertising budget among a score of national newspapers in as many Republics. By contrast, the United States, at any rate in a neighbouring market like Mexico, Cuba or Puerto Rico, enjoyed some of the advantages Britons themselves experienced in the colonies and Dominions. Leay noted how British newspapers were never seen in Mexico in the early 1900s, while American magazines were everywhere; American newspapers and heavy trade journals were entering on the ½d. post, crammed with advertising.[1] In Canada the position for newspapers and journals was much the same, while in the Western provinces foreign advertising became by degrees almost exclusively North American. The records kept by one of the largest advertising agencies in Winnipeg showed, at the end of the war, that Canadian firms took 60% of the space, American 35% and British only 5%.[2]

The inclination of British manufacturers to continue trading through import houses in Latin America rather than direct naturally reduced the number of commercial travellers canvassing markets in the Republics. No complaint is more frequent in British consular reports than of the shortage of British commercial travellers, by which, in the words of one consul, 'the expansive power of British trade was seriously crippled'. Admittedly British consuls were not always aware of the number of travellers passing through their districts; travellers were not expected to call automatically at the consulate and the majority never had reason to do so. In the lace trade more travellers were sent out from England than from her competitors, and consular complaints are known to have been entirely misleading.[3] But there was a sense in which anxiety was justified for Latin America, not because British manufacturers did not know their business but because in many lines travellers could not earn their keep. British travellers were to be found in any line of trade within Britain's own enclosed markets. Continental travellers were practically unknown in a

---

[1] Leay's report on Vera Cruz for 1903, P.P. 1905, XC, 716.
[2] Quoted in Beale's report on Western Canada for 1919, P.P. 1920, XXXIII, 492.
[3] The point is discussed in the Tariff Commission's *Report on the Textile Trades (Lace Industry)* (London, 1905), para. 2637.

British colony like Nigeria, where the trade was handled almost exclusively by Britons. English commercial travellers frequently visited the British West Indies and did excellent business in textiles, soaps, toilet articles, spirits and canned provisions. Yet in a neighbouring Spanish Caribbean market, in the Central American Republics, Colombia and Venezuela, the poverty of the consumer, the national taste in foodstuffs and alcohol, made it uneconomic to support travellers except in the few, big-selling lines—cotton and woollen textiles, cotton laces and possibly hardware. In drugs, perfumery, hats, leather, stationery, provisions, British representation was practically nil; the trade was handled by a few large firms, normally German, with their resident partners or buying agents in Europe.

The infrequency or otherwise of travellers was very much a function of type of trade, location of market, comparative costs and anticipated results of alternative sales methods. Consular complaints of wilful neglect of certain markets often failed to take these into account. British travellers were frequent enough in Latin America on the well-beaten routes, through Pernambuco to Rio, Montevideo and Buenos Aires, through Panama to Guayaquil, Callao and Valparaiso. Even at the end of the '90s, when such complaints reached a crescendo, the Britsh vice-consul in Panama felt that nothing could be said on the score of a lack of travellers.[1] Chambers reported from Ecuador's port, Guayaquil, that 'many respectable travelling agents representing British firms have visited the country at various times during the year [1897], and have as a rule expressed their satisfaction with their share of the import trade'[2]; yet Söderström complained from the national capital that whereas a few commercial travellers from France, Germany, and the United States had visited Quito during the year, none had come from England.[3] But Guayaquil was a natural place to call, lying as it did on the sea route south from Panama; Quito was a long ride up in the mountains and was in any case supplied from Guayaquil in all the main lines of trade. On the east coast of the Continent, Pernambuco was the first port of call for the Royal Mail and Pacific Steam Navigation steamers when outward bound, and the last port of call when homeward bound.

[1] Dolby-Tyler's report on Panama for 1896, P.P. 1897, XC, 268.
[2] Chambers' report from Guayaquil for 1897, P.P. 1898, XCV, 110.
[3] Söderström's report on Quito for 1897, ibid., 124.

It was amply served by British travellers right up to the First World War; they called annually and they frequently took Pernambuco as their base of operations for trips north and south as required. But few if any British travellers felt it worth their while, even during the height of the rubber boom, to pay special visits to the Amazon ports of Pará and Manaos, where the trade was handled by resident British import houses.

It was a straight commercial calculation, expenses against sales. Even at a nearby outlet like La Rochelle in France, the British consul calculated that travelling with samples for ten months in the year would cost £400 in expenses alone, in addition to salary. A very fair average for orders taken in circuit would be £6,000, and about half as much more by post. The profit, as he said, was a matter of speculation, and for some years would be very small.[1] Taxation could add formidably to costs in many Latin American markets, as it did in Europe and in many of Britain's own colonies.[2] No taxes existed for Rio or São Paulo in the 1900s, but both Bahia and Porto Alegre imposed a tax on visiting travellers of £62. 10s. There was no tax in Chile, Peru, Colombia and Ecuador. In most of the other Republics, a range of municipal, state and federal taxes had to be built into any calculations. In a great market like Argentina, high provincial taxation on commercial travellers meant that few firms could afford to send representatives further afield than Buenos Aires and Rosario, and the greater part of the business was handled through the larger importing houses at the capital.

Much the same arithmetic applied in other respects. Some British traders were less efficient and up to date than others. But this was as true of traders of all nationalities. British merchants had long experience of the markets, and there is no reason to suppose that they were, in general, any less efficient than others in making use of this experience. A long-established trader is likely to be more cautious in offering extended facilities when he knows the problems to which these may lead. British traders and manufacturers were sometimes criticized for failing to quote prices in local currency, or for refusing to give as generous credit facilities

[1] Report of March 1898, *Opinions on Trade Methods*, P.P. 1899, XCVI, 654.
[2] The rates are given in a *Memorandum summarising the Regulations with Regard to British Commercial Travellers*, P.P. 1906, CXXI, 219-65.

as some of their competitors. Yet the sharp fluctuations and heavy depreciation of so many Latin American currencies in the last decades of the century meant that incaution in this respect could and often did lead to bankruptcy. In normal times British traders, no less than anyone else, could afford to ignore current commercial practice, and long credit remained standard for the Latin American import trade throughout the period.

In such matters as packaging, measurements, f.o.b. or c.i.f. terms, each man made his own decisions according to the conditions of the market, and no rule could be laid down for Latin America as a whole. Britain was in advance of most competitors in the development of specialist export packing. The metric system was generally advisable for measurements, but there were certain lines of trade where British and American manufacturers held so large a portion of the market that yards, feet and inches were the measures in common use. C.i.f. terms may have seemed an obvious improvement on f.o.b., but for inland markets with irregular transport by river or mule it was better to quote at most to the nearest large port, after which local agents could negotiate the best terms; any alternative arrangement meant either an excessive covering charge or the possibility of serious loss to the vendor. If the greater part of sales were in practice made through import houses or resident foreign engineers, it did not always make sense to translate sales literature, sometimes of a technical nature, into poor Spanish or worse Portuguese. Some of the catalogues reaching Spain in the late '90s were 'calculated to increase hilarity rather than business'; 'Anglo-Spanish catalogues are often as funny and incomprehensible as Germano-English'.[1] National feeling was so strong within the Austro-Hungarian Empire that while Italian, German and Slav languages were all spoken, those who could read a catalogue in one language would simply refuse to look at it in another.[2] Many of the catalogues reaching Brazil were printed in Spanish, but, said Churchill from Pará, the Brazilian or Portuguese importer would prefer to read them in English or French rather than Spanish; they were proud of their nationality and race and resented being taken for what they were not. Churchill had seen some British attempts at corresponding in Portuguese. He thought that they took longer to decipher than

[1] *Opinions on Trade Methods*, P.P. 1899, XCVI, 672, 675.
[2] *Ibid.*, 680.

the originals written in English which in any case was a language generally understood in commercial circles at Pará.[1]

Indeed, the barrage of complaints against the distribution of sales literature, against the 'catalogue selling' so popular in and after the '80s, was the response of an amateur to a process which he imperfectly understood. In the first place, a large part of the trade literature reaching Latin America was simply the surplus of a considerable sales effort in the British Empire, sent out on the off-chance of picking up some orders, just as American trade literature, printed in Spanish, was the surplus of a sales effort in neighbouring Mexico and Cuba. In colonial markets, catalogue selling was very common. The Trade Commissioner in South Africa pointed out that 'trade in South Africa follows the catalogue, and money spent upon them and upon clear popular advertisements is rarely wasted'.[2] Britons were on the look out for markets for many of their new industries. Home and colonial consumers provided the main outlet, but it cost little to circulate catalogues to a wider public in any country of the world. A catalogue, even if it never led to a direct sale, might introduce consumers to manufactures of which they could not otherwise have known; they might then take steps to order through the normal channels of import houses in Rio, Buenos Aires, Montevideo, Valparaiso or Lima.

Blanket coverage of Latin American markets by sales managers in the United Kingdom had some curious results. Costly and elaborate catalogues were sent out to tropical Matto Grosso in the heart of Brazil offering 'new systems of heating for houses and factories, as also of gas, oil and electric heating stoves quite useless in this climate'.[3] To Haiti, where it was as much as anybody could do to survive, British manufacturers despatched illustrated price lists of 'gold and silversmiths' wares, jewellery, motor cars, kinematographs, machinery, laundry machines, athletic goods, games, wines, photographic and other expensive goods'.[4] They could have made no sales. But the interesting thing is that they tried at all, and that they were promoting so wide a range of the new generation of consumer goods. These were the products

[1] Churchill's report on Pará for 1902, P.P. 1904, XCVII, 260-1.
[2] Birchenough's report on South Africa for 1903, P.P. 1904, LXI, 73.
[3] Atkinson's report on Cuyabá for 1909, P.P. 1910, XCVI, 625.
[4] Murray's report on Haiti for 1909, P.P. 1910, XCIX, 479.

which were already making such an impression on the colonial trade. No businessman in his senses would have sent out travellers in such lines except, perhaps, to Rio and Buenos Aires. But it was not so unreasonable to test new markets with trade literature at minimal cost, to follow up a response only where it seemed promising, and to hope, over time, to create consumer demand where none had existed before. Whatever the individual failures, British manufacturers continued to circulate trade literature and to advertise in British export journals like *El Guardian Mercantil* published specifically for the Latin American market. Is it reasonable to expect that they would have done so if it had not paid its way?

CHAPTER VIII

Latin American Imports

LITTLE 'neutrality' existed in the circumstances under which nations competed for world markets before 1914. Quite apart from the peculiar advantages enjoyed by one or other of the manufacturing nations in individual markets by reason of resources, experience, aptitudes, tastes, ease of access or national preference, some allowance must be made for the combinations, trusts, price conventions, market-sharing agreements which effectively limited international competition well before the First World War. Even by 1896 Liefmann found competition to be restricted or eliminated altogether in 'borax, bicarbonate of ammonia, uranium dyes, muriatic acid, soda, caffeine, lactic sugar, alizarin, chloralhydrate, oxalic acid, iodine, strontianite, bromides, cyanide of potassium, chromates, phosphates, imitation gold leaf, potter's earth, fertilizers, saline products, dynamite, small arms ammunition, rails, tubes, iron bars, gas piping, rolled wire, needles, wooden screws, coke, raw zinc, rolled zinc, bismuth, lead, copper, enamelled ware, cement, looking-glass, parchment and thread'[1]—and his list was not exhaustive.

The organization of international trade was taken further during the 1900s and further still during and after the war. Yet it remains a comfortable illusion among Englishmen that cartels, trusts and combinations were an unpleasant development in German or North American industrialization with which British manufacturers were unfamiliar before 1914. The fact was that twenty-two

[1] Robert Liefmann, *International Cartels, Combines and Trusts* (London, 1927), pp. 32-3.

of Liefmann's forty international producer cartels were Anglo-German, while within British industry itself organization took forms which, though less obvious than the great consolidations of Germany or the United States, were better suited to British conditions and hardly less effective. John Hilton, Secretary to the Committee on Trusts (1919), warned that it should not too readily be assumed that British industries were behindhand in this respect.

> Individuality has counted for more in British manufacture than in foreign, and if amalgamation has proceeded cautiously there has been reason in the caution. British combines and consolidations may not rank as prodigies, but among them are some that can vie in efficiency with any in the world. British trade associations make little parade of their existence or achievements, but there are few corners of British industry in which some kind of trade association is not to be found, and some of them can show a thoroughness of organization not easily surpassed. What is notable among British consolidations and associations is not their rarity or weakness so much as their unobtrusiveness. There is not much display in the window, but there is a good selection inside.

Although, for many industries, trades and services in Britain, combination had made hardly any headway before 1914, Hilton identified considerably more than five hundred associations, all exerting a substantial influence on the course of industry and prices. He concluded that competition was 'no longer a reliable regulator of prices over a very considerable field'.[1]

The effect on British trading performance in Latin America was felt in several directions. Perhaps the majority of pre-war combinations in British industry were formed during the final twenty years, in response to the threat of foreign competition in home and overseas markets. One of their functions, once sufficiently powerful to control and maintain prices in the home market, was to enable participants to extend their output by selling their products at lower prices, even at a loss, in foreign markets—in other words, to practise precisely that 'dumping' of which British

---

[1] Hilton's study of trade organizations and combinations in the United Kingdom is printed as an Appendix to the *Report of the Committee of the Ministry of Reconstruction on Trusts*. P.P. 1918, XIII, 805-20.

manufacturers themselves complained so loudly in the context of the German or North American steel cartels or Continental silk, linen, linen yarn, cotton hosiery and lace manufacturers.

The difficulty, then, of speaking realistically of 'open' competition or 'neutral' markets is compounded in many lines of trade by the artificial prices attached to export products. Further, and this was an important element in emphasizing the trend in British exports towards Empire markets, international market-sharing agreements like the steel-rail or tobacco concordats naturally gave British producers priority in traditionally British markets, at home and overseas. The circumstance that British imports of tobacco into New Zealand rose from virtually nothing before 1903 to challenge American imports by the late 1900s, or that China in 1913 was taking almost as much (in value) of tobacco and snuff manufactured in the United Kingdom as the entire British Possessions, tells us no more about British competitive 'success' in those markets than does Britain's 'failure' to make any impression on manufactured tobacco imports into Latin America. The figures merely reflect a parcelling-out of world markets after the epic struggle between the American Tobacco Trust and Imperial Tobacco. British American Tobacco, a joint enterprise in business after 1902, brought competition to an end in home markets and ensured that sales and production effort overseas was distributed thereafter along the 'natural' lines of trade.

In any case, few national industries could hope to organize and control all international markets all the time, and even without market-sharing agreements the natural tendency was to organize first of all the home and colonial markets with which contact was closest. 'One cannot conceal from oneself', said Birchenough from South Africa in 1904, 'that the free play of competition in South Africa is more or less paralysed by the influence of "rings", not necessarily organized combinations of any kind, but more or less powerful interests. The shipping "conference" is a common and well-known example, but there are in all branches of trade influences which keep both wholesale and retail prices and profits at a very high level.'[1] This, in turn, made these markets even more attractive to British manufacturers, and reduced their interest in those over which their control was less complete.

[1] Birchenough's report on South Africa for 1903, P.P. 1904, LXI, 41.

Cotton Manufactures

While the proportion of cotton piece goods to total imports from the United Kingdom was far higher for some Republics than it was for others, cotton manufactures remained the largest single element in British exports to Latin America before 1914. Cotton manufactures accounted for over half the value of Britain's total exports in 1830. Diversification and expansion in British industry gradually reduced this proportion to about a quarter in 1914, but it was a quarter of a vastly expanded overseas trade. In linear yards, which in a century of falling prices serve as a better measure than values, British exports of cotton piece goods rose from a yearly average of 476 million yards in 1830-4 to 6,479 million yards in 1910-14.[1]

Table XI

World Trade in Cotton Textiles, 1882-4 to 1936-8
(yearly averages, million yards)

	1882-4	1910-13	1926-8	1936-8
United Kingdom	4,410	6,650	3,940	1,720
Europe	770	1,900	2,320	1,490
U.S.A.	150	400	540	250
India	50	90	170	200
Japan	—	200	1,390	2,510
Other Countries	—	260	190	290
Total	5,380	9,500	8,550	6,460

Source: R. Robson, *The Cotton Industry in Britain* (London, 1957), p. 4.

Britain's position in the world trade in cotton manufactures was not seriously challenged before the war. Other countries took a larger percentage as they outgrew their own home markets, gained access through the Suez Canal to supplies of Indian cotton, and developed new markets in adjacent territories—in Central America and the Caribbean for the United States, in the Near East for Germany and Italy, in Mongolia for Japan. Britain's 82% of world trade in 1882-4 had fallen to 58% by 1910-13. But the rate of growth of the British cotton industry still averaged about $1\frac{1}{4}$% per annum for the half-century before 1914, and the industry was expanding up to the war. Robson's figures for world

[1] Maurice G. Kendall (ed.), *The Sources and Nature of the Statistics of the United Kingdom* (London, 1952), I, 116.

trade in cotton textiles show the overwhelming lead of British industry before the war, just as they show its sad collapse before Japanese competition during the inter-war years (Table XI).

Certainly, neither Japan nor India were factors to be reckoned with in Latin American markets before 1914, and such competition as there was came largely from the United States and Europe. National taste and fashion sold substantial quantities of French dyed and printed cottons in the new Republics, and it was on this basis that French cottons continued to find some sale throughout the period. But even in the early years British manufacturers did not regard France, in general, as a formidable competitor. The low price of English cottons had ruined the manufacturers of Bengal, and if we were alarmed by anybody in the 1820s, it was by the United States and even then only in a single article, American coarse, strong 'domestics' which commanded a good market in Mexico, Brazil, Argentina and Chile. By 1833 the challenge was already met. Joshua Bates thought that it was a case of the American manufacturer using, in his ignorance, nothing but the very best cotton; 'they put more of the raw material into it; this has given them an advantage for a time; at Manchester they now make an imitation of the American domestic which is nearly as good, and at rather a less price'.[1]

It was this adaptability, this readiness to make for any market, which maintained the leading position of British cotton piece goods in Brazil and the Republics. If a local design commanded a market, a sample was sent home to Lancashire, the design copied, and a cheaper substitute introduced. In the early '70s, when brown and bleached cottons from the United States were selling well in the Northern Republics, goods of an identical description were manufactured and supplied by British manufacturers at much lower prices, and North American imports came to an end.[2] Even in the British home market wholesalers and retailers were always on the look out for novelties, and no manufacturer could hope to anticipate every new direction of taste and fashion. A German printed calico in a tobacco colour slightly different from Manchester work was for a short while in great demand in the home trade, where 'the shopkeepers would have the German stuff because it

---

[1] Minutes of Evidence, *Select Committee on Manufactures, Commerce and Shipping*, P.P. 1833, VI, Q.892.
[2] Middleton's report on Venezuela for 1873, P.P. 1874, LXVII, 468.

was smaller in supply and could not be obtained from British competitors'; within weeks Manchester calico printers had precisely the same tints of tobacco colour for the ground work and the competition was over.[1] British manufacturers reproduced and replaced American checks in Haiti at the turn of the century, Italian trousering and American grey drills in Colombia, 'Tessuti Italiani' and 'Tela Florida' in Brazil.[2] In cotton goods Lancashire had no difficulty in meeting the complaint that Britons would not make cheap qualities for pauper markets. What Germany was prepared to do in other lines, Britain did for cottons, and more than 50% of British cotton goods imported by Nicaragua at the turn of the century consisted of the 'cheapest, flimsiest kind of grey cloths, drills, prints, lawns, muslins, shirtings, etc., it is possible to obtain'.[3]

Specialization among British manufacturers, the advantages of narrow geographical concentration, the skill of Britain's textile workers, the experience of her export houses, her packers, her Lancashire travellers, enabled her to match requirements in what was still, before the war, a localized, fragmented market with an enormous range and variety of demand. Zimmern describes how, especially before the days of the Calico Printers' Association (1899), an exporter could go to a calico printer and pick out styles suitable not merely for Brazil or Peru or Colombia, but for Rio and São Paulo but not for Ceará and Maranhao; for Arequipa, Lima, or Piura; for Barranquilla but not for Bogotá.[4] And this applied not only to printed goods but to the finish and even the length and make-up of white calico.

Each market—often each district or department—had its own special requirements of width, length, folding, stamping, etc. Thus, according to their destination, white shirtings for Colombia were shipped in 20, 24, 30, 40 yard pieces. . . . The pieces were made up long-fold, lapped or plaited, print-way,

[1] Thomas Stuttard's evidence, 11 February 1886, printed as Appendix A (6), *Second Report of the Royal Commission on the Depression of Trade and Industry*, P.P. 1886, XXI, 601.
[2] Wardrop's report on Haiti for 1902, P.P. 1904, XCIX, 573-4; Dickson's report on Colombia for 1901, P.P. 1902, CVI, 357; Worthington's second report on Brazil, 20 December 1898, P.P. 1899, XCVI, 566.
[3] Chambers' report on Nicaragua for 1898, P.P. 1899, CI, 226.
[4] W. H. Zimmern, 'Lancashire and Latin America', *Manchester School of Economic and Social Studies*, XIII (1944), 58.

silk fold or French fold, book-fold, Dutch fold. . . . In some places goods bore the importer's name or trade-mark; in others complete anonymity was the practice.[1]

Straight price competition was not at issue; differences in the first price of manufactured products, even after the improvement of communications, could often be lost in the commissions and profits of intermediaries. In the smaller individual markets, sales were rather the outcome of intimate and long-standing connections between client and merchant house. Zimmern, speaking particularly of the Colombia and Venezuela of the 1890s and 1900s which he knew so well, explained that there were few importing firms and little real competition; each importer had his pet connections in Manchester and he stuck to them largely on account of credit and as an insurance against the currency fluctuations, tariff changes and new regulations with which at any moment he might need assistance and accommodation.

Among overseas suppliers, competition in the decade before 1914 came largely from the United States in the Caribbean and Germany and Italy in South America. Britain lost two of her best markets to the United States when Cuba and Puerto Rico fell to American control in 1898. Puerto Rico imported £511,814 of cotton goods from the United States in 1909; £3,667 from Britain.[2] In Cuba, British manufacturers managed to maintain about half of the trade in cotton goods, but it was against a preferential tariff of 30 to 40% in favour of the United States. In the Central American Republics, Nicaragua, Honduras, El Salvador, the natural lines of trade were with the United States. Almost daily steamer communication was maintained with New Orleans and Mobile in connection with the banana trade, and by the mid-1900s the United States had gained a near monopoly of imported dry goods, principally cheap grey and white shirtings, prints, printed ducks and drills, and hosiery. But she was able to make little impression elsewhere. Americans manufactured first and foremost for the home market; their strength was in large-scale production of standardized goods. While the domestic market continued to offer such opportunities for expansion, American manufacturers were not prepared to compete in the diverse, sometimes miniature

---

[1] *Ibid., Manchester School*, XXVIII, 43-4.
[2] The 1908 figures were £403,052 and £4,706 respectively: Churchward's report on Puerto Rico for 1909, P.P. 1910, CIII, 600, 604.

markets so well worked already by Britons and Germans. Fashion, taste and proximity sold American cottons in Canada. Manchuria, before the Japanese arrived, offered a large but erratic outlet for the range of heavy grey goods of plain texture which the United States could supply in large quantities at small labour cost. To Canada and Central America, American exports of cotton manufactures rose steadily from $3 million in 1891 to $12·5 million in 1910. In Asia they touched $32·9 million in 1906, though they were down to $7·5 four years later. Over the whole of *South* America, total exports were a mere $2·2 million in 1891 and $3·3 in 1910, reaching a single peak of $4·1 million in 1905.[1]

Hinrichsen, a Manchester merchant in business shipping cottons to all parts of the world, put the position plainly for the mid-'80s. He was asked whether British cotton goods met German or French in 'neutral' markets. He replied:

> Very seldom, some where taste is in question, but very few, and we see them even here in this country ; but staple goods, plain goods such as grey and bleached goods we do not; it is more in fancy goods of high value and quality, that we meet them sometimes, but in the staples it is impossible for any of those countries to compete with us.[2]

His opinion was shared by every Lancashire witness before the Royal Commission on the Depression of Trade and Industry (1886). Germany captured individual markets at particular times, and the strength of her mercantile representation in the Republics meant that an increasing proportion of the cotton goods reaching Latin America before 1914 came through German ports. The German component, however, could be quite small. It is difficult or impossible to arrive at any precise figures, but the extent of re-exports in 'German' trade was indicated by a heavy fall in German cotton imports into Venezuela from 23·6% in 1909-10 to 10·9% in 1910-11 while British cottons rose from 47·6% to 61·5%, accounted for by a shift in the trade in drills, formerly imported through German houses in Hamburg and now shipped direct from the country of origin.[3]

---

[1] Melvin T. Copeland, *The Cotton Manufacturing Industry of the United States* (Cambridge, Mass., 1912), p. 222.

[2] Minutes of Evidence, *Report of the Royal Commission on the Depression of Trade and Industry*, P.P. 1886, XXI, Q.6062.

[3] Milne's report on Venezuela, 1913, P.P. 1913, LXVIII, 160.

Imports of Italian textiles, too, included an element of semi-manufactured black goods from Manchester, dyed in Switzerland and exported through Genoa. But the Italians were claiming a share of Latin American markets in their own right, particularly in Argentina. The Italian textile industry advanced rapidly after the introduction of protective tariffs in 1878 and of a prohibitive tariff in 1887. Italian manufacturers were adaptable and ready to suit any market. They had the advantage of rapid and direct communication with the Republics, on immigrant ships, at half the freight from northern Europe. They were helped by the demand of hundreds of thousands of Italian immigrants for the heavy yarn-dyed qualities for the men's shirts and suits and the women's blouses and skirts which Italians wore at home.

Table XII

British, Italian, German and United States
Exports of Cotton Piece Goods to
Argentina and Brazil, 1909-13
(annual averages, metric tons)

	Argentina	Brazil
United Kingdom	14,650	8,567
Italy	6,884	686
Germany	2,102	1,162
United States	106	215

Source: S. B. Saul, *Studies in British Overseas Trade 1870-1914* (Liverpool, 1960), p. 34.

Yet whatever the circumstances and even without taking account of quality of fabrics or proportion of re-exports, Britain remained well ahead as a supplier of cotton goods to the two leading markets of South America, Argentina and Brazil. Italy approached her most nearly in Argentina, Germany in Brazil, while the United States was not a serious competitor in either. Table XII shows the position as it was in the last years before the war.

Yet for all Britain's obvious competitiveness in world trade and despite a rise in British exports of cotton piece goods to all destinations from 5,033 million yards in 1895 to 7,075 million yards in 1913, British exports to Latin America, which had reached their peak in 1895 at 876·5 million yards, had fallen to 703·9 million yards by 1913. This was a period of rising demand for cotton piece goods in Latin America as a whole. Clearly foreign competition on its own can supply no satisfactory explanation, and an answer must be looked for in the development of Latin America's own cotton manufacturing industry.

Cotton manufacturing was unevenly distributed among the Republics, and despite one or two attempts to develop a trade, there was no traffic to speak of between them. Some indication of the scale of cotton manufacturing is given in Table XIII. Cotton manufacturing was well advanced in Brazil and Mexico, and

Table XIII
The Cotton Manufacturing Industry: Size and Distribution in Latin America, 1910-11

	Factories	Spindles	Looms
Brazil	137	1,000,000	35,000
Mexico	139	726,278	25,325
Peru	7	52,250	1,750
Colombia	5	20,000	300
Venezuela	2	11,000	250
Argentina	6	9,000	1,200
Guatemala	1	6,000	150
Chile	3	5,000	400
Ecuador	4	5,000	200
Uruguay	3	—	300
Total	307	1,834,528	64,877

Source: *The Times*, South American Supplement, 29 August 1911, 4a.

expansion continued in Brazil at a rate which brought spindles up to 1,500,722 and looms to 50,449 by 1915.[1] Manufacturing made less progress elsewhere, but the limited capacity of markets could mean that a relatively small industry was sufficient to satisfy local demand. Scholfield estimated in the '70s that among the Indian population of Guatemala two to three yards of grey cotton per person satisfied the annual requirement for such clothing as was not already supplied by the local handicraft industry.[2] When the Cantel Company was formed in 1909-10 to manufacture the blue denim so widely used not only by the Guatemalan army and police but also for schools and by the people generally, its promoters

[1] Hambloch's report on Brazil for 1919, P.P. 1920, XLIII, 128.
[2] Scholfield's report on Guatemala for 1871, P.P. 1873, LXIV, 317-18.

confidently expected to be able to meet the entire national demand by a production of 40 pieces (of 72 yards) per day.[1]

It was capacity, indeed, which so attracted Britons to Argentina. Argentina was a comparatively large market. Her cotton manufacturing industry was still at an early stage of development. Textiles were the largest single element in her import trade, and it was in textiles that Britain was most firmly established and best represented. Table XIV shows the extent to which expansion in exports of piece goods to Argentina enabled Lancashire to fill the gap created by import substitution in Brazil, Mexico and Peru.

Table XIV
British Exports of Cotton Piece Goods to Argentina, Brazil, Mexico and Peru in selected years 1880-1913
(million yards)

	1880	1885	1890	1895	1900	1905	1910	1913
Argentina	62	66	65	157	131	159	185	199
Brazil	233	190	213	194	105	131	155	97
Mexico	35	27	40	51	38	21	22	23
Peru	7[1]	20	34	37	28	39	27	29

[1] A year of political disturbance to trade. The average for 1880-84 was 23 million.

Source: *U.K. Trade and Navigation Accounts*, rounded to the nearest million.

From an early date mill production in Mexico exceeded British imports. By the mid-'60s, Middleton estimated mill production at about 54 million yards of *manta* ('grey domestic'), and the incomplete official returns for 1878, which Carden regarded as seriously understating production, gave an annual mill production of 120 million yards of *manta* and 12 million yards of prints.[2] By contrast, British exports of cotton goods to Mexico, entered by the yard, averaged 30·8 million yards annually both in 1861-5 and in 1874-8. Local production, sheltered by heavy protective tariffs, made it impossible for British manufacturers to compete either in *manta* or in the inferior kinds of cotton prints. At the turn of the century (1901) local production in 124 cotton factories had risen to 353,794,464 yards, while British exports to Mexico were down to 21,533,800 yards. Biorklund, in supplying the

[1] Haggard's report on Guatemala for 1909, P.P. 1911, XCIII, 315.
[2] Carden's report on Mexico, 5 July 1883, P.P. 1883, LXXV. 525-6.

Mexican figures, added that the qualities produced by the better-equipped factories were equal to those imported.[1] Import substitution was virtually complete by 1911. 97·2% of consumption in plain and printed goods, excluding luxury goods, was produced at home. The Mexican cotton industry in 1910 manufactured a total of 15 million pieces (approximately 450 million yards)[2]; British exports of piece goods to Mexico for 1910 were still a mere 21·5 million yards. Similarly in Brazil cotton cloth production rose from about 20 million metres in 1885 to 378,619,000 metres in 1911.[3] British exports to Brazil were 190,096,700 yards in 1885, 160,068,100 yards in 1911, and 96,537,900 yards in 1913. Certainly, Brazil still found room for British imports in the finer counts and in prints, where the range was impossible to match, but no openings remained in the mass market.

Among those of the smaller Republics which developed a cotton manufacturing industry, the cheaper ranges of imported cottons were naturally the first to be replaced. Few grey domestics were imported into Peru by the turn of the century, 'so that this branch of trade, which has been monopolized by British manufacturers, may be considered as almost totally lost to them'.[4] In Colombia, although there was no competition to speak of in staple Manchester goods (white shirtings, printed cottons, white and dyed cotton dress goods), local manufacturing had developed sufficiently since the turn of the century to displace imported grey domestics, grey drills, striped drills and Oxfords; by 1913 British imports in this range were reduced to 'a negligible quantity'.[5] Even in Venezuela, where there was no sign of a cotton factory in the '90s and only four mills in operation by 1914, the local manufacture of greys, with which imported goods could not compete, had displaced a similar quality of United States manufactures universally on sale throughout Central America.[6]

Lancashire found some compensation for lost exports in the rising demand for cotton machinery and yarn. Indian yarns competed successfully with British in the Far East, but Britain

[1] Biorklund's report on Mexico for 1901, P.P. 1903, LXXVIII, 186.
[2] Rosenzweig in Cosío Villegas, *Mexico: La Vida Económica*, I, 342.
[3] Stanley J. Stein, *The Brazilian Cotton Manufacture* (Cambridge, Mass., 1957), p. 100.
[4] St John's report on Peru for 1901, P.P. 1902, CIX, 112.
[5] Badian's report on Antioquia for 1913, P.P. 1914-16, LXXI, 870-1.
[6] Milne's report on Venezuela, 1913, P.P. 1913, LXVIII, 602.

was still a major supplier of fine cotton yarns to the world's manufacturing industries. Germany took 90·8% (£4,570,000) of her total imports of fine cotton yarns from Britain in 1912; Austria-Hungary, 59·7%.[1] The Fine Cotton Spinners' and Doublers' Association, founded in 1898 by the amalgamation of 31 British firms, soon virtually controlled the whole of English fine yarn production. With a capital of over £7 million it was one of England's largest industrial combines, and it gained a comfortable leadership in world markets. Colombia, for example, bought £84,000 worth of British yarn in 1911 to feed her new mills; Germany supplied £3,940 and the United States £2,007.[2]

Table XV

British Exports of Cotton Yarn to selected Cotton Manufacturing Countries in Latin America for selected years, 1880-1913
(thousand lb)

	1880	1885	1890	1895	1900	1905	1910	1913
Brazil	—[1]	779	1,386	2,654	1,872	1,338	1,114	1,338
Mexico	102	136	209	181	189	177	198	89[2]
Peru	—[1]	29	—[1]	—[1]	—[1]	—[1]	109	107
Colombia	—[1]	—[1]	229	464	26[2]	83	993	2,708
Argentina	—[1]	—[1]	—[1]	1,384	1,794	3,482	2,342	1,872

[1] Not separately distinguished.
[2] Figures seriously distorted by political troubles.

Source: *U.K. Trade and Navigation Accounts*, rounded to the nearest thousand.

Table XV shows the development of British trade in yarns to the leading cotton manufacturers in Latin America. The normal pattern was expansion in the earlier stages of manufacturing, followed by decline in response to the development of local spinning capacity. As raw cotton producers, Brazil and the Republics soon developed cotton spinning for themselves, and Latin America consequently never approached the huge German or Dutch demand for English yarn (52 million and 39 million lb respectively in 1913).

In sewing-thread Britain was virtually unbeatable. The Germans and Italians were beginning to challenge her in Latin American

[1] Committee on Commercial and Industrial Policy, *Interim Report on the Treatment of Exports from the United Kingdom*, P.P. 1918, XIII, 235, 237 (Tables I and IIa).
[2] Milne's report on Colombia, 1913, P.P. 1913, LXVIII, 575.

markets by the end of the 1900s, while local manufacturing in Brazil was cutting into British imports. But British manufacturers had almost a monopoly of cotton thread imports into Mexico in the 1900s (£175,245 in 1905-6 out of an import of £194,645), and thread formed a substantial part of the trade in cotton products remaining to the United Kingdom (£597,544); by the end of the decade, 1909-10, Britain still supplied £189,063 of cotton thread out of total Mexican imports of £214,559, with Germany's share rising from £8,345 to £13,868.[1] British exports in sewing-thread were dominated by two great combines, J. &. P. Coats (capital, £11,181,000) and English Sewing Cotton (capital, £3,101,000). The 'English thread trust' operated as one in many respects, held a commanding interest in an American thread trust (the American Thread Company), and owned factories in the United States, Spain, Russia and Canada.

The operation of the thread combines shows how difficult it is, on trade figures alone, to get any true picture of Britain's competitive position after the '80s. At the end of the century by far the larger part of J. &. P. Coats' profits were derived not from its British mills but from shares in foreign manufacturing companies, and a 'decline' in British exports of thread to some of the main markets meant simply that British companies were now safely manufacturing behind foreign tariff barriers. In the specific case of exports of thread to Cuba, the English Sewing Company had enjoyed large profits from its Barcelona factory under the Spanish protective tariff. When Barcelona lost the Cuban market after the Spanish-American War, the company agreed to reallocate the trade to J. & P. Coats' American mill. 'Spanish' imports of cotton thread into Cuba were replaced by 'American', when both, in fact, might equally have been described as 'British'.

Woollen Manufactures

Britain's salvation as an exporter of cotton manufactures before 1914 lay first in a huge Indian market (which, in 1912-13, accounted for 36% of her total production of cotton piece goods), and then in the steadily expanding outlets of the Dominions and Colonies.

---

[1] Biorklund's memorandum on Mexican imports from the United Kingdom and Germany, 1907, P.P. 1907, LXXXVII, 635-8; Biorklund's memorandum for 1905-10, P.P. 1912-13, XCVII, 736.

British woollen manufacturers, on the other hand, had always been able to depend on a strong home demand. The home market absorbed between 60 and 70% of production, and it was supported by a rising Empire market. Demand for British woollen manufactures in Latin America, while sustaining a useful trade which in the years before 1914 enjoyed exceptionally healthy circumstances, lagged well behind the demand for cottons. The hot climate of many Republics favoured cottons at the expense of wool. In the mountains, a long-established handicraft industry continued to meet the general, low/medium level of demand. British manufacturers were quick to react to orders which were big enough to give some advantage to power looms or to the superior organization of manufacturing and sales in the Yorkshire woollen districts. They made brightly coloured striped blankets for the Mexican and South American markets; they were very ready to meet the particular demands of customers provided that the runs were of a reasonable length; they specialized in *bayetas* (woollen baizes in imitation of native cloth) which they marketed under brand names and special markings designed to attract the Latin American peasant—'Aroma Encendido', 'Sangre de Toro', 'Dragon', 'Cresto de Gallo', 'Ojo de Cielo'. There was a good sale among the better-off Latin Americans for the high-quality worsteds and, later, for the all-wool fabrics in which Britain specialized. Yet locally manufactured ponchos, in brilliant colours, were still the normal dress for the Indians of Ecuador, serving also, said Haggard, as a bed by night, a basket, a wheel-barrow, a pocket-handkerchief and a cradle.[1] The Peruvian Indians had replaced Bradford *bayetas* by local baizes, and in the early 1900s imports had fallen off to a tenth part of their former size.[2] In Central America and in Mexico, a long tradition of hand-loom manufacturing for the ponchos, blankets and the woollen materials in general use in Indian households was barely disturbed by English imports.

Factory production of woollens was everywhere slow to develop, and no equivalent existed of the great cotton manufacturing industries of Mexico and Brazil. Yet Mexican official returns gave a mill production in 1878 of over two million yards of cassimere and cloth, in addition to carpeting, baize, and woollen thread for

[1] Haggard's report on Ecuador for 1891-2, P.P. 1893-4, XCIII, 103.
[2] Robilliard's report on Mollendo for 1902, P.P. 1904, C, 509.

making up into blankets, when British exports of woollen cloth to Mexico amounted to 641,600 yards. Writing in the mid-'80s, Lionel Carden reported that Mexican manufacturers had since made great progress, 'not only in the amount turned out, but also in the quality of the goods, which has been so much improved that the cloth is now extensively used in tailoring establishments even in the capital'.[1] So far, increased prosperity in Mexico had maintained the level of imports, but the decline in woollen piece goods imported in the mid-'90s (£310,792 in 1895, £267,398 in 1896 and £225,562 in 1897) was explained by Carden, in a later report, as 'without doubt due to the great improvement both as regards quantity and quality in the output of the Mexican woollen mills'.[2] The Mexican woollen manufacturing industry developed only gradually, more as a result of the competitiveness of local handicraft production than of imports. Imports of woollen cloth continued to decline, although the reduced flocks in Mexico and the competition of handloom weavers for local wools meant an increase in imported wools to supply the Mexican mills.

The natural dress for Brazil was cotton, and a small woollen industry survived on imported raw material; in the 1900s its production, slight as it was, was about equal in value to imports.[3] Peruvian woollen mills were reported in 1902-3 to be supplying a large proportion of the cheap class of goods, while the quality was generally admitted to be improving.[4] In the wool-producing Republics of the South a wool manufacturing industry anticipated the cotton industry. The Retiro cloth factory in Buenos Aires in the early '90s was employing 200 hands and consuming 400 tons of wool per annum. Local consumption, in weight of unwashed wool, rose from 2,000 tons in 1895 to 4,700 tons in 1913. In kilos of washed wool, Argentine consumption in 1913 reached 2·9 million, of which 1·5 million kilos went to the textile industry and 1·4 million to 'mattresses and other uses'.[5] Using a conversion factor of 365 grammes of washed wool to the square metre of medium/coarse quality cloth, Argentine woollen cloth production

---

[1] Carden's report on Mexico, 5 July 1883, P.P. 1883, LXXV, 526.
[2] Carden's report on Mexico for 1897, P.P. 1899, CI, 18.
[3] Cheetham's report on Brazil for 1908, P.P. 1909, XCII, 636-7.
[4] Reid's report on Salaverry and Trujillo for 1902, P.P. 1904, C, 514.
[5] The figures for local wool consumption are from Ernesto Tornquist & Co. Ltd., *The Economic Development of the Argentine Republic in the last Fifty Years* (Buenos Aires, 1919), pp. 72-3.

just before the war can be estimated at 4·1 million metres, in contrast to British exports to Argentina of 12·0 million yards.[1]

In Chile the Indians manufactured large quantities of woollen ponchos and blankets. When Worthington visited the Republic in April 1898 there was still no sign of a cotton factory, yet the Fabrica Nacional de Tejidos at Santiago manufactured woollen cloth for use particularly by the Chilean armed services, and the Tomé factory was in business in the Concepción district. Neither was on a large scale, and Worthington estimated their combined output at not more than 100,000-120,000 metres a year (Britain exported 1,864,800 yards of woollen cloth to Chile in 1898).[2] As for Uruguay, although no woollen mills were in existence in the '80s, by the early 1900s local manufacturing had replaced the imported British 'poncho' altogether, enough woollen baize was made to satisfy local demand, and local manufacturers were able to undersell imported flannel and woollen goods, ladies' shawls, and the cheaper materials for men's suits.[3]

Climate, however, rather than local manufacturing was the chief restraint on exports of British woollen goods to the Republics. Among competing foreign woollen manufactures in the limited market which still existed, fashion and design were often the critical elements in determining a sale. Consumers of imported woollens came generally from a higher social and economic class than those for imported cottons; first price was less important, mark-ups and commissions were higher, and taste counted for more. Latin American society followed the fashions of France, and France was producing fine quality fabrics of a notably superior design and dye. Britain was improving in this respect. She copied good designs as soon as they were published. She imported French and German designers and trained her own in the new colleges of art and design. Yet at the end of 1889 the *Bradford Observer* complained that British manufacturers were still dependent on

---

[1] The conversion factor for blankets, a large element in Argentine production, is about 450 grammes per square metre. If not counterbalanced in turn by understatement for finer qualities, this may reduce Argentine production in terms of square metres. However, the production figures are not available in any form, let alone broken down by quality and type of product.

[2] Worthington's report on Chile, 1898, P.P. 1899, XCVI, 469, 475.

[3] Kestell Cornish's report on Uruguay for 1902 and 1903, P.P. 1904, CI (Part II), 444.

the Continent for guidance and inspiration, 'and however we may congratulate ourselves upon the advances we have made in Bradford during recent years, a glance through a French pattern book is enough to leave one sick with envy and to make it clear that while we are going forward, others are not standing still'.[1]

A serious crisis hit the British woollen industry in the late '70s and early '80s, the result in part of a change of fashion from the harder bright lustre fabrics of Bradford to the soft, all-wool tissues of France, in part of the exclusion of British woollens by tariffs from their best markets in Europe and North America. But Britain had long taken only a comparatively modest share in Latin American imports. The Paris houses had the Latin American market well under control. Travellers sold the cheaper woollens, in which Britain was still competitive, to Paris, whence they were exported in company with the finer French fabrics to Brazil and the Republics—a process, incidentally, which worked in the opposite direction for French woollens reaching British colonial markets through London wholesalers. The routing of the trade distorts the figures, and the lower class goods appearing as 'French' or 'German' in Latin American imports were as often as not British. But the change of fashion and the superiority of Continental design undoubtedly lost Britain a large part of the Latin American market from the late '70s. In Argentina, where imports of woollens increased over 130% between 1876 and 1884, British imports remained stationary so that their share fell from 21 to 11%.[2] At Rio in the early '90s, except in baizes, cloths, blankets and other coarse materials in which Britain still excelled, the Germans had a monopoly of woollen goods; 'in cheapness, suitability, tasteful get-up and finish, they are far in advance of English manufactures'.[3] In Chile, although British manufacturers had 72·44% of the cotton textile imports in 1896 to Germany's 21·92%, the Germans supplied 49·24% of all woollen and mixed wool/cotton imports to Britain's 43·54%.[4]

The manufacturers, however, had been reacting to the new position since the early '80s. Sir Jacob Behrens, an expert witness

[1] Quoted by Sigsworth, *Black Dyke Mills*, p. 93.
[2] Bridgett's report on Argentina (to the Royal Commission on the Depression of Trade and Industry), 24 December 1885, P.P. 1886, XXIII, 643.
[3] Ancell's report on Rio for 1894, P.P. 1895, XCVI, 415.
[4] Croker's report on Valparaiso for 1896-7, P.P. 1898, XCIV, 482-3.

before the Royal Commission on the Depression of Trade and Industry (1886), was in no doubt that Bradford would soon be fully capable of meeting up to French competition in soft tissues. He explained that it was slow business capturing a long-established trade from another country; until recently the Bradford manufacturers had had no incentive to do so, since they were as well and as profitably employed on mixed fabrics as any Frenchman on all-wool goods; meanwhile, they had a staple trade in mixed goods to themselves.[1] The experience thereafter was of a continued decline in the exports of worsted tissues, particularly mixed goods, from an annual average of 159,862,000 linear yards in 1885-9 to 78,724,000 yards in 1909-13, compensated for by a rise in the export of yarn from 43,457,000 lb (1885-9) to 61,854,000 lb (1909-13) and of tops from 9,543,000 lb (1890-4) to 41,851,000 lb (1909-13). Meanwhile, woollen tissues, by now fully competitive, rose from a trough of 50,224,000 yards in 1890-4 to 95,621,000 in 1909-13.[2]

Clearly, the sound progress of the British wool textile industry over the period 1870-1914, with recessions in the early '80s and early 1900s, owed more to the home trade, the Empire trade, the Argentine trade, and the expanding export of yarns and tops than to the recapture of the general market in Latin America. Yet recapture that market it did. Sigsworth and Blackman explain that rising prices for both raw wool and cotton gave British manufacturers a price advantage over their competitors; the ability of the woollen industry to blend increasing amounts of rag wool with virgin wool was a large element in keeping down costs.[3] Certainly the whole tone of reports changed for British competition in Latin America. Design, colour and fashion continued to preserve a share of the high-class market for France. The Tariff Commission reported in 1905 that Germany had made large inroads into the trade in vesting cloths, that skilled manufacturers had for years been complaining that they could do nothing in tweeds and serges, and that the blanket trade with Brazil, Argentina and Uruguay

---

[1] Minutes of Evidence, *Report of the Royal Commission on the Depression of Trade and Industry*, P.P. 1886, LXXI, QQ.6721-988.
[2] Figures from E. M. Sigsworth and J. M. Blackman, 'The Woollen and Worsted Industries', in D. H. Aldcroft (ed.), *The Development of British Industry and Foreign Competition 1875-1914* (London, 1968), pp. 135-6.
[3] *Ibid.*, pp. 153-7.

was lost.[1] Yet in Brazil in the mid-1900s alpacas and woollen textiles appear in the category of imports described as 'still chiefly British'.[2] In Uruguay about half of the imported woollen goods came from Britain, well over twice the share of her nearest rivals, Germany and France.[3] Britain supplied 59·9% of the 'woollen cloth' imports into Argentina in 1912, 16·5% of the 'woollen goods', 72·1% of the 'woollen and mixed goods', and 54·9% of the 'cotton and woollen goods'; the German percentages were 17·4, 41·3, 15·7 and 24·1 respectively.[4] British manufacturers maintained a handsome lead in textiles in Central America and in an open market like Panama, with no competition either in linen or wool.[5] In Venezuela in 1911-12, in spite of a commercial representation which was entirely German, Britain supplied between half and two-thirds of imported woollen goods, compared with a sixth each from Germany and France.[6] These encouraging percentages were the Latin American expression of a general trend towards reduced foreign competition in the British home market and towards a marked advance in British competitiveness overseas. The annual average for British exports of wool textiles rose from £15·8 million in 1900-4 to £24·6 million in 1909-13; German exports over the same period rose only slightly from £11·5 million to £12·8 million and French exports actually fell from £8·7 million to £8·2 million.[7]

Silk, Linen and Jute Manufactures

As for the remainder of the textile industry, Britons were unfortunate in silks. The British silk industry could survive in the home market only under the shelter of a protective tariff; it was in no condition to enter into competition overseas. The 1860 Commercial Treaty with France, by opening the home market to unrestricted French competition, put most British silk manufacturers

---

[1] Tariff Commission, *Report on the Textile Trades* (*Woollen Industry*) (London, 1905), para. 1430.
[2] Mark's report on Santos for 1902-4, P.P. 1906, CXXIII, 46-7.
[3] Dunlop's report on Uruguay for 1911, P.P. 1912-13, CI, 558-61.
[4] Mackie's report on Buenos Aires for 1912-13, P.P. 1914, LXXXIX, 573.
[5] Chalkley's report on Panama for 1911, P.P. 1912-13, XCVIII, 669-71.
[6] Gilliat-Smith's report on Venezuela for 1911-12, P.P. 1913, LXXIII, 707.
[7] Figures from Saul, *Overseas Trade*, p. 33.

out of business. On the other hand, the enormously successful rayon and artificial silk industry, for which production on a commercial scale began only with Messrs Courtauld's Coventry factory in 1905, enjoyed so rich a field for its enterprise in the home and colonial markets, and so promising and concentrated a profit opportunity in branch factory production in the principal protected countries, that it made no serious efforts to develop direct sales to Latin America before the war.

Latin America, however, was a useful outlet for the British linen industry. In the early years, most of the linens reaching Brazil and the new Republics were Continental, a continuation of an extensive colonial trade. Dundee and Belfast manufacturers, the first with coarse linens, the second with finer, lighter qualities, gradually drove German and French linens from the market. The transfer of importing and retailing services to German or French houses helped promote a revival of Continental competition in the '70s and '80s. The better designs, the 'novelties' and the fashionable fabrics from Germany, Austria, Belgium and France had always kept a share of the Latin American market, while access to local supplies of raw material, cheaper labour and longer hours gave German, Belgian and Austrian lower-class linens a price advantage in the late '70s and early '80s. Imports into the biggest market for linens, the United States, showed a five and a half fold increase in Continental linens between 1870 and 1884, compared with a $12\frac{1}{2}\%$ fall in the value of British imports—a trend which left Britain still with imports valued in 1884 at £2,699,000 compared with a combined import of £680,000 from Germany, Belgium, Austria, France and Russia. The trend was naturally reflected in the markets of Latin America, always more open to lower class imports than to the higher prices and qualities.

All the same, outside the protected home markets of other producers the British linen industry was able to hold its own even during these relatively depressed years in overseas trade. It was more skilled. It had a better climate with the more equable temperatures and the higher degree of moisture necessary for the production of bleached linens, shirtings, table linens and handkerchiefs, if they were wanted pure white.[1] Signs of a return to British linens were detected in Colombia even in the early '80s,

[1] Minutes of Evidence, *Report of the Royal Commission on the Depression of Trade and Industry*, P.P. 1886, XXI, QQ.7068-76.

and Bridgett reported from Buenos Aires at the end of 1885 that 'in linen goods the old position is well maintained'.[1] National production was never a problem, although in Mexico local factories succeeded in reducing linen imports by 56% between 1888-9 and 1910-11, from 1,760,000 pesos to 779,000.[2] Nor was there any real competition after the '80s from foreign manufacturers; the competition was between Belfast and Dundee. More serious for low-price outlets in Latin America was the substitution of cheaper cottons, often locally manufactured, for imported linens. This was the likely explanation for the static pattern of British exports of linen piece goods to Brazil, where the normal yardage remained within the range of 2·5 to 3·5 million for the entire period 1880-1913.

Latin American manufacturers were more successful in replacing imported hessian. Dundee, drawing its supplies of jute from the only source, British India, kept the world market almost to itself in the '70s. Tariff barriers in Germany, France and Italy killed Dundee's European market, and Germany became the largest consumer of jute outside the British Empire. But Germany's surplus for export was negligible, perhaps 10% of production, practically all of which went to her neighbours in Europe.[3] Among the Republics, Brazil, with her large demand for coffee and sugar sacks, was the first to replace imported sacking, and even by the mid-'80s imported Dundee sacks at Pernambuco were reported as 'much cut into by native manufacturers'.[4] By the end of the century British exports of jute piece goods to Brazil had almost ceased, falling from nearly 18 million yards in 1885 to 1·3 million in 1900. Reduced exports of piece goods were part compensated for, as was so often the case, by a substantial increase in Brazilian demand for British yarn, from 12½ million lb in 1894

---

[1] White's report on Medellín for 1882, P.P. 1884, LXXIX, 533; Bridgett's report on Argentina, 24 December 1885, P.P. 1886, XXIII, 643.

[2] Stevenson's report on Cartagena for 1897, P.P. 1898, XCV, 23; Mark's report on Santos for 1902-4, P.P. 1906, CXXIII, 46-7; Cartwright's report on Ecuador for 1906, P.P. 1908, CXI, 132; Chalkley's report on Panama for 1911, P.P. 1912-13, XCVIII, 669-71; Biorklund's memorandum on Mexican imports 1905-10, P.P. 1912-13, XCVII, 740-2; Rosenzweig in Cosío Villegas (ed.), *Mexico: La Vida Económica*, I, 346-7.

[3] *Report of the Departmental Committee on the Textile Trades*, P.P. 1918, XIII, 676, 678.

[4] Rickett's report on Rio for 1885, P.P. 1886, LXV, 334.

to 32 million lb in 1902, and Brazil in 1913 was still Britain's largest market for jute yarn (14·5 million lb at nearly £300,000).

Naturally enough, the other Republics experiencing a large local demand for sacking made some effort to meet their own needs. The main difficulty was the failure to find a completely satisfactory substitute for the raw material, jute. Mexico was unable to replace imported jute, but a large factory at Orizaba, opened in 1894, was reported a few years later as 'turning out large quantities of hemp and jute sacks of a very good quality, and also sacking, which is used for the export of coffee and ores'.[1] A high proportion of the bags used in Argentina by 1891-2 was locally produced by steam factories in Buenos Aires and Rosario, with one factory accounting for 11½ million bags; the hessian continued to be imported almost entirely from Dundee.[2] Argentina was capable of meeting home demand by the late '90s, producing, in the five main factories, 38¼ million sacks in 1897.[3] It was only the phenomenal rise in Argentine grain production which kept demand ahead of local supply, and Argentina remained Britain's best Latin American market, in 1913, for bags and sacks (£317,733) and jute piece goods (£275,000).

Ultimately, it was Britain's own colony, India, which replaced her in jute and hessian. Only four jute mills were in operation in India in 1873, manufacturing exclusively for the home market. By the mid-'80s there were 20 mills, with an aggregate of about 8,000 looms and 150,000 spindles. With the advantage of cheap labour, longer hours and direct access to raw material, Indian mills captured the 'heavy goods' market from Dundee first in Australia, and then in the Cape of Good Hope, Egypt and San Francisco. They could outsell British manufacturers in any market to which direct shipments were cheap and easy, and although superior transport connections kept open Britain's markets in the West Indies, Central America and the east coast of South America, she faced severe competition on the west coast, where India could supply Valparaiso direct with its needs for grain and nitrate sacks.[4] India's competitive position continued

[1] Biorklund's report on Mexico for 1898, P.P. 1899, CI, 69.
[2] Bridgett's report on Argentina for 1891, P.P. 1892, LXXXI, 153.
[3] Appendix to Worthington's report on Argentina, 18 August 1898, P.P. 1899, XCVI, 519-20.
[4] Minutes of Evidence, *Report of the Royal Commission on the Depression of Trade and Industry*, P.P. 1886, XXI, QQ.6185-91.

O

to improve, and only the great increase in world demand and heavy investment in machinery for the production of the lighter goods enabled Dundee to keep its head above water. In 1913 British exports of bags and sacks were valued at £1,224,675 and of jute piece goods, etc., at £3,333,362. Indian exports of gunny bags for the trade year 1913-14 reached £8,353,417 and of gunny cloth £10,396,146, of which Argentina took £115,795 and £1,847,947 respectively. Indian producers enjoyed a comfortable lead in a west coast market like Chile, to which they exported £673,702 of bags and cloth, to Britain's £41,315 of bags and sacks and £34,203 of jute manufactures.[1]

Boots and Shoes, Ready-made Clothing, Hosiery, Furniture and Carpets

Whatever the state of Britain's commercial representation in Latin America, the competitiveness of her cotton, woollen and linen manufactures made it impossible for her trade to be replaced, unless artificially by local manufactures sheltered behind high tariff barriers. German, French or Italian importers were business-men first, patriots second; they could not afford to turn away a profitable line of trade, and orders continued to come to Britain. Where Britain's competitive position was less secure, where the trade was smaller or more fragmented—whether in hosiery, haber-dashery, chemists' supplies, hardware, china and glass, small arms, paper and stationery, jewellery and silverware—she was likely to lose orders to those with direct commercial connections, just as she had held exactly the same lines of trade, without necessarily herself being fully competitive at the time, when she serviced Latin America's import/export trade in the early years of indepen-dence.

In each of the smaller lines of trade, the same characteristic pattern recurred—the growth of Continental, North American and then local competition; the shift of British traders and manu-facturers to expanding home and colonial markets; the develop-ment of more sophisticated or higher quality products, less suited to Latin America yet better adapted to a new demand in more easily exploitable markets. Examples may certainly be given of straight failure to match up to foreign competition—in cotton

---

[1] *Tables relating to the Trade of British India*, P.P. 1916, XXI, 921-2.

hosiery, in cheap glassware, in ready-made clothes, in ammunition, rifles and sporting guns, in watches and clocks, in optical glass and dye-stuffs. In some other industries the development of a new process, such as the substitution of wood fibre for rags in paper making after the '60s, turned the tables; where Britain, with her ready supply of rags, had had the advantage in the first half of the nineteenth century, the forests of Germany and Sweden gave *them* the advantage thereafter. Normally, however, a competitive 'failure' in Latin America was made up elsewhere; it was a decision to look for higher returns, to switch to a more modern line of products, to exploit such limited resources as could be mustered in more promising markets. Even if re-exports are deducted, Britain was supplying Australia, in 1909, with 38·7% of her imported jewellery, time pieces and instruments, 35·6% of her india rubber and leather goods, 56·3% of her drugs and chemicals, 57·7% of her building materials, 59·6% of her paper and stationery, 67·7% of her apparel and textiles, 67·8% of her metals and machinery, 70·4% of her groceries.[1] The percentages even for the best Latin American markets were much smaller. Was one, then, a 'success' and the other a 'failure'? Or was it simply that no man could hope, in the expanding world markets of the late nineteenth and early twentieth centuries, to hold the lead in every location, trade and product at all times?

The competition offered by local industry was always at its strongest for the lesser items, for those in which no great manufacturing industries were competing, no large or established import/export business likely to be threatened. Even in Honduras, where local industries were 'quite in their infancy', a brewery was in operation in Tegucigalpa by the late '90s and a soap and candle factory in Amapala, boots and shoes were made all over the country, and the pita grass hats of the north had an established reputation dating back over many years.[2] Each replaced a line in imports. Beer imports, indeed, were one of the first to go. British beer lost ground after the middle of the century to the lighter German and Danish beers more suited to hot climates; by 1900 these in turn had been replaced by local beers in nearly every Republic, selling often at less than half the price of imported beer. The same

[1] Hamilton Wickes' report on Australia for 1909, P.P. 1911, LXXXVII, 570-1.
[2] Campbell's report on Honduras for 1896-7, P.P. 1898, XCVI, 554.

substitution was natural for any of the basic consumer goods—foodstuffs, boots and shoes, soaps, candles, matches, earthenware, ready-made clothes, hosiery, furniture. For each of these British manufacturers were likely to turn their attention to those home and colonial markets which they knew best, rather than fight for a share of an alien trade where profits were cut to the bone.

Even if the Republics continued to import tanned leather, textiles or cotton yarn, there was little to prevent them replacing imported boots and shoes, ready-made clothing or hosiery by local manufactures. As one correspondent complained to *The Times* in 1880, a 50% *ad valorem* protective tariff was on its way to converting the citizens of Argentina from good sheep farmers into bad bootmakers and execrable tailors.[1] Most of the Republics by the 1900s were meeting their basic requirements in shoes, saddlery and harness, and some had developed good tanneries of their own. In the early '90s a large boot factory in Buenos Aires, employing 900 persons, was turning out 400,000 pairs of boots and shoes per annum, quite equal to the imported article; the working classes were wearing rope-soled 'alpargatas', also locally manufactured.[2] Under a 60% protective tariff, the boot and shoe industry made rapid progress in Argentina. A Buenos Aires factory in the late 1900s was manufacturing 5 million pairs of shoes a year.[3] Argentina still found room for good quality imported English boots and shoes; British exports amounted to 59,296 dozen pairs of leather boots and shoes in 1913. But local manufacturing in Brazil had put a stop to the trade. The 56,000 dozen pairs imported in 1890-4 had fallen to just over 2,000 dozen pairs a decade later (1905).[4] Chile was manufacturing all her needs for boots and shoes by 1914, with the exception of some ranges of children's shoes; her imports were limited to small quantities of high class boots and shoes (12,453 dozen pairs from the United Kingdom in 1913).[5] Even Colombia's four factories, with the aid of leased machinery from the United Shoe Machinery Company of Boston, had a manufacturing capacity of about 12,000 pairs a month just

[1] *The Times*, 7 July 1880, 8a.
[2] Bridgett's report on Argentina for 1891, P.P. 1892, LXXXI, 152-3.
[3] *The Times*, South American Supplement, 28 December 1909, 52c.
[4] P. Head, 'Boots and Shoes', in Aldcroft (ed.), *Development of British Industry*, pp. 159-60.
[5] Dept. of Overseas Trade, *Report on the Financial and Commercial Condition of Chile* (H.M.S.O., 1922), p. 39.

before the war; ready-made shoes continued to be imported from the United States and France, but the market was small since probably five-sixths of the population either wore locally manufactured rope-soled alpargatas or no shoes at all.[1] Virtually no boots and shoes were imported into Venezuela by 1913, where local factories, under the protection of a prohibitive tariff and with the aid of American machinery, met local needs; the largest, Messrs Boccardo in Caracas, obtained most of its leather from its own tannery and manufactured at the rate of about 500 pairs per day.[2]

So far as there *was* a market for imported shoes in the Republics, Britain held on in the south while losing out to the United States in the north, particularly in Cuba and Mexico. In the first years of this century, 1901-4, British manufacturers were badly shaken in every market, at home and overseas, by an irruption of American footwear, stylish, mass-produced and in a wide range of fittings. But their recovery, based primarily on home and colonial markets, was remarkably rapid, and *The Economist* could congratulate itself, by 1913, on the 'Victory of British Boots'.[3] 1,044,849 dozen pairs of leather boots and shoes out of a total export of 1,442,815 found a sale in British possessions in 1913; for New Zealand, the home country's share of the market was as high as 95%.[4]

Britain led the field in the competitive manufacture of textiles, but she could not prevent these textiles from being made-up by others. In part, as for boots and shoes, it was a matter of fashion and taste; however well they sold at home or in the Empire, British ready-made clothes were not suited to the Latin taste of the southern Republics or to the North American taste of the United States' neighbours in Canada, Mexico and the Caribbean. Britain supplied about 85% of the clothing imported by South Africa in 1912 and 1913, and in the woollen trade British manufacturers had long been accustomed to sending three-quarters of their ready-made clothing exports to the Empire.[5] More suitable

---

[1] Bowle's report on Bogotá for 1909-13, P.P. 1914-16, LXXI, 859-60.
[2] Milne's report on Venezuela, 1913, P.P. 1912-13, LXVIII, 593, 600.
[3] Head in Aldcroft (ed.), *Development of British Industry*, pp. 161, 183.
[4] Wickham's report on New Zealand for 1913, P.P. 1914-16, XLVI, 626.
[5] Sothern Holland's report on South Africa for 1913, P.P. 1914-16, XLV, 609; Minutes of Evidence, *Report of the Royal Commission on the Depression of Trade and Industry*, P.P. 1886, XXI, Q.3778.

styles and cheaper labour had lost the bulk of the South American markets to France and Germany after the middle of the nineteenth century, and Spanish, Italian and Portuguese immigrants preferred the rough, workman's clothes to which they were accustomed. Britain could always keep some part of the snob trade, in hats with sought-after West End labels, in ready-made clothing for the fashionable male in Rio, Montevideo, Buenos Aires, even in Bogotá where one high-class house was still importing its ready-made clothing and trouser lengths exclusively from the United Kingdom in the 1900s. In the south, where British manufacturers were well represented, where tradition was strong and the climate more rigorous, they could stand up to competition in a few lines; in Uruguay at the turn of the century they supplied about a quarter of the imported clothing ($420,000 worth).[1] But local tailors were perfectly capable of meeting demand, labour was cheap, and workshop production an obvious development. Ultimately, local manufacturing took over the major part of the market from all importers. The Tariff Commission reported in 1905 that the ready-made clothing trade to Latin America was to a large extent lost, partly as a result of the deliberate tariff policy of the Republics, partly because of the independent development of competing native industries. Brazil had once provided a large trade in ready-made clothing. 'This is now entirely gone. The Brazilians make a large quantity themselves, and the little that is left is said to be divided between Germany, France and England.'[2] Argentina, while supplying only 22·6% of her home consumption of textiles in 1911-15, manufactured 87·9% of the category described in her industrial census statistics as 'clothing and cosmetics'.[3]

Hosiery was another line, like clothing, which was likely to pass into the control of local manufacturers. With their lead in power-driven machinery, British hosiery manufacturers had little to fear from competition before the '70s. They lost the lead, so far as cotton hosiery was concerned, when this machinery was introduced first to the Continent (and Saxony in particular), and then to the larger Republics. In woollen hosiery, the superior quality of

[1] Hervey's report on Uruguay for 1899-1900, P.P. 1900, XCVII, 524.
[2] Tariff Commission, *Report on the Textile Trades* (*Woollen Industry*) (London, 1905), paras. 1430-2.
[3] Table IV above.

British products maintained sales even in protected markets, so that exports rose from £420,000 in 1881-5 to £1,415,000 in 1906-10 and £1,966,717 in 1913; it was a high-quality product for a high-quality market, principally in the Dominions.[1] By 1913, the Dominions' share of total British exports of woollen hosiery to British Possessions (£1,532,752) was £1,370,635. Argentina was the only significant Latin American market, taking £50,379 out of total exports to foreign countries of £433,965. As for cotton hosiery, which had formerly enjoyed large sales in the lower-quality markets of Latin America, German products cut the ground from under British feet in the '80s, while the bulk of stockings, socks and underclothes on sale in Argentina by the late '90s were locally manufactured.[2] The Tariff Commission observed that Britain's main South American customers, Chile, Brazil, Uruguay and Argentina, had taken £48,000 worth of cotton hosiery (stockings and socks) in 1886; this had been reduced to £4,000 in 1904.[3] Argentina and Chile were the only Latin American markets of any significance for British cotton stockings and socks by 1913, at £2,139 and £1,290 respectively, at a time when Australia took £52,635 and South Africa £41,356. However, Brazil and Argentina were leading foreign markets for other kinds of cotton hosiery, with sales of £16,645 and £16,649 out of a total export to foreign countries of £152,029 in 1913, again in contrast to a much larger export total to British Possessions of £320,143. Cotton manufacturing countries like Mexico developed factories for the manufacture of all kinds of hosiery, not only in the capital but in many of the larger cities of the Republic; Mexican products were reported as 'of a very fair quality, and superior to the common grades of imported goods, while their price is more in keeping with the resources of the people'.[4]

Furniture, again, was a line in which British manufacturers were not likely to compete with locals. Although pianos and looking glasses, the indispensable 'props' of Society, continued to reach

[1] F. A. Wells, *The British Hosiery Trade: its history and organization* (London, 1935), pp. 178-82.

[2] Worthington's report on Argentina, 18 August 1898, P.P. 1899, XCVI, 498-9.

[3] Tariff Commission, *Report on the Textile Trades (Hosiery)* (London, 1905), paras. 2327, 2360, 2367.

[4] Biorklund's report on Mexican imports, July 1905 to June 1910, P.P. 1912-13, XCVII, 738.

Bogotá on the backs of mules right up to the arrival of the railway, transport costs normally put imported furniture, except of the lightest kind, out of the market as soon as systematic local manufacturing began. Britain had something of a monopoly of iron bedstead imports into Latin America over the last decades before 1914. 'Knock-down' and wicker furniture was imported from the United States, and reasonably large sales were achieved for cheap bentwood furniture from Austria and Germany. In the ordinary classes of furniture, local manufacturing met most needs. Chapman reported from Brazil at the turn of the century that furniture was now mostly manufactured in the country, and duties on Austro-Hungarian bentwood furniture had been raised heavily.[1] In Mexico in 1900 two furniture factories were encroaching on high-class imports, manufacturing fine furniture of all styles at prices very much lower than the cost of imported furniture from Europe.[2] Out of £142,174 of furniture imported into Mexico in 1909-10, only £4,911 came from Britain; 75% of the common imported furniture came from the United States and 15% from Austria, while France supplied 57% of the small imports of 'choice and fancy furniture, gilt, etc.'.[3] In Argentina, 70% of consumption in the industry broadly described as 'furniture, cars, etc.' was met by local production just before the war, and the percentage for furniture on its own must have been much higher;[4] a limited import of £553,000 in 1912 was divided primarily between the United States (22%), the United Kingdom (19·2%), Austria-Hungary (19·1%) and France (18·3%).[5] Britain continued to export small quantities of furniture to Latin America. Maples had a branch in Buenos Aires in the late 1900s, and Harrods (of Buenos Aires), Gath & Chaves, Thompson Muebles imported some of the latest styles principally to satisfy the demand of a large British and Anglo-Argentine resident community. The British component in furniture imports into Dominion and colonial markets other than Canada was naturally higher; 30 to 35% in Australia in 1910-12. But the incentive to manufacture locally was

---

[1] Chapman's report on Brazil in 1902, P.P. 1903, LXXVI, 483.
[2] Biorklund's report on Mexico for 1899, P.P. 1901, LXXXIII, 535.
[3] Biorklund's report on Mexican imports, 1905-10, P.P. 1912-13, XCVII, 726.
[4] Table IV above.
[5] Mackie's report on Buenos Aires for 1912-13, P.P. 1914, LXXXIX, 575.

as strong here as in Latin America, and total Australian imports of furniture amounted only to £303,000 in 1912. Milne explained that furniture manufacturing had become quite an important industry throughout Australia, 'many of the beautiful timbers of this country lending themselves to cabinet-making and work of this kind'.[1]

It was the same with carpets, where tariffs in Europe and the United States had virtually killed British exports by the end of the century, and manufacturers like John Crossley and Sons Ltd. of Halifax had been compelled to get in behind the tariff wall and set up factories in Russia and Austria. Taste was important, as were the natural lines of trade in meeting competition in the lower grades—British manufacturers could hold their own in the higher qualities—from German, Belgian or North American manufacturers. In a market primarily open to cheap and medium qualities, the United Kingdom kept a 90% share of the carpets used in Australia in the mid-1900s.[2] Just before the war, Britain was exporting about a third of her total output of some £4½ million. The Empire was her principal export market, with Canada alone taking £449,101 and Australia £334,045. Argentina, characteristically, was her largest foreign market (with £71,937) and Chile fourth after the Netherlands and the United States with £50,938.

The British carpet industry was a highly specialized branch of the woollen trade. It had lost some of its old markets as a result of tariffs in Europe and the United States, but it found sufficient outlets for its exportable surplus before the war, and opened branch factories in the larger protected markets. Carpet manufacturing was a good trade, but it had neither the resources nor the will for continuous expansion into increasingly marginal, competitive markets. It found itself in a parallel situation to the 140 British manufacturers of pianos, who could produce cheap pianos to compete with the Germans, but who were not competing in Latin America because it was all they could do to produce enough for an expanding demand at home, in neighbouring France and in the Dominions.[3]

---

[1] Milne's report on Australia for 1913, P.P. 1914, LX, 133.

[2] Tariff Commission, *Report on the Textile Trades* (*Carpet Industry*) (London, 1905), paras. 2924-5.

[3] *Report of the Departmental Committee on the Engineering Trades*, P.P. 1918, XIII, 401-2.

Armaments and Warships

The decision to compete in a particular market, among those manufacturers big enough even to think of developing an export trade, was determined by taste, habit, existing contacts and connections. Taste, habit, contacts and connections led Britons in one direction, Germans, French and North Americans in another. In overseas sales of small arms and ammunition, Birmingham manufacturers were seriously affected by the tendency of all major governments, Latin American included, to establish their own manufactories of military supplies, to make themselves (for strategic reasons, rather than economic) independent of imports, and to develop in turn into competitors in world export markets. State arsenals, dockyards and private manufacturers in the larger Latin American Republics, especially Brazil, went some way towards replacing normal day-to-day orders for imported small arms and ammunition, powder, cannon and river gunboats. British gunsmiths sold few sporting guns to the Republics, where the market was pre-empted by ornamental Belgian guns more suited to Latin taste. 'No Englishman,' one Birmingham exporter explained in 1885, 'would buy a Belgian gun to go sporting with, a gun of £20 or £30, because it would not suit his view of the shape or form, he would look upon it pretty much as he would buying a French saddle, it is a question of foreign taste.' 'The Latin nations,' said another, 'will prefer a showy gun to a really good quality one.'[1]

In the middle decades of the century Britain lost her military trade on the Continent and in North America. British manufacturers were fully competitive again by the '80s, and Birmingham machinery for standardization and mass production was as up to date as American.[2] Vickers Sons and Maxim, Armstrong Whitworth, William Beardmore were among the more formidable steel, shipbuilding and armament combines of their day. Yet except for the navies, where Britain supplied naval advisers, warships, guns and torpedoes to Brazil, Argentina, Chile and Peru, Latin America was not a good customer for military equipment. Chile in 1913 led the way by taking £146,913 of British arms,

---

[1] Minutes of Evidence, *Report of the Royal Commission on the Depression of Trade and Industry*, P.P. 1886, XXI, QQ.1607, 1623.

[2] *Ibid.*, Q.1817. Also Clive Trebilcock, 'Spin-Off in British Economic History: Armaments and Industry, 1760-1914', *Economic History Review*, 2s. XXII (1969), 474-90.

ammunition, military and naval stores, to Brazil's £134,214, Argentina's £61,762 and Peru's £26,695. By contrast, British manufacturers sold £1,061,267 to Australia, £420,809 to South Africa and £185,169 to New Zealand. Of total British exports amounting to £4,706,546, nearly half went to British Possessions, while the best foreign customers were Italy (£531,724), Japan (£465,313) and Spain (£283,453). French officers trained the Peruvian navy and the armies of Brazil, Peru, Mexico and Bolivia. Germans drilled the Chilean army, and German military influence was strong in Argentina and Central America. Foreign military and naval advisers directed orders towards their own countries, just as the United Kingdom met the Service requirements of the white Dominions.

The explanation for relative lack of success in Latin American markets in the years before 1914 is to be found in order books already filled by rearmament at home, by the Anglo-German naval race, and by the pressure on British shipyards maintained by continued modernization in the world's largest and most up-to-date mercantile marine. The sale of £4,721,000 of war vessels to Brazil in 1910 was the only substantial warship export to Latin America after the £518,700 Peruvian sale of 1907. A British ship-builder explained the circumstances which had lost an Argentine order for two large battleships, the *Rivadavia* and the *Moreno*, to the Fore River Shipbuilding Company of Massachusetts in January 1910. He pointed out that the American yards, which had quoted £78·3 per ton to Armstrong's £87·4, were desperately short of work. American shipping, other than in the lake, river and coastal trade, could not compete internationally, and naval orders were restricted. When it came to tendering

On the one side stood a group of American firms hungry for work and having little prospect of considerable orders from the United States Navy Department; on the other side were two British firms [Armstrong and Vickers] already in possession of large orders from the British Admiralty and Brazil, and secure in their expectation of further large and profitable orders— especially for guns, gun-mountings, ammunition and *matériel* of various kinds—in view of the coming enlargement of British shipbuilding programmes.[1]

[1] *The Times*, Engineering Supplement, 16 February 1910, 13 b, c.

Glass and Pottery

For some lines of trade the United Kingdom could not put up much of a fight outside home and colonial markets. She had never had much of a tradition in glass, and her manufacturers were in competition on the Continent with a long-established industry, a large pool of cheap semi-skilled and skilled labour, and, in the 1900s, powerful international cartels in the looking-glass and bottle-glass industries. They could compete only in areas where skill, capital or technical innovation played a major part, or in home and Empire markets where national taste or imperial preference gave them a special advantage. They took the best class trade in all ranges in South Africa at the beginning of the century, while the cheaper qualities of window glass, general table and ornamental goods were imported from Belgium, Germany and America. Canada, where German imports were blocked and an imperial preference in operation, became Britain's most important single overseas market. Of total glass exports amounting to £1,813,765 in 1913, £1,101,616 went to British Possessions (£355,114 to Canada). Argentina (£131,398) and Brazil (£41,973) took second and fourth place respectively in British exports to foreign countries.

By contrast, the pottery industry had long taken a prominent place in export markets. Here too Britain had lost the common trade to Germany. But her manufacturers built up both the better class of trade and a range of specialities such as sanitary ware, principally within the Empire. The Tariff Commission found that British manufacturers, in the mid-1900s, looked to Canada and New Zealand, and in a lesser degree to South Africa and Australia, for their most promising export markets. While the export trade to foreign countries had remained more or less static at about £1·4 million over the past twenty-five years, the share to the Colonies and India had risen from 25% (£524,000) of Britain's whole export in 1875-9 to 40% (£878,000) in 1900-4. Practically no export trade survived outside the Empire in common china, and the Commission observed that 'trade in common earthenware plates, bowls, teas, jugs and chambers, white, sprayed and painted, has decreased very much indeed with Mexico and South America, specially Brazil, and is now being done principally by German manufacturers'. It is characteristic that here, as always, Britain showed herself at her strongest in Argentina. Her exports of pottery to Brazil had averaged £115,000 in 1875-9; they declined thereafter to £75,000 in 1900-4, but rose to £120,000 in 1906. To Argentina she exported an average of only £23,000 in 1875-9, after which exports rose steadily to £185,000 in 1906.[1] In 1913 her Argentine exports of chinaware or porcelain, earthenware and pottery had reached the respectable total of £348,279 and her Brazilian £284,218, making them her next most important foreign market after the United States (£417,125). Although with Chile (£261,760) the only markets of any importance among the Latin American Republics, they compared reasonably well with Dominion markets where Canada took £493,674, Australia £323,047, South Africa £133,329 and New Zealand £128,030.

Chemicals, Explosives, Paints and Soaps

In the rapidly expanding chemical industry, which in any case was widely organized into cartels, monopolies, associations, international price and market sharing agreements, the pattern was rather one of a natural division of labour, specialities and markets than of outright competition. Britain may have supplied only 8% of the drugs reaching Guatemala just before the war, and only 5% of the patent medicines and drugs for Venezuela.[2] Her consuls were right to draw attention to the hard-sell methods of American travellers in patent medicines, to the leading position of Germany in drugs, and to the fact that, in these smaller Latin American markets, she seemed to be making no effort to build up a trade. Yet she was leading the market with about 25% of the medicines and pharmaceutical products reaching Peru in 1910, presumably because of her strong commercial representation in that Republic.[3] To New Zealand her share of drugs and druggist sundries actually increased from 44% of the market in 1912 to 47% in 1913.[4] H. W. Richardson has pointed out how in some lines Britain and Germany 'carved up the world's markets between

[1] Tariff Commission, *Report on the Pottery Industries* (London, 1907), paras. 55, 65 and Table 2.
[2] Milne's reports on Central America and Venezuela, 1913, P.P. 1913, LXVIII, 472, 606.
[3] Byrne's report on Peru for 1911-12, P.P. 1913, LXXII, 38-9.
[4] Wickham's report on New Zealand for 1913, P.P. 1914-16, XLVI, 627.

them'. Britain dominated exports in the soap trade to the Dominions and the United States, while Germany took the lead in South America and the Dutch East Indies. British and German exports of drugs and medicines just before the war were roughly equal in value at about £2·3 million, 'but whereas Britain was unchallenged in Empire markets and China, Germany was dominant in Russia, the United States and most parts of Western Europe'.[1] After the 'Bleaching Powder War' of 1900-4, for example, United Alkali (British) surrendered its European markets to a German syndicate while reserving comfortable sales to itself in the Colonies and Japan.[2]

Over the chemical industry as a whole, Britain was slow, for reasons of high existing capital commitments, to abandon the old Leblanc soda process in favour of the Solvay process adopted on the Continent in and after the '70s. Her manufacturers made no effort to compete with Germany in synthetic dye-stuffs before 1914; they were 'quite prepared to allow German concerns to act as a highly specialized and skilled ancillary to the great British textile industries, rather than to embark themselves upon such a speculative enterprise'.[3] The joint capital of the six principal German dye firms was only £2·5 million, and it was, indeed a small, service industry, best left to specialists. Nor did British manufacturers see any reason to compete with Germany before the war in a number of other specialities, in the salts of bromine, refined bismuth, potash, cocaine, iodine.

The British chemical industry held its own in a range of drugs of great importance, such as the general anaesthetics, chloroform and ether, and the alkaloids of opium, where it produced enough not only to supply the home market but to export in large quantities. Germany's success in essential medicinal chemicals before the war, as the National Health Insurance Commission argued in 1916, had depended on the large scale of German industrial organization, on many years of experience, and on the ability, unrestricted by Britain or by British industry, to obtain large quantities of raw material, especially coal tar, from the United

---

[1] H. W. Richardson, 'Chemicals', in Aldcroft (ed.), *Development of British Industry*, p. 298.

[2] L. F. Haber, *The Chemical Industry 1900-1930* (Oxford, 1971), p. 139.

[3] D. W. F. Hardie, 'The Emergence of the German Dye Industry', *Business History*, 5 (1963), 120.

Kingdom.[1] Miall has pointed out how the country that neglects its dye-stuff industry, with its research on the complex substances derived from benzene, naphthalene, phenol and other coal-tar products, will be very much handicapped in its efforts to discover or make new drugs. The Bayer Company of Leverkusen, a principal manufacturer of aniline dyes, was the first to develop and manufacture the new synthetic medicinal chemicals in quantity. The research done by British manufacturers of drugs and chemicals was 'almost confined to the study of alkaloids'.[2] Enforced import-substitution during the First World War showed that the essential medicinal chemicals could be made commercially by British manufacturers; before the war, they had had no incentive to compete, no reason, under Free Trade, to replace existing low-cost suppliers.

Ivan Levinstein, one of the leading dye-stuffs manufacturers, complained with some reason in 1886 that the development of industrial enterprise in the United Kingdom over the previous thirty years had been 'practically confined to cotton, wool, iron and coal, to the lamentable neglect of other industries of apparently minor importance'.[3] Manufacturers, like traders, put their money where they saw the best opportunities for a reasonable, non-speculative rate of return. The range of opportunities, in the chemical industry as elsewhere, was vastly increased by the last decade of the century. Britain took little part in the development of organic chemicals or in electro-chemicals, where the leadership went to Germany and the United States respectively. But she was strong in heavy chemicals, where her exports were 70% higher in value than Germany's in 1913, and in fertilizers where they were higher by 65 to 70%.[4] Where she failed was in broadening the base of her industry to include the fastest growing sector, organic chemicals; she continued to produce in the area of heavy inorganic chemicals where growth was slower and foreign competition

---

[1] *Memorandum on the Supply of Essential Drugs*, 2 October 1916, printed as an Appendix to the Committee on Commercial and Industrial Policy, *Interim Report on certain Essential Industries*, P.P. 1918, XIII, 217-20.

[2] Stephen Miall, *A History of the British Chemical Industry* (London, 1931), p. 124.

[3] Quoted by L. F. Haber, *The Chemical Industry during the Nineteenth Century* (Oxford, 1958), p. 168.

[4] Richardson in Aldcroft (ed.), *Development of British Industry*, p. 298.

always increasing. It was a relative rather than absolute failure. Britain's exports under the heading 'Chemicals' rose from £8 million in 1880 to £24 million in 1913; her percentage of world trade in chemicals fell from 29·4% to 21·9%.[1]

Although Britain was second only to Germany in overseas markets for chemicals, the scale of each industry was entirely different. The British chemical industry's sales in 1907 may have been in the region of £24-29 million, compared with German sales estimated in 1913 at £120 million.[2] Naturally, the United Kingdom's performance in Latin American markets was a function of her specialities in the chemical industry, and of market preferences in many individual lines. She continued to sell explosives to the mining Republics, Chile, Peru, Bolivia, Colombia, although local production reduced dynamite imports into Mexico. Explosives were one of the many areas where international competition could not really be said to exist after the '80s. The Nobel Dynamite Trust Co., a holding company, had been created in 1886 formally to unite the German and Glasgow companies and reinforce an amicable agreement already reached a couple of years before. The Trust bought shares in other dynamite and explosives companies, and subsidiary companies were formed all over the world in the late '90s. In fact, the whole international trade in dynamite, for use in armaments and mining, was regulated at least from the beginning of the 1900s (and possibly a decade earlier) by the Nobel Dynamite Trust Company representing English, German and British colonial manufacturers, by du Pont in the United States, and by the Société Centrale de Dynamite in Paris, formed by the amalgamation of French, Swiss, Spanish and Italian firms. The three Groups made arrangements to share out world markets between them, more especially for South Africa, but also for the valuable mining business in Mexico and for the dynamite required for canal construction in Panama.[3] Elsewhere in the Republics Britain had specialities in chemicals for the textile industries, in sheep dips, in certain fertilizers, and in the cyanides widely used after the beginning of the '90s for processing gold and silver.

---

[1] S. B. Saul, 'The Export Economy 1870-1914', *Yorkshire Bulletin of Economic and Social Research*, 17 (1965), 13.
[2] Haber, *The Chemical Industry 1900-1930*, p. 135.
[3] Liefmann, *International Cartels*, p. 76.

British preferences in the overseas chemical trade are indicated by the most successful industries, the manufacture of paints, varnishes and soaps. Britain had almost a monopoly of imported paints in the main Dominion markets before 1914, and the whole trend just before, during and after the war and in the 1920s was to set up works and depots in Australasia, Canada, India, South Africa, France, Italy and Spain. Latin America was largely ignored, although Reckitt and Sons, Ltd. had a works at São Paulo in the 1920s. Similarly, Britain enjoyed a strong position in world exports of soap, and in those markets which she chose to enter the only competition was between her own manufacturers. Raw materials were an overwhelmingly large element in the cost of producing soap, and the United Kingdom's status as a free trade market for the world's fats and oils gave her an excellent base from which to compete. Latin American markets were not promising. As large tallow producers the Republics had always been able to meet a large part of local demand in hard soaps and later in the common lines of toilet soap. It was an experience shared among tallow producers in Empire markets; British imports of common soap into South Africa, as a direct result of the development of local competitive industries, fell from £213,258 in 1906 to £46,169 in 1913.[1]

The point was that British manufacturers had at home, in Europe, in the United States and in the Dominions accessible, high-quality markets amply capable of absorbing the direct sales and investment effort of what were still, before the war, relatively small industrial empires. In December 1888, when William Lever started looking overseas for markets for his Sunlight soap, his first trips were to Europe, then to Canada, two years later to America, Canada again, New Zealand, Australia, and later still to South Africa. Lever's overseas business in the mid-1900s was in Canada and the United States, South Africa, Australia and the Pacific Islands, Switzerland, Germany, Belgium, France and Holland. These were the most concentrated markets, those in which he might hope to *explain* to housewives and shopkeepers, through direct sales and advertising, the peculiar merits of his branded product—an indispensable element in the new generation of brand sales, where it was no longer simply a case of producing good value

[1] Sothern Holland's report on South Africa for 1913, P.P. 1914-16, XLV, 612.

P

for money in basic, easily understood, and interchangeable commodities. Although Lever had developed contacts with Far
Eastern markets by 1914, he made no effort independently to
develop any business in Latin America, Central or South, and
such sales as he achieved, in highly priced toilet soap, were through
the agency of import houses in the capitals. It was only in the
1920s that Levers felt it worth extending into branch factories in
Latin America, and not surprisingly the factories were established
in Britain's four traditionally strong markets, in Buenos Aires in
1928, São Paulo in 1930, and Uruguay and Chile a few years later.[1]
Gossage and Crosfield, the other main soap exporters, followed
precisely the same pattern. Crosfields' export sales, which were
about a third of their soap production, nearly doubled between
1898 (6,623 tons) and 1911 (12,394 tons). Unlike Levers, most of
their overseas sales were in bar soaps, in the mottled soaps, in the
cheaper household pale and brown soaps, and in lower quality
toilets like Old Brown Windsor. Latin America at least paid them
the compliment of imitation, and spurious Brown Windsor was
to be found all over the continent in the 1900s. But Crosfields'
main outlets were the lower-caste 'colonial' markets, the West
Coast of Africa, Gibraltar, India, the West Indies, Hong Kong,
China, South Africa, where they were promoting their products
under a number of suitable brand names—Pyramid, Crescent,
Camel, Elephant. Their total export sales, as Britain's third largest
exporter of soaps, were only about £108,000 in 1908, with the
West Coast of Africa leading at over £19,000. Little remained to
encourage thoughts of direct representation in Latin America, and
indeed when Crosfields first appointed their own salaried representatives, in 1911-12, it was in China, India, the West Indies, the
Middle East and the West Coast of Africa.[2]

Hardware

Soaps, cosmetics, perfumes, pharmaceuticals fell within that
category of products, ordered in multiple kinds and qualities, for
which the nationality and location of trader and wholesaler were
generally more important than a small difference in price ex-works.

---

[1] Charles Wilson, *The History of Unilever* (London, 1954), I, 89, 110;
II, 358-60.
[2] A. E. Musson, *Enterprise in Soap and Chemicals: Joseph Crosfield &
Sons, Limited, 1815-1965* (Manchester, 1965), pp. 181-5.

The same was true of the thousand and one different elements in the hardware trade. If demand could not be met by local manufacturers, an English retailer or import house abroad ordered through his wholesaler in London, a German through Hamburg. Unless some good reason existed for doing otherwise, these orders were filled in the country to which they first came. Naturally Britain found herself steadily replaced as the automatic, first resort supplier of hardware to Latin America as German houses took over from British after the middle of the nineteenth century. From the 1850s cheap hardware from Hamburg was beginning to make an impression on the British monopoly, but as yet it was of such poor quality that it seemed unlikely to have any permanent effect. The quality improved, the price remained low, and the depreciation of Latin American currencies, by raising import prices, put an additional premium on cheapness, even at the cost of quality. During the '90s the Chilean dollar fell from 3s. to 1s. 6d., the Brazilian milreis from 2s. 3d. to 7¾d. The fall in purchasing power left the Latin American consumer with no choice; he had to take the cheapest on the market.

Depreciation encouraged import-substitution in hardware, as it had in textiles, foodstuffs, building materials. Nails and wire, iron rivets and screws, iron bedsteads, chests and boxes, scales were being manufactured in Argentina by the late '90s.[1] About a third of Argentina's consumption of household utensils was met by local production in the years before the war.[2] Nearly every Republic had some rudimentary ironworks and foundries by the beginning of this century, if only for the processing and re-use of scrap metal. There was a foundry near Bogotá, a small ironworks at Pacho and at Samaca. Plough bars, planting bars, hoes, adzes and coffee diggers were locally manufactured in Colombia, although of a very inferior quality. Dickson reported that foreign tools were much preferred, and the native article bought only where means were lacking for imports.[3] This was probably as far as most of the smaller Republics were able to get, beyond providing for their needs in the cruder pots and pans, kitchen utensils and cutlery.

---

[1] 'Memorandum on the Leading Argentine Industries', printed as Appendix V to Worthington's report on Argentina, 18 August 1898, P.P. 1899, XCVI, 519-31.

[2] Table IV above.

[3] Dickson's report on Colombia for 1903, P.P. 1904, XCVII, 607.

But Brazil and the major Republics could take substitution much further. Brazil's Minister of Agriculture reported in the later '70s that there were eighteen iron and copper foundries in the Empire belonging to private individuals or companies; they employed 700 workmen and produced about £500,000 worth of manufactured goods in the year.[1] By the end of the century Rio de Janeiro was supplying outlying markets, under a protective tariff, with mule shoes, tin ware, lead piping and lead shot at prices lower than they could be imported; the hardware trade was gradually being invaded, competition from local manufacturers was constantly growing, and 'every now and then one more article disappears from the foreign importers' list'.[2] At the National Exhibition at Rio de Janeiro in 1908 the locally produced iron exhibits included 'cooking ranges, flat irons, cooking pans and other domestic utensils, safes, ironmongery, ornamental iron work, etc.'.[3] Progress was rapid over the next few years, and just before the war Brazilian manufacturers were competing successfully in sanitary fittings, enamelled iron baths, steel plate work, tanks, girders and foundry work of all kinds for both iron and yellow metal.[4]

Nevertheless, it was European and North American competition which was more generally effective in hardware. Britain lost her trade altogether in one of the largest single lines of business, wrought enamelled goods, and she was threatened in the cast-iron trade. Cheap German cutlery worried Sheffield from time to time. In tools and implements, where local taste often had more to do with sales than price or quality differences, British manufacturers gained some markets and lost others. In 1913 Guatemalans, Salvadoreans and Venezuelans favoured British *machetes*; the peasants of Honduras, Costa Rica and Panama preferred American; most Colombians liked German; while the Nicaraguans divided their favours between German (33%), American (32%) and British (30%).[5] On the whole, averaged over hardware generally, there is enough evidence to suggest that British competitiveness reasserted itself by the mid-'90s, and that subsequently the markets

---

[1] O'Conor's report on Brazil, 15 May 1877, P.P. 1877, LXXXI, 352.
[2] Chapman's report on Brazil for 1902, P.P. 1903, LXXVI, 483; Archer's report on Porto Alegre for 1902, *ibid.*, 463.
[3] Cheetham's report on Brazil for 1908, P.P. 1909, XCII, 677.
[4] Birch's report on Brazil for 1912-13, P.P. 1914-16, LXXI, 185.
[5] Milne's reports on Central America and the northern Republics, 1912-13, P.P. 1913, LXVIII, 447, 469, 490, 508, 527, 545, 578, 605.

in which Britons continued to make a poor impression were those in which they were not sufficiently interested to compete. Britain was sending £171,954 of general hardware to Brazil in 1913 and £112,618 to Argentina. Her exports to Brazil in this line had risen from £118,091 in 1909, and by 1913 Brazil and Argentina were her leading foreign markets, if still some distance behind Australia, South Africa and India. Imports of tools and implements into Brazil in 1913 were twice as high from Britain (£381,000) as they were from Germany (£149,000) or the United States (£191,000).[1] If further evidence is needed of the renewed competitiveness of the hardware trade, it can be found in the continued strength of British hardware imports even to a German enclave like Porto Alegre and Rio Grande do Sul in Southern Brazil, where the import trade was dominated by strong German and Brazilian houses. It is difficult to get precise figures, since so many British imports appeared as German when shipped via Hamburg. But Archer, who was one of the more competent consular observers in Latin America, was confident that British hardware retained the lead in the 1890s and 1900s. In his 1908 report he explained that hardware, ironmongery, cutlery, tools, etc., were imported on a considerable scale, the better and more expensive qualities usually from the United Kingdom. Archer's enquiries from the most important firms engaged in the trade supported the view that imports from Britain equalled German in value, and 'one of the most important hardware firms (German) estimates that its imports from the United Kingdom exceed those from Germany in value though not in quantity'.[2]

The problem was rather lack of interest than of competitiveness. British manufacturers held these markets in South Brazil without any commercial representation or direct sales; they were dependent on the commercial good sense of German, Portuguese and Brazilian importers. Hervey, commenting on the infrequency of British ironmongery in Guatemala in the mid-1900s, explained that it was not, in his opinion, due to inferiority of workmanship or difference of price; the reason was simply that not a single British merchant was engaged in this line of business.[3] Nevertheless,

[1] P.P. 1918, XIII, 418.
[2] Archer's reports on Porto Alegre for 1896, P.P. 1897, LXXXIX, 516; for 1900, P.P. 1901, LXXXI, 306; for 1908, P.P. 1909, XCII, 528.
[3] Hervey's report on Guatemala for 1905, P.P. 1906, CXXV, 719.

Milne's mission in 1912-13 showed that British hardware continued to be reasonably competitive in Central America, Venezuela and Colombia just before the First World War, except for blue and white enamelled ware of cheap quality where the Germans swept the board. The trade in British hardware to these areas seems to have been in the hands of one or two Birmingham houses who were presumably satisfied with what they got; travellers directly representing British hardware firms were few and far between, and British manufacturers rarely tried to introduce novelties. By contrast, British commission houses were strongly entrenched, perhaps too strongly for their own good, in the Australian market, with the result that in general hardware Britain held on to no less than 65·64% of the Australian trade in 1910.[1]

Bicycles, Motor Cycles and Automobiles

Lack of interest accounted for a large part of the 'failure' in hardware exports to some of the more marginal markets; it was certainly the case for Central America. But there had also been a shift of direction in the Midland industries towards products less suited to lower class outlets. Competition naturally increased in world markets for the standard lines of hardware, and profit margins narrowed. An obvious course of action for the Midland manufacturer, as G. C. Allen explained long ago in his classic study *The Industrial Development of Birmingham and the Black Country 1860-1927* (London, 1929), was to abandon the cheap bulk trade in favour either of specialized lines in which competition was less, or of new lines where the home market could offer prospects unknown overseas. Rifle, tinplate and stamping concerns switched over to the manufacture of bicycles. Instrument-makers, gasfittings manufacturers, brass founders, tube-makers, the nonferrous trades, malleable iron foundries and general engineers turned to the new electrical industry. Bicycle manufacturing led on to rubber tyres, cars, machine tools, each of which drew new recruits from the old hardware and metal trades. Weighing and measuring apparatus was developed for the home market, primarily to meet scientific developments, changes in commercial

[1] Hamilton Wickes' report on Australia for 1911, P.P. 1912-13, XCIII, 923.

methods and legislation in the United Kingdom. There was rapid growth in the chemical industry, particularly at Oldbury, where industrial, agricultural and photographic chemicals were manufactured very largely for the home market. A strong local market for paints and enamels for the bicycle and motor trades stimulated the paint and varnish industry. Spectacular development took place in the food and drink trades, almost entirely to satisfy the demand created by higher real wages, new habits of consumption, and advertising at home and in the Empire—Messrs Cadbury Brothers, employing only a few hundred persons in the early '80s, had 6,000 on their books by 1914, far more than in many of the ancient staples of the area, buttons, guns, locks, glass and tinplate wares. Manufacturers supplied the paper bags and boxes needed to meet expansion in local food producing firms; they provided the office equipment associated with changes in business organization in the United Kingdom and with the multiplication of office staff; they became interested in a whole range of products suited to a rising home and colonial market, the new artificial silks and rayons, wholesale clothing, fancy leather goods, sports equipment and travelling bags.

The whole industrial structure of the area, Professor Allen concluded, had been modified so as to make it 'a centre, not so much of small metal articles, but of finished products of a highly composite character'. The effect on British trade with the Latin American Republics, still in the market only for the old staples, was profound. Outside a few major cities, no market to speak of existed for any of these new manufactures. They were directed first towards the home market, then to the Empire, and finally to such sophisticated markets in Europe and North America as were not already closed by tariffs. Any which trickled through the mercantile house system to the Republics, other than to the 'white dominion' Argentina, got there almost by accident.

The bicycle and automobile industries illustrate the trend. When a man like George Accles gave up manufacturing Gatling guns and turned to bicycles, he was leaving a trade which had had some interest to Latin American markets and entering another which had virtually none. The hot climate and the appalling roads made a bicycle something of an urban toy in the Republics. In Britain, the development of the rear-chain-driven 'safety' in 1885 and the invention of the pneumatic tyre in 1888 had diverted cycling from the sport of athletes to the carriage of ordinary men. In the rapid expansion which followed, the British bicycle industry satisfied a large home market and took the initiative in developing a comfortable export trade to Europe, the Empire and the United States. In export markets Britain soon met severe competition from the United States, France and Germany, and her prices and qualities, founded on a strong home demand among the middle classes for high-quality expensive cycles, put her at an immediate disadvantage in the poorer outlets. Certainly the bicycles reaching even the favourite Latin American markets, Brazil and Argentina, at the end of the '90s were chiefly from America, with Germany as the runner up.[1] The collapse of the cycle boom in 1898 brought a sharp fall in British prices. The £30 bicycle of the '90s was replaced by the first ten-guinea machine in 1898; in the early 1900s bicycles could be bought for as little as £5. At this level British cycles, in quality and durability, priced foreign competitors off the market. The United States, which had reached her highest point in 1898 with 37·9% of world exports, to the United Kingdom's 25·7% and Germany's 20·3%, lost her trade to Germany and Britain over the next five years. German exports, which had 48% (£461,122) of the world market in 1906 to Britain's £431,122, had fallen to £353,250 in 1913. Britain by now was well ahead with £609,482.[2] What is more, her exports of bicycle *parts*, principally for assembly overseas, had reached £1,477,716. The new competitiveness of British cycles was shown in Latin America. Brazil in 1913 imported approximately £15,000 of British bicycles and parts, and the nearest competitor was Germany with £5,000; Argentina took £26,000 from Britain, with France next at £12,000.[3] But it was trivial. Taking the 1912 British export figures, £11,114 of complete bicycles are shown as shipped to Brazil and £12,018 to Argentina, together with an unenumerated but relatively small quantity of parts. That same year, total exports of British bicycles and parts to the Netherlands were valued at £274,565, to British India £186,289, and to Australia £164,882.

The expansion of British motor cycle exports from 880 motor

---

[1] Archer's report on Porto Alegre for 1898, P.P. 1899, XCVIII, 369-70; Worthington's report on Argentina, 18 August 1898, P.P. 1899, XCVI, 505; Rhind's report on Rio for 1899, P.P. 1900, XCII, 363.

[2] A. E. Harrison, 'The Competitiveness of the British Cycle Industry, 1890-1914', *Economic History Review*, 2s. XXII (1969), 293.

[3] P.P. 1918, XIII, 415, 418.

cycles in 1907 to 16,850 in 1913 was again a development in which Latin America could take no share.[1] Road and climatic conditions were unfavourable, as they were for the motor trade, and the £150,026 of motor cycles and parts despatched to New Zealand in 1913 found no parallel in British exports to the Republics. The trade was largely an Empire trade, with £663,777 out of a total of £991,035 of motor cycles and parts exported to British Possessions in 1913. Latin American import statistics record only £4,000 of British motor cycles and parts as entering Argentina in 1913 and £5,000 for Brazil, although in each case Britain headed the list of importers.[2]

In the motor trade, however, although it would be difficult to speak of a market in Latin America until the years just before the First World War—and even then only in the immediate environment of the larger cities—Brazil and Argentina were supplying opportunities for rapid expansion. Automobiles were not separately distinguished in Brazilian import returns before 1906, but in that year imports were valued at £79,595, with France heading the list at £47,208 and the United Kingdom second at £12,969.[3] By 1913 imports were up to £1·1 million, and of the 3,785 vehicles disembarked only 205 were of British make.[4] Argentina was the best Latin American market, taking 304 British cars in 1913, whereas India imported 1223, Australia 1055, South Africa 934 and New Zealand 829. France, in fact, still led the way by a long margin in the supply of automobiles to Argentina and Brazil, although the United States was gaining ground rapidly.

The explanation for Britain's poor performance must be taken on at least two levels. The motor industry, starting from virtually nothing in the late '90s (the first motor company was launched in 1896), had become a major force in British engineering by 1913. In 1908 it was producing 10,500 cars and commercial vehicles; by 1913 employment in the industry was over 100,000 and production had reached 34,000.[5] As Professor Saul says, 'in their own speciality of medium priced cars costing £300 and more, British makers

[1] Figures from S. B. Saul, 'The Engineering Industry', in Aldcroft (ed.), *Development of British Industry*, p. 224.
[2] P.P. 1918, XIII, 415, 418.
[3] Chapman's report on Brazil for 1906, P.P. 1907, LXXXVIII, 225.
[4] Birch's report on Brazil for 1912-13, P.P. 1914-16, LXXI, 181.
[5] S. B. Saul, 'The Motor Industry in Britain to 1914', *Business History*, 5 (1962), 25.

were surpassed by only one or two American firms in size of output, and in technical quality and value for money there was little to
choose between them'.[1]

It seems clear that in this range the loss of markets in Latin
America was more a case of concentration of sales, by what were
still a large quantity of relatively small producers, on a limited
number of promising outlets. S. F. Edge, speaking for Napier cars
in the late 1900s, explained that his export business was with New
Zealand and Australia, where the preferential duties made all the
difference to American competition, and with the United States
herself where, in spite of a 40-45% tariff, orders were received
from 'the class of people who are prepared to pay an abnormal sum
for something which they think is the best'; at the time the United
States was taking all Napier's surplus output, while the home
demand was growing faster than the company's ability to supply
it.[2] W. A. Smith, chairman of the Hozier Engineering Co. of
Glasgow, which was currently producing about 20 finished cars
a week, told the Tariff Commission that he did not care how much
tariffs were raised against him; 'we are so overwhelmed with work
that we do not require to cater for any particular trade'.[3] Neither
Napier nor Hozier were likely to put much effort into promoting
sales for the occasional car in Latin America; servicing and spare
parts were creating enough problems in the few export markets
worth developing, without taking on others. Among medium-
priced four-cylinder cars produced by Napier for export after 1907
was one 'built particularly for the "colonial" trade', with a high
enough clearance 'to ford fairly deep streams and to avoid all but
the most formidable obstacles on unmade roads'. These cars, with
a list price of between £500 and £700, were as well suited to Latin
American as colonial conditions. But the point was that the company itself had the colonial market in mind, and it was towards
the colonies that Napier's sales effort was directed; if and when
the cars reached Latin America, they did so in response to isolated
orders through one of the mercantile houses. Napier, which after
1906 was the leading motor car manufacturer in the United
Kingdom and one of the first makers in the world, made only

---

[1] Saul in Aldcroft (ed.), *Development of British Industry*, p. 226.
[2] Tariff Commission, *Report on the Engineering Industries* (London,
1909), paras. 609, 613.
[3] *Ibid.*, para. 604.

4,258 cars over its whole period of production 1906-1924,[1] and the scale of production is obviously the first point to bear in mind for British motor sales to the Republics.

The failure was to anticipate development at the lower end of the market. The British motor industry manufactured cheap, low-powered cars adequate for city use in the colonies and Dominions, or for modest touring on relatively good roads in the United Kingdom. It made good quality medium and high-powered cars for long distance touring over reasonably rough conditions. What it did not even try to do until just before the First World War was to meet the demand, as the conveniences of motoring became more apparent and motors more reliable, for a cheap, medium-powered car for use out in the 'camp'. No such market existed at home, as it did for American manufacturers developing their own home market; British manufacturers were unable to find a home base for mass production, and the colonial demand for rough, cheap cars was not large enough to encourage investment in an entirely new line. It was at this level that the Ford Model T cut into the colonial market, and extinguished what hopes Britain had for more than specialised sales in Latin America. Up to the end of 1911, she had much the largest share of the motor car imports into colonial Singapore. Then Ford came on the market with a five-seater car at a retail price of £195, weighing little over half the £400 British car of the same seating capacity. The American car was rougher and machined up only when required in the bearings, while the English car was largely hand-worked, heavy and substantial; but 'what is required here and in the Federated Malay States is a car of light structure, low-priced, and parts easy to replace at reasonable cost'.[2]

No doubt this slowness in meeting the new demand for cheap, tough, medium-powered cars in mass production was in part a product of the demand for higher quality cars in Britain's home market, and in part the outcome of continued large sales in the Empire—neither of which helped or encouraged competition for Latin American sales. British exports of complete motor cars to

---

[1] Charles Wilson and William Reader, *Men and Machines: a History of D. Napier and Son, Engineers, Ltd., 1808-1958* (London, 1958), pp. 60, 86-91.

[2] Stuart's report on Singapore, 9 September 1912, P.P. 1913, LXVIII, 407.

British Possessions rose from 1,919 in 1909 to 5,054 in 1913, and of chassis from 79 to 886. The motor industry encountered formidable competition even here from Fords, amongst others. But it still supplied over half of the 3,000 cars imported by India in 1913-14.[1] Although Morris and Austin finally took the plunge, it took a great deal to persuade businessmen that they should 'sink the very large capital in machinery and stock which is absolutely necessary for the production of a very cheap car. . . . A car which can be sold at £80 in the States can hardly be kept out of this country except by direct prohibition.[2]

Iron and Steel

The remaining elements in British exports to the Republics were those more directly associated with the local expansion of transport, industry, agriculture and services in and after the 1860s—iron and steel, machinery and coal. Even in the early '70s, the small but well-situated city of Montevideo was importing coal from England at an average of about £220,000 p.a.; it was a coaling station for upwards of thirty ocean steamers a month, in addition to coasters. But the most striking change was in the manufactured iron trade, which now for the first time challenged the overwhelming lead of textile imports into the Republic. Consul Munro, in a breathless account of progress at Montevideo, observed the notable increase in the consumption of British productions in the hardware and manufactured iron trades

> to which a very rapid extension has been given in the last seven years in the rapid enlargement of this city and its suburbs, and the planting, progress, and completion of railways, tramways, gasworks, docks, and waterworks, the last-named conveying the supply of water for the Capital a distance of over forty miles in iron pipes, with corresponding reservoirs, and huge machinery, all the iron-work, machinery, rolling-stock of railways, tramways, gasworks, and waterworks being English, as well as the iron work in the construction of houses, and stores, as also of two commodious iron built market-places; and, as the

[1] Saul, *Overseas Trade*, p. 201.
[2] *Report of the Departmental Committee on the Engineering Trades*, P.P. 1918, XIII, 392.

introduction of railway material may be said to be but yet in its commencement, this class of English trade is certain to increase yearly, and in large amount.[1]

Britain could not have preserved this monopoly for long, and the same broad pattern of preferences established itself in these major lines of trade as for the minor. Increased competition, declining profit margins, a demand rising higher than ability to supply, encouraged British manufacturers to shift into more specialized lines of production, to trade increasingly within home and imperial markets.

Local manufacturing was not a serious factor in the iron and steel trades other than at the lowest level of iron cooking-pots and basic cutlery and hardware. The larger Republics developed some manufacturing capacity. Perhaps two-thirds of the pig-iron used in Brazil in the late 1900s was produced locally, even if all the steel and wrought iron had still to be imported.[2] Mexico, as a result of heavy investment, improved transport and power, was able at least to check the expansion of iron and steel imports by the end of the 1900s; iron and steel railway material, imported to the extent of 80,000 tons in 1903-4, rose to 97,000 tons in 1907-8 and then fell to 84,000 tons in 1910-11. Production at Mexico's leading iron and steel works, the Cia. Fundidora de Fierro y Acero of Monterrey, rose from 21,583 tons of iron and 8,823 tons of steel ingots in 1903, to 71,337 tons and 84,697 tons respectively in 1911[3]; British exports of 'iron, steel and manufactures thereof' to Mexico in 1911 were only 23,951 tons.

The expansion of demand prevented local manufacturing from cutting back imports, if averaged over *all* forms of iron and steel manufactures. But for both Mexico and Brazil local production of structural iron, commercial iron, and large items like boilers or storage tanks, for which transport costs formed so large an element in the final price, made more progress towards meeting national needs. The same was true of ironworks and foundries in Argentina and Chile, even if the raw material was still largely imported. Elsewhere, British manufacturers had nothing much to worry about, and indeed the anxiety of Latin American

[1] Munro's report on Uruguay, 1873, P.P. 1874, LXVIII, 400.
[2] Cheetham's report on Brazil for 1908, P.P. 1909, XCII, 677.
[3] Rosenzweig in Cosío Villegas (ed.), *Mexico: La Vida Económica*, I, 381-2.

governments to encourage the development of transportation and industry meant that basic iron and steel, though not manufactures, could almost always be imported at minimal tariff rates.

Competition came from suppliers in Europe and the United States, but the issue was far from straightforward. 'Dumping', accidental advantages in transport rates, preferential tariffs, price and market-sharing agreements, make it difficult to speak realistically of 'competition' in the world's iron and steel trade before 1914. Every manufacturing nation was prepared, at one time or another, to quote lower rates for exports than for local consumption. British consuls and journalists tended to see the motes in German or North American eyes, yet it was well known in the trade that British steel manufacturers in the 1900s were quoting a reduction on home prices of as much as twenty shillings a ton on steel for direct export.[1] Terms might vary from market to market according to the preferences, contacts and expectations of suppliers, and from one day to another with variations in the disposable surplus after meeting home demand. Nobody knew for certain when United States Steel would next decide to off-load, or at what price, and the uncertainty was particularly evident in neighbouring Latin American markets. Pricing policies, in any case, were often determined by long-term strategic considerations rather than current costs. In 1910 Haggard reported from Guatemala a decline in Britain's share of imported galvanised iron sheets, a product in which she remained fully competitive elsewhere until 1914. America's share had risen sevenfold in 1909, and she took a further 11% in 1910. Haggard put this down to United States Steel's habit in these markets of quoting prices (including insurance and freight to Guatemala) which were 2% lower, more when necessary, than those published by German and British firms.[2] Milne, visiting Central America a few years later, found a similar situation. He quoted a 'confidential' circular issued by the United States Steel Products Export Company, 12 January 1912, in which it was noted that prices for tubes—which Britain was manufacturing at very competitive prices at the time—were

[1] Messrs Denny & Co.'s letter to the press of 11 November 1902, quoted by Henry W. Macrosty, *The Trust Movement in British Industry* (London, 1907), p. 68; *Report of the Departmental Committee on the Engineering Trades*, P.P. 1918, XIII, 378.

[2] Haggard's report on Guatemala for 1910, P.P. 1912-13, XCVII, 102.

not given, but were regulated by those ruling in the United Kingdom, subject to discounts of 55-80%. Milne was told of another case where 'Flat head bright screw nails, $\frac{3}{4}$ inch' were on offer from an American manufacturer at the English price less $82\frac{1}{2}\%$.[1]

It was in part to avoid rate-cutting of this kind that attempts were made periodically to syndicate the whole international steel trade. Even if these failed, international market-sharing and price agreements certainly existed for a number of principal products. British and German gas pipe makers came to an agreement over price maintenance in 1881.[2] Anglo-German competition in screws, at least in home markets, was brought to an end by mutual agreement in September 1905.[3] For steel rails, the agreements were older and, from the point of view of trade with Latin America, more influential. British steel rail manufacturers were naturally anxious, as competing industries developed overseas, to eliminate unnecessary competition in the home market and to maintain as large a share of the export trade as they could. The result was an agreement between the British Rail Makers' Association and the German and Belgian Associations in 1884, extended to the American and French Associations in 1904, and renewed again in 1912. The British Rail Makers' Association admitted quite frankly that although the results were disappointing, with the allotted British share of the pooled export trade reduced from 65% in 1884 to 37% in 1904 and 34% in 1912, it was by this means alone that the British rail trade was kept alive for many years.[4] Home and colonial markets were allocated to local manufacturers wherever they could meet national demand and delivery dates, while the remaining world markets were syndicated on a percentage basis. The effect, for Latin America, was to extinguish any genuine competition.

For much of the international steel trade before 1914 it would be absurd to claim, on the basis of a larger percentage share in a particular market, any competitive 'victory' for one nation's

[1] Milne's report on Central America, 1912-13, P.P. 1913, LXVIII, 472-3.
[2] J. C. Carr and W. Taplin, *History of the British Steel Industry* (Oxford, 1962), p. 167.
[3] Macrosty, *The Trust Movement*, p. 79.
[4] Statement by the British Rail Makers' Association, attached to the *Report of the Iron and Steel Trades Committee*, P.P. 1918, XIII, 429-30.

industry over another. Britain supplied 43·7% of the steel rails reaching Argentina in 1912, to Germany's 26·4%,[1] yet this can hardly be taken to prove an overwhelming contemporary lead in the world's market for British steel rails. All the same, it is possible to identify certain developments in the British steel industry which account in part for a shift in interest away from the Republics. It was inescapable that the steel industries of Germany and the United States, based on a strong, protected home market, should take over neighbouring markets as soon as they reached a point of development where their prime manufacturing costs were comparable with Britain's. Lower transport costs, which for iron and steel formed so important an element in the final market price, gave them an immediate advantage, quite apart from the benefits derived from ease of access, rapid deliveries, matching specifications, direct sales and engineering services. The result was that Germany by 1913 was supplying 62·8% of steel imports into Western Europe to Britain's 16·6% and the United States' 3·7%. On the other hand, the United States took 85·7% of the important Canadian market to Britain's 8·3% and Germany's 4·8%, and 84·5% of the neighbouring markets to the south, Mexico, Cuba and Panama (to Britain's 5·5% and Germany's 4·8%). As for the British Empire market, where transport advantages and national preferences were British, if Canada is excluded the British steel industry held on to 63·4% to Germany's 16·0% and America's 9·7%.[2]

It was Britain's misfortune that she found herself at such a disadvantage in Western Europe and Canada, which accounted between them for 51·6% of world trade in steel, and there was little that her manufacturers could do about it. To some extent the loss was compensated for by so large a share of the growing Empire market, which even without Canada amounted to 18·1% of world trade. But British manufacturers were also looking increasingly to the home market. Whereas in 1885 they had exported 2,169,800 tons of finished iron and steel, consuming only 3,626,200 tons at home, the totals for 1896 were 2,490,200 tons and 5,100,000

---

[1] The percentage distribution, of a total import of £1,054,600, is given in Mackie's report on Buenos Aires for 1912-13, P.P. 1914, LXXXIX, 572.

[2] Percentages from Peter Temin, 'The Relative Decline of the British Steel Industry, 1880-1913' in H. Rosovsky (ed.), *Industrialization in Two Systems* (New York, 1966), p. 148.

tons respectively. Sinclair makes the point that whereas the Bessemer steel firms, for which the main product was rails, were facing severe problems of over-capacity and foreign competition, the open-hearth steel firms made great progress based first and foremost on the home demand of the British shipbuilders; in fact, by 1894 more open-hearth steel was being produced annually than Bessemer.[1]

Furthermore, from an early date the tendency among Britain's leading steel manufacturers had been to abandon bar and sheet steel, rails and railway material, in which competition had now become formidable and where protective tariffs were excluding Britons from their former markets in Europe and North America, in favour of more specialized lines. Thomas Vickers explained to the Royal Commission in 1886 that foreign tariffs had been felt far more severely for those products where cheap labour could be employed than for those where quality and excellence of manufacture were necessary. Vickers, Sons and Company, Ltd., like many Sheffield manufacturers, had been moving away from the wrought iron trade to a business in heavy steel manufactures—marine shafting and ordnance—where knowledge and experience gave them the advantage.[2] The Consett Iron Company, enjoying an average return of 19·1% on capital employed over its first half-century of operation 1864-1914, owed its prosperity to good management and a sensible decision to turn from rails to plates, with a special line in shipbuilding materials—'an obvious choice to be made by a firm long producing rails and plates once the rail trade had collapsed'. At the turn of the century Consett was one of the biggest steel plate makers in the world, and although it exported plates as far as India, China and Australia, the greater part of its production went to the home shipbuilding industry.[3] A handsome business in steel tubes developed out of the home demand of the new cycle and motor car industries, and out of what was virtually a protected industry in Britain—the battleship industry on contract to the Admiralty. In shipbuilding generally,

---

[1] W. A. Sinclair, 'The Growth of the British Steel Industry in the Late Nineteenth Century', *Scottish Journal of Political Economy*, VI (1959), 34-5.

[2] Minutes of Evidence, *Report of the Royal Commission on the Depression of Trade and Industry*, P.P. 1886, XXI, QQ.3430, 3444, 3492-3502.

[3] H. W. Richardson and J. M. Bass, 'The Profitability of Consett Iron Company before 1914', *Business History*, VII (1965), 72, 89-90.

Q

Germany was the sole competitor in the late 1900s, and then only in cargo carriers and ordinary passenger steamers; no country could touch British shipbuilders for the larger type of war vessels or for the best class of tramp steamers and liners.[1] The implications of all this for British exports to Latin America are obvious. Latin America's demand for steel was still associated principally with the railways, and the rail manufacturers were the weakest element in the British steel industry. The strength of the open hearth industry and of specialized producers in the heavy trades could not be reflected in export statistics to the Republics,

Table XVI

British Exports of new Iron or Steel Steam Ships (other than War Vessels), Hull, Fittings and Machinery, to Argentina, Brazil, Chile and Peru, 1905-13

	1905 £	1906 £	1907 £	1908 £	1909 £
Argentina	143,863	236,902	267,683	177,989	210,028
Brazil	139,398	204,487	562,984	438,566	610,307
Chile	42,000	258,533	53,231	59,546	89,859
Peru	34,830	24,207	11,770	2,830	232,500

	1910 £	1911 £	1912 £	1913 £
Argentina	33,064	249,822	325,776	294,272
Brazil	534,418	318,675	509,548	160,435
Chile	620	31,094	17,165	28,608
Peru	13,756	3,582	8,550	1,104

Source: *U.K. Trade and Navigational Accounts.*

where the demand for such sophisticated products was slight. Indeed, it might not be unreasonable to insist that if any judgement *must* be passed on the British steel industry's performance in Latin American markets before 1914, it cannot be done independently of the export figures for its main customer, British shipbuilders. Steel by this route would certainly show a different pattern of performance. Warship orders have been referred to already on pp. 204-5. The British mercantile marine, in the extensive modernization programmes of the pre-war years, sold

[1] From the evidence given by Francis Elgar of the Fairfield Shipbuilding and Engineering Co. Ltd. and by John Thornycroft of John I. Thornycroft & Co., Ltd.: Tariff Commission, *Report on the Engineering Industries* (London, 1909), paras. 500-3, 529-30.

many of its older ships abroad, and some of these were bought by shipowners in Latin America. Table XVI shows the fluctuating but valuable exports of *new* British merchant ships to the Republics.

For reasons such as these, although all exports of 'iron and steel and manufactures thereof' rose sharply in the period 1909-13 with the United Kingdom taking a good share, relatively she was falling behind (Table XVII). Taking a single Latin American market, Brazil, the distribution for 1912—which is the last useful year for comparison before the 1913 slump—was $23\frac{1}{2}$ million milreis (about £1·6 million) imported from the United Kingdom, 22 million from Germany, 16 million from Belgium, and $15\frac{1}{2}$

Table XVII

Exports of Iron and Steel and Manufacturers thereof, 1909-13
(£000)

	United Kingdom	Germany	United States
1909	38,690	28,465	12,768
1910	43,441	33,871	16,585
1911	44,172	40,344	21,311
1912	48,996	48,036	26,555
1913	54,692	55,683	30,275

Source: Appendix B, Section VI, *Report of the Iron and Steel Trades Committee*, P.P. 1918, XIII, 446.

million from the United States. Belgium led the way in rails and railway accessories; Germany took first place for iron and steel wire, cutlery, axles, enamelled iron, manufactures of tin plate and structural iron for building; and Britain continued to be the largest supplier of iron pipes, nails and screws, tin-plated sheets and galvanized sheets.[1]

Machinery

It was the engineering industry which accounted for so much of the general expansion of British trade after the middle of the nineteenth century. In 1850 no less than 63% of total exports consisted of textiles, and only 18% were described as 'metal and engineering'; by 1913 the percentages of a vastly expanded trade were 34 and 27 respectively.[2] Professor Saul points out how exports

[1] Birch's report on Brazil for 1912-13, P.P. 1914-16, LXXI, 181-2.
[2] E. A. G. Robinson, 'The Changing Structure of the British Economy', *Economic Journal*, LXIV (1954), 460.

of textiles, after rising consistently since 1815, halted in 1888 and did not exceed that level for another seventeen years; exports of machinery doubled over the '80s and rose in volume by another 50% during the '90s.[1]

In the normal run of business, British manufacturers did not meet competition in machinery outside the 'protected' countries until the late '80s. J. A. Crowe, who had been Commercial Attaché in Europe since the post was first established in 1880, told the Royal Commission on the Depression of Trade, late in 1885, that he was not aware of any country, even Belgium, which was an exporter of machinery. The utmost that could be said was that there was some traffic on the Alsace frontier. But the main current of the trade remained English, an English trade in France and an English trade in Germany. Machinery was certainly manufactured much more widely in Germany and France now than formerly, but it was made for self-supply and not for exportation.[2]

Crowe was over-simplifying, and his mind was running on the weaving, spinning and agricultural machines which were still the normal machinery exports of the day. In fact Britain was finding herself challenged in a number of different directions. But at this stage conditions had to be peculiarly favourable to allow foreign manufacturers to make such impact on the leading position of British machinery exporters in all but their own protected home market. In the mid-'90s (1894) Britain was still supplying a useful market like Chile with nearly 80% of her total imports of 'engines, machinery, instruments and other Articles for Industries and Trade'.[3] Table XVIII gives a breakdown for machinery over the decade 1884-1894.

Where they chose to compete, European and North American manufacturers were capturing their home trade, and to a limited extent the same was beginning to be true for Latin Americans. Big ports created their own demand for local work shops. MacGregor reported in the 1840s that Messrs Starr and Co.'s works at Pernambuco for the manufacture of steam engines, machinery, etc., were extensive and prosperous, while two other English

---

[1] Saul, *Yorkshire Bulletin of Economic and Social Research*, 17 (1965), 9.
[2] Minutes of Evidence, *Report of the Royal Commission on the Depression of Trade and Industry*, P.P. 1886, XXI, QQ.1053-5.
[3] Hayes Sadler's report on Valparaiso for 1895, P.P. 1897, LXXXIX, 577.

establishments of a similar description had lately been formed, with good prospects of success.[1] Government arsenals and associated private manufactories had always provided some basis for expansion, even if only by training apprentice metal workers and

Table XVIII

Imports of Classes of Machinery into Chile from Britain, Germany, France and the United States, 1884, 1889 and 1894
($000 at 3s. 2d to the dollar)

Articles	Britain			Germany		
	1884	1889	1894	1884	1889	1894
Engines and machinery in general	433·5	1,404·8	750·7	18·2	73·3	145·6
Machinery for refining nitrate	168·7	9·8	54·8	22·8	—	182·1
Assorted machinery	200·8	560·0	524·1	38·4	161·5	198·8
Sewing machines	24·0	26·4	18·1	135·0	158·6	75·2
Ploughs	14·1	4·5	5·7	0·1	2·9	0·8
Engines and Articles for railways	1,146·1	2,318·4	1,752·2	116·4	312·3	161·6

Articles	France			United States		
	1884	1889	1894	1884	1889	1894
Engines and machinery in general	34·5	64·1	32·9	102·3	122·4	223·8
Machinery for refining nitrate	—	—	—	—	—	19·9
Assorted machinery	15·4	11·6	36·4	64·5	33·3	56·2
Sewing machines	3·4	0·3	0·2	3·0	10·1	14·9
Ploughs	0·1	0·3	—	18·4	39·5	28·3
Engines and Articles for railways	0·6	216·0	10·9	1,116·8	259·1	263·5

Source: Hayes Sadler's report on Valparaiso for 1895, P.P. 1897, LXXXIX, 583.

engineers; Viscount Mauá's Niteroi establishment actually manufactured 72 steam engines in its first years of operation, 1846-60.[2] Repair shops were attached to all the major railways, public utilities, manufacturing plants, and mines; intended at first to cope simply with the problem of slow deliveries on replacement parts

[1] John MacGregor, Commercial Statistics: a digest (London, 1847), IV, 187.
[2] M. G. and E. T. Mulhall, Handbook of Brazil (Buenos Aires, 1877), pp. 97-8.

for imported machinery, they developed often enough into manufacturers in their own right. Then, the main exporting industries,
whether mines or processing plants for agricultural products,
were certain in Latin America as in Australia or Canada to encourage the development of locally manufactured machinery at
the level where transport costs made foreign imports of simple
machines uncompetitive. Brazil in the 1900s was manufacturing
coffee and rice cleaning machinery, maize and mandioca mills, and
sugar machinery, although the more complex items were still
imported from Britain, North America and Germany.[1] Several
large engineering works were in operation in Valparaiso by the
end of the century manufacturing locomotives, railway rolling
stock, marine engines, mining machinery, bridges and every other
kind of engineering work; the mining machinery was reported to
be 'of a very high class'. According to the consul-general, Sir
Berry Cusack-Smith, these establishments were able to tender for
Government and other contracts at prices which almost prohibited
competition by manufacturers in the United Kingdom.[2] Worthington found that the two large foundries at Iquique were turning
out a certain amount of machinery; the nitrate works themselves,
being comparatively isolated, generally maintained machine shops
capable of coping with a good part of their own renewals. He had
been told that everything for two large modern nitrate works,
Chilean-owned, had been manufactured in Valparaiso except for
the engines and pumps imported from England; mining machinery,
reportedly very good, was produced by the Caldera works of the
Caldera and Copiapó Railway.[3] Several important manufacturers
in Argentina were constructing the smaller items of machinery for
general use. But an enquiry agency, reporting these activities,
made the necessary distinction when it pointed out that

> At the same time it is impossible to consider the manufacture of
> machinery in Argentina as of any importance, for the simple
> reason that, although the machinery might be made, it is not
> worth while to turn out only two or three machines after pre-
> paring the moulds; and as there would be no market for a

[1] Cheetham's report on Brazil for 1908, P.P. 1909, XCII, 677.
[2] Cusack-Smith's report on Chile for 1899, P.P. 1900, XCII, 475, 493,
503.
[3] Worthington's report on Chile, 24 May 1898, P.P. 1899, XCVI,
466.

greater quantity those required by the country continue to be imported.[1]

The implication, perfectly correct, was that Latin American manufacturers had no hope of developing an export market. British manufacturers could not expect to be so fortunate in competition with Continental and North American manufacturers, and it was not long before international competition developed outside the 'protected' home markets. Britons had no difficulty in holding their lead in textile machinery, and the cotton manufacturing industries of Latin America continued to operate largely with British machinery up to the First World War. Even in Mexico, which in most respects had fallen within the North American trading area, the machinery for the substantial mills of Puebla, Mexico City, Guadalajara, Atlixco and Orizaba was still, just before the Revolution, 'almost all of British manufacture'.[2] Brazil was Britain's biggest market, and the machinery for the new mills in construction in the Pernambuco consular district in 1913-14 was 'mostly British'.[3] Of enumerated textile machinery imported into Brazil in 1913, £25,000 was British, and only £100 from the United States. At Medellín, the centre of the Colombian cotton manufacturing industry, the machinery for the six cotton weaving and spinning mills in operation in 1914 was 'all imported from the United Kingdom'.[4] British exports of textile machinery in 1913 were 'three times those of the nearest and only serious competitor, Germany, and . . . much the largest single area of export engineering products'.[5] But it was far more difficult, at any rate outside the favoured home and colonial markets, to maintain sales in agricultural, mining and electrical machinery.

Much of Britain's continued strength in the export of cotton machinery was built on the size of the home market, and the experience gained from it. The same factors, combined with proximity, favoured her competitors equally in many other branches of machinery production. Britain, as the first country to use

---

[1] Included as Appendix V to Worthington's report on Argentina, 18 August 1898, P.P. 1899, XCVI, 523.
[2] Dept. of Overseas Trade, *Report on the Financial and Commercial Condition of Mexico* (H.M.S.O., 1921), p. 10.
[3] Macray's report on Alagoas for 1913, P.P. 1914-16, LXXI, 164.
[4] Badian's report on Antioquia for 1913, P.P. 1914-16, LXXI, 871.
[5] Saul in Aldcroft (ed.), *The Development of British Industry*, p. 195.

and appreciate agricultural machinery, began with a good command over world markets. She was able to preserve this lead in the range of machinery which had developed out of her strong position in steam and iron technology—in traction engines, boilers, steam threshing sets, steam excavators, pumps. Here her exports were limited by productive capacity rather than foreign competition. Clayton and Shuttleworth of Lincoln even at their peak never produced more than twenty-five threshing sets a week, and Britain's total production of threshing sets, in which she had an acknowledged technical lead before the war, had reached only a hundred sets weekly by 1913.[1] Her exports naturally went primarily to easily serviced markets in Europe and Russia, to the Dominions where she could afford to be well represented, and to the labour-starved pampas of Argentina where no less than ten English agricultural machinery firms were represented at the grain centre, Rosario, even by the beginning of the '80s. British firms saw no point in serving a market like Mexico, where Biorklund was complaining at the turn of the century that English threshing machines, though recognized throughout the country as superior to those from the United States, lost sales for lack of servicing and spare parts.[2] Carden reported a characteristic reaction. A wealthy Cuban planter wished to try out a British appliance in place of an American. He offered, if the manufacturers would send out one of their machines, to pay all expenses and give it a good trial.

> To this they replied that the only terms on which they could send one out would be those of purchase, adding that the demand for their machines was so great that it was impossible for them to cope with it, an observation which only admitted of the inference that their correspondent must consider himself as very fortunate to have the opportunity of buying one at all.[3]

The same considerations, of course, applied to manufacturers of any nationality, and it is worth remembering that the successful North American manufacturers of agricultural machinery were as anxious as the British to concentrate their sales effort on a single

---

[1] *Ibid.*, pp. 207-8, and S. B. Saul, 'The Market and the Development of the Mechanical Engineering Industries in Britain, 1860-1914', *Economic History Review*, 2nd ser. XX (1967), 119.

[2] Biorklund's report on Mexico for 1899, P.P. 1901, LXXXIII, 539.

[3] Carden's report on Cuba for 1903, P.P. 1905, LXXXVIII, 283.

promising market, rather than disperse it among many of individually small capacity. Argentina was overrun with salesmen from the United States, Canada, even Australia. The giant International Harvester Company provided both extended credit facilities for the sale of its harvesting machinery and a staff of technical experts to see that the machines were properly set up and operated during the reaping season. But for sound business reasons the effort was not matched elsewhere. Argentina was by far the largest Latin American importer of U.S. agricultural implements and twine in 1910, taking $8,560,000 out of a total of $10,810,000; a further $900,000 went to Cuba and Mexico, while $1,350,000 had to be distributed among all the remaining Republics.[1]

British manufacturers of agricultural machinery lost ground in Argentina, where they were in other respects capable of matching American sales representation, in lines such as hay rakes, reaping and mowing machines for which the sheer volume of Argentine demand, the size and similarity of the American home market, even the low cost of the wood which formed so large an element in these early agricultural machines, gave United States manufacturers an overwhelming advantage. Argentina, like Empire grain producers in Canada and Australia, was in this respect a mere extension of the American home market. Argentine statistics give an importation of £562,200 of reapers in 1912 and £314,400 of threshing machines, of which the United States supplied 71·7% and 80% respectively; Britain could hold only 11·8% even of the threshers.[2]

British manufacturers were not entirely supine in this or any other branch of agricultural machinery. British ploughs, constructed specifically to suit local conditions and copied from local patterns, forced down the price of home-made ploughs at Odessa by 20%, in spite of protective tariffs.[3] Soon after the Boer War, the 'improved' No. 75 plough was driving the old American No. 75 off the Kaffir market; an English agent had bought an American plough, sent it home to his principals, and prepared a new version which had since sold in hundreds throughout South Africa.[4] Even

[1] Downs, *Quarterly Journal of Economics*, XXVI (1912), 129.
[2] Mackie's report on Buenos Aires for 1912-13, P.P. 1914, LXXXIX, 573.
[3] Report from Odessa, August 1898, in *Opinions of H.M. Diplomatic and Consular Officers on British Trade Methods*, P.P. 1899, XCVI, 633.
[4] Birchenough's report on South Africa for 1903, P.P. 1904, LXI, 96.

in harvesting machinery, Harrison, McGregor and Co. Ltd. had increased their sales of mowing and self-binding machines from 2,357 in 1886 to 9,227 in 1906. They introduced up-to-date plant and reorganized manufacturing and sales. But they were not likely to look much further than home, Continental and Empire markets. W. Harrison pointed out in his evidence to the Tariff Commission that there was no branch of the agricultural machinery industry where the supply of spare parts was so great as for harvesting machines; an ordinary mowing machine averaged ten shillings worth a year. This in turn meant the development and maintenance of an elaborate sales and servicing organization.[1] Besides, in Dominion and other major markets, agricultural machinery, large in bulk and comparatively inexpensive, was a natural candidate for import substitution. Canada became a large *exporter* of agricultural machinery well before the war, and Australia was already meeting a substantial share of her home demand.

Yet in the markets where they might expect to compete, British manufacturers were doing good business in agricultural machinery before the war. Russia was by far and away the largest outlet. The other leading markets are shown on Table XIX. British firms were even recapturing some of the lost ground in Dominion markets. They had 'every reason to be congratulated on the enterprise they [were] showing in meeting the wants of South African farmers'; this enterprise, Sothern Holland observed, had been brought prominently to his notice in the course of his travels in outlying districts. They enjoyed no preferential tariff in this respect, yet they supplied 38% of South Africa's imported agricultural machinery in 1913 to 37·61% from the United States and 19·99% from Canada; in 1912 the percentages had been 33·22, 43·09 and 18·87 respectively.[2]

The United Kingdom had an acknowledged lead in the main branches of processing machinery for agricultural products, in sugar and coffee machinery and flour mills. This was an area where the nationality of capital often determined sales, and the preponderance of French capital in the Brazilian and Peruvian

---

[1] Tariff Commission, *Report on the Engineering Industries* (London, 1909), paras. 643-50.
[2] Sothern Holland's report on South Africa for 1913, P.P. 1914-16, XLV, 601.

sugar industries was said to give France the bulk of machinery orders. Similarly, American capital in Cuban and Puerto Rican sugar production makes it difficult to speak of competition in machinery supplies, quite apart from the tariff advantages enjoyed by American manufactures in these markets. Yet much of the new machinery ordered for Cuba during the substantial expansion of the sugar industry in and after the autumn of 1912 was British, and a consular officer reported, after a trip through the island, that 'sentiment was quite strongly in favour of British sugar

Table XIX
British Exports of Agricultural Machinery[1] to Selected Countries, Annual Averages for 1909-13

Country	Annual Average 1909-13 £	Country	Annual Average 1909-13 £
Russia	724,613	Egypt	59,969
British Possessions	322,096	Romania	47,641
Argentina	310,029	Netherlands	39,421
Germany	304,419	Belgium	36,754
France & Algeria	234,012	Brazil	33,324
Italy	172,945	Spain	30,641
Chile	104,102	Denmark	28,473

[1] Prime movers and non-prime movers, excluding electrical machinery.
Source: *U.K. Trade and Navigation Accounts.*

machinery which bears a reputation for durability possessed by no other'.[1] Although direct representation gave United States manufacturers orders for the bulk of the small sugar-crushing plants in use in Central America, the larger installations were generally British, and in Mexico the sugar growers were said to have learned by experience the superiority of British machinery.[2] Further south there could be no doubt where the competitive advantage lay. French capital and what British representatives described derogatorily as their 'pretty' machinery, took a share of the trade, particularly for distilleries, but Britain was doing a handsome and increasing trade with Argentina, where an order for plant placed with an English manufacturer by the Compañía

[1] Cowan's report on Cuba for 1911-12, P.P. 1914, XC, 654.
[2] Milne's report on Central America and Venezuela, 1913, P.P. 1913, LXVIII, 449, 509, 606; Tariff Commission, *Report on the Engineering Industries* (London, 1909), paras. 137-8.

Azucarera y Refinería de Ledesma in 1911-12 was said to have established a world record for size.[1] British manufacturers were as strongly placed in machinery for cleaning and preparing coffee, and their machinery, which was lower in price and of a better finish than competing American machinery, was preferred throughout the coffee-producing Republics of Central and northern South America. Where they lost the trade to Northern American suppliers, as in Nicaragua, it was because they lacked the direct contact with the customer, the cheaper freights and quicker communications, the ready replacement of spare parts enjoyed by their American competitors, for none of which, given the existing lines of trade, was there any simple commercial solution.[2]

For mining machinery, again, the determining forces were often geographical situation, experience with like conditions at home, and nationality of management and ownership, rather than quality or list price. Britain, as a nation of miners with wide experience and large investments overseas, was well-placed to hold a lead in mining machinery. Johannesburg, perhaps the most exciting of international markets for mining machinery in the early 1900s, was an outlet in which every producer of mining machinery found it worth while to compete, and a breakdown of competition in 1903-4 shows the areas in which British manufacturers had to watch their trade. For coal and diamond mining machinery competition was unimportant, except in electrical plant. For the machinery employed in gold-mining on the Rand, the position was less straightforward. Birchenough explained that British manufacturers were strong in some departments, weak in others.

They take the lead in boilers, winding machines, auxiliary engines, steel head gears, economisers, pumps, wire ropes, electrical cables; they are either run very hard or are beaten (1) by the Americans in mill engines, air compressors, rock drills, crushers, stamp batteries, belt conveyors, electrical plant and machine tools; (2) by the Germans and Belgians in cyanide tanks, trucks and rails, shoes and dies, electrical plant; and (3) by the Swiss in hauling engines and electrical plant.

[1] Mackie's report on Buenos Aires for 1911, P.P. 1912-13, XCIV, 140.
[2] Milne's report on Central America and Venezuela, 1913, P.P. 1913, LXVIII, 449, 509, 606; Venable's report on Nicaragua for 1910, P.P. 1912-13, XCVIII, 503.

Birchenough found it difficult to make any general comparison between British, American and foreign machinery, but on the basis of information from one of the Government Inspectors of Machinery, confirmed in discussion with many engineers, he concluded that value for value British manufacturers could hold their own, although their tenders were generally higher because of their habit of reading their specifications more liberally than their competitors. There was little to choose between the best British and foreign work in quality, but in average work the British machinery was superior and British machines always excelled in materials. No great difference in efficiency could be detected when both were new, but if cost of maintenance and length of life were taken into account, British work had a decided advantage.[1] Of course, whatever the competitive advantage on one side or the other, Johannesburg came comfortably within the British trading area. Most of the mines were British, and most of the machinery, although made to specifications drawn up in South Africa, was put out to tender in London. Britain's share, taken over the whole range of machinery imports, was far larger than that of any single competitor.

Britons were interested in Latin American mines, but to nothing like the same extent. British capital in Latin American mines, exclusive of copper and nitrates, reached a peak of £25·68 million in 1911; contemporary British investment in African mining was in the order of £165 million.[2] However, in Chilean nitrates, in gold dredging in the South, in mining in Bolivia and Colombia, Britain's capital and the genuine competitiveness of her mining machinery gave her the lead. In spite of a growing North American interest in Chilean copper, Chilean import statistics show that Britain sold £21,000 of mining machinery to Chile in 1913, compared with £20,000 from the United States and £11,000 from Germany.[3] In Mexico and the Central American Republics, ease of access, similarity of conditions with those experienced in mining further north, and United States capital and management gave the advantage to American manufacturers. As far back as the 1860s,

---

[1] Birchenough's report on South Africa for 1903, P.P. 1904, LXI, 107-8, 114.
[2] A. P. Tischendorf, 'British Investments in Latin American and African Mines: a study in Contrasts', *Inter-American Economic Affairs*, 6 (1953), 31-35.
[3] P.P. 1918, XIII, 418.

modern machinery was much more in evidence in the northern-most Mexican mining states of Sonora and Chihuahua than elsewhere in the interior of Mexico, 'owing to the facility of obtaining it from the numerous manufactories established at San Francisco'.[1] American manufacturers were always to enjoy this advantage both in supplying new machinery and in servicing old. Aided by the similarity of their own mines, they were able also to corner the Mexican market for quartz mills in the '80s and '90s with which British manufacturers and mining engineers had no experience.[2] The British mining machinery industry began to manufacture in these lines, and in any others which promised sales. But again it found itself at a disadvantage as electrification progressed in Mexico, while the United States' leadership in mining machinery was strengthened by her experience in the oil industry. In 1910 no less than 400 well-drilling plants were imported through Tampico for the new oil-fields, nearly all of which came from America.[3]

For *mining* machinery the division of British interest in 1913 between South Africa (£360,406), Chile (£27,545), Mexico (£13,203), Brazil (£13,191), Colombia (£11,389) and Peru (£2,292), shows where the balance of effort lay. Yet for machinery (non-electrical) in general, Argentina (£1,946,251) was Britain's most important foreign market after Russia (£3,946,547) and France (£2,395,783), with Japan and Germany close behind. She sold £12,850,927 to British Possessions, of which no less than £5,396,803 went to British India.

Locomotives

In nearly every branch of the engineering trade it was not on any difference of skill or ability, whether in manufacturing or marketing, that sales overseas depended. Success came first and foremost from the suitability of a foreign market to the manufacturing practices of a particular national industry, and from the similarity of its demand to large markets elsewhere at home or abroad. British manufacturers were perfectly capable of making railway locomotives to suit every variety of conditions. It was, as a witness

---

[1] Middleton's report on Mexican mines, 10 July 1866, P.P. 1867, LXIX, 227.

[2] Jerome's report on Mexico for 1902, P.P. 1903, LXXVIII, 246.

[3] Wilson's report on Tampico for 1910, P.P. 1911, XCIV, 121.

from the locomotive industry told the Tariff Commission, an 'exploded idea' that the American locomotive adapted itself better to a bad road. Britain had built engines exactly similar to those built by the Americans, but she preferred in general to turn out a more durable and expensive, custom-built locomotive priced perhaps at 15 to 20% more than an 'off the shelf' American engine.[1] It was a policy which often paid good dividends. British engines proved their value in the rough conditions experienced in Colombia; 'their durability is a matter of peculiar importance where scant facilities for repair exist'.[2]

An American manufacturer like Baldwins did not rely for its success in export markets on any peculiar ability in building the most suitable engines for poorly ballasted and new lines. On the basis of a large home market, Baldwins were able to sell a relatively small number of standard locomotives abroad—292 out of a total production of 2,374 in 1906—at very competitive prices. Their place in the Argentine market, as Worthington explained, developed out of their sales organization, with good agents and engineers to attend to complaints, remedy defects, and watch out for new requirements; in any case, of the locomotives imported into Argentina in 1912, 84·4% came from the United Kingdom, in company with 69·5% of the railway waggons, 90·9% of the passenger cars, and 92% of the wheels and axles.[3] British manufacturers, on the other hand, were excluded from a rich home market, since English railways preferred to build locomotives for themselves in their own workshops. In the absence of a large, standardized home production-run on which to base a cheap, mass-produced locomotive for the general export trade, the business of British locomotive manufacturers was to act as contractors to British railway engineers overseas, building to detailed, individual specifications. The result, not unnaturally, was that of the 13,899 British locomotives sold to overseas railways between 1890 and 1913, 8,558 went to the Empire (of which 5,542 were supplied to India alone).[4] Central and South America, with a total

[1] Tariff Commission, *Report on the Engineering Industries* (London, 1909), para. 591.
[2] Bowle's report on Bogotá for 1909-13, P.P. 1914-16, LXXI, 850.
[3] Worthington's report on Brazil, November 1898, P.P. 1899, XCVI, 547; Mackie's report on Buenos Aires for 1912-13, P.P. 1914, LXXXIX, 573.
[4] Saul in Aldcroft (ed.), *The Development of British Industry*, p. 200.

of 3,090, was the next largest market—the outcome of heavy British investment in, and management of, Latin American railway systems. Every developed nation made its own locomotives, totally or in part, in Europe, Canada, Australia, New Zealand, Argentina, Chile or Brazil. Such overseas markets as remained were shared out, according to nationality, custom, means and accessibility, between the specialist manufacturers and the makers of a cheap standard model, between the locomotive builders of the United Kingdom, Germany and the United States.

Electrical Products

Among the engineering industries, it was only in the electrical industry that British manufacturers began at a disadvantage which they were long in overcoming. Progress in the British electrical industry was inhibited by restrictive legislation on electrification and tramways, by the abundance of cheap gas, by Britain's highly developed steam technology (and consequently, by a delay in the industrial use of electricity), by small power stations and lack of experience in high voltage transmission. German and North American manufacturers had been able to build themselves up on the basis of a strong home market. By the time the British home market showed signs of developing, foreign manufacturers were well established and British manufacturers had to compete, in an unprotected home market, with such giants as the Siemens-Schuckert group, the Allgemeine Elektricitäts Gesellschaft (A.E.G.), Westinghouse and General Electric, acting, in the case of A.E.G. and General Electric after 1901, on a market-sharing basis overseas. The Americans and the Germans, naturally, pioneered electrification in Latin America; it was as much as Britain could do to keep her head above water in her home and colonial markets.

The sparsity of British commercial representation in so many of the Republics reacted particularly unfavourably on exports of any entirely new line of goods not understood or tested in these markets before, where the customer had to be convinced personally and directly of its virtues. It was probably in this respect that Germany made most progress with electrical goods. By far the greater part of United States' exports of electrical machinery and instruments to Latin America—$5 million out of a total of $7 million in 1910—

went to Brazil and Mexico, where the United States and Canada were strongly entrenched in electric traction, lighting and power; of the rest, $750,000 went to Cuba, again as a result of capital investment.[1] Britons too could depend on the influence of their investment—on the British-owned and managed tramway systems of Buenos Aires, Montevideo, Pernambuco, Caracas, Mexico City, on telephone, light and cable companies scattered throughout the Republics. But neither Britons nor Americans were well represented at the commission house/retail level at which the bulk of ordinary electrical sales were made. The many German retailers, on the other hand, were well placed to accept and promote business, and they were supported by the experience and resources of what was, after the Baghdad Railway, Germany's largest foreign enterprise, the Deutsche Ueberseeische Elektricitäts Gesellschaft. In 1913 Germany supplied 75% of imports of electrical machinery and apparatus to Chile, 50% to Argentina; British imports were next, and the United States well behind both.[2]

As usual, precisely the reverse was true of Empire markets. No doubt many of the electrical products reaching Empire markets from the United Kingdom were Continental re-exports, or manufactured by German or North American branch plants in Britain. But the fact was that no less than 65·83% of Australia's imports of electrical material in 1910 came from the United Kingdom, with Germany as the nearest competitor (17·2%) and the United States following at 5·7%.[3] British manufacturers were hard-pressed by the Germans in South Africa; German imports of electrical machinery were substantially higher. But if all 'electrical' imports into South Africa in 1913 are grouped together (fittings and posts, machinery, wires and cables), British imports were valued at £467,053 to Germany's £390,670 and the United States' £85,612.[4] As for India, the British share of imports of electrical apparatus and machinery in 1913 was 78%.[5] Not surprisingly, these were the markets on which the sales effort was concentrated. Byatt remarks that over the years 1908-13, 48% of British exports of electrical

---

[1] Downs, *Quarterly Journal of Economics*, XXVI, 131.
[2] Saul, *Overseas Trade*, p. 39 fn. 2.
[3] Hamilton Wickes' report on Australia for 1911, P.P. 1912-13, XCIII, 920.
[4] Sothern Holland's report on South Africa for 1913, P.P. 1914-16, XLV, 643.
[5] Saul, *Overseas Trade*, 201.

R

machinery, 53% of electric light and power cables, and 63% of electric lamps went to British Possessions, mainly to India, Australia, and South Africa, while the best outlet for the remainder was Japan and South America.[1] In fact, of total exports in 1913 under the heading electrical goods and apparatus (other than machinery and insulated wire), British Possessions accounted for £3,317,490 out of £5,386,273. Argentina (£386,087), Brazil (£259,490), the United States (£205,802), Japan (£118,956), China (£114,943) and Chile (£77,581) were the leading foreign markets.

The relative position of Britain and Germany for 1913 in electrical plant, mains and appliances was set out by the Departmental Committee on the Electrical Trades (Table XX). The

Table XX
Relative Performance of the British and German Electrical
Industries, 1913
(£000)

	United Kingdom	Germany
Total electrical products	22,500	60,000
Exports	7,500	15,000
Imports	2,933	631
Consumption of home-made machinery	15,000	45,000

Committee added that the approximate annual consumption of home-made electrical machinery in Germany before the war was about £70 per 100 people, compared with only £33 in the United Kingdom.[2]

For the whole engineering trade in the decades before 1914, Germany's geographical position gave her a most advantageous position in Europe, just as it gave the United States her advantage in Canada. These, as Professor Saul so rightly points out, were precisely the areas where the demand for the products of the newer industries, and for electrical goods above all, was so high.[3] Of Germany's total exports of machinery (excluding electrical

[1] I. C. R. Byatt, 'Electrical Products', in Aldcroft (ed.), *The Development of British Industry*, p. 268.
[2] *Report of the Departmental Committee on the Electrical Trades*, P.P. 1918, XIII, 361.
[3] S. B. Saul, *The Myth of the Great Depression 1873-96* (London, 1969), p. 49.

Table XXI

Engineering Products imported into Argentina from the United Kingdom, France, Belgium, the United States and Germany, 1913

	U.K. £	France £	Belgium £	U.S.A. £	Germany £
Agricultural	133,000	5,000	1,000	806,000	24,000
Arms, ammunition, etc.	33,000	20,000	52,000	107,000	47,000
Boilers	188,000	2,000	4,000	3,000	16,000
Cutlery	17,000	24,000	2,000	14,000	83,000
Cycles and parts	26,000	12,000	1,000	4,000	9,000
Electrical machinery	105,000	5,000	1,000	37,000	129,000
Implements and tools (except machine tools)	85,000	40,000	10,000	176,000	118,000
Locomotives	528,000	400	15,000	13,000	139,000
Machine tools	2,000	6,000	500	1,000	3,000
Motor cars, chassis and parts	158,000	397,000	73,000	208,000	176,000
Motor cycles and parts	4,000	2,000	1,000	4,000	1,000
Pumping machinery	11,000	3,000	100	40,000	14,000
Railway carriages and trucks	763,000	3,000	283,000	254,000	185,000
Scientific instruments	5,000	11,000	1,000	4,000	34,000
Sewing machines and parts	47,000	400	3,000	145,000	49,000
Typewriters and parts	1,000	—	—	38,000	6,000
Unenumerated machinery	441,000	128,000	104,000	585,000	756,000
Total Engineering products imported in 1913	2,547,000	658,000	551,000	2,439,000	1,789,000

Source: Report of the Departmental Committee on the Engineering Trades, P.P. 1918, XIII, 415.

machinery) amounting to £37·2 million in 1913, no less than £29·2 million went to Europe. The main markets for British machinery in 1913, out of an export totalling £34·7 million, were Europe (£13·5 million), the Empire (£10·0 million), Argentina, Brazil, and Chile (£3·6 million).[1] The competitive pattern for engineering products to Britain's principal Latin American market, Argentina, is shown in Table XXI.

Coal

Coal remains as the last of Britain's principal exports to Latin America. To some of the Republics, to Uruguay and Argentina in 1913, it was the largest single element in British trade, exceeding even British exports of cotton piece goods. The United Kingdom had exported very little coal before the middle of the last century, but the substitution of steam for sail, the extension of overseas railway systems, of gas production and of powered industry accounted for a steady increase in world consumption averaging 4% per annum for many years before 1914.[2] Total exports under the heading 'coal, coke, cinders and patent fuel' amounted to a bare £1,284,000 in 1850; they reached £38,619,856 in 1900, £53,659,660 in 1913. With only a 2% share of British total exports in 1850, coal accounted for 10% of the value of a hugely increased trade by 1913.[3] What is more, British coal exports had expanded most rapidly at a period, 1880-1900, when most of the major export groups were stagnant or in decline (Table XXII).

Britain's leading position among European coal producers in output per man per shift was maintained right up to the First World War, giving British producers, according to a Political and Economic Planning estimate, a favourable margin in export markets of not much less than two shillings per ton.[4] The British shipping industry, with its return freights of bulk primary produce from Latin America, Africa and the East, could offer low outward freights for coal where the only alternative was ballast. Above all, British coal mines were placed to best advantage for the export trade, with an average length of haul for export coal of not more

[1] Saul, *Overseas Trade*, p. 31.
[2] W. H. B. Court, 'Problems of the British Coal Industry between the Wars', *Economic History Review*, XV (1945), 4.
[3] Robinson, *Economic Journal*, LXIV, 460.
[4] Political and Economic Planning, *Report on the British Coal Industry* (London, 1936), p. 156.

than 25 miles, compared with 50 miles for Belgian coal fields, 35-70 miles for French, 100-150 miles for the Ruhr, and 400 miles for Upper Silesia. In fact, even in the more competitive conditions of the 1930s, when extensive mechanization in Continental coal fields had put Britain well behind in output per man shift (1,195 kg in 1936, to the Polish 2,073 kg, the German 1,710 kg and the Dutch 1,781 kg), P.E.P. concluded that the natural advantages of the British coal industry were still such that under conditions of free competition it could land coal on the German North Sea Coast or the American North Atlantic ports at a rather lower price than the coal supplied from native mines.[1]

Table XXII
Main Classes of British Exports, 1880, 1890 and 1900
(£000)

	1880	1890	1900
Cotton yarn and manufactures	75,564	74,431	69,751
Woollen and worsted yarns and manufactures	21,488	25,679	21,806
Linen yarn and manufactures	6,814	6,577	6,159
Iron, steel and other metals, and manufactures thereof	32,000	38,304	37,638
Machinery and mill work	9,264	16,411	19,620
Coal, coke, cinders and patent fuel	8,373	19,020	38,620

Source: Board of Trade, *British and Foreign Trade and Industrial Conditions*, P.P. 1903, LXVII, 299-300.

Transport costs were so large an element in competition that Britain's relative position in overseas trade for coal was bound to decline as coal mining developed in distant areas, as transport costs fell within coal producing nations (including the Republics), and as the shipping services of international competitors like Germany and the United States improved. The virtual monopoly enjoyed by British producers in the overseas coal trade for the late nineteenth century was reduced to about 85% in 1900, to 80% in 1906 and to 71% during the national coal miners' strike year of 1912.[2] Freight costs and local competition ensured that out of the 76·2 million tons of British coal shipped in 1913, 65·6 million went to Europe and the Mediterranean, and only 10·6

[1] *Ibid.*, p. 152.
[2] H. Stanley Jevons, *The British Coal Trade* (London, 1915), p. 682.

million to countries outside Europe, distributed between South America (7·6), West and South Africa and the Islands (1·9), countries east of Suez (0·9), Central America (0·1), and North America (0·1).[1]

It is worth taking a closer look at performance in the separate Republics. Britain had lost her markets to the United States in Canada, Mexico, the Caribbean and Central America. She barely held her own on the West Coast, and then only on the basis of a steady demand for the best Welsh steam coal; in ordinary qualities, it was practically impossible to compete with local production or with imported Japanese and Australian coal.[2] Chile was meeting rather under half its own consumption in the early 1900s. Accurate figures for local production are unobtainable, but one estimate put production at about 750,000 tons in 1904, compared with imports of 914,085 tons (445,742 from Britain, 457,020 from Australia, and 11,323 from the United States). Imported coal, either on its own or mixed with local coal, had to supply most needs for steam coal and smelting coal; the soft native coal, with a relatively low thermal output, was not competitive for mining, shipping or rail purposes at any great distance from the coal mining areas of the south.[3] British and Australian coal continued to be used by the nitrate oficinas in the north, replaced increasingly in the 1900s by imported oil at first from Talara in Peru and later from California. Peruvian oil had nearly replaced coal at Caleta Buena by as early as 1907, and its use was spreading south; Iquique's oil imports rose from £208,698 in 1908 to £406,453 in 1910, while coal fell from £508,842 to £468,555, and the Antofagasta oficinas were experimenting with fuel oil in place of coal early in 1912.[4]

In Peru herself, oil and coal production combined to keep a check on imported coal. Britain sent 58,703 tons of coal, coke and manufactured fuel to Peru in 1913. Peru's oil production was 214,947 tons in 1912, and her Goyllarisquisca and Quishuarcancha coal-mines extracted 1,000 tons of coal per day in late 1913.[5]

---

[1] *Report of the Departmental Committee on Shipping and Shipbuilding*, P.P. 1918, XIII, 548, 551.

[2] Jevons, *Coal Trade*, p. 687.

[3] Rowley's report on Chile for 1904, P.P. 1905, LXXXVII, 559.

[4] Danks' report on Caleta Buena for 1907, P.P. 1908, CX, 94; Hudson's report on Iquique for 1911, P.P. 1912-13, XCIV, 548; Bird's report on Antofagasta for 1911, *ibid.*, 526.

[5] Wilson's report on Peru for 1913, P.P. 1914, XCIII, 725, 737.

Mexico, among the Republics, made the most progress towards self sufficiency. She had always used water power, and she was the first of the Latin American Republics to make use of hydro-electricity in quantity. Acccording to Dr Antonio Peñafiel's calculations of power in use in Mexico in 1902, 66,008 horse power was steam, 32,147 water and 17,828 electric.[1] Mexican coal production rose from some 350,000 tons at the beginning of the century to about a million tons in 1911. But high transport costs within Mexico limited its market to the factories of Chihuahua and Nuevo León and to the railway lines within reach of the Sabinas coal-fields.[2] Electricity and above all the large Mexican oil strikes in and after 1908 cut back the expected expansion of Mexican coal imports during a period of rapid industrialization. Imports of coal, which had reached £695,293 in 1907-8 principally from the United States, fell to £499,783 in 1909-10.[3] British exports of coal, coke and patent fuel to Mexico fell from 238,171 tons in 1907 to 156,013 tons in 1910, 54,997 tons in 1911, and 22,545 tons in 1913. In some parts of Mexico the substitution was rapid and complete. Nunn reported from Vera Cruz early in 1912 that the use of petroleum as a fuel was rapidly supplanting coal in all branches of commerce; all the railways based on Vera Cruz had converted to oil, and the coal trade had practically ceased.[4]

Nevertheless, a *Times* engineering correspondent was not incorrect for *South* America in dismissing local production as 'trifling as compared with the needs of the people', and native petroleum as 'of no appreciable importance at present as a factor in the power problem'. His conclusion, in an article on 'Power resources in South America', was that power for industrial purposes was obtained from imported coal, native wood, wind, water and oil, in that order. South America had imported coal to the value of £12,300,000 during the three years 1903-5; this had risen by 46·3% to £18 million for 1906-8 and by a further 22·2% for 1909-11; 'of this coal Great Britain supplied practically 90%, the United States, Australia, and South Africa contributing the

---

[1] Quoted in Jerome's report on Mexico for 1904, P.P. 1905, XC, 789.
[2] Guadalupe Nava Oteo in Cosío Villegas (ed.), *Mexico: La Vida Económica*, I, 247-8.
[3] Biorklund's report on Imports into Mexico from July 1905 to June 1910, P.P. 1912-13, XCVII, 732.
[4] Nunn's report on Vera Cruz for 1911, *ibid.*, 792.

rest'.[1] (Table XXIII). In fact, Argentina, which was the most important market for imported coal, took no less than 94·4% of her coal from Britain in 1912.[2] Again it was the rapid expansion of British exports to Argentina which formed by far the largest element in the trade. Argentina had no accessible coal and very little wood. Her capacity for employing water power or generating

Table XXIII

British Coal, Coke and Manufactured Fuel Exports to Selected Republics
(000 tons)

	1890	1895	1900	1905	1910	1913
Argentina	567·3	909·3	771·2	1,802·3	2,920·7	3,769·9
Brazil	660·5	839·1	793·6	1,107·6	1,710·1	2,124·8
Uruguay	275·0	294·4	460·0	359·7	1,013·0	793·9
Chile	356·7	400·2	298·0	593·9	1,048·1	755·8

Source: *U.K. Trade and Navigation Accounts*, rounded to the nearest hundred.

hydro-electricity was limited. Oil had been discovered in several parts of the Republic, but the 19,000 tons produced by the Comodoro Rivadavia oil-fields in 1912 went no way towards meeting the 2 million tons estimated as needed to displace coal imports.[3] The result was a healthy trade for South Wales, and a substantial boost to the general level of exports to Argentina.

[1] *The Times*, South American Supplement, 29 October 1912, 6a.
[2] Mackie's report on Buenos Aires for 1912-13, P.P. 1914, LXXXIX, 571.
[3] *Ibid.*, 548.

CHAPTER IX

Latin American Exports

PERHAPS the strongest element in Britain's success as a world trader before 1914 was the importance of the British market for foreign produce. In 1850 British net imports (exclusive of products intended for re-export) formed as much as 28% (£79·2 million) of the world's aggregate non-British exports (£287 million). In 1913, Britain still took 19% of a very much enlarged total, £659·2 million out of £3,530 million; if re-exports are included, the share was 22%.[1] On the other hand, if these imports are broken down, 44% in 1913 came from Europe and the Mediterranean. The remaining 56% was itself divided as follows—40% from North America, 22% from east of Suez, 14% from Australasia, 5% from Africa, 16% from South America and 3% from Central America.[2] In 1913, out of the £659·2 million of imports retained in the United Kingdom, £64·8 million came from Latin America.

Figure IV (p. 277) shows that for Latin American exports, even more than for imports, trade with the United Kingdom was dominated after the '80s by Argentina. Britain was a selective market for Latin American exports, both in the quality demanded and in the range of products imported. By nineteenth-century standards, Britons were high-quality consumers; only the better qualities of imported meat, grain, coffee, tobacco, wool, cotton, could be sure of a sale. The quality of Latin American produce, for one

---

[1] Albert H. Imlah, *Economic Elements in the Pax Britannica* (Cambridge, Mass. 1958), pp. 190-1.

[2] S. G. Sturmey, *British Shipping and World Competition* (London, 1962), p. 24.

reason or another, seldom approached the best qualities available on world markets, and indifferent quality control normally disqualified products for the British consumer. Then, Britain was interested only in a limited range of the traditional Latin American exports; she bought meat and grain, rubber, tin and copper. She was either never, or no longer, a significant factor in world markets for many of the more important Latin American products in the decades before the First World War, for coffee, nitrates, cocoa, sugar, tobacco, wool, cotton, hides and skins. With some it was a question of taste, with others of quality, with others of alternative products to which the British market was more accustomed or better suited.

The tendency, in any case, was to substitute an Empire product where possible, often as an unplanned outcome of the natural swing towards colonial trade so evident in British exports. Dr Wolff has pointed out that the share of Britain's food imports from imperial sources rose from 19·8% in 1870 to 30·3% in 1913; Empire sources of raw materials never provided less than a third of Britain's raw material imports over the same period.[1] This was bound to affect interest in Latin American products, even if it often meant that British custom was not as good as it might have been rather than that it was redirected altogether. The process was evident for two of the traditional, monopoly products of Latin America, in cinchona bark (a source of quinine) and coca (for the local anaesthetic, alkaloid cocaine). Cinchona bark, of first importance to the Colombian export economy, arrived at its maximum development in 1881-2 when the value exported reached some $30 million. A decade later the trade had completely collapsed under competition from India and Java.[2] Britain's total demand for cocaine for legitimate medicinal purposes did not exceed 4 cwt a year before the war, and it was only the convenience of obtaining manufactured cocaine from Germany which prevented her from developing an entirely independent source of supply in Ceylon.[3]

The same was likely to be true of any product for which the

---

[1] Richard D. Wolff, 'Economic Aspects of British Colonialism in Kenya, 1895-1930', *Journal of Economic History*, XXX (1970), 274.

[2] Thomson's report on the Agricultural Products of Tolima, 1895, P.P. 1895, CII, 102-3.

[3] 'Memorandum on the Supply of Essential Drugs', printed as Appendix to the Committee on Commercial and Industrial Policy, *Interim Report on certain Essential Industries*, P.P. 1918, XIII, 219.

conditions were right within the Empire. Britain was a good customer for Central American and Caribbean bananas. Of the 10·2 million bunches shipped from Costa Rica, the largest Central American producer, in 1914, 7·1 million went to the United States and 3·1 million to Britain.[1] But naturally the British government attempted, without much success, to develop banana production as an alternative to sugar in the depressed colonies of the British West Indies. Even in the world sugar market, British capacity was limited by cheap European beet sugar and by existing suppliers in Java, the West Indies, Guiana, India and Mauritius, so that Latin America found a place only when the beet-sugar crop fell short of demand. The United Kingdom took a bare 21,150 cwt of unrefined Cuban sugar in 1909, 1,926,730 cwt in 1910 and 76,957 cwt in 1911, and parallel fluctuations were experienced by each of the Latin American suppliers, Haiti and San Domingo, Brazil, Peru and Mexico, over years for which Britain's total imports of sugar were rising steadily. In the case of cocoa, so large an element in the exports of Brazil, Ecuador, Venezuela and the Dominican Republic to the markets of France, Germany and the United States, Britain was meeting much of her needs by the end of the century from her own colonies. Chambers reported from Guayaquil for 1890 that cocoa, which had formerly gone to Britain for consumption or re-export, was now finding its way direct to Amsterdam, Rotterdam, Antwerp and Hamburg; 'as the English market is principally supplied with cocoa from her own colonies, a very much smaller supply goes there than used to be the case in previous years'.[2] Development of cocoa production on the Gold Coast undermined both Ecuadorian and Brazilian production, and swamped the English home market. In 1900 the Gold Coast exported 545 tons to Brazil's 16,916 and Ecuador's 18,922. Gold Coast exports were greater than either by 1914, with 53,735 tons to Brazil's 40,766 and Ecuador's 47,210.[3] Britain in 1913 was importing very nearly twice as much raw cocoa from British Possessions (principally West Africa and the West Indies) as she was from foreign countries.

A British industrialist, anxious to control his sources of raw materials, was likely to look to his neighbours in Europe, to the

[1] Cox's report on Costa Rica for 1914, P.P. 1914-16, LXXI, 939.
[2] Chambers' report on Guayaquil for 1890, P.P. 1890-91, LXXXV, 633.
[3] Ivar Erneholm, *Cacao Production in South America* (Gothenburg, 1948), p. 90.

Empire, perhaps to the disciplined suppliers of other colonial Powers. At the turn of the century Levers were developing plantations in the British Solomon Islands, British West Africa and the Belgian Congo. Both Crosfields and Gossages had West African interests, while Crosfields were in business in Fiji. Guest, Keen and Nettlefolds, Consett, Dowlais, Coltness, Dorman Long, William Baird, John Brown, Cammells, Bolckow Vaughan, and Millom and Askam owned extensive foreign hematite ore supplies, particularly in Spain but also in Sweden and Newfoundland. The United Alkali Company acquired copper properties in Spain in 1903 and 1904 to secure its supply of pyrites. The Tharsis Copper and Sulphur Company, formed by a number of manufacturing chemists in 1867 to safeguard sulphur supplies, took its sulphur from its own mines in Spain. Pilkingtons bought an interest in a Belgian silver sand supplier in 1903. No physical or political obstacles existed to prevent the development of a similar pattern for Latin America, but simple convenience was likely to put the Republics low on the list.

Three of Latin America's most important exports, tobacco, coffee and nitrates, made little impression in the United Kingdom. Britain was an excellent market for high-quality Cuban cigars, but the main outlets for Cuban tobacco were Bremen, Hamburg, Antwerp and the United States. Mexican tobacco found some sale in Britain, but exports were never large. Germany had always bought most of Brazil's exported tobacco. Of the 1860 exports, 41,274 bales were listed as for Germany, 23,758 to Channel 'for orders', and 2,114 for Britain; Consul Morgan pointed out that almost all the Channel shipments and even the small shipment to Great Britain ultimately reached Germany.[1] Hamburg and Bremen in turn acted as distributing centres not only for the German hinterland but also for much of Northern Europe and European Russia. Whatever the final destination, and there is no doubt that the major part remained in Germany, 24,473 tons out of the 29,388 tons of Brazilian unmanufactured tobacco exported in 1913 went to Germany.[2]

As late as the 1913-14 crop Britain took 75·64% of Costa Rican coffee exports.[3] Costa Rican coffee enjoyed a high reputation, and

---

[1] Morgan's report on Bahia for 1860, P.P. 1862, LVIII, 636.
[2] Hambloch's report on Brazil for 1919, P.P. 1920, XLIII, 120.
[3] Cox's report on Costa Rica for 1914, P.P. 1914-16, LXXI, 944.

a trading connection had developed over the years; otherwise the United Kingdom proved to be no market for Latin American coffee. Britons never had much taste for it, a fact which consuls in Brazil found unsurprising since 'certainly, a more unpalatable beverage than the mixture ordinarily presented [in England] as coffee cannot well be imagined'.[1] So long as Britain maintained her commercial connections, some part of the world's coffee crop continued to pass through her ports, but of the 80,287 tons of coffee of all sorts imported into the United Kingdom in 1870, 64,652 tons were re-exported, and only 13,674 tons were absorbed by the home market.[2] The United States was far and away the best market for Brazilian coffee exports, and a rapidly rising consumption of coffee per head, in contrast to a static or even declining *per capita* consumption in the United Kingdom, kept her well in the lead. Of Brazilian coffee exports in 1913, 294,884 tons went to the United States, 111,938 tons to Germany, 110,817 tons to France and only 14,770 tons to the United Kingdom.[3] By this time Britain had lost her re-export trade, and virtually the whole of the Brazilian import was intended for home consumption.

As for fertilizers, Britain was the best market for Peruvian guano in the mid-nineteenth century, and about 50% came to the United Kingdom for consumption or re-export. Guano imports reached their highest point at 302,207 tons in 1858, but exaggerated prices of up to £13 a ton and the development of specialized substitute fertilizers halved Peruvian earnings from British sales over the next twenty years.[4] Nitrates replaced guano on the West Coast, and Germany took the greater part of Chilean nitrates as a fertilizer for the beet-sugar crop. British firms continued to handle a substantial part of the nitrate trade, and much of the nitrate was shipped to Channel ports 'for orders'. But a sizeable competitive supply of nitrates developed as a by-product of the British gas industry, while superphosphates were in any case more popular with English farmers so that demand for Chilean nitrates was comparatively low. In 1905 Britain took 1,222,528 quintals to France's 3,368,603, Germany's 8,622,210 and North America's

---

[1] Phipps' report on Brazil, 24 June 1872, P.P. 1872, LIX, 645.
[2] *Ibid.*, 646.
[3] Hambloch's report on Brazil for 1919, P.P. 1920, XLIII, 121.
[4] W. M. Mathew, 'Peru and the British Guano Market, 1840-1870', *Economic History Review*, 2s. XXIII (1970), 112-13, 125.

7,703,786.[1] Chilean government statistics, which contain a large 'for orders' element, are not very helpful in this context. Atlee explained that the Chilean statistics for 1911 showed 1,086,483 metric tons as exported to the United Kingdom, whereas it was known from other sources that the nitrate consumed did not exceed 150,000 tons.[2] The amounts recorded in the English statistics as imported from Chile in 1910 and 1911, 121,642 tons and 125,281 tons respectively, confirm his point.

Raw Cotton and Wool

Latin America was not even significantly placed among the suppliers of raw material to the British textile industry. At the end of the 1780s, $2\frac{1}{2}$ million lb of cotton were said to have come from the Portuguese settlements in Brazil out of a total British import of about $22\frac{1}{2}$ million lb.[3] The expansion of the cotton manufacturing industry created a comfortable demand for Brazilian cotton, and some 20% of the cotton used in the United Kingdom in 1801-10 was supplied by Brazil, rising as a result of the break in North American supplies to about 31% in the decennial period 1811-20.[4] Thereafter a decline in European prices and the attraction of alternative crops to the producer in Brazil meant that, apart from the sudden expansion of demand for Brazilian cotton during and immediately after the American Civil War, Brazil's production remained more or less static, her home demand increased so as to absorb much of that production, and her position in British imports sank to insignificance. Table XXIV shows the situation for the nineteenth century. Britain remained easily the most important market for such raw cotton as Brazil could spare after meeting the demand of her own considerable cotton textile industry. Of a total export of 16,733,942 kilos in 1912, 13,670,130 kilos went to the United Kingdom.[5] But although Brazilian cotton exports were expanding rapidly at the time, it was a drop in the ocean. An average of only 1·7% of British annual imports of cotton for the

[1] Rowley's report on Chile for 1905, P.P. 1906, CXXIII, 191.
[2] Atlee's report on Valparaiso for 1910-11, P.P. 1912-13, XCIV, 589.
[3] Sydney J. Chapman, *The Lancashire Cotton Industry* (Manchester, 1904), p. 143.
[4] Phipps' report on Brazil, 24 June 1872, P.P. 1872, LIX, 647.
[5] Birch's report on Brazil for 1912-13, P.P. 1914-16, LXXI, 199.

five years 1910-14 came from Brazil, with another 1·3% from Peru. The rest was divided almost entirely between the United States (74·3%) and the British Empire (21·9%).[1]

Traditionally England had always herself been a large wool producer, while Spain and Prussia supplied most of the imported wool at the beginning of the nineteenth century. Australian wool was insignificant until 1814, after which an improvement in quality and the introduction of Merino sheep brought Australia rapidly

Table XXIV

Raw Cotton: Sources of Supply for European and North American Manufacturing, 1836-1900

(million lb, annual averages)

Years	America	Brazil	West Indies	East Indies	Egypt, Smyrna	Total
1836-40	585·7	25·3	13·4	56·5	30·1	711·0
1841-45	816·3	18·9	9·4	72·6	23·8	941·0
1846-50	964·2	23·8	6·3	86·7	29·7	1,110·7
1851-55	1,254·7	27·1	6·3	134·8	60·0	1,482·9
1856-60	1,633·7	27·7	7·2	207·9	57·0	1,933·5
1861-65	531·7	36·2	14·6	491·3	191·4	1,265·2
1866-70	1,108·6	99·9	33·2	576·5	190·9	2,009·1
1871-75	1,682·3	108·8	42·3	538·5	238·0	2,609·9
1876-80	2,231·5	43·7	15·9	407·4	268·7	2,967·2
1881-85	2,717·2	54·1	11·6	540·3	292·5	3,615·7
1886-90	3,170·0	52·2	13·6	583·1	301·7	4,120·6
1891-95	3,773·6	50·5	13·6	453·4	455·7	4,746·8
1896-1900	4,594·5	24·6	15·6	300·4	575·4	5,510·5

Source: Board of Trade, *Comparative Trade Statistics*, P.P. 1903, LXVII, 755.

to the front. Henry Hughes, giving evidence as a wool broker before the 1833 Committee, commented on the remarkable improvement in the cleanliness and quality of Australian wool. He could sell as much as he could import; there was 'no other wool known to spin so well as the Australian wool from its length of staple and peculiar softness'. Hughes predicted that it would eventually entirely displace Spanish and German wool in British imports.[2] Latin American wool, on the other hand, was nothing like as well

[1] *Report of the Departmental Committee on the Textile Trades*, P.P. 1918, XIII, 649.
[2] Minutes of Evidence, *Report of the Select Committee on Manufactures, Commerce and Shipping*, P.P. 1833, VI, Q.1260.

suited to the British market. The 'long, lustrous fibres of the alpaca', in which Peru and Chile had a monopoly, sold well to the West Riding worsted industry, and Peruvian exports increased from 5,700 lb in 1834 to nearly 4 million lb in the early '70s; an alpaca weft combined with a cotton warp produced a lustrous fabric well suited to the light, bright ladies' dress goods in fashion during the middle years of the century.[1] Argentina, by crossing her coarse-wooled native 'freollas' with imported Merinos from Spain, Saxons from Germany and Rambouillets crossed with Negrettis from France, had produced a reasonable, fine-wooled sheep, so that her exports of wool increased from 1,609,650 kilos in 1840 to 97,518,089 kilos in 1880.[2] But she was selling a short wool unsuited to the British trade.

La Plata wools, and the merino wools generally of the southern hemisphere (South America, South Africa and Australia), experienced a revival of interest on the British market with the shift of fashion in the third quarter of the century. Britain's traditional worsted stuffs, now out of favour, had employed long, lustrous wools; the all-wool goods of France were manufactured from short merino wool. La Plata wool acquired an unfortunate reputation for arriving in a dirty condition, with an excessive proportion of burr and scab, and Australian merino was generally preferred by British manufacturers. But Sir Jacob Behrens, a leading figure in the Bradford wool trade, felt sure that the 'great prejudice against Buenos Ayres wool' was dying out by the mid-'80s:

> there is one feature which gives me great hope for Bradford, and that is that every year we are employing more and more of a class of wool of which France in 1884 worked up 220,000,000 lbs. weight, that is to say, the South American wool, of which in the fleece we imported only 6,000,000 lbs. I believe that the large employment of that wool has been one of the causes of the French being able to undersell us in many of their all-wool goods. They have worked that wool extensively whilst our spinners did not like to meddle with it, but every one now, I find, is trying it.[3]

[1] Sigsworth, *Black Dyke Mills*, pp. 234-5.
[2] Simon G. Hanson, *Argentine Meat and the British Market* (Stanford, 1938), pp. 15-16.
[3] Minutes of Evidence, *Report of the Royal Commission on the Depression of Trade and Industry*, P.P. 1886, LXXI, QQ.6731, 6870.

Undoubtedly, British imports of South American wool—largely Argentine and Uruguayan—increased very considerably after the 1880s. Yet Britain still accounted for only 17% of the South American clip in 1913, 35% of which went to France and Belgium (partly for re-export to Germany), and 30% direct to Germany and Austria. South America, in turn, was contributing only 32% of the world's production for export, in contrast with 68% from the British Empire. 85% of the world's exportable production of merino came from the British Empire, and 45% of the cross-bred, while the proportions for South America were 15% and 54% respectively.[1] In aggregate, the United Kingdom imported 641·6 million lb of Empire wool in 1913, to South America's 94·7 million lb.

Beef and Mutton

By the early years of the twentieth century, Britain's main interest in Latin American produce was in certain minerals, particularly copper and tin, in rubber, and, above all, in Argentine meat, maize and wheat. It was meat and grain which gave Argentina so disproportionate a share in the expansion of Latin American exports to the United Kingdom after the mid-'80s.

Britain had always taken a part of the traditional pastoral products of Latin America, tallow, hides, bones, horns and hoofs, hair, tongues, sheepskins and wool, even if British consumers never quite reached the level of desperation which might have sold the local dried salt beef, 'macerated caoutchouc lumps of tasajo, [which] required soaking for something like twenty-four hours and boiling for twelve hours more, and after all was little more palatable than good white leather'.[2] Britain was still an importer of animal products in 1913. She had lost her re-export trade in hides, so that of the £881,522 of raw hides imported from Argentina in 1913 almost the entire amount, £860,649, was retained for home consumption; she took and retained £291,028 of Argentine tallow, £44,637 of bones for manufacturing and manure, £34,282 of sheepskins, £22,027 of horse hair, £718 of horns and hoofs. But whereas before the '80s virtually no meat had been imported from Latin

[1] *Report of the Departmental Committee on the Textiles Trades*, P.P 1918, XIII, 664-9.
[2] *Chambers's Journal*, January 1867, 39-40.

S

America, other than beef extract from the mid-'60s and small quantities of canned meat in the '70s, by 1912 meat had completely displaced the traditional products in order of magnitude. A rising *per capita* consumption of meat in the United Kingdom, from an annual 108 lb in 1880 to over 130 lb in 1900-4, together with a continual expansion of population, created a demand which had to be filled by ever-increasing imports. Domestic production responded in spite of falling prices, and in 1913 British producers were still supplying 63·22% of local consumption of beef and veal and 52·58% of mutton and lamb. But room remained for an import, in chilled and frozen beef alone, of 9,200,884 cwt, no less than 7,171,875 cwt of which were coming from Argentina.[1]

Argentina's difficulty was to supply a product of sufficient quality to compete in British markets. An attempt was made as early as 1869 to ship live cattle from Uruguay to England, but mortality on the voyage and the poor quality of the cattle in comparison with home and North American stock prevented repeat shipments. These and similar problems continued to place a restraint on the competitive position of Argentine livestock right up to the closure of British ports to Argentine cattle in 1900, as a precaution against endemic foot-and-mouth disease. Only the low initial price of Argentine cattle could account for a sudden expansion from 653 head exported to Britain in 1890 to an average of about 70,000 head in the late '90s. The journey was nearly three times the length of the North Atlantic crossing, with correspondingly higher expenses for attendance, fodder and incidentals; freight was double; losses of weight *en route* were estimated at 12-25% compared with a maximum of 7-10% from the United States; mortality was ten times as high.[2] The real opportunity came with the first successful shipments of frozen meat from Argentina at the end of the '70s. Mutton was the first to benefit, since it suffered less than beef in quality, flavour and appearance. Frozen Argentine mutton had to compete only with the mutton of Australia and New Zealand, and once Argentine breeders were able to change the prevailing strain from the small, lean Merino with an average weight of less than 40 lb to the 55-60 lb Lincoln favoured in English markets, Argentine exports made rapid progress. New

---

[1] Street's report on the Meat Export Trade of Australia, P.P. 1914-16, XLVI, 17-18.
[2] Hanson, *Argentine Meat*, pp. 80-2.

Zealand maintained her lead in the best imported mutton, but Argentine mutton overtook Australian in volume in 1885 and in quality by the end of the decade.[1] Australian mutton recovered, and Argentina's lead was maintained neither in quality nor quantity. British imports of Argentine mutton reached 1,114,800 cwt in 1900, rose to a peak of 1,782,066 cwt in 1911, and were down to 1,012,347 cwt in 1913; New Zealand in 1913 supplied Britain with 2,200,525 cwt to Australia's 1,665,859 cwt, Uruguay's 164,983 cwt and Chile's 160,543 cwt. Argentine expansion was checked by the competing claims of wool production within Argentina herself and by the spread of agricultural land at the expense of sheep grazing, as much as it was by any superiority in quality and value for Australasian and home-grown mutton on the English market.

Frozen Argentine beef, which in any case lost much of its juiciness in freezing, had to compete with imported live cattle from the United States, with American chilled beef, and with the higher quality frozen beef of New Zealand and Australia. The result was that the Argentine *frigoríficos* found it impossible to develop a market until the quality of Argentine beef was raised sufficiently to compete with Australian, and until the successful application of the new chilling process to Argentine beef had given Argentina a competitive advantage over Australia which no effort could overcome. Quality was the first problem. The native cattle were 'small, long-horned, thick-hided, slow growing beasts, of every conceivable colour', well suited to the trade in jerked beef, hides, tallow, etc., but not to a more sophisticated meat consumption, at home or abroad. The first short-horn bull was imported into Argentina in 1848, and continued attempts were made, more particularly after the formation of Sociedad Rural in 1866, to improve quality. But progress was slow, more attention was paid to the improvement of sheep than of cattle, and F. R. St John was right in complaining, as late as the mid-'70s, of the 'insignificance [£752 in 1874] in the amount of that item of imports which of all others is the most needed in this country, namely, blood-stock'.

The all but total disregard of the first principle in cattle-breeding, viz., judicious selection, has, in spite of the many natural advantages offered by this country, left that portion of

[1] *Ibid.*, pp. 84-5.

the live stock which comprises horned cattle and horses very much in the same condition in which it was probably first introduced by the early Spaniards.[1]

The higher quality demanded by Argentina's own home market, while no prospect yet existed of quality exports, must undoubtedly have provided the foremost incentive for improvement, and in the '70s Durham short horns were the favourite cross with local cattle, at least among the English cattle breeders of northern Santa Fé.[2] Arthur Peel, reporting in 1895 on the agricultural and pastoral industries of Argentina, remarked on the 'brisk reformation' over the last twenty years in cattle breeding; few herds in the main cattle provinces had no English blood. The Durham short horn was still most in demand, but the Hereford, a more hardy animal, was tried on the frontier lands, and the polled Angus had attracted some attention for the newly developed live export trade.[3]

The improved quality of Argentine beef won over English markets temporarily lost to Queensland beef during the droughts of 1900-02. Argentine beef was able to establish a firm place in British tastes and preferences. But it was the chilling process which gave Argentina a decisive lead. Chilled beef was first shipped from Argentina in commercial quantities in 1901, and the Argentine product soon took over from declining North American chilled beef exports, now diverted to an insatiable home market. Chilled beef had the advantage over frozen beef of preserving its juices. It needed more space and attention in shipment, but it commanded a better price; Ross reported only a few months after the first shipments that Argentine chilled beef was selling at about $\frac{1}{2}$d. per lb more than frozen beef for the forequarters and 1d. more for the hindquarters.[4] Above all, the length of the voyage, while just suited by a small margin to the River Plate trade, made Australian competition impracticable on a commercial scale. The chilling process, in turn, demanded a higher quality of beef and provided a strong stimulus for improved breeding. In the decade ending in 1910, Argentine imports of pedigree stock, mainly cattle, with horses, sheep, asses and pigs in descending order, amounted to a

---

[1] St John's report on Argentina for 1874, P.P. 1876, LXXIII, 198.
[2] Barnett's report on Rosario for 1876, P.P. 1877, LXXXIII, 8.
[3] Peel's report on the Agricultural and Pastoral Industries in Argentina, 14 May 1895, P.P. 1895, CII, 37-8.
[4] Ross's report on Buenos Aires for 1901, P.P. 1902, CV, 129.

grand total of £2,187,454. Mackie commented on the marked change in the style and scale of pastoral activity in Argentina.

The old-fashioned ranch or *estancia* is fast disappearing to make room for the large skilfully managed farm. To the uninitiated it would be difficult to realise that an *estancia* such as that of San Jacinto extends over an area of no less than 244 square miles, of which some 65 square miles are covered by carefully enclosed pastures of rich lucerne grass, where 100,000 cattle, bred from pedigree stock, a similar number of highly bred Lincoln sheep and some 10,000 horses represent the livestock; while what used to be a modest farmhouse is now a mansion standing in its own park and gardens.[1]

Argentina never developed into a significant competitor in the world's dairy industry before 1914. It was difficult to match the quality of Danish and Australian dairy products, and quality remained a barrier to the Argentine dairy industry, as it did to any appreciable development of meat exports to the United Kingdom from any of the competing Latin American cattle lands. Although efforts were made to develop frozen beef exports from Brazil and Venezuela in the last years before 1914, and frozen mutton from Southern Chile, the 61·18% of British imports in 1913 labelled as 'South American' was almost entirely Argentine. In fact, Argentina was well ahead over a wide area of meat imports. It had long been obvious that the home demand in the United States was overtaking production and that the surplus for export was on the decline. But as Mr Justice Street pointed out at the time, the actual cessation of American exports to Britain had come more suddenly and dramatically than anyone anticipated. In 1907 the United States was still the largest supplier of meat to Britain (in the shape of beef and live cattle in weight equivalent to 231,599 tons). By the end of 1913 the United States had actually taken 6,621 tons of re-exported meat from Britain to meet the requirements of the New York and Boston markets, and was now a free importer of Australian and South American meat. South America in 1913 supplied virtually *all* the chilled beef imported by the United Kingdom, 262,400 tons out of 262,801 tons, leaving only 401 tons from the United States and Canada; of beef in general, frozen

---

[1] Mackie's report on Buenos Aires for 1911, P.P. 1912-13, XCIV, 126-7.

and chilled, she supplied 82·62% of British imports (29·97% of total consumption); of mutton and lamb, 25·82% (11·96% of total consumption).[1]

Grain

South America—and again 'South America' might almost as well read 'Argentina'—did not provide for anything like so large a share of British wheat comsumption. Britain imported a total of 105·9 million cwt in 1913, of which 50·7 million came from British Possessions (Canada, India and Australasia). Argentina (14·8 million cwt) was Britain's second largest foreign supplier after the United States (34·1 million); Chile (0·8 million) was fourth, but well behind Russia at 5·0 million cwt. Argentina, however, led the way for maize by a large margin, supplying 38·9 million cwt in 1913 out of a total import of 49·2 million.

Nobody really believed in Argentina's potential as a grain exporter until the '70s, and doubts persisted to the end of the century. 'There never was a greater mistake made here,' wrote *The Economist's* Buenos Aires Correspondent on 31 December 1897, 'than the fad of supplanting pastoral industry by tillage, exclusively of wheat. . . . Argentina will always be a very spasmodic and uncertain factor in the world's grain supply. . . .'[2] The interior provinces traditionally supplied their own wants for wheat and maize. The littoral provinces, Buenos Aires, Santa Fé, Entre Rios and Corrientes, were dependent on imports from Chile and the United States, and they remained so until mass immigration in the '60s and the settlement of the land showed that grain could be produced in great quantities without the artificial irrigation believed indispensable on the pampas.

Even then, nobody quite knew *which* grain would prove exportable. A cargo of wheat was sent to England in 1872 at the point when Argentina first managed to produce enough wheat to cease herself to be an importer, but 'the result was very unsatisfactory, as the quality was not appreciated by the millers'.[3] Consul Joel thought that the future lay with maize, and possibly with barley

---

[1] Street's report on the Meat Export Trade of Australia, P.P. 1914-16, XLVI, 17, 23.

[2] *The Economist*, 5 February 1898, 195.

[3] Bridgett's report on Buenos Aires for 1872, P.P. 1874, LXVI, 188.

and linseed. An unusually large crop of maize in 1873 left a surplus on the local market, and a trial shipment of 80 tons was despatched to Liverpool early in September with such good results that 2,000 tons had been shipped by the end of the year. Joel doubted whether wheat, subject as it was to so many vicissitudes (locusts, smut, too much or too little rain) had ever made a profit for its Argentine cultivators, except in a particularly good year. He agreed that

> The uncertainty as to what kind of grain can be profitably exported may appear strange, but it must be borne in mind that no more than fifteen years have elapsed since agriculture was first thought of in this province [Santa Fé] . . . and it was only during the past year that the absolute necessity of seeking a foreign market for the surplus forced itself upon the attention of those interested in this trade.[1]

Thereafter, the success of Argentine wheat depended, rather as it had for beef, on exceptionally low production costs and a slow improvement in quality. Locusts and hailstorms in particular, but also rain, frost, drought, even Indians (until the end of the '70s), added to the troubles of the 'colonists'. Ocean freight rates to the United Kingdom in 1890 were less than a shilling a quarter from the Baltic, three shillings from the Black Sea, two shillings from New York. The rate was five shillings a quarter from the River Plate (Paraná), and the South American freight factor was still a serious disadvantage right up to 1913.[2] But good wheat growing land, after the collapse of land speculations in 1890-91, was very cheap indeed in Argentina, with an average value for ploughed land, including animals, machines, utensils and rough buildings, of only £18 a hectare; the land alone in France fetched £80 a hectare.[3] Rent in Argentina varied considerably according to quality of land and distance from railway and port of shipment, while the rate for hired labour was high in season and often unpredictable. But Argentina could produce at a profit when wheat growing elsewhere was totally uneconomic. The price of wheat in Europe in the 1894-5 season was down to £1 a quarter. Even at this price the Argentine producer could make a modest profit. Within a 10-15

---

[1] Joel's report on Rosario for 1873, P.P. 1874, LXVII, 485-6.
[2] Douglass North, 'Ocean Freight Rates and Economic Development, 1750-1913', *Journal of Economic History*, XVIII (1958), 545-6, 551-2.
[3] Gastrell's report on Argentina for 1893, P.P. 1893-4, XCII, 292.

mile radius of a railway station, the hiring expenses of a family, the bags, threshing and cartage might in a good year be about nine shillings a quarter, to which railway and ocean freight charges added another seven shillings; four shillings were left to be divided between the landlord and his tenant.[1]

Quality control was more of a problem, and lack of capital among small producers, ignorance of or inattention to scientific farming, the absence of covered storage at depots, the shortage of grain elevators, made it difficult for Argentine wheat to compete with the graded, quality wheats of Canada and the United States. Even just before the war elevators existed only at the ports, and grain was taken to the quayside in bags; without elevators, classification

Table XXV

Argentine Wheat and Maize Imports into the United Kingdom, five-year averages 1886-90, 1901-5, 1909-13
(cwt)

	1886-90	1901-5	1909-13
Wheat	1,176,478	14,238,546	16,691,620
Maize	2,843,893	16,955,170	22,747,757

Source: *U.K. Trade and Navigation Accounts.*

was impossible. Yet the naturally good conditions for wheat production in the Republic made up for many deficiencies, both in quality and quantity. In a dry season like 1891 or 1892, Argentine wheat fetched prices in Europe on a par with American 'Red Winter'. Naturally, grain shipments were subject to large annual variations. The United Kingdom took 3·6 million quarters of Argentine maize in 1911, 38·9 million in 1913. But taken over five-year periods, the figures for Argentine grain imports into Britain show the healthy condition of the trade.

Copper, Tin and Rubber

For copper, tin and rubber, Britain's other main points of interest in Latin American exports before the war, she was both a re-exporter and a substantial consumer. In the early years the United Kingdom had served as a market-place for most Latin American

[1] Gastrell's report on Argentina for 1894, P.P. 1895, XCVI, 106, 109; *The Times*, 18 June 1894, 10b.

products. The development of Continental and North American mercantile houses and shipping services in and after the middle of the nineteenth century encouraged direct shipments and sales. But there were advantages in centralized selling, and although the hide market was lost to Antwerp, the cocoa market to Le Havre, the Caribbean sugar and tobacco market to New York, the wool market in part to the producers themselves at their own sales in Argentina and Australia, services were offered which continued to attract many of the world's products to the United Kingdom. Cecil Gosling explained how Bolivia, by 1910, was second only to the Malay Peninsula as a producer of tin; rubber, to about half the value of tin, was her second export. The United Kingdom took the bulk of both, but Bolivian tin and rubber were consigned to Liverpool, Swansea and London more for the free selling price than for use, 'though doubtless an appreciable amount finds its way to British works after sale'.[1] Tin and copper would normally have left the United Kingdom in a manufactured or semi-manufactured state, so that the figure for ores retained do not reveal the extent of re-exports; in 1913 Britain exported £1·1 million of copper ingots and £2·4 million of unwrought tin. Table XXVI shows the position for British imports and re-exports in 1913, with the reservation that since the exports included a manufactured component, the two columns can only give an idea of the flow without accurately representing the amount retained for home consumption.

Before Charles Goodyear discovered the vulcanization process in 1839, rubber had had little commercial value; some was used experimentally for crude waterproofing, and Brazilian india-rubber was exported in small quantities chiefly as shoes. Vulcanization made it possible to extend the applications to railway mechanicals, general engineering, and later to insulating material for the new electrical industries. Production in the Amazon Valley rose from a few tons in the early '20s to 8,635 tons in 1880. As demand increased in the engineering and electrical industries, production doubled over the next decade to 16,890 tons in 1890. The acceleration to 26,693 tons in 1900 owed much to the reapplication by the Dunlop patent of 1888 of a forty-year-old idea, the pneumatic tyre, at a time when conditions were right for a great extension first of the

[1] Gosling's report on Bolivia for 1910, P.P. 1911, XC, 342.

Table XXVI

British Imports of Brazilian, Peruvian and Bolivian Rubber, Chilean Copper Ore and Bolivian Tin Ore, total and retained, 1909–13

(£000)

	1909		1910		1911		1912		1913	
	Amount imported	Amount retained	Amount imported	Amount retained	Amount imported	Amount retained	Amount imported	Amount retained	Amount imported	Amount retained
Rubber, Brazilian	8,626·6	3,291·0	14,434·8	6,075·7	7,935·6	1,440·8	6,791·7	636·3	5,940·7	1,337·3
Rubber, Peruvian	731·4	319·9	1,117·3	699·7	711·9	296·3	701·5	405·3	445·7	272·5
Tin ore, Bolivian	1,026·9	909·0	1,081·5	979·0	1,353·4	1,156·8	1,389·7	1,139·0	2,082·6	1,839·1
Rubber, Bolivian	30·3	−52·3[1]	116·7	64·8	40·2	−11·5[1]	26·6	−6·9[1]	7·5	−17·0[1]
Copper ore, Chilean	493·5	470·6	468·0	467·9	428·6	428·5	450·8	450·2	419·6	418·4

[1] Re-exports in excess of Consigned Imports.

Source: *U.K. Trade and Navigation Accounts*, rounded to the nearest hundred.

bicycle industry and then of the new motor industry.[1] Demand exceeded supply. Prices rose from approximately 2s. 6d. per lb in 1889 to 4s. 6d. a lb in 1899. Of a world production amounting to 57,500 tons in 1899, 25,000 tons came from the Amazon district (Brazil, Peru and Bolivia), 3,500 tons from the rest of South America, and 2,500 tons from Central America and Mexico; the remainder was almost entirely West African. North America (the United States and Canada) and the United Kingdom took 21,000 tons each, and Continental Europe 15,500 tons.[2]

Unfortunately, higher prices attracted competition, and a familiar pattern recurred of replacement by colonial plantation production. All Latin American rubber producers experienced the same problems. Production costs were relatively high and irreducible. The wild rubber trees were widely dispersed and irregularly distributed. The great distance separating trees from packing and marketing centres not only raised transport costs but added to the wages and maintenance of labour; labour costs in the Amazon region in 1914 were calculated at the equivalent of 8s. 8d. a day compared with less than a shilling in the Far East.[3] In the Amazon, flooding restricted the tapping season to six months in the year.

Up to the end of the 1900s wild rubber producers were shielded from the worst effects of competition both by the constantly rising world demand for rubber and by the time taken for the new plantations to reach maturity. But just before the war the Brazilian government, faced with sharply falling prices and a predictable plantation output of 75,000 tons in 1914 rising to 200,000 tons in 1917, was desperately anxious for the future of the wild rubber industry. The Peruvians, whose costs were probably the highest of major producers, could console themselves only with the hope that plant disease and an increase in the cost of Singalese and Malayan plantation labour might yet reduce competition to equality with the Amazon.[4] It was a delusion. Although synthetic rubber did not become a serious factor in world markets until the Second

[1] Figures from Temple's report on Pará for 1900, P.P. 1901, LXXXI, 263.
[2] Temple's report on Amazonas, 1900, P.P. 1900, XCI, 41-2, 63.
[3] Birch's report on Brazil for 1912-13, P.P. 1914-16, LXXI, 194.
[4] *Ibid.*, 194; Michell's report on Iquitos for 1911, P.P. 1912-13, XCIX, 12.

World War, Table XXVII shows the shift against wild rubber as the plantations came into full production.

Britain's selective interest in Latin American exports, the loss of her entrepôt trade, and the decline of her commercial representation meant that, for the majority of Republics, the proportion of exports despatched to the United Kingdom after the middle of the nineteenth century fell to relative insignificance. From a coffee port like Santos in 1908, Britain accounted for only £399,787 out of a total export of £17,313,956; the previous year it had been

Table XXVII

World Rubber Production, Wild and Plantation, selected years, 1900-49
(000 tons)

	Wild	Plantation
1900	44·5	0·5
1910	82·5	12·5
1920	35·0	307·5
1925	37·5	490·0
1929	25·0	845·0
1932	7·5	702·5
1941	27·5	1,572·5
1947	35·0	1,225·0
1949	27·5	1,455·0

Source: M. G. Kendall (ed.), *The Sources and Nature of the Statistics of the United Kingdom* (London, 1952), I, 100.

£748,190 out of £21,418,023.[1] The natural destination for the export trade of Mexico, Central America and the Northern Republics was the United States. Out of a total Mexican export of £29,987,351 in 1910-11, £22,917,544 went to the United States, when Britain took only £3,662,990.[2] Ecuador's exports to the United Kingdom in 1909 were valued at £250,000, to the United States £683,000, and to France, as the principal entrepôt for Ecuadorian cocoa, £892,000.[3]

Further south, Argentina sent Britain the greater part of her exports, grain and meat. The United Kingdom still provided a

[1] Sandall's report on Santos for 1908, P.P. 1909, XCII, 575.
[2] Stringer's report on Mexico for 1911, P.P. 1912-13, XCVII, 867-8.
[3] Cartwright's report on Ecuador for 1909, P.P. 1910, XCVII, 798.

good market for Peruvian and Chilean copper, even if United States interest in low-grade copper ores had deprived Britain of her lead as an export market. Rubber maintained a respectable total for Brazil. But British consumers had little interest in the conventional exports of the smaller Republics. In 1910, a representative year, they took only $3½ million out of Uruguay's total exports of $41 million, half of which was in one line—preserved and frozen meats, meat extracts and tongues.[1] From Paraguay, direct exports to the United Kingdom in 1911 and 1912 were £164 and £210, in contrast to a direct export to Germany of £204,096 and £174,810[2]; with no British export house in business in Paraguay, German and Spanish resident exporters sent Paraguayan hides, tobacco and quebracho to their home market for disposal, perhaps for re-export.

It was the reversal of the pattern experienced by Britain in her trade with the Empire. As much as 50% of South African imports into the United Kingdom just before the First World War may have been re-exported, but in the first instance 94·79% of South African exports were directed to Britain in 1907, 92·33% in 1911, 92·21% in 1913 and 94·32% in 1914.[3]

Naturally, unless there were strong reasons for doing otherwise, Britain creamed off the home market with Empire produce before she even thought of Latin America. Table XXVIII indicates the proportion of British imports supplied by each of the principal Latin American exports in 1913, the lines of particular interest, and the products in which the Empire had substituted wholly or in part for Latin America.

[1] Dunlop's report on Uruguay for 1911, P.P. 1912-13, CI, 553-5.
[2] Oliver's report on Paraguay for 1912, P.P. 1914, XCIII, 331.
[3] Sothern Holland's report on South Africa for 1911, P.P. 1912-13, XCIII, 900; Gauntlett's report on South Africa for 1914, P.P. 1914-16, XLV, 691-2.

Table XXVIII

British Market for the main Latin American Exports; distribution between Latin American and alternative suppliers, 1913

(£000)

Product	Total British imports	Total from British Possessions	Principal Latin American and other foreign suppliers
Bananas, raw	2,172·7	132·6	Costa Rica (681·1), Colombia (603·0), Canary Is. (750·4)
Beef, chilled	9,785·4	—	Argentina (9,729·4)
Beef, frozen	6,278·8	2,539·3	Argentina (3,085·6), Uruguay (650·8)
Cocoa, raw	2,282·6	1,162·6	Brazil (387·9), Ecuador (284·7)
Coffee, raw	2,920·9	362·4	Brazil (793·6), Costa Rica (719·1), Guatemala (315·7), Colombia (299·4), Mexico (118·4)
Copper, ore	1,005·1	282·7	Chile (419·6)
Copper, regulus and precipitate	1,449·4	635·6	Mexico (357·8), Spain (190·0), Chile (105·4), Portugal (104·8)
Copper, unwrought, in bars, blocks, slabs, cakes and ingots	7,345·7	1,542·6	U.S.A. (3,718·1), Japan (600·4), Chile (477·4), Spain (400·0), Mexico (205·6)
Cotton, raw	70,570·5	1,932·0	U.S.A. (47,307·8), Egypt (17,642·4), Brazil (1,992·3), Peru (1,280·2)
Hides, raw dry	2,554·2	1,549·4	Russia (207·8), France (159·8), Brazil (69·4)
Hides, raw wet	3,014·4	803·7	Argentina (868·9), Italy (513·3), Russia (259·8)
Mutton, frozen	10,583·9	8,093·7	Argentina (1,908·3), Chile (293·1), Uruguay (288·8)

Nitrate of Soda	1,490·7	—	Chile (1,439·9)
Rubber	20,524·0	11,739·8	Brazil (5,940·7), Peru (445·7)
Seeds, Flax or Linseed	7,195·4	4,358·4	Argentina (2,398·6), Russia (228·2)
Sugar, refined	12,351·1	3·7	Germany (6,161·4), Austria-Hungary (2,632·7), Netherlands (2,477·3), Belgium (668·8), Russia (357·3)
Sugar, unrefined	10,715·5	9273	Germany (4,733·4), Cuba (2,249·1), Austria-Hungary (1,618·0), Denmark (307·8), Brazil (266·1)
Tin, ore	3,308·9	604·2	Bolivia (2,082·6), Chile (348·0)
Tin in blocks, ingots, bars and slabs	9,252·0	8,770·2	Dutch East Indies (254·4), Germany (73·7), Bolivia (55·6)
Tobacco, unmanufactured	6,709·1	63·4	U.S.A. (5,657·5), Turkey (429·8), Netherlands (287·5), Germany (180·6)
Tobacco, manufactured (cigars)	1,138·0	41·5	Cuba (978·1)
Wheat	43,849·2	21,252·3	U.S.A. (13,953·1), Argentina (6,137·5), Russia (1,985·0), Uruguay (326·2)
Wool, Sheep's or Lamb's	34,226·1	27,465·2	Argentina (2,140·6), Chile (789·0), Uruguay (397·0), Turkey (274·1), Peru (212·3)
Maize	13,769·8	175·5	Argentina (10,851·9), U.S.A. (1,922·8), Russia (490·0)
Oats	5,672·0	795·3	Argentina (1,892·2), Germany (1,137·5), Russia (865·2), U.S.A. (465·0), Chile (268·8)

Source: *United Kingdom Trade and Navigation Accounts*, rounded to the nearest hundred.

CHAPTER X

Elements in the Survival of British Trade

THE general trend in patterns and preferences for British trade was against Latin American markets for half a century before 1914. Yet a stable percentage, 11-12%, of a vastly increased export trade continued to find an outlet in Latin America. What was it that concealed the trend in the overall trade figures for the Continent? Why did the total continue to expand in spite of an obvious preference for trade elsewhere? A part of the answer may certainly be found in the recovery of British competitiveness in and after the late '90s. But far more influential were the strength of Britain's trading relations with Argentina, the size of her investments, her leadership in the world's cotton trade, and the buoyant demand for her coal.

It is difficult to exaggerate the importance of Argentina to British trade with Latin America, in imports or exports. Anglo-Argentine trade was not peculiar in this respect. Germany too, although prepared to spread the range of her trading connections far further in the smaller Republics, was finding the same irresistible attractions in Argentina. Over the turn of the century, the balance of Germany's trading interest shifted sharply from Brazil to Argentina, and Argentina by 1908 accounted for nearly 50% of German/South American trade, imports and exports combined. Figure III shows the high proportion of British exports directed to Argentina. British exports to Argentina supported the whole Latin American trade. Two of the three points of real expansion, 1885-9 and 1902-6, were heavily dependent on Argentina. The third, the burst of trade in 1909-12, reflected an investment boom

Figure III. British Exports to Latin America (A) and to Argentina (B), 1880-1913 (declared values).

£ million

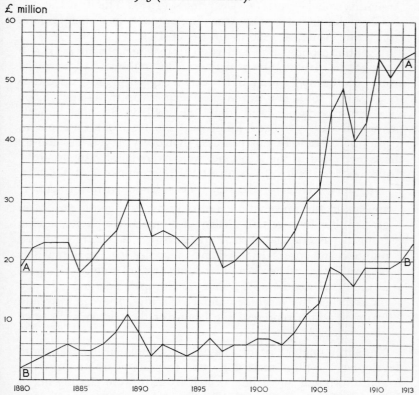

Source: U.K. Trade and Navigation Accounts, *rounded to the nearest million pounds.*

T

in several Republics and an isolated advance in British exports to Brazil, attributable in the main to a single £4,721,000 order for warships. Thereafter, Argentine expansion carried the trade until the outbreak of war.

British imports from Latin America show a similar pattern. If allowance is made for a 60% share in 'for orders' shipments as shown in Argentine statistics, Britain was taking over 35% of Argentina's total exports (£74,525,200) in 1910.[1] The British statistics show the share taken by Argentine products in British imports from Latin America, 1880 to 1913 (Fig. IV).

Argentina's population had risen from 2,680,000 in 1881-4 to 7,203,000 in 1910-14. Over thirty years her railways had increased from 3,000 km to 31,100 km, her cereal exports from 131,000 tons to 5,294,000 tons, her frozen meat exports from nil to 376,000 tons, her exports per head from $23 (gold) to $56, her imports per head from $27 to $50.[2] There was some truth in the complaint, in the first decade of this century, that every Argentine, and all those interested in the Republic, were overwhelmed by progress, drunk with statistics. In contrast to the commerce of Western Europe the Argentine trade, said a *Times* leader writer in 1912,

> appeals to the imagination, not only by its gigantic strides in growth, but by a certain quality of dignified simplicity, arising from its pastoral and agricultural pursuits. It is a trade of vast numbers and spaces, handled on a magnificent scale; the surplus of great flocks and herds, and far-flung fields of grain, exchanged, in the grand manner, for a share of Europe's hoarded gold and for some of the machines and clever toys, the comforts and luxuries, which represent the labour of the Old World's town bred masses.[3]

Not surprisingly, Britain was putting almost all her effort into developing the three most important markets of South America, Argentina, Brazil and Chile, which by 1910 were sharing about 85% of the foreign trade of the Continent. In each she was meeting with German and, increasingly, United States competition, but in each she was holding on to between 25 and 30% of total imports. In Mexico, Britain had long surrendered trade supremacy to

---

[1] Mackie's report on Buenos Aires for 1911, P.P. 1912-13, XCIV, 153.
[2] I owe these five-year average figures to the courtesy of Professor A. R. Ford, University of Warwick.
[3] *The Times*, South American Supplement, 30 May 1912, 5a.

Figure IV. British Imports from Latin America (A) and from Argentina (B), 1880-1913 (computed values).

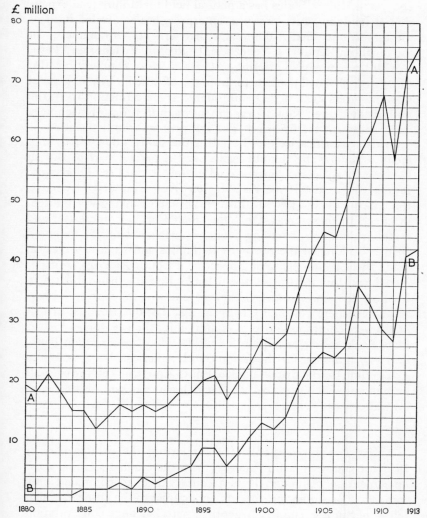

Source: U.K. Trade and Navigation Accounts, *rounded to the nearest million pounds.*

America. In Central America, as a *Times* Washington Correspondent explained in a general survey of Latin American trade in 1909, 'the United States has a natural field for commercial expansion at its doors, and American enterprise has so availed itself of the opportunity that it dominates that territory throughout'.[1] In the northern Republics, Venezuela, Colombia, Ecuador and Peru, British trade was also meeting severe American competition. But these were all small markets for imports, of little interest to general manufacturers even if they still offered some attraction to textile mills in the United Kingdom and to the manufacturers of machinery and equipment for British-owned railways and public utilities.

British priorities were reflected in the distribution of banking facilities among the Republics. By far the greater part of British banking by 1914 was concentrated in four Republics. There were four banks in the River Plate region (Argentina and Uruguay), three in Brazil, and two in Chile, and branch banking was limited, in effect, to these areas. Only the small Cortés Commercial and Banking Company, a trading house as much as a bank, represented British banking in the northern Republics and Central America, while the London Bank of Mexico and South America, amalgamated with one of the southern banks in 1912, had affiliates in Mexico, Peru and elsewhere. Expansion during the 1900s was rapid and comprehensive, and by 1914 the assets of the principal British banks were enormous—over £32 million for the London and River Plate Bank, over £22 million for the London and Brazilian Bank, nearly £20 million for the Anglo South American Bank, and over £14 million for the British Bank of South America. Yet 'the over-all impression which remains', as David Joslin has said, 'is of a concentration rather than a geographical widening of effort'.[2]

*

A few Republics, then, were supporting the greater part of British trade with Latin America, with the emphasis falling most on Argentina. Although Britain could expect to command only some 30% of Argentine imports, in contrast to the 50-60% which fell to her in the Empire, Argentina, with her huge concentration of British investments, settlement and trade, and her high *per*

---

[1] *The Times*, South American Supplement, 28 December 1909, 43f.
[2] David Joslin, *A Century of Banking in Latin America* (London, 1963), pp. 108-9.

capita imports, had more in common with Dominion markets than with the general run of markets in Latin America. Trade with Argentina, in turn, was supported by heavy investments, and the same, to a lesser degree, was true of the rest of Latin America where British investments in the whole apparatus of transport and services after the middle of the nineteenth century brought solid returns in orders for British products.

British financiers seldom 'tied' their loans to the purchase of British products. H.M. Government was careful not to intervene in the direction and control of British investment in Latin America before 1914, and the traditional division of interest between British finance and manufacturing made it unusual, though not impossible, for investments or loans to carry the 'tying' clauses so often found in French or German overseas loans. The money raised from London bankers to carry out the extension of the Brazilian state-owned Estrada de Ferro de Bragança in 1906-7 was said, at the time, to be provided on condition that the material was bought in the United Kingdom.[1] But Frank Dudley Docker, the great Birmingham manufacturer, when calling for more direction and 'tying' of investment in a letter to *The Economist* of 31 January 1914, complained that Britain was ill-organized in this respect, 'and in regard to the broad national aspects of our commercial policy, the three great divisions of the business world—industrial, mercantile, and financial—pay little regard to one another's interests'.[2]

However, the effect of British investments on trade, even without 'tying', was direct. Follett Holt, who agreed with Docker that something more might be done to organize Britain's foreign trade 'upon which so much of our future as the dominant race depends', drew on his experience as an authority on Latin American railways to quote a typical case of an English company, the owners of a South American railway, for which over the past eight years £3,700,000 had been raised in London.

The value of stores and materials purchased during the same period was £1,700,000. Of this amount £1,360,000, or 80%, was expended in Great Britain and £340,000, or 20%, abroad, mainly in the United States of America and the Continent.[3]

[1] Southgate's report on Pará for 1905-6, P.P. LXXXVIII, 207.
[2] *The Economist*, 7 February 1914, 293.
[3] *Ibid.*, 7 March 1914, 599.

Holt added that it need hardly be said that those responsible for placing the 20% abroad did so with no particular pleasure and only because the interests of their shareholders seemed to demand it; and certainly, the relationship between the general investment of British capital and the ebb and flow of British trade is so close as to leave no doubt of the connection. It arose most directly out of orders for capital goods required for construction and operation. In turn, the wealth and employment created by investment increased demand among Latin Americans for imports of all kinds. Even at company level, British firms extended their preference from capital goods to consumer goods. Big establishments like the Liebigs works at Fray Bentos in Uruguay, the Lautaro Nitrate Company and the Copiapó Mining Company in Chile, operating in relatively isolated conditions, imported the greater part of the cotton goods for their working people and the specialized provisions for their expatriate staff direct from the United Kingdom, in addition to whatever materials and machinery they needed for their operations. Others, more centrally placed, gave the same preference to British importers and manufacturers, through the ordinary channels. Figure V shows the pattern taken by British exports to and investment in Argentina over the period 1882 to 1913, with British exports (curve A) normally following investments (curve B) after a one to two-year interval during which work started and orders accumulated.

In general, the boom periods for British investment in Latin America were the mid-'60s to the depression of the mid-'70s, the late '80s to the Baring Crisis of 1890-1, and the mid-1900s to 1912 when political troubles in the Balkans put a check on further overseas lending. The first period saw the opening-up of the Continent by the great railway systems, and it brought immediate returns to British trade. In 1862, only three British ships from abroad entered the port of Rosario in Argentina; four years later, in 1866, 52 ships, of which 43 were British-registered, brought 20,382 tons of material for the new Central Argentine Railway, including rails, sleepers, iron for bridges, electric telegraph apparatus, coals, stores and rolling stock, nearly all of which came from Britain.[1] British exports of wrought and unwrought iron to the Argentine Confederation rose from 7,300 tons in 1862 to 35,628 tons in 1865; of coal from 16,177 tons to 34,767 tons.

[1] Hutchinson's report on Rosario for 1866, P.P. 1867-8, LXVIII, 257.

Figure V. British Exports to (A), and Capital Issues for (B), Argentina,
1882-1913.

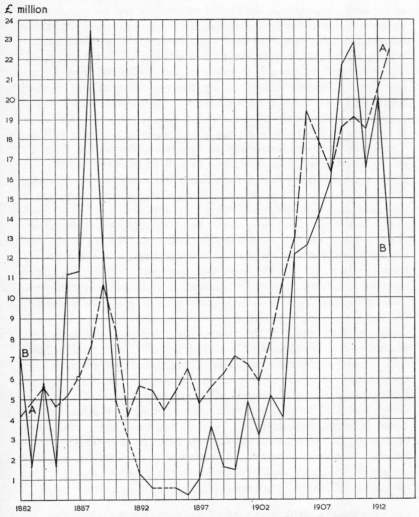

Source: (A) U.K. Trade and Navigation Accounts; *(B) A. G. Ford,* The Gold
Standard 1880-1914: Britain and Argentina *(Oxford, 1962), table XXV. Figures
rounded to the nearest hundred thousand pounds.*

At this point, there was little serious competition from Europe or the United States for those lines of trade in which Britain was interested. Competition developed in the '70s and early '80s to an extent which created great alarm in Britain and overseas. But there is evidence that, aided no doubt by the renewal of heavy investments, British manufacturers were matching up to that competition satisfactorily enough in many of the traditional lines by the late '80s. Consuls were reporting the regaining of lost ground particularly in Manchester and Birmingham goods and Dundee linen,[1] and the rush of investment brought heavy orders for machinery and railway materials. *The Economist*, a convinced Free Trader inclined professionally to optimism, concluded from its examination of total German and British exports for 1879, 1881, 1883, 1885 and 1887 that Britain had shown a marked gain under every head, with the exception of pig-iron, where there was a decrease, and woollen goods, where the increase was slight. Germany had made rapid progress in some directions, cotton goods, glass, paper, woollen manufactures, silk, but British trade had gained most in others, and on the whole the result was in Britain's favour.[2] In spite of vigorous German competition, especially directed at Latin America, British traders and manufacturers were holding their own very well in Argentina where, said *The Economist*, the competition had, perhaps, been keenest.[3]

The tone changed in the 1890s, when 'almost universal complaints [were] heard about the decadence of British trade'. Consular reports at this time paid particularly close attention to foreign competition, more especially German competition since the United States had yet to make much of an impression, and France, the chief rival for most of the nineteenth century in the markets of Latin America, was dropping behind. This was the period, too, of Joseph Chamberlain's well-known enquiry into foreign competition in colonial markets, of renewed investigations into the means by which H.M. Government might promote trade, of the formation of the Commercial Intelligence Committee, and of

[1] For example, Hampshire's report on Santos for 1887, P.P. 1888, C, 46; de Lemos's report on Ciudad Bolívar for 1888, P.P. 1889, LXXXI, 372; Cowper's report on Santos and São Paulo for 1889, P.P. 1890, LXXIV, 149.

[2] 'German v. British Trade', *The Economist*, 27 July 1889, 959.

[3] Leading article on British trade with Argentina, *The Economist*, 20 July 1889, 927.

Thomas Worthington's official tour of 1898 to report on the 'Conditions and Prospects of British Trade in certain South American Countries'.[1]

No doubt the alarm was overdone, and Sir Courtenay Boyle did well to point out that although the United States and Germany were gaining ground in home and neutral markets, Britain was still greatly ahead of both in her capacity to manufacture for export, so much so that up to date (January 1897) the gains of neither had had any very serious effect on her trade; it was simply that 'beginning from a lower level, each country is for the moment travelling upwards more rapidly than we are who occupy a much higher eminence'.[2] But in Latin America, British trade was undoubtedly experiencing a lean period. The Baring crisis, a crisis in the Argentine economy created by excessive imports of capital, over-rapid development and wild speculation in land, brought a disastrous collapse in confidence in Latin American investments. By August 1891, it was estimated that no less than £40 million had been lost out of the £53 million paid by the public for Argentine *cedulas* (land mortgage bonds).[3] Between August 1889 and June 1891, Provincial Cedulas fell from 74 to 30, National Bank shares from 347 to 30, Banco Constructor shares from 152 to 4, Catalinas Warehouses from 365 to 9. Herbert printed the figures for the principal Argentine government stocks and railways (Table XXIX).

The Baring crisis, so far as the emphasis and direction of British trade were concerned, could hardly have come at a more unfortunate time. It dried up investment for a decade at a moment when British interest was increasing in Empire markets. It helped accelerate the shift of trading interest away from Latin America to home markets and the Dominions. It forced Latin America to look elsewhere for capital and develop investment and trading links with other competing nations. It encouraged the Republics, deprived of imports, to expand local industries; it gave them a depreciated currency to protect those industries; and it made available unemployed mercantile capital for local industrial development. Much of the ground lost to British imports during the '90s could never

---

[1] Worthington's reports were published in P.P. 1899, XCVI, 449-613.
[2] Memorandum of Comparative Statistics, 16 January 1897, P.P. 1897, LXXXIII, 733.
[3] Estimate from 'a leading Argentine paper', 4 August 1891, quoted in Herbert's report on the Finances of the Argentine Republic, P.P. 1892, LXXXI, 56.

be recovered. Local industry, under the protection first of a heavily depreciated currency and then of increased tariffs, blocked further imports in a number of traditional lines. The recovery of British trade in the late '90s and early 1900s owed much to its greater competitiveness in the new lines for which local industry was not yet in a position to compete; it owed more to the continued superiority of British textiles and to the rising sales of British coal; it owed most to a renewed interest in Latin America as an opening for profitable investment.

Table XXIX
Market Price of Argentine Government Bonds and
Railway Stock, 1889-91

	March 1889	March 1891	July 1891
Loan of 1889	92	53	33
Loan of 1884	100	54	31
Great Southern Railway	220	153	129
Rosario Railway	185	120	74
Pacific Railway	145	100	70
Central Argentine Railway	219	79	47
Buenos Aires and Ensenada Railway	211	116	65
Western Railway	107	88	70
Great Western Railway	98	55	46
East Argentine Railway	110	74	53

Source: *Report on the Finances of the Argentine Republic, 31 August 1891*, P.P. 1892, LXXXI, 82.

By the turn of the century British capitalists were interested not only in the traditional investment opportunities of Latin America—the railways, the public utilities, and government bonds —but also in the full range of new promotions reaching the market. In Chile in the late '90s, British syndicates were getting into copper and borax. In Cuba in 1898-9, they were buying railways and cigar factories. In Brazil, they were taking up sugar and coffee plantations. The incentive was the attractive rate of return on a portfolio of Latin American investments. The net return on an Argentine railway investment totalling £74 million in 1891 was down to $1\frac{1}{4}\%$, and 13 of the 27 railways were said to be running at a loss.[1] Yet only a couple of years later, when conditions were

[1] Figures from the Argentine official railway report for 1891, quoted in P.P. 1893-4, XCII, 104.

still depressed, *The Economist* drew attention to the attractions of the better lines. At the current market price, Buenos Ayres Great Southern debentures were yielding 3·74%, Rosario 4·21%, Western 4·08%, and Central Argentine 4·35%. An investment in the main home lines, the Great Northern, the Great Western, the North Western and the Midland, would not have brought more than 2·85%. *The Economist* pointed out that Argentine debentures were equally or better secured than British, and yielded far more interest. Making every allowance for the glamour attached to trustee stock and the feeling of security given by a line in the United Kingdom, the price at which Argentine debentures might be obtained was unreasonably depreciated:

> While the Argentine companies are liable to currency crises, and possible revolutions, the British companies have their difficulties before them. The labour question may affect them most materially, and cause a continual increase in their wages bills, while their habit of consistently issuing further debenture stock will at the same time raise their fixed charges.[1]

These were returns on debentures, and the position was less agreeable for the holders of Argentine ordinary stock. But the general revival of the Latin American economies towards the end of the decade brought up returns everywhere. At the end of August 1910, the £600 million of South America securities quoted on the London Stock Exchange were yielding an *average* return of 4·73%, while the tendency of quotations had for years been upwards with a record of capital appreciation agreeably different from that experienced by investors in home or colonial enterprises. Of the £174½ million in the stocks of the various Anglo-Argentine railways, nearly £30 million were receiving 7%, over £23 million 6%, nearly £40 million 5%, and only £7 million were in receipt of no dividend at all. *The Times* thought that it would be difficult to find a group of securities in any part of the world in which so small a percentage of the total capital invested was not receiving a dividend, while the capital appreciation even on this 7% over the last few years had been so great that the holders had reason to be content with their investment.[2]

Latin American investments were attractive both to the ordinary

[1] *The Economist*, 10 June 1893, 692-3.
[2] *The Times*, South American Supplement, 27 September 1910, 9a.

investor looking for something better than the two to three per cent obtainable on safe British investments, and to the more adventurous with an eye to the premium for insecurity. Over the years 1900 to 1904, fixed interest home investments promised an average return of 3·18%; for 1905 to 1909, 3·61%. Similar investments in the Colonies could offer little more, with 3·33% and 3·94% respectively. But foreign investments, in which Latin Americans formed a large element, promised 5·39% for 1900 to 1904, and 4·97% for 1905 to 1909.[1] United Kingdom Consols in 1912, at 75¼, were yielding £3. 6s. 6d.; Argentine 5 per cents at 104 brought £4. 15s. 0d.; Brazilian 5 per cents, at 101½, £5. 0s. 6d.; Chilean 4½ per cents, at 93, £4. 19s. 6d.[2] The average return in 1913 on all British investments in Latin American government bonds was 4·4%, 4·2% on railways, 5·5% on miscellaneous investments and 10·1% on banks and shipping.[3] A mixed portfolio of Argentine industrial and mortgage stock should have brought a return of between 10 and 15%.

The effect of these rates is shown in Professor Simon's figures for new British portfolio investment. £7·1 million of new British capital went to South America in 1904; the total for 1907 was £30 million, and a peak of nearly £46 million was reached in 1912.[4] Argentina, over the seven years 1907 to 1913, attracted new British subscriptions totalling £118,339,585; Brazil, £88,227,036.[5]

*

It is probably impossible to compute at all accurately total British investment in Latin America before 1914. The existing estimates are most unsatisfactory and misleading, based as they are, for lack of other data, simply on easily accessible figures for public issues. Professor Stone's attempt, the last in the line, continues to exclude all British-owned assets in Latin America other

[1] R. A. Lehfeldt, 'The Rate of Interest on British and Foreign Investments', *Journal of the Royal Statistical Society*, LXXVI (1912-13), 201.
[2] *The Economist*, 1 February 1913, 213.
[3] As calculated by the *South American Journal*, 3 December 1927, 1242.
[4] Matthew Simon, 'The Pattern of New British Portfolio Foreign Investment, 1865-1914' in A. R. Hall (ed.), *The Export of Capital from Britain, 1870-1914* (London, 1968), p. 40.
[5] Sir George Paish, 'The Export of Capital and the Cost of Living', *Transactions of the Manchester Statistical Society* (1913-14), 81.

than public issues.[1] Naturally, government bonds, railways and public utilities were the big consumers of capital, and such capital, practically without exception, was raised publicly. But it is a long step from here to the dismissal of land ownership, industrial or trading capital as 'insignificant' in British interest in Latin America. Matthew Simon, for example, solemnly calculated the fifty-year totals for money calls 1870-1914, and discovered that 69% of British overseas investment could be described as 'social overhead', 12% as in the extractive industries and only 4% in 'manufacturing', from which he concluded that it was 'abundantly clear that British funds did not directly foster the development of extensive overseas industrialization'.[2] But he excluded direct investment by individuals, partnerships and the companies themselves, and obviously the normal pattern for investment in manufacturing, in which British capital was heavily interested in the Dominions, was in branch plants or in private small-scale investments by individuals or commercial firms. To a lesser extent, this was true also of British interest in the more important Republics of Latin America, and Irving Stone's assurance, based on his few, public industrial enterprises, that 'as was the case in other areas of British overseas investment, British capital in manufacturing in Latin America was insignificant', is worthless. Precisely the same applies to any estimates of British participation in the production of certain kinds of raw materials, where, for instance, coffee and rubber 'companies' were the exception to the rule. It applies to land-ownership generally, where British-owned estates in Latin America were seldom, in practice, the property of public companies.

However, Professor Stone's totals (Table XXX) may still serve as the lower limit of British interest in Latin American investment before 1914, above which any sum to be added for participation in commerce, industry, and land-ownership can be calculated, if at all, only by an exhaustive survey of local taxation returns and valuations. In a small Republic like Uruguay, for which Britons, as it happened, had always had a strong partiality, the lands and buildings owned by British subjects in 1910 were valued, for taxation purposes, at $12,259,749 (£2,608,457); their agricultural estates covered over 750,000 acres; and their commercial

---

[1] Irving Stone, 'British Long-Term Investment in Latin America, 1865-1913', *Business History Review*, XLII (1968), 211-37.
[2] Simon in Hall (ed.), *Export of Capital*, pp. 23-6.

undertakings, paying taxes upon the capital declared, were assessed at \$17,588,000 (£3,742,127).[1] A substantial element of under-valuation is likely for any such figures; they take no account of the large properties owned by British subjects born in Uruguay, which appear as 'Uruguayan' in the statistics, nor can they allow for a deliberate under-valuation of up to a third in tax declarations. All the same, even without such allowances they could add as much as 15% to a total based on public issues alone, and if figures of this order may be obtained for Uruguay, what must they have been for Argentina, Brazil and Chile?

Table XXX

British Investment in Government Bonds and Public Issues,
Latin America, 1865-1913
(£000)

	1865	1875	1885	1895	1905	1913
Government loans	61,781	129,360	161,160	262,377	307,760	445,481
Railways	9,551	24,085	55,184	199,926	237,288	404,535
Public utilities	848	8,406	10,500	17,801	40,235	139,092
Financial	2,012	3,352	4,154	39,502	50,864	94,446
Land, mines and oil	2,708	2,504	7,831	18,373	27,613	36,185
Industrial and miscellaneous	1,044	2,082	4,837	11,432	18,527	37,396
Shipping companies	2,926	4,820	2,953	3,095	5,981	18,330
Total	80,869	174,611	246,620	552,505	688,268	1,177,462

Source: Irving Stone, 'British Long-Term Investment in Latin America, 1865-1913', *Business History Review*, XLII (1968), 323. (The totals do not add because of rounding of individual items.)

Professor Stone arrives at a total of £1,177·5 million for British investment in Latin America by 1913. *The South American Journal*, taking into account simply issues on the London Stock Exchange, gave £999·2 million, for which the geographical distribution is shown in Table XXXI. United States' investments, next after British in Latin America, have been estimated at £339 million, French at £329 million, and German at £185 million.[2] Over the

[1] Taken from Kennedy's report on Uruguay for 1910, P.P. 1911, XCVII, 746.
[2] Woodruff, *Impact of Western Man*, p. 154.

entire world, British investments in 1914 may have aggregated £4,004 million, French £1,766 million, German £1,376 million and United States' £513 million.[1]

If account is taken simply of government bonds and public companies, British investments in Latin America just before the

Table XXXI

British Investments in Latin America at the end of 1880, 1890, 1913
(Public Issues, nominal values, £)

Country	1880	1890	1913
Argentina	20,338,709	156,978,788	357,740,661
Bolivia	1,654,000	503,003	419,720[1]
Brazil	38,869,067	68,669,619	223,895,435
Chile	8,466,521	24,348,647	63,938,237
Colombia	3,073,373	5,399,383	6,654,094
Costa Rica	3,304,000	5,140,840	6,660,060
Cuba	1,231,600	26,808,000	44,444,618
Dominican Republic	714,300	1,418,300	n.a.
Ecuador	1,959,380	2,189,480	2,780,974
El Salvador	n.a.	294,000	2,224,700
Guatemala	544,200	922,700	10,445,220
Honduras	3,222,000	3,888,250	3,143,200
Mexico	32,740,916	59,883,577	159,024,349[1]
Nicaragua	206,570	411,183	1,239,100
Paraguay	1,505,400	1,913,424	2,995,730
Peru	36,177,070	19,101,315	25,658,298
Uruguay	7,644,105	27,713,280	46,145,393
Venezuela	7,564,390	9,846,219	7,950,009
General	10,274,660	10,297,702	33,876,767
Total	179,490,261	427,727,710	999,236,565

[1] The Mexican and Bolivian totals for 1913 are particularly unreliable; £100 million and £5 million respectively may be nearer the mark.

Source: J. Fred Rippy, British Investments in Latin America, 1882-1949 (Minneapolis, 1959) and the South American Journal.

First World War were fully a quarter of Britain's total overseas investments. The distribution is misleading since it is clear that so much larger a proportion of Empire investment was in private industrial, commercial and landholding enterprise and in branch plants of home manufacturers, none of which are recorded in these statistics. But whatever the qualifications—and some allowance

[1] Sidney Pollard, The Development of the British Economy, 1914-64 (London, edn. 1969), p. 186.

should be made for a parallel understatement for Latin American investment—the total figures are impressive. Investment on this scale could not have failed to support British trade, however unfavourable conditions may have been in so many other respects for the development of British trade with the Republics.

*

Table XXXI has given some idea of priorities for British investment (public issues). Argentina in 1913 stood well at the head of the list with £357·7 million, compared with Brazil's £223·9 million and Chile's £63·9 million.

Even at the end of the 1880s it was said that between £150 million and £200 million of British capital was interested in Argentina in one shape or another; a revised and corrected estimate put the total for British capital in 1890 at £174,768,000.[1] A decade later £200 million had become the 'lowest calculation' for British capital invested in public and private enterprises in the Republic.[2] The collapse of Argentine credit in 1890 put a stop to further external loans. Confidence in public issues was slow to revive and *The Times* warned investors towards the end of the '90s that they 'would do well to look at the situation all round with a cool and discriminating eye before they are induced again to stake their money on the prospect of a coming period of prosperity'.[3] But private capital from abroad and resident British capital continued to be attracted by the low prices of Argentine land after the Baring crisis, and by the opportunities for industrialization created by a depreciated currency and the fall in imports. In the 1900s Argentine credit experienced a remarkable recovery. In his report to Congress of September 1910 the Minister of Finance (Dr Iriondo) explained how, at the beginning of 1900, Argentine 4 per cent external bonds stood at 54, the 5 per cent bonds at 72, and the 6 per cents at 90: in the local market the 6 per cents were down to about 73. By 1904, the 4 per cent bonds were quoted at 85 to 87¾, the 5 per cents from 96 to 100 and the 6 per cents at 100¾; 6 per cent bonds were quoted even in Buenos Aires at about 99.[4] Britain had always

---

[1] Jenner's report on Argentina, 13 May 1889, P.P. 1889, LXXVIII, 37; *The Times*, 22 May 1890, 12a; Ferns, *Britain and Argentina*, p. 493.
[2] *The Economist*, 3 September 1898, 1288.
[3] *The Times*, 20 September 1897, 7d, e.
[4] Quoted in P.P. 1911, XC, 33.

held an overwhelmingly large proportion of Argentina's bonded debt. Pillado calculated that of the total foreign obligations contracted by the Republic from its emancipation to the mid-1900s, 82% came from Britain; at the end of the 1900s, of the current bonded debt, Britain still held something like two-thirds of the total.[1]

Taking account again simply of public issues, the distribution of Argentina's debt to Britain was as shown in Table XXXII.

Table XXXII
Distribution of British Investment in
Argentina, 1910
(Public issues, £)

Government	33,768,000
Municipal	4,571,000
Railways	186,126,000
Banks	1,850,000
Breweries and distilleries	993,000
Canals and docks	1,941,000
Commercial and industrial	6,922,000
Electric lighting and power	889,000
Financial, land and investment	8,060,000
Gas and water	3,854,000
Mines	832,000
Telegraphs and telephones	1,390,000
Tramways	18,612,000
Total	269,808,000

Source: George Paish, 'Great Britain's Capital Investments in Individual Colonial and Foreign Countries', *Journal of the Royal Statistical Society*, LXXIV (1911), 182.

There is no way of arriving at the total for all British capital invested, public and private. H. C. Allen, a director of the Buenos Ayres Great Southern Railway, in a lecture to the Chartered Institute of Secretaries on 18 April 1912, told his audience that more than 80% of the railways in Argentina were British and 70% of the ocean-going ships, while no less than 67 English joint-stock companies were quoted on the London Stock Exchange for

---

[1] *The Economist*, 11 September 1909, 512; *The Economist*, 27 November 1909, 1085.

U

Argentina with a total capital of £224 million. Allen estimated that the British capital invested 'in every way' in Argentina was between £400 million and £500 million.[1] The *South American Journal's* total for Argentine issues on the London Stock Exchange at the end of 1913 was £357,740,661. And the figure for all British capital freely quoted in Argentina herself just before the First World War, no doubt exaggerated, was somewhere in the region of £500 million.[2]

It was as true of Brazil as of Argentina that the pace of British trade in the decade before 1914 was forced by massive investment. In 1855-9 British exports to Brazil had averaged £4 million; the average was £5 million in 1860-4, fluctuating between £6 million and £7·5 million until 1900, with a single peak of £8 million in the early years of the Republic, 1891-93. In 1901, British exports were back to £4·2 million, and £5·5 million in 1902 and 1903. The pattern, then, had been relative stagnation, with the trade promoted on the one hand by imports of material for railways, public utilities and industry, but held back on the other by import substitution in cotton textiles. By 1913, British exports were up to nearly £12½ million. Britain was still holding on to a 24·5% share of a vastly increased total import trade (the percentage in 1902 had been 30%).[3] Import substitution had continued at every point below a certain level of sophistication in industry, and British manufacturers were steadily losing their position in cotton goods, hardware, iron work, etc. But Brazil, on the strength of her great exports, coffee and rubber, and of a most favourable visible balance of trade (exports in 1906-9 totalling £215,955,900 compared with imports of £146,277,799),[4] was making every effort to bring herself up to date. She was extending her railway system, improving her harbours and docks, her water supply and drainage, her tramways, light and power, and expanding her merchant navy. The greatest inflow of foreign capital followed the recession of 1907-8, falling off sharply again with the Balkan crisis and the cut-back in European investment in 1913. In the seven years 1908 to 1914 no less

[1] *The Times*, South American Supplement, 30 April 1912, 7a.
[2] Mackie's report on Buenos Aires for 1912-13, P.P. 1914, LXXXIX, 525. The same figure had been mentioned as far back as 1909 in *The Times*, South American Supplement, 28 December 1909, 45d.
[3] Hambloch's report on Brazil for 1919, P.P. 1920, XLIII, 94, 96.
[4] Grant-Watson's report on Brazil for 1909, P.P. 1910, XCVI, 541.

than £190,125,533 of foreign capital, raised largely in London and Paris, entered Brazil[1]:

1908	£28,000,000
1909	20,277,176
1910	32,787,143
1911	37,661,331
1912	24,754,550
1913	40,645,333
1914	6,000,000

In London alone, £34 million of new Brazilian issues were floated in 1908-10, and nearly £50 million over the next three years, 1911-1913.[2] Rippy's figures for total nominal British investment (public issues) in Brazil are £38·8 million at the end of 1880, £90·6 million in 1900, £151·4 million in 1910 and £223·8 million at the end of 1913.[3]

In terms of nominal British investment (public issues), Brazil was next after Argentina as destination for British capital in Latin America. No basis exists at present for estimating the scale of *private* British investment in Brazil, but the restricted size of the British community and the range of its interests suggest that this must have been far less important in Brazil than it was in Argentina. Furthermore, the fact that a high proportion of British investment was out of British control in Brazilian government bonds (more than half of nominal investment compared with about one-seventh in Argentina), and that a fair proportion of the remainder came under the management and control of North American and Canadian railway and public utility companies in the years immediately preceding the First World War, meant that the returns brought to British trade were less generous in proportion to capital invested than they were further south. The result was reflected in British exports to Brazil in 1913, at £12,465,115 not much more than half those to Argentina (£22,640,921).

On the whole, North America's interest was in Brazilian land development, railways and public utilities rather than in the import or commission business, and although her percentage of the rapidly

---

[1] *Ibid.*, 67.
[2] A. H. John, *A Liverpool Merchant House* (London, 1959), p. 109.
[3] J. Fred Rippy, 'A Century and a Quarter of British Investment in Brazil', *Inter-American Economic Affairs*, VI (1952), 83-6.

developing Brazilian import trade rose from 12% in 1902 to 16% in 1910, it was down again to 15·5% in 1913. Germany, with her strong interest in nearly every aspect of the Brazilian market, was Britain's most serious rival, with a share of the import trade rising from 11% in 1902 to 17% in 1913.[1] British engineers and industrialists were themselves making increased efforts to hold on to the promising trade in engineering and associated products, and of the 44 foreign companies formed for trading in Brazil in 1911, 20 were British. There had been more evidence over the past few years, Hambloch reported from Rio in 1913, 'of a proper appreciation of the fact that trade in Brazil cannot be secured by merely spending a few hours on shore in Rio de Janeiro *en route* to Buenos Aires'.[2]

In the two southern Republics of Chile and Uruguay, where British trade retained a handsome proportion of the market right up to the war, the trade was encouraged by relatively strong British communities, by good representation, by established tastes and connections, and by the distance of those markets from, and the difficulty of communication with, the United States. But in both Uruguay and Chile, a strong element in British imports was provided by heavy investment and by the orders which accompanied it; indeed, without that investment, Uruguay would have had a totally insignificant place in British trade.

From the earliest years of independence, Britons were large landowners in Uruguay. Perpetual civil war had restrained and reduced this interest over the years, but British interest had developed in other directions so that by the beginning of the '80s, with the exception of a French company working the mines at Cunapiru, all the industrial enterprises of any importance—the railways, the tramways, the telegraphs, the banks, the docks, the gas and water supplies—were in English hands, established with British capital and managed by Englishmen.[3] In the late 1900s Britons owned all the railways, the Montevideo gasworks and waterworks, the telephones, most of the electric tramways and the transatlantic telegraph service; four large London banks had branches in the Republic; British shipping accounted for nearly half of the foreign shipping entering Montevideo. R. J. Kennedy

---

[1] Hambloch's report on Brazil for 1919, P.P. 1920, XLIII.
[2] Hambloch's report on Rio for 1911-12, P.P. 1913, LXIX, 209.
[3] Monson's report from Montevideo, 19 September 1881, P.P. 1882, LXIX, 133-4.

estimated that over £50 million of British capital was invested in Uruguay, and, as he said in a later report, 'the preponderance of British investments over those of other countries is too well-known to require comment'.[1] Issues quoted on the London Stock Exchange for 1913 amounted to £46,145,393, and it was this heavy investment, together with ease of access to the huge commercial and financial resources of the British community at Buenos Aires, which made Uruguay, as distinct from the other small Republics, so promising and substantial a market.

The £64 million of British capital in Chile quoted on the London Stock Exchange for 1913 had the same effect, although for Chile as for Uruguay over half was invested in government bonds. A railway investment of £20·5 million and perhaps £11 million in nitrates brought direct returns to British trade. Investment by resident Britons in Chile, or by private commercial partnerships, must in any case have added very considerably to the Stock Exchange total. Mercantile and finance houses like Antony Gibbs & Sons, Williamson Balfour, Duncan Fox, and Weir Scott had large industrial, land and mining interests, beyond the considerable capital they could call on for their trading and financial transactions. Much of the capital described as 'Chilean' in nitrates, in sheep-farming in the south, in manufacturing, and possibly also in Bolivian tin-mines was British; with British-owned sheep farms changing hands, during the speculative boom of 1905, at as much as £200,000 there was plenty of money on hand for promising adventures. A trade which had remained steady at between £2 million and £3 million worth of British imports over the last thirty years of the nineteenth century had, under the influence primarily of British investment, reached £6 million by 1913.

In each of the smaller South American Republics, in Peru, Colombia, Venezuela, Ecuador, Bolivia and Paraguay, where Britain's import trade at the best of times was exiguous, her trading position depended first on the superiority of her cotton goods and then on the extent and variety of her investments. A single railway, in a small import trade, could determine Britain's place among the principal importers. Of the £219,147 of British exports to Paraguay in 1910, well over half (£122,741) was made up of cotton manufactures, but £48,800 of the remainder came from

[1] Kennedy's reports on Uruguay for 1908 and 1909, P.P. 1909, XCIX 625, and P.P. 1910, CIII, 1087.

extensions and improvements in progress on the British-owned
Paraguay Central Railway Company. Where a railway changed
hands, the effect was seen immediately in the international distribution of a small import trade. The Speyer & Co. railway enterprises
(North American) in Bolivia were bought up by the Antofagasta
Railway Co. (British) in 1908-9. United States trade had been
heavily supported by the increased imports of railway material,
and the result of the takeover can be seen in import figures for
1909 and 1910 (Table XXXIII). Cecil Gosling pointed out, in this
context, that it would probably continue to be the case for Bolivia
that the sales of British goods would follow in the wake of heavy
British investment, rather than that British traders would attempt,

Table XXXIII
British and United States Imports into Bolivia, 1907-10

		1907	1908	1909	1910
Britain	£	488,000	528,000	670,000	805,000
U.S.A.	£	624,000	648,000	870,000	440,000

Source: P.P. 1911, XC, 360.

on their own initiative, to work up a business for themselves in
urban centres.[1] As it was, a total of rather over £6 million of
British capital interested in Bolivia in 1911, in contrast to under
£3 million French, under £1 million German and scarcely £500,000
American ensured that Britain held on to over 20% of the import
trade in a Republic where her commercial representation, in comparison with Germany, was negligible.[2]

By something of an historical accident, the United Kingdom
was well represented by British houses in Peru up to the First
World War. The relative position of her trade was affected rather
by an inflow of United States capital into Peruvian copper mines,
coal and oil, raising North American imports from £591,566 in

[1] Gosling's report on Bolivia for 1910, P.P. 1911, XC, 342, 360; also
Moore's report on Sucre for 1911, P.P. 1912-13, XCIV, 423. £500,000
has been deducted from the official import figure of £1,305,000 for Britain
in 1910 to allow for the exceptional bullion imports from London in that
year.
[2] The estimates are from Adams' report on Bolivia for 1911, P.P. 1912-
1913, XCIV, 412-13. These take account of railway and mining investments
included in the totals for other countries in the *South American Journal*
estimates in Table XXXI.

1902 to £1,105,749 in 1912. Imports from the United Kingdom, using the Peruvian figures, were on average only £1 million annually for the last half of the nineteenth century; they reached £1,720,133 in 1911 and were back down to £1,198,632 in 1912.[1] Britain's record would have been worse but for the fact that the decline in her cotton textile and coal imports under local competition was matched by new demand created by resident British capital and by British ownership, through the Peruvian Corporation, of over 90% of the Peruvian railway system.

British trade in the northern Republics depended almost entirely, as it had for Bolivia and Paraguay, on Manchester goods and British capital. Ecuador, Colombia and Venezuela were within easy reach of the United States, and swifter deliveries, lower freights, more suitable equipment, greater canvassing made it far less automatic here than further south for a British enterprise to order only from the United Kingdom. For the extensive schemes on hand in Caracas in 1905-6 for the establishment of electric trams, telephones, etc., accounting for over £200,000 of British capital, the managers explained that in spite of their wish to buy their material in the United Kingdom, the class of goods offered and the undue delay before delivery (amounting often to more than six months) had forced a decision in favour of the United States where the goods were cheap, of sufficient quality, and delivered within about three weeks of the date of the order.[2]

The first inclination for a British firm, in this case as in others, was to buy British, and in a British import trade worth only, on average, £840,523 p.a. in the five years before the war, a British investment of £2,400,000 in Venezuelan public utilities and industrial enterprises and nearly £3 million in railways obviously had its effect. Furthermore, Britons were showing a new interest in Venezuelan gold, copper and petroleum, and total British investment in public companies just after the war (by which time nearly £2 million of British capital was invested in oil) was calculated by Beaumont at £8 million; additional British capital was interested privately in the Venezuelan textile industry, in real estate, and in the cattle industry.[3]

[1] Figures from P.P. 1908, CXV, 10, and P.P. 1914, XCIII, 734.

[2] Haggard's report on Caracas for 1905, P.P. 1906, CXXIX, 917.

[3] Dept. of Overseas Trade, *Report on the Financial and Commercial Condition of Venezuela* (H.M.S.O., 1921), pp. 14, 28.

The British railways in Venezuela bought mainly British coal and rolling stock, just as the Gran Ferrocarril de Venezuela, a German line, bought German, and the same applied, with the occasional exceptions imposed by local conditions, to the British railways, gold and silver mines in Colombia. 60% (539 kilometres) of the Colombian railway system at the close of 1909 was in the hands of companies incorporated under British laws; a considerable amount of British capital, just before the war, was engaged in the gold and silver mines under British management; and South African and London groups were associated in gold and platinum explorations in the Choco district.[1]

From the last decade of the nineteenth century the United States had taken the lead in trade with the whole Mexican, Central American and Caribbean area. Many of her exports were foodstuffs which were not in competition with Britain. But her manufactures, with so many advantages in access, deliveries and suitability to neighbouring markets, could meet British products in practically any direction. Such trade as Britons maintained was in certain specialized lines of machinery, in a miscellany of small lines of hardware, in tools where they still maintained the advantage of an established preference among conservative consumers, and above all in cotton goods. Investment here as elsewhere helped to preserve a trade which, without it and in such unfavourable conditions, showed every sign of disappearing altogether.

Mexico, by the end of the Porfiriato (1911), had become one of the leading consumers of British capital in Latin America. British interest in Mexican investment was slight until the late '80s, when the restoration of diplomatic relations and an arrangement of the External Debt revived confidence in Mexican securities. This was a period when, as for Argentina, the lack of promising opportunities for capital increments at home in the United Kingdom was driving speculative capital abroad. Sir Francis Denys, reporting on the finances of Mexico at the end of 1889, noted how since 1886 the registered capital of companies formed in London for undertakings in Mexico had amounted to £32,990,190. Money was still flooding into Mexican railways, lands, mines, public securities, banks—

---

[1] Huckin's report on the Railways of Colombia, P.P. 1910, XCVI, 3; Milne's report on Colombia for 1913, P.P. 1913, LXVIII, 567.

Great Britain has assumed a hold on the railway system of Mexico which it will be difficult to throw off. The Mexican Railway is an English Corporation; the control of the National Railway is in English hands, the Interoceanic and Mexican Southern are also English companies. The Tehuantepec Railway is being constructed with British capital. It is stated that the majority of the first mortgage bonds of the Central Railway have passed into English hands.[1]

To Denys and others at the time it seemed that, except in mining, British capital was taking over the position gained by United States capital in the early '80s—at the time of the first railway boom. But Mexico, like Canada, was the natural *point d'appui* for American trade and investment. It was an extension of the American home market along the new railways; it was cheaply accessible for commercial canvassing; it was easily surveyed for investment. United States investment picked up again in the 1890s, and substantial progress was made in railway building, in mines, in plantations and in industrial enterprises at a time when British capital was still licking its wounds after the Baring crisis. There may have been £40 million of British capital in Mexico in the early '90s, but nearly every mining enterprise floated in the late '80s had ended in disaster, and the large British holdings of stock in the two trunk lines of Mexico, the Central and the National, were passing into American hands. New British investment in Mexico in the 1890s, directly through the Stock Exchange, amounted in total to £1,833,843 for the whole decade,[2] whereas United States investment by 1900 was estimated to have reached over £100,000,000.[3] The Mexican government, alarmed at the political threat implicit in heavy American investment and by the spread of American citizens throughout the Republic—over 50,000 Americans were said to be in Mexico just before the Revolution, in contrast to some 15,000 in 1900[4]—took steps to limit further American investment, in particular by buying back a controlling interest in the principal railways. It attempted also to encourage a new flow of investment from Europe. The result, in D'Olwer's

[1] P.P. 1890, LXXVI, 145.
[2] Luis d'Olwer in Cosío Villegas (ed.), *Mexico: La Vida Económica*, II, 1158.
[3] Leay's report on Vera Cruz for 1902, P.P. 1903, LXXVIII, 259.
[4] *The Times*, 5 November 1913, 7d.

figures (which are the best we have), was that out of a total of £340 million of foreign capital in Mexico in 1911, £129 million came from the United States, £99 million from Britain, £91 million from France, £65½ million from Germany and £3½ million from Holland. British capital was distributed chiefly in railways (£40 million), public utilities (£21 million), mines (£11½ million), real estate (£9 million), the public debt (£8 million) and oil (£5¾ million).[1]

It might be expected that an investment of this size should bring a large return in trade, especially since the public debt component was relatively small. Obviously British investment was a factor in keeping British imports into Mexico at a respectable level in competition with German. Although Germany's commercial representation in Mexico was far stronger than Britain's and her shipping services incomparably better, especially to the West Coast, her total investment was two-thirds the size, and over 40%, in D'Olwer's calculations, was in that industrial expansion and import substitution within Mexico herself which so seriously restricted the import trade for all manufacturing countries. Mexico, with her large cotton-manufacturing industry and a variety of smaller industries developed with the full support of Díaz's 'científicos', was a relatively small market for imports; her imports in five years before the 1911 Revolution averaged only about £21 million in comparison with Argentina's average for 1909-11 of £68 million. Of this, Britain could barely hold 11·5%, while the United States provided 55-60%. By 1911 American capitalists and entrepreneurs had found their way into every important sector of the Mexican economy—the railway interests under the umbrella of J. P. Morgan & Co., the smelting and mining interests controlled by Guggenheim, Senator Aldrich's rubber interests, the oil interests of Standard Oil operating through Waters Pierce. But it was not simply the competitive presence of American capital; trading returns from British capital invested in Mexico were limited by the fact that so much of it consisted of bonds, debentures or shares in enterprises under North American or Canadian management and control. In Mexico as in Brazil, the so-called 'Canadian Octopus' (the Montreal and Toronto group under the control of Dr Pearson)

[1] D'Olwer in Cosío Villegas (ed.), *Mexico: La Vida Económica*, II, 1154. These figures are certainly a more reliable guide than those quoted in the *South American Journal* and printed above in Table XXXI.

had bought its way into a dominant share in the traction, light and power undertakings, and its shares, which offered better opportunities for improvement than many of the fixed-interest securities currently on the market, were taken up readily in London. In fact, of the leading Mexican securities quoted in the Stock Exchange List just before the Revolution—the Mexico 5 per cent External Loan, the Interoceanic Railway of Mexico, the Mexico North-Western Company, the National Railways of Mexico, the Mexican Railway, the Mexican Light and Power Company, Monterrey Railway Light & Power, Mexican Eagle Oil, and the Mexican Tramways Company—only the Mexican Railway was under purely British management. *The Economist*, looking back on this period, explained how the Stock Exchange had taken a 'rosy view of the future of Mexico', and British capital, which for a long time had not been active in the development of Mexican resources, was flowing in once more. But American and Canadian entrepreneurs had done most of the pioneer work, so that nearly all the Mexican companies which appealed to the British investor were of North American origin.[1]

British investments were scattered throughout Central America and the Caribbean. The fact that Britain had large investments in Cuba and owned most of the railways helped to preserve a part of her Cuban trade against the overwhelmingly strong position gained by the United States since the war of 1898. But she was not interested to any extent in the sugar industry, and there were only five or six British plantations in the whole of Cuba in 1910-11. In every Central American and Caribbean Republic, Britain's trade depended very largely on the superiority of certain lines of Manchester cotton goods; such investments as she had were a small element in what was still a primitive market. She was only marginally interested in the sugar and coffee plantation and export business. The huge 'banana empire' of the United Fruit Company channelled trade through the United States. American railway, light and power interests took over many of the enterprises which Britons had initiated. The Costa Rica Railway experienced two changes of management. Built by the American entrepreneur, Minor Keith, with American materials and equipment, it was handed over to the Costa Rica Railway Company (English) in 1891 and imported its materials as far as possible thereafter from Britain. In 1907 it

[1] *The Economist*, 15 February 1913, 329.

was leased to the Northern Railway Company of Costa Rica, an American corporation. British imports of railway material fell at once from £27,955 in 1907 to £225 in 1908. Coal soon followed; nearly all the coal coming into Costa Rica before 1908 came from the United Kingdom and after 1908 from the United States.[1]

In the circumstances Britain did well to hold on to a 21·7% average share of total imports into the Central American Republics, 1906-11, even if the United States were providing 49·2%. Germany was lagging behind, and it was only the size of her investments in Guatemala—where she was said to have 250 million marks invested principally in coffee plantations in 1914[2]—which kept her up to 13·4%. The United States figures are inflated by imports, like flour and petroleum, in which she was in no sense in competition with Britain. Taking simply the competition in manufactured goods, over the years 1906-11 Britain supplied Central America on average with £1,150,000 of imports; the United States provided £1,715,000 and Germany only £645,000. Comparable figures for the northern Republics of South America, Colombia and Venezuela, in manufactured goods, were £1,710,000 from Britain, £965,000 from the United States and £755,000 from Germany.[3]

*

Three main elements preserved the British trading position in Latin America against a strong trend towards home and Empire markets and towards a greater emphasis on more sophisticated products less marketable and less easily promoted by Englishmen in the Republics. These were the size of Britain's investments, her continued strength and competitiveness as an exporter of textiles in general and of cotton manufactures in particular, and the importance of her trade in coal. Figure V (p. 281) indicates the relationship between British investment in, and exports to, Argentina. British trade with Argentina was supported further by exports of cotton manufactures rising from £991,465 in 1880 to £3,728,396

[1] Sharpe's report on Costa Rica for 1891, P.P. 1892, LXXXI, 782; Cox's report on Costa Rica for 1908, P.P. 1909, XCIII, 571; Milne's report of 1913, P.P. 1913, LXVIII, 521-2.

[2] Dept. of Overseas Trade, *Report on Economic and Financial Conditions in Guatemala* (H.M.S.O., 1922), p. 14.

[3] Milne's report on Central America, Colombia and Venezuela, P.P. 1913, LXVIII, 428-9.

Figure VI. Cotton Manufactures as a Proportion of total British Exports to Colombia, Ecuador and Venezuela, 1890-1913.

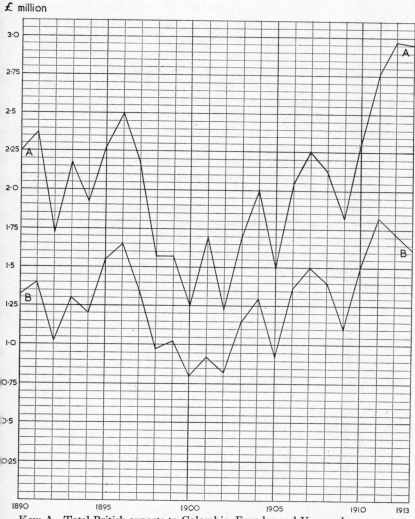

Key: A – Total British exports to Colombia, Ecuador and Venezuela
 B – British exports of cotton manufactures to Colombia, Ecuador and Venezuela.

Source: U.K. Trade and Navigation Accounts, *rounded to the nearest twenty-five thousand pounds.*

in 1913, and of coal from £48,300 to £3,191,900. Import substitution in Brazil displaced British cottons in the cheaper ranges, but Britain still sent £2,235,052 of cotton manufactures to Brazil in 1913 (£3,498,688 in 1880), and her coal exports had risen from £194,693 in 1880 to £1,900,920 in 1913. In her relations with the smaller Republics, investments in railways and public utilities helped generate trade, particularly after 1905, but cotton manufactures remained by far the most important element. Taking the three northern Republics, Colombia, Ecuador and Venezuela, Figure VI illustrates the proportion of total British exports (curve A) supplied by cotton manufactures, principally piece-goods (curve B).

Without investment, without cotton manufactures or coal the general pattern of retreat from these markets to better opportunities elsewhere, which was to show itself so clearly in the inter-war period, would have been evident long before 1914. All its elements had been present from at least the beginning of the 1890s, and they can be traced in one form or another to the first serious challenge to Britain's leadership in foreign trade and investment in Latin America in and after the third quarter of the nineteenth century.

CHAPTER XI

Conclusion

PROFESSOR SAUL, in passing judgment on Britain's competitive performance in world markets before 1914, felt that we could see Britain's relative decline most clearly by examining the condition of trade in South America, 'the most truly competitive area of all'; he referred later to 'the importance of the struggle for the truly competitive market of South America'.[1] But a market can only be truly competitive if all feel an equal urge to compete, and it is obvious that the trend in British trade was strongly against Latin America almost from the beginning.

It would be easy to exaggerate the drift to home and Empire markets, and as easy, in reaction against a common view, to over-state the extent of local industrialization and import substitution in the Republics. Latin America was still, in many respects, a pastoral, agricultural and mining community before 1914. It offered opportunities to a limited group of import/export houses. It provided good profits for a fair number of British commercial banks, financial houses, insurance and mortgage companies. It was a satisfactory customer for some branches of Britain's mercantile marine. It gave work to Britain's textile mills and large and increasing orders to British coal-mines. It was an excellent outlet for investment, better often than the Colonies and Dominions, and investment in turn generated a substantial trade, brought Britons to the Continent, and encouraged further enterprise. If Latin America ceased to be, or never was, of prime interest either to British exports or to imports, it could certainly offer much to some

[1] Saul, *Overseas Trade*, pp. 38, 219.

elements in British enterprise, and at least one of the Republics, Argentina, became after 1880 a most promising partner in trade.

Yet the total impression of British trading interest in Latin America is of withdrawal, a withdrawal which was *not* symptomatic of a general, world-wide decline in Britain's competitive power but of a deliberate refining of effort. The explanation for British attitudes to the Republics should be looked for in the options open to British traders and manufacturers elsewhere, in the changing structure of British industry, in priorities and preferences among manufacturers and sellers, producers and consumers.

Britain had enjoyed a profitable trade with colonial Latin America, whether legitimately through Spain and Portugal, or illegitimately by contraband. The end of the Spanish Empire brought new business to British traders and manufacturers as tastes enlarged, as the existing trading classes were displaced, and as British substitutes were found for the traditional imports from the Continent. For a short period, when an accumulated demand had still to be satisfied and the markets of Europe and North America were closed by war, Brazil and the Republics seemed to offer an answer to every prayer. But the poverty of the market soon brought traders to their senses, and British manufacturers returned to a primary emphasis on production for the home market, for Europe and for the United States. A second honeymoon followed in the '60s and '70s. Rising production at home, industrialization and import substitution within Britain's traditional export markets, increased the attractions of non-industrial outlets further afield, while the steady fall in the prices of manufactured goods made British manufacturers better equipped to undercut local handicraft producers. Demand now existed for the primary produce of the Republics in an urban and industrial Europe, and capital, attracted by the new market opportunities, flowed into Latin American railways, port works, utilities, processing plants and mines, opening the way for a vastly enlarged market for British manufactured goods. At a point when Britain still led the world in iron and steel, railway materials and machinery, the new demand was entirely to her advantage, and once again Latin America seemed to offer a most promising relief outlet for British trade.

European industry, however, was bound to challenge British manufacturing before long as each home market reached saturation and as manufacturers began to look for outlets for their surplus products overseas. Britons, no more than anyone else, had infinite capacity for expansion and exploitation, either in men or money, and as Latin America became a battleground among competing industrial nations, British traders and manufacturers naturally concentrated their resources on markets where profits were higher, trade and distribution easier, and long-term prospects more encouraging. The first resort, obviously, was to the home market, after which they turned to their neighbours in Europe, to North America, to British India, the Colonies and the Dominions. Latin America enjoyed some priority among the manufacturers and traders of Germany and the United States. It came low on the list for Britain, and the trend which gave Empire markets nearly half of British exports by 1938 in contrast to 7·7% for Central and South America, was well under way by 1914. The critical importance of Argentina, the influence of heavy investment, the continued competitiveness of British cotton manufactures, and the rising demand for British coal, delayed and obscured, but did nothing to alter, the general drift of British trade and manufactures towards home and Empire markets, towards more specialised and sophisticated production less suited for sale to the second rank of primary producers.

Competing industrialization in Europe and North America naturally worried British manufacturers, and it is difficult to keep some sense of proportion amidst the clamour of criticism and complaint. The United Kingdom was the first industrial nation, and it is not surprising that she found herself always on the watch for those in pursuit. A. J. Mundella, in an address to the Statistical Society in February 1878, drew attention to a recurrence of all the old fears that Britain's trade was leaving her, that her prosperity had passed its summit and would henceforth decline.

We have grown so accustomed to our pre-eminence that any new evidence of foreign enterprise, or any fresh indication of successful foreign competition, excites our fears. It would be easy to recall many instances of those periodical alarms during the past thirty years. In my own experience, I cannot recollect a time of depression when this anxiety as to the stability of our trade has not shown itself. So far back as 1848, German competition was the dread of our manufacturers of textiles, hosiery,

x

and small-wares ... Belgian coal, iron, and calico, American machinery, hardware, and cotton-cloths, have all played their part in turn, have all in succession contributed to our alarm. In the majority of instances our fears have been entirely groundless. Not a single cargo of Belgian coal ever reached this country, although largely advertised for sale; more American cottons have been made in the neighbourhood of Manchester than have been imported, and in nearly every instance the fact of this competition has been greatly exaggerated and its cause wholly misunderstood.[1]

British manufacturers were bound to feel challenged as step by step foreign competitors entered markets in which they had enjoyed as much or as little trade as they cared to handle. Inevitably, the chronic fright at foreign competition ran over into the decade before 1914, when Britain's trade was healthy and her prospects fair. She found it difficult then, and she finds it difficult still, to rid herself of an attitude of mind. She had, after all, so much to lose.

Businessmen are reticent about success. They can see no point in calling attention to an opportunity for further profit. Disaster, on the other hand, is recorded and analysed, and it is easy to get the impression, when returning to the archives many years later, that the commercial history of a period consists simply of a succession of crises. The Master Cutler of Sheffield, commenting on the exaggerated alarm of the mid-'80s, pointed out that much prominence was given to foreign competition by those who suffered from it, while those unaffected quietly pursued their trade[2]; and in fact, reading between the lines, this was the burden of most of the industrial evidence taken by the Royal Commission on the Depression of Trade and Industry. Again, if consular complaints are studied in detail, it will be found that after the first big scare in the '80s and early '90s, when alarm was almost universal, the bulk of the criticism came either from British officers in Europe and North America, where tariffs and local industry had already destroyed much of the traditional trade, or from those serving in the smaller Republics of Central and South America, in which British businessmen were making no effort to compete. 'It cannot be too

---

[1] Mundella, *Journal of the Statistical Society*, XLI, 87-8.
[2] Minutes of Evidence, *Second Report of the Royal Commission on the Depression of Trade and Industry*, P.P. 1886, XXI, Q.2659.

strongly insisted,' said Wardrop in his report on Haiti for 1902, 'that where we have lost the trade in any particular article in this country, it is not generally because the foreigner has produced something cheaper or better, but because our own manufacturers have not taken the trouble to push the trade.'[1] And who could have blamed them?

The interesting point is that from the early 1900s in the Trade Commissioners' reports on the Dominions, and from the later 1900s in the diplomatic and Consular reports from Latin America, foreign competition lost its terrors. Germany and the United States had captured a substantial share of the trade. But the trade itself was vastly increased, Britain still held a comfortable proportion, and the steady drain on her trading position had been halted and often reversed. If any nation had cause to worry in the years immediately before 1914, it was Germany, not the United Kingdom.

*

It would be pleasant to believe that one of the results of this book might be to extend the common ground between economic historians and businessmen. Businessmen know their trade, and their livelihoods depend on making the right decision at the right time. As historians, we would be unwise to assume that we can judge business decisions by a kind of macro-economic hindsight, by broad economic trends, by developments which may be clear enough to us now but which at the time covered more than a man's working lifetime. Throughout this book care has been taken, so far as possible, to present the decisions and options as they would have appeared to businessmen at the time; the intention is to show that within contemporary experience and conditions of trade, the decisions were those which any qualified man might, and probably should, have taken. British traders and manufacturers were established men with solid financial connections and a century of experience behind them. Could they all have been so misguided? Did Britain's industrial leadership 'fall from their ineffectual grasp'? Is it sensible to expect British traders and manufacturers, as first in the field, to keep all to themselves indefinitely? Could they have done so, even if they had tried? Nothing is perfect. Individuals make mistakes and go bankrupt. Whole generations do not.

[1] P.P. 1904, XCIX, 574.

Britons came to Latin America as businessmen, and whether or not they remained depended ultimately not only on the rate of return to be expected from this capital, but on comfort, on security, on the opportunity to earn an honest living. They withdrew from Latin America when, for a number of separate reasons, it was no longer worth their while to continue, not when the trade had ceased to make any profit at all. Many Victorians preferred, quite legitimately, to take a smaller profit with less risk in a colonial trade, or to wind up their businesses altogether and retire to the respectable status of rentier in their own home country. To the Victorian trader as to the working man, a lifetime of labour in Latin America needed to offer special rewards to compete with the more congenial opportunities nearly always at hand among his compatriots in North America, South Africa and Australasia. The same was true, in general, for British manufacturers, though the motives were more simply economic. More obvious candidates presented themselves for branch factory development and the opening of direct sales campaigns than the Republics. British manufacturers were operating branch factories throughout Europe and North America in and after the '70s, primarily to maintain a share of rich markets now enclosed behind high tariff barriers. Tariff barriers were often as formidable in the Republics, but the relative poverty and unfamiliarity of the markets, the distance from home, and the difficulty of maintaining a satisfactory control, meant that it was not until the 1920s and 1930s that British branch factories spread so far outside the traditional markets. Indeed, it is not easy to quote an example of a branch plant in Latin America opened by a British manufacturer before the First World War, other than a single shoe factory in Brazil. Others, presumably, must have existed, but if they did they have sunk without trace.

If Britons had been gifted with infinite wisdom, if they had enjoyed clear prevision of the post-war world, they might have used their great resources to better effect. They were dangerously dependent, in Latin America as elsewhere, on a continued trade in cotton and coal, and in a perfect world they would, no doubt, have switched their investment to more promising lines well before the collapse of both markets between the wars. But it is absurd to think that they could have done so. Both cotton and coal were doing exceptionally well just before the war. No mine-owner, manufacturer or trader could have been expected to abandon a good line of trade while it lasted, all in the remote prospect of the emergence of the Japanese textile industry, of a new wave of state-promoted competition from European coal, of a long-term substitution of oil for coal. Even if some far-sighted businessmen were moving into newer, more sophisticated lines, it was inconceivable that in either cotton textiles or coal Britain should have ceased large-scale production until the times had actually and decisively changed. This itself is no exception to the rule that there is almost always, as one might expect, a rational explanation for those business practices and decisions which economic historians are accustomed to describe as criminally negligent or ignorant, as outstanding examples of entrepreneurial failure—for a refusal to give credit here, a reluctance to quote c.i.f. there, a decision to mount a campaign of catalogue sales somewhere else. Allowing for individual failure, there is no reason to suppose that businessmen in general were blind to what may now seem so obvious to commercial novices such as ourselves.

Trade depends, as often as not, on the natural advantages of proximity and access, both to markets and to raw materials. It follows the lines laid down by the existence of shipping and rail connections, by the nationality of traders and by their knowledge, experience and traditional contacts. Trade may develop out of the existence of a return product by which alone a two-way traffic may pay for itself. Jerome explained, early in this century, that from what he had been able to learn the greatest difficulty in the way of extending British trade with Mexico was the want of quick direct communication, and the absence in the United Kingdom of an acknowledged mart for Mexican products.[1] This was the point. When Britons were not represented in a trade, it was not necessarily because they were inept, or blind to their own best interests. It was not because they were experiencing what has come to be known, among academic theorists, as 'third-generational entrepreneurial decline'. The reason was simply that the basis of a satisfactory trade, in resources, in return on capital, in existing services, did not exist for British businessmen, even when such a basis may well have existed, under a different combination of circumstances, for one or other of their competitors. Wickham, the Trade Commissioner in New Zealand, complained in a moment of exasperation that those who were currently (1913-14) condemning

[1] Jerome's report on Mexico for 1903, P.P. 1905, XC, 760.

the British manufacturer in sweeping terms were rarely able, when challenged, to give particular instances; those cited were usually 'prehistoric'.

> Instances, on the other hand, are quoted where the British manufacturer fails to compete, or has allowed his competitors to establish a long lead; and here it is generally found that there is some explanation not far to seek in the natural resources, or in the social and industrial conditions of the various competing industrial countries.[1]

*

This book is the first attempt to place British trade with Latin America firmly in the context of import substitution within the Republics, of the increased concentration of British interest in home and Empire markets, and of the changing character of British industry. The result is a picture of British trading performance formidably different from impressions developed simply from area studies, taken in isolation.

It may not be too much of a caricature to describe the textbook version of the British connection with Latin America in the following terms. After independence, an irresistible flood of British goods entered Brazil and the Republics. Local industries were 'destroyed', and British traders and manufacturers consolidated a strong and unchallengeable monopoly over a significant import trade. During the first three-quarters of the century Britain assumed a major role both as a supplier of manufactured goods and as a consumer of Latin America's raw materials. These were the years of Britain's 'hegemony', of the 'imperialism of Free Trade', of a total dependence in the Republics on British manufacturers for imports and on British consumers for exports. Britain was first challenged by Germany only in the early '80s. The challenge was wholly successful, and Britain's steady competitive decline faithfully reflected, in this 'neutral' market, the general malaise of British industry in competition with the new industrial nations.

The actual position was entirely different in nearly every respect. The implications for the pattern of British commercial and financial contact with Latin America, before and after the First World

[1] Wickham's report on New Zealand for 1913, P.P. 1914-16, XLVI, 631.

War, are interesting enough. But in the wider context of Britain's performance in world markets before 1914, the effect of a closer analysis of the options open to British trade throws doubt on the whole notion of Britain's competitive 'decline'. Every economic historian would give much to discover some genuinely 'neutral' market, some 'truly competitive' area where one nation's performance may be measured accurately against another's. When Latin America is struck off the list—as it must be—where else is one to look? And if generalizations on Britain's competitive position have been based even in part on the supposed 'neutrality' of Latin American markets before 1914, we shall obviously have to think again.

Appendixes

APPENDIX I

Exports of Produce and Manufactures of the United Kingdom to Latin America, 1850-1913
(Declared Value, £ million)

	1850	1851	1852	1853	1854	1855	1856	1857
Argentina	0·8	0·5	0·8	0·6	1·3	0·7	1·0	1·3
Bolivia	—	—	—	—	—	—	—	—
Brazil	2·5	3·5	3·5	3·2	2·9	3·3	4·1	5·5
Chile	1·2	1·2	1·2	1·3	1·4	1·3	1·4	1·5
Colombia	0·3	0·3	0·5	0·5	0·3	0·6	0·5	0·6
Central America	0·3	0·3	0·3	0·2	0·2	0·3	0·3	0·3
Costa Rica[1]	—	—	—	—	—	—	—	—
El Salvador[1]	—	—	—	—	—	—	—	—
Guatemala[1]	—	—	—	—	—	—	—	—
Honduras[1]	—	—	—	—	—	—	—	—
Nicaragua[1]	—	—	—	—	—	—	—	—
Panama[2]	—	—	—	—	—	—	—	—
Cuba and Puerto Rico[3]	0·9	1·2	1·1	1·1	1·1	1·1	1·4	1·9
Dominican Republic and Haiti[4]	0·3	0·2	0·3	0·1	0·2	0·2	0·2	0·3
Ecuador	—	0·1	—	—	—	—	—	—
Mexico	0·5	0·6	0·4	0·8	0·4	0·6	0·9	0·6
Paraguay	—	—	—	—	—	—	—	—
Peru	0·8	1·2	1·0	1·2	0·9	1·3	1·0	1·2
Uruguay	0·1	0·2	0·6	0·5	0·5	0·3	0·4	0·5
Venezuela	0·3	0·3	0·3	0·2	0·3	0·4	0·4	0·4

	1872	1873	1874	1875	1876	1877	1878	1879
Argentina	3·9	3·7	3·1	2·4	1·5	2·1	2·3	2·1
Bolivia	—	0·1	0·1	0·1	0·2	0·1	0·1	0·1
Brazil	7·5	7·5	7·7	6·9	5·9	6·0	5·6	5·7
Chile	3·1	3·2	2·8	2·2	1·9	1·5	1·2	1·0
Colombia	3·2	3·1	2·6	0·9	0·8	0·9	1·0	0·9
Central America	0·3	0·3	0·2	0·8	0·7	0·9	0·7	0·7
Costa Rica[1]	—	—	—	—	—	—	—	—
El Salvador[1]	—	—	—	—	—	—	—	—
Guatemala[1]	—	—	—	—	—	—	—	—
Honduras[1]	—	—	—	—	—	—	—	—
Nicaragua[1]	—	—	—	—	—	—	—	—
Panama[2]	—	—	—	—	—	—	—	—
Cuba and Puerto Rico[3]	3·0	2·8	1·9	2·6	2·0	2·2	1·9	1·8
Dominican Republic and Haiti[4]	0·6	0·5	0·4	0·7	0·4	0·4	0·3	0·2
Ecuador	0·8	0·1	0·1	0·1	0·2	0·3	0·2	0·3
Mexico	0·8	1·2	1·1	0·9	0·5	1·0	0·8	0·7
Paraguay	—	—	—	—	—	—	—	—
Peru	2·9	2·5	1·6	1·6	1·0	1·3	1·4	0·7
Uruguay	1·8	1·8	1·2	0·7	1·0	1·1	1·0	0·9
Venezuela	0·5	0·5	0·5	0·7	0·7	0·6	0·5	0·5

59	1860	1861	1862	1863	1864	1865	1866	1867	1868	1869	1870	1871
1·0	1·8	1·4	0·9	1·3	1·8	2·0	2·8	2·8	1·9	2·3	2·3	2·5
3·7	4·4	4·6	3·7	4·0	6·2	5·7	7·2	5·7	5·4	7·0	5·4	6·3
1·5	1·7	1·4	1·0	1·4	1·7	1·6	1·9	2·5	2·0	2·0	2·7	2·0
0·7	0·8	0·8	0·8	1·6	2·1	2·4	2·9	2·4	2·7	2·1	2·1	2·6
0·2	0·2	0·2	0·2	0·1	0·2	0·1	0·2	0·2	0·2	0·2	0·4	0·3
—	—	—	—	—	—	—	—	—	—	—	—	—
—	—	—	—	—	—	—	—	—	—	—	—	—
—	—	—	—	—	—	—	—	—	—	—	—	—
—	—	—	—	—	—	—	—	—	—	—	—	—
1·7	1·5	1·4	1·9	2·1	3·0	2·2	2·2	2·3	2·5	1·1	2·5	2·9
0·2	0·4	0·3	0·5	0·5	0·5	0·3	0·4	0·3	0·2	0·1	0·4	0·3
—	0·1	0·2	—	—	—	—	—	—	0·1	0·1	0·1	—
0·6	0·5	0·6	0·8	1·7	1·8	1·9	1·3	0·8	0·8	0·6	0·9	1·1
0·9	1·4	1·2	0·8	1·0	1·3	1·2	1·4	1·4	1·1	1·4	1·8	2·2
0·7	0·9	0·6	0·5	0·5	1·0	0·8	1·4	1·5	0·9	1·1	0·8	1·0
0·3	0·3	0·4	0·2	0·4	0·5	0·4	0·4	0·3	0·1	0·4	0·1	0·3

81	1882	1883	1884	1885	1886	1887	1888	1889	1890	1891	1892	1893
3·3	4·2	4·9	5·8	4·7	5·2	6·2	7·7	10·7	8·4	4·2	5·7	5·5
0·1	0·1	0·1	0·1	0·1	0·1	0·1	0·1	—	—	—	—	—
6·7	6·9	6·6	6·5	5·3	6·1	5·8	6·3	6·2	7·5	8·3	7·9	7·8
2·5	3·0	2·1	2·1	1·4	1·6	2·0	2·2	2·9	3·1	2·0	3·7	2·4
1·2	1·0	1·2	1·2	0·7	0·9	1·2	1·1	1·2	1·1	1·3	1·1	1·0
0·9	0·7	0·8	0·9	0·7	0·7	1·0	0·9	1·0	1·0	1·1	—	—
—	—	—	—	—	—	—	—	—	—	—	0·1	0·2
—	—	—	—	—	—	—	—	—	—	—	0·3	0·2
—	—	—	—	—	—	—	—	—	—	—	0·3	0·3
—	—	—	—	—	—	—	—	—	—	—	0·1	—
—	—	—	—	—	—	—	—	—	—	—	0·1	0·1
2·2	2·3	2·2	1·4	1·5	1·7	1·5	1·6	1·8	1·9	1·5	1·5	1·3
0·4	0·2	0·3	0·5	0·4	0·3	0·4	0·3	0·2	0·5	0·3	0·2	0·3
0·3	0·2	0·2	0·4	0·1	0·3	0·4	0·4	0·3	0·3	0·3	0·3	0·3
1·6	1·9	1·6	1·0	0·8	0·9	1·1	1·3	1·5	1·9	1·7	1·3	1·2
0·8	1·0	0·7	1·1	0·7	0·9	0·7	1·1	1·0	1·1	1·0	0·8	0·8
1·4	1·5	1·3	1·6	1·4	1·3	1·8	1·8	2·4	2·0	1·2	1·3	1·5
0·5	0·5	0·6	0·6	0·3	0·5	0·8	0·6	0·8	0·8	0·8	0·4	0·9

[*continued overleaf*

APPENDIX I—*Continued*

	1894	1895	1896	1897	1898	1899	1900	190
Argentina	4·5	5·4	6·6	4·8	5·6	6·2	7·1	6
Bolivia	—	—	—	—	—	—	—	·
Brazil	7·5	7·3	6·7	5·4	6·2	5·4	5·8	4
Chile	2·2	3·2	2·6	2·2	1·7	2·2	3·3	3
Colombia	1·0	1·2	1·3	1·2	0·8	0·7	0·3	0
Central America	—	—	—	—	—	—	—	·
Costa Rica[1]	0·2	0·2	0·2	0·2	0·1	0·1	0·2	0
El Salvador[1]	0·3	0·4	0·4	0·3	0·1	0·2	0·2	0
Guatemala[1]	0·3	0·4	0·4	0·2	0·2	0·1	0·2	0
Honduras[1]	0·1	—	—	—	—	—	0·1	0
Nicaragua[1]	0·2	0·2	0·2	0·1	0·1	0·1	0·2	0
Panama[2]	—	—	—	—	—	—	—	·
Cuba and Puerto Rico[3]	1·1	0·9	0·7	0·6	0·3	{ 1·1 / 0·3	1·2 / 0·1	1
Dominican Republic and Haiti[4]	0·3	0·4	0·3	0·3	0·2	0·2	0·3	0
Ecuador	0·3	0·3	0·4	0·4	0·3	0·4	0·3	0
Mexico	1·2	1·5	1·5	1·6	1·8	2·0	2·0	1
Paraguay	—	—	—	—	—	—	—	·
Peru	0·6	0·7	0·9	0·7	0·8	0·8	0·9	1
Uruguay	1·5	1·3	1·4	0·8	1·3	1·3	1·7	1
Venezuela	0·7	0·8	0·8	0·7	0·5	0·5	0·6	0

[1] Included with Central America prior to 1892.
[2] First distinguished from Colombia in 1905.
[3] Taken together under heading 'Spanish West Indies' prior to 1899.
[4] Not distinguished until 1913, when the totals were £162,217 and £167,310 respectively.

Source: *U.K. Trade and Navigation Accounts*, rounded to nearest hundred thousand.

902	1903	1904	1905	1906	1907	1908	1909	1910	1911	1912	1913
5·9	8·0	10·8	13·0	19·0	17·8	16·4	18·7	19·1	18·6	20·5	22·6
—	—	—	—	—	—	—	0·2	0·2	0·3	0·3	0·4
5·4	5·6	6·0	6·6	7·6	10·2	8·1	8·5	16·4	11·9	12·7	12·5
2·8	3·0	3·3	4·5	6·1	7·4	4·0	4·6	5·5	6·1	6·2	6·0
0·6	0·8	0·9	0·6	0·9	1·0	0·9	0·9	1·2	1·1	1·4	1·7
0·1	0·2	0·2	0·1	0·2	0·3	0·2	0·2	0·2	0·3	0·2	0·2
0·2	0·2	0·3	0·3	0·3	0·3	0·4	0·3	0·3	0·4	0·4	0·3
0·2	0·1	0·3	0·3	0·3	0·3	0·2	0·2	0·2	0·3	0·4	0·3
—	0·1	0·1	0·1	0·1	0·1	0·1	0·1	0·1	0·1	0·1	0·1
0·1	0·1	0·2	0·2	0·2	0·2	0·2	0·2	0·1	0·4	0·2	0·2
—	—	0·2	0·3	0·3	0·3	0·3	0·3	0·4	0·5	0·4	0·5
1·2	1·5	1·8	1·9	1·9	2·1	1·7	1·9	1·9	2·2	2·6	2·2
0·1	0·1	—	—	—	0·1	0·1	0·1	0·1	0·1	0·1	0·1
0·2	0·3	0·3	0·3	0·3	0·3	0·3	0·3	0·4	0·4	0·3	0·3
0·3	0·3	0·3	0·4	0·4	0·5	0·5	0·4	0·3	0·6	0·6	0·4
2·2	1·8	1·9	1·9	2·3	2·9	2·2	2·1	2·4	2·3	2·5	2·2
—	0·1	0·1	0·1	0·2	0·1	0·1	0·1	0·2	0·1	0·1	0·2
0·9	1·0	1·1	1·2	1·3	2·0	1·4	1·3	1·3	1·4	1·4	1·5
1·5	1·6	1·3	2·0	2·2	2·5	2·6	2·3	2·9	2·9	2·9	2·9
0·3	0·6	0·7	0·5	0·7	0·8	0·7	0·5	0·8	1·1	1·0	0·8

APPENDIX II

Imports of Latin American Produce into the United Kingdom, 1854-1913
(Real Value, £ million)

	1854	1855	1856	1857	1858	1859	1860	186
Argentina	1·3	1·1	1·0	1·6	1·2	1·7	1·1	1·
Bolivia	—	—	—	—	—	0·2	0·2	0·
Brazil	2·1	2·3	2·2	3·5	2·3	2·8	2·3	2·
Chile	1·4	1·9	1·7	1·9	1·9	2·0	2·6	2·
Colombia	0·4	0·4	0·5	0·5	0·5	0·6	0·6	0·
Central America	0·1	0·2	0·2	0·3	0·2	0·3	0·2	0·
Costa Rica[2]	—	—	—	—	—	—	—	—
El Salvador[2]	—	—	—	—	—	—	—	—
Guatemala[2]	—	—	—	—	—	—	—	—
Honduras[2]	—	—	—	—	—	—	—	—
Nicaragua[2]	—	—	—	—	—	—	—	—
Panama[3]	—	—	—	—	—	—	—	—
Cuba and Puerto Rico	3·4	2·3	2·7	3·5	3·8	3·5	3·3	4·
Cuba[4]	—	—	—	—	—	—	—	—
Puerto Rico[4]	—	—	—	—	—	—	—	—
Dominican Republic and Haiti[5]	0·1	0·1	0·2	0·1	0·1	0·1	0·1	0·
Ecuador	—	0·1	—	0·1	0·1	—	0·1	0·
Mexico	0·2	0·2	0·2	0·3	0·3	0·4	0·5	0·
Paraguay[6]	—	—	—	—	—	—	—	—
Peru	3·1	3·5	3·0	4·4	4·8	1·6	2·6	3·
Uruguay	0·4	0·4	0·6	0·7	0·5	0·7	0·9	0·
Venezuela	—	—	—	—	—	—	—	—

	1874	1875	1876	1877	1878	1879	1880	188
Argentina	1·3	1·4	1·7	1·7	1·1	0·8	0·9	0·
Bolivia	0·3	0·5	0·4	0·4	0·6	0·3	0·3	0·
Brazil	7·0	7·4	5·2	6·3	4·7	4·7	5·3	6·
Chile	4·7	4·2	3·6	3·3	2·2	3·7	3·5	2·
Colombia	1·0	1·0	0·7	0·5	0·9	0·9	0·8	1·
Central America	1·1	1·3	0·9	1·4	1·0	1·4	1·3	1·
Costa Rica	—	—	—	—	—	—	—	—
El Salvador[2]	—	—	—	—	—	—	—	—
Guatemala[2]	—	—	—	—	—	—	—	—
Honduras[2]	—	—	—	—	—	—	—	—
Nicaragua[2]	—	—	—	—	—	—	—	—
Panama[3]	—	—	—	—	—	—	—	—
Cuba and Puerto Rico	3·8	3·7	2·9	1·5	1·8	2·9	1·8	1·6
Cuba[4]	—	—	—	—	—	—	—	—
Puerto Rico[4]	—	—	—	—	—	—	—	—
Dominican Republic and Haiti[5]	0·3	0·4	0·4	0·2	0·2	0·1	0·2	0·1
Ecuador	0·3	0·2	0·2	0·2	0·3	0·5	0·6	0·3
Mexico	0·5	0·7	0·7	0·8	0·5	0·6	0·6	0·6
Paraguay[6]	—	—	—	—	—	—	—	—
Peru	4·5	4·9	5·6	4·7	5·2	3·4	2·7	2·2
Uruguay	1·4	1·2	0·8	0·7	0·6	0·4	0·7	0·5
Venezuela	0·1	—	0·1	0·1	0·1	0·1	0·2	0·2

1862	1863	1864	1865	1866	1867	1868	1869	1870	1871	1872	1873
1·1	1·2	1·2	1·0	1·1	0·9	1·5	1·3	1·5	2·0	1·9	2·6
0·3	0·3	0·2	0·2	0·2	0·1	0·2	0·1	0·1	0·3	1·0	0·8
4·4	4·5	7·0	6·8	7·2	5·9	7·5	7·3	6·1	6·7	9·5	7·4
2·9	2·3	3·2	3·8	2·9	4·4	4·4	3·6	3·8	3·8	5·6	4·8
0·8	0·8	1·7	1·6	1·5	1·0	1·1	1·1	0·9	1·0	1·0	1·1
0·5	0·5	0·4	0·7	0·6	0·8	0·9	1·1	1·1	1·1	1·1	1·4
—	—	—	—	—	—	—	—	—	—	—	—
—	—	—	—	—	—	—	—	—	—	—	—
—	—	—	—	—	—	—	—	—	—	—	—
—	—	—	—	—	—	—	—	—	—	—	—
4·2	4·3	6·3	5·1	3·0	4·3	4·8	4·8	5·4	2·6	5·2	5·1
—	—	—	—	—	—	—	—	—	—	—	—
0·2	0·3	0·3	0·2	0·2	0·2	0·1	0·2	0·2	0·2	0·4	0·3
0·1	0·1	—	—	0·1	0·1	0·1	0·2	0·1	0·3	0·2	0·3
0·6	2·3	3·1	3·2	0·3	0·3	0·4	0·4	0·3	0·4	0·4	0·5
2·4	3·6	2·7	4·0	3·0	3·7	3·4	4·0	4·9	4·0	4·2	5·2
1·0	1·2	1·1	1·2	1·5	1·2	1·1	0·8	1·0	1·2	1·4	1·3
—	—	0·2	0·2	0·2	0·1	—	0·1	0·1	0·1	0·1	0·1

1882	1883	1884	1885	1886	1887	1888	1889	1890	1891	1892	1893
1·2	0·9	1·2	1·9	1·6	2·2	2·7	2·0	4·1	3·5	4·5	4·8
0·4	0·4	0·2	0·2	0·2	0·1	0·1	—	—	—	—	—
6·5	6·1	4·7	4·1	3·5	5·4	5·2	5·1	4·4	4·2	3·5	4·6
3·4	3·4	2·6	2·5	2·3	2·2	3·1	3·3	3·5	3·7	3·9	3·8
1·1	0·8	0·4	0·2	0·3	0·3	0·4	0·2	0·3	0·3	0·5	0·6
1·5	1·1	1·3	1·1	1·1	1·3	1·1	1·2	1·3	1·4	—	—
—	—	—	—	—	—	—	—	—	—	0·5	0·5
—	—	—	—	—	—	—	—	—	—	0·2	0·2
—	—	—	—	—	—	—	—	—	—	0·3	0·4
—	—	—	—	—	—	—	—	—	—	—	—
—	—	—	—	—	—	—	—	—	—	0·1	0·1
1·8	1·1	0·9	1·0	0·1	0·2	0·3	0·1	0·1	0·1	0·1	0·1
—	—	—	—	—	—	—	—	—	—	—	—
0·1	0·1	0·2	0·1	0·1	—	0·1	—	0·1	—	—	0·1
0·2	0·3	0·2	0·2	0·2	0·2	0·1	0·1	0·1	0·1	0·1	0·2
0·6	0·7	0·7	0·7	0·6	0·5	0·5	0·5	0·5	0·5	0·5	0·6
2·7	2·3	2·1	1·9	1·7	1·6	2·0	1·3	1·1	1·0	1·6	1·4
0·8	0·6	0·7	0·6	0·4	0·3	0·5	0·5	0·3	0·4	0·3	0·1
0·3	0·3	0·3	0·2	0·1	0·1	0·3	0·3	0·3	0·3	0·3	0·1

[continued overleaf

APPENDIX II—*Continued*

	1894	1895	1896	1897	1898	1899	1900	190
Argentina	6·2	9·1	9·0	5·8	7·8	10·9	13·1	12
Bolivia	—	—	—	—	—	—	—	-
Brazil	3·9	3·6	4·1	3·7	4·6	4·0	5·9	5
Chile	3·7	3·4	3·6	3·2	3·6	4·2	4·8	4
Colombia	0·6	0·4	0·6	0·6	0·6	0·6	0·3	0
Central America	—	—	—	—	—	—	—	-
Costa Rica[2]	0·4	0·3	0·3	0·3	0·6	0·2	0·3	0
El Salvador[2]	0·2	0·2	0·2	0·2	0·2	0·1	0·1	0
Guatemala[2]	0·3	0·4	0·4	0·4	0·3	0·2	0·1	0
Honduras[2]	—	—	—	—	—	—	—	-
Nicaragua[2]	0·1	0·1	0·1	0·1	0·1	—	0·1	-
Panama[3]	—	—	—	—	—	—	—	-
Cuba and Puerto Rico	0·2	0·1	—	—	—	—	—	-
Cuba[4]	—	—	—	—	—	—	—	-
Puerto Rico[4]	—	—	—	—	—	—	—	-
Dominican Republic and Haiti[5]	0·1	0·1	0·1	0·1	0·1	0·1	0·1	0
Ecuador	0·2	0·1	0·2	0·1	0·3	0·2	0·2	0
Mexico	0·6	0·5	0·6	0·6	0·3	0·5	0·5	0
Paraguay[6]	—	—	—	—	—	—	—	-
Peru	1·1	1·4	1·3	1·5	1·5	1·3	1·3	1
Uruguay	0·3	0·5	0·3	0·3	0·4	0·3	0·5	0
Venezuela	0·1	0·1	0·1	0·1	—	—	0·1	0

[1] Import figures in the annual Statements in and after 1909 were based on records of countri
of consignment, not as previously on countries of shipment.
[2] Included with Central America prior to 1892.
[3] First distinguished from Colombia in 1905.
[4] Taken together prior to 1899.
[5] Not distinguished until 1913, when the totals were £154,492 and £115,542 respectively.
[6] Imports never in excess of £50,000.

Source: *U.K. Trade and Navigation Accounts*, rounded to nearest hundred thousand.

1902	1903	1904	1905	1906	1907	1908	1909[1]	1910[1]	1911[1]	1912[1]	1913[1]
14·0	19·1	23·0	25·0	23·8	26·5	35·7	32·7	29·0	27·3	40·8	42·5
—	—	—	—	—	—	—	1·2	1·4	1·6	1·6	2·3
6·2	6·7	6·2	8·1	9·1	9·7	6·9	11·3	17·5	10·9	9·4	10·0
4·5	4·6	5·4	6·1	6·3	6·0	7·4	5·5	5·2	4·3	5·0	5·4
0·4	0·6	0·7	0·3	0·3	0·3	0·3	0·8	1·0	1·0	1·2	1·1
0·3	0·4	0·6	0·8	0·8	1·0	1·0	0·9	0·8	1·2	1·3	1·4
0·1	0·1	0·3	0·2	0·1	—	0·1	0·1	0·1	0·1	0·1	0·1
0·2	0·1	0·3	0·2	0·1	0·2	0·1	0·2	0·2	0·3	0·4	0·4
0·1	0·1	0·1	0·1	0·1	0·1	0·1	0·1	0·1	0·1	0·1	0·1
—	—	—	—	—	—	—	—	—	—	—	0·1
—	—	—	—	—	—	—	—	—	—	—	—
—	0·3	0·2	0·2	0·2	0·3	0·3	1·3	2·7	1·3	2·5	3·7
—	—	—	—	—	—	—	—	—	—	—	—
0·1	—	0·1	—	—	0·2	0·1	0·3	1·2	0·5	0·8	0·3
0·2	0·1	0·2	0·2	0·1	0·2	0·4	0·5	0·6	0·6	0·4	0·5
0·3	0·7	0·6	0·9	0·8	2·0	1·9	2·2	2·3	2·2	2·5	1·9
1·4	1·6	2·4	2·4	1·7	2·8	2·9	3·0	3·7	3·2	3·3	3·2
0·7	0·9	0·6	0·8	0·5	1·0	1·0	1·3	1·7	1·4	2·4	2·7
—	0·1	0·2	0·2	0·2	0·2	0·2	0·4	0·6	0·7	0·7	0·6

Y

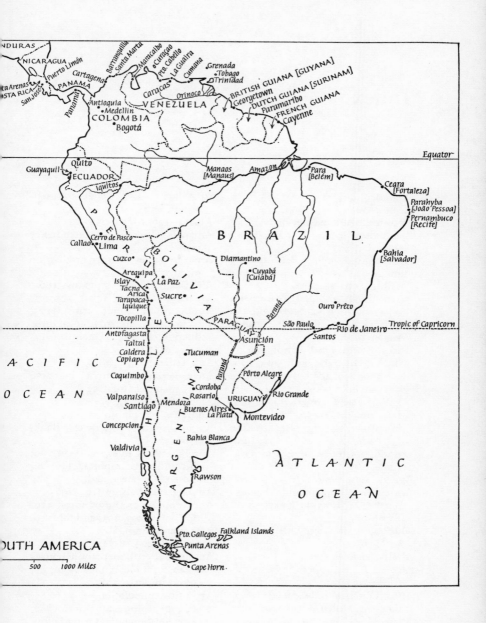

Index

Acapulco, 8
Accles, George, 217
Accoutrements, military, 48
Admiralty, British, and shipbuilding, 205, 227
Advertising, and Br. trading methods, 166-72; and catalogue selling, 170-1
Africa, East, and Br. investment, 135; and German shipping, 162
Africa, Equatorial, and German trade, 101, 120
Africa, South, local manufacturing in, 86; Br. trade with, 103, 106-16, 159, 199, 201, 205-7, 210-12, 215, 219, 235-40, 243-4, 248, 258-9; and German trade, 114; Br. emigration to, 131-2; Br. investments, 135; Br. trading methods, 138, 166, 171; and trade combines, 175; and L.A. trade, 249
Agents, commission, 50-1, 54
Agricultural implements, U.S. exports of, 102, 235; Br. exports of, 233-8
Aldrich, Senator, and U.S. interests in Mexico, 300
Alfalfa, 127
Algeria, Br. exports to, 237
Alizarin, 173
Allen, G. C., on industrial development of Midlands, 216-17
Allen, H. C., and Br. investments in Argentina, 291-2

Allgemeine Elektricitäts Gesellschaft, 242
Alpaca, 146-7, 192, 258
Amapala (Honduras), local industry in, 197
Amazon Valley, rubber production in, 267, 269
American Thread Company, 186
American Tobacco Trust, 175
Ammunition, small arms, 173; competition in, 197; local production of, 204; Argentine imports of, 245
Amsterdam, 253
Anaesthetics, Br. trade in, 208; raw materials for, 252
Ancon Bay (Peru), 25
Andrews, Joseph, 40
Anglo South American Bank, 278
Antofagasta (Chile), port at, 69; and Bolivian imports, 159; oil and coal imports, 248
Antofagasta Railway Co., 296
Antwerp, and transport rates, 129, 162; and cocoa, 253; and tobacco, 254; and hides, 267
Archer, A., 215
Arequipa (Peru), mercantile houses at, 42, 147; local industry in, 92; cotton imports, 178
Argentina, population of, 5, 6, 89, 96, 276; as importer before 1860, 7-22; local manufacturing before 1860, 9-22; cottons, 13, 21, 82,

326

z